Rick Steves

Emma + Benjamin

GREECE:
ATHENS & THE
PELOPONNESE

CONTENTS

SIGHTS

1. Acropolis
2. Acropolis Museum
3. Adrianou Street
4. Agora Museum
5. Ancient Agora
6. Apostolou Pavlou Street
7. Arch of Hadrian
8. Benaki Museum of Greek History & Culture
9. Benaki Mus. of Islamic Art
10. Byzantine & Christian Mus.
11. Cathedral (Mitropolis)
12. Central Market
13. Church of Agios Eleftherios
14. Church of Kapnikarea
15. Dionysiou Areopagitou St.
16. Dora Stratou Theater
17. Ermou Street
18. Flea Market
19. Jewish Museum
20. Keramikos Cemetery
21. Library of Hadrian
22. Mars Hill (Areopagus)
23. Museum of Cycladic Art
24. Museum of Greek Folk Art (Ceramics)
25. Museum of Greek Folk Art (Main)
26. Museum of Greek Popular Instruments
27. To Mus. of the City of Athens
28. To National Archaeological Museum & Exarchia District
29. National Garden
30. National War Museum
31. Odeon of Herodes Atticus
32. Panathenaic (Olympic) Stadium
33. Parliament
34. Parthenon
35. Roman Forum
36. Syntagma Square
37. To Technopolis & Gazi District
38. Temple of Olympian Zeus
39. Theater of Dionysus
40. Tomb of the Unknown Soldier & Evzone Guards
41. Tower of the Winds
42. Zappeion

KOLOKOTRONI

SYNTAGMA

PERIKLEOUS

ERMOU

CATHEDRAL (MITROPOLIS)

APOLLONOS

NIKIS

Bus #X80 to / from Piraeus

HOTEL GRANDE BRETAGNE

Syntagma Square 36

POST

MITROPOLEOS

Syntagma

Bus #040 to Piraeus

Bus #X95 to Airport

Bus #040 from Piraeus

JEWISH MUSEUM

PLAKA 19

Filomousou Square

ARCH OF HADRIAN 7

Bus #X80 from Piraeus

Bus #X80 to Piraeus

TEMPLE OF OLYMPIAN ZEUS 38

ATHANASIOU DIAKOU

Bus #040 to Piraeus

KALLIRROIS

VOULIAGMENIS

SARGOUS

KOLONAKI

To Lykavittos Hill

BENAKI MUSEUM OF GREEK HISTORY & CULTURE 8

VASILISSIS

MUSEUM OF CYCLADIC ART 23

To Evangel- ismos

NATIONAL WAR MUS. 30

SOFIAS

BYZANTINE & CHRISTIAN MUSEUM 10

LYKIOU

To Airport

VASILEOS GEORGIOU

VASILISSIS AMALIAS

29 NATIONAL GARDEN

ZAPPEION (EXHIBITION HALL)

42

VASILISSIS OLGAS

IRODOU ATTIKOU

Stadium Square

PANATHENAIC STADIUM 32

ARDITTOU

ARDITOS

VASILEOS KONSTANTINOU

PANGRATI

ERATOSTHENOUS EFFRANOROS

ARHIMIDOUS

N

200 Meters
200 Yards

PROFITIS

Cemetery

IMMITOU

Rick Steves®

GREECE:
ATHENS & THE
PELOPONNESE

DELPHI

NATIONAL ARCHAEOLOGICAL MUSEUM

ACROPOLIS

OLYMPIA

HYDRA

NAFPLIO

EPIDAVROS

KARDAMYLI

MYKONOS

MYCENAE

MONEMVASIA

MANI PENINSULA

SANTORINI

INTRODUCTION

Democracy and mathematics. Medicine and literature. Theater and astronomy. Mythology and philosophy. All of these, and more, were first thought up by a bunch of tunic-clad Greeks in a small village huddled at the base of the Acropolis. The ancient Greeks—who reached their apex in the city of Athens—have had an unmatched impact on European and American culture. For many North American travelers, coming to Greece is like a pilgrimage to the cradle of our civilization.

A century and a half ago, Athens was a humble, forgotten city of about 20,000 people. Today it's the teeming home of nearly four million Greeks—nearly half of the 10 million people in all of Greece. Athens is famous for its sprawl, noise, graffiti, and pollution. The best advice to tourists has long been to see the big sights, then get out. But over the last decade or so, the city has made a concerted effort to curb pollution, clean up and pedestrianize the streets, spiff up the museums, and invest in one of Europe's better public transit systems. All of these urban upgrades reached a peak as Athens hosted the 2004 Olympic Games.

And yet, the conventional wisdom still holds true: Athens is a great city to see...but not to linger in. This book also includes the best Greek destinations outside the capital, including the highlights of the Peloponnese—Greece's heartland peninsula, the site of the ancient oracle at Delphi, and the castaway islands of Hydra, Mykonos, and Santorini.

Greece's economic woes continue to make headlines, but for travelers the news is (almost) all good. The occasional strike or protest rarely interferes with the sightseer's Greece, and anywhere outside of the islands, hotel prices are low. Now is a great time to visit.

In this book, I'll give you all the information and opinions necessary to wring the maximum value out of your limited time

Map Legend

⅄ Viewpoint	✈ Airport	Tunnel
↑ Entrance	Ⓣ Taxi Stand	Pedestrian Zone
⊕ Tourist Info	Ⓣ Tram Stop	Railway
WC Restroom	Ⓑ Bus Stop	Ferry/Boat Route
⊕ Church	Ⓜ Metro Stop	Tram
▪ Statue/Point of Interest	Ⓟ Parking	Stairs
	)(Mtn. Pass	Walk/Tour Route
⊠ Elevator	Park	Trail

Use this legend to help you navigate the maps in this book.

and money. If you plan two weeks or less in this part of Greece and have a normal appetite for information, this book is all you need. If you're a travel-info fiend, this book sorts through all the superlatives and provides a handy rack upon which to hang your supplemental information.

The destinations covered in this book are balanced to include a comfortable mix of cities and villages, ancient sites and Byzantine churches, great museums and relaxing beaches. While you'll find the predictable biggies (such as the Acropolis and ancient Olympia), I've also mixed in a healthy dose of Back Door intimacy (workaday towns such as Kardamyli, rustic seaside viewpoints, and neighborhood tavernas where you'll enjoy a warm welcome).

The best is, of course, only my opinion. But after spending much of my life exploring and researching Europe, I've developed a sixth sense for what travelers enjoy. The places featured in this book will make anyone want to shout, *"Opa!"*

ABOUT THIS BOOK

Rick Steves Greece: Athens & the Peloponnese is a personal tour guide in your pocket. This book is organized by destinations. Each is a minivacation on its own, filled with exciting sights, strollable neighborhoods, affordable places to stay, and memorable places to eat.

The first half of this book focuses on Athens and contains the following chapters:

Greece offers an introduction to this mesmerizing land, including a crash course in the Greek alphabet.

Orientation to Athens has specifics on public transportation, helpful hints, local tour options, easy-to-read maps, and tourist information. The "Planning Your Time" section suggests a schedule for how to best use your limited time.

Key to This Book

Updates

This book is updated regularly—but once you pin down Greece, it wiggles. For the latest, visit www.ricksteves.com/update.

Abbreviations and Times

I use the following symbols and abbreviations in this book:

Sights are rated:

▲▲▲	Don't miss
▲▲	Try hard to see
▲	Worthwhile if you can make it
No rating	Worth knowing about

Tourist information offices are abbreviated as **TI,** and bathrooms are **WC**s. To categorize accommodations, I use a **Sleep Code** (described on page 472).

Like Europe, this book uses the **24-hour clock.** It's the same through 12:00 noon, then keeps going: 13:00, 14:00, and so on. For anything over 12, subtract 12 and add p.m. (14:00 is 2:00 p.m.).

When giving **opening times,** I include both peak-season and off-season hours if they differ. So, if a museum is listed as "May-Oct daily 9:00-16:00," it should be open from 9 a.m. until 4 p.m. from the first day of May until the last day of October (but expect exceptions).

A 🛦 symbol in a sight listing means that the sight is described in greater detail elsewhere—either with its own self-guided tour, or as part of a self-guided walk. A 🎧 symbol indicates that a free, downloadable self-guided Rick Steves audio tour is available.

For **transit** or **tour departures,** I first list the frequency, then the duration. So, a bus connection listed as "2/hour, 1.5 hours" departs twice each hour and the journey lasts an hour and a half.

Sights in Athens describes the top attractions and includes their cost and hours.

Self-Guided Walks and **Tours** take you through interesting neighborhoods, pointing out sights and fun stops. In Athens these include a city walk, the Acropolis, the Ancient Agora, the Acropolis Museum, and the National Archaeological Museum.

Sleeping in Athens describes my favorite hotels, from good-value deals to cushy splurges.

Eating in Athens serves up a buffet of options, from inexpensive tavernas to fancy restaurants.

Shopping and Nightlife in Athens gives you tips for shopping painlessly and enjoyably, and guides you to music, folk dances, outdoor movies, and bustling nighttime neighborhoods.

Greece at a Glance

These attractions are listed (as in this book) starting with Athens, moving to the Peloponnese, and then covering other regions.

▲▲▲**Athens** Greece's capital, featuring the ancient world's most magnificent sight—the Acropolis—a pair of world-class museums, an atmospheric Old Town, and funky neighborhoods bursting with avant-garde nightlife.

▲▲▲**Nafplio** Greece's first capital and finest midsized town, with a cozy port, an elegant Old Town, a cliff-topping fortress, and energetic street life; handy to nearby ancient sites (Mycenae and Epidavros).

▲**Epidavros** Best-preserved theater of the ancient world, with unbelievable acoustics.

▲**Mycenae** Legendary mountaintop palace/fortress with iconic Lion Gate, massive beehive tomb, and mythic links to the Trojan War.

▲▲**Olympia** Birthplace of the Olympic Games, with stunning temple ruins, a still-functional stadium, and an intimate museum of ancient masterpieces.

▲**Kardamyli** Cozy, unspoiled beach town, providing a handy jumping-off point for the Mani Peninsula.

Athens Connections outlines your options for traveling to destinations by car or bus, and includes information on getting to and from Athens' airport.

The **Peloponnese** section includes in-depth chapters on the historic peninsula's top sights: **Nafplio, Epidavros, Mycenae, Olympia, Kardamyli** and the **Mani Peninsula,** and **Monemvasia.**

The **Beyond Athens & the Peloponnese** section covers the ancient oracle site at **Delphi** and the idyllic islands of **Hydra, Mykonos,** and **Santorini.**

The **Greek History and Mythology** chapter gives you a quick overview of the country's past.

Practicalities is a traveler's tool kit, with my best tips about money, sightseeing, sleeping, eating, staying connected, and transportation (buses, boats, car rentals, driving, and flights).

The **appendix** has the nuts-and-bolts: useful phone numbers and websites, a holiday and festival list, recommended books and films, a climate chart, a handy packing checklist, and Greek survival phrases.

▲**Mani Peninsula** Remote, rustic region with dramatic hill towns, spectacular caves (Pyrgos Dirou), and breathtaking jagged coastlines.

▲▲**Monemvasia** Greece's Gibraltar-like fortress on an imposing rock peninsula jutting out into the sea, blending Venetian and Byzantine charm, traffic-free cobbled lanes, and million-dollar views.

▲▲**Delphi** Mountainside draped with the Sanctuary of Apollo and other once-grandiose structures, where ancients came to consult the oracle.

▲▲▲**Hydra** Idyllic island getaway, convenient to Athens and the Peloponnese, with picturesque harbor, casual beaches, enticing coastal hikes, and no cars (but plenty of donkeys).

▲▲**Mykonos** Quintessential (and very popular) Greek isle with postcard-perfect whitewashed village, old-fashioned windmills, and pulsating nightlife; ruins on nearby Delos mark the birthplace of Apollo and a once-mighty shipping center.

▲▲**Santorini** Romantic island destination built on the remains of a volcano crater, renowned for cliff-clinging white villages punctuated by blue-domed churches, volcanic black-sand beaches, and spectacular sunsets.

Browse through this book, choose your favorite destinations, and link them up. Then have a great trip! Traveling like a temporary local, you'll get the absolute most of every mile, minute, and dollar. And, as you visit places I know and love, I'm happy that you'll be meeting some of my favorite Greeks.

Planning

This section will help you get started on planning your trip—with advice on trip costs, when to go, and what you should know before you take off.

TRAVEL SMART

Your trip to Greece is like a complex play—it's easier to follow and really appreciate on a second viewing. While no one does the same trip twice to gain that advantage, reading this book in its entirety before your trip accomplishes much the same thing.

Design an itinerary that enables you to visit sights at the best

Athens and the Peloponnese in Two Weeks

Outside of Athens, this region is best visited by car. If you'd rather get around by bus, you'll see less in virtually the same amount of time (or you can add more days to your itinerary to see it all).

Best Trip by Car

Day	Plan	Sleep
1	Arrive Athens	Athens
2	Athens	Athens
3	Athens	Athens
4	Boat to Hydra	Hydra
5	Hydra	Hydra
6	Boat back to Athens, pick up rental car, drive to Delphi	Delphi
7	Sightsee Delphi, drive to Olympia	Olympia
8	Sightsee Olympia, drive to Kardamyli	Kardamyli
9	Relax in Kardamyli	Kardamyli
10	Mani Peninsula loop drive, on to Monemvasia	Monemvasia
11	Monemvasia	Monemvasia
12	See Mycenae en route to Nafplio	Nafplio
13	Nafplio, side-trip to Epidavros	Nafplio
14	Return to Athens, drop off rental car	Athens
15	Fly home, or continue to Mykonos and/or Santorini by plane or boat	

Best Trip by Bus

Day	Plan	Sleep
1	Arrive Athens	Athens
2	Athens	Athens
3	Athens	Athens
4	Morning in Athens, afternoon bus to Delphi	Delphi
5	Sightsee Delphi	Delphi
6	Morning bus to Athens, then boat to Hydra	Hydra
7	Hydra	Hydra
8	Morning boat back to Athens, then bus to Olympia	Olympia
9	Sightsee Olympia	Olympia
10	Morning bus to Nafplio	Nafplio
11	Day trip to Mycenae	Nafplio
12	Day trip to Epidavros	Nafplio
13	Bus to Athens	Athens
14	Fly home, or continue to Mykonos and/or Santorini by plane or boat	

Best Trip by Car

GREECE

Delphi

Athens

Mycenae

Olympia

Nafplio

Aegean Sea

Hydra

Epidavros

Ionian Sea

To Mykonos
& Santorini →

Kardamyli

Monemvasia

Mani
Peninsula

Sea of Crete

50 Kilometers

50 Miles

Bus Notes: Research and consider your bus connections carefully (usually easier to do on site than online); these can be limited and complicated, especially on the Peloponnese.

Two nights in Delphi offer a fine escape from big-city Athens, but if you have limited time, you can see Delphi either as a day trip on Day 4 (return to Athens to spend the night) or as a single overnight (bus from Athens to Delphi on the morning of Day 4, afternoon sightseeing and overnight in Delphi, then bus to Athens and boat to Hydra on Day 5).

The bus itinerary leaves out the hardest-to-reach destinations: Kardamyli/Mani Peninsula (best by car or with a hired local driver) and Monemvasia.

If you've seen enough ancient sites, you could skip Olympia (which is time-consuming to reach by bus), and instead visit Monemvasia (reachable by bus, with an extra transfer and more travel time than Olympia) or enjoy more beach time on Hydra.

The easiest connection from Hydra to the Peloponnese is via Athens, but adventurous travelers might want to tackle the cheaper and shorter—though more complicated—boat-taxi-bus connection to Nafplio instead; for tips, see page 234.

With an extra week and a bunch of patience, you could include all of the recommended destinations.

possible times. Note festivals, holidays, specifics on sights, and days when sights are closed. To connect the dots smoothly, read the tips in Practicalities on taking buses or renting a car and driving. Designing a smart trip is a fun, doable, and worthwhile challenge.

Make your itinerary a mix of intense and relaxed stretches. To maximize rootedness, minimize one-night stands. It's worth taking a long drive after dinner (or a bus ride with a dinner picnic) to get settled in a town for two nights. Every trip—and every traveler—needs slack time (laundry, picnics, people-watching, and so on). Pace yourself. Assume you will return.

Reread this book as you travel, and visit local tourist information offices (abbreviated as TI in this book). Upon arrival in a new town, lay the groundwork for a smooth departure; confirm the bus, road, or boat you'll take when you leave.

Even with the best-planned itinerary, you'll need to be flexible. Update your plans as you travel. Get online or call ahead to double-check tourist information, learn the latest on sights (special events, tour schedules, and so on), book tickets and tours, make reservations, reconfirm hotels, and research transportation connections.

Enjoy the hospitality of the Greek people. Connect with the culture. Set up your own quest for the best baklava, Byzantine church, or secluded beach. Slow down and be open to unexpected experiences. Ask questions—most locals are eager to point you in their idea of the right direction. Keep a notepad in your pocket for noting directions, organizing your thoughts, and confirming prices. Wear your money belt, learn the currency, and figure out how to estimate prices in dollars. Those who expect to travel smart, do.

TRIP COSTS

Five components make up your trip costs: airfare, surface transportation, room and board, sightseeing and entertainment, and shopping and miscellany.

Airfare: A basic round-trip flight from the US to Athens can cost, on average, about $1,000-2,000 total, depending on where you fly from and when (cheaper in winter). If your trip extends beyond Greece, consider saving time and money by flying into one city and out of another; for instance, into Paris and out of Athens. Overall, Kayak.com is the best place to start searching for flights on a combination of mainstream and budget carriers. Note that if you're visiting only Greece, the airport at Athens is your most convenient way in and out of the country.

Surface Transportation: If you're just touring Athens, you can get around easily on foot and on the Metro (plan on $25 for three full days in Athens and a round-trip ticket to/from the airport). If you're venturing beyond the capital—say, doing a two-week loop of this book's destinations—figure per-person costs of

$150 by public transit (boat to Hydra, bus to everything else) or $460 by car (not including tolls, gas, and insurance). Car rentals and leases are cheapest if arranged from the US. For more on public transportation and car rentals, see "Transportation" in Practicalities. For information on flights, see "See "Getting Around the Greek Islands" (page 365).

Room and Board: You can thrive in Greece on $100 a day per person for room and board (less on the Peloponnese). This allows $15 for lunch, $20 for dinner, and $65 for lodging (based on two people splitting the cost of a $130 double room that includes breakfast). Students and tightwads can enjoy Greece for as little as $60 a day ($30 for a bed, $30 for meals and snacks).

Sightseeing and Entertainment: In Athens, figure about $12-24 per major sight (Acropolis, National Archaeological Museum), $8-10 for minor ones (Benaki Museum of Greek History and Culture, Byzantine and Christian Museum), and $40-90 for splurge experiences (such as walking tours, concerts, special art exhibits, and big-bus tours). An overall average of $30 a day works for most people. Don't skimp here. After all, this category is the driving force behind your trip—you came to sightsee, enjoy, and experience Greece.

Shopping and Miscellany: Figure 50 cents per postcard and $3-4 per coffee or ice-cream cone. Shopping can vary in cost from nearly nothing to a small fortune. Good budget travelers find that this category has little to do with assembling a trip full of lifelong memories.

SIGHTSEEING PRIORITIES
So much to see, so little time. How to choose? Depending on the length of your trip, and taking geographic proximity into account, here are my recommended priorities.

2-3 days:	Athens
5 days, add:	Hydra
7 days, add:	Delphi
10 days, add:	Nafplio, Epidavros, Mycenae
12 days, add:	Olympia, Monemvasia
14 days, add:	Kardamyli and the Mani Peninsula, and slow down

Although this book focuses on Athens and the Peloponnese, I've also included Mykonos and Santorini—two of Greece's best islands—for travelers with more time. The "Greece at a Glance" sidebar can help you decide where to go (page 4).

For a suggested itinerary, see page 6.

INTRODUCTION

🎧 Rick Steves Audio Europe 🎧

My free **Rick Steves Audio Europe app** is a great tool for enjoying Europe. This app makes it easy to download my audio tours of top attractions, plus hours of travel interviews, all organized into destination-specific playlists.

My self-guided **audio tours** of major sights and neighborhoods are free, user-friendly, fun, and informative. Among the sights in this book, these audio tours include my Athens City Walk, and my Acropolis, Ancient Agora, and National Archaeological Museum tours. Sights covered by my audio tours are marked with this symbol: 🎧. You can choose whether to follow the written tour in this book, or pop in your headphones and listen to essentially the same information—freeing up your eyes to appreciate the sights. These audio tours are hard to beat: Nobody will stand you up, the quality is reliable, you can take the tour exactly when you like, and the price is right.

The Rick Steves Audio Europe app also offers a far-reaching library of insightful **travel interviews** from my public radio show with experts from around the globe—including many of the places in this book.

This app and all of its content are entirely free. You can download Rick Steves Audio Europe via Apple's App Store, Google Play, or the Amazon Appstore. For more information, see www.ricksteves.com /audioeurope.

WHEN TO GO

The "summer" and "winter" seasons can vary, but summer is roughly Easter through October, when Athens can be crowded.

Peak Season: In summer, Athens is packed with tourists, and hotel prices can be correspondingly high. July and August are the hottest months.

Shoulder Season: Late spring and fall are pleasant, with comfortable weather, no rain, and lighter crowds (except during holiday weekends).

Winter Season: Weather from late October through mid-March is colder. Though rain is rare in Athens, this is the time for it. Some sights close for lunch, TI offices keep shorter hours, and some tourist activities vanish altogether. Hotel rates are soft; look for bargains.

KNOW BEFORE YOU GO

Check this list of things to arrange while you're still at home.

You need a **passport**—but no visa or shots—to travel in Greece. You may be denied entry into certain European countries

---

How Was Your Trip?

Were your travels fun, smooth, and meaningful? If you'd like to share your tips, concerns, and discoveries, please fill out the survey at www.ricksteves.com/feedback. To check out readers' hotel and restaurant reviews—or leave one yourself—visit my travel forum at www.ricksteves.com/travel-forum. I value your feedback. Thanks in advance.

---

if your passport is due to expire within three months of your ticketed date of return. Get it renewed if you'll be cutting it close. It can take up to six weeks to get or renew a passport (for more on passports, see www.travel.state.gov). Pack a photocopy of your passport in your luggage in case the original is lost or stolen.

Book rooms well in advance if you'll be traveling during peak season (summer) or any major holidays or festivals (see page 510), or are hoping to land a particular hotel on Mykonos or Santorini, where perennial visitors often book their favorite rooms months ahead.

Call your **debit- and credit-card companies** to let them know the countries you'll be visiting, ask about fees, request your PIN code (it will be mailed to you), and more. See page 464 for details.

Do your homework if you want to buy **travel insurance.** Compare the cost of the insurance to the cost of your potential loss. Also, check whether your existing insurance (health, homeowners, or renters) covers you and your possessions overseas. For more tips, see www.ricksteves.com/insurance.

If you're planning on **renting a car** in Greece, bring your driver's license and get an International Driving Permit (see page 496).

If you plan to hire a **local guide,** reserve ahead by email. Popular guides can get booked up.

If you're bringing a **mobile device,** consider signing up for an international plan for cheaper calls, texts, and data (see page 486). Download any apps you might want to use on the road, such as translators, maps, transit schedules, and **Rick Steves Audio Europe** (see previous page).

Traveling as a Temporary Local

We travel all the way to Greece to enjoy differences—to become temporary locals. You'll experience frustrations. Certain truths that we find "God-given" or "self-evident," such as cold beer, ice in drinks, bottomless cups of coffee, "the customer is king," and bigger being better, are suddenly not so true. One of the benefits of travel is the eye-opening realization that there are logical, civil, and even better alternatives. A willingness to go local ensures that you'll enjoy a full dose of Greek hospitality.

Europeans generally like Americans. But if there is a negative aspect to the Greek image of Americans, it's that we are loud, wasteful, ethnocentric, too informal (which can seem disrespectful), and a bit naive.

While the Greek people look bemusedly at some of our Yankee excesses—and worriedly at others—they nearly always afford us individual travelers all the warmth we deserve.

Judging from all the happy feedback I receive from travelers who have used this book, it's safe to assume you'll enjoy a great, affordable vacation—with the finesse of an independent, experienced traveler.

Thanks, and *kalo taxidi!*

Rick Steves

Back Door Travel Philosophy

From *Rick Steves Europe Through the Back Door*

Travel is intensified living—maximum thrills per minute and one of the last great sources of legal adventure. Travel is freedom. It's recess, and we need it.

Experiencing the real Europe requires catching it by surprise, going casual..."through the Back Door."

Affording travel is a matter of priorities. (Make do with the old car.) You can eat and sleep—simply, safely, and enjoyably—anywhere in Europe for $100 a day plus transportation costs. In many ways, spending more money only builds a thicker wall between you and what you traveled so far to see. Europe is a cultural carnival, and time after time you'll find that its best acts are free and the best seats are the cheap ones.

A tight budget forces you to travel close to the ground, meeting and communicating with the people. Never sacrifice sleep, nutrition, safety, or cleanliness to save money. Simply enjoy the local-style alternatives to expensive hotels and restaurants.

Connecting with people carbonates your experience. Extroverts have more fun. If your trip is low on magic moments, kick yourself and make things happen. If you don't enjoy a place, maybe you don't know enough about it. Seek the truth. Recognize tourist traps. Give a culture the benefit of your open mind. See things as different, but not better or worse. Any culture has plenty to share. When an opportunity presents itself, make it a habit to say "yes."

Of course, travel, like the world, is a series of hills and valleys. Be fanatically positive and militantly optimistic. If something's not to your liking, change your liking.

Travel can make you a happier American, as well as a citizen of the world. Our Earth is home to seven billion equally precious people. It's humbling to travel and find that other people don't have the "American Dream"—they have their own dreams. Europeans like us, but with all due respect, they wouldn't trade passports.

Thoughtful travel engages us with the world. It reminds us what is truly important. By broadening perspectives, travel teaches new ways to measure quality of life.

Globetrotting destroys ethnocentricity, helping us understand and appreciate other cultures. Rather than fear the diversity on this planet, celebrate it. Among your most prized souvenirs will be the strands of different cultures you choose to knit into your own character. The world is a cultural yarn shop, and Back Door travelers are weaving the ultimate tapestry. Join in!

GREECE

Hellas / Ελλάς

Slip a coaster under that rickety table leg, take a sip of wine, and watch the sun extinguish itself in the sea. You've arrived in Greece.

Greece offers sunshine, seafood, whitewashed houses with bright-blue shutters, and a relaxed, Zorba-the-Greek lifestyle. As the cradle of Western civilization, it has some of the world's greatest ancient monuments. While it's a late bloomer in the modern age and retains echoes of a simpler time-passed world, contemporary Greece has one of Europe's fastest-changing cultural landscapes. With its classical past, hang-loose present, and edgy future, Greece offers something for every traveler.

This is a great time to travel to Greece. The financial crisis—while making life difficult for most Greeks—is a boon for budget travelers. Hotel prices are down, the normally warm Greek hospitality has ratcheted up a few notches, and roads outside of Athens are essentially traffic-free, as higher gas prices have caused locals to cut down on any inessential driving. The downsides (shorter hours at minor sights, reduced long-distance bus service, occasional strikes) are noticeable, but not reason enough for you to postpone a trip to Greece. Concerns about travelers' safety are wildly unfounded (for my take on this issue, see the sidebar on page 21). All the things you're looking for in a Greek trip—deep-blue water, mouth-watering food, striking scenery, and the thrill of connecting with ancient history—are all here waiting for you...at a cheaper price.

Start in Athens, a microcosm of the country. By day, tour the Acropolis, the Agora, and the history-packed museums. Light a candle alongside an old lady in black at an icon-filled church. Haggle with a sandal maker at the busy market stalls, or have coffee with the locals in a Plaka café. At night, Athens becomes a pan-European party of Greeks, Germans, Brits, and Swedes eating, drinking, and dancing in open-air tavernas. In the colorful This-sio or rickety-chic Psyrri neighborhoods, rub elbows with a trendy new breed of Athenians to get a taste of today's urban Greece.

With its central location, Athens is the perfect launch pad for farther-flung Greek destinations. Commune with ancient spir-

its at the center of the world: the oracle near the picturesque mountain hamlet of Delphi. Take a vacation from your busy vacation on one of the best and easiest-to-reach Greek isles, traffic-free Hydra. For longer island getaways, the picture-perfect, whitewashed village of Mykonos and the dramatically-situated towns overlooking the flooded volcano crater at Santorini are tops.

An hour's drive west of Athens, the Peloponnese is the large peninsula that hangs from the rest of the Greek mainland by the narrow Isthmus of Corinth. Its name, which means "the Island of Pelops," derives from the mythical hero Pelops. This wild, moun-tainous landscape is dotted with the ruins of Mycenaean palaces,

Greece Almanac

Official Name: It's the Hellenic Republic (*Elliniki Dhimokratia* in Greek). In shorthand, that's Hellas—or Greece in English.

Population: Greece is home to 10.8 million people (similar to the state of Ohio). About 93 percent are Greek citizens, and 7 percent are citizens of other countries—mainly Albania, Bulgarian, and Romania. Greece does not collect ethnic data. More than 95 percent are Greek Orthodox, the state religion. A little more than 1 percent are Muslim. The dominant language is Greek.

Latitude and Longitude: 39°N and 22°E. The latitude is the same as Maryland.

Area: With 51,485 square miles, Greece is a bit smaller than Alabama.

Geography: Greece is a mountainous peninsula that extends into the Mediterranean Sea between Albania and Turkey in southern Europe. It includes the Peloponnesian Peninsula—separated from the mainland by a canal—and 3,000 rugged islands (227 are inhabited). Nearly four-fifths of the country's landscape is covered by mountains, the highest of which is Mount Olympus (9,570 feet). About 30 percent of the land is forested. Flat, arable plains are centered in Macedonia, Thrace, and Thessaly. Greece's coastline is the 10th longest in the world at 9,246 miles.

Biggest Cities: One in three Greeks lives in the capital of Athens (about 664,000 in the city, 3.7 million including the greater metropolitan area). Thessaloniki has 385,000 (one million in its urban area).

Economy: Greece has a GDP of $284 billion, with a GDP per capita of $25,000. A European Union member, Greece has used the euro as its currency since 2002. At first, its economy—based

ancient temples, frescoed churches, and countless medieval hilltop castles built by the Crusaders and the Venetians. At Mycenae, visit the hub of a civilization that dominated Greece from 1600 to 1200 B.C. Hike up the stone rows of the world's best-preserved ancient theater, at Epidavros. Run a lap at Olympia, site of the first Olympic Games. To round things out, enjoy the stunning landscapes of the wild Mani Peninsula and the charming old Venetian towns of Monemvasia (a fortified, village-topped giant rock hovering just offshore) and Nafplio (the first capital of independent Greece). As you hop from town to town, compare Greek salads and mountains-and-olive-grove views.

Greece possesses a huge hunk of human history. It's the place that birthed the Olympics; the mischievous gods (Zeus, Hermes, Dionysius); the tall tales of Achilles, Odysseus, and the Trojan War; the rational philosophies of Socrates, Plato, and Aristotle; democracy, theater, mathematics...and the gyro sandwich.

heavily on tourism, shipping, and agriculture—benefited from an infusion of EU cash. But by the end of the decade the country was in a severe recession. In 2010, 2012, and again in 2015, Greece accepted huge bailout packages from the EU and was forced to adopt severe (and controversial) spending cuts and tax increases.

Government: Greece is a parliamentary republic, headed by a largely ceremonial president elected by the parliament. Power resides with the prime minister, chosen from the majority political party. Left-wing coalition leader Alexis Tsipras became prime minister in January 2015.

Flag: A blue square bears a white cross (the symbol of Greek Orthodoxy) in the upper-left corner, against a field of horizontal blue-and-white stripes. The blue is said to stand for the sky and seas, while the white represents the purity of the push for Greek independence. Each of the nine stripes is said to symbolize a syllable in the Greek motto, *Eleutheria e Thanatos,* which translates as "Freedom or Death."

The Average Zorba: The average Greek is 43 years old, will live to be 80, and has 1.4 children. About 80 percent of Greeks have mobile phones. A typical local eats over 60 pounds of cheese a year (mostly feta)—the highest per capita cheese consumption in the world.

Besides viewing impressive remnants of its Golden Age (450-400 B.C.), you'll see Byzantine churches, Ottoman mosques, and Neoclassical buildings marking the War of Independence—all part of Greece's 3,000-year history.

Greece is easy on travelers. Tourism makes up 18 percent of the gross domestic product, and the people are welcoming and accommodating. Greeks pride themselves on a concept called *filotimo* ("love of honor"), roughly translated as openness, friendliness, and hospitality. Social faux pas by unwary foreigners are easily overlooked by Greeks. The food is uncomplicated, the weather is good, and the transportation infrastructure is sufficient.

Greece's geography of mountains, peninsulas, and 3,000 islands divides the Greek people into many regions, each with its distinct cultural differences. "Where are you from?" is a common conversation-starter among Greeks.

Greece is also divided by a severe generation gap. Up until late

GREECE

1974 (when the military junta was ousted), Greek society was traditional, economically backward, and politically repressed. Then the floodgates opened, and Greece has gone overboard trying to catch up with the modern world.

You'll find two Greeces: the traditional/old/rural Greece and the modern/young/urban one. In the countryside, you'll still see men on donkeys, women at the well, and people whose career choice was to herd goats across a busy highway. In the bigger cities, it's a concrete world of honking horns and buzzing mobile phones. Well-dressed, educated Greeks listen to hip-hop music and thumb text messages. As the rural exodus continues, the urban environment is now home to a majority of Greeks. Young Greeks seem to

overcompensate for their country's conservative past with excessive consumerism, trendiness, and antiauthoritarianism.

Still, Greece is unified by language and religion. The Greek Orthodox Church—a rallying point for Greeks during centuries of foreign occupation—remains part of everyday life. Ninety-five percent of all Greeks declare themselves Orthodox, even if they rarely go to church. The constitution gives the Orthodox Church special privileges, blurring church-state separation.

Orthodox elements appear everywhere. Icon shrines dot the highways. Orthodox priests—with their Old Testament beards, black robes, necklaces, cake-shaped hats, and families in tow—mingle with parishioners on street corners and chat on their mobile phones. During the course of the day, Greeks routinely pop into churches to light a candle, asking for favors. Even the young celebrate feast days with their families and make the sign of the cross when passing a church. Greek lives are marked by the age-old rituals of baptism, marriage, and funeral.

It seems like every man in Greece shares the same few names: Georgios, Kostas, Nikos, Vassilis, Dimitris, Constantinos, and Yiannis. That's because many still follow the custom of naming boys after their grandfathers using the names of Orthodox saints. Most surnames seem to have the same endings: -polous, -aikis, or -idis; all mean "son of." Names ending in -ous or -os are usually male; -ou names are female.

Despite modern changes, men and women still live in somewhat different spheres. Women rule the home and socialize at open-air marketplaces. Fewer women join the workforce than in other European countries.

Men rule the public arena. You'll see them hanging out endlessly at coffee shops, playing backgammon, watching soccer games on TV (basketball is also popular), and arguing politics with loud voices and dramatic gestures.

Greeks are family-oriented, with large extended families. Kids live at home until they're married, and then they might just move into a flat upstairs in the same apartment building. The "family" extends to the large diaspora of emigrants. Three million Greek-Americans (including George Stephanopoulos, Pete Sampras, and Tina Fey) keep ties to the home country through their Orthodox faith and their Big Fat Greek Weddings.

The pace of life in Greece remains relaxed. People work in the mornings, then take a midafternoon siesta, when they gather with

their families to eat the main meal of the day. On warm summer nights, even the kids stay up very late. Families spill into the streets to greet their neighbors on the evening stroll. For entertainment, they go out to eat (even poor people), where they order large amounts and share it family-style.

Later, they might gather to hear folk songs sung to a bouzouki, a long-necked mandolin. These days the music is often amplified, fleshed out with a synthesizer, and tinged with pop influences. People still form a circle to dance the traditional dances, with arms outstretched or thrown across one another's shoulders. A few might get carried away, "applaud" by throwing plates or flowers, and dance on the tables into the wee hours.

While pollution still plagues traffic-choked cities and dirty beaches, there are signs of change. Greeks everywhere took great pride in the 2004 Olympics. The country's capital has recently converted traffic-free pedestrian zones, modern public transport, a state-of-the-art airport, a fledgling recycling program, and the stunning Acropolis Museum.

It's easy to surrender to the Greek way of living. With its long history and simple lifestyle, Greece has a timeless appeal.

GREECE'S ECONOMIC CRISIS AND OTHER CHALLENGES

This is a particularly rocky time for the Greeks. Sharing a beer or a coffee with a talkative native can provide you with a lesson in contemporary Greece that's every bit as fascinating as the Classical stuff.

In recent years, Greece has become infamous as one of the world's most troubled economies. Embarrassingly high national debt figures prompted foreign investors to abandon Greek bonds; now, after several hefty EU/International Monetary Fund bailouts, the country is struggling to put its economy back together.

In the view of many observers (and many Greeks), the Greeks have lived beyond their means, worked too little, retired too early, consumed too much, produced too little, enjoyed too much job security, created a real-estate bubble with overvalued properties, and funded too much on a growing deficit. The black market has thrived, and many Greeks practice tax evasion as if it were a fine art (with the predictable effect of limiting tax revenue).

The government itself has been notoriously corrupt and nepotistic. Government employees, with cushy jobs, 100 percent job security, and great benefits, were seen as luxuriating away their work lives in worry-free comfort. Stories of fiscal scandal and fraud fill the news almost daily, sparking public anger. Over the past couple of years, Greece's young people have taken to the streets in constant demonstrations challenging every public institution.

Now the Greek government is scrambling to salvage the economy by raising taxes, cutting back staff, selling off public agencies, and getting more serious about tax collection. This means everything people consume costs more, with a significant chunk of people's income going to the government to rescue the economy. Many businesses have gone bankrupt during the crisis, so there's less competition—which also means higher consumer prices.

The Greek people are also feeling the pinch of cuts to social benefits. For example, Greeks who turned 60 in 2009 are comfortably retired; those who turned 60 in 2010 will need to work seven more years. These austerity measures have triggered strikes and more civil unrest.

Many other countries—including the US—are plagued by similar problems, but Greece is an extreme case, with extreme consequences. If there's a positive outcome from all of this, it's that Greece's economic irresponsibility has sparked a sweeping realization among politicians and political movements across Europe that government pork, corporate corruption, and personal production relative to consumption all need to be recalibrated.

Greece is also grappling with other, somewhat-related issues. Young, well-educated, multilingual Greeks feel that they're

Visiting Greece Despite Unrest and Rumors

I'm sometimes asked if Greece is "safe" for travelers—a question that feels absurd the instant you arrive here. (A magazine I write for didn't want to run my article on Greece, fearing that it would inspire its traveling readers to venture into trouble.) Ask anyone who's been to Greece recently, and you'll learn that safety concerns have been played up by both Greek and international media outlets.

Political protests are indeed a common occurrence, and not just in Athens. You're likely to see plenty of political posters and graffiti, experience a strike or two, and you may even be in town on the same day as an organized demonstration. Like the rest of Europe, Greece has an anarchist fringe element that sees any peaceful demonstration or rally by teachers or doctors at Athens' Parliament building as an opportunity to get media coverage—and it works. Like back home, when it comes to TV news, "If it bleeds, it leads." But most rallies involve zero violence. When violence has broken out, it's all been strictly between police and protesters, not bystanders... and certainly not tourists out for a stroll.

On my last trip here, if it hadn't been for the blaring headlines and shrill news reports calling the demonstrations "riots," I probably wouldn't have been aware of them at all—I was too busy pondering the ancients at the Acropolis and nibbling olives at dinner. I found Greece to be the same old wonderful place...with, perhaps, a few more minor headaches.

Protest rallies are generally scheduled in advance: Your hotelier can tell you if anything's likely to be afoot in a main city square during your visit. Strikes are another nuisance, but generally not prolonged—just a day or two here and there. (Strikes have long been a way of life in Greece; most Greeks see a general strike as an excuse for an impromptu holiday.) If the Metro isn't running, taxis or buses can fill the gaps. Boats to the islands are mostly unaffected, and museums generally remain open. Although strikes have indeed closed the Acropolis once or twice, such closures are rare and are often announced in advance. Check with your hotelier for the latest, and don't leave any must-see sights for the end of your stay.

Travelers are more likely to notice other effects of Greece's economic upheaval: cheaper hotel rates, shorter sightseeing hours, and reduced bus service. But the biggest impact of the crisis on anyone visiting Greece is the satisfaction you'll get from contributing to the economy of a nation dealing with tough times, and the joy that comes with a tourist industry that really appreciates your presence.

overqualified for what their country has to offer and are tempted to go abroad for employment. This "brain drain" of bright young people—which has only been exacerbated by the recent economic woes—is a threat to Greece's future.

At the same time, Greece's once-homogeneous populace is feeling threatened by recently arrived immigrants happy to take low-paying jobs—the woman cleaning your hotel room is likely an immigrant. The culture that gave us the word "xenophobic" is suspicious of threats from abroad. Like other European countries, Greece must figure out how to keep its own cultural identity even as it becomes more of a melting pot. Beyond the cultural issues, Greece is concerned about the financial costs involved. The country is bearing the brunt of the huge wave of immigrants and refugees fleeing the Middle East and North Africa, for whom Greece is the most logical stepping stone into the rest of Europe. Meanwhile, the country's inefficient, underfunded bureaucracy has done a poor job of accommodating the basic needs of the new arrivals.

Greece has, it seems, more than its share of troubles right now. Still, Greeks are optimistic by nature. Most believe that they'll get through these tough economic times. They're quick to point out that, regardless of the economy, the olives remain just as tasty, the water just as blue, and the sun—like the Greek people—just as warm.

GREEK LANGUAGE

Even though the Greek alphabet presents challenges to foreign visitors, communication is not hard. You'll find that most people in the tourist industry—and almost all young people—speak fine English. Many signs and menus (especially in Athens and major tourist spots) use both the Greek and our more familiar Latin alphabet. Greeks realize that it's unreasonable to expect visitors to learn Greek (which has only 14 million speakers worldwide). It's essential for them to find a common language with the rest of the world—especially their European neighbors to the west—so they learn English early and well.

Of course, not everyone speaks English. You'll run into the most substantial language barrier when traveling in rural areas and/or dealing with folks over 60, who are more likely to have learned French as a second

language. Because signs and maps aren't always transliterated into our alphabet (i.e., spelled out using a Latin-letter equivalent), a passing familiarity with the basics of the Greek alphabet is helpful for navigating—especially for drivers (see "Greek Alphabet," below).

There are certain universal English words all Greeks know: hello, please, thank you, OK, pardon, stop, menu, problem, and no problem. While Greeks don't expect you to be fluent in their tongue, they definitely appreciate it when they can tell you're making an effort to pronounce Greek words correctly and use the local pleasantries.

It's nice to learn "Hello" (*"Gia sas,"* pronounced "yah sahs"), "Please" (*"Parakalo,"* pronounced "pah-rah-kah-LOH"), and "Thank you" (*"Efharisto,"* pronounced "ehf-hah-ree-STOH"). Watch out for this tricky point: The Greek word for "yes" is *ne* (pronounced "neh"), which sounds a lot like "no" to us. What's more, the word for "no" is *ohi* (pronounced "OH-hee"), which sounds enough like "OK" to be potentially confusing. For more Greek words, see the "Greek Survival Phrases" on page 519.

Don't be afraid to interact with locals. You'll find that doors open a little more quickly when you know a few words of the language. Give it your best shot.

Greek Alphabet

Most visitors find the Greek alphabet daunting, if not indecipherable. At first, all the signs look like...well, Greek to us. However,

Greek has more in common with English than may be immediately apparent. Technically the world's oldest complete alphabet (Phoenician, its predecessor, had no vowel symbols), Greek is the parent of our own Latin alphabet—itself named for the first two Greek letters (alpha and beta). Because it's used worldwide among mathematicians and scientists (not to mention frat guys), you may recognize some letters from your student days—but that doesn't help much when you're trying to read a map or a menu.

Fortunately, with a little effort the alphabet becomes a lot less baffling. Many uppercase Greek letters look just like their Latin counterparts (such as A, B, and M), and a few more look similar with a little imagination (Δ, Ξ, and Σ look a little like D, X, and S, if you squint). A few look nothing like anything in our alphabet, and a couple are particularly confusing (Greek's P is our R, and Greek's H is our I).

Getting comfortable with the lowercase letters is more chal-

GREECE

Greek from A to Ω

Transliterating Greek to English is an inexact science, but here is the Greek alphabet, with the most common English counterparts for the Greek letters and letter combinations.

Greek	English Name	Common Transliteration	Pronounced
A α	alpha	a	A as in father
B β	beta	b or v	V as in volt
Γ γ	gamma	y or g	Y as in yes or G as in go*
Δ δ	delta	d or dh	TH as in then
E ε	epsilon	e	E as in get
Z ζ	zeta	z	Z as in zoo
H η	eta	i	I as in ski
Θ θ	theta	th	TH as in theme
I ι	iota	i	I as in ski
K κ	kappa	k	K as in king
Λ λ	lambda	l	L as in lime
M μ	mu	m	M as in mom
N ν	nu	n	N as in net
Ξ ξ	xi	x	X as in ox
O o	omicron	o	O as in ocean
Π π	pi	p	P as in pie
P ρ	rho	r	R as in rich (slightly rolled)
Σ σ, ς	sigma	s or c	S as in sun
T τ	tau	t	T as in tip
Υ υ	upsilon	y	Y as in happy
Φ φ	phi	f or ph	F as in file
X χ	chi	ch, h, or kh	CH as in loch (gutturally)
Ψ ψ	psi	ps	PS as in lapse
Ω ω	omega	o or w	O as in ocean

*Gamma is pronounced, roughly speaking, like the English "hard" G only when it comes before consonants, or before the letters a, o, and ou.

lenging. Just like in our alphabet, most lowercase letters are similar to their uppercase versions, but a few bear no resemblance at all.

Once you're familiar with the letters, it's less of a challenge to learn how each is said. Nearly every letter (except P and H) is pronounced roughly like the Latin letter it most resembles. As for the handful of utterly unfamiliar characters, you'll just have to memorize those.

Most Greek words have one acute accent that marks the stressed vowel (such as ά rather than α, έ rather than ε, ί rather than ι, ό rather than ο, and ύ rather than υ). These accents are worth paying attention to, as a change in emphasis can bring a change in meaning. Also, note the list of letter combinations below—pairs of letters that, when together, sound a little different than expected (similar to our own "th" or "ch" combinations).

Learn to recognize and pronounce each letter, and you'll be able to sound out the words you see around you: Μάνη = M-a-n-i, Mani (the peninsula, pronounced MAH-nee). Greek is phonetic—it has rules of pronunciation, and it sticks to them. As you stroll the streets, practice reading aloud—you may be surprised how quickly you'll be able to sound out words.

Certain Greek letter combinations create specific sounds. These include:

Greek		Transliteration	Pronounced
ΑΙ	αι	e	E as in get
ΑΥ	αυ	av/af	AV as in have, or AF as in after
ΕΙ	ει	i	I as in ski
ΕΥ	ευ	ev/ef	EV as in never, or EF as in left
ΟΙ	οι	i	I as in ski
ΟΥ	ου	ou/u	OU as in you
ΓΓ	γγ	ng	NG as in angle
ΓΚ	γκ	ng/g	NG as in angle, or G as in go (at start of word)
ΜΠ	μπ	mb/b	MB as in amber, or B as in bet (at start of word)
ΝΔ	νδ	nd/nt/d	ND as in land, or D as in dog (at start of word)
ΤΣ	τσ	ts	TS as in hats
ΤΖ	τζ	dz	DS as in lands, or DG as in judge

Greek Place Names

One Greek word can be transliterated into English in many different ways. For example, the town of Nafplio may appear on a map or road sign as Navplio, Naufplio, or Nauvplio. Even more confusing, there are actually two different versions of Greek: proper Greek, which was used until the 1950s (and now sounds affected to most Greeks); and popular Greek, a simplified version that is the norm today. This means that even Greeks might use different names for the same thing (for example, the city names Nafplio and Patra are popular Greek, while Nafplion and Patras are formal Greek).

The following list includes the most common English spelling and pronunciation for Greek places. If the Greeks use their own differently spelled transliteration, it's noted in parentheses.

English	Pronounced	Greek Transliteration
Greece (Ellada or Hellas)	eh-LAH-thah, eh-LAHS	Ελλάδα or Ελλάς
Athens (Athina)	ah-THEE-nah	Αθήνα
Delphi	dell-FEE	Δελφοί
Epidavros	eh-PEE-dah-vrohs	Επίδαυρος
Hydra	EE-drah	Ύδρα
Kardamyli	kar-dah-MEE-lee	Καρδαμύλη
Mani	MAH-nee	Μάνη
Monemvasia	moh-nehm-VAH-see-ah	Μονεμβασιά
Mycenae (Mikenes)	my-SEE-nee (mee-KEE-nehs)	Μυκήνες
Mykonos	MEE-koh-nohs	Μύκονοσ
Nafplio	NAF-plee-oh	Ναύπλιο
Olympia	oh-leem-PEE-ah	Ολυμπία
Peloponnese (Peloponnisos)	PEL-oh-poh-neez (pel-oh-POH-nee-sohs)	Πελοπόννησος
Piraeus	pee-reh-AHS	Πειραιάς
Santorini (Thira)	sahn-toh-REE-nee (THEE-rah)	Θήρα

Note that these are the pronunciations most commonly used in English. Greeks might put the emphasis on a different sylla-ble—for example, English-speakers call the Olympics birthplace oh-LEEM-pee-ah, while Greeks say oh-leem-PEE-ah.

ATHENS
ΑΘΉΝΑ / Αθήνα

ORIENTATION TO ATHENS

Though sprawling and congested, Athens has a compact, pleasant tourist zone capped by the famous Acropolis—the world's top ancient site. In this historic town, you'll walk in the footsteps of the great minds that created democracy, philosophy, theater, and more...even when you're dodging motorcycles on "pedestrianized" streets. Romantics can't help but get goose bumps as they kick around the same pebbles that once stuck in Socrates' sandals, with the floodlit Parthenon forever floating ethereally overhead.

Many tourists visit Athens without ever venturing beyond the Plaka (Old Town) and the ancient zone. With limited time, this is not a bad plan, as greater Athens offers few sights (other than the excellent National Archaeological Museum). But for a more authentic taste of the city, visit the fun, thriving districts of Thissio, Psyrri, and Gazi.

Because of its prominent position on the tourist trail and the irrepressible Greek spirit of hospitality, the city is user-friendly. It seems that virtually all Athenians speak English, major landmarks are well-signed, and most street signs are in both Greek and English.

ATHENS: A VERBAL MAP

Ninety-five percent of Athens is noisy, polluted modern sprawl, jammed with characterless, poorly planned, and hastily erected concrete suburbs that house the area's rapidly expanding population. The construction of the Metro for the 2004

Athens Landmarks

Area	Description	Pronounced (Greek Name)
Syntagma	Main square	SEEN-dag-mah
Plaka	Old town	PLAH-kah
Adrianou	Old town's main street	ah-dree-ah-NOO
Akropoli	Acropolis	ah-KROH-poh-lee
Dionysiou Areopagitou / Apostolou Pavlou	Pedestrian walkways near Acropolis	dee-oo-nee-SEE-oo ah-reh-oh-pah-GEE-too / ah-poh-STOH-loo PAW-loo
Archaea Agora	Ancient market	ar-HEH-ah ah-goh-RAH
Monastiraki	Market district	moh-nah-stee-RAH-kee
Psyrri	Nightlife district	psee-REE
Thissio	Western dining district	thee-SEE-oh
Gazi	Artsy district	GAH-zee
Makrigianni / Koukaki	Southern residential and hotel districts	mah-kree-YAH-nee / koo-KAH-kee
Kolonaki	Wealthy museum and residential area	koh-loh-NAH-kee
Exarchia	Edgy student district	ex-AR-hee-yah
Piraeus	Athens' port	pee-reh-AHS

ORIENTATION

Olympics was, in many ways, the first time urban planners had ever attempted to tie the city together and treat it as a united entity.

But most visitors never see that part of Athens. In fact, you can pretend that Athens is the same small charming village at the foot of the Acropolis as it was a century ago. Almost everything of importance to tourists is within a few blocks of the Acropolis. As you explore this city-within-a-city on foot, you'll realize just how small it is.

A good map is a necessity for enjoying Athens on foot. The fine map the TI gives out works great. Get a good map and use it.

Athens by Neighborhood

The Athens you'll be spending your time in includes the following districts:

The Plaka (PLAH-kah, Πλάκα): This neighborhood at the foot of the Acropolis is the core of the tourist's Athens. One of the only parts of town that's atmospheric and Old World-feeling, it's also the most crassly touristic. Its streets are lined with souvenir shops, tacky tavernas, a smattering of small museums, ancient Greek and Roman ruins, and pooped tourists. The Plaka's narrow, winding streets can be confusing at first, but you can't get too lost with a monument the size of the Acropolis looming overhead to keep you oriented. Think of the Plaka as Athens with training wheels for tourists. While some visitors are mesmerized by the Plaka, others find it obnoxious and enjoy venturing outside it for a change of scenery.

Monastiraki (moh-nah-stee-RAH-kee, Μοναστηρακι): This area ("Little Monastery") borders the Plaka to the northwest, surrounding the square of the same name. It's known for its handy Metro stop (where line 1/green meets line 3/blue), seedy flea market, and souvlaki stands. The Ancient Agora is nearby (roughly between Monastiraki and Thissio).

Psyrri (psee-REE, Ψυρή): Formerly a dumpy ghetto just north of Monastiraki, Psyrri is now a cutting-edge nightlife and dining district. Don't be put off by the crumbling, graffiti-slathered buildings...this is one of central Athens' most appealing areas to explore after dark, and for now, locals still outnumber tourists here.

Syntagma (SEEN-dag-mah, Σύνταγμα): Centered on Athens' main square, Syntagma ("Constitution") Square, this urban-feeling zone melts into the Plaka to the south. While the Plaka is dominated by tourist shops, Syntagma is where local urbanites do their shopping. Syntagma is bounded to the east by the Parliament building and the vast National Garden.

Thissio (thee-SEE-oh, Θησείο): West of the Ancient Agora, Thissio is an upscale, local-feeling residential neighborhood with piles of outdoor cafés and restaurants. It's easily accessible thanks to the handy pedestrian walkway bordering the base of the Acropolis.

Gazi (GAH-zee, Γκάζι): At the western edge of the tourist's Athens (just beyond Thissio and Psyrri), Gazi is trendy, artsy, and gay-friendly. Its centerpiece is a former gasworks-turned-events center called Technopolis.

Makrigianni (mah-kree-YAH-nee, Μακρυγιάννη) and **Koukaki** (koo-KAH-kee, Κουκάκι): Tucked just behind (south of) the Acropolis, these overlapping, nondescript urban neighborhoods have a lived-in charm of their own. They're so nondescript that many locals just call Makrigianni the "south Plaka." If you want to escape the crowds of the Plaka, this area—with fine hotels and restaurants within easy walking distance of the ancient sites—makes a good home base.

Kolonaki (koh-loh-NAH-kee, Κολωνάκι): Just north and east of the Parliament/Syntagma Square area, this upscale diplomatic quarter is home to several good museums and a yuppie din-

Athens Neighborhoods

NATIONAL ARCHAEOLOGICAL MUSEUM

OMONIA SQUARE

EXARCHIA

LYKAVITTOS HILL

NAT'L LIBRARY

PANEPISTIMIOU/ ELEFTHERIOU VENIZELOU

ATHINAS

← To Gazi

KOLONAKI

PSYRRI

ERMOU

SYNTAGMA

VASILISSIS SOFIAS

MONASTIRAKI

AGORA

SYNTAGMA SQUARE

PARLIAMENT

THISSIO

ADRIANOU

PLAKA

APOSTOLOU PAVLOU

ACROPOLIS

DIONYSIOU AREOPAGITOU

VASILISSIS AMALIAS

Nat'l Garden

FILOPAPPOS HILL

ACROPOLIS MUSEUM

TEMPLE OF OLYMPIAN ZEUS

MAKRIGIANNI

SYNGROU

KOUKAKI

To Piraeus & Cruise Port

Not to Scale

ORIENTATION

ing zone. It's huddled under the tall, pointy Lykavittos Hill, which challenges the Acropolis for domination of the skyline.

Exarchia (ex-AR-hee-yah, Εξάρχεια): Just beyond Kolonaki is a rough-and-funky student zone. The home of many protesters grabbing Greek headlines, it's a fascinating but not-for-everyone glimpse into an Athens that few tourists experience.

Major Streets: Various major streets define the tourist's Athens. The base of the Acropolis is partially encircled by a broad traffic-free walkway, named **Dionysiou Areopagitou** (Διονυσίου Αρεοπαγίτου) to the south and **Apostolou Pavlou** (Αποστόλου Παύλου) to the west; for simplicity, I call these the "**Acropolis Loop.**" Touristy **Adrianou** street (Αδριανού) curves through the Plaka a few blocks away from the Acropolis' base. Partly pedestrianized **Ermou** street (Ερμού) runs west from Syntagma Square, defining the Plaka, Monastiraki, and Thissio to the south and Psyrri to the north. Where Ermou meets Monastiraki, **Athinas** street (Αθηνάς) heads north to Omonia Square.

The tourist zone is hemmed in to the east by a series of major highways: The north–south **Vasilissis Amalias** avenue (Βασιλίσσης Αμαλίας) runs between the National Garden and the Plaka/Syntagma area. To the south, it jogs around the Temple of Olympian Zeus and becomes **Syngrou** avenue (Συγγρού). To

ORIENTATION

Greek Words and English Spellings

Any given Greek name—for streets, sights, businesses, and more—can be transliterated many different ways in English. Throughout this book, I've used the English spelling you're most likely to see locally, but you will definitely notice variations. If you see a name that looks (or sounds) similar to one in this book, it's likely the same place. For example, the Ψυρρή district might appear as Psyrri, Psyrrí, Psyri, Psirri, Psiri, and so on.

Most major streets in Athens are labeled in Greek in signs and on maps, followed by the transliteration in English. The word ΟΔΟΣ (*odos*) means "street," ΛΕΩΦΟΡΟΣ (*leoforos*) is "avenue," and ΠΛΑΤΕΙΑ (*plateia*) is "square."

If a name used in this book appears locally only in Greek, I've included that spelling to aid your navigation.

the north, at the Parliament, it forks: The eastward branch, **Vasilissis Sofias** (Βασιλίσσης Σοφίας), heads past some fine museums to Kolonaki; the northbound branch, **Panepistimiou** (usually signed by its official name, **Eleftheriou Venizelou**, Ελευθερίου Βενιζέλου), angles northwest past the library and university buildings to Omonia Square.

PLANNING YOUR TIME

Although Athens is a big city, its sights can be seen quickly. The top sights—the Acropolis/Ancient Agora, the Acropolis Museum, and the National Archaeological Museum—deserve a half-day each. Two days total is plenty of time for the casual tourist to see the city's main attractions. To enhance your experience, consider downloading my 🎧 free audio tours of the Athens City Walk and the major sights (see page 10).

Day 1: In the morning, follow my Athens City Walk. Grab a souvlaki lunch near Monastiraki, and spend midday in the markets (shopping in the Plaka, browsing in the Central Market, and wandering through the flea market—best on Sun). After lunch, as the crowds (and heat) subside, visit the ancient biggies: First tour the Ancient Agora, then hike up to the Acropolis (confirming carefully how late it's open). Be the last person off the Acropolis. Stroll down the Dionysiou Areopagitou pedestrian boulevard, then promenade to dinner—in Thissio, Monastiraki, Psyrri, or the Plaka.

Day 2: Spend the morning visiting the Acropolis Museum and exploring the Plaka. After lunch, head to the National Archaeological Museum.

Day 3: Museum lovers will want more time to visit other archaeological sites (especially those included with your Acropolis

Daily Reminder

Sunday: Most sights are open, but the Central Market is closed. The Monastiraki flea market is best to visit today. An elaborate changing of the guard—including a marching band—usually takes place at 11:00 in front of the Parliament building. State-run sights and museums, including the Acropolis, are free on the first Sunday of the month during off-season (Nov-March).

Monday: Many museums and galleries are closed, including the Benaki Museum of Greek History and Culture, Benaki Museum of Islamic Art, Byzantine and Christian Museum, Museum of Greek Popular Instruments, and National War Museum. The Keramikos Cemetery Museum is closed on Mondays off-season (Nov-March).

Tuesday: These sights are closed today: Benaki Museum of Greek History and Culture, Benaki Museum of Islamic Art, Museum of Cycladic Art, and Museum of the City of Athens.

Wednesday: The Benaki Museum of Islamic Art is closed.

Thursday: All major sights are open.

Friday: All major sights are open.

Saturday: All major sights are open, except the Jewish Museum.

Evening Sightseeing: Many sights are open late in summer, often until 20:00. Some sights are open until 20:00 year-round, including the Acropolis Museum (Tue-Sun) and Museum of Cycladic Art (Thu only). The Benaki Museum of Greek History and Culture is open Thursday and Saturday until 24:00. The Acropolis Museum is open Friday until 22:00.

ORIENTATION

Ticket), museums, and galleries. The city has many "also-ran" museums that reward patient sightseers. I'd suggest heading out toward Kolonaki to take in the Benaki Museum of Greek History and Culture, Museum of Cycladic Art, and Byzantine and Christian Museum (and the nearby National War Museum, if you're interested).

Note that a third (or fourth) day could also be used for the long but satisfying side-trip by bus to Delphi or a quick getaway by boat to the isle of Hydra—each more interesting than a third or fourth day in Athens. But these sights—and many others—are better as an overnight stop. For suggestions on an itinerary that gets you out of Athens, see page 6.

TOURIST INFORMATION

The Greek National Tourist Organization (EOT), with its main branch near the Acropolis Museum, covers Athens and the rest of the country. Although their advice can be hit-or-miss, it's worth a stop to pick up their free city map, pocket public transportation

Athens Overview

ORIENTATION

map, *Athens Live* booklet, and their slick, glossy book on Athens. They also have information on museums and hours, entertainment options, and bus and train connections (April-Sept Mon-Fri 8:00-20:00, Sat-Sun 10:00-16:00; Oct-March Mon-Fri 9:00-19:00 or possibly earlier, Sat-Sun 10:00-16:00; on pedestrian street leading to Acropolis Museum at Dionysiou Areopagitou 18-20, Metro: Akropoli; tel. 210-331-0392, www.visitgreece.gr, info@gnto.gr).

Helpful Websites: Though not officially part of the TI, **Matt Barrett's Athens Survival Guide** (www.athensguide.com) is a great resource for anyone visiting Greece. Matt, who splits his time between North Carolina and Greece, splashes through his adopted hometown like a kid in a wading pool, enthusiastically sharing his discoveries and observations on his generous website. While his practical information isn't always the most up-to-date, his perspectives and advice are top-notch. Matt covers emerging neighborhoods that few visitors venture into, and offers offbeat angles on the city and recommendations for vibrant, untouristy restaurants. He also blogs about his latest impressions of the city.

Other useful websites include **Athens Today** (www.athens-today.com) and the online version of the bimonthly Greek lifestyle magazine *Odyssey* (www.odyssey.gr).

ARRIVAL IN ATHENS

For information on arriving in (or departing from) Athens by plane, boat, bus, train, or car, see the Athens Connections chapter.

GETTING AROUND ATHENS

Because Athens is such a huge city, you'll likely use public transportation to reach farther-flung destinations (such as the National Archaeological Museum, the port of Piraeus, or the airport). But most travelers on a short visit find they don't need to take any public transit at all, once they're settled into their hotel—the tourists' core of Athens is surprisingly walkable.

For information on all of Athens' public transportation, see www.oasa.gr. Beware of pickpockets on public transportation.

By Metro

The Metro is the most straightforward way to get around Athens. Just look for signs with a blue M in a green circle. The Metro—mostly built, renovated, or expanded for the 2004 Olympics—is slick and user-friendly. Signs are in both Greek and English, as are announcements inside subway cars. Trains run every

(left margin, rotated) ORIENTATION

Athens Transit

- ▬▬▬ Metro Line 1 (Green)
- ▬▬▬ Metro Line 2 (Red)
- – – – Metro Line 3 (Blue)
- ‑ ‑ ‑ Bus Line w/#
- ┝━┥ Rail
- ▬▬▬ Coastal Tram w/#

Trains to Thessaloniki & Northern Greece

Kifissia

Irini

Line 1 (Green)

Bus Terminal B (Liossion)

Anthoupoli

To Piraeus   #X96

Airport

Aghia Marina

Larissis (Train Stn.)

Attiki

Victoria

NATIONAL ARCHAEO-LOGICAL MUSEUM

Line 3 (Blue)

Egaleo

Omonia

Keramikos

LYKAVITTOS HILL

To Airport

Evangelismos

#X95

Monastiraki

Syntagma

#X96

Thissio

ACROPOLIS

Akropoli

Syngrou-Fix

Neo Faliro

#040 & #X80

Neos Kosmos

N

Piraeus

CRUISE PORT

NEA SMYRNI

Line 2 (Red)

Saronic Gulf

Ferries & Hydrofoils to Islands

Helliniko

To Voula

Not to Scale

ORIENTATION

few minutes on weekdays, and slightly less frequently on weekends (5:00-24:00, later on Fri-Sat, www.stasy.gr).

You can buy tickets at machines or from ticket windows. The **basic ticket** (€1.20, half price if over 65 or under 18) is good for 70 minutes on all public transit, including buses and trams, and covers transfers. Note that you'll need a pricier €8 ticket to go all the way to the airport (cheaper for multiple tickets—see page 197). If planning more than three rides in a day, consider the **24-hour ticket** (€4; doesn't include airport). For a longer visit using lots of public transit, you might get your money's worth with a **five-day ticket** (€10; no airport). If starting and finishing at the airport, consider the **three-day tourist ticket** (€20), which includes a round-trip airport transfer on the Metro or Express bus #X95 as well as unlimited in-city travel on all Metro lines, the suburban railway *(Proastiakos)*, the tram, and bus.

Be sure to stamp your ticket in a validation machine, usually located near the ticket booth, before you board (tickets only need to be stamped the first time). Those riding without a ticket (or with an unstamped ticket) are subject to stiff fines. A multiride ticket is convenient as you just validate it once, tuck it away, and travel with no ticket concerns.

The three Metro lines are color-coded and numbered. Use the end-of-the-line stops to figure out which direction you need to go.

Line 1 (green) runs from the port of Piraeus in the southwest to Kifissia in the northern suburbs. Because this is an older line—officially called ISAP or electrical train *(elektrikos)* rather than Metro—it's slower than the other two lines. Key stops include **Piraeus** (boats to the islands), **Thissio** (enjoyable neighborhood with good restaurants and nightlife), **Monastiraki** (city center), **Victoria** (10-minute walk from National Archaeological Museum), and **Omonia** (15-minute walk from National Archaeological Museum). You can transfer to line 2 at Omonia and to line 3 at Monastiraki (sometimes labeled "Monastirion").

Line 2 (red) runs from Anthoupoli in the northwest to Helliniko (Elliniko) in the southeast. Important stops include **Larissis** (train station), **Syntagma** (city center), **Omonia** (National Archaeological Museum), **Akropoli** (Acropolis and Makrigianni/Koukaki hotel neighborhood), and **Syngrou-Fix** (Makrigianni/Koukaki hotels). Transfer to line 1 at Omonia and to line 3 at Syntagma.

Line 3 (blue) runs from Aghia Marina in the west to the airport in the east. Important stops are **Keramikos** (near Keramikos Cemetery and the lively Gazi district), **Monastiraki** (city center), **Syntagma** (city center), **Evangelismos** (Kolonaki neighborhood, with Byzantine and Christian Museum and National War Museum), and the **Airport** (requires a separate ticket). Transfer to line 1 at Monastiraki and to line 2 at Syntagma.

By Bus and Tram

The usefulness of Athens' other forms of public transit is limited for visitors sticking to the city center sightseeing zone.

Public **buses** can help connect the dots between Metro stops, though the city center is so walkable that most visitors never ride one. A one-way, bus-only ticket costs €1.20; buy tickets at a kiosk or Metro station (unavailable from driver). Some of the newsstands that dot Athens' streets also sell bus tickets. Tickets must be validated in the orange machines as you board. In general, I'd avoid Athens' slow and overcrowded buses, with a few exceptions: Bus **#035** takes you from Athinas street near Monastiraki to the National Archaeological Museum, and bus **#224** links to the museum from Syntagma Square. Bus **#040** goes from Piraeus' cruise-terminal area to Syntagma Square, express bus **#X80** links the cruise terminal to Dionysiou Areopagitou (near the Acropolis Museum), express bus **#X95** zips between the airport and Syntagma Square, and express bus **#X96** connects the airport with Piraeus (airport buses are €5 each, bus info: www.oasa.gr).

The **Athens Coastal Tram**—essentially worthless to tourists—starts at Syntagma and runs 18 miles through the neighborhoods of Neos Kosmos and Nea Smyrni, emerging at the sea near Paleo Faliro. From there it splits: One branch heads north, to the modern stadium and Olympic coastal complex in Neo Faliro; the other runs south, past the marinas and beaches to the Voula neighborhood. The price depends on how many stops you're going (www.stasy.gr).

The city also has various **suburban rail lines,** but you're unlikely to need them. For details, talk to the TI or your hotelier.

By Taxi

Despite the vulgar penchant some cabbies here have for ripping off tourists (especially at the cruise terminals), Athens is a great taxi town. Its yellow taxis are cheap and handy (€3.50 minimum charge covers most short rides in town; after that it's €0.74/km—tariff 1 on the meter, plus surcharges: €1.20 from Piraeus ports and train and bus stations, €4 from the airport—already included in airport flat rate). Between midnight and 5:00 in the morning or outside the city limits, prices are about 50 percent higher (tariff 2). Outside the city limits, you're better off negotiating a rate with your driver rather than using the meter, and you are responsible for any tolls. Baggage costs €0.45 for each large suitcase (generally items over 10 kilograms—about 22 pounds). To avoid rip-offs, make sure the meter is on (unless traveling out of the city) and set to tariff 1 (unless it's the middle of the night). Find out in advance about how much the fare should be (ask at hotel or restaurant).

Hotels and restaurants can call to order a taxi ("radio-taxi"), but there's a €2-4 surcharge. Warning: Cabbies may try to cheat you with a higher surcharge. Hold firm.

Uber is also an option for people who use it at home.

By Private Car with Driver

These companies offer excursions from the cruise terminal for individuals and small groups, as well as transfers and tours from Athens: **George's Taxi,** run by George Kokkotos and his sons, has a solid reputation (tel. 210-963-7030, www.taxigreece.com, georgetaxitours@yahoo.com). **Olympic Traveller** car service, run by Christos Dorzioti, has cars and minivans in Athens and Olympia (tel. 262-402-3908, www.olympictraveller.com, info@olympictraveller.com).

HELPFUL HINTS

Theft Alert: Be wary of pickpockets, especially in crowds. Avoid carrying a wallet in your back pocket, and hold purses or small day bags in front, particularly at the following locations: Monastiraki flea market, Central Market, changing of the guard at the Tomb of the Unknown Soldier, major public transit routes (such as the Metro between the city and Piraeus), at the port, and on the main streets through the Plaka, such as Adrianou and Pandrossou.

Emergency Help: The Tourist Police have a 24-hour help-line in English and other languages for emergencies (tel. 171). Their office, south of the Acropolis in the Makrigianni/Koukaki district, is open 24 hours daily (Veikou 43, tel. 210-920-0724). The American Embassy may also be able to help (business hours tel. 210-720-2414; after-hours tel. 210-729-4444).

Traffic Alert: Streets that appear to be "traffic-free" often are shared by motorcycles or moped drivers weaving their vehicles through the crowds. Keep your wits about you, and don't step into a street—even those that feel pedestrian-friendly—without looking both ways.

Slippery Streets Alert: Athens (and other Greek towns) have some marble-like streets and red pavement tiles that become very slick when it rains. Watch your step.

Check Sight Hours Locally: The hours for sights in Greece are often in flux, and with government spending cuts, some sights have reduced hours. I've listed the posted hours, but check locally for the most up-to-date information.

Free Sights: The Museum of Greek Popular Instruments, National Garden, and all of Athens' churches have no entry fee. The Benaki Museum of Greek History and Culture is free on Thursdays.

Sights and museums run by the state, including the Acropolis, are free on all national holidays and on the first Sunday of the month during off-season (Nov-March).

Internet Access: Bits and Bytes, in the heart of the Plaka, has plenty of terminals, a peaceful ambience, and air-conditioning (€2 minimum, €2.50/hour, can burn your digital photos to DVD, open 24 hours daily, just off Agora Square at Kapnikareas 19, tel. 210-325-3142).

Post Offices: The most convenient post office for travelers is at Syntagma Square (Mon-Fri 7:30-20:30, Sat 7:30-14:30, Sun 9:00-13:30, bottom of the square, at corner with Mitropoleos). A smaller neighborhood office is in Makrigianni (Mon-Fri 8:00-14:00, closed Sat-Sun, Dionysiou Areopagitou 7).

Bookshops: Eleftheroudakis (ΕΛΕΥΘΕΡΟΥΔΑΚΗΣ) is Greece's answer to Barnes & Noble, with a great selection of travel guides and maps, along with a lot of English books (Mon-Fri 9:00-21:00, Sat 9:00-16:00, closed Sun, three blocks north of Syntagma Square at Panepistimiou/Eleftheriou Venizelou 15, tel. 210-305-8440). **Public** at Syntagma Square offers a reasonable variety of English books (tel. 210-324-6210). For locations, see the map on page 187.

Laundry: A full-service **launderette** in the heart of the Plaka will wash, dry, and fold your clothes (about €15/load, same-day service if you drop off by noon; Mon and Wed 8:00-17:00, Tue and Thu-Fri 8:00-20:00, closed Sat-Sun; Apollonos 17, tel. 210-323-2226). **Athens Studios,** one of my recommended accommodations near the Acropolis Museum, operates a self-service launderette (€5 wash, €2 dry, includes soap, daily 8:00-23:00, Veikou 3A—see map on page 170, tel. 210-922-4044).

Updates to This Book: For the latest, see www.ricksteves.com/update.

Tours in Athens

🎧 To sightsee on your own, download my **free audio tours** that illuminate some of Athens' top sights and neighborhoods, including the Acropolis, the Agora, the National Archaeological Museum, and my Athens City Walk (see sidebar on page 10).

ON WHEELS
Bus Tours

Various companies offer half-day, bus-plus-walking tours of Athens that include a guided visit to the Acropolis (about €55). Longer tours also include a guided tour of the Acropolis Museum (€68).

Some companies also offer a night city tour that finishes with dinner and folk dancing at a taverna (€63) and a 90-mile round-trip afternoon drive down the coast to Cape Sounion and the Temple of Poseidon (€43, not worth the time if visiting ancient sites elsewhere in Greece). These buses pick up passengers at various points around town and near most hotels.

The most established operations include the well-regarded **Hop In** (modern comfy buses, narration usually English only, tel. 210-428-5500, www.hopin.com), **CHAT Tours** (tel. 210-323-0827, www.chatours.gr), **Key Tours** (tel. 210-923-3166, www.keytours.gr), and **GO Tours** (tel. 210-921-9555, www.gotours.com.gr). It's convenient to book tours through your hotel; most act as a booking agent for at least one tour company. While hotels do snare a commission, some offer discounts to their guests.

Beyond Athens: Some of these companies also offer day-long tours to Delphi and to Mycenae, Nafplio, and Epidavros (either tour €98 with lunch, €86 without), two-day tours to the monas-

ORIENTATION

teries of Meteora (from €165), and more. **Greek Travelling** offers day trips from Athens to the Peloponnese and mainland, as well as customized private tours of Athens (reasonable rates, mobile 697-320-1213, www.greektravelling.com, info@greektravelling.com; with-it, charming guides Christos and Niki).

Hop-on, Hop-off Bus Tours

Several hop-on, hop-off bus tour companies offer 1.5-hour loops and 24-hour tickets, including **CitySightseeing Athens** (€18, tel. 210-922-0604, www.citysightseeing.gr) and **Athens Open Tour** (€17, tel. 210-881-5207, www.athensopentour.com). The main stop is on Syntagma Square, though you can hop on and buy your ticket at any stop—look for signs around town. Because most of the major sights in Athens are within easy walking distance of the Plaka, I'd use this only if I wanted an overview of the city or had extra time to get to the outlying sights.

Tourist Trains

Two different trains do a sightseeing circuit through Athens' tourist zone. As these goofy little trains can go where big buses can't, they can be useful for people with limited mobility. You can catch the **Sunshine Express** train on Aiolou street along the Hadrian's Library fence at Agora Square, or near the entrance to the Acropolis Museum (€5, hourly 9:30-22:00, Oct-April Sat-Sun only, 50-minute loop, tel. 211-405-5373, www.athensbytrain.gr, info@athensbytrain.com). The **Athens Happy Train** is similar, but offers hop-on, hop-off privileges at a few strategic stops (€6, 2/hour 9:00-24:00, 1-hour loop; catch it at the bottom of Syntagma Square or at Monastiraki Square; tel. 213-039-0888, www.athenshappytrain.com).

ON FOOT
Walking Tours

Athens Walking Tours offers several walks, including just the Acropolis (€29, daily at 11:15, 1.5 hours), the Acropolis and City Tour (€38 plus entry fees, daily at 9:30, 3 hours), and their combo Acropolis, City Tour, and Acropolis Museum Tour (€54 plus entry fees, daily at 9:30, 5.5 hours, reserve in advance, tel. 210-884-7269, mobile 694-585-9662, www.athenswalkingtours.gr, Despina). They also offer a food tour, wine tasting tour, and cooking lesson with dinner (see page 182).

  Context Athens' "intellectual by design" walking tours are geared for serious learners and led by "docents" (historians, architects, and academics) rather than by guides. They cover ancient sites and museums and offer themed walks with topics ranging from food to architecture to the Byzantine era. Their Orientation to Athens tour touches on most of these themes while giving you an overview of the city's highlights (€80 plus entry fees, 2 hours, US tel. 800-691-6036, www.contexttravel.com/city/athens).

Food Tours

A good way to experience Greek culture is through its cuisine. Several companies offer culinary walking tours around Athens (see page 182 for a rundown).

Local Guides

A good private guide can bring Athens' sights to life. While the formal rate is €50 per hour and guides respect this, in practice they often charge less. I've enjoyed working with each of these guides: **Effie Perperi** (mobile 697-739-6659, effieperperi@gmail.com); **Angelos Kokkaliaris** (mobile 697-412-7127, www.athenswalkingguide.com, angelo@athenswalkingguide.com); **Dora Mavrommati** (mobile 694-689-9300, mavrom.dor@gmail.com); **Faye Georgiou** (mobile 697-768-5503, fayegeorgiou@yahoo.gr); and **Anastasia Gaitanou** (mobile 694-446-3109, anastasia2570@yahoo.com).

ORIENTATION

SIGHTS IN ATHENS

The sights listed in this chapter are arranged by neighborhood for handy sightseeing. When you see a 📖 in a listing, it means the sight is covered in much more depth in my Athens City Walk or in one of my self-guided tours. This is why Athens' most important attractions get the least coverage in this chapter—we'll explore them later in the book. A 🎧 means the walk or tour is available as a free audio tour (via my Rick Steves Audio Europe app—see page 10). Some walks and tours are available in both formats—take your pick.

Be aware that open hours at some sights may vary from those printed in this book. Check locally before planning your day.

Note that most of Athens' top ancient sites are covered by the Acropolis combo-ticket (see sidebar). All museums and archaeological sites run by the Ministry of Greek Culture, including the Acropolis, are free on national holidays and the first Sunday of the month from November through March. Children under 18 always get in free to these sights. For more tips on sightseeing, see page 468.

ACROPOLIS AND NEARBY

A broad pedestrian boulevard that I call the "Acropolis Loop" strings together the Acropolis, Mars Hill, Theater of Dionysus, Acropolis Museum, and the Ancient Agora. The Acropolis, the Acropolis Museum, and the Agora are covered in more detail in their respective tour chapters.

▲▲▲Acropolis

The most important ancient site in the Western world, the Acropolis (which means "high city" in Greek) rises gleaming like a beacon above the gray concrete drudgery of modern Athens. This is where the Greeks built the mighty Parthenon—the most famous temple

Acropolis Tickets

A basic Acropolis ticket costs €20 (€10 Nov-March) and covers entry to the Acropolis, as well as access to sights on the north and south slopes, including the Theater of Dionysus. If you plan to visit Athens' other major ancient sites, the €30 Acropolis combo-ticket is the better deal, as it covers not only the Acropolis and Theater of Dionysus, but also the Ancient Agora (€8), Roman Forum (€6), Temple of Olympian Zeus (€6), Library of Hadrian (€4), and Keramikos Cemetery (€8; individual entry prices are cut in half for all of these sights in winter; no winter discount on combo-ticket). The combo-ticket is valid for five days, and since you can buy it at any participating sight, it allows you to skip the ticket-buying line at the Acropolis. The Acropolis-only ticket must be purchased at the Acropolis ticket office.

Note that these sights are always free for those 18 and under. They're also free on national holidays and on the first Sunday of the month from November through March.

on the planet and an enduring symbol of ancient Athens' glorious Golden Age from nearly 2,500 years ago.

This icon of Western civilization was built after a war with Persia. The Athenians had abandoned their city when the Persian king's troops invaded Greece; his soldiers destroyed everything on the Acropolis. But in the naval Battle of Salamis (480 B.C.), the outnumbered Athenians routed the Persians, reclaiming their city. Now at the very peak of its power, Athens became the most popular kid on the block. Other city-states and islands paid cash tributes to be on the winning side. The Athenian ruler, Pericles, spared no expense as he set about rebuilding the Acropolis, transforming it into a complex of lavishly decorated temples to honor the city's patron goddess, Athena.

The four major monuments built during this time—the Parthenon, Erechtheion, Propylaea, and Temple of Athena Nike—survive in remarkably good condition given the battering they've taken over the centuries. Although the Persians, Ottomans, and Lord Elgin were cruel to the Acropolis in the past, the greatest dangers it faces now are acid rain and pollution. Ongoing restoration means that you'll see some scaffolding—but even that can't detract from the greatness of this sight.

Cost and Hours: €20, €10 off-season, €30 Acropolis combo-

SIGHTS

Athens Center

SIGHTS

ticket covers other current sights—see sidebar; open daily May-Sept 8:00-20:00, April and Oct 8:00-19:00, Nov-March 8:00-15:00; main entrance at western end of the Acropolis—from the Ancient Agora, signs point uphill; tel. 210-321-4172, www.culture.gr.

⬐ See the Acropolis Tour chapter or ⌂ download my free audio tour.

▲▲"Acropolis Loop"
(a.k.a. Dionysiou Areopagitou and Apostolou Pavlou)

One of Athens' best attractions, this wide, well-manicured, delightfully traffic-free pedestrian boulevard borders the Acropolis to the south and east. It's composed of two streets with tongue-twisting names—Dionysiou Areopagitou and Apostolou Pavlou (think of them as Dionysus Street and Apostle Paul's Street); for simplicity, I refer to them collectively as the "Acropolis Loop." One of the city's many big improvements made in preparation for its 2004 Olympics-hosting bid, this walkway immediately became a favorite local hangout, with vendors, al fresco cafés, and frequent special events enlivening its cobbles.

Dionysiou Areopagitou, wide and touristy, runs along the southern base of the Acropolis. It was named for Dionysus the Areopagite, first bishop and patron saint of Athens and a member of the ancient Roman-era senate that met atop Mars Hill (described next). The other section, **Apostolou Pavlou**—quieter, narrower, and tree-lined—curls around the western end of the Acropolis and the Ancient Agora. It feels more local and has the best concentration of outdoor eateries (in the Thissio neighborhood). This section was named for the Apostle Paul, who presented himself before Dionysus the Areopagite at Mars Hill.

Where Apostolou Pavlou meets the Thissio Metro stop, you can head west on Ermou—a similarly enjoyable pedestrianized boulevard—to reach the Gazi district's Technopolis and the Keramikos Cemetery. If you head east on Ermou (with traffic), you'll come to Syntagma Square. Or, if you want to encircle the base of the Acropolis, head east on Adrianou, the pedestrian street you'll hit just before the Thissio Metro stop, and stroll through the Plaka on your way back to Dionysiou Areopagitou.

▲Mars Hill (Areopagus)

The knobby, windswept hill crawling with tourists in front of the Acropolis is Mars Hill, also known as Areopagus (from

Areios Pagos, "Ares Hill," refer-ring to the Greek version of Mars). While the views from the Acropolis are more strik-ing, rugged Mars Hill (near the Acropolis' main entrance, at the western end) makes a pleasant perch. As you're climbing Mars Hill, be warned: The stone stairs (and the top of the rock) have been polished to a slippery shine by history, and can be treacherous even when dry. Watch your step and use the metal staircase.

This hill has an interesting history. After Rome conquered Athens in 86 B.C., the Roman overlords wisely decided to extend citizenship to any free man born here. (The feisty Greeks were less likely to rise up against a state that had made them citizens.) Whereas Rome called the shots on major issues, minor matters of local governance were determined on this hill by a gathering of leaders. During this time, the Apostle Paul—the first great Chris-tian missionary and author of about half of the New Testament—preached to the Athenians here on Mars Hill. Paul looked out over the Agora and started talking about an altar he'd seen—presumably in the Agora (though archaeologists can't confirm)—to the "Un-known God." (A plaque embedded in the rock near the stairs con-tains the Greek text of Paul's speech.) Although the Athenians were famously open-minded, Paul encountered a skeptical audience and only netted a couple of converts (including Dionysus the Areop-agite—the namesake of the pedestrian drag behind the Acropolis). Paul moved on to Corinth where he enjoyed a better reception.

Theater of Dionysus

The scant remains of this theater are scattered southeast of the Acropolis, just above the Dionysiou Areopagitou walkway. Dur-ing Roman times, the theater was connected to the Odeon of Herodes Atticus (see page 96) by a long, covered stoa, creating an

ensemble of inviting venues. But its illustrious history dates back well before that: It's fair to say that this is where our culture's great tradition of theater was born. During Athens' Golden Age, Sophocles and others watched their plays performed here. Originally just grass, with a circular dirt area as the stage, the theater was eventually expanded, and stone seating added, to accommodate 17,000 patrons in about 330 B.C., during the time of Alexander the Great. Later the Romans added a raised stage. Because the theater is included in your Acropolis ticket, consider a stroll through its rubble. Plans are afoot to restore the theater to its former greatness.

Cost and Hours: Covered by €20 Acropolis ticket and €30 Acropolis combo-ticket, same hours as the Acropolis, main gate across from Acropolis Museum, tel. 210-322-4625.

▲▲▲Acropolis Museum

This museum is a modern-day temple to the Acropolis. Located at the foot of Athens' famous ancient hill, it contains relics from the Acropolis, including statues of young men and women, gods and goddesses, reliefs that once adorned the hilltop temples, and five of

the six original Caryatids (lady-columns) that once held up the roof of the prestigious Erechtheion temple. But the highlight is a life-size re-creation of the frieze that once wound all the way around the outside of the Parthenon, blending original pieces with copies of panels housed in the British Museum and other collections. Completed in 2009, the stunning glass building is a work of art in itself. The top floor sits slightly askew, like a graduation cap, mimicking the orientation of the Parthenon. The glass walls are designed not only to flood the place with natural light, but also to disappear into the background so that the architecture plays second fiddle to the real stars: the statues and the views of the Acropolis.

Cost and Hours: €5; Mon 8:00-16:00, Tue-Sun 8:00-20:00, Fri until 22:00. The museum faces the south side of the Acropolis from across the broad Dionysiou Areopagitou pedestrian drag, and is right at the Akropoli Metro stop; tel. 210-900-0900, www. theacropolismuseum.gr.

   📖 See the Acropolis Museum Tour chapter.

ANCIENT AGORA AND BEYOND

These sights are listed in geographic order, starting with the Agora and fanning out from there (mostly to the west—see the map on page 35). You can walk to the cemetery and the Gazi district via the wide, pedestrianized Ermou street.

▲▲▲Ancient Agora: Athens' Market

If the Acropolis was Golden Age Athens' "uptown," then the Ancient Agora was "downtown." Although literally and figuratively overshadowed by the impressive Acropolis, the Agora was for eight centuries the true meeting place of the city—a hive of commerce, politics, and everyday bustle. Everybody who was anybody in ancient Athens spent time here, from Socrates and Plato to a visiting missionary named Paul. Built upon, forgotten, and ignored for centuries, the Agora was excavated in the 1930s. Now it's a center of archaeological study and one of the city's top tourist attractions. A visit here lets you ponder its sparse remains, wander through a modest museum in a rebuilt stoa (the Agora Museum), admire its beautifully preserved Temple of Hephaistos, and imagine sharing this hallowed space with the great minds of the ancient world.

Cost and Hours: €8, covered by Acropolis combo-ticket; daily May-Sept 8:00-20:00, April and Oct 8:00-19:00, Nov-March 8:00-15:00; Agora Museum opens at 11:00 on Mon; main entrance on Adrianou—from the Monastiraki Metro stop, walk a block south (uphill, toward the Acropolis); tel. 210-321-0180, www.culture.gr.

☐ See the Ancient Agora Tour chapter or ∩ download my free audio tour.

▲▲Thissio and Psyrri

These two neighborhoods, just west and north (respectively) of the Ancient Agora, offer a real-world alternative to the tourist-clogged, artificial-feeling Plaka. **Thissio,** around the far side of the Acropolis (just follow the main pedestrian drag), has a trendy yuppie vibe and a thriving passel of cafés and restaurants with Acropolis views (see page 193). It also has an appealing open-air cinema. **Psyrri**—the yang to Thissio's yin—is grungy and run-down, but increasingly populated by a wide range of eateries, cafés, and clubs, with everything from dives to exclusive dance halls to crank-'em-out chain restaurants (for details on where to eat, see page 178). While enjoyable at any time of day, both neighborhoods are ideal in the evening—either for dinner or for a stroll afterward.

Benaki Museum of Islamic Art

Sometimes it seems the Greeks would rather just forget the Ottoman chapter of their past...but when you're talking about nearly 400 years, that's difficult to do. If you're intrigued by what Greeks consider a low point in their history, pay a visit to this branch of the prominent, private Benaki Museum (see listing for main branch on page 63). The 8,000-piece collection, displayed in two renovated Neoclassical buildings, includes beautifully painted ceram-

SIGHTS

Athens at a Glance

Sights generally keep consistent morning opening hours but can close earlier than listed in the afternoon. Many closing times depend on the sunset. Check locally.

▲▲▲**Acropolis** The most important ancient site in the Western world, where Athenians built their architectural masterpiece, the Parthenon. **Hours:** Daily May-Sept 8:00-20:00, April and Oct 8:00-19:00, Nov-March 8:00-15:00. See page 44.

▲▲▲**Acropolis Museum** Glassy modern temple for ancient art. **Hours:** Mon 8:00-16:00, Tue-Sun 8:00-20:00, Fri until 22:00. See page 50.

▲▲▲**Ancient Agora** Social and commercial center of ancient Athens, with a well-preserved temple and an intimate museum. **Hours:** Same hours as the Acropolis. See page 50.

▲▲▲**National Archaeological Museum** World's best collection of ancient Greek art, displayed chronologically from 7000 B.C. to A.D. 500. **Hours:** April-Oct daily 8:00-20:00; Nov-March Mon 12:00-17:00, Tue-Sun 8:00-15:00. See page 61.

▲▲**"Acropolis Loop"** Traffic-free pedestrian walkways ringing much of the Acropolis with vendors, cafés, and special events. **Hours:** Always open. See page 48.

▲▲**Thissio and Psyrri** Vibrant nightlife neighborhoods near the center, great for eating, exploring, and escaping other tourists. **Hours:** Always open. See page 51.

▲▲**Anafiotika** Delightful village-like neighborhood draped across the hillside north of the Acropolis. **Hours:** Always open. See page 54.

▲▲**Temple of Olympian Zeus** Remains of the largest temple in ancient Greece. **Hours:** Same hours as the Acropolis. See page 58.

▲▲**Benaki Museum of Greek History and Culture** Exquisite collection of artifacts from the ancient, Byzantine, Ottoman, and modern eras. **Hours:** Wed and Fri 9:00-17:00, Thu and Sat 9:00-24:00, Sun 9:00-15:00, closed Mon-Tue. See page 63.

▲▲**Museum of Cycladic Art** World's largest compilation of Cycladic art, from 4,000 years ago. **Hours:** Mon and Wed-Sat 10:00-17:00, Thu until 20:00, Sun 11:00-17:00, closed Tue. See page 64.

SIGHTS

▲▲**Byzantine and Christian Museum** Fascinating look at the Byzantines, who put their own stamp on Greek and Roman culture. **Hours:** April-Oct daily 8:00-20:00; Nov-March Tue-Sun 9:00-16:00, closed Mon. See page 65.

▲**Mars Hill** Historic spot—with a classic view of the Acropolis— where the Apostle Paul preached to the Athenians. **Hours:** Always open. See page 48.

▲**Gazi** Former industrial zone, now the colorful and kinetic heart of Athens' gay community. **Hours:** Always open. See page 54.

▲**Roman Forum and Tower of the Winds** Ancient Roman marketplace with wondrously intact tower. **Hours:** Daily 8:00-15:00, possibly open later in summer. See page 55.

▲**Museum of Greek Popular Instruments** Musical instruments from the 18th century to today. **Hours:** Tue and Thu-Sun 10:00-14:00, Wed 12:00-18:00, closed Mon. See page 55.

▲**Jewish Museum of Greece** Triumphs—and persecutions—of Greek Jews since the second century B.C. **Hours:** Mon-Fri 9:00-14:30, Sun 10:00-14:00, closed Sat. See page 56.

▲**Syntagma Square** Famous public space with a popular changing-of-the-guard ceremony. **Hours:** Always open, guards change five minutes before the top of each hour. See page 56.

▲**Church of Kapnikarea** Small 11th-century Byzantine church with symbols of Greek Orthodox faith. **Hours:** Likely open daily 8:30-13:30 plus Tue and Thu-Fri 17:00-19:30. See page 57.

▲**Church of Agios Eleftherios** Tiny Byzantine church decorated with a millennia of Christian bric-a-brac. **Hours:** Likely open daily 8:30-13:30 & 17:00-19:30. See page 58.

▲**Panathenaic (a.k.a. "Olympic") Stadium** Gleaming marble stadium restored to its second-century A.D. condition. **Hours:** Daily March-Oct 8:00-19:00, Nov-Feb 8:00-17:00. See page 60.

▲**Museum of the City of Athens** Exhibits about Athenian history, housed in a former royal residence. **Hours:** Mon and Wed-Fri 9:00-16:00, Sat-Sun 10:00-15:00, closed Tue. See page 67.

SIGHTS

ics, a rare 14th-century astrolabe, and an entire marble room from a 17th-century Cairo mansion.

Cost and Hours: €7, Thu-Sun 9:00-17:00, closed Mon-Wed, northeast of Keramikos Cemetery at Agion Asomaton 22, on the corner with Dipilou, Metro: Thissio, tel. 210-325-1311, www.benaki.gr.

Keramikos Cemetery

Named for the ceramics workshops that used to surround it, this is a vast place to wander among marble tombstones from the seventh century B.C. onward. While the sprawling cemetery provides more exercise than excitement—and requires a good imagination to take on much meaning—the small, modern museum is a delight. With a wealth of artifacts found right here, it explains the evolution of ancient burial rituals one age at a time.

Cost and Hours: €8, covered by Acropolis combo-ticket; daily May-Sept 8:00-20:00, April and Oct 8:00-19:00, Nov-March 8:00-15:00 except closed Mon; air-con, Ermou 148, Metro stops: Thissio or Keramikos, tel. 210-346-3552.

▲Gazi

Just beyond Keramikos Cemetery, this former industrial zone is now the center of the city's gay community. Recent gentrification is transforming it into one of central Athens' most interesting neighborhoods. For a visit, try one of my recommended eateries (see page 180).

Gazi huddles around the Technopolis events center complex, built in the remains of a 19th-century gasworks. Technopolis hosts an eclectic assortment of cultural happenings, including art exhibits, rock concerts, and experimental theater. After dark, the still-standing smokestacks are illuminated in red, giving an eerie impression of its former industrial activity (Pireos 100, Metro: Keramikos—as you exit, walk to the square brick smokestacks, tel. 210-346-1589, www.technopolis-athens.com).

IN THE PLAKA AND MONASTIRAKI

These sights are scattered around the super-central Plaka neighborhood. The first three sights are covered in more detail in the Athens City Walk 📖 chapter and 🎧 audio tour.

▲▲Anafiotika

Clinging to the northern slope of the Acropolis (just above the Plaka), this improbable Greek-island-on-a-hillside feels a world apart from the endless sprawl of concrete and moped-choked streets that stretch from its base. For a break from the big city, escape here for an enjoyable stroll.

▲Roman Forum
(a.k.a. "Roman Agora")
and Tower of the Winds

After the Romans conquered Athens in 86 B.C., they built their version of an agora—the forum—on this spot. Today it's a pile of ruins, watched over by the marvelously intact Tower of the Winds. Panels circling the top of the tower depict the eight winds that shape Athenian weather. The ticket office and entry gate are near the tallest standing colonnade, and the tower is explained on a plaque.

Cost and Hours: €6, covered by Acropolis combo-ticket, daily 8:00-15:00, possibly open later in summer, corner of Pelopida and Aiolou streets, Metro: Monastiraki, tel. 210-324-5220.

Library of Hadrian

About a block from the Roman Forum, down Aiolou street, is an area of Roman ruins containing what's left of the Library of Hadrian (erected A.D. 132-131), along with a few remains of various churches that were built in later periods, including a fifth-century tetraconch church (with four semicircular apses) and a simple 12th-century church. Tucked away in a corner building is a 10-foot statue of Nike stepping on a globe, uncovered in 1988.

Cost and Hours: €4, covered by Acropolis combo-ticket, daily 8:00-15:00, possibly open later in summer, across from Agora Square, Metro: Monastiraki, tel. 210-324-5220.

▲Museum of Greek Popular Instruments

Small but well-presented, this charming old place is one of the most entertaining museums in Athens. On its three floors, you can wander around listening (on headphones) to different instruments and styles of music. Examine instruments dating from the 18th century to today, including flutes, clarinets, bagpipes, drums, fiddles, violins, mandolins, bells, and even water whistles. Photos and paintings illustrate the instruments being played, and everything is described in English. This easily digestible collection is an enjoyable change of pace from more of the same old artifacts.

Cost and Hours: Free, Tue-Sun 8:00-15:00, closed Mon, near Roman Forum at Diogenous 1, Metro: Monastiraki, tel. 210-325-0198, www.culture.gr.

Museum of Greek Folk Art (Ceramics Collection)

Housed in the old mosque overlooking Monastiraki Square, this museum contains mostly pieces from the early 20th century, with an emphasis on traditional Greek and Cypriot workshops. Each item is accompanied by a brief description of the artist who crafted it. With its rainbow-painted niche, the mosque interior is more interesting than the collection.

Cost and Hours: May be closed for renovation—call ahead or check locally for updates, just off Monastiraki Square—entrance along fence to right of mosque, Metro: Monastiraki, tel. 210-322-9031, www.culture.gr.

Museum of Greek Folk Art (Main Collection)

This museum, reopening in 2017 in a new location near Monastiraki Square, displays four centuries (17th-20th) of items relating to Greek life. The collection includes traditional artwork, folk costumes, plus a look at religion, food, and where and how Greeks lived in earlier times.

Cost and Hours: Closed for renovation—call ahead or check locally for updates, tel. 210-322-9031, www.culture.gr.

▲Jewish Museum of Greece

Many Jewish communities trace their roots back to medieval Spain's Sephardic diaspora and, before that, to classical Greece. (Before the Nazis invaded, Greece had 78,000 Jews; more than 85 percent of them perished in the Holocaust.) This collection of more than 8,000 Jewish artifacts—thoughtfully displayed on four floors of a modern building—traces the history of Greek Jews since the second century B.C. Downstairs from the entry, you can visit a replica synagogue with worship items. Then spiral up through the split-level space (borrowing English descriptions in each room) to see exhibits on Jewish holidays, history, Zionism, the Nazi occupation and Holocaust, traditional dress, and the everyday lives of Greek Jews.

Cost and Hours: €6, Mon-Fri 9:00-14:30, Sun 10:00-14:00, closed Sat; Nikis 39, at the corner with Kidathineon—ring bell to get inside; Metro: Syntagma, tel. 210-322-5582, www.jewishmuseum.gr.

IN SYNTAGMA

The Syntagma area borders the Plaka to the north and east. All of these sights are covered in detail in the Athens City Walk 📖 chapter and 🎧 audio tour. I've listed only the essentials here.

▲Syntagma Square (Plateia Syntagmatos)

The "Times Square" of Athens is named for Greece's historic 1843 constitution, prompted by demonstrations right on this square. A major transit hub, the square is watched over by Neoclassical masterpieces such as the Hotel Grande Bretagne and the Parliament building.

Parliament

The former palace of King Otto is now a house of democracy. In front, colorfully costumed evzone guards stand at attention at the

Tomb of the Unknown Soldier and periodically do a ceremonial changing of the guard to the delight of tourists (guards change five minutes before the top of each hour, less elaborate crossing of the guard around :25 after, full ceremony with marching band Sundays at 11:00—get there early as they may start a bit before 11:00).

Ermou Street

This pedestrianized thoroughfare, connecting Syntagma Square with Monastiraki (and on to Thissio and Keramikos Cemetery), is packed with top-quality international shops. While most Athenians can't afford to shop here, it's enjoyable for people-watching and is refreshingly traffic-free in an otherwise congested area.

CHURCHES IN THE PLAKA AND SYNTAGMA AREA

All of these sights are covered in detail in the Athens City Walk 📖 chapter and 🎧 audio tour. Only the basics are listed here.

▲Church of Kapnikarea

Sitting unassumingly in the middle of Ermou street, this small 11th-century Byzantine church offers a convenient look at the Greek Orthodox faith.

Cost and Hours: Free, likely open daily 8:30-13:30 plus Tue and Thu-Fri 17:00-19:30.

Cathedral (Mitropolis)

Dating from the mid-19th century, this big but stark head church of Athens—and therefore of all of Greece—is covered in scaffolding. The cathedral is the centerpiece of a reverent neighborhood, with a pair of statues out front honoring great heroes of the Church, surrounding streets lined with religious paraphernalia shops (and black-cloaked, long-bearded priests), and the cute little Church of Agios Eleftherios (described next).

Cost and Hours: Free, generally open daily 8:00-13:00 & 16:30-19:00, no afternoon closure in summer, Plateia Mitropoleos.

▲Church of Agios Eleftherios

This tiny church, huddled in the shadow of the cathedral, has a delightful hodge-podge of ancient and early Christian monuments embedded in its facade. Like so many Byzantine churches, it was partly built (in the late 12th century) with fragments of earlier buildings, monuments, and even tombstones. Today it's a giant *Da Vinci Code*-style puzzle of millennia-old bits and pieces.

Cost and Hours: Free, likely open daily 8:30-13:30 & 17:00-19:30, Plateia Mitropoleos.

EAST OF THE PLAKA

These two sights, dating from Athens' Roman period, overlook a busy highway at the edge of the tourist zone (just a few steps up Dionysiou Areopagitou from the Acropolis Museum and Akropoli Metro stop, or a 10-minute walk south of Syntagma Square). Both are described in greater detail in the Athens City Walk 📖 chapter and 🎧 audio tour.

▲Arch of Hadrian

This stoic triumphal arch stands at the edge of the new suburb of ancient Athens built by the Roman Emperor Hadrian in the second century A.D. (always viewable).

▲▲Temple of Olympian Zeus

Started by an overambitious tyrant in the sixth century B.C., this giant temple was not completed until Hadrian took over seven centuries later. Now 15 of the original 104 Corinthian columns stand evocatively over a ruined base in a field. You can get a good view of the temple ruins through the fence by the Arch of Hadrian, but if you have purchased the Acropolis combo-ticket, you can easily drop in for a closer look.

Cost and Hours: €6, covered by Acropolis combo-ticket;

daily May-Sept 8:00-20:00, April and Oct 8:00-19:00, Nov-March 8:00-15:00; Vasilissis Olgas 1, Metro: Akropoli; tel. 210-922-6330, www.culture.gr.

SOUTH AND EAST OF THE PARLIAMENT AND SYNTAGMA SQUARE

The busy avenue called Vasilissis Amalias rumbles south of Syntagma Square, where you'll find the following sights. Note that the Arch of Hadrian and the Temple of Olympian Zeus (both described earlier) are just south of the National Garden and Zappeion.

National Garden

Extending south from the Parliament, the National Garden is a wonderfully cool retreat from the traffic-clogged streets of central Athens. Covering an area of around 40 acres, it was planted in 1839 as the palace garden, created for the pleasure of Queen Amalia. Opened to the public in 1923, the garden has many pleasant paths, a café, WCs, scattered picturesque ancient columns, a playground, and several zoo-type exhibits of animals.

Cost and Hours: Free, open daily from dawn to dusk.

Zappeion

At the southern end of the National Garden stands the grand mansion called the Zappeion, surrounded by formal gardens of its own. To most Athenians, the Zappeion is best known as the site of the Aigli Village outdoor cinema in summer (behind the building, on the right as you face the colonnaded main entry; for details, see page 192). But the building is more than just a backdrop. During Ottoman rule, much of the Greek elite, intelligentsia, and aristocracy fled the country. They returned after independence and built grand mansions such as this. Finished in 1888, it was designed by the Danish architect Theophilus Hansen, who was known (along with his brother Christian) for his Neoclassical designs. The financing was provided by the Zappas brothers, Evangelos and Konstantinos, two of the prime movers in the campaign to revive the Olympic Games. This mansion housed the International Olympic Committee during the first modern Olympics in 1896 and served as a media center during the 2004 Olympics. Today the Zappeion is a conference and exhibition center.

Cost and Hours: Gardens free and always open, building only open during exhibitions for a fee, Vasilissis Amalias, Metro: Akropoli or Evangelismos.

▲Panathenaic (a.k.a. "Olympic") Stadium

In your travels through Greece, you'll see some ruined ancient stadiums (including the ones in Olympia and Delphi). Here's your chance to see one intact. This gleaming marble stadium has many names. Officially it's the Panathenaic Stadium, built in the fourth century B.C. to host the Panathenaic Games. Sometimes it's referred to as the Roman Stadium, because it was rebuilt by the great Roman benefactor Herodes Atticus in the second century A.D., using the same prized Pentelic marble that was used in the Parthenon. This magnificent white marble gives the place its most popular name: Kalimarmaro ("Beautiful Marble") Stadium. It was restored to its Roman condition in preparation for the first modern Olympics in 1896. It saw Olympic action again in 2004, when it provided a grand finish for the marathon and a wonderful backdrop for the Paralympics opening ceremony. Today, it's occasionally used for ceremonies and concerts. In ancient times, around 50,000 spectators filled the stadium; today, 45,000 people can pack the stands.

Cost and Hours: €5, includes good audioguide, daily March-Oct 8:00-19:00, Nov-Feb 8:00-17:00, southeast of the Zappeion off Vasileos Konstantinou, Metro: Akropoli or Evangelismos, tel. 210-752-2985, www.panathenaicstadium.gr.

NORTH OF MONASTIRAKI

Athinas street leads north from Monastiraki Square to Omonia Square. Walking this grand street offers a great chance to feel the pulse of modern workaday Athens, with shops tumbling onto broad sidewalks, striking squares, nine-to-fivers out having a smoke, and lots of urban energy. Central Market is on the way to Omonia Square (see map on page 35). Farther up Athinas street past Omonia Square is the superb National Archaeological Museum.

Central Market

Take a vibrant, fragrant stroll through the modern-day version of the Ancient Agora. It's a living, breathing, and smelly barrage on all the senses. You'll see dripping-fresh meat, livestock in all stages of dismemberment, still-wriggling fish, exotic nuts, and sticky figs. It may not be Europe's most colorful or appealing market, but it offers a lively contrast to Athens' ancient sites.

Hours: Mon-Sat 7:00-15:00, closed Sun, on Athinas between Sofokleous and Evripidou, between Metro stops Omonia and Monastiraki.

Visiting the Market: The entire market square is a delight to explore, with colorful and dirt-cheap souvlaki shops and a carnival of people-watching. The best and cheapest selection of whatever's in season is at the fruit and vegetable stalls, which spread across Athinas street downhill to the west and are flanked by shops selling a dozen different kinds of olives and feta from the barrel. Meat and fish markets are housed in the Neoclassical building to the east, behind a row of shops facing Athinas street that specialize in dried fruit and nuts. Try the roasted almonds and the delicious white figs from the island of Evia. For a memorable drink and snack, seek out the **Karayiannis Ouzo Bar** in the market's fish section (see listing on page 184 for details).

▲▲▲National Archaeological Museum

This museum is the single best place on earth to see ancient Greek artifacts. Strolling through the chronologically displayed collection—from 7000 B.C. to A.D. 500—is like watching a time-lapse movie of the evolution of art. You'll go from the stylized figurines of the Cycladic Islands, to the golden artifacts of the Mycenaeans (including the so-called Mask of Agamemnon), to the stiff, stoic kouros statues of the Archaic age. Then, with the arrival of the Severe style (epitomized by the *Artemision Bronze*), the art loosens up and comes to life. As Greece enters the Classical Period, the *Bronze Statue of a Youth* is balanced and lifelike. The dramatic *Artemision Jockey* hints at the unbridled exuberance of Hellenism, which is taken to its extreme in the *Statue of a Fighting Gaul*. Rounding out the collection are Roman statuary, colorful wall paintings from Thira (today's Santorini), and room upon room of ceramics.

Cost and Hours: €10, €5 off-season; April-Oct daily 8:00-20:00; Nov-March Mon 12:00-17:00, Tue-Sun 8:00-15:00; live guides available for hire in lobby; 28 Oktovriou (a.k.a. Patission) #44, a 15-minute walk from Metro: Omonia Metro or 10 minutes from Metro: Victoria—see page 36 for transit options; tel. 213-214-4800, www.namuseum.gr.

📖 See the National Archaeological Museum Tour chapter or 🎧 download my free audio tour.

SIGHTS

Exarchia

For an edgier taste of Athens, wander into Exarchia, just a short walk behind the National Archaeological Museum. Wedged be-

tween the National Technical University, Omonia Square, and Lykavittos Hill, Exarchia is nicknamed the city's "New Berlin." As you roam its colorful streets, you'll begin to under-stand why.

Populated mostly by stu-dents, immigrants, and coun-terculture idealists, Exarchia is defiant, artsy, coated in graffiti,

and full of life. According to locals, many of the anarchists who are the firepower behind Athens' violent protests call this area home. While Exarchia sounds intimidating—and is a bit farther afield than other areas described in this book—with a sense of adventure and an extra helping of common sense, it can be a fascinating and worthwhile area to wander.

From the small Exarchia Square, side streets spin off into grungy neighborhoods. Mainstream businesses tend to steer clear

of this area; instead, streets are lined with alternative boutiques, record stores, and cafés. About two blocks south of the main square—at the corner of Mesolongiou and Tzabella streets—is a memorial to Alexandros Grigoropou-los, a local teen who was shot and killed here in

December 2008 when police fired into a crowd of protestors. The incident sparked an attention-grabbing wave of riots across Greece, and ever since, frustrated neighbors keep the cops out and do their own policing. The juxtaposition between Exarchia and the adja-cent, very ritzy Kolonaki district makes the tragedy even more poi-gnant. (You might notice that Exarchia's border with Kolonaki is marked by Athens police vans.)

With its penchant for riots and protests, Exarchia feels less safe than other Athens neighborhoods. It can be dangerous. For some people this is the seedy underbelly of Athens they came to see; others can't wait to get back to the predictable souvlaki stands and leather salesmen of the Plaka. If you do venture here, exer-cise caution, try to avoid conflict, and, unless you're street-smart

SIGHTS

and comfortable in gritty urban neighborhoods, think twice before wandering around after dark.

THE KOLONAKI MUSEUM STRIP, EAST OF SYNTAGMA SQUARE

The district called Kolonaki, once the terrain of high-society bigwigs eager to live close to the Royal Palace (now the Parliament), is today's diplomatic quarter. Lining the major boulevard called Vasilissis Sofias are many embassies, a thriving local yuppie scene, and some of Athens' top museums outside the old center. These are listed in the order you'd reach them, heading east from the Parliament (see map on page 35).

▲▲Benaki Museum of Greek History and Culture

This exquisite collection takes you on a fascinating walk through the ages. And, as it's housed in a gorgeous Neoclassical mansion, it gives a peek at how Athens' "one percent" lived back in the 19th century. The mind-boggling array of artifacts—which could keep a museum lover busy for hours—is crammed into 36 galleries on four floors, covering seemingly every era of history: antiquity, Byzantine, Ottoman, and modern. The private collection nicely complements the many state-run museums in town. Each item is labeled in English, and it's all air-conditioned. The Benaki gift shop is a fine place to buy jewelry (replicas of museum pieces).

Cost and Hours: €7, free entry on Thu; open Wed and Fri 9:00-17:00, Thu and Sat 9:00-24:00, Sun 9:00-15:00, closed Mon-Tue; classy rooftop café where some of today's high society hang out, across from back corner of National Garden at Koumbari 1, Metro: Syntagma, tel. 210-367-1000, www.benaki.gr.

Visiting the Museum: The first exhibit kicks things off by saying, "Around 7000 B.C., the greatest 'revolution' in human experience took place: the change from the hunting-and-gathering economy of the Paleolithic Age to the farming economy of the Neolithic Age..." You'll see fine painted vases, gold wreaths of myrtle leaves worn on heads 2,300 years ago, and evocative Byzantine icons and jewelry. Look for Byzantine icon art, including two pieces by Domenikos Theotokopoulos before he became El Greco (glass case in center of room).

Upstairs, the first floor picks up where most Athens museums leave off: the period of Ottoman and Venetian occupation. Here you'll find traditional costumes, furniture, household items, farm implements, musical instruments, and entire rooms finely carved from wood and lovingly transplanted from Northern Greece. In Rooms 22 and 23, a fascinating exhibit shows Greece through the eyes of foreign visitors, who came here in the 18th and 19th centuries

SIGHTS

(back when Athens was still a village, spiny with Ottoman minarets) to see the same ruins you're enjoying today.

Climb up through smaller rooms to the café and exhibit hall (which has good temporary exhibits). On the top floor, Romantic art depicts Greece's stirring and successful 19th-century struggle for independence. Finally, one long hall brings you into the 20th century.

▲▲Museum of Cycladic Art

This modern, cozy, enjoyable, and manageable museum shows off the largest exhibit of Cycladic art anywhere, collected by one of Greece's richest shipping families (the Goulandris clan). While you can see Cycladic art elsewhere in Athens (such as in the National Archaeological Museum), it's displayed and described most invitingly here. While the first floor is all Cycladic, there are four floors—each with a fine exhibit. Note that the museum's entrance is a few steps up the side street (Neophytou Douka); the more prominent corner building, fronting Vasilissis Sofias, is their larger annex (or "New Wing"), hosting special exhibits. A pleasant café is near the gift shop on the ground floor.

Cost and Hours: €7, half-price on Mon and off-season; open Mon and Wed-Sat 10:00-17:00, Thu until 20:00, Sun 11:00-17:00, closed Tue and many religious holidays; Neophytou Douka 4, Metro: Evangelismos, tel. 210-722-8321, www.cycladic.gr.

Visiting the Museum: The **first floor** up focuses on art from the Cycladic Islands, which surround the isle of Delos, off the coast southeast of Athens. The Aegean city-states here—predating Athens' Golden Age by 2,000 years—were populated by a mysterious people who left no written record. But they did leave behind an ample collection of fertility figurines. These come in different sizes but follow the same general pattern: skinny, standing ramrod-straight, with large alien-like heads. Some have exaggerated breasts and hips, giving them a violin-like silhouette. Others (likely symbolizing pregnancy) appear to be clutching their midsections with both arms. These items give an insight into the matriarchal cultures of the Cycladic Islands. With their astonishing simplicity, the figurines appear almost abstract, as if Modigliani or Picasso had sculpted them.

While that first floor is the headliner, don't miss three more floors of exhibits upstairs: ancient Greek art, Cypriot antiquities, and scenes from daily life in antiquity. The highlight—for some, even better than the Cycladic art itself—is the engrossing **top-floor exhibit** that explains ancient Greek lifestyles. Artifacts, engaging illustrations, and vivid English descriptions resurrect a fun cross-section of the fascinating and sometimes bizarre practices of the ancients: weddings, athletics, agora culture, warfare, and various female- and male-only activities (such as the male-bonding/dining ritual called the symposium). Listen for the music that accompanies the exhibit—historians' best guess at what the ancients listened to. One movie uses actors and colorful sets to dramatize events in the life of "Leon," a fictional young man of ancient Greece. Another movie demonstrates burial rituals (for the dearly departed Leon), many of which are still practiced by Orthodox Christians in Greece today.

▲▲Byzantine and Christian Museum

This excellent museum displays key artifacts from the Byzantine Empire, covering the chapters of the Greek story that come after

its famed Golden Age. It traces the era from Emperor Constantine's move from Rome to Byzantium (which he renamed Constantinople, now known as Istanbul) in A.D. 330 until the fall of Constantinople to the Ottomans in 1453. While the rest of Europe fell into the Dark Ages, Byzantium shone brightly. And, as its dominant language and education were Greek, today's Greeks proudly consider the Byzantine Empire "theirs." Outside of the Golden Age of antiquity, the Byzantine era is considered the high-water mark for Greek culture.

Cost and Hours: €8; April-Oct daily 8:00-20:00; Nov-March Tue-Sun 9:00-16:00, closed Mon; excellent café/restaurant, Vasilissis Sofias 22, Metro: Evangelismos, tel. 210-213-9501, www.byzantinemuseum.gr.

Visiting the Museum: The museum consists of two buildings around an entry courtyard. The building in the center sells tickets and hosts temporary exhibits, while the one on the left features the permanent collection, which sprawls underground through the complex and is thoughtfully described in English.

The permanent exhibit—organized both chronologically and thematically—traces the story of the Byzantine Empire, from the waning days of antiquity through the fledgling days of early Christianity and on to the glory days of Byzantium. It's divided into two sections.

The **first section,** "From the Ancient World to Byzantium," explains how the earliest Byzantine Christians borrowed artistic forms from the Greek and Roman past and adapted them to fit their emerging beliefs. For example, the classical Greek motif of the calf bearer became the "good shepherd" of Byzantine Christianity, while early depictions of Jesus are strikingly similar to the Greek "philosopher" prototype. You'll also view mosaics and capitals from the earliest "temples" of Christianity and see how existing ancient temples were "Christianized" for new use. Other topics include Coptic art (from Egyptian Christians) and graves and burial customs.

The **second section**, "The Byzantine World," delves into various facets of Byzantium—the administration of a vast empire, the use of art in early Christian worship, wall paintings transplanted from a Byzantine church, the role of Athens (and the surrounding region of Attica) in the Byzantine Empire, the introduction of Western European artistic elements by Frankish and Latin Crusaders during the 13th century, everyday countryside lifestyles (to balance out all that stuffy ecclesiastical art), the final artistic flourishing of the 13th and 14th centuries, and the fall of Constantinople (and the Byzantine emperor) to Ottoman Sultan Mehmet the Conqueror. Altogether, it's a fascinating place to learn about a rich and often-overlooked chapter of Greek history.

National War Museum

This imposing three-story museum documents the history of Greek warfare, from Alexander the Great to today. The overtly patriotic exhibit, staffed by members of the armed forces, stirs the Greek soul. Start by riding the elevator upstairs to the first floor. Here you'll get a quick chronological review of Greek military history, including replicas of ancient artifacts you'll see for real in other museums—fine history lessons in early war technology. The mezzanine level focuses on the Greek experience in the 20th century, including World War I (with amazing video clips) and World War II (Nazi occupation, resistance, and liberation). Back on the ground floor you'll parade past military uniforms, browse an armory of old weapons, and (outside) ogle modern military machines—tanks, fighter jets, and more (visible from the street, even when the museum is closed).

Cost and Hours: €3, May-Oct Tue-Sat 9:00-19:00, Sun 9:00-17:00, closed Mon, closes two hours earlier off-season, Rizari 2 at Vasilissis Sofias, Metro: Evangelismos, tel. 210-725-2975, www.warmuseum.gr.

NORTH OF SYNTAGMA SQUARE

A few blocks up from Syntagma Square and the traffic-free Ermou street thoroughfare are more museums, including the impressive National History Museum, the Numismatic Museum (i.e., coins), and this place:

SIGHTS

▲Museum of the City of Athens

Housed in the former residence of King Otto and Queen Amalia (where they lived from 1836 to 1843), this museum combines an elegant interior with a charming overview of the 19th- and early 20th-century history of Athens.

Cost and Hours: €5, Mon and Wed-Fri 9:00-16:00, Sat-Sun 10:00-15:00, closed Tue, free Clio Muse app provides more info on various stops in museum—download beforehand as there's no Wi-Fi at the museum, outdoor café, Paparigopoulou 5, Metro: Panepistimio, tel. 210-323-1397, www.athenscitymuseum.gr.

Visiting the Museum: The ground floor has two highlights. In the first room is a giant panoramic late 17th-century painting of Louis XIV's ambassador and his party, with Athens in the background. The work shows a small village occupied by Ottomans (with prickly minarets rising from the rooftops), before the Parthenon was partially destroyed (it's the only painting depicting an intact Athens and Parthenon).

In the next room, a large model shows Athens circa 1842, just as it was emerging as the capital of Greece. A touchscreen computer lets you choose various locations on the model, read more about those sights, virtually circle around them, and watch videos.

Upstairs are lavishly decorated rooms and exhibits that emphasize King Otto's role in the fledgling Greek state following the Ottoman defeat. Throughout the place you'll see idyllic paintings of Athens as it was a century and a half ago: a red-roofed village at the foot of the Acropolis populated by Greek shepherds in traditional costume. Stepping back outside into the smog and noise after your visit, you'll wish you had a time machine.

SIGHTS

ATHENS CITY WALK

From Syntagma Square to Monastiraki Square

Athens is a bustling metropolis of nearly four million people, home to one out of every three Greeks. Much of the city is unappealing, cheaply built, poorly zoned 20th-century sprawl. But the heart and soul of Athens is engaging and refreshingly compact. This walk takes you through the striking contrasts of the city center—from chaotic, traffic-clogged urban zones, to sleepy streets packed with bearded priests shopping for a new robe or chalice, to peaceful, barely-wide-enough-for-a-donkey back lanes that twist their way up toward the Acropolis. Along the way, we'll learn about Athens' rich history, the intriguing tapestry of Orthodox churches that dot the city, and the way that locals live and shop.

The walk begins at Syntagma Square, meanders through the fascinating old Plaka district, and finishes at lively Monastiraki (near the Ancient Agora, markets, good restaurants, and a handy Metro stop). This sightseeing spine will help you get a once-over-lightly look at Athens, which you can use as a springboard for diving into the city's various colorful sights and neighborhoods.

Orientation

Churches: Athens' churches are free but keep irregular hours—generally open daily 8:30-13:30 & 17:00-19:30. If you want to buy candles at churches (as the locals do), be sure to have a few small coins.

Cathedral: Free, generally open daily 8:00-13:00 & 16:30-19:00, no afternoon closure in summer.

Temple of Olympian Zeus: €6, covered by Acropolis combo-ticket, daily May-Sept 8:00-20:00, April and Oct 8:00-19:00, Nov-March 8:00-15:00, Vasilissis Olgas 1, Metro: Akropoli, tel. 210-922-6330, www.culture.gr.

Roman Forum: €6, covered by Acropolis combo-ticket, daily 8:00-15:00, possibly open later in summer, corner of Pelopida and Aiolou streets, Metro: Monastiraki, tel. 210-324-5220.

Library of Hadrian: €4, covered by Acropolis combo-ticket, daily 8:00-15:00, possibly open later in summer, across from Agora Square, Metro: Monastiraki.

When to Go: Do this walk early in your visit, as it can help you get your bearings in this potentially confusing city. Morning is best, since many churches close for an afternoon break, and other sights—such as the Acropolis—are too crowded to enjoy.

Dress Code: Wearing shorts inside churches is frowned upon, though usually tolerated.

Getting There: The walk begins at Syntagma Square, just northeast of the Plaka tourist zone. It's a short walk from the recommended Plaka hotels; if you're staying away from the city center, get here by Metro (stop: Syntagma).

Audio Tour: ∩ Download my free Athens City Walk **audio tour.**

Length of This Walk: Allow plenty of time. This three-part walk takes two hours without stops or detours. But if you explore and dip into sights here and there—pausing to ponder a dimly lit Orthodox church, or doing some window- (or actual) shopping—it can enjoyably eat up a half-day or more. If you find this walk too long, it's easy to break up—stop after Part 2 and return for Part 3 at a different time or on another day.

Starring: Athens' top squares, churches, and Roman ruins, connected by bustling urban streets that are alternately choked with cars and mopeds, or thronged by pedestrians, vendors... and fellow tourists.

CITY WALK

The Walk Begins

This lengthy walk is thematically divided into three parts: The first part focuses on modern Athens, centered on Syntagma Square and the Ermou shopping street. The second part focuses on Athens' Greek Orthodox faith, with visits to three different but equally interesting churches. And the third part is a wander through the charming old core of Athens, including the touristy Plaka and the mellow Greek-village-on-a-hillside of Anafiotika.

Athens City Walk

1. Syntagma Square
2. Tomb of the Unknown Soldier & Evzone Guards
3. Parliament
4. Hotel Grande Bretagne
5. Ermou Street
6. Church of Kapnikarea
7. Cathedral & Square
8. Church of Agios Eleftherios
9. Agia Filotheis Street
10. Church of Agia Filotheis
11. Adrianou Street
12. Arch of Hadrian & Temple of Olympian Zeus
13. Lysicrates Monument & Square
14. View of Lykavittos Hill
15. Anafiotika
16. Roman Forum & Tower of the Winds
17. Agora Square
18. Library of Hadrian
19. Monastiraki Square
20. "Souvlaki Row"
21. Former Mosque & Ceramics Museum
22. Ancient Agora
23. Flea Market
24. Monastiraki Metro Stn.

CITY WALK

PART 1: MODERN ATHENS

This part of our walk lets you feel the pulse of a European capital.

• *Start at Syntagma Square. From the leafy park at the center of the square, climb to the top of the stairs (in the middle of the square) and stand across the street from the big, Neoclassical Greek Parliament building.*

❶ Syntagma Square (Plateia Syntagmatos)

As you look at posh hotels and major banks, you are standing atop the city's central Metro stop, surrounded by buses, cars, and taxis.

Facing the Parliament building (east), get oriented to the square named for Greece's constitution (*syntagma;* SEEN-dag-mah). From this point, sightseeing options spin off through the city like spokes on a wheel.

Fronting the square on the left (north) side are high-end hotels, including the opulent Hotel Grande Bretagne (with its swanky rooftop garden restaurant—see page 167).

Directly to the left of the Parliament building is the head of Vasilissis Sofias avenue, lined with embassies and museums, including the Benaki Museum of Greek History and Culture, Museum of Cycladic Art, Byzantine and Christian Museum, and National War Museum. This boulevard leads to the ritzy Kolonaki quarter, with its funicular up to the top of Lykavittos Hill. Extending to the right of the Parliament building is the National Garden, Athens' "Central Park." Here you'll find the Zappeion mansion-turned-conference-hall (with a fine summer outdoor cinema nearby) and, beyond the greenery, the evocative, ancient Panathenaic Stadium.

On your right (south) is one of Athens' prime transit hubs, with stops for bus #X95 to the airport, and the Athens Coastal Tram. Beneath your feet is the Syntagma Metro station, the city's busiest.

Behind you, at the west end of the square, stretches the traffic-free shopping street called Ermou, which heads to the Plaka neighborhood and Monastiraki Square. (We'll be heading that way soon.) Nearby is the terminus for one of Athens' two tourist trains (see page 42).

Take a moment to look at the square and modern Athens: People buzz about on their way to work, handing out leaflets, feeding pigeons, or just enjoying a park bench shaded by a variety of trees. Plane trees, cypress, and laurel make Syntagma a breezy and restful spot. Breathe deeply and ponder the fact that until 1990,

Athens was the most polluted city in Europe. People advertising facial creams would put a mannequin outside on the street for three hours and film it turning black. The message: You need our cream.

But over the last two decades, "green" policies have systematically cleaned up the air. Traffic, though still pretty extreme, is limited: Even- and odd-numbered license plates are prohibited in the center on alternate days (though downtown residents are exempt). Check the license plates of passing cars (not taxis or motorcycles): The majority end with either an even or an odd number, depending on the day of the week. While car traffic is down, motorcycle usage is up (since bikes are exempt). Central-heating fuel is more expensive and much cleaner these days (as required by European Union regulations), more of the city center is pedestrianized, and the city's public transport is top-notch.

• *Using the crosswalk (one on either side of Syntagma Square), cross the busy street. Directly in front of the Parliament you'll see the...*

❷ Tomb of the Unknown Soldier and the Evzone Guards

Standing amid pigeons and tourists in front of the imposing Parliament building overlooking Syntagma Square, you're at the center of Athens' modern history. Above the simple marble-slab tomb—marked only with a cross—is a carved image of the Unknown Soldier, a heavily armed dying Greek, inspired by the statue of a dying nude from the ancient Aphaia temple on the island of Aigina, very close to Athens. Etched into the stone on each side of the tomb are the names of great battles in Greek military history from 1821 forward (practice your Greek alphabet by trying to read them: Cyprus, Korea, Rimini, Crete, and so on).

The tomb is guarded by the much-photographed evzone, an elite infantry unit of the Greek army. The guard changes five min-

utes before the top of each hour, with a less elaborate crossing of the guard at :25 after. They march with a slow-motion, high-stepping march to their new positions, then stand ramrod straight, where you can pose alongside them. A full changing-of-the-guard ceremony, complete with marching band, takes place every Sunday at 11:00 (arrive a bit early).

These colorful characters are clad in traditional pleated kilts *(fustanella)*, white britches, and pom-pom shoes. (The outfits may look a little goofy to a non-Greek, but their mothers and girlfriends are very proud.) The uniforms, worn everywhere in

Greece, were made famous by the Klephts, ragtag bands of mountain guerrilla fighters. After nearly four centuries under the thumb of the Ottoman Empire (from today's Turkey, starting in 1453), the Greeks rose up. The Greek War of Independence (1821-1829) pitted the powerful Ottoman army against the lowly but wily Klephts. The soldiers' skirts have 400 pleats...one for each year of Ottoman occupation (and don't you forget it). Although considered heroes today for their courage, outrageous guerrilla tactics, and contribution to the Liberation Army in the 19th century, the Klephts were once regarded as warlike bandits (their name shares a root with the English word "kleptomania").

As the Klephts and other Greeks fought for their independence, a number of farsighted Europeans (including the English poet Lord Byron)—inspired by the French Revolution and their own love of ancient Greek culture—came to their aid. In 1829, the rebels finally succeeded in driving their Ottoman rulers out of central Greece, and there was a movement to establish a modern democracy. However, the Greeks were unprepared to rule themselves, and so, after the Ottomans came...Otto.

• *For the rest of the story, take a step back for a view of the...*

❸ Parliament

The origins of this "palace of democracy" couldn't have been less democratic. The first independent Greek government, which had its capital in Nafplio, was too weak to be viable. As was standard operating procedure at that time, the great European powers forced Greece to accept a king from established European royalty.

In 1832, Prince Otto of Bavaria became King Otto of Greece. A decade later, after the capital shifted to Athens, this royal palace was built to house King Otto and his wife, Queen Amalia. The atmosphere was tense. After fighting so fiercely for its independence from the Ottomans, the Greeks now chafed under royal rule from a dictatorial Bavarian monarch. The palace's over-the-top luxury only angered impoverished locals.

On September 3, 1843, angry rioters gathered in the square to protest, demanding a democratic constitution. King Otto stepped onto the balcony of this building, quieted the mob, and gave them what they wanted. The square was dubbed Syntagma (Constitution), and modern Athens was born. The former royal palace has been the home of the Greek parliament since 1935. Today this is where 300 Greek parliamentarians (elected to four-year terms) tend to the business of the state—or, as more cynical locals would say, become corrupt and busily get themselves set up for their cushy, post-political lives.

• *Cross back to the heart of Syntagma Square, and focus on the grand building fronting its north side.*

❹ Hotel Grande Bretagne and Neoclassical Syntagma

Imagine the original Syntagma Square (which was on the out-skirts of town in the early 19th century): a big front yard for the

new royal palace, with the country's influential families building mansions around it. Surviving examples of 19th-century architecture—as well as more modern buildings renovated in a neo-Neo-classical style so they'd fit in—include Hotel Grande Bretagne, the adjacent

Hotel King George Palace, the Zappeion in the National Garden (not visible from here), and the stately architecture lining Vasilis-sis Sofias avenue behind the palace (now embassies and museums).

Many of these grand buildings date from Athens' Otto-driven Neoclassical makeover. Eager to create a worthy capital for Greece, Otto imported teams of Bavarian architects to draft a plan of broad avenues and grand buildings in what they imagined to be the classical style. This "Neoclassical" look is symmetrical and geometrical, with pastel-colored buildings highlighted in white trim. The windows are rectangular, flanked by white Greek half-columns (pilasters), fronted by balconies, and topped with cornices. Many of the buildings are also framed at the top with cornices. As you continue on this walk, notice not only the many Neoclassical buildings, but also the more modern buildings that try to match the same geometric lines.

Syntagma Square is also worth a footnote in American Cold War history. In December 1944, Greek communists demonstrated here, inducing the US to come to the aid of the Greek government. This became the basis (in 1947) for the Truman Doctrine, which pledged US aid to countries fighting communism and helped shape American foreign policy for the next 50 years.

• *Head down to the bottom of Syntagma (directly across from the Parliament). Stroll down the traffic-free street near the McDonald's.*

❺ Ermou Street

The pedestrian mall called Ermou (AIR-moo) leads from Syntagma down through the Plaka to Monastiraki, then continues westward to the ancient Keramikos Cemetery and the Gazi district. Not long ago, this street epitomized all that was terrible about Athens: lousy building codes, tacky neon signs, double-parked trucks, and noisy traffic. When Ermou was first pedestrianized in 2000, merchants were upset. Now they love the ambience created as countless locals stroll through what has become a people-friendly shopping zone.

This has traditionally been the street of women's shops. However, these days Ermou is dominated by high-class international chain stores, which appeal to young Athenians but turn off older natives, who lament the lack of local flavor. For authentic, hole-in-the-wall shopping, many Athenians prefer the streets just to the north, such as Perikleous, Lekka, and Kolokotroni.

Even so, this people-crammed boulevard is a pleasant place for a wander. Do just that, proceeding gradually downhill and straight ahead for seven blocks. As you window-shop, notice that some of Ermou's department stores are housed in impressive Neoclassical mansions. Talented street performers provide an entertaining soundtrack. All of Athens walks along here: businesspeople, teenage girls with iPhones, Orthodox priests, activists gathering signatures, illegal vendors who sweep up their wares and scurry when they see police, and, of course, tourists. Keep an eye out for vendors selling various snacks—including pretzel-like sesame rings called *koulouri* and slices of fresh coconut.

After six short blocks, on the right (at the intersection with Evangelistrias/Ευαγγελιστριασ), look for the little **book wagon** selling cheap lit. You'll likely see colorful, old-fashioned alphabet books (labeled ΑΛΦΑΒΗΤΑΡΙΟ, *Alphabetario*), which have been reprinted for nostalgic older Greeks. Remember that the English word "alphabet" comes from the first two Greek letters (alpha, beta).

PART 2: THE GREEK ORTHODOX CHURCH

This part of our walk introduces you to the Orthodox faith of Greece, including stops at three different churches. The Greek faith is one denomination of Eastern Orthodox Christianity; for more information, see the sidebar on page 82.

• *Stranded in the middle of both Ermou street and the commercial bustle of the 21st century is a little medieval church.*

The Story of Modern Athens

By the time of the Greek War of Independence (1821-1829), Athens had declined, becoming little more than a rural backwater on the fringes of the Ottoman Empire. Its population had shrunk to about 2,000 people occupying a cluster of red-tiled Turkish houses on the northern side of the Acropolis (the area now known as the Plaka).

When it came to choosing a capital for the new nation, Athens wasn't even considered. The first choice was Nafplio on the Peloponnese, which the Ottomans had also favored as a seat of government. It would probably have stayed that way, if it weren't for the assassination of Greece's first president, Ioannis Kapodistrias, in 1831. His death led to international pressure to install an outsider, 17-year-old Prince Otto of Bavaria, as the first king of Greece.

Otto was as wet behind the ears as any teenager, and was heavily influenced by his forceful father, King Ludwig I of Bavaria (grandfather of "Mad" King Ludwig, of Neuschwanstein Castle fame). These Bavarians—great admirers of classical Athens—insisted that the city become the capital in 1834. They also were responsible for the shape of the new Athens, ferrying in teams of Bavarian architects to create a plan of broad avenues and grand Neoclassical buildings—much as they had done in Munich.

The character of Athens changed once more after 1922, when the defeat of the occupying Greek army in Turkey resulted in a forced population exchange between the two rivals. Athens' population doubled almost overnight, and any thought of town planning went out the window as authorities scrambled to build cheap apartment blocks to house the newcomers.

Greece's belated industrialization in the 1950s, coupled with the hard times of the Nazi occupation and civil war (when villagers, who could no longer afford to feed themselves, flocked to the city), sparked a wave of migration from rural areas. It's amazing to think that the city with less than a million inhabitants in 1950 now has about four million. The trend continues to this day: More than a third of Greece's population now lives in greater Athens.

When they hosted the Olympic Games in 2004, the Greeks turned over a new leaf and showed a passion for city planning. Improvements in infrastructure, public transportation, and an overall beautification program quickly pulled the city up to snuff, making it an increasingly attractive tourist destination.

CITY WALK

❻ Church of Kapnikarea

After the ancient Golden Age, but before Otto and the Ottomans, Athens was part of the Byzantine Empire (A.D. 323-1453). In the 11th and 12th centuries, Athens boomed, and several Eastern Orthodox churches like this one were constructed.

The Church of Kapnikarea is a classic 11th-century Byzantine church. Notice that it's square and topped with a central dome. Telltale signs of a Byzantine church include tall arches over the windows, stones surrounded by a frame of brick and mortar, and a domed cupola with a cross on top. The large white blocks are scavenged from other, earlier monuments (also typical of Byzantine churches from this era). Over the door is a mosaic of glass and gold leaf, which, though modern, is made in the traditional Byzantine style.

Step inside if the church is open (if it's closed, don't fret—we'll be visiting a couple of similar churches later). Notice the Greek-cross floor plan and the early 20th-century, modern-yet-still-medieval art. It's decorated with standing candelabras, hanging lamps, tall arches, a wooden pulpit, and a few chairs. If you wish, you can do as the Greeks do and follow the standard candle-buying, icon-kissing ritual (see sidebar on page 82). The icon displayed closest to the door gets changed with the church calendar. You may notice lipstick smudges on the protective glass and a candle-recycling box behind the candelabra.

Look up into the central dome, lit with windows, which symbolizes heaven. Looking back down is the face of Jesus, the omnipotent *Pantocrator* God blessing us on Earth. He holds a Bible in one hand and blesses us with the other. On the walls are iconic murals of saints. Notice the focus on the eyes, which are considered a mirror of the soul and a symbol of its purity.

• *When you leave the church, turn south toward the Acropolis and proceed downhill on Kapnikareas street. Up ahead, catch a glimpse of the Acropolis. Go two blocks to the traffic-free Pandrossou shopping street. Turn left and walk up the pedestrian street to the cathedral.*

❼ Cathedral (Mitropolis) and Cathedral Square (Plateia Mitropoleos)

Built from 1842 to 1862, this "metropolitan church" (as the Greek Orthodox call their cathedrals) is the most important in Athens, which makes it the head church of the Greek Orthodox faith. Unfortunately, it's unremarkable and oddly ramshackle inside

and out...and has been decorated with scaffolding since the
earthquake of 1999.

If it's open, head inside.
Looking up, you'll notice balconies. Traditionally, women
worshipped apart from men in
the balconies upstairs. Women
got the vote in Greece in 1952,
and since about that time, they've been able to worship in the
prime, ground-floor real estate alongside the men.

When you're back outside on the square, notice the statue facing the cathedral. This was erected by Athens' Jewish community

as thanks to **Archbishop Damaskinos** (1891-
1949), the rare Christian leader who stood up
to the Nazis during the occupation of Greece.
At great personal risk, Damaskinos formally
spoke out against the Nazi occupiers on behalf
of the Greek Jews he saw being deported to
concentration camps. When a Nazi commander threatened to put Damaskinos before a firing
squad, the archbishop defiantly countered that
he should be hanged instead, in good Orthodox tradition. After the occupation, Damaskinos served as regent and then prime minister
of Greece until the king returned from exile.

Here Damaskinos is depicted wearing the
distinctive hat of an archbishop (a kind of fez
with cloth hanging down the sides). He carries a staff and blesses
with his right hand, making a traditional Orthodox sign of the
cross, touching his thumb to his ring finger. This gesture forms the
letters ICXC, the first and last letters of the Greek name for Jesus
Christ (ΙΗΣΟΥΣ ΧΡΙΣΤΟΣ—traditionally C was substituted
for Σ). Make the gesture yourself with your right hand. Touch the
tip of your thumb to the tip of your ring finger and check it out:
Your pinkie forms the I, your slightly crossed index and middle
fingers are the X, and your thumb and ring finger make a double-
C. Jesus Christ, that's clever. If you were a priest, you'd make the
sign of the cross three times, to symbolize the Father, the Son, and
the Holy Spirit.

The double-headed eagle that hangs around Damaskinos' neck
is an important symbol of the Orthodox faith. It evokes the Byzantine Empire, during which Orthodox Christianity was at its peak
as the state religion. Appropriately, the eagle's twin heads have a
double meaning: The Byzantine Emperor was both the secular and
spiritual leader of his realm, which exerted its influence over both

East and West. (Historically, any power that wanted to be considered the successor of the ancient Roman Emperor—including the Holy Roman Empire and the Austro-Hungarian Empire—used this symbol.)

At the far end of the square from the cathedral is another statue, this one of a warrior holding a sword. This is **Emperor Constantine XI Palaeologus** (1404-1453), the final ruler of the Byzantine Empire. He was killed defending Constantinople from the invading Ottomans, led by Mehmet the Conqueror. Considered the "last Greek king" and an unofficial saint, Constantine XI's death marked the ascension of the Ottomans as overlords of the Greeks for nearly four centuries. On his boots and above his head, you'll see the double-headed eagle again.

• *The small church tucked behind the right side of the cathedral is the...*

❽ Church of Agios Eleftherios

A favorite of local church connoisseurs, the late 12th-century Church of Agios Eleftherios (St. Eleutherius) is also known as

Panaghia Ghorghoepikoos ("Virgin Mary, quick to answer prayers") and is sometimes referred to as "the old cathedral." It was used by the archbishops of Athens after the Ottomans evicted them from the church within the Parthenon. It's a jigsaw-puzzle hodgepodge of B.C. and A.D. adornments (and even tombstones) from earlier buildings. For example, the carved marble reliefs above the door were scavenged from the Ancient Agora in the 12th century. They are part of a calendar of ancient Athenian festivals, thought to have been carved in the second century A.D. The frieze running along the top of the building depicts a B.C. procession.

Later, Christians added their own symbols to the same panels, making the church a treasure trove of medieval symbolism. There are different kinds of crosses (Maltese, Latin, double) as well as carved rosettes, stars, flowers, and griffins feeding on plants and snakes. Walk around the entire exterior. Then step inside to sample unadorned 12th-century Orthodox simplicity.

• *Exit the church, go up to the main sidewalk level, and walk around to the back side of the church where you'll find a religious gear shop and the start of...*

❾ Agia Filotheis Street

This neighborhood is a hive of activity for Orthodox clerics. The priests dress all in black, wear beards, and don those fez-like hats. Despite their hermetic look, most priests are husbands, fathers, and well-educated pillars of the community, serving as counselors and spiritual guides to Athens' cosmopolitan populace.

Notice the stores. Just behind and facing the little church is the shop of the **Theodoropoulos** family—whose name manages to use nearly every Greek character available (ΘΕΟΔΩΡΟΠΟΥΛΟΣ). They've been tailoring priestly robes since 1907.

This is the first of many **religious objects stores** that line the street. Cross the busy Apollonos street and continue exploring the shops of Agia Filotheis street. The Orthodox religion comes with ample paraphernalia: icons, gold candelabras, hanging lamps, incense burners, oil lamps, chalices, various crosses, and gold objects worked in elaborate repoussé design.

Pop into the **stoa** (arcades) at #17 (on the left) to see workshops of the artisans who make these objects—painters creating or restoring icons in the traditional style, tailors making bishops' hats and robes, and carvers making little devotional statuettes.

A few more steps up on the left, the ❿ **Church of Agia Filotheis** (named, like the street, for a patron of Athens—St. Philothei) is adjacent to an office building (at #19) that serves as the headquarters for the Greek Orthodox Church. Athenians come here to file the paperwork to make their marriages (and divorces) official.

PART 3: ATHENS' "OLD TOWN" (THE PLAKA AND ANAFIOTIKA)

This part of our walk explores the atmospheric twisty lanes of old Athens. Remember, back before Athens became Greece's capital in the early 1800s, the city was a small town consisting of little more than what we'll see here.

• *Continue up Agia Filotheis street until you reach a tight five-way intersection. The street that runs ahead and to your right (labeled ΑΔΡΙΑΝΟΥ)—choked with souvenir stands and tourists—is our next destination. Look uphill and downhill along...*

⓫ Adrianou Street

This intersection may be the geographical (if not atmospheric) center of the neighborhood

The Eastern Orthodox Church

In the fourth century A.D., the Roman Empire split in half, dividing Eastern Europe and the Balkan Peninsula down the middle. Seven centuries later, with the Great Schism, the Christian faith diverged along similar lines, into two separate branches: Roman Catholicism in the west (based in Rome and including most of Western and Central Europe), and Eastern or Byzantine Orthodoxy in the east (based in Constantinople—today's Istanbul—and prevalent in far-eastern Europe, Russia, the eastern half of the Balkan Peninsula, and Greece). The root *orthos* is Greek for "right," and *dogma* is "faith," making orthodoxy the "right belief." And it seems logical that if you've already got it right, you're more conservative and resistant to change.

Over the centuries the Catholic Church shed old traditions and developed new ones. Meanwhile, the Eastern Orthodox Church—which remained consolidated under the stable and wealthy Byzantine Empire—stayed true to the earliest traditions of the Christian faith. Today, rather than having one centralized headquarters (such as the Vatican for Catholicism), the Eastern Orthodox Church is divided into about a dozen regional branches that remain administratively independent but share the same rituals. Some branches include the Russian Orthodox Church, the Serbian Orthodox Church, the Bulgarian Orthodox Church, and the Greek Orthodox Church, which is based at Athens' cathedral. The Greek constitution recognizes Orthodox Christianity as the "prevailing" religion of Greece. The Archbishop of Athens is Greece's "pope."

The doctrine of Catholic and Orthodox churches remains very similar, but many of the rituals are different. As you enter any Greek Orthodox church, you can join in the standard routine: Drop a coin in the wooden box, pick up a candle, say a prayer, light the candle, and place it in the candelabra. Make the sign of the cross and kiss the icon.

Where's the altar? Orthodox churches come with an altar screen covered with curtains and icons (the "iconostasis"). The standard design of the iconostasis calls for four icons flanking the central door, with Jesus to the right, John the Baptist to Jesus' right, Mary and the Baby Jesus on the left, and an icon featuring the saint or event that the church is dedicated to on the far left.

This iconostasis divides the lay community from the priests— the material world from the spiritual one. Following Old Testament Judeo-Christian tradition, the Bible is kept on the altar behind the iconostasis. The spiritual heavy lifting takes place behind the iconostasis, where the priests symbolically turn bread and wine into the body and blood of Jesus. Then they open the doors or curtains and serve the Eucharist to their faithful flock—spooning the wine from a chalice while holding a cloth under each chin so as not to drop any on the floor.

Notice that there are few (if any) pews. Worshippers stand through the service as a sign of respect (though some older parishioners sit on the seats along the walls). Traditionally, women stand on the left side, men on the right (equal distance from the altar, to represent that all are equal before God).

The Orthodox faith tends to use a Greek cross, with four equal arms (like a plus sign, sometimes inside a circle), which focuses on God's perfection. The longer Latin cross, more typically used by Catholics, more literally evokes the Crucifixion, emphasizing Jesus' death and sacrifice. This also extends to the floor plans of church buildings: Many Orthodox churches have Greek-cross floor plans rather than the elongated nave-and-transept designs that are common in Western Europe.

Unlike many Catholic church decorations, Orthodox icons (golden paintings of saints) are not intended to be lifelike. Packed with intricate symbolism and often cast against a shimmering

golden background, they're meant to remind viewers of the metaphysical nature of Jesus and the saints rather than their physical form, which is considered irrelevant. You'll almost never see statues, which are thought to overemphasize the physical world—and, to Orthodox people, feel a little too close to the forbidden worship of graven images.

Most Eastern Orthodox churches have at least one mosaic or painting of Christ in a standard pose—as *Pantocrator,* a Greek word meaning "Ruler of All." The image, so familiar to Orthodox Christians, shows Christ as King of the Universe, facing directly out, with penetrating eyes. Behind him is a halo divided by a cross, with the bottom arm of the cross hidden behind Christ—an Orthodox symbol for the Crucifixion, hinting of the Resurrection and salvation that follow.

Orthodox services generally involve chanting (a dialogue that goes back and forth between the priest and the congregation), and the church is filled with the evocative aroma of incense, combining to heighten the experience for the worshippers. While many Catholic and Protestant services tend to be more of a theoretical and rote covering of basic religious tenets (come on—don't tell me you understand every phrase in the Nicene Creed), Orthodox services are about creating a religious experience. Each of these elements does its part to help the worshipper transcend the physical world and enter into communion with the spiritual one.

called the Plaka. Touristy Adrianou street is a main pedestrian drag that cuts through the Plaka, running roughly east–west from Monastiraki to here. Adrianou offers the full gauntlet of Greek souvenirs: worry beads, sea sponges, olive products, icons, carpets, jewelry, sandals, knock-off vases and Greek statues, profane and tacky T-shirts, and on and on. It also offers plenty of cafés for tourists seeking a place to sit and rest their weary feet.

• *Bear left onto Adrianou and walk uphill several blocks. Finally, the street dead-ends at a T-intersection with Lysikratous street. (There's a small square ahead on the left, with palm trees, the Byzantine church of Agia Aikaterini, and an excavated area showing the street level 2,000 years ago.)*

From here you can turn right and take a few steps uphill to the Lysicrates Monument and Square (and skip ahead to the section on the Lysicrates Monument). But if you've got more time and stamina, it's worth a two-block walk to the left down Lysikratous street to reach the remains of the Arch of Hadrian.

⑫ Arch of Hadrian and Temple of Olympian Zeus

After the Romans conquered the Greeks, Roman emperor Hadrian (or Adrianos) became a major benefactor of the city of Athens. He built a triumphal arch, completed a temple beyond it (now ruined), and founded a library we'll see later. He also created a "new Athens" in the area beyond the arch (sometimes known as Hadrianopolis). The grand archway overlooks the bustling modern Vasilissis Amalias avenue, facing the Plaka and Acropolis. (If you turned left and followed this road for 10 minutes, you'd end up back on Syntagma Square—where we began this walk.)

Arch of Hadrian

The arch's once-brilliant white Pentelic marble is topped with Corinthian columns, the Greek style preferred by the Romans. Hadrian built it in A.D. 131 to celebrate the completion of the Temple of Olympian Zeus (which lies just beyond—described next). Like a big gate marking the entrance to a modern Chinatown, this arch represented the dividing line between the ancient city and Hadrian's new "Roman" city. An inscription on the west side informs the reader that "This is Athens, ancient city of Theseus," while the opposite frieze carries the message, "This is the city of Hadrian, and not of Theseus."

• *Look past the arch to see the huge (and I mean huge) Corinthian columns remain-*

ing from what was once a temple dedicated to the Olympian Zeus. For a closer look, cross the busy boulevard (crosswalk to the right). You can pretty much get the gist by looking through the fence. But to get close to those giant columns and wander the ruins, you can enter the site (covered by Acropolis combo-ticket—buy it here to avoid the Acropolis line). To reach the entrance (a five-minute walk), curl around the left side of the arch, then turn right (following the fence) up the intersecting street called Vasilissis Olgas. The entrance to the temple is a few minutes' walk up, on the right-hand side.

Temple of Olympian Zeus (Olympieion)

This largest ancient temple in mainland Greece took almost 700 years to finish. It was begun late in the sixth century B.C. during

the rule of the tyrant Peisistratos. He died before the temple was completed, and his successors were expelled from Athens. The temple lay abandoned, half-built, for centuries until the Roman emperor Hadrian arrived to finish the job in A.D. 131. This must have been a big deal for Hadrian, as he came here in person to celebrate its inaugura-

tion. Romans did things big. When completed, the temple was 360 feet by 145 feet, consisting of two rows of 20 columns on each of the long sides and three rows of eight columns along each end (counting the corners twice). Although only 15 of the original 104 Corinthian columns remain standing, their sheer size (a towering 56 feet high) is enough to create a powerful impression of the temple's scale. The fallen column—which resembles a tipped-over stack of bottle caps—was toppled by a storm in 1852. The temple once housed a suitably oversized statue of Zeus, head of the Greek gods who lived on Mount Olympus, and an equally colossal statue of Hadrian.

• Return to Lysikratous street and backtrack two blocks, continuing past the small square with the church you passed earlier. After another block, you'll run into another small, leafy square with the Acropolis rising behind it. In the square is a round, white, col-umned monument.

⑬ Lysicrates Monument and Square

This elegant marble monument has Corinthian columns that support a

CITY WALK

dome that once held an ornamental vase on top. A frieze runs along the top, representing Dionysus turning pirates into dolphins. The monument is the sole survivor of many such monuments that once lined this ancient "Street of the Tripods." It was so called because the monuments came with bronze tripods that displayed cauldrons (like those you'll see in the museums) as trophies. These ancient "Oscars" were awarded to winners of choral and theatrical competitions staged at the Theater of Dionysus on the southern side of the Acropolis. This now-lonely monument was erected in 334 B.C. by "Lysicrates of Kykyna, son of Lysitheides"—proud sponsor of the winning choral team that year. Excavations around the monument have uncovered the foundations of other monuments, which are now reburied under a layer of red sand and awaiting further study.

The square itself, shaded by trees, is a pleasant place to take a break before climbing the hill. Have a frappé or coffee at the café tables, grab a cheap cold drink from the cooler in the hole-in-the-wall grocery store to the left, or just sit for free on the benches under the trees.

• *From here you're only two blocks from the TI—you may want to detour there if you haven't stopped by yet (on pedestrian street leading to Acropolis Museum at Dionysiou Areopagitou 18). Otherwise, pass the Lysicrates Monument on its left-hand side, then head uphill toward the Acropolis, climbing the staircase called Epimenidou street. At the top of the stairs, turn right onto Stratonos street, which leads around the base of the Acropolis. As you walk along, the Acropolis and a row of olive trees are on your left. The sound of the crickets evokes for Athenians the black-and-white movies that were filmed in this area in the 1960s. To your right you'll catch glimpses of another hill off in the distance.*

⓮ View of Lykavittos Hill

This cone-shaped hill (sometimes spelled "Lycabettus") topped with a tiny white church is the highest in Athens, at just over 900 feet above sea level. The hill can be reached by a funicular, which leads up from the Kolonaki neighborhood to a restaurant, café, and view terrace at the top. Although it looms high over the cityscape, Lykavittos Hill will always be overshadowed by the hill you're climbing now.

• *At the small Church of St. George of the Rock (Agios Georgios, generally closed), go uphill, along the left fork. As you immerse yourself in a maze of tiny, whitewashed houses, follow signs that point to the Acropolis (even if the path seems impossibly narrow). This charming "village" is a neighborhood called...*

⑮ Anafiotika

These lanes and homes were built by people from the tiny Cycladic island of Anafi, who came to Athens looking for work after Greece gained its independence from the Ottomans. (Many stoneworkers and builders hired to construct the modern city of Athens built these higgledy-piggledy residences after-hours.) In this delightful spot, nestled beneath the walls of the Acropolis, the big city seems miles away. Keep following the *Acropolis* signs as you weave through narrow paths lined with flowers and dotted with cats dozing peacefully in the sunshine (or slithering luxuriously past your legs). Though descendants of the original islanders still live here, Anafiotika (literally "little Anafi") is slowly becoming a place for wealthy locals to keep an "island cottage" in the city. As you wander through the oleanders, notice the male fig trees—no fruit—that keep flies and mosquitoes away. Smell the chicken-manure fertilizer (and cat poop), peek into delicate little yards, and enjoy the blue doors and maroon shutters... it's a transplanted Cycladic world. Posters of Anafi hang here and there, evoking the sandy beaches of the ancestral home island.

• *Follow the narrow walkway until you emerge from the maze of houses and hit a wider, cobbled lane. Turn right (downhill) and continue down the steep incline. When you hit a wider road (Theorias), turn left and walk toward the small, Byzantine-style Church of the Metamorphosis. (Note: To reach the Acropolis entry from here, you would continue along this road as it bends left around the hill. For more on the Acropolis, take my Acropolis Tour, available as a 📖 chapter in this book and as a free 🎧 audio tour. For now, though, let's continue our walk.)*

Just before the church, turn right and go down the steep, narrow staircase (a lane called Klepsidras, labeled ΚΛΕΨΥΔΡΑΣ*). You'll pass the first university of Athens (with a free little museum) on the right. Cross the street called Tholou and continue down Klepsidras. Enjoy the graffiti. The lane gets even narrower (yes, keep going between the plants). You'll pass a charming little café a block before you emerge at a railing overlooking some ruins.*

⑯ The Roman Forum and the Tower of the Winds

The rows of columns framing this rectangular former piazza were built by the Romans, who conquered Greece around 150 B.C. and stayed for centuries. This square—sometimes called the "Roman Agora"—was the commercial center, or forum, of Roman Athens, with a colonnade providing shade for shoppers browsing the many

CITY WALK

stores that fronted it. Centuries later, the Ottomans made this their grand bazaar. The mosque was built upon a church that was built upon a Roman temple. The mosque, one of the oldest and best-preserved Ottoman structures, survives (although its minaret, like all minarets in town, was torn down by the Greeks when they won their independence from the Ottomans in the 19th century).

Take a few steps to the right to see the octagonal, domed **Tower of the Winds.** The carved reliefs depict winds as winged

humans who fly in, bringing the weather. Built in the first century B.C., this building was an ingenious combination of clock, weather-vane, and guide to the planets. The beautifully carved reliefs represent male personifications of the eight winds of Athens, with their names inscribed. As you walk down the hill (curving right, then left around the fence, always going downhill), you'll see reliefs depicting Lips, the southwest wind, holding a ship's steering rudder; Zephyros, the mild west wind, holding a basket of flowers; Skiron, scattering glowing coal from an inverted bronze brazier, indicating the warmer winter winds; and Boreas, the howling winter wind from the north, blowing a conch shell. The tower was once capped with a weathervane in the form of a bronze Triton (half-man, half-fish) that spun to indicate which wind was blessing or cursing the city at the moment. Bronze rods (no longer visible) protruded from the walls and acted as sundials to indicate the time. And when the sun wasn't shining, people told time using the tower's sophisticated water clock, powered by water piped in from springs on the Acropolis. Much later, under Ottoman rule, dervishes used the tower as a place for their whirling worship and prayer.

• *It's possible but unnecessary to enter the ruins: You've seen just about everything from this vantage point. Don't confuse the Roman Forum with the older, more interesting Ancient Agora, which is near the end of this walk.*

Otherwise, from just below the Tower of the Winds, head to the right down Aiolou street one block to...

⓱ Agora Square (Plateia Agoras)

This leafy, restaurant-filled square is the touristy epicenter of the Plaka.

On the left side of the square you'll see the second-century A.D. ruins of the ⓲ **Library of Hadrian** (open to the public). The four lone columns that sit atop the apse-like foundations are the remains of a fifth-century church. The ruins around it are all that's left of a big rectangular complex that once boasted 100 marble columns. Destroyed in the third century A.D., it was a cultural center (library, lecture halls, garden, and art gallery), built by the Greek-loving Roman em-

peror for the Athenian citizens. Notice how the excavated stones rest neatly in stacks awaiting funding for reconstruction.

• *Continue downhill alongside the ruins to the next block, where Aiolou intersects with the claustrophobic Pandrossou market street (which we walked along earlier). Remember that this crowded lane is worked by expert pickpockets—be careful. Look to the right up Pandrossou: You may see merchants sitting in folding chairs with their backs to one another, competition having soured their personal relationships. Turn left on Pandrossou and wade through the knee-deep tacky tourist souvenirs. Several shops here (including one we just passed on Aiolou, and two more on Pandrossou) supply fans of the "Round Goddess"—a.k.a. soccer (each team has its own store). Continue until you spill out into Monastiraki Square.*

⓳ Monastiraki Square Spin-Tour

We've made it from Syntagma Square—the center of urban Athens—to the city's *other* main square, Monastiraki Square, the gateway to the touristy Old Town. To get oriented to Monastiraki Square, stand in the center, face the small church with the cross on top (which is north), and pan clockwise.

The name Monastiraki ("Little Monastery") refers to this square, the surrounding neighborhood, the flea-market action nearby...and the cute **Church of the Virgin** in the square's center (12th-century Byzantine, mostly restored with a much more modern bell tower).

Beyond that (straight ahead from the end of the square), **Athinas street** heads north to the Central Market, Omonia Square, and (after about a mile) the National Archaeological Museum.

Just to the right (behind the little church) is the head of

Ermou street—the bustling shopping drag we walked down earlier (though no longer traffic-free here). If you turned right and walked straight up Ermou, you'd be back at Syntagma Square in 10 minutes.

Next (on the right, in front of the little church) comes Mitropoleos street—Athens' ❷⓿ **"Souvlaki Row."** Clogged with outdoor tables, this atmospheric lane is home to a string of restaurants that serve sausage-shaped, skewered meat—grilled up spicy and tasty. The place on the corner—Bairaktaris (ΜΠΑΪΡΑΚΤΑΡΗΣ)— is the best known, its walls lined with photos of famous politicians and artists who come here for souvlaki and pose with the owner. But the other two joints along here—Thanasis and Savas—have a better reputation for their souvlaki. You can sit at the tables, or, for a really cheap meal, order a souvlaki to go for €2. (For details, see the Eating in Athens chapter.) A few blocks farther down Mitropoleos is the cathedral we visited earlier.

Continue spinning clockwise. Just past Pandrossou street (where you entered the square), you'll see a ❷❶ **former mosque** (look for the Arabic script under the portico and over the wooden door). Known as the Tzami (from the Turkish word for "mosque"), this was a place of worship from the 15th to 19th century. Today it houses the Museum of Greek Folk Art's **ceramics collection** (see page 56).

To the right of the mosque, behind the fence along Areos street, you might glimpse some huge Corinthian columns. This is the opposite end of the **Library of Hadrian** complex we saw earlier. Areos street stretches up toward the Acropolis. If you were to walk a block up this street, then turn right on Adrianou, you'd reach the ❷❷ **Ancient Agora**—one of Athens' top ancient attractions (for more, take my Ancient Agora Tour, available 📖 as a chapter in this book and 🎧 as a free audio tour). Beyond the Agora are the delightful Thissio neighborhood, ancient Keramikos Cemetery, and Gazi district.

As you continue panning clockwise, next comes the pretty yellow building that houses the **Monastiraki Metro station.** This was Athens' original, 19th-century train station—Neoclassical with a dash of Byzantium. This bustling Metro stop is the intersection of two lines: the old line 1 (green, with connections to the port of Piraeus, the Thissio neighborhood, and Victoria—near the National Archaeological Museum) and the modern line 3 (blue, with connections to Syntagma Square and the airport). The stands in front of the station sell seasonal fruit and are popular with commuters.

Just past the station, Ifestou street leads downhill into the ❷❸ **flea market** (antiques, jewelry, cheap clothing, and so on—for more details, see page 188). If locals need a screw for an old lamp, they know they'll find it here.

Keep panning clockwise. Just beyond busy Ermou street (to the left of Athinas street, behind the A for Athens hotel—which has a rooftop bar popular for its views) is the happening **Psyrri** district. For years a run-down slum, this zone is being gentrified by twentysomethings with a grungy sense of style. Packed with cutting-edge bars, restaurants, cafés, and nightclubs, it may seem foreboding and ramshackle, but it is actually fun to explore. (Wander through by day to get your bearings, then head back at night when it's buzzing with activity.) For more on Psyrri, see pages 51 and 178.

❷❹ Monastiraki Metro Station

Finish your walk by stepping into the Monastiraki Metro station and riding the escalator down to see an exposed bit of ancient Athens. Excavations for the Metro revealed an ancient aqueduct, which confined Athens' Eridanos River to a canal. The river had been a main axis of the town since the eighth century B.C. In the second century A.D., Hadrian and his engineers put a roof over it, turning it into a more efficient sewer. You're looking at Roman brick and classic Roman engineering. A cool mural shows the treasure trove archaeologists uncovered with the excavations.

This walk has taken us from ancient ruins to the Roman era, from medieval churches and mosques to the guerrilla fighters of Greek Independence, through the bustling bric-a-brac of the modern city, and finally to a place where Athens' infrastructure—both ancient and modern—mingles.

• *Our walk is over. If you're ready for a break, savor a spicy souvlaki on "Souvlaki Row." If you're looking for local color, head four blocks up Athinas street to the Central Market (described on page 60).*

CITY WALK

ACROPOLIS TOUR

Ακρόπολη

Even in this age of superlatives, it's hard to overstate the historic and artistic importance of the Acropolis. Crowned by the mighty Parthenon, the Acropolis ("high city") rises above the sprawl of modern Athens, a lasting testament to ancient Athens' glorious Golden Age in the fifth century B.C.

The Acropolis has been the heart of Athens since the beginning of recorded time. This limestone plateau, faced with sheer, 100-foot cliffs and fed by per-

manent springs, was a natural fortress. The Mycenaeans (c. 1400 B.C.) ruled the area from their palace on this hilltop, and Athena—the patron goddess of the city—was worshipped here from around 800 B.C. on.

But everything changed in 480 B.C. when Persia invaded Greece for the second time. As the Persians approached, the Athenians evacuated the city, abandoning it to be looted and vandalized. All the temples atop the Acropolis were burned to the ground. The Athenians fought back at sea, winning an improbable naval victory at the Battle of Salamis. The Persians were driven out of Greece, and Athens found itself suddenly victorious. Cash poured into Athens from the other Greek city-states, which were eager to be allied with the winning side.

By 450 B.C., Athens was at the peak of its power and the treasury was flush with money...but in the city center, the Acropolis still lay empty, a vast blank canvas. Athens' leader at the time, Pericles, was ambitious and farsighted. He funneled Athens' newfound wealth into a massive rebuilding program. Led by the visionary architect/sculptor Pheidias (490-430 B.C.), the Athenians transformed the Acropolis into a complex of supersized, ornate temples worthy of the city's protector, Athena.

The four major monuments—the Parthenon, Erechtheion, Propylaea, and Temple of Athena Nike—were built as a coherent ensemble (c. 450-400 B.C.). Unlike most ancient sites, which have layer upon layer of ruins from different periods, the Acropolis we see today was started and finished within two generations—a snapshot of the Golden Age set in stone.

Orientation

Cost: €20 for Acropolis ticket, €10 off-season, €30 Acropolis combo-ticket also covers other major ancient sites—see page 45. If you buy an Acropolis combo-ticket at a different site, you can bypass the ticket booth.

Hours: Daily May-Sept 8:00-20:00, April and Oct 8:00-19:00, Nov-March 8:00-15:00. Be aware that open hours are subject to change; check locally before planning your day.

Crowd-Beating Tips: Arrive early or late to avoid the crowds and midday heat. The place is miserably packed with tour groups from 10:00 to about 12:30 (when you might have to wait up to 45 minutes to get a ticket). On some days, as many as 6,000 cruise passengers converge on the Acropolis in a single morning. Buying an Acropolis combo-ticket at another sight may save ticket-buying time, but doesn't ensure a speedy entry: The worst lines are caused by the bottleneck of people trying to squeeze into the site through the Propylaea gate. Late in the day, as the sun goes down, the white Parthenon stone gleams a creamy golden brown, and what had been a tourist war zone is suddenly peaceful. On my last visit, I showed up late and had the place to myself in the cool of early evening.

Getting There: There's no way to reach the Acropolis without a lot of climbing (though wheelchair users can take an elevator—see below). Figure a 10- to 20-minute hike from the base of the Acropolis up to the hilltop archaeological site. There are multiple paths up, but the only ticket office and site entrance are at the western end of the hill (to the right as you face the Acropolis from the Plaka).

If you're touring the Ancient Agora, you can hike directly up to the Acropolis entrance along the Panathenaic Way. The approach from the Dionysiou Areopagitou pedestrian zone behind (south of) the Acropolis is slightly steeper. From this walkway, various well-marked paths funnel visitors up to the entrance; the least steep one climbs up from the parking lot at the western end of the pedestrian zone. You can reach this path either by taxi or by tourist train (the Athens Happy Train—see page 42), but it still involves quite a bit of uphill hiking.

If you use a **wheelchair,** you can take the elevator that ascends the Acropolis (from the ticket booth, go around the left side of the hilltop). However, once you are up top, the site is not particularly level or well-paved, so you may need help navigating the steep inclines and uneven terrain.

ACROPOLIS

Information: Supplement this tour with the free information brochure (you may have to ask for it when you buy your ticket) and info plaques posted throughout. Tel. 210-321-4172, www.culture.gr.

Tours: If you'd like a live **guide,** consider making advance arrangements with one of my recommended local guides (see page 43). You can hire your own tour guide at the entrance, but I wouldn't—the guides here tend to be rude, overpriced, and underqualified.

☊ Download my free Acropolis **audio tour.** This sight is particularly suited to an audio tour, as it allows your eyes to enjoy the wonders of the Acropolis while your ears learn its story.

Length of This Tour: Allow two hours. Visitors with more time can easily precede this tour with the Ancient Agora Tour (see the next chapter).

Baggage Check: Backpacks are allowed; baby strollers are not. There's a checkroom just below the ticket booth near Mars Hill.

Services: There are WCs at the Acropolis ticket booth and more WCs and drinking fountains atop the Acropolis in the former museum building (behind the Parthenon). Also inside the turnstiles are machines selling cheap, cold bottles of water. Picnicking is not allowed on the premises. Near the ticket booth are a juice/snack stand (which sells overpriced sparkling water but not plain bottled water), a drinking fountain, a post office, and a museum shop.

Plan Ahead: Wear sensible shoes—Acropolis paths are steep and uneven. In summer, it gets very hot on top, so take a hat, sunscreen, sunglasses, and a bottle of water.

Starring: The Parthenon and other monuments from the Golden Age, plus great views of Athens and beyond.

The Tour Begins

• *Climb up to the Acropolis ticket booth and the site entrance, located at the west end of the hill.*

Near this entrance (below and toward the Ancient Agora) is the huge, craggy boulder of **Mars Hill** (a.k.a. Areopagus). Consider

climbing this rock for great views of the Acropolis' ancient entry gate, the Propylaea (described later) and the Ancient Agora. Mars Hill's bare, polished rock is extremely slippery—a metal staircase to the left helps somewhat. (For more on Mars Hill and its role in Christian history, see page 48.)

Before you show your ticket and enter the Acropolis site, make sure you have everything you'll need for your visit. Remember, after you enter the site, there are no services except WCs and water fountains.

• *Enter the site and start climbing the paths that switchback up the hill, following signs on this one-way tourist route (bearing to the right). Before you reach the summit, peel off to the right for a bird's-eye view of the...*

The Acropolis

① *Odeon of Herodes Atticus*
② *Propylaea (Entrance Gate)*
③ *Temple of Athena Nike*
④ *Monument of Agrippa*
⑤ *Beulé Gate*
⑥ *Statue of Athena Promachos*
⑦ *Parthenon*
⑧ *Porch of the Caryatids*
⑨ *Erechtheion*
⑩ *Greek Flag*
⑪ *Views of Athens (2)*

Mars Hill

To Ancient Agora, Monastiraki & Plaka

Cliffs

PROPYLAEA

BEULÉ GATE

TICKETS, WC & JUICE/SNACKS

ACROPOLIS ENTRANCE

TEMPLE OF ATHENA NIKE

ODEON OF HERODES ATTICUS

⋯⋯ STANDING RUINS
— ORIGINAL FOOTPRINT

DIONYSIOU AREOPAGITOU

To Acropolis Museum

ACROPOLIS

❶ Odeon of Herodes Atticus

The grand Odeon huddles under the majestic Propylaea. Tourists call it a "theater," but Greeks know it's technically an *odeon*, as it was mainly used for musical rather than theatrical performances. (*Odeon*—like the English word "ode"—comes from the Greek word for "song.")

A large 5,000-seat **amphitheater** built during Roman times, it's still used for performances. From this perch you get a good look at the stage setup: a three-quarter-circle orchestra (where musicians and actors performed in Greek-style theater), the overgrown remnants of a raised stage (for actors in the Roman tradition), and an intact stage wall for the backdrop. Originally it had a wood-and-tile roof as well.

The Odeon is sometimes called the Herodion, after Herodes Atticus, a wealthy landowner who had the building erected in A.D.

161 in memory of his wife. Herodes Atticus was a Greek with Roman citizenship, a legendary orator, and a friend of Emperor Hadrian. This amphitheater is the most famous of the many impressive buildings he financed around the country.

Destroyed by the invading Herulians a century after it was built, the Odeon was reconstructed in the 1950s to the spectacular state it's in today. It's open to the public only during performances, such as the annual Athens & Epidavros Festival, when an international lineup of dance, music, and theater is performed beneath the stars. If there's something on tonight, you may see a rehearsal from here. Athenians shudder when visitors—recalling the famous "Yanni Live at the Acropolis" concert—call this stately place "Yanni's Theater."

ACROPOLIS

• *After climbing a few steps, you'll see two gates: On the right, steps lead down to the Theater of Dionysus (described on page 49); on the left is the actual entry uphill into the Acropolis. Stay left and continue up to reach the grand entrance gate of the Acropolis: the Propylaea. Stand at the foot of the (very) steep marble staircase, facing up toward the big Doric columns.*

As you face the Propylaea, to your left is a tall, gray stone pedestal with nothing on it: the Monument of Agrippa. On your right, atop the wall, is the Temple of Athena Nike. Behind you stands a doorway in a wall, known as the Beulé Gate.

❷ The Propylaea

The entrance to the Acropolis couldn't be through just any old gate; it had to be the grandest gate ever built. Ancient visitors would stand here, catching their breath before the final push to the summit, and admire these gleaming columns and steep steps that almost fill your field of vision. Imagine the psychological impact this awe-inspiring, colonnaded entryway to the sacred rock must have had on ancient Athenians. The odd mix of **stairs**

here shows how the way up looked in different eras. The original ascent, a ramp that allowed sacrificial animals to make the climb, was replaced with a grand marble staircase in Hellenistic times, and then with a zigzag road (partly still intact) in the Middle Ages. (A few original stairs survive under the wooden ramp.)

The Propylaea (pro-PEE-leh-ah) is U-shaped, with a large central hallway (the six Doric columns), flanked by side wings that reach out to embrace the visitor. The central building looked like a mini-Parthenon, with Doric columns topped by a triangular pediment. Originally, the Propylaea was painted bright colors.

The left wing of the Propylaea was the **Pinakotheke,** or "painting gallery." In ancient times this space contained artwork and housed visiting dignitaries and VIPs.

The buildings of the Acropolis were all built to complement one another. The Propylaea was constructed in five short years (437-432 B.C.), just after the Parthenon was finished. Its design (by Mnesicles) was meant to give the visitor a hint of the Parthenon to come. Both buildings are Doric (with Ionic touches) and are aligned east-west, with columns of similar width-to-height ratios.

• *Before ascending, notice the monuments flanking the entryway. To the right of the Propylaea, look up high atop the block wall to find the...*

❸ Temple of Athena Nike

The Temple of Athena Nike (Greeks pronounce it "NEEK-ee") was started as the Propylaea was being finished (c. 427-421/415 B.C.). It was designed by Callicrates, one of the architects of the Parthenon. This little temple—nearly square, 11 feet tall, with four columns at both ends—had delightful proportions. Where the Parthenon and Propylaea are sturdy Doric, this temple pioneered the Ionic style in Athens, with elegant scroll-topped columns.

The Acropolis was mainly dedicated to the **goddess Athena,** patron of the city. At this temple, she was worshipped for bringing the Athenians victory ("Nike"). A statue of Athena inside the temple celebrated the turning-point victory over the Persians at the Battle of Plataea in 479 B.C. It was also meant to help ensure future victory over the Spartans in the ongoing Peloponnesian War. The statue was never given wings because Athenians wanted Athena to stay and protect their city—hence the place became known as the Temple of Wingless Athena.

The Temple of Athena Nike has undergone **extensive restoration.** From 2001 to 2010, it was completely disassembled, then cleaned, shored up, and pieced back together. This was the third time in its 2,500-year history that the temple had been entirely taken apart. The Ottomans pulled it down at the end of the 17th century and used the stone elsewhere, but Greeks reassembled the temple after regaining their independence. In 1935 it was taken apart for renovation and put back together in 1939. Unfortunately, that shoddy work did more harm than good—prompting the most recent restoration. Now it's been done the right way and should hold for another 2,500 years.

• *To the left (as you face the Propylaea) is the...*

❹ Monument of Agrippa

This 25-foot-high pedestal, made of big blocks of gray marble with yellow veins, reaches as high up as the Temple of Athena Nike. The (now-empty) pedestal once held a bronze statue of the **four-horse chariot** owned by Eumenes II, king of Pergamon—the winner of the race at the 178 B.C. Panathenaic Games.

Over the centuries, each ruler of Athens wanted to put his mark on the mighty Acropolis. When Rome occupied the city, Marc Antony placed a statue of himself and his girlfriend Cleopatra atop the pedestal. After their defeat, the Roman general Agrippa (son-in-law of Augustus) replaced it with a statue of himself (in 27 B.C.).

• *Before entering, look downhill. Behind you is the...*

❺ Beulé Gate

This **ceremonial doorway** was built by the Romans, who used the rubble from buildings that had recently been destroyed in the barbarian Herulian invasion of A.D. 267. (The gate's French name comes from the archaeologist who discovered it in 1852.) During Roman times, this gate was the official entrance to the Acropolis, making the Propylaea entry even grander.

• *Climb the steps (or today's switchback ramps for tourists) and go...*

Inside the Propylaea

Imagine being part of the grand parade of the Panathenaic Festival, held every four years (see page 128). The procession started at Athens' city gate (near the Keramikos Cemetery), passed through the Agora, then went around Mars Hill, through the central hall of the Propylaea, and up to the glorious buildings atop the summit of the Acropolis. Ancient Greeks approached the Propylaea by proceeding straight up a ramp in the middle, which narrowed as they ascended, funneling them into the central passageway. There were five doorways into the Propylaea, one between each of the six columns.

The Propylaea's **central hall** was once a roofed passageway. The marble-tile ceiling, now partially restored, was painted sky blue and studded with stars. Floral designs decorated other parts of the building. The interior columns are Ionic, a bit thinner than the Doric columns of the exterior. You'll pass by some big column drums with square holes in the center, where iron pins once held the drums in place. (Greek columns were not usually made from a single piece of stone, but from sections—"column drums"—stacked on top of one another.)

• *Pass through the Propylaea. As you emerge out the other end, you're on top of the Acropolis. There it is—the Parthenon! Just like in the books (except for the scaffolding). Stand and take it all in.*

The Acropolis

The "Acropolis rock" is a mostly flat limestone ridge covering seven acres, scattered with ruins. There's the Parthenon ahead to the right. To the left of that, with the six lady pillars (Caryatids), is the Erechtheion. The Panathenaic Way ran between them. The processional street and the buildings were aligned east–west, like the hill.

Ancient visitors here would have come face-to-face with a welcoming 30-foot ❻ **Statue of Athena Promachos,** which stood between the Propylaea and the Erechtheion. (Today there's just a field

of rubble, the statue's former location marked by three stones forming a low wall.) This was one of three statues of Athena on the Acropolis. The patron of the city was worshipped for her wisdom, purity, and strength; here she appeared in her role as "Frontline Soldier" *(promachos),* carrying a shield and spear. The statue was cast by Pheidias, the visionary sculptor/architect most responsible for the design of the Acropolis complex. The bronze statue was so tall that the shining tip of Athena's spear was visible from ships at sea. The statue disappeared in ancient times, and no one knows its fate.

Two important buildings, now entirely gone, flanked this statue and the Panathenaic Way. On the right was the **Chalkotheke,** a practical storage area for the most precious gifts brought to the temple—those made of copper and bronze. On the left stood the **Arrephorion,** a house where young virgins called *ergastinai* worked at looms to weave the *peplos,* the sacred dress given to Athena on her birthday.

• *Move a little closer for the classic view of the...*

❼ Parthenon
West End

The Parthenon is the hill's showstopper—the finest temple in the ancient world, standing on the highest point of the Acropolis, 490 feet above sea level. It's now largely in ruins, partly from the ravages of time, but mostly from a direct mortar-shell hit sustained in 1687 (launched by a Venetian army aiming for the gunpowder stored inside by the Ottomans).

It's impressive enough today, but imagine how awesome the Parthenon must have looked when it was completed nearly 2,500 years ago (much of the west end is behind scaffolding for now—if it's still up during your visit, circle around to the east side). This is Greece's largest **Doric temple:** 228 feet long and 101 feet wide. At each end were 8 outer and 6 inner fluted Doric columns, with 17 columns along each side, plus 23 inner columns in the Doric and 4 in the Ionic style. The outer columns are 34 feet high and 6 feet in diameter. In its heyday, the temple was decorated with statues and carved reliefs, all painted in vivid colors. It's considered Greece's greatest Doric temple—but not its purest example because it incorporates Ionic columns and sculpture.

The Parthenon served the **cult of Virgin Athena.** It functioned as both a temple (with a cult statue inside) and as the treasury of Athens (safeguarding the city's funds, which included the treasury of the Athenian League).

This large temple was completed in less than a decade (447-438 B.C.), though the sculptural decoration took a few years more (finished c. 432). The project's overall look was supervised by the master sculptor-architect Pheidias, built by well-known architects Ictinus and Callicrates, and decorated with carved scenes from Greek mythology by sculptors Agoracritos and Alcamenes.

It's big, sure. But what makes the Parthenon truly exceptional is that the architects used a whole bagful of **optical illusions** to

AS IT APPEARS   AS IT WAS BUILT

AS IT WOULD LOOK
WITHOUT OPTICAL CORRECTIONS

give the building an ever-so-subtle feeling of balance, strength, and harmonious beauty. Architects know that a long, flat baseline on a building looks to the human eye like it's sagging, and that parallel columns appear to bend away from each other. To create a building that looked harmonious, the Parthenon's ancient architects calculated bends in the construction. The base of the Parthenon actually arches several inches upward in the middle to counteract the "sagging" illusion. Its columns tilt ever so slightly inward (one of the reasons why the Parthenon has withstood earthquakes so well). If you extended all the columns upward several miles, they'd eventually touch. The corner columns are thicker to make them appear the same size as the rest; they're also spaced more closely. And the columns bulge imperceptibly halfway up (an effect called "entasis"), giving the subconscious impression of stout, barrel-chested men bearing the weight of the roof. For a building that seems at first to be all about right angles, the Parthenon is amazingly short on straight, structural lines.

All these clever refinements form a powerful subconscious impression on the viewer that brings an otherwise boring architectural box to life. It's amazing to think that all this was planned and implemented in stone so long ago.

The statues and carved reliefs that once decorated the outside of the Parthenon are now mostly faded or missing, but a few remain. Look up at the crossbeam atop the eight columns, decorated with panels of relief carvings called **metopes,** depicting Athenians battling Amazons. Originally there were 92 Doric-style metopes in high relief, mostly designed by Pheidias himself.

The crossbeams once supported a triangular pediment (now gone). This area was once filled in with statues, showing Athena with her olive tree competing with Poseidon and his trident to be Athens' patron god. Today just one statue remains (and it's a reconstruction).

Approach closer and look between the eight columns. Inside, there's another row of eight columns, supporting a covered entrance porch. Look up above the inner eight columns. Decorating those crossbeams are more relief carvings—the "frieze." Originally, a 525-foot-long **frieze** of panels circled the entire building. It showed the Panathenaic parade—women, men on horseback,

ACROPOLIS

musicians, sacrificial animals being led to the slaughter—while the gods looked on. All of the sculptures—metopes, pediment, and frieze—were originally painted in bright colors.

Today, most of the originals are in museums across Europe. In the early 1800s, the cream of the crop, the famous Elgin Marbles (you'd better call them the Parthenon Marbles in Greece), were taken by Lord Elgin to England, where they now sit in the British Museum. The Acropolis Museum (which stands at the base of the hill—you'll see it from a distance later on this tour) was built to house the fragments of the Parthenon sculpture that Athens still owns...and to try to entice the rest back from London.

• *Continue along the Panathenaic Way, walking along the long left (north) side of the Parthenon.*

North Side

This view of the Parthenon gives you a glimpse into how the temple was constructed and how it is being reconstructed today by modern archaeologists.

Looking between the columns, you can see remnants of the interior walls, built with thousands of rectangular blocks. The columns formed an **open-air porch** around the main building, which had an entry hall and *cella* (inner sanctum). Large marble roof tiles were fitted together atop wooden beams. These tiles were carved so thin that the interior glowed with the light that shone through it.

The Parthenon's columns are in the Doric style—stout, lightly fluted, with no base. The simple capital on top consists of a convex plate topped with a square slab. The capitals alone weigh eight to nine tons. The crossbeams consist of a lower half ("architrave") and an upper half, its metopes interspersed with a pattern of grooves (called triglyphs).

The Parthenon (along with the other Acropolis buildings) was constructed from the very finest materials, including high-quality, white Pentelic marble from Penteliko Mountain, 16 miles away. Unlike the grand structures of the Egyptians (pyramids) and the Romans (Colosseum), the Parthenon was built not by slaves but by free men who drew a salary (though it's possible that slaves worked at the quarries).

Imagine the engineering problems of quarrying and transporting more than 100,000 tons of marble. Most likely the **column drums** (5-10 tons each) were cut at the quarry and rolled here. To hoist the drums in place, the builders used four-poster cranes (and Greek mathematics), centering the drums with a cedar peg in the middle. The drums were held together by metal pins that were coated in lead to prevent corrosion, then fitted into a square hole cut in the center of the drum. (The Ottomans scavenged much of this lead to make bullets, contributing to the destruction of the temple over the ages.) Because the Parthenon's dimensions are not mathematically precise (intentionally so), each piece had to be individually cut and sized to fit its exact place. The Parthenon's stones are so well-crafted that they fit together within a thousandth of an inch. The total cost to build the Parthenon (in today's dollars) has been estimated at over a billion dollars.

• *Continue on to the...*

East End and Entrance

This end was the original entrance to the temple. Over the doorway, the triangular pediment depicted the central event in Athenian history—the **birth of Athena,** their patron goddess.

Today, the pediment barely survives, and the original statues of the gods are partly in the British Museum. Originally, the gods were gathered at a banquet (see a copy of the reclining Dionysus at the far left—looking so drunk he's afraid to come down). Zeus got a headache and asked Hephaistos to relieve it. As the other gods looked on in astonishment, Hephaistos split Zeus' head open, and—at the peak of the pediment—out rose Athena. The now-missing statues were surprisingly realistic and three-dimensional, with perfect anatomy and bulging muscles showing through transparent robes.

Imagine this spot during the age of Pericles and Socrates. Stand back far enough to take it all in, imagine the huge statue of Athena that once stood inside (see next page), and picture the place in all its glory on the day of the **Panathenaic parade.** The procession would have traveled through the Agora, ascended the Acropolis, passed through the Propylaea, and arrived here at the altar of Athena in front of the entrance of the Parthenon. People gathered on the surrounding grass (the hard stone you see today was once covered with plants). Musicians played flutes and harps, young women carried gifts, and men on horseback reined in their restless animals. On open-air altars, the priests offered a sacrifice of 100 oxen (a hecatomb—the ultimate sacrificial gift) to the goddess Athena.

Here at the Parthenon entrance, a select few celebrants were chosen to go inside. They proceeded up the steps, passed through the majestic columns into the foyer *(pronaos),* and entered the main hall, the *cella*—100 feet long, 60 feet wide, and 4 stories tall. At the far end of the room stood an enormous, 40-foot-tall statue of **Athena Parthenos** (Athena the Virgin). This was a chryselephantine statue, meaning "of gold and ivory"—from the Greek *chrysos,* "gold," and *elephantinos,* "ivory." Its wooden core was plated with ivory to represent her skin and a ton of pure gold to define her garments (or so say local guides). Dressed as a warrior, she wore a helmet and rested her shield at her side. Her image was reflected in a pool in the center of the room. (The pool also served a practical purpose—the humidity helped preserve the ivory treasures.) In Athena's left hand was a spear propped on the ground. In her upturned right hand was a statuette of Nike—she literally held Victory in the palm of her hand.

The statue—the work of the master Pheidias—was either carried off in A.D. 426 to Constantinople, where it subsequently vanished, or was burned by the Herulians in A.D. 267. (A small-scale Roman copy is on display in Athens' National Archaeological Museum; see page 152.) Another famous chryselephantine statue by Pheidias—of a seated Zeus—was considered one of the Seven Wonders of the Ancient World (see sidebar on page 266).

The culmination of the Great Panathenaic parade every four years was the presentation of a newly woven *peplos* to Athena. The dress was intended for the life-size wooden statue of Athena kept at the Erechtheion (described later).

• *The modern brown-brick building behind you once housed the* ***former Acropolis museum****—its collection has been painstakingly moved into the modern Acropolis Museum down the hill. The old museum building may reopen someday as a coffee shop, but for now, it has just WCs and a drinking fountain alongside.*

Across the street from the Parthenon stands the Erechtheion, where the Panathenaic parade ended. Start by enjoying its famous...

❽ Porch of the Caryatids

An inspired piece of architecture, this balcony has six beautiful maidens functioning as columns that support the roof. Each

of the **lady-columns** has a base beneath her feet, pleated robes as the fluting, and a fruit-basket hat as the capital. Both feminine and functional, they pose gracefully, exposing a hint of leg—a combination of architectural elements and sculpture.

These are faithful copies of

the originals, five of which are on display in the Acropolis Museum. The sixth was removed (c. 1805) by the sticky-fingered Lord Elgin, who shipped it to London. The Caryatids were supposedly modeled on *Karyatides*—women from Karyai (modern Karyes, near Sparta on the Peloponnese), famous for their upright posture and noble character.

The Erechtheion (c. 421-406 B.C.) is sometimes ascribed to Mnesicles, the man who designed the Propylaea. Whereas the Propylaea and Parthenon are both sturdy Doric, the Erechtheion is elegant Ionic. In its day, it was a stunning white building (of Pentelic marble) with painted capitals and a frieze of white relief on a darker blue-gray background.

Near the porch (below, to the left) is an **olive tree,** a replacement for the one Athena planted here in her face-off with Poseidon (described later). Olive trees have been called "the gift of Athena to Athens." Greece has more than 140 million of these trees.

• *Walk around to the right and view the Erechtheion from the east end, with its six Ionic columns in a row.*

❾ Erechtheion

Though overshadowed by the more impressive Parthenon, the Erechtheion (a.k.a. Erechtheum) was perhaps more prestigious. It

stood on one of the oldest sites on the hill, where the Mycenaeans had built their palace. (It lay mainly on the south side, facing the Parthenon, under the huge scattered stones—all that's left of the seventh-century Athena Temple.) Inside the Erechtheion was a life-size, olive-wood statue of Athena in her role of **Athena Polias** ("Protector of the City").

Pericles took the statue with him when the Athenians evacuated their city to avoid the invading Persians. Dating from about 900 B.C., this statue, much older and more venerable than either of

Pheidias' colossal statues, supposedly dropped from the sky as a gift from Athena.

This unique, two-story structure fits nicely into the slope of the hill. The east end (with the six Ionic columns) was the upper-level entrance. The lower entrance was on the north side (on the right), 10 feet

Acropolis Now: The Renovation Project

The scaffolding, cranes, and modern construction materials you see here are part of an ongoing renovation project. The challenge is to save what's left of the Parthenon from the modern menaces of acid rain and pollution, which have already caused irreversible damage. Funded by Greece and the EU, the project began in 1976, which means that they've been at it more than three times as long as it took to build the Parthenon in the first place.

The project first involves cataloging every single stone of the Parthenon—blocks, drums, capitals, bits of rock, and pieces lying on the ground or in museums around the world. Next, archaeologists hope to put it back together, like a giant 70,000-piece jigsaw puzzle. Along the way, they're fixing previous restorations that were either inaccurate or problematic. For example, earlier restorers used uncoated iron and steel rods to hold things together. As weather fluctuations caused the metal to expand, the stone was damaged. This time around, restorers are using titanium rods.

Whenever possible, the restorers use original materials. But you'll also see big blocks of new marble lying on the

ground—freshly cut from the same Pentelic quarries that supplied the original stone. The new marble is being used to replace damaged and missing pieces. Many of the columns have light-colored "patches" where the restorers have installed the new stone, cut to fit exactly. Though it looks much whiter, in time the newly cut marble will age to match the rest of the Parthenon.

When complete, the renovated Parthenon won't look like a fully restored building—just a shored-up version of the ruin we see today. If you want to see what the Parthenon temple looked like in its heyday, there's a full-scale replica open to visitors...in Nashville, Tennessee.

lower, where you see six more Ionic columns. (These columns are the "face of the Acropolis" that Athenians see from the Plaka.) The **Porch of the Caryatids** is attached to the south side of the building. Looking inside the temple, you can make out that the inner worship hall, the *cella*, is divided in two by walls.

This complex layout accommodated the worship of various gods who had been venerated here since the beginning of time. Legend says this was the spot where Athena and Poseidon fought for naming rights to the city. Poseidon threw his trident, which opened a gash in the earth to bring forth water. It left a diagonal crack that you can still see in the pavement of the entrance farthest from the Parthenon (although lightning is a more likely culprit). But Athena won the contest by stabbing a rock with her spear, sprouting an olive tree near the Porch of the Caryatids. The twin *cellas* of the Erechtheion allowed the worship of both gods—Athena and Poseidon—side by side to show that they were still friends.

• *Look to the right (beyond the Plaka-facing porch). The modern **elevator** carries people with limited mobility up to the Acropolis. The north wall of the Acropolis has a retaining wall built from **column drums**. This is about all that remains of an earlier half-finished Parthenon that was destroyed after the Persian invasion of 480 B.C. The Persians razed the entire Acropolis, including an unfinished temple then under construction. The Athenians rebuilt as fast as they could with the scattered material to fortify the city against Sparta.*

Walk to the far end of the Acropolis. There you'll find an observation platform with a giant...

❿ Greek Flag

The blue-and-white Greek flag's nine stripes symbolize the nine syllables of the Greek phrase for "Freedom or Death." That phrase

took on new meaning when the Nazis entered Athens in April 1941. According to an oft-repeated (but unverified) story, the evzone (member of a select infantry unit) guarding the flag flying here was ordered by the Nazis to remove it. He calmly took it down, wrapped himself in it...and jumped to his death. About a month later, two heroic teenagers, Manolis Glezos and Apostolis Santas, scaled the wall, took down the Nazi flag and raised the Greek flag. This was one of the first well-known acts of resistance against the Nazis, and the boys' bravery is honored by a plaque near the base of the steps.

After the Golden Age: The Acropolis Through History

Classical: The Parthenon and the rest of the Acropolis buildings survived through classical times largely intact, despite Herulian looting (A.D. 267). As the Roman Empire declined, precious items were carried off, including the 40-foot Athena statue from the Parthenon.

Christian: The Christian emperor Theodosius II (Theodosius the Great) labored to outlaw pagan worship and to close temples and other religious sites. After nearly a thousand years as Athena's temple, the Parthenon became a Christian church (fifth century A.D.). It remained Christian for the next thousand years, first as the Byzantine Orthodox Church of Holy Wisdom, then as Mother Mary of Athens (11th century), and at the end as a Roman Catholic cathedral of Notre Dame (dedicated to Mary in 1205 by Frankish Crusaders). Throughout medieval times it was an important stop on the pilgrimage circuit.

The Parthenon's exterior was preserved after its conversion to a church, but pagan sculptures and decorations were removed (or renamed), and the interior was decorated with colorful Christian frescoes. The west end of the building became the main entrance, and the interior was reconfigured with an apse at the east end.

Muslim: In 1456, the Turks arrived and converted the Parthenon into a mosque, adding a minaret. The Propylaea gateway was used as a palace for the Turkish ruler of Athens. The Turks had no respect for the sacred history of the Acropolis—they even tore down stones just to get the lead clamps that held them in place in order to make bullets. (The exasperated Greeks even offered

To this day, Greeks can see this flag from just about anywhere in Athens and think of their hard-won independence.

• *Walk out to the end of the rectangular promontory to see the...*

⓫ View of Athens

The Ancient Agora spreads below the Acropolis, and the sprawl of modern Athens whitewashes the surrounding hills. In 1830, the population of Athen's core was about 5,000. By 1900, it was 600,000, and during the 1920s, with the influx of Greeks from Turkey, the population surged to 1.5 million. The city's expansion them bullets to stop destroying the temple.) The Turks also used the Parthenon to store gunpowder, unfortunately leading to the greatest catastrophe in the Acropolis' long history. It happened in...

1687: A Venetian army laid siege to the Acropolis. The Venetians didn't care about ancient architecture. As far as they were concerned, it was a lucky hit of mortar fire that triggered the massive explosion that ripped the center out of the Parthenon, rattled the Propylaea and the other buildings, and wiped out the Turkish defenders. Pieces of the Parthenon lay scattered on the ground, many of them gathered up as souvenirs by soldiers.

Lord Elgin: In 1801, Lord Elgin, the British ambassador to the Ottomans in Constantinople, got "permission" from the sultan to

gather sculptures from the Parthenon, buy them from locals, and even saw them off the building (Greeks scoff at the idea that "permission" granted by an occupying power should carry any weight). He carted half of them to London, where the "Elgin Marbles" are displayed in the British Museum to this day, despite repeated requests for their return. Although a few original frieze, metope, and pediment carvings still adorn the Parthenon, most of the sculptures are on display in museums, including the Acropolis Museum.

From Independence to the Present: In the 19th century, newly independent Greece tore down the Parthenon's minaret and the other post-Classical buildings atop the Acropolis, turning it into an archaeological zone. Since then the site has been excavated and subjected to several renovations. Today, the Acropolis strikes wonder in the hearts of visitors, just as it has for centuries.

ACROPOLIS

could barely keep up with its exploding population. With the boom times in the 1950s and 1980s, the city grew to nearly four million. Pan around. From this perch you're looking at the homes of one out of every three Greeks.

Looking down on the **Plaka,** find (looking left to right) the Ancient Agora, with the Temple of Hephaistos. Next comes the Roman Forum (the four columns and palm trees) with its round, white, domed Temple of the Winds monument. The **Anafiotika** neighborhood clings to the Acropolis hillside directly below us. About eight blocks beyond that, find the dome of the cathedral.

Lykavittos Hill, Athens' highest point, is crowned with the Chapel of St. George (and an expensive view restaurant; cable car up the hill). Looking farther in the distance, you'll see lighter-colored bits on the mountains behind—these are **Pentelic quarries,** the source of the marble used to build (and now restore) the monuments of the Acropolis.

As you continue panning to the right, you'll spot the beige Neoclassical **Parliament** building, marking Syntagma Square; the **National Garden** is behind and to the right of it. In the garden is the yellow **Zappeion,** an exhibition hall. The green area in the far distance contains the 60,000-seat, marble **Panathenaic Stadium**—an ancient venue (on the site where Golden Age Athens held its games), which was rehabbed in 1896 to help revive the modern Olympics.

• *Complete your visual tour of Athens at the south edge of the Acropolis. To reach the viewpoint, walk back toward the Parthenon, then circle along its left side, by the cliff-top wall. Belly up to that wall for...*

More Views of Athens

Look to the left. In the near distance are the huge columns of the **Temple of Olympian Zeus.** Begun in the sixth century B.C., it wasn't finished until the time of the Roman emperor Hadrian,

700 years later. It was the biggest temple in all of Greece, with 104 Corinthian pillars, housing a 40-foot seated statue of Zeus, a replica of the famous one created by Pheidias in Olympia. This area was part of Hadrian's "new Athens," a planned community in his day, complete with the triumphal **Arch of Hadrian** near the temple.

The **Theater of Dionysus**—which hosted great productions (including works by Sophocles) during the Golden Age—lies in ruins at your feet (a visit to these ruins is covered by your Acropolis ticket). For some background on Greek theater, see the sidebar on page 238.

Beyond the theater is the wonderful **Acropolis Museum,** a black-and-gray modern glass building, with three rectangular floors stacked at irregular angles atop each other. The top floor, which houses replicas and some originals of the Parthenon's art, is angled to match the orientation of that great temple.

Looking right, you see **Filopappos Hill**—the green, tree-dotted hill topped with a marble funerary monument to a popular Roman senator, Philopappos, who died in the early second century. This hill is where the Venetians launched the infamous mortar attack of 1687 that destroyed the Parthenon. Today, a theater here hosts popular folk-dancing performances (described in the Nightlife in Athens chapter).

Farther in the distance, you get a glimpse of the turquoise waters of the **Aegean** (the only island visible is Aegina). While the Persians were burning the Acropolis to the ground, the Athenians watched from their ships as they prepared to defeat their foes in the history-changing Battle of Salamis. In the distance, far to the right, is the port of Piraeus (the main departure point for boats to the islands).

• *Our tour is finished. Enjoy a few final moments with the Acropolis before you leave. If you're not yet ready to return to modern Athens, you can continue your sightseeing at several nearby sights.*

To reach the Theater of Dionysus ruins and the Acropolis Museum: Head left when you exit the Acropolis site, and walk down to the Dionysiou Areopagitou pedestrian boulevard. Turn left and follow this walkway along the base of the Acropolis. You'll pass (on the left) the Theater of Dionysus ruins, and (on the right) the Acropolis Museum (see the 📖 *Acropolis Museum Tour chapter).*

To reach the Ancient Agora: Turn right as you exit the Acropolis site, pass Mars Hill, and follow the Panathenaic Way down to the Ancient Agora (possible to enter through the "back door," facing the Acropolis). My Ancient Agora Tour is covered in the next 📖 *chapter and is also available as a free* 🎧 *audio tour.*

ANCIENT AGORA TOUR

Αρχαία Αγορά

While the Acropolis was the ceremonial showpiece, the Agora was the real heart of ancient Athens. Although used as a residential and burial area since 3000 B.C., it became a public space around 600 B.C. For some 800 years, until its destruction by barbarians in A.D. 267, it was the hub of all commercial, political, and social life in Athens, as well as home to much of its religious life.

Agora means "gathering place," but you could call this space by any of the names we typically give to the busiest part of a city— downtown, main square, forum, piazza, marketplace, commons, and so on. It was a lively place where the pace never let up—much like modern Athens.

Little survives from the classical Agora. Other than one very well-preserved temple and a rebuilt stoa, it's a field of humble ruins. But that makes it a quiet, uncrowded spot—nestled in the shadow of the Acropolis—to wander and get a feel for the ancients.

Orientation

Cost: €8, covered by €30 Acropolis combo-ticket (which you can buy here; see page 45).

Hours: Daily May-Sept 8:00-20:00, April and Oct 8:00-19:00, Nov-March 8:00-15:00. The Agora Museum inside has the same hours, except on Monday, when it opens at 11:00.

Getting There: From the Monastiraki Metro stop, walk a block south (uphill, toward the Acropolis). Turn right on Adrianou street, and follow the pedestrian-only, café-lined street along the railroad tracks for about 200 yards. The Agora entrance is on your left, across from a small, yellow church. The entrance can be hard to spot: It's where a path crosses over the railroad tracks (look for a small, pale-yellow sign that says *Ministry of Culture—Ancient Agora*).

Compass Points: The Agora entrance is north; the Acropolis is south.

Information: Panels with printed descriptions of the ruins are scattered helpfully throughout the site. Tel. 210-321-0180, www.culture.gr.

Tours: ∩ Download my free Ancient Agora audio tour.

Services: Machines behind the ticket booths sell bottled water. The only WCs on the site are inside the Stoa of Attalos, at its northernmost end.

Eating: Picnicking is not allowed in the Agora. Plenty of cafés and tavernas line busy Adrianou street near the entrance, and more good eateries front the Apostolou Pavlou pedestrian walkway that hems in the western edge of the Agora, in the district called Thissio (see the Nightlife in Athens chapter).

Starring: A well-preserved temple, a rebuilt stoa, three monumental statues, and the ruins of the civilization that built the Western world.

The Tour Begins

Entering the site from Adrianou street, belly up to the illustration at the top of the ramp that shows the Athenian Agora at the peak

of its size. Face the Acropolis (to the south), look out over the expanse of ruins and trees, and get oriented.

The long column-lined building to the left is the reconstructed Stoa of Attalos (#13 on the illustration). To your right, atop a hill (the view is likely blocked by trees) is the well-preserved Temple of Hephaistos (#20). The pathway called the Panathenaic Way (#21) runs from the Agora's entrance up to the Acropolis. Directly ahead of you are three tall statue-columns (also probably obscured by trees)—part of what was once the Odeon of Agrippa (#12).

In the distance, the Agora's far end is bordered by hills. From left to right are the Acropolis (#1), the Areopagus ("Hill of Ares," or Mars Hill, #2), and Pnyx Hill (#3).

Although the illustration implies that you're standing somewhere behind the Stoa Poikile ("Painted Stoa," #28), in fact you are located in front of it, closer to the heart of the Agora, to the left of the Altar of the Twelve Gods (#26). In ancient times, that altar

AGORA

The Agora at Its Peak

ACROPOLIS

MARS HILL

- **Ⓐ** Stoa of Attalos
- **Ⓑ** Temple of Hephaistos
- **Ⓒ** Panathenaic Way
- **Ⓓ** Odeon of Agrippa
- **Ⓔ** Current Entrance

was considered the geographical center of Athens, from which distances were measured. Today, the area north of the altar (and north of today's illustration) remains largely unexcavated and inaccessible to tourists, taken over by the railroad tracks and Adrianou street.

This self-guided tour starts at the Stoa of Attalos (with its museum), then crosses the Agora to the Temple of Hephaistos, returning to the Panathenaic Way via three giant statues. Finally, we'll head up the Panathenaic Way toward the Acropolis.

• *Walk to the bottom of the ramp at your left for a better view. Find a shady spot to ponder...*

❶ The Agora

What lies before you now is a maze of ruins—the remains of many centuries of buildings.

A millennium before the time of Socrates, during the Mycenaean Period (around 1600-1200 B.C.), this area held the oldest cemetery in Athens. Later, the Agora was developed into a political forum—the center for speeches, political announcements, and demonstrations. The rectangular area (about 100 yards by 200 yards, bordered by hills) naturally evolved into a marketplace, with sellers lured by the crowds. Over time, that central square became

↑To Plaka, Mars Hill
& Acropolis

30 Meters

30 Yards

TOUR ENDS

Ancient Agora

⚫ STANDING RUINS
◦◦◦◦ ONLY FOUNDATIONS

To
Apostolou
Pavlou
Entrance

STOA OF
ATTALOS

PANATHENAIC WAY

WC

**MAIN
ENTRANCE**

AGORA
←ILLUSTRATION

TICKETS

TEMPLE OF
HEPHAISTOS

ADRIANOU

To Monastiraki
Square & Ⓜ

● TOUR BEGINS

IFESTOU

MONASTIRAKI

To Ermou Street
& Psyrri District ↓

To Thissio Ⓜ

❶ Agora	❾ Statue of Hadrian
❷ Stoa of Attalos	❿ Odeon of Agrippa
❸ Agora Museum	⓫ Panathenaic Way
❹ Middle Stoa	⓬ Post-Herulian Wall
❺ Corinthian Capital	⓭ Church of the
❻ Great Drain	Holy Apostles
❼ Tholos	⓮ South Gate
❽ Temple of Hephaistos	

surrounded by buildings, then filled in with more buildings. There were stoas like the (reconstructed) Stoa of Attalos (above on the left), used for shops and offices; temples such as the Temple of Hephaistos; and government buildings. Imagine the square framed by these buildings—decorated with painted statues and friezes, fronted with columns of gleaming white marble, topped with red-tile roofs. The square itself was studded with trees and dotted with statues, fountains, and altars. Merchants sold goods from wooden market stalls.

The square buzzed with people—mostly men and lower-class working women, as the place was considered a bit vulgar for genteel matrons. Both men and women would be dressed in simple tunics

AGORA

(men's were knee-length, women's to the ankle). The Agora was the place to shop—to buy clothes, dishes, or to get your wagon wheel fixed. When a perishable product was available—for example, a catch of fresh fish—a certain bell was rung to announce its arrival. If you needed a zoning permit for your business, you came to the courthouse. You could make an offering to the gods at a number of temples and altars. At night people attended plays and concerts, and nearby tavernas hummed with excited drinkers. Many people passed through here on their way to somewhere else, as this was the main intersection in town (and ancient Athens probably had a population of at least 100,000). On holidays, the procession ran down main street, the Panathenaic Way. At any time, this was the place to come to run into your friends, to engage in high-minded discussion with philosophers such as Socrates or Diogenes, or just to chat and hang out.

• *Now go to the long, intact, colonnaded building on your left (entrance at the south/far end), which is the...*

❷ Stoa of Attalos

This stoa—an ancient shopping mall—was originally built by the Greek-loving King Attalos II of Pergamon (in modern-day Turkey, 159-138 B.C.) as a thank-you gift for the education he'd received in Athens. That structure is long gone, and the building we see today is a faithful reconstruction built in the 1950s by the American School of Classical Studies.

This is a typical two-story stoa. Like many of the Agora's buildings, it's made of white Pentelic and gray-blue Hymettus marble from the quarries northeast of the city. The portico is supported on the ground floor by 45 Doric columns (outer layer) and 22 Ionic columns (inner layer). The upper story uses Ionic columns. This mix of Doric and Ionic was typical of buildings from the period.

Stoas, with their covered walkways, provided protection from sun and rain for shoppers and merchants. This one likely served as a commercial mall. The ground floor was divided by walls into 21 rooms that served as shops (it's now the museum). Upstairs were offices (which today house more of the Agora Museum and research facilities of the American School of Classical Studies).

Like malls of today, the Agora's stoas were social magnets. Imagine ancient Greeks (their hard labor being done by slaves and servants) lounging here, enjoying the shade of the portico. The design of the pillars encourages people to lean against them (just as you may be doing right now)—with fluting starting only above six feet for the comfort of philosophers. (These smooth-bottomed columns were typical for pub-

lic buildings, whereas temple columns—which the hoi polloi didn't loiter around—always had fluting all the way to the base.)

• *Inside, the Stoa of Attalos houses the...*

❸ Agora Museum

The Agora is mostly ruins, but the excellent little museum displays some choice rubble that helps bring the place to life. Before entering, enjoy the arcade. Near the fifth column, find the impressive sculpted head of a bearded man with a full head of hair. This **Head of a Triton** (c. A.D. 150) comes from one of the statues that decorated the Odeon of Agrippa. Three of his fellow statues are still standing (we'll see them soon).

Walk halfway down the arcade and step inside the museum (included with your Agora ticket). Its modest but engaging collection fills a single long hall and part of the next level up. Look in the corner for the 1952 photo showing this spot before the reconstruction.

This well-described chronological stroll through art from 3200 B.C. gives you a glimpse of life in ancient Athens. Along the hall on the left, big panels show the Agora and Acropolis during each age, allowing you to follow their physical evolution. It's hard to believe that everything on display was found right here at the grounds of the Agora.

The first few cases show off **jars** from various eras, including Neolithic (when the Agora was first inhabited) and Geometric (1050-700 B.C.). One of the oldest pieces found here is the female figure displayed in the glass case in the center (from the fourth millennium B.C.). Much of this exhibit shows how Greek pottery evolved over time. Pottery was a popular export product for the seafaring Greeks, and by tracing local styles of pottery manufacture and decoration, archaeologists have learned about their trading habits. The earliest pottery featured geometric patterns, then came floral and animal motifs, and finally painted human silhouettes—first showing black figures on the natural orange clay, then red figures on a black background. Also in this display is what the Greeks received in return for their pots: ivory and gold, both likely from Egypt.

In case 26 (on the right), look for the cute little baby's **commode,** with a photo showing how it was used. Case 24 has a comb—notable as one of the very rare surviving wooden items found here. Nearby (case 69, on left) are Archaic-era statues with smiling faces.

Cases 30-32 (on right), with items from **early democracy,** are especially interesting. The "voting machine" (*kleroterion*, case 31) was used to choose judges. Citizens put their name in the slots, then black and white balls went into the tube to randomly select who would serve (much like your turn in jury duty). Below the machine are bronze ballots from the fourth century. The pottery shards with names painted on them (*ostrakan*, case 30) were used as ballots in

voting to ostracize someone accused of corruption or tyranny. Find the ones marked ΘEMIΣΘOKLES NEOKLEOS (item #37) and ARISSTEIΔES (item #17, see photo). During the Golden Age, Themistocles and Aristides were rivals (in both politics and romance) who served Athens honorably, but were exiled in political power struggles.

In case 32, see the *klepsydra* ("water thief")—a water clock used to time speeches at Council meetings. It took six minutes for the 1.7 gallons to drain out. A gifted orator truly was good to the last drop...but not a second longer.

Across the hall (under the banner, between cases 68 and 67) is the so-called **"Stele of Democracy"** (c. 336 B.C.). This stone monument is inscribed with a decree outlawing tyranny. Above, a relief carving shows Lady Democracy crowning a man representing the Athenian people.

Next to that (in case 67) is a **bronze shield** captured from defeated Spartans in the tide-turning Battle of Sphacteria, which gave Athens the upper hand in the first phase of the Peloponnesian War. The next case over (case 66) displays herm heads. With news and directions attached, these functioned as signposts along roads.

In the middle of the room,

find the case of **coins**. These drachms and tetradrachms feature Athena with her helmet. In Golden Age times, a drachm was roughly a day's wage. The ancients put coins like these in the mouth of a deceased person as payment for the underworld ferryman Charon to carry the soul safely across the River Styx. Coin #7, with the owl, was a four-drachm piece; that same owl is on Greece's €1 coin today.

For a reminder that the ancients weren't so different from us, look for the two **barbecue grills** (case 61, left; and case 42, right).

The downstairs exhibit winds up with **Roman sculptural heads** (cases 58 and 56, left), which show how the Romans were more honest than the Greeks when it came to portraying people with less-than-ideal features, and even more pottery items—including various toys (case 48, right).

• *Exit this room at the far end of the arcade (where there's a WC and water fountain), and turn left to find the stairway leading up to the second level.*

The best part of this open-air upper floor is the **nice views** it affords down into the Agora and across to the Temple of Hephaistos. While you're up here, study the models of the Agora from various eras. The statues displayed here aren't much different from those you'll see at the Acropolis Museum and the National Archaeological Museum, but their well-written English descriptions and striking setting make them worth at least a quick visit. Before heading downstairs, peer into the storage cases at the back: shelf upon shelf holds pottery shards, all of them dug up right here in the Agora.

• *Back downstairs, leave the stoa through its southern end (where you entered), then cross the main road and continue straight (west) along the lane, across the middle of the Agora. You're walking alongside the vast ruins (on your left) of what once was the...*

❹ Middle Stoa

Stretching clear across the Agora, this was part of a large complex of what were likely shops and office buildings. It was a long, narrow rectangle (about 500 by 60 feet), similar to the reconstructed Stoa of Attalos you just left. You can still see the two lines of stubby column fragments that once supported the roof, a few stone steps, and (at the far end) some of the reddish foundation blocks. Constructed around 180 B.C., this stoa occupied what had been open space in the center of the Agora.

• *Midway down the lane (near the wooden ramp), you'll come across a huge and frilly upper cap, or capital, of a column.*

❺ Corinthian Capital

This capital (dating from the fourth century B.C.) once stood here atop a colossal column, one of a dozen columns that lined the monumental entrance to the Odeon of Agrippa, a theater that extended northward from the Middle Stoa. (We'll learn more about the Odeon later on this tour.) The capital's elaborate acanthus-leaf decoration is a nice example of the late Corinthian style. Rarely used in Greek buildings, the Corinthian style became wildly popular with the Romans.

From here look back toward the entrance, overlooking what was once the vacant expanse at the center of the Agora. In 400 B.C., there was no Middle Stoa and no Odeon—this was all open space. As Athens grew, the space was increasingly filled in with shops and monuments. Now imagine the place in its heyday (see sidebar on page 124).

• *Continue westward across the Agora. Near the end of the Middle Stoa, you'll see a gray well—still in its original spot and worn by the grooves of ropes. From here look up at the Acropolis, where the towering but empty pedestal once sported the Monument of Agrippa, a grand statue with four horses. Mars Hill, likely topped with tourists, is where the Apostle Paul famously preached the Gospel (described on page 48). Below the Erechtheion are broken columns shoring up the side of the hill. These were rubble from temples destroyed by the Persians.*

Just beyond the well to the right is a big drain and a round foundation—the tholos. *Backtrack from the well a few steps to cross the wooden ramp, and go left to find the ditch that was once part of the...*

❻ Great Drain

Dug in the fifth century B.C. and still functioning today, these ditches channel rainwater runoff from the southern hills through the Agora. Here at the southwest corner of the Agora, two main collection ditches meet and join. You can see exposed parts of the stone-lined ditch. The well we just passed was also part of this system.

• *Passing across the ditch and through the line of shrubbery, take the left fork toward a 60-foot–across round footprint with a stubby column in its center. This is the...*

❼ Tholos

This rotunda-shaped building was an assembly place for the administrators of Athens' City Council. Built around 465 B.C., it originally had six inner Ionic columns that held up a conical roof. In the middle was an altar (marked today by the broken column).

AGORA

The fundamental unit of Athenian democracy was the Assembly, made up of the thousands of adult male citizens who could vote. Athenian citizens were organized into 10 tribes; in order to prevent the people living in any one geographical area from becoming dominant, each tribe was composed of citizens from city, coastal, and inland areas. Each man in the Assembly was considered to be from one of these tribes.

All of Athens' governing bodies met in the Agora. Though some Assembly meetings were held in the Agora's main square, the main assemblies took place just uphill, on the slope of Pnyx Hill. The City Council also met in the Agora. The Council consisted of 500 men (50 from each of the 10 tribes) who were chosen from the Assembly by lottery to serve a one-year term. The Council proposed and debated legislation, but because Athens practiced direct (not representational) democracy, all laws eventually had to be approved by the whole Assembly. The Council chose 50 ministers who ran the day-to-day affairs.

As part of the civic center complex, the *tholos* served several functions. It was the headquarters, offices, and meeting hall for the 50 administrators. Many lived and ate here, since the law required that at least a third of these ministers be on the premises at all times (they served for terms of only 36 days). The *tholos* also housed the city's official weights and measures. Any shopper in the Agora could use these to check whether a butcher or tailor was shortchanging them. As the center of government, the *tholos* of any ancient Greek city was also a kind of temple. The altar in the middle held an eternal flame, representing the hearth of the extended "family" that was Athens.

• *Beyond and above the* tholos *is the hill-capping Temple of Hephaistos. To reach it, climb the stairs to the left and go through the trees, pausing along the way at a viewpoint with a chart.*

❽ Temple of Hephaistos

One of the best-preserved and most typical of all Greek temples, this is textbook Golden Age architecture. Started in 450 B.C.—just before the Parthenon—it was built at Athens' peak as part of the massive reconstruction of the Agora after invading Persians destroyed the city (480 B.C.).

But the temple wasn't completed and dedicated until 415 B.C., as work stalled when the Greeks started erecting the great buildings of the Acropolis. Notice how the frieze around the outside of the building

AGORA

The Agora in Action

Think of thousands of angry Athenian citizens assembled here, listening to speeches as they voted to ostracize a corrupt or tyrannical leader. Other than ostracisms, general assemblies usually were not held here, but rather on Pnyx Hill, which rises southwest of the Agora.

The roving philosopher **Socrates** (469-399 B.C.) spent much of his life simply hanging out in the Agora, questioning passersby, and urging people to "know thyself." Socrates discussed the meaning of piety, as recorded by Plato in the dialogue called the Euthyphro. "The lover of inquiry," said Socrates, "must follow his beloved wherever it may lead him." Shortly after, Socrates was tried and condemned to death here for "corrupting the youth"...by encouraging them to question Athenian piety.

Plato, Socrates' disciple and chronicler of his words, spent time teaching in the Agora, as did Plato's disciple **Aristotle.** (Their schools—Plato's Academy and Aristotle's Lyceum—were located elsewhere in Athens.)

The great statesman **Pericles**—whose Funeral Oration over the Greek dead from the first year of the Peloponnesian War is a famous expression of Athenian ideals—must have spent time here, since he oversaw the rebuilding program after the Persian invasion.

was only decorated on the side facing the Agora (it's blank on the other three sides, as were most temples of this kind—the Parthenon is unusual for its continuous, wrap-around frieze).

This is a classic peristyle temple (like the Parthenon)—meaning that the building is surrounded by columns—six on each end, 13 on the long sides (counting the corners twice). Also like the Parthenon, it's made of Pentelic marble in the Doric style, part of Pericles' vision of harking back to Athens' austere, solid roots. But the Temple of Hephaistos is only about half the size of the grand Parthenon and with fewer refinements (compared to the Parthenon's elaborate carvings and fancy math).

The temple's entrance was on the east end, facing the Agora. Priests would enter through the six columns here, crossing through a covered portico (note the coffered ceiling) and a three-sided alcove, called the *pronaos* or "pre-temple," before reaching the central hall *(cella).* Large bronze statues of Hephaistos, the blacksmith god,

When Athens triumphed over Sparta in one battle during the Peloponnesian War (425 B.C.), **General Cleon** displayed the shields of captured prisoners in the Agora. This action mocked the Spartans for their surrender, since brave Spartans were always supposed to die with their shields on.

Diogenes the Cynic lived as a homeless person in the Agora and shocked the Athenians with his anti-materialist and free lifestyle. He lived in a wooden tub (in disregard for material comfort), masturbated openly (to prove how simply one's desires could be satisfied), and wandered the Agora with a lighted lamp in daylight (looking for one honest man in the corrupt city). According to legend, Alexander the Great was intrigued by this humble philosopher who shunned materialism. One day he stood before him and said, "Diogenes, I will give you whatever you want. What would you like?" History's first hippie looked at the most powerful man on earth and replied, "Please get out of my sunshine."

The earliest Greek plays and concerts were performed here in the open air and, later, in theaters (including the Odeon of Agrippa). The playwright **Aristophanes** set scenes in the Agora, and the tragedian **Sophocles** spent time here.

Imagine the buzz in the Agora at key points in Athens' history—as Athenians awaited the onslaught of the Persians and debated what to do, or as they greeted the coming of Alexander the Great, the conquering Romans, and the invasions of the Herulians and Slavs.

The **Apostle Paul** likely talked religion here in the Agora on his way to Corinth in A.D. 49 (Acts 17:17). He would have seen the various altars dedicated to pagan gods, which he decried from Mars Hill, overlooking the Agora.

and Athena, patroness of Athens and of arts and crafts, once stood in this central hall. In ancient times, metalworking and pottery shops surrounded the temple, but in the third century B.C. some were replaced with gardens, similar to today's. Behind the *cella* (the west end) is another three-sided alcove, matching the *pronaos*.

The carved reliefs (frieze and metopes) that run around the upper part of the building are only partly done; some panels may have been left unfinished.

At the end overlooking the Agora, look between the six columns and up at the frieze above the *pronaos* to find scenes of the mythical hero Theseus battling his enemies, trying to unite Athens. Theseus would go on to free Athens from the dominance of Crete by slaying the bull-headed Minotaur. The frieze decorations led Athenians to mistakenly believe that the temple once held the remains of Theseus—and to this day, they call it the Theseion.

Walk around behind the temple, to the far (west) end. The

AGORA

frieze above the three-sided alcove depicts the mythological battle between the Lapith tribe and centaurs during a wedding feast.

Other scenes you'll see around the building (there are many interpretations) include Hercules (his labors and deification) and the birth of Erichthonios (one of Athens' first kings, who was born when spurned Hephaistos tried to rape Athena, spilled semen, and instead impregnated Gaia, the earth).

In the seventh century A.D., the temple was converted into the Church of Agios Georgios, and given the vaulted ceiling that survives today. During the Ottoman occupation, the Turks kept the church open but permitted services to be held only once each year (on St. George's Day). Because it was continually in use, the temple-turned-church is remarkably well preserved—but notice the bullet holes, damage sustained mostly in the 1820s, when the Greeks resisted the Turks.

• *Note that there's a "back door" exit nearby for those wanting to take the smooth, paved walkway up to the Acropolis, rather than the rough climb above the Agora. (To find the exit, face the back of the temple, turn right, and follow the path to the green gate, which deposits you on the inviting, café-lined Apostolou Pavlou pedestrian drag. From here you could turn left and walk up toward the Acropolis.*

But there's still more to see in the Agora. Wind your way down the hill (northeast) and find the headless...

❾ Statue of Hadrian

The first Roman emperor to wear a beard (previously a Greek fashion), Hadrian (r. A.D. 117-138) was a Grecophile and benefactor of Athens. Get close to this second-century A.D.

statue and notice the insignia on the breastplate. There's Romulus and Remus, being suckled by the she-wolf who supports Athena on her back. This was Hadrian's vision—that by conquering Greece, Rome actually saved it. Hadrian was nicknamed Graecula ("The Little Greek") for his love of Greek philosophy, literature, and a handsome Greek teenager named Antinous (see the story on page 355). Hadrian personally visited Athens, where he financed a comprehensive building program, including the Arch of Hadrian, Library of Hadrian, Temple of Olympian Zeus (which had been started by the Greeks), and a whole new master-planned neighborhood. (For more on these sights, see the 📖 Athens City Walk chapter or 🎧 download my free audio tour.) Hadrian's legacy endures. The main street through the Plaka is now called Adrianou—"Hadrian's" street.

• *Continuing on, head straight down the lane (to the left of Hadrian) and you'll pass three giants on four pedestals, which once guarded the...*

⓾ Odeon of Agrippa

This theater/concert hall (a.k.a. the "Palace of the Giants"), once fronted by a line of six fierce Triton and Giant statues, was the centerpiece of the Agora during the Roman era.

A plaque explains the history of this building: During the Golden Age, this site was simply open space in the very center of the Agora. The *odeon* (a venue designed mainly for musical performances) was built by the Roman general and governor Marcus Agrippa in the time of Caesar Augustus (around 15 B.C.), when Greece was a Roman-controlled province. For the theater-loving Greeks and their Greek-culture-loving masters, the *odeon* was a popular place. Two stories tall and built into the natural slope of the hill, it could seat more than a thousand people.

Back then, the entrance was on the south side (near the Middle Stoa), and these Triton and Giant statues didn't yet exist. Patrons entered from the south, walking through two rows of monumental columns, topped by Corinthian capitals. After the lobby, they emerged at the top row of a 20-tier, bowl-shaped auditorium, looking down on an orchestra and stage paved with multicolored marble and decorated with statues. The sightlines were great because the roof, spanning 82 feet, had no internal support columns. One can only assume that, in its heyday, the *odeon* hosted concerts, poetry readings, and more lowbrow Roman-oriented entertainment.

Around A.D. 150, the famously unsupported roof collapsed. By then Athens had a bigger, better performance venue (the Odeon of Herodes Atticus, on the other side of the Acropolis—described on page 96), so the Odeon of Agrippa was rebuilt at half the size as a 500-seat lecture hall. The new entrance was here on the north side, fronted by six colossal statues serving as pillars. Only two Tritons (with fish tails), a Giant (with a snake's tail), and an empty pedestal remain.

The building was burned to the ground in the Herulian invasion of A.D. 267 (explained later, under "Post-Herulian Wall").

AGORA

Around A.D. 400, a large palace was built here, which also served as the university (or "gymnasium," which comes from the Greek word for "naked"—young men exercised in the buff during PE here). It lasted until the Constantinople-based Emperor Justinian closed all the pagan schools in A.D. 529. A plaque under the first statue gives you more information.

· *Continue to the main road, where you'll see we've made a loop. Now turn right and start up toward the Acropolis on the...*

⓫ Panathenaic Way

The Panathenaic Way was Athens' main street. It started at the main city gate (the Dipylon Gate, near the Keramikos Cemetery),

cut diagonally through the Agora's main square, and wound its way up to the Acropolis—two-thirds of a mile in all. The Panathenaic Way was the primary north-south road, and here in the Agora it intersected with the main east-west road to the port of Piraeus. Though some stretches were paved, most of it (then as now) was just packed gravel. It was lined with important temples, businesses, and legal buildings.

During the Panathenaic Festival held in the summer, this was the main parade route. Every four years on Athena's birthday, Greeks celebrated by giving her statue a new dress, called a *peplos*. A wheeled float carrying the *peplos* was pushed up this street. Thousands participated—some on horseback, others just walking—while spectators watched from wooden grandstands erected along the way. When the parade reached the Acropolis, the new dress was ceremonially presented to Athena and used to adorn her life-size statue at the Erechtheion. Today's tourists use the same path to connect the Agora and the Acropolis.

· *Continue up the Panathenaic Way, past the Stoa of Attalos. Along the left-hand side of the Panathenaic Way are several crude walls and column fragments.*

⓬ Post-Herulian Wall

This wall marks the beginning of the end of Roman Athens.

In A.D. 267, the barbarian Herulians sailed down from the Black Sea and utterly devastated Athens. (The crumbling Roman Empire was helpless to protect its provinces.) The Herulians burned most of the Agora's buildings to the ground, leaving it in ashes.

As soon as the Herulians left, the surviving Athenians began hastily throwing up this wall—cobbled together from rubble—to keep future invaders at bay. They used anything they could find: rocks, broken columns, statues, frieze fragments, all thrown together without mortar to make a wall 30 feet high and 10 feet thick. Archaeologists recognize pieces scavenged from destroyed buildings, such as the Stoa of Attalos and the Odeon of Agrippa.

Up until this point, the Agora had always been rebuilt after invasions (such as the Persians in 480 B.C. and Romans in 89 B.C.); but after the Herulians, the Agora never recovered as a public space. What remained suffered through a Slavic invasion in A.D. 580. By A.D. 700, it was a virtual ghost town, located outside the city walls, exposed to bandits and invaders. Only the hardiest of souls used it as a residence. Considering how accessible the Agora was over the centuries as a quarry for pre-cut stones, it's no wonder that so little of it survives today.

• *Next came the Christians. On the right is the...*

⓭ Church of the Holy Apostles

This charming little church with the lantern-like dome marks the Agora's revival. Built around A.D. 1000, it commemorates St. Paul's

teaching in the Agora (see information about Mars Hill on page 48). Under protection from the Christian rulers of Byzantium (in Constantinople, modern-day Istanbul), Athens—and the Agora— slowly recovered from centuries of invasions and neglect. The church was built

on the ruins of an ancient nymphaeum, or temple atop a sacred spring, and became one of many Christian churches that served the booming populace of Byzantine Athens.

This church was the prototype for later Athenian churches: a Greek-cross floor plan with four equal arms, topped by a dome and featuring windows with tall horseshoe-shaped arches. (The narthex, or entrance, was added later, spoiling the four equal arms.) The church was built of large, rectangular, finished stone blocks rather than small bricks. Ringing the eaves is a decorative pattern of bricks shaped into calligraphic Kufic script (developed in the city of Kufa).

AGORA

Enter (if the church is open) around the far side. It contains some interesting 17th-century Byzantine-style frescoes. The windows are in flower and diamond shapes. From the center, look up at Jesus as *Pantocrator* ("ruler over all") at the top of the dome, and see the icon on the altar and the faded frescoes on

the walls. Notice the remains of the marble altar screen with wide-open spaces—frames that once held icons.

• *End your tour by continuing up the Panathenaic Way to the south exit gates and looking back over the Agora and modern Athens.*

Legacy of the Agora

By the 18th century, the Agora had become a flourishing Turkish residential district. The Church of the Holy Apostles was only one

of many churches serving the populace. In the early 20th century, outdoor movies were shown in the Agora. In the 1930s, the American School of Classical Studies purchased and demolished buildings that had stood for centuries, forcing everyone from their houses and

businesses—all so they could dig here. The Church of the Holy Apostles was the only structure left standing, and it was heavily renovated by the American School to return it to its original state. Excavation in the Agora has continued nearly without pause for the past 70-some years.

Now that the ancient Agora has become a museum, the role of city center has shifted to Athens' many modern neighborhoods. Produce is bought and sold at the Central Market. The government center is at Syntagma Square. Multiple neighborhoods—the Plaka, Psyrri, Thissio, and Gazi—harbor nightlife. Monastiraki and a dozen other squares have become the new social-center "agoras." And the Metro has replaced the Panathenaic Way as the city's main artery.

• *Your tour is finished. There are three exits from the Agora: the gate through which you entered, at Adrianou street; the "back door" gate behind the Temple of Hephaistos; and the ⓮ south gate next to the Church of the Holy Apostles (where you are now).*

AGORA

To head straight up to the Acropolis (to complete your own Panathe-naic Festival), exit through the gate by the church, head straight up the hill, and turn to the 📖 *Acropolis Tour* chapter, which is also available as a 🎧 free audio tour.

ACROPOLIS MUSEUM TOUR

Μουσείο Ακρόπολης

Athens' Acropolis Museum is a custom-built showcase for artifacts from the Acropolis, complemented by modern exhibits about the site. The state-of-the-art 2009 building—housing the Parthenon sculptures still in Greek hands, the original Caryatids from the Erechtheion, and much more—is the boldest symbol yet of today's Athens.

The museum also serves as a sort of 21st-century Trojan horse, intended to lure the famous "Elgin Marbles" (the Parthenon sculp-

tures taken to London in the 1800s) away from the British Museum and back to Athens. For years the Greeks have asked for the marbles back, and for years the Brits have claimed that Greece can't give them a suitable home. Even now, with this ultramodern facility ready and waiting, Britain is reluctant to give in, for fear of setting a precedent...and getting "me, too" notices from Italy, Egypt, Iran, Iraq, and all the other nations who'd like to reclaim the missing pieces of their cultural heritage.

With or without the Elgin Marbles, this new museum has trumped the National Archaeological Museum as the most exciting exhibit in town, and is definitely worth your time.

Orientation

Cost: €5.

Hours: Mon 8:00-16:00, Tue-Sun 8:00-20:00, Fri until 22:00.

Getting There: It's the giant, can't-miss-it modern building facing the south side of the Acropolis from across the broad Dionysiou Areopagitou pedestrian drag. The museum is next to the Akropoli Metro stop on Makrigianni, a street lined with restaurants.

Information: Museum guards (with red badges) can answer questions, and a 13-minute video plays continuously in the atrium (level 3). Tel. 210-900-0900, www.theacropolismuseum.gr.

Baggage Check: There's a free bag check at the counter near the turnstiles at the base of the ramp (required for big bags). If you're dining at the museum's restaurant after your visit, note that the bag check closes when the museum does.

Length of This Tour: Allow 1.5 hours.

Photography: No photos are allowed on the ground floor (level 0) or of level 1's Archaic statues. It's OK to take photos without flash in the rest of the museum (of the scale models, Caryatids of the Erechtheion, and Parthenon sculptures).

Services: A café and gift shop are on the ground floor; level 2 has a pricey but well-regarded restaurant, a bookstore, and great views. Wheelchairs and strollers are available. You can enter the gift shop and the restaurant without a museum ticket.

Starring: Marble masterpieces from one of the most influential archaeological sites in human history.

The Tour Begins

Even as it echoes the ancient history all around it, the Acropolis Museum's striking, glassy building—designed by Swiss-born, New York-based architect Bernard Tschumi—gives a postmodern jolt to Athens' otherwise staid, mid-century-concrete cityscape. Its two lower levels are aligned with the foundations of ancient ruins discovered beneath the building (which are exposed

and still being excavated). The top floor sits askew, imitating the orientation of the Parthenon. A long terrace extends over the main entry, with café tables stretching toward panoramic views of the Acropolis. The museum's glass walls maximize the natural light inside the building and also "disappear," focusing attention on the statuary and views of the Acropolis itself.

Visitors enter into a grand lobby. The ground floor (level 0) has the ticket office, WCs, museum shop, and temporary exhibits. To proceed chronologically through the exhibits, you'd start with the

Archaic collection on level 1, then go upstairs (to the top floor—level 3) for the Parthenon section, then back down to level 1 for Hellenistic and Roman sculpture. But for this tour, we'll do the small Hellenistic and Roman section as an out-of-chronological-sequence side-trip from the Archaic and Classical sections, and let the top-floor Parthenon sculptures be our finale.

• *Near the ticket desk, start by getting a good look at the models that show the Acropolis as it looked from 1200 B.C. to 1500 A.D. Then, after going through the turnstiles, head up the long, glass...*

RAMP

Pause to look through the glass floor at the ancient ruins being excavated beneath the museum. The major buildings of ancient Athens were at the Acropolis and Agora—this was a neighborhood of everyday houses and shops. Appropriately, the ramp is lined with artifacts that were found in the sanctuaries and houses on the slopes leading up to the Parthenon. Many of these artifacts, dating from the fourth millennium B.C. to the fifth century A.D., owe their well-preserved state to having been buried with their owners.

Among the ramp's highlights is case #5 (on the left), which takes you step-by-step through marriage rituals in ancient Athens. Freestanding cases midramp give insight into the similarities between ancient Greek pagan worship rituals and later Christian styles. One has Christian-looking votives thanking the gods for prayers answered. On the right, just below the stairs, is an offering box (like you see in churches today); this one stood at the Sanctuary of Aphrodite. To assure a good marriage, you'd have been wise to pop in a silver drachma.

LEVEL 1

• *Climb the stairs at the top of the ramp toward a collection of statues.*

❶ Pediment of the Hekatompedon

Throughout the centuries, three temples of Athena have occupied the spot where the Parthenon stands today. The fragments assembled here, from 570 B.C., once adorned the Hekatompedon ("100 feet"), the first of those temples. The still-under-construction building was leveled by invading Persians in 480 B.C., paving the way for the Parthenon to be built. On the left, Hercules fights the sea monster Triton. In the center are the scant remains of two lions

Acropolis Museum—Level 1

20 Meters
20 Yards

N

POST-PARTHENON GALLERY

ROMAN PERIOD GALLERY

ESCALATORS TO LEVELS 2 & 3

ELEVATORS

ERECHTHEION

Open to below

Open to below

STAIRS

ARCHAIC GALLERY

❶ Pediment of the Hekatompedon
❷ Kore & Kouros Statues
❸ Pediment of the Archaios Naos & Kritios Boy
❹ Pensive Athena Relief
❺ Temple of Athena Nike & Nike Adjusting Her Sandal Reliefs
❻ Side-Trip to Hellenistic & Roman Art
❼ Caryatids from the Erechtheion

killing a bull. On the left is Hercules struggling with a sea snake. To the right is a three-headed demon with a snake tail. Each figure holds an object in its hand, representing the elements of wind, water, and fire. While their expressions are more goofy than demonic, they illustrate the struggle of man versus nature. Traces of the original paint are still apparent.

• *Turn right and enter a gallery flooded with daylight.*

❷ Kore and Kouros Statues

In this column-lined gallery stand several kore (female) and kouros (male) statues. They sport the characteristic stiff poses, braided hair, generic faces, and mysterious smiles of the Archaic era (c. 700-480 B.C.). For more on Archaic statues, see page 148.

The men are generally naked, showing off buff and toned bodies. The bearded dudes are adults, and boys are beardless. The women are modestly clothed, but pull their robes to

ACROPOLIS MUSEUM

the side. Before the coming-of-Golden-Age realism and the "wet drapery" technique that enabled sculptors to portray the bodies beneath robes, this was a crude way to lend some motion and to show a little of their figures. The kore statues are almost always holding something: The Greeks believed women shouldn't approach the gods without a gift of some kind. The equestrian statues represent the upper class, those wealthy elites who owned horses and liked to show them off.

• *Halfway down the gallery, on the right against the interior wall, is the...*

❸ Pediment of the Archaios Naos and Kritios Boy

These sculptures once decorated the temple to Athena next to the Hekatompedon. The temple, damaged after the Persian Wars, was used until the new Parthenon was completed. In the center, Athena, dressed in an ankle-length cloak, strides forward, brandishing a snake as she attacks a giant, who sprawls backward onto his bum. The figures were part of a scene depicting the "Gods Versus Giants" battle atop the temple. The pesky Persians invaded Greece several times over a 50-year period (c. 499-449 B.C.). On the plus side, the wars forced Greeks to band together, and Athens emerged as a dominant naval power. Athenians rebuilt the Acropolis as a symbol of rebirth, with the Parthenon as its centerpiece. In just a few short decades, Greek society—and art—evolved rapidly and remarkably.

Enjoying the statuary in this hall, you can trace the evolution of Greek art from the static Archaic period to the mastery of the body as a living thing, free and full of movement, in the Golden Age. In the Classical style of fifth-century B.C. Greece, the spine moves realistically with the hips. This is nicely illustrated by the nearby Kritios Boy, ten steps away. Look up at, and then circle, the Kritios Boy as he gracefully seems to step into Greece's Golden Age.

• *Continue down the gallery. Near the up escalator, look for a small well-preserved marble relief.*

❹ Pensive Athena Relief

The goddess, dressed in a helmet and belted *peplos*, rests her forehead thoughtfully on her spear (460 B.C.). Although she was called "pensive," some think she was actually meant to be mourning the deaths of her citizens in the Persian War.

• *Backtrack a tad, then veer left past a bank of elevators. Continue past an open gallery with some statuesque women (we'll visit them in a minute). After the second bank of elevators, look for a series of four squarish marble slabs on your left.*

❺ Temple of Athena Nike and Nike Adjusting Her Sandal Reliefs

This set of reliefs (c. 410 B.C.) originally decorated the parapet of the Temple of Athena Nike (which stands near the entrance to the Acropolis). Nike figures had a better chance of survival through the ages than other statues because anti-pagan Christian vandals mistook the winged Nikes for angels. Nearby is a display containing more chunks of the Temple of Athena Nike. You'll see toes gripping rocks, windblown robes, and realistically twisted bodies—exuberant, life-filled carvings signaling Athens' emergence from the Persian War.

• *Turn right and go up the long gallery for a...*

❻ Side-Trip to Hellenistic and Roman Art

Before heading upstairs for the highlight of the collection, continue around on this floor to the small stretch of statues from the Hellenistic and Roman period. The head of Alexander the Great, on a square pillar in the center of the gallery, is a rare original, likely sculpted from life (336 B.C.). Alexander's upper lip curls, and his thick hair sprouts from the center of his forehead—immediately identifying this remarkable man. When he died, in 323 B.C., this Macedonian had conquered the rest of Greece, and spread Greek culture throughout the Mediterranean world and as far east as India.

Farther back, visit the spooky "magic sphere" that resembles a dirty soccer ball covered with graffiti. It's actually a marble sphere etched with mysterious symbols (Roman, second or third century A.D.).

• *Now turn around, retracing your steps, and turn left at the bank of elevators. Around the corner, on their own, as if starring in their own revue on a beautifully lit stage, are the...*

❼ Caryatids from the Erechtheion

Here stand five of the original six lady-columns that once supported the roof of the prestigious Erechtheion temple. (The six on the Acropolis today are copies; another original is in London's British Museum.) Despite their graceful appearance, these sculptures were structurally functional. Each has a fluted column for a leg, a capital-like hat, and buttressing locks of hair in the back. The Caryatids were modeled on and named after the famously upright women of Karyai, near Sparta.

Time and the elements have ravaged these maidens. As recently as the 17th century (see the engravings), they had fragile arms holding ritual bowls for libations. Until the 1950s (before modern smog), their worn-down faces had crisp noses and mouths. In a half-century of Industrial Age pollution, they experienced more destruction than in the previous 2,000 years. But their future looks brighter now that they've been brought indoors out of the acidic air, cleaned up with a laser, and safely preserved for future generations. (For more on the Caryatids in their original location, see page 106.)

There's a glass floor overhead, but you may not want to look up, out of respect for any visitors wearing dresses above you.

• *From the Caryatid gallery, walk to the end of the building. At the relief of Pensive Athena, ride the escalators up. Pause at level 2 to enjoy the view down over the Archaic statues we just visited (the second level has a restaurant and terrace with awesome Acropolis views). Then head for the top floor—it's the reason you're here.*

LEVEL 3

• *The escalator deposits you at the "cella"—symbolizing in actual size the inner sanctum of the Parthenon. Before entering the Parthenon Gallery, sit in the atrium and enjoy the video on the Parthenon, which covers the temple's 2,500-year history, including a not-so-subtle jab at how Lord Elgin got the marbles and made off with them to England. For more on Lord Elgin, see page 111.*

Parthenon Models

Two models show how the west and east pediment statues (which are mostly fragments today) would have looked in their prime.

The east pediment (the model on the right) features Nike crowning newly-born Athena with a wreath of olive branches. Zeus allowed Athena, the goddess of wisdom, to rise from his brain fully grown and fully armed, to inaugurate the Golden Age of Athens. The other gods at this Olympian banquet—naked men and clothed women—are astounded by the amazing event. At the far left, Helios' four horses are doing their morning chore, dragging the sun out of the sea. And on the far right, Selene, the moon goddess, follows the horses back as she sets into the sea.

The west pediment model (on the left) shows Athena and Poseidon competing for Athens' favor by giving gifts to the city. Poseidon spurts water (beneath him) and Athena presents an olive tree (behind). A big, heavenly audience looks on. Had Poseidon bested Athena, you'd be in Poseidonia today instead of Athens.

• *Leave this central zone and enter the huge gallery that rings the* cella.

The Parthenon Frieze

This top floor re-creates the exact dimensions of the Parthenon—with the frieze (mounted lower for easier viewing), the metopes, and the east and west pediments, all in their proper positions. The stainless steel columns mark the location of each marble column. Feel the impetus to stroll. Go with the flow, following the Panathenaic procession to the east.

Study the museum's highlight—a life-size mock-up of the 525-foot frieze that once wrapped all the way around the outside of the Parthenon. The relief panels depict the Great Panathenaia, the procession held every four years in which citizens climbed up to the Parthenon to celebrate the birth of the city. Circle the perimeter and watch the parade unfold.

Men on horseback, gods, chariots, musicians, priests, riders, officers, warriors, and sacrificial animals are all part of the grand parade, all heading in the same direction—uphill. Prance on. At the heart of the procession are maidens dressed in pleated robes. They shuffle along, carrying gifts for the gods, including incense burners, along with jugs of wine and bowls to pour out offerings. The procession culminates in the presentation of a new *peplos* to Athena, as the gods look on.

Notice the details—for example, the muscles and veins in the horses' legs and the intricate folds in the cloaks and dresses. Some panels have holes drilled in them, where accessories such as gleaming bronze reins were fitted to heighten the festive look. Of course, all these panels were originally painted in realistic colors. As you move along, notice that, despite the bustle of figures posed every which way, the frieze has one unifying element—most of the people's heads are at the same level, creating a single ribbon around the Parthenon.

Of the original marble frieze, the museum owns only 32 feet. These panels were already so acid-worn in 1801 that Lord Elgin didn't bother taking them. Filling in the gaps in this jigsaw puzzle are white plaster replicas of panels still in London's British Museum (marked BM), in Paris' Louvre, and in Copenhagen. Blank spaces represent panels that are forever lost. Small 17th-century engravings show how the frieze looked before the 1687 explosion that devastated the Parthenon.

• *Now stroll through the gallery and look out the windows. Take a moment to...*

Ponder the Parthenon

There's the Parthenon itself, perched on the adjacent hilltop. Let the museum disappear around you, leaving you to enjoy the art and the temple it once decorated. The Parthenon is one of the most influential works humankind has ever created. For 2,500 years it's inspired generations of architects, sculptors, painters, engineers, and visitors from around the globe. Here in the Acropolis Museum, you can experience the power of this cultural landmark. The people of Athens relish the Acropolis Museum. Local guides grow taller with every visit, knowing that Greece finally has a suitable place to preserve and share the best of its artistic heritage.

• *On your way down, stop by the restaurant on level 2 for its exterior terrace and the awesome view of the Acropolis.*

ACROPOLIS MUSEUM

NATIONAL ARCHAEOLOGICAL MUSEUM TOUR

Εθνικό Αρχαιολογικό Μουσείο

The National Archaeological Museum is far and away the top ancient Greek art collection anywhere. Ancient Greece set the tone for all Western art that followed, and this museum lets you trace its evolution—taking you in air-conditioned comfort from 7000 B.C. to A.D. 500 through beautifully displayed and described exhibits on one floor. You'll see the rise and fall of Greece's various civilizations: the Minoans, the Mycenaeans, those of Archaic Greece, the Classical Age and Alexander the Great, and the Romans who came from the west. You can also watch Greek sculpture evolve, from prehistoric Barbie dolls, to stiff Egyptian-style, to the *David*-like balance of the Golden Age, to wet T-shirt, buckin'-bronco Hellenistic, and finally, to the influence of the Romans. Walk once around fast for a time-lapse effect, then go around again for a closer look.

This museum is a great way to either start or finish off your sightseeing through Greece. It's especially worth visiting if you're

traveling beyond Athens, because it displays artifacts found all around Greece, including Mycenae, Epidavros, Santorini, and Olympia— and the treasures displayed here are generally better than those remaining at the sites themselves. The sheer beauty of the statues, vases, and paintings helps bring the country's dusty ruins to life.

Orientation

Cost: €10, €5 off-season.

Hours: April-Oct daily 8:00-20:00; Nov-March Mon 12:00-17:00, Tue-Sun 8:00-15:00.

Getting There: The only major Athens sight outside the city center, the museum is a mile north of the Plaka at 28 Oktovriou (a.k.a. Patission) #44. Your best bet is to take a **taxi,** which costs about €6 from the Plaka. By **Metro,** use the Omonia stop (as you exit, follow signs to *28 Oktovriou/28 October Street,* and walk seven blocks to the museum—about 15 minutes) or the Victoria stop (about a 10-minute walk). You can also hop a **bus** to the Polytechneio stop: The #035 leaves from a stop on Athinas street, just north of Monastiraki, and drops you off around the corner from the museum. Bus #224 leaves from Vasilissis Sofias avenue (near Syntagma Square) and stops kitty-corner from the museum.

Information: Tel. 213-214-4800, www.namuseum.gr.

Tours: There are no audioguides, but live **guides** hang out in the lobby waiting to give you a €50, hour-long tour.

⌒ Download my free National Archaeological Museum **audio tour.**

Length of This Tour: Allow, at the very least, two hours for this tour; more if you want to dig deeper into this world-class museum.

Baggage Check: Free and required, except for small purses.

Services: A museum shop, WCs, and an inviting café surround a shady and restful courtyard in the lower level (to access from the main entrance lobby, take the stairs down behind ticket desk); these are easiest to access at the beginning or end of your museum tour.

Photography: Photos are allowed, but no flash and no goofy poses in front of statues. The Greek museum board considers this disrespectful of the ancient culture and is very serious about it—you'll hear, "No posing!" from stern guards if someone stands in front of the Zeus/Poseidon statue and tries to match his thunderbolt-/trident-throwing pose.

Cuisine Art: The **Museum Garden** café in front of the building is pricey, but the generous portions are shareable, and it stays open after the museum closes.

Starring: The gold Mask of Agamemnon, stately kouros and kore statues, the perfectly posed *Artemision Bronze,* the horse and jockey of Artemision, and the whole range of Greek art.

The Tour Begins

The collection is delightfully chronological. To sweep through Greek history, simply visit the numbered rooms in order. From the entrance lobby (Rooms 1-2), start with the rooms directly in front of you (Rooms 3-6), containing prehistoric and Mycenaean artifacts. Then circle clockwise around the building's perimeter on the ground floor (Rooms 7-33) to see the evolution of classical Greek statuary. Breeze through the rooms at the back of the building, then go upstairs to see several more exhibits. Keep track of your ticket—you'll need to scan it again to enter some of the exhibits.

The following self-guided tour zeroes in on a few choice pieces (out of many) that give an overview of the collection. See these items, then browse to your heart's content. Note that my descriptions here are brief—for more detail, read the excellent posted English information in each room.

• *From the entrance lobby, go straight ahead into the large central hall (Room 4). This first area—Rooms 3-6—is dedicated to prehistory (7000-1050 B.C., including the treasures of the Mycenaeans. Start in the small side room to the right, Room 6. In several of this room's cases—including the one directly to the right as you enter—you'll find stiff marble figures with large heads. Look closely into that first case, filled with...*

❶ Cycladic Figurines

Goddess, corpse, fertility figure, good-luck amulet, spirit guide, beloved ancestor, or Neolithic porn? No one knows for sure the purpose of these female figurines, which are older than the Egyptian pyramids. Although these statuettes were made only in the Cycladic Islands, well-traveled ones have been found all over Greece. The earliest Greeks may have worshipped a Great Mother earth goddess long before Zeus and company (variously called Gaia, Ge, and other names), but it's not clear what connection she had, if

ARCH. MUSEUM

National Archaeological Museum

EGYPTIAN ARTIFACTS

41 42 43 44 47
37 36 45 46
40 37A
38 BRONZE STATUES
39
35
To ❷③
34

11 17 18 14
16 ❶❶ ❶③ ❶④
20 *To Café & WCs* 19 21
EPIDAVROS PEDIMENT RELIEFS
22 23 24
❶⑤
15 10 CLAY TABLETS 3 ❹ 25 28
❶⑥
12 ❶② FRESCOES ❸ WARRIOR KRATER 26 29 ❶⑦
14 10 5 4 6
13 10 BASES ❷ 27 30
❾ CAFÉ & WCS ❶ 19 ❶⑨
9 *To Café & WCs* ❶⑧
KOUROI ❺ 30A
11 8 7 2 33 32 31
❽ ❼ ❻ ❷❷ ❷① ❷⓪
12 ROOM 1

ENTRANCE

VASIL. IRAKLEIOU

CAFÉ

To Ⓜ *Victoria* *To 28 Oktovriou (Patission)* *To Plaka & Acropolis*

❶ Cycladic Figurines
❷ Mask of Agamemnon, Etc.
❸ More Mycenaean Artifacts
❹ Vapheio Cups
❺ Dipylon Vase
❻ Kore Statue, c. 650 B.C.
❼ Kouros from Sounion
❽ Kore Statue, c. 550 B.C.
❾ More Kouroi & Bases
❿ The Artemision Bronze
⓫ Attic Funerary Monuments
⓬ The Athena Varvakeion

⓭ Funeral Steles
⓮ The Artemision Jockey
⓯ Grave Relief of a Horse
⓰ Bronze Statue of a Youth
⓱ Philosopher Portrait Head
⓲ Fighting Gaul
⓳ Aphrodite, Pan & Eros
⓴ Emperor Augustus
㉑ Sleeping Maenad, Antinous & Asklepios
㉒ Various Busts
㉓ Upstairs to Wall Paintings & Ceramics Collection

any, with these statuettes. The ladies are always naked, usually with folded arms. The figures evolved over the years from flat-chested to violin-shaped, to skinny. There is evidence that the eyes, lips, and ears were originally painted on.

The map on the wall (straight across from the entry) demarcates the Cycladic region, showing how the sacred island of Delos marks the center of the circle, or cycle, formed by the Cycladic Islands (for more on Delos, see page 407). As these islands were in close proximity, there was plenty of trade and contact between them. In the glass case to the right of the map are two interesting figurines: one playing the harp, the other a flute—proof that humans have been making music for at least 5,000 years.

Before returning to the main room, stroll the long, dead-end Cycladic Hall. You'll see more figurines, painted vases, and tools such as knives and spears made of worked obsidian. Obsidian objects like these were probably exportable treasures, as the Cycladic society was a relatively peaceful culture with an artistic sense of style. Notice the finely painted bathtub on the left. You'll see carved marble bowls so thin and delicate that light shines through, along with bronze blades, tweezers, and needles. All of these artifacts are from around 2500 B.C., roughly 1,000 years before Mycenae and 2,000 years before Greece's Golden Age.

• *Return to the long central hall (Room 4), divided into four sections. Here you'll find the...*

❷ Mask of Agamemnon and Other Mycenaean Treasures

Room 4 displays artifacts found in the ruins of the ancient fortress-city of Mycenae, 80 miles west of Athens. You'll see finely decorated swords, daggers, body armor, and jewelry, all found buried alongside bodies in Mycenaean graves. Many items were discovered in the cemetery that archaeologists call "Grave Circle A." (For more on the history of this site, see the Mycenae chapter.) The objects' intricately hammered detail and the elaborate funeral arrangements point to the sophistication of this early culture.

In a glass case in the middle of the second section is the so-called **Mask of Agamemnon** (c. 1550 B.C.). Made of beaten gold and showing a man's bearded face, this famous mask was tied over the face of a dead man—note the tiny ear-holes for the string.

The Mycenaeans dominated southern Greece a thousand years before the Golden Age (1600-1200 B.C.). Their (real) history was lost in the misty era of Homer's (fanciful) legends of the Trojan War. Then Mycenae was unearthed in the 19th century by the German businessman Heinrich Schliemann (the Indiana Johann of his era). Schliemann, fascinated by the works of Homer, had recently discovered the real-life ruins of Troy (in western Turkey), and he was convinced that Mycenae was the city of the Greeks who'd conquered Troy. That much, at least, may be historically true. Schliemann went on to declare this funeral mask to be that of the legendary King Agamemnon, which *isn't* true, because the mask predates the fall of Troy (c. 1300 B.C.).

You're surrounded by 30 pounds of gold pounded into decorative funerary objects, excavated from the graves of 19 bodies found in a circular tomb. Notice the two babies whose bodies were completely covered in a blanket of gold leaf.

On the back side of the Mask of Agamemnon case, look closely at the knife and sheath with a warrior-versus-lions scene. Compared with the Minoan and Cycladic civilizations, Mycenaean society was warlike, and their weapons were artfully rendered.

· *In the next section of Room 4, you'll find...*

❸ More Mycenaean Artifacts

A **model of the Acropolis of Mycenae** (left side) shows the dramatic hilltop citadel where many of these objects were unearthed. Find the famous Lion Gate entrance (#1 on the model), the round cemetery known as Grave Circle A (#2), and the king's royal palace crowning the hill (#8). Also in Room 4 are **frescoes** from the royal palace, done in bright colors in the Minoan style. **Clay tablets** show the Mycenaean written language known as Linear B, whose syllabic script (in which marks stand for syllables) was cracked only in the 1950s.

Other colorful wall frescoes, from nearby Tiryns, show a Minoan influence and feature scenes such as men with dogs hunting

wild boar and men ritually leaping over bulls.

· *Look at the back side of the display case in the center of this section.*

The painted, two-handled vase known as the **House of the Warrior Krater** (#1426) was Schliemann's favorite find. A woman (far left) waves goodbye to a line of warriors heading off to war, with their fancy armor and duffle bags hanging from their spears. Although this provided the world with its first glimpse

ARCH. MUSEUM

of a Mycenaean soldier, it's a timeless scene with countless echoes across the generations.

• In the center of the last section of Room 4 is a glass case displaying the...

❹ Vapheio Cups

These gold cups (c. 1600-1550 B.C.), found with other precious items in a Mycenaean tomb, are metalwork masterpieces. The intri-

cate worked detail on #1 shows a charging bull sending a guy head over heels. On #2 you'll see a bull and a cow making eyes at each other, while the hind leg of another bull gets tied up by one good-looking cowboy. These realistic, joyous scenes are the product of the two civilizations that made 15th-century B.C. Greece the wonder of Europe—the Mycenaeans and the Minoan culture of Crete.

Note also the light and flexible bone helmet (14th-13th century B.C.) in this room. Made from many pieces of boar tusk, a helmet such as this was a prized possession.

Between roughly 1450 and 1150 B.C., the Minoan society collapsed, and Minoan artisans had to find work painting frescoes and making cups for the rising Mycenaean culture. Then, around 1100 B.C., the Mycenaeans disappeared from history's radar screen. Whether from invasion, famine, internal strife, or natural disaster, these sudden disappearances plunged Greece into 500 years of Dark Ages (c. 1200-700 B.C.). Little survives from that chaotic time, so let's pick up the thread of history as Greece began to recover a few centuries later.

• Backtrack to the entrance lobby and begin circling clockwise around the perimeter of the building, starting in Room 7. After scanning your ticket again to enter this room, look for the tall vase on your right.

❺ Dipylon Vase

This monumental ocher-and-black vase (c. 750 B.C.), as tall as a person, is painted with a funeral scene. Vases such as this marked the graves of well-off Greeks; the belly-handled shape of this one tells us it likely honored a woman (men's graves were typically marked by pedestalled vases).

In the center, the deceased lies on a funeral bier, flanked by a line of mourners who pull their hair in grief. It's far from realistic. The triangular torsos, square arms, circular heads, and bands of geometric patterns epitomize the style of what's known as the Geometric Period (9th-8th century B.C.). A few realistic notes pop through, such as the raw emotions of the mourners and some grazing antelope and ibex (on the neck of the vase). Note the one little child in attendance. Discovered in Athens' Keramikos Cemetery, the vase gets its name from the nearby Dipylon Gate, the ancient city's renowned main entrance.

After four centuries of Dark Ages and war, the Greeks of the eighth century B.C. were finally settling down, establishing cities, and expanding abroad (as seen on the map behind the big vase), with colonies in western Turkey (Ionia), southern Italy (Magna Graecia), and Sicily. They were developing a written language and achieving the social stability that could afford to generate art. This vase is a baby step in that progression. Next, large-scale statues in stone were developed.

• *In Rooms 7-14 you'll get a look at some of these giant statues, including the early Greek statues called...*

KORE AND KOUROS

Some of the earliest surviving examples of post-Mycenaean Greek art (c. 700-480 B.C.) are these life-size and larger-than-life statues of clothed young women (kore/korai) and naked young men (kouros/kouroi). Influenced by ancient statues of Egyptian pharaohs, the earliest of these are big and stiff, with triangular faces and arms at their sides. As you walk through the next few rooms, you'll see the statues become more realistic and natural in their movements, with more personality than we see in these earlier rigid shells.

• *Take a closer look at a few particular statues. First, facing the vase in the middle of Room 7 is a...*

❻ Kore, c. 650 B.C.

With hands at her sides, a skinny figure, a rectangular shape, and dressed in a full-length robe (called a chiton), this kore looks as much like a plank of wood as a woman. Her triangular lion-mane hairstyle resembles an Egyptian headdress. The writing down her left leg says she's dedicated to Apollo. Stroll around. The Egyptian influence is clear.

• *In the next room (Room 8), your eyes go right to a very nice pair of knees that belong to a...*

❼ Kouros from Sounion, c. 600 B.C.

A typical kouros from the Archaic period (c. 700-480 B.C.), this young naked man has braided dreadlocks and a stable forward-facing pose, and is stepping forward slightly with his left leg. His fists are clenched at his sides, and his scarred face obscures an Archaic smile—a placid smile that suggests the inner se-cret of happiness. His anatomy is strongly geo-metrical and stylized, with almond-shaped eyes, oval pecs, an arched rib cage, cylindrical thighs, and a too-perfect symmetry. While less plank-like than earlier statues, he's still much flatter than an actual person. The overdeveloped mus-cles (look at those quads!) and his narrow waist resemble those of an athletic teenager.

Rather than strict realism, kouros statues capture a geometric ideal. The proportions of the body parts follow strict rules—for example, most later kouros statues are precisely seven "heads" tall. Although this kouros steps forward slightly, his hips remain even (think about it—the hips of a real person would shift forward on one side). The Greeks were obsessed with the human body—remember, these statues were of (idealized) humans, not gods. Standing naked and alone, these statues represented a microcosm of the rational order of nature.

Statues were painted in vivid, lifelike colors. Notice that the rough surface of the marble lacks the translucent sheen of Classi-cal Age statues. (Archaic chisels were not yet strong or efficient enough to avoid shattering the crystalline marble.)

Kouros statues were everywhere, presented as gifts to a god at a sanctuary or to honor the dead in a cemetery. This one was dedicated to Poseidon at the entrance to the temple at Sounion. As a funeral figure, a kouros symbolized the deceased in his prime of youth and happiness, forever young.

• *Continue into the next room (Room 11). On the left, hold-ing a flower, is a...*

❽ Kore, c. 550 B.C.

Where a male kouros was naked and either life-size or larger than life (emphasizing masculine power), a fe-male kore was often slightly smaller than life and mod-estly clothed, capturing feminine grace (males were commonly naked in public, but women never were). This petite kore stands with feet together, wearing a pleated chiton belted at the waist. Her hair is braided

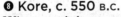

The Four Stages of Greek Sculpture

Archaic (c. 700-480 B.C.): Rigid statues with stylized anatomy, facing forward, with braided hair and mysterious smiles (see photo).

Severe (c. 480-460 B.C.): More realistic and balanced statues (with no smiles), capturing a serious nobility. Works from this transitional period are sometimes described as Early Classical.

Classical (c. 460-323 B.C.): Realistic statues of idealized beauty with poses that strike a balance between movement and stillness, with understated emotion. (Within this period, the Golden Age was roughly 450-400 B.C.)

Hellenistic (c. 323-30 B.C.): Photorealistic (even ugly) humans engaged in dramatic, emotional struggles, captured in snapshot poses that can be wildly unbalanced.

and held in place with a diadem (a wreath-like headdress), and she wears a necklace. Her right hand tugs at her dress, indicating motion (a nice trick if the artist lacks the skill to actually show it), while her left hand holds a flower. Like most ancient statues, she was painted in lifelike colors, including her skin. Her dress was red—you can still see traces of the paint—adorned with flower designs and a band of swastikas down the front. (In ancient times—before German archaeologist Schliemann's writings popularized it and Hitler appropriated it—the swastika was a harmless good-luck symbol representing the rays of the sun.) This kore, like all the statues in the room, has that distinct Archaic smile (or smirk, as the Greeks describe it). Browse around. Study the body types—the graceful, Avatar-like builds, those mysterious smirks, and the rigid hairdos.

• *The next room—a long hall labeled Room 13—has...*

❾ More Kouroi and Bases for Funerary Kouroi

These statues, from the late Archaic period (around 500 B.C.), once decorated the tombs of hero athletes—perhaps famous Olympians. (The map just inside the door shows the continued expansion of Greek civilization in the sixth century B.C.) Notice that these young men are slightly more relaxed and realistic, with better-formed thighs and bent elbows. Some kouros statues stood on pedestals, like the two square marble bases located farther down Room 13 (left side). The indentations atop each base held a kouros statue that represented an idealized version of the deceased. On the first base, the carved relief shows wrestlers and other athletes. Perhaps this was an excuse for the artist to show off a new ability to depict the body in a twisting pose. Notice the cute dog-and-cat fight. The second base features a field hockey-like game, each scene reflecting the vigor of the deceased man in his prime.

During the Archaic period, Greece was prospering, growing, expanding, trading, and colonizing the Mediterranean. The smiles on the statues capture the bliss of a people settling down and living at peace. But in 480 B.C., Persia invaded, and those smiles soon vanished.

• *Pass through Room 14 and into Room 15, which is dominated by one of the jewels of the collection...*

❿ The *Artemision Bronze*

This statue was discovered amid a shipwreck off Cape Artemision (north of Athens) in 1928. The weapon was never found, so no one

knows for sure if this is Zeus or Poseidon. The god steps forward, raises his arm, sights along his other arm at the distant target, and prepares (if it's Zeus) to hurl his thunderbolt or (if Poseidon) his trident.

The god stands 6'10" and has a physique like mine. His hair is curly and tied at the back, and his now-hollow eyes once shone white with inset bone. He plants his left foot and pushes off with the right. Even though every limb moves in a different direction, the whole effect is one of balance. The statue's dimensions are a study in Greek geometry. His head is one Greek foot high, and he's six heads tall (or one Greek fathom). The whole figure has an "X" shape that would fit into a perfect circle, with his navel at the center and his fingertips touching the rim. Although the bronze statue—cast with the "lost wax" technique (explained on page 154)—is fully three-dimensional, it's most impressive from the front. (Later Greek statues, from the Hellenistic era, seem fully alive from every angle, including the three-quarter view.)

This Zeus/Poseidon, from c. 460 B.C., is an example of the transition into the Classical style, as sculpture evolved beyond the so-called Severe style (480-460 B.C.). (The famous charioteer of Delphi, pictured on page 355, is textbook Severe: far more lifelike than a kouros, but still frontal and unmoving.) Historically, the Severe/Early Classical Period covers the time when Greece battled the Persians and emerged victorious—the era when ordinary men had also just shaken off tyrants and taken control of their own destiny through democracy. The Greeks were entering the dawn of the Golden Age. During this time of horrific war, the Greeks made art that was serious (no more Archaic smiles), unadorned, and expressed the noble strength and heroism of the individuals who had carried them through tough times. The statues are anatomically realistic, celebrating the human form.

With his movements frozen, as if Zeus/Poseidon were posing for a painting, we can examine the wonder of the physical body. He's natural yet ideal, twisting yet balanced, moving while at rest. (Later Greek sculptures would improve upon this, with figures that look almost as if they've been caught mid-motion with the click of a camera.) With his geometrical perfection and godlike air, the figure sums up all that is best about the art of the ancient world.

Browse the rest of the art in this room from this generation, including a mini-Zeus in the early Severe style with a thunderbolt and a sacred eagle (just to the right of Zeus/Poseidon), painted vases, and funeral monuments.

Next we enter the Golden Age. Room 16 is filled with big, tall vases made of marble, labeled ⓫ **Attic Funerary Monuments.** These grave markers take the shape of the ceramic urns used for the ashes of cremated bodies in ancient times. One of these vases (#4485) is particularly touching: A grieving family looks on as Hermes (with his winged sandals) leads a young woman to the underworld.

• *Continue through Room 16 and into Room 17. The WCs and café are out the door and downstairs, in the courtyard. From Room 17, turn right into Rooms 19 and 20 (then right again, then left). At the dead end is a small glass case containing...*

⓬ The *Athena Varvakeion*

This marble statue, known as the *Athena Varvakeion* (c. A.D. 250), is considered the most faithful copy of the great *Athena Parthenos* (438 B.C.) by Pheidias. It's essentially a one-twelfth-size replica of the 40-foot statue that once stood in the Parthenon. Although a miniature copy of the glorious original, it provides a good look at Greek art at its Golden Age pinnacle. Athena stands dressed in flowing robes, holding a small figure of Nike (goddess of victory) in her right hand and a shield in her left.

Athena's helmet sprouts plumes with winged horses and a sphinx. To give a sense of scale of the original, the tiny Nike in Athena's hand was six feet tall in the Parthenon statue. Athena's covered in snakes. She wears a snake belt and bracelet; coiled snakes decorate her breastplate and one is curled up inside her shield, representing the goddess' connection to her half-snake son, who was born out of the earth and considered to be one of the ancestors of the Athenians. The snake-headed Medusa (whom Athena helped Perseus slay) adorns the center of her chest. (For more on the statue's original location, see my Acropolis Tour, available 📖 as a chapter in this book and 🎧 as a free audio tour.)

• *Backtrack to Room 17, turn right, and continue circling the museum clockwise into Room 18, which has...*

⑱ Funeral *Steles*

The tombstones that fill this room, all from the fifth century B.C., are more good examples of Golden Age Greek art. With a mastery of the body, artists show poignant scenes of farewell, as loved ones bid a sad goodbye to the dead, who are seated. While the dead are often just shaking hands, there's usually a personal meaning with each scene. For example, on the tombstone on the left wall, a woman who died in childbirth looks at her baby, held by a servant as it reaches for its dead mother. Other scenes include a beautiful young woman, who died in her prime, narcissistically gazing into a mirror. Servants are shown taking part in the sad event, as if considered part of the family. In the center of the room, a rich and powerful woman ponders which treasure from her jewel box to take with her into eternity. Though shallow reliefs, these works are effectively three-dimensional. There's a timeless melancholy in the room, a sense that no matter who you are—or how powerful or affluent your family is—when you go, you go alone...and shrouds have no pockets.

• *Pass into Room 21, a large central hall. We'll take a temporary break from the chronological sequence to see statues dating from the second century B.C., when Greece was ruled by Rome. The hall is dominated by...*

⑲ The *Artemision Jockey*

In this bronze statue (c. 140 B.C.), the horse is in full stride, and the young jockey looks over his shoulder to see if anyone's gaining on them. The statue was recovered in pieces from the seafloor off Cape Artemision. Missing were the reins the jockey once held in his left hand and the whip he used with his right to spur the horse to go even faster—maybe too fast, judging by the look on his face.

Greeks loved their horse races, and this statue may celebrate a victory at one of the Panhellenic Games. The jockey is dressed in a traditional short tunic, has inlaid eyes, and his features indicate that he was probably ethnically part Ethiopian.

The statue, like other ancient bronzes created by Greeks in Roman times, was made not by hammering sheets of metal, but with the classic "lost wax" technique. The artist would first make a rough version of the statue from clay, cover it with a layer of wax, and then cover that with another layer of clay to make a form-fitting mold. When heated in a furnace to harden the mold, the wax would melt—or be "lost"—leaving a narrow space between the clay model and the mold. The artist would then pour molten bronze into the space, let it cool, break the mold, and—*voilà!*—end up with a hollow bronze statue. This particular statue was cast in pieces, which were then welded together. After the cast was removed, the artist added a few surface details and polished it smooth. Notice the delightful detail on the rider's spurs, which were lashed to his bare feet.

Stylistically, we've gone from stiff Archaic, to restrained Severe, to balanced Classical...to this wonderful example of the unbridled emotion of Hellenism. Like other Hellenistic sculptures, this one doesn't sit primly, as the poised Classical statues did, but dominates its space.

The other statues in the room are second-century B.C. Roman copies of fifth-century B.C. Greek originals. The Romans were great warriors, engineers, and administrators, but they had an inferiority complex when it came to art and high culture. For high-class Romans, Greek culture was the ideal, which created a huge demand for Greek statues. As demand exceeded supply, making copies of Greek originals became a big industry, and the Romans excelled at it. In fact, throughout Europe today, when you see a "Greek" statue, it's likely a Roman copy of a Greek original. Thanks to excellent copies like the ones in this room, we know what many (otherwise lost) Golden Age Greek masterpieces looked like.

While the Greeks could cast a freestanding bronze statue with no problem, when the Romans tried to re-create it in marble, the statue needed extra support. Here's a tip: When you see a tree trunk buttressing some statue...it's a Roman copy.

• *To return to our chronological tour (picking up back before the Romans arrived), head into Room 22, with pediment reliefs (Sack of Troy on the right, Greeks vs. Amazons on the left) that once decorated the Temple of Asklepios at Epidavros (see page 242). Pass through a couple of rooms displaying funeral monuments with progressively higher relief and more monumental scale until you reach the long Room 28, where you'll come face-to-face with a large...*

⓯ Grave Relief of a Horse

The spirited horse steps lively and whinnies while an Ethiopian boy struggles with the bridle and tries to calm him with food. The

realistic detail of the horse's muscles and veins is astonishing, offset by the panther-skin blanket. The horse's head pops out of the relief, becoming fully three-dimensional. The boy's pose is slightly off-balance, anticipating the "unposed poses" of later Hellenism (this relief is from the late fourth century B.C.). We sense the emotions of both the overmatched boy and the nervous horse. We also see a balance between the horse and boy, with the two figures creating a natural scene together rather than standing alone.

To the left, the *stele* labeled *#738* is the last masterpiece of this style—in such deep relief that it's barely attached to the stone behind it.

• *Farther down Room 28 stands the impressive, slightly-larger-than-life-size...*

⓰ Bronze Statue of a Youth

Scholars can't decide whether this statue (c. 340-330 B.C.) is reaching out to give someone an apple or demonstrating a split-finger fastball. He may be Perseus, holding up the head of Medusa, but he's most likely the mythical Paris, awarding a golden apple to the winner of a beauty contest between goddesses (sparking jealousies that started the Trojan War). Imagine how striking this statue would have been in its original full shine, before the bronze darkened with age.

The figure is caught in midstep as he reaches out, gazing intently at the person he's giving the object to. Split this youth vertically down the middle to see the *contrapposto* (or "counter-poise") stance of so many Classical statues. His left foot is stable, while the right moves slightly, causing his hips to shift. Meanwhile, his right arm is tense while the left hangs loose. These subtle, contrary motions are in perfect balance around the statue's vertical axis.

In the Classical Age, statues reached their peak of natural realism and balanced grace. During the following Hellenistic Period, sculptors added to that realism, injecting motion and drama. Statues are fully three-dimensional (and Hellenistic statues even more so, as they have no "front": You have to walk around them to see the whole picture). Their poses are less rigid than those in the Archaic period and less overtly heroic than those of the Severe. The beauty of the face, the perfection of the muscles, the balance of elegant grace and brute power—these represent the full ripeness of the art of this age.

• *Continue into the small Room 29. To the left of the following door, find a black bronze head in a glass case. Look into the wild and cynical inlaid eyes of this...*

⓱ Head from a Statue of a Philosopher

This philosopher was a Cynic, part of a movement of non-materialist nonconformists founded in the fourth century B.C. by Diogenes.

The term "cynic" aptly describes these dislikable, arrogant guys with unkempt hair. The statue's aged, bearded face captures the personality of a distinct individual and is considered a portrait likeness. From c. 240 B.C., it's typical of the Hellenistic Period, the time after the Macedonian Alexander the Great conquered the rest of Greece and proceeded to spread Greek values across much of the Mediterranean and beyond. Hellenistic Greek society promoted a Me-Generation individualism, and artists celebrated everyday people like this. Rather than Photoshop out their eccentricities, they presented their subjects warts and all. For the first time in history, we see human beings in all their gritty human glory: with wrinkles, male-pattern baldness, saggy boobs, and middle-age spread, all captured in less-than-noble poses.

The glass case to the left shows other parts of his body. The statue was likely shipped in pieces (like an Ikea self-assembly kit) for practical purposes.

This statue, like a number of the museum's statues, was found by archaeologists on the seabed off the coast of Greece. Two separate shipwrecks in ancient times have yielded treasures now in this museum: At the wreck off Cape Artemision, Zeus/Poseidon and the bronze horse and jockey were found. Another wreck, off the

tiny island of Antikythira (near the southern tip of the Peloponnesian Peninsula), is the source of this statue, as well as the bronze statue of a youth (the one that's either Paris or Perseus).
• *Continue into the long Room 30 and head to the far end to find the...*

⑱ Statue of a Fighting Gaul

Having been wounded in the thigh (note the hole), this soldier has fallen to one knee and reaches up to fend off the next blow. The style of his helmet indicates that he's not a Greek, but a Gaul (from ancient France). The artist catches the exact moment when the tide of battle is about to turn. The face of this Fighting Gaul says he's afraid he may become the Dying Gaul.

The statue (c. 100 B.C.) sums up many of the features of Hellenistic art: He's frozen in motion in a wild, unbalanced pose that dramatizes his inner thoughts. The diagonal pose runs up his left leg and out his head and outstretched arm. Rather than a noble, idealized god, this is an ordinary soldier caught in an extreme moment. His arms flail, his muscles strain, his eyes bulge, and he cries out in pain. This statue may have been paired with others in a theatrical mini-drama that heightened emotion. Hellenism shows us the thrill of victory, and—in this case—the agony of defeat.

• *To the right, on the other side of a doorway, is a...*

⑲ Statue of Aphrodite, Pan, and Eros

In this playful marble ensemble (c. 100 B.C.) from the sacred island of Delos, Aphrodite is about to whack Pan with her sandal. Strik-

ing a classic *contrapposto* pose (with most of her weight on one foot), Aphrodite is more revealing than modest, her voluptuous body polished smooth. There's a bit of whimsy here, as Aphrodite seems to be saying, "Don't! Stop!"...but may instead be saying, "Don't stop." The actions of the (literally) horny Pan can also be interpreted in two ways: His left arm is forceful, but his right is gentle—holding her more like a dance partner. Eros, like an omnipresent Tinkerbell, comes to Aphrodite's aid—or does he? He has the power to save her if she wants help,

but with a hand on Pan's horn and a wink, Eros seems to say, "OK, Pan, this is your chance. Come on, man, go for it." Pan can't believe his luck. This marble is finer than those used in earlier statues, and it has been polished to a sheen with an emery stone. As you walk around this delightful statue, enjoy the detail, from the pudgy baby feet and the remnants of red paint on the sandal to the way the figures all work together in a cohesive vignette.

Across the room, another sculpture shows the ability of the artists of this age to capture action and tell a story. Find the carved relief showing two hairy men stomping grapes in big stone bins. Between them, like wrestlers dancing, two other brutes are toting a giant two-handled vase (krater) filled with grape juice, hauling it off to the next step in the process of becoming wine.

• *Now, enter Room 31 to see a...*

⓴ Statue of the Emperor Augustus

This statue of Augustus, founder of the Roman Empire and its first emperor (c. 12-10 B.C.), is the only known statue of him on horse-

back, although it is missing its lower half. He holds the (missing) reins in his left hand and raises his right hand in a gesture of blessing or of oration—an expression of the emperor's power. Although Greece was conquered by the Romans (146 B.C.), Greek culture ultimately "conquered" the Romans, as the Grecophile Romans imported Greek statues to Italy to beautify their villas. They preserved Greece's monuments and cranked out high-quality copies of Greek art. When the Roman Emperor Augustus began remaking the city of Rome, he used Greek-style Corinthian columns—a veneer of sophistication on buildings erected with no-nonsense, brick-and-concrete Roman-arch engineering. It's largely thanks to the Romans and their respect for Greek culture that so much of this ancient art survives today.

• *Step into Room 32 and find a portrait of a beautiful woman asleep on a rock.*

㉑ Sleeping Maenad (and Friends)

In the center of the room is a marble statue (c. A.D. 120) featuring a sleeping Maenad, a female follower of the god Dionysus. This Roman copy was made during the reign of Emperor Hadrian. Like a sleeping beauty, this slumbering Maenad lies exposed atop a rock on a soft skin of a panther. As if being mooned by the Maenad, a **bust** of the emperor himself stands on the nearby wall.

Hadrian was a Grecophile in two senses—he not only loved Greek culture, but he also had a hunky young Greek boyfriend named Antinous. Just to Hadrian's left is a fine portrait bust of **An-**

tinous—look into his disarmingly beautiful eyes. After the young man drowned in the Nile in A.D. 130, the depressed Hadrian had him deified and commissioned statues of him throughout the empire.

At the (missing) feet of the Maenad stands a statue of the Greek god of medicine, **Asklepios,** from the renowned ancient Sanctuary of Epidavros. Asklepios is portrayed with his snake and stick—back then, snakes were involved in healing procedures in the sanctuaries of the god. This statue is a Roman copy (A.D. 160) of a fourth-century Greek original.

• *Continue into Room 33 to see...*

㉒ Busts from the Late Roman Empire

These busts (A.D. 300-500) capture the generic features and somber expressions of the late Roman Empire. As Rome decayed and fell

to barbarians, the empire shifted its capital eastward to Constantinople (modern Istanbul). For the next thousand years, the Byzantine Empire, which included Greece, lived on as an enlightened, Christian, Greek-speaking enclave, while Western Europe fell into poverty and ignorance. During that time, Greek culture was mostly lost to the West and lay hidden until it was rediscovered during Europe's Renaissance (c. 1500). Gradually, Greek sites were unearthed, its statues cleaned up and repaired, and Greek culture once again was revived in all its inspirational glory.

• *Exit into the entrance lobby and take a breath. You've seen the core of this museum and its highlights. If you have an appetite for more, stay on the ground level, return to the boy on the horse, and pass straight to the back-left corner of the building (passing through Rooms 4, 21, and 34). You'll find bronze statues in Rooms 36-39 and devotional offerings—statuettes and intricate artifacts—from the Sanctuary of Olympia. Egyptian artifacts are in Rooms 40 and 41.*

The museum's upper level holds one more major set of works that you should muster up the energy for: prehistoric wall paintings. Find the ㉓ staircase in Room 35. At the top of the stairs, continue straight into Room 48, and go to the far end of the room to see the best of Santorini...

Cycladic Wall Paintings

These magnificent paintings were uncovered on the walls of homes at the ancient settlement of Akrotiri on the island of Thira (better known today as Santorini). When the island's volcano blew in a massive, bigger-than-Krakatoa eruption (c. 1630 B.C.), it preserved these frescoes in a thick blanket of ash. (Luckily, the town's inhabitants escaped, probably having been encouraged by a large earthquake and previous minor eruption to pack up their more-portable treasures and find a less-cranky island.) For more about Akrotiri and the eruption, see the Santorini chapter.

Akrotiri's people shared an artistic tradition with the Minoans (centered on the isle of Crete), but gave it their own twist. Un-

like most early peoples, the Thirans were not fighters but traders, and their work made them prosperous. Their unfortified homes and palaces housed elaborate furniture (see the bed, cast in plaster from a hole in the ash) and were decorated with colorful frescoes like these, which celebrate life in rolling springtime landscapes and everyday scenes. Flirting swallows soar over hillsides of lilies. An antelope buck turns to make eyes at a doe. Two boys, perhaps a prince and his servant, box (notice their mostly shaved heads). The frescoes are vivid, featuring primary colors of red, yellow, and blue, with thick black outlines. These are probably "secco" frescoes, started while the plaster wall was wet but continued even after it had dried. Those pigments absorbed by the plaster create the glowing translucent effect that distinguishes these paintings. Remember that most early cultures used art only as propaganda for a king, to commemorate a famous battle, or to represent a god. But the Aegeans were among the first to love beauty for its own sake. That love of beauty became part of the legacy of ancient Greece.

• *As long as you're upstairs, you might as well enter Room 49 (turn left as you exit) to browse a world-class...*

Ceramics Collection

Starting in this room, you can walk clockwise through eight rooms showing the evolution of pottery from the Bronze Age, to

Geometric/Archaic, to Severe, to Classical. In the sixth century B.C., artists painted black figures on a red background. During the Classical Age, the trend was red-on-black (with the occasional red-and-black on white). It's amazing to see how these ancient potters mastered the art of creating three-dimensional scenes on a two-dimensional surface, and a curvy one at that. Along the way you can also see two well-preserved skeletons from the Keramikos Cemetery.

• *Whew! Our tour is over. It's time to leave the ancients and make your way back to central Athens and the modern world.*

SLEEPING IN ATHENS

Greece's economic struggles translate into good values at Athens hotels. Prices are soft, and if you show up without a reservation, you'll often get a deep discount. Still, small, inexpensive hotels in the Plaka and Syntagma area are relatively scarce, listed in all the guidebooks, and filled with other tourists. Be willing to expand your search beyond the old center. I've found several gems in the Makrigianni and Koukaki neighborhoods, behind the Acropolis and a short walk from the Plaka action. These typically offer better value and a more sedate and authentic (rather than bustling and touristy) experience. Reserve ahead, especially for the summer months.

Check the hotel's website for special deals, and try asking for a lower price. Local travel agencies also have access to discount rates for many hotels (including some listed here). But don't be sucked in by *very* cheap, too-good-to-be-true deals: Most of those hotels are located in sleazy districts around Omonia Square, or down in the coastal suburbs of Glyfada and Voula—far from the places you've come to see. You'll pay a premium to stay near the Acropolis...and it's worth it. Many hotels have Acropolis-view rooms—some for no extra charge, but usually for a higher rate.

In general, lower your expectations. In ramshackle Athens, any room less than €75 will likely be clean, but expect well-worn bathrooms and furnishings.

If you want a bathtub, ask about one when you reserve, as most hotel bathrooms have just a shower. All over Greece, including Athens, most bathrooms have ancient plumbing that clogs easily. Rather than flushing toilet paper, dispose of it in the wastebasket next to the toilet. This may seem unusual, but it keeps the sewer system working and prevents you from getting cozy with your hotel janitor.

Sleep Code

Abbreviations   **(€1=about $1.10, country code: 30)**
S=Single, **D**=Double/Twin, **T**=Triple, **Q**=Quad, **b**=bathroom
Price Rankings
  $$$ **Higher Priced**—Most rooms €100 or more
   $$ **Moderately Priced**—Most rooms €75-100
    $ **Lower Priced**—Most rooms €75 or less
Unless otherwise noted, breakfast is included, English is spoken, and free Wi-Fi and/or a guest computer is generally available. Many places accept credit cards, and rooms generally have air-conditioning. Prices can change; verify current rates online or by email. For the best prices, always book directly with the hotel.

Athens is a noisy city, and Athenians like to stay out late. This, combined with the abundance of heavy traffic on city streets, can make things challenging for light sleepers. I've tried to recommend places in quieter areas, but finding a peaceful corner isn't always possible. Many hotels were renovated for the Olympics, adding "soundproof" doors and windows that can be successful at blocking out noise. Still, be ready to use earplugs.

For information and tips on pricing, getting deals, making reservations, and much more, see page 470.

IN THE PLAKA AND SYNTAGMA
Business-Class Hotels

These interchangeable places, scattered between the Plaka and Syntagma Square, were spiffed up for the 2004 Olympics. Today they offer predictable business-class comfort and fairly new-feeling rooms.

$$$ Hotel Plaka has a rooftop bar/terrace and 67 modern rooms (some with Acropolis views) with updated bathrooms. Its classy management adds some nice touches, such as a staff member on hand at breakfast to answer travel questions (Sb-€80-110, Db-€110-130, Tb-€85-145, rooms with balconies and Acropolis views may cost a bit more; 10 percent discount if you reserve direct and show this book at check-in, prices are soft—check website for deals, mostly for early bookings and longer stays—and lower Nov-March; elevator, at the corner of Mitropoleos and Kapnikarea, reservation tel. 210-322-2706, reception tel. 210-322-2096, www.plakahotel.gr, plaka@athenshotelsgroup.com).

$$$ Central Hotel has 84 sleek rooms, even sleeker public spaces, and an anonymous business-class vibe. There are several classes of rooms, based on whether they have balconies and/or views. If you stick with the cheaper rooms, it's a good value

SLEEPING

1 Hotel Plaka
2 Central Hotel &
   Hotel Hermes
3 Hotel Acropolis House
4 Niki Hotel
5 Hotel Adonis
6 Pan Hotel
7 Hotel Phaedra
8 Hotel Kimon
9 Student & Travellers' Inn
10 To Athens International
   Youth Hostel
11 Hotel Grande Bretagne
12 Hotel Electra Palace
13 Hotel Electra
14 Athens Center
   Square Hotel
15 Hotel Attalos
16 Hotel Cecil
17 Hotel Phidias
18 Hotel Tempi
19 Launderette
20 Internet Café

Central Athens Hotels

(Sb–€90–€110, superior Sb–€130–€150, Db–€110–€130, superior Db–€150–€170, rates depend on size and condition of room, often €10-20 less in slower times; elevator, swanky rooftop terrace with café and Jacuzzi; Apollonos 21, tel. 210-323-4357, www.centralhotel.gr, reservation@centralhotel.gr).

$$$ Hermes Hotel, professionally run by the folks at Hotel Plaka, is nearly as nice, located on a quiet street closer to Syntagma and a little less convenient to the ancient sites. Many of its 45 rooms have balconies, and guests share a pleasant lounge, a kids' activity room, and a rooftop patio with a peek at the Acropolis (Sb–€70-100, Db–€90-120, possible to add child's cot; 10 percent discount if you reserve directly with the hotel and show this book at check-in, prices are soft—check website for deals, mostly for longer stays—and lower Nov-March; elevator, Apollonos 19, reservation tel. 210-322-2706, reception tel. 210-323-5514, www.hermeshotel.gr, hermes@athenshotelsgroup.com).

Budget Hotels

$$ Hotel Acropolis House was once a wealthy lawyer's villa, and it still feels homey. You'll find antiques scattered amid the dark-wood furnishings in its lobby and 23 rooms, offered at what its owners call "realistic prices." Many rooms have balconies—ask when you reserve. Rooms without a bath have a private bathroom across the hall (S–€57, Sb–€60, D–€69, Db–€75, Tb–€99, 20-25 percent less off-season, check website for deals, reserve with credit card but pay in cash, breakfast-€7.50, no elevator, Kodrou 6, tel. 210-322-2344, www.acropolishouse.gr, hotel@acropolishouse.gr, run by Emmanuella with help of charmingly gregarious Jasmine, Andreas, and others).

$$ Niki Hotel has 23 tight-but-trendy rooms with artistic touches. Rooms in the back are a bit darker, and, hence, cheaper (back Db–€84, front Db–€94, superior view Db with balcony-€98, Qb view suite available, much cheaper off-season, no single rooms/rates, elevator, café, Nikis 27, tel. 210-322-0913, www.nikihotel.gr, info@nikihotel.gr).

$$ Hotel Adonis, with 26 retro-simple rooms, stands on the quiet, traffic-free upper reaches of Kodrou, right in the heart of the Plaka. A couple of rooms on the fourth floor have good views of the Acropolis, as does the rooftop bar (Sb–€70, Db–€85, Tb–€105, 40 percent cheaper Nov-March, check website for deals, reserve with credit card but pay in cash; rates include breakfast on roof terrace—which is also open at night for drinks and snacks, elevator, public areas can be smoky, Kodrou 3, tel. 210-324-9737, www.hotel-adonis.gr, info@hotel-adonis.gr, owner Spiros, assisted by Nikos).

$$ Pan Hotel is an old-school business hotel centrally located just below Syntagma Square. The 33 rooms are well maintained, with modern bathrooms (Sb-€70, Db-€85, Tb-€110, €10 cheaper Oct-April, check website for deals, elevator, Mitropoleos 11, tel. 210-323-7816, www.panhotel.gr, reservations@panhotel.gr).

$ Hotel Phaedra is simple but wonderfully located, overlooking a peaceful Plaka square with ancient ruins and a Byzantine church. The institutional hallways lead to 21 nicely appointed rooms—most with balconies and all but three of them with views. Six rooms have private bathrooms across the hall (Sb-€60-65, D with private bath across hall-€65-70, smaller twin Db-€70, Db with balcony-€75-80, Tb-€90, 20-30 percent less off-season, breakfast-€5, Acropolis-view rooftop terrace, elevator, 2 blocks from Hadrian's Arch at Herefondos 16, at intersection with Adrianou, tel. 210-323-8461, www.hotelphaedra.com, info@hotelphaedra.com; brothers Kostas and Stamatis, and their kids Marianna, Periklis, and Natalia).

$ Hotel Kimon is a crank-'em-out hotel with little character. However, the 15 rooms are well maintained, the location—in the Plaka, near the cathedral—is handy, and the prices are affordable (Sb-€30-60, Db-€55-80, Tb-€80-90, Qb suite available, 10-20 percent less off-season, continental breakfast-€5, Greek breakfast-€8, no elevator, top-floor terrace with a corner that looks up at the Acropolis, Apollonos 27, tel. 210-331-4658, www.kimonhotel.com).

Hostels

$ Student & Travellers' Inn by Greco Hostel is a good backpacker place in the Plaka, and the perfect spot to meet up with other young travelers. The 33 renovated rooms range from dorms with communal bathrooms to private rooms. An in-house travel agency specializes in trips to the Greek islands (bed in dorm room-€16-20, Sb-€50, D-€50, Db-€57, T-€60, Tb-€65, prices vary with demand, cheaper Nov-March; breakfast extra, open 24 hours, elevator, pay laundry service, courtyard bar, kitchen; Kidathineon 16, tel. 210-324-4808, www.studenttravellersinn.com, info@studenttravellersinn.com, managed by Pericles, a.k.a. Perry).

Athens International Youth Hostel (a.k.a. "Hotel Victor Hugo") has more beds at a cheaper price. This high-rise hostel just outside the tourist zone near the Metaxourghio Metro stop has recently renovated, Greek island-themed rooms and a guest kitchen (16 Victor Hugo, tel. 210-523-2540, www.athens-international.com, info@athens-international.com).

Cream of the Crop

$$$ Hotel Grande Bretagne, a five-star splurge with 320 sprawling and elegantly furnished rooms, is considered the best hotel in

Greece and ranks among the grand hotels of the world. It's *the* place to stay if you have royal blood—or wish you did and feel like being treated like royalty for a few days. Built in 1862 to accommodate visiting heads of state, it became a hotel in 1874 and still retains its 19th-century elegance. No other hotel in Athens can boast such a rich history (Sb/Db-generally around €350, buffet breakfast-€33, continental breakfast-€27, elevator, free Wi-Fi in lobby and pricey pay Wi-Fi in rooms, overlooking Syntagma Square at Vassileos Georgiou 1, tel. 210-333-0000, www.grandebretagne.gr, info.gb@starwoodhotels.com). If you'd rather just eat here, consider their recommended rooftop restaurant.

$$$ Hotel Electra Palace is a luxury five-star hotel with 155 rooms in a quiet corner of the Plaka, not far from Syntagma. It's pricey but plush, if a bit snooty, with top-notch service and elegance (Db-€220, "superior" Db with Acropolis view and balcony-€275, Db suite-€450; in slow times rates can drop to Db-€160 or less, superior Db-€225; check website for deals, elevator, garden patio, indoor pool, Acropolis-view outdoor pool; Nikodimou 18, tel. 210-337-0000, www.electrahotels.gr, salesepath@electrahotels.gr). Their second hotel—**Hotel Electra,** at #5 on the busy pedestrian Ermou street—has four stars and lower rates.

IN AND NEAR PSYRRI

$$ Athens Center Square Hotel is part of the Plaka and Hermes Hotel chain but is much less expensive, mostly because it's farther away from the main sightseeing action, and over a very seedy square. Inside, however, its 54 modern rooms are fresh, minimalist, and colorfully painted. The wonderful roof garden has commanding Acropolis views (Sb-€50-70, Db-€70-90, 10 percent discount when you reserve directly with the hotel and show this book at check-in, across from market hall just off Athinas street at Aristogitonos 15, reservation tel. 210-322-2706, reception tel. 210-321-1770, www.athenscentersquarehotel.gr, acs@athenshotelsgroup.com).

$$ Hotel Attalos, an 80-room budget standby, is a bit tired but peaceful, friendly, well-run, and conveniently close to Monastiraki Square. Their roof garden offers commanding Acropolis views and a great bar (Sb-€82, Db-€92-98, Tb-€114, Qb-€139, €10-15 more with balcony, soft prices, cheaper Oct-April, 10 percent discount for Rick Steves readers when you book directly with the hotel via email, breakfast-€9, elevator, Athinas 29, tel. 210-321-2801, www.attaloshotel.com, info@attaloshotel.com).

$$ Hotel Cecil has 36 rooms in a formerly grand, then faded, and now lightly updated old building. The rooms can be a bit worn, but the price is decent, the breakfast is generous, and the location—between Monastiraki and the Central Market, on the edge of the

Psyrri neighborhood—is convenient. Its antique iron-cage elevator is so rare that the manufacturer wanted it for the company museum and offered to replace it for free—but the owners declined (Sb-€55, Db-€75, Tb-€90, family room-€120, about 20 percent less off-season, prices fluctuate with demand, ask for quieter room in back, Athinas 39, tel. 210-321-7079, www.cecil.gr, info@cecil.gr, Trevlakis family).

$$ Hotel Phidias, in the Thissio neighborhood behind the Ancient Agora, has a charming location right on the delightful Apostolou Pavlou pedestrian drag. The 15 simple, unfussy rooms are reasonably priced for this location. Streetside rooms get some noise from nearby cafés—especially on weekends—ask for a quieter back room (Sb-€65, Db-€80, Tb-€95, at least €10 less off-season, elevator, Apostolou Pavlou 39, tel. 210-345-9511, www.phidias.gr, phidiasa@otenet.gr).

$ Hotel Tempi, run by friendly Yiannis and Katerina, offers old-fashioned hospitality at old-fashioned prices. The 24 rooms are Spartan, and the bathrooms are cramped and minimal (especially the shared ones)—but the rates are just right. It's well-situated on lively Agia Irini Square, which is filled with trendy cafés and bars. Rooms in front come with balconies overlooking the square and with views of the Acropolis (S-€37, Sb-€42, D-€47, Db-€55, Tb-€64, cheaper Nov-March; lots of stairs, elevator is for luggage only, kitchen/breakfast room, optional breakfast at café next door-€6 and up; Aiolou 29, tel. 210-321-3175, www.tempihotel.gr, info@tempihotel.gr).

IN MAKRIGIANNI AND KOUKAKI, BEHIND THE ACROPOLIS

The Plaka has abundant charm...and abundant noise, crowds, and higher prices. Instead, consider making the adjoining residential Makrigianni and Koukaki neighborhoods, just south of the Acropolis, your home base in Athens. With the Acropolis Museum standing boldly as its gateway, this typically Athenian urban area—full of six-story concrete apartment buildings, colorful grocery stores, and corner cafés—offers tourists the chance to become a temporary Athenian. Most importantly, it allows easy access to the sights (all of the following hotels are within a 10-minute walk of the Dionysiou Areopagitou pedestrian boulevard under the Acropolis, and the edge of the Plaka). Be aware that some locals call Makrigianni the "south Plaka" instead.

These hotels are all located between the Akropoli and Syngrou-Fix Metro stops.

$$$ Hotel Hera is a tempting splurge, with 38 plush rooms above a classy lobby. With helpful service, lots of thoughtful little touches, an air of elegance, and a handy location near the Acropolis

SLEEPING

Makrigianni & Koukaki Hotels & Restaurants

1 Hotel Hera
2 Hotel Acropolis Select
3 Art Gallery Hotel
4 Athens Studios & Launderette
5 Marble House Pension
6 Athens Backpackers Hostel
7 Mani Mani Restaurant
8 Strofi Athenian Restaurant
9 To Kati Allo Restaurant
10 Konstantinidis Ice Cream
11 Swift/Avanti Car Rental

end of this neighborhood, it's a great value for this price range (Sb-€95-110, Db-€100-€130 depending on size, €20 extra for Acropolis-view room on fourth floor, cheaper Nov-March; breakfast-€15, check website for deals, elevator, rooftop Acropolis-view restaurant open only in evening for dinner or drinks; Falirou 9, tel. 210-923-6682, www.herahotel.gr, info@herahotel.gr).

$$$ Hotel Acropolis Select has 72 rooms over a stylish lobby, a can-do staff, and a generous breakfast. Their service ethic goes way beyond the norm—they've been known to send a guide on a motorbike to lead lost drivers to the hotel (Db-roughly €80-120 depending on size and season, elevator, Falirou 37—look for flags out front, tel. 210-921-1610, www.acropoliselect.gr, select3@otenet.gr, run by Yannis).

$$ Art Gallery Hotel is a comfy, cozy, well-run small hotel with 21 rooms near the top of a pleasant, pedestrian stair-step lane. The original artwork in the halls and rooms adds charm (Sb-€40-70, Db-€50-80, Tb-€70-100, higher prices are for peak season, breakfast-€7, elevator, fourth-floor bar open 20:00-24:00, Erechthiou 5, tel. 210-923-8376 or 210-923-1933, www.artgalleryhotel.gr, artgalleryhotel@gmail.com). Say hello to Artie, the hotel's cat.

$$ Athens Studios, run by the gang at Athens Backpackers (described later), rents nicely appointed, good-value apartments with retro-mod decor, kitchens, and other nice touches (Db/Tb-€55-95, Qb-€80-125, 6b-€90-155, check website for deals; elevator; sports bar, fish café, and public launderette on ground floor; pay long-term luggage storage available, Veikou 3A, tel. 210-923-5811, www.athensstudios.gr, info@athensstudios.gr, Daniel).

$ Marble House Pension is a small, family-run place hiding at the end of a little cul-de-sac, a few minutes' walk past my other listings in this area. The 16 cozy rooms are simple but well cared for, and (true to its name) it's decorated with real marble. If you don't mind the more remote location, it's an excellent deal (D-€40, Db-€45, Tb-€55, Qb-€65, these prices if you book directly with the hotel, cheaper Nov-mid-March, reserve with credit card but pay in cash, may be closed Jan-Feb; breakfast-€5, air-con-€5/day by request, 3 floors—no elevator; 5-minute walk from Syngrou-Fix Metro at Zini 35a—from Zini street take the alley to the left of the tidy Catholic church, tel. 210-923-4058, www.marblehouse.gr, info@marblehouse.gr; Thanos, Nancy, and Christos).

$ Athens Backpackers is the best place in town for backpacker bonding. Youthful and fun-loving (with two bars, including one on the rooftop), and well-run by gregarious Aussies, it offers good bunks and an opportunity to meet up with other travelers (bed in dorm room-€15-25, all rooms have 3-6 beds and bathroom; big communal kitchen, public launderette at Athens Studios; €6 city walking tours offered daily in summer, less frequent off-season; Makri 12, tel. 210-922-4044, www.backpackers.gr, info@backpackers.gr).

EATING IN ATHENS

Greek food is just plain good. And Athens has a lively restaurant scene. Locals and tourists alike fill endless tavernas, *mezedopolio*s (eateries selling small plates called *mezedes*), *ouzeries* (bars selling ouzo liquor and pub grub), and other traditional eateries dishing up the basics. For much more on Greek cuisine, see page 479.

I've listed these restaurants by neighborhood. You probably won't be able to resist dining in the touristy Plaka at least once—it's fun, folkloric, and full of clichés (but beware the tourist traps). But don't be afraid to venture elsewhere. For a trendy and youthful local scene, target Psyrri and Gazi—just beyond the tourist zone. For those staying near the Acropolis Museum in Makrigianni or Koukaki, I've listed a couple of convenient options (including my two favorite elegant restaurants in all of Athens).

THE PLAKA

Diners—Greeks and tourists alike—flock to the Plaka. In this neighborhood, the ambience is better than the food. I've avoided the obvious, touristy joints on the main pedestrian drag—with shards of broken plates in the cobbles and obnoxious touts out front luring diners with a desperate spiel—in favor of more authentic-feeling eateries huddled on the quieter hillside just above. Eat at one of my recommendations, or simply choose the place with your favorite view of an ancient monument, on a square that appeals to you, or with live music. Prices are pretty consistent and painless.

At the top of the Plaka, the stepped lane called Mnisikleous (stretching up toward the Acropolis) is lined with eateries featuring interchangeable food and delightful outdoor seating. Many of these places have live music and/or rooftop gardens.

Xenios Zeus (ΞΕΝΙΟΣ ΖΕΥΣ) sits proudly at the top of the Mnisikleous steps. Exuberant Eleni offers good, traditional, home-cooking Greek food inside or out on a terrace overlooking Athens' rooftops (€1.50 toasted village bread with garlic and olive oil, €3-8 appetizers, €9-20 main dishes, €13-18 fixed-price meals, daily 11:00-24:00, closed Nov-March, Mnisikleous 37, tel. 210-324-9514, http://xenioszeus.com.gr). Eleni promises a free bottle of ouzo to diners with this book (be sure to ask).

Geros tou Moria Tavern is a sprawling and venerable place with three eating areas. The tour-group-friendly, powerfully air-conditioned indoor dining hall features a more-formal menu and live Greek music and dance (no cover, nightly from 20:15). The more intimate Palio Tetradio ("Old Notebook") has a terrace, cozy-in-the-winter indoor seating, and more *mezedes*. Maybe best of all are the tables along

the steps under grapevines (€4-9 starters and salads, €9-20 main dishes, daily 12:00-24:00, Mnisikleous 27, tel. 210-322-1753, www.gerostoumoria-restaurant.com).

Palia Taverna tou Psara ("Old Fisherman's Tavern") is a big, slick, pricey eatery that enjoys bragging about the many illustrious guests they've hosted since opening in 1898. It's the kind of place

where a rowdy, rollicking group of a hundred can slam down a dish-'em-up Greek meal. While often dominated by tour groups, it can be enjoyable. There's live folk music in the lower building and, kitty-corner across the way, a grand rooftop terrace (€3-14 *mezedes*, €10-25 main dishes, daily 12:00-24:00, Eretheos 16, tel. 210-321-8734, www.psaras-taverna.gr).

Scholarhio Ouzeri Kouklis Mezedes Restaurant, at the intersection of Tripodon and Epicharmou streets, serves only small plates. While jammed with tourists, it's fun, inexpensive, and ideal for small groups wanting to try a variety of traditional *mezedes* (€3-6/plate) and drink good, homemade booze on an airy perch at the top of the Plaka. Since 1935, the Kouklis family has been making ouzo liquor and feeding people here—maintaining a 1930s atmosphere. Waiters present a big platter of dishes, and you choose. Drinks are cheap, and the stress-free €14 meal deals (including dessert) are worth considering, especially for a group. Many wait for a spot to open up on the lively front terrace, but you can instead climb to the upstairs dining room with its romantic balconies for two (daily 11:00-24:00, Tripodon 14, tel. 210-324-7605, www.scholarhio.gr). Vasilis and his gang welcome anyone with this book with free homemade ouzo—if you ask.

Klepsidra Café is parked on a characteristic corner high in the Plaka with an island ambiance and a young local crowd. With tiny tables littering the ramshackle steps, they serve light bites (€5-12), good desserts, traditional coffee, and lots of booze (daily 9:00-24:00, Thrasivoulou 9, tel. 210-321-2493).

CHEAP EATS NEAR MONASTIRAKI SQUARE

Souvlaki Row: Monastiraki Square (where it meets Mitropoleos street) is souvlaki heaven, with three frantic restaurants—**Thanasis, Savvas,** and **Bairaktaris**—spilling into the street and keeping hordes of hungry eaters happy. The dominant operation, **Bairaktaris,** while not necessarily the best eating value, has a boisterous, fun-loving interior. These places also sell meat shaved from gyros, hearty Greek salads, other standard Greek dishes, wine, beer, and ouzo. You can get your souvlaki to go or at a table. They're all open daily until very late.

Take-Out: A gyro or souvlaki sandwich to go costs about €2. For these cheap carry-out prices, order and pay at the cashier, then take your receipt to the counter to claim your meal. It can be tricky to find a comfortable bench or other suitable perch in this crowded neighborhood—plan to munch as you walk.

Table Service: All three places sell souvlaki to go really cheaply. You'll pay basic restaurant prices and get much bigger portions when you sit. The ambience is lively, especially at the outdoor tables. A big plate of four souvlaki (plus pita bread, onions, and tomatoes) costs €9-10; a smaller helping of two souvlaki—plenty for most eaters—runs about €5-6.

Agia Irini Square: Kosta Souvlaki is a beloved hole-in-the-wall that's been serving up good souvlaki pitas since the 1940s. This is a classic place—no gyro slices...just traditional €2 skewer-roasted souvlaki. You can get it to go or grab a stool on the tiny square facing St. Irene's Church to enjoy

Souvlaki: A Quick and Cheap Meal in Athens

My favorite fast-food meal in Greece is souvlaki—fast, cheap, and filling. As international fast-food places move in, the traditional souvlaki stand is harder to find...but more worthwhile than ever to seek out and enjoy.

Souvlaki is meat grilled on a skewer and served on a plate or wrapped in pita bread to make a sandwich. When you get it "to go," the meat (often pork or lamb) is tucked into a wonderful greasy pita pocket with lettuce, tomato, onions, and *tzatziki* (the famous cucumber-yogurt-garlic sauce). It's often sprinkled with red pepper, bulked up with doughy French fries (which you can opt out of if you speak up), and wrapped in wax paper that you peel back as you eat. If you order souvlaki in a restaurant, insist on a "souvlaki sandwich" or you'll generally get a big meaty plate, which costs four times as much.

The **gyro** *(yee-row)* is a virtually identical type of sandwich made with meat cooked on a spinning vertical rotisserie (also called a gyro, meaning "turn"). The meat—usually pork, chicken, or a combination—is shaved into a steamy, tasty pile and then tucked into a pita with the usual accompaniments. The words souvlaki and gyro might be used interchangeably, depending where you are or who you're talking to.

Which is the best souvlaki stand in Athens? There are famous places—big restaurants with a to-go counter and venerable holes-in-the-wall. But my favorites are the simple, no-name neighborhood joints that lurk in the back streets.

(This sidebar was written with the help of Matt Barrett, whose Greece Travel.com website is a wonderful resource.)

EATING

the almost Parisian ambience of the emerging St. Irene district (daily 9:00-17:00, Agia Irini, off Aiolou Street a block north of Ermou).

Picnics: To assemble a cheap meal of your own, head 500 yards north of Monastiraki (on Athinas) to the **Central Market.** For details, see page 60. Plenty of small shops in the neighborhood offer what you need to throw together a decent picnic.

NEAR SYNTAGMA SQUARE

Tzitzikas and Mermigas ("The Ant and the Cricket") serves modern, regional Greek cuisine. Choose between two levels of indoor seating in a fun, mod, retro-grocery-store atmosphere, or grab a sidewalk table. It's named for the folktale about a hardworking ant and the lazy cricket who goofs off...only to come asking for help

EATING

1 Xenios Zeus
2 Geros tou Moria Tavern
3 Palia Taverna tou Psara
4 Scholarhio Ouzeri Kouklis Mezedes Restaurant
5 Klepsidra Café
6 "Souvlaki Row": Thanasis, Savvas & Bairaktaris
7 Kosta Souvlaki
8 Central Market
9 Tzitzikas and Mermigas
10 Kimolia Art Café
11 Avocado Vegetarian Café
12 Ariston
13 Athinaikon Restaurant
14 2Mazi Restaurant Wine Bar
15 Roof Garden Restaurant
16 Taverna tou Psyrri
17 O Nikitas
18 Avli
19 Ta Karamanlidika
20 James Joyce Irish Pub
21 Koulouri of Psyrri
22 To Gazi Eateries
23 Konstantinidis Ice Cream
24 Bougatsadiko Thessaloniki
25 Krinos Loukoumades
26 Mokka Coffee
27 By the Glass Wine Bar
28 Brettos Distillery
29 Karayiannis Ouzo Bar

EATING

when winter arrives (€5-9 starters, €8-14 main dishes, daily 13:00-24:00, Mitropoleos 12, tel. 210-324-7607).

Kimolia (Κιμωλία) Art Café is a cute little pastel place serving light café fare with reasonable prices, a relaxing vibe, free Wi-Fi, and friendly service. It's a nice place to take a break (€5-7 sandwiches and salads, daily 10:00-late, Ypereidou 5, tel. 211-184-8446).

Avocado Vegetarian Café is a good bet if you need a yoga-friendly eatery with lots of energy juices, a passion for organic farming, and nothing with eyeballs (€10-12 plates, Mon-Sat 11:00-22:00, Sun 12:00-19:00, Nikis 30, tel. 210-323-7878).

Ariston (ΑΡΙΣΤΟΝ), in business for more than a century, is one of Athens' top spots for a wide range of savory and sweet pastries (€2 apiece). Choose between *spanakopita* (spinach pie), *tiropita* (cheese pie), *kreatopita* (minced pork meat pie), *meletzanitopita* (eggplant pie), and lots more (leek, shrimp, olives and feta, and so on...all labeled in English). They also have lovely sweet desserts made with flaky phyllo (Mon, Wed, and Sat 7:30-18:00; Tue and Thu-Fri 7:30-21:00; closed Sun, 2 blocks from Syntagma toward the Plaka at Voulis 10, tel. 210-322-7626).

FINER DINING BETWEEN SYNTAGMA AND THE CATHEDRAL

Athinaikon Restaurant, with a heritage going back to the 1930s, is a venerable businessman's favorite, serving a variety of traditional *mezes* and Greek and Mediterranean recipes. You'll dine in a no-nonsense art-deco/modern interior with professional service and a local crowd (€5-8 *mezes*, €10-15 main dishes, Mon-Sat 12:00-24:00, Sun until 19:00, a block from the cathedral at Mitropoleos 34, tel. 210-325-2688).

2Mazi Restaurant Wine Bar gets its name from a play on the Greek word for "together," and is the collaboration of two well-known local chefs. It's a good place to enjoy modern Greek gourmet cooking in a stylish setting with equally stylish locals (€10-15 salads, €20-25 main dishes, "12 Surprises" tasting menu for €50, daily 13:00-24:00, Nikis 48, tel. 210-322-2839, reservations smart, http://www.2mazi.gr).

Hotel Grande Bretagne's Roof Garden Restaurant is posh as can be. Considered by many the finest place in town to dine on Greek and Mediterranean cuisine, it's pure fancy-hotel-restaurant elegance—in a rooftop garden with spectacular Acropolis views (€20-25 pastas, €30-50 main dishes, plan on spending €60/person for dinner, daily 13:00-24:00, reservations required for meals, "smart casual" dress code, on Syntagma Square, tel. 210-333-0766, www.grandebretagne.gr). If you don't want such an expensive meal, drop by their swanky bar for a pricey beer or cocktail.

PSYRRI

The thriving Psyrri district, just north of Monastiraki, is one of Athens' most enjoyable areas to explore. The mix of trendy and crusty gives the area a unique charm. Your options include slick, touristy tavernas with live traditional music (many are painted in the same Greek saloon style—these places are fresh, formulaic, and part of a chain), highly conceptual café/bars catering to cool young Athenians, and clubs with DJs or live music for partying the night away.

While I've listed a few restaurants to consider, the scene is ever-changing and the vibe is different each night—you might just wander and see what feels best.

Iroon Square is the lively hub of the action. From there the streets called Agiou Dimitriou and Agion Anargyron are lined with the most accessible and fun places. The third street, Miaouli, which extends from Iroon Square toward Monastiraki, is a younger, university scene—packed with the outdoor tables of unpretentious, local-feeling pubs and tavernas. Lepeniotou and Aisopou streets have the most creatively themed café/bars—most of them mellow and colorful—great spots to relax with a drink and appreciate the decor (Oineas Restaurant, at Aisopou 9, is particularly fun). Each one has its own personality and idiosyncratic sense of style (from Lebanese to Argentinian).

Taverna tou Psyrri is right in the heart of the restaurant action, with checkerboard tablecloths, a garden terrace hidden in the back, a straightforward menu, and good prices (€3-6 starters, €7-10 main dishes, daily 12:00-24:00, Eschilou 12, tel. 210-321-4923).

O Nikitas (Ο Νικήτας) sits on a peaceful square, serving mainly *mezedes* and good food to a local crowd (€3 starters, €6-8 main dishes, Sun-Tue 12:00-18:00, Wed-Sat 12:00-23:00, across from church on Agion Anargyron 19, tel. 210-325-2591).

Avli (αυλή; "the courtyard") is for the adventurous. Stepping through its speakeasy door you'll find a long, skinny, and thriving courtyard with a jumble of tiny tables and Greeks wondering, "How did that tourist find this place?" They have no menu, instead serving a daily *meze* plate for €8-10 (daily 12:00-24:00, Agiou Dimitriou 12). Look for the small doorway labeled αυλή.

Ta Karamanlidika, just outside of Psyrri near the market, is my favorite in the area. It's a quality meat-and-cheese shop that doubles as a restaurant. With its mix of authentic Byzantine and Cappadocian flavors, aged cheese, and cured meats, it's a tasty reminder that many Greek Turks were expelled in the 1920s and settled here in Athens—bringing their Anatolian cuisine with them. You'll enjoy tasty plates for €5-7 and the friendly service of Maria and her gang (Mon-Sat 12:00-23:00, closed Sun, a block off Athinas at Evripidou 52, tel. 210-325-4184).

James Joyce Irish Pub (just outside of Psyrri facing the Agora) offers travelers an escape from Greece. The complete Irish-pub menu (€8-12 main dishes), Irish beers on tap, air-conditioned freshness, and rock 'n' roll ambience combine to transport you to Ireland (between the Thissio temple and Ermou street at Astiggos 12, tel. 210-323-5055, Tom Cameron).

Fresh Koulouri: These sesame bread rings, sold at corner carts throughout the city, are a popular Athenian on-the-run snack, especially in the morning. For the best, visit **Koulouri of Psyrri,** which supplies most of the street vendors in the city and where you can try one fresh out of the oven (Karaiskaki 23, tel. 210-321-5962).

GAZI

Residents here must be dizzy at the rapid change sweeping through what was recently a depressed industrial zone. Towering overhead are the square, brick smokestacks of Technopolis, a complex of warehouses, old gasworks, and brick factory buildings that now host galleries and theaters with a world of cutting-edge culture.

Simply ride the Metro to Keramikos. Exiting the Keramikos Metro station, you'll emerge at the top of the main square—a delightful park surrounded by streets lined with super-stylish restaurants, clubs, bars, and cafés. While wild-and-alternative places to eat and drink dot the back lanes, the main square is busy with options accessible to any tourist. Stand looking downhill, with the gasworks smokestacks to your back. On the right is a line of clubs and cocktail bars. On the left is a line of happening restaurants. I've listed my favorite three (starting just steps away and working downhill).

Kazani Meze Restaurant is a modern, stylish place with a sleek yet classic feel and an enjoyable and accessible menu of *mezes* featuring dishes from all over Greece (€5-10/plate, daily 13:00-24:00, just steps from the Metro station at Persefonis 39, tel. 210-346-4984).

Kandavlos Souvlaki, a thriving student hangout with white tables and a clubby crowd, serves the best €2.50 souvlaki in Gazi (daily 11:00-24:00, left of Gazi College Eatery at Persefonis 47, tel. 210-342-4725).

Gazi College Eatery is a fresh, modern, and inviting place for a light meal or drink in the company of a student crowd that's typical of the area. It offers a fun and affordable menu all day and evening (€6-8 pizzas, pastas, salads, and sandwiches; daily 8:00-24:00, Persefonis 53, tel. 210-342-2112).

MAKRIGIANNI AND KOUKAKI,
NEAR THE ACROPOLIS MUSEUM

New development in this area, including the Akropoli Metro stop, has brought with it a trendy and touristy row of restaurants, cafés, and ice-cream shops along pedestrian Makrigianni street, facing the Acropolis Museum. The other pedestrian street, Dionysiou Areopagitou, also has plenty of tourist-friendly options between the museum and the Arch of Hadrian, including a good souvlaki joint and a yogurt bar.

While there are countless hardworking eateries along these streets, these three restaurants are worth serious consideration: my two favorite places in town for a fine dinner, and a delightful home-cookin' hole-in-the-wall. For locations, see the map on page 170.

Mani Mani offers a touch of class for reasonable prices, with cuisine from the Mani Peninsula and typical Mani ingredients. The dining is indoors only, and the food, like the decor, is thoughtfully updated Greek. Chef Alex cooks, Yolanda (his wife) greets you, and their staff provides great service and a description of your beautifully presented plates as they land. Alex offers a tasting menu a few days a month, which lets him lavish you with his favorite dishes *meze*-style. With wine, dessert, and an after-dinner drink—the entire experience to the max—it's highly recommended. Each of the starters are gourmet treats (€6-9 starters—available as half-portions for half-price until 18:00 on Mon-Fri, €10-15 main dishes, daily 14:00-23:00 in summer, shorter hours in winter, reservations smart, go upstairs at Falirou 10, tel. 210-921-8180, www.manimani.com.gr).

Strofi Athenian Restaurant is my choice in Athens for white-tablecloth, elegantly modern, rooftop-Acropolis-view dining. Niko Bletsos and his staff offer attentive service, gorgeously presented plates, and classic Greek cuisine—especially lamb. And though they have a fine air-conditioned interior, the rooftop is comfortable regardless of how hot or cool the evening. For a floodlit Acropolis view, you'll be glad you made reservations (€7-10 starters, €13-20 main dishes, Tue-Sun 12:00-late, closed Mon, about 100 yards down Propyleon street off Dionysiou Areopagitou at Rovertou Galli 25, tel. 210-921-4130, www.strofi.gr).

To Kati Allo Restaurant, immediately under the far side of the Acropolis Museum, lacks tourists and is the quintessential neighborhood hole-in-the-wall. Run by English-speaking Kostas Bakatselos and his family (including Jennifer, the American daughter-in-law), this place offers both sidewalk seating and fan-cooled inside tables. The menu, written on a blackboard, features a short list of cheap, fresh, and tasty local options (€6-10 main

Food Tours

Food tours are a great way to get to know Greeks, who love to cook and love to eat. With a good tour, you'll learn a lot about Greek history and culture through food, plus you'll get to sample classic dishes. Here are a few good choices:

Shorter Walks: Alternative Athens and **Athens Walking Tours** both offer three-hour tours and include similar stops (Central Market, olive stand, Greek sweets, meat-and-cheese shop, specialty grocery store, and so on). I prefer Alternative Athens' food walk, which dips into more local-feeling places and offers a few more bites and insight (€45/person, Mon-Sat at 10:00, none on Sun, 3 hours, 12-person max, mobile 694-840-5242, www.alternativeathens.com; they also offer home-cooked meal experiences). Athens Walking Tours is a perfectly fine alternative (€49/person, Mon-Sat at 9:30, none on Sun, 14-person max, averages 8 people, tel. 210-884-7269, www.athenswalkingtours.gr; they also offer cooking lessons and wine-tasting tours).

Longer Walks: Culinary Backstreets' tours are for people who love to eat. They offer two tours: Backstreet Plaka and Downtown Athens. The groups are smaller, and you'll stop at more places (from family-run holes-in-the-wall to trendier eateries), linger longer at stops, and eat more unique food—and a lot more of it. You won't want to eat for the rest of the day ($135/person, both run 9:30-15:00 but on different days—check their schedule, 2-7 people, www.culinarybackstreets.com).

dishes, daily 11:00-24:00, just off Makrigianni street at Chatzichristou 12, tel. 210-922-3071).

SUGAR, CAFFEINE, AND OTHER DRUGS
Sweets

Yogurt Bars: For a fun treat, look for fast-food joints selling create-a-dream yogurt desserts. This is just good (un-frozen) Greek yogurt with your choice of decadent toppings. They generally have several types of yogurt to choose from (low-cal or traditional—from cow's milk, extra rich—a mix of cow and sheep milk, and sheep milk), honey, nuts, and an array of "spoon sweets" (fancy jams) and sprinkles (a hit with kids). They'll also blend in ice and milk to make smoothies. Frozen Greek yogurt is also popular. Look for these stores across town: **Froyo, Yasu, Chillbox, Snoyo,** and **Fresko Yogurt Bar.**

Great Ice Cream and Baklava: Konstantinidis is a local favorite for both ice cream and baklava and, after my discerning taste test, I enthusiastically agree. While a chain, they do a good job of embracing their "good old days" heritage. You'll find two branches in the town center: Stadiou 3 (3 blocks northwest of Syntagma; see map on page 177) and Syngrou Ave 98 (the biggest and best, just beyond the Syngrou-Fix Metro station; see map on page 170).

Bougatsa and *Loukoumades:* Locals say that **Bougatsadiko Thessaloniki** makes some of the best *bougatsa*—thin pastry with cream inside. Watch the pastry master at work, then order a plate (if not on display just ask for it, 1 Iroon Square, tel. 210-322-2088). **Krinos** is famed for its *loukoumades*—fried Greek doughnuts (closed Sun, 87 Aiolou, tel. 210-321-6852). See the map on page 177 for locations.

Coffee

If you want good local coffee for half the price of Starbucks and want your money to stay in Greece, you'll find handy branches of

Grigoris Coffee Right (a Greek gourmet coffee chain) all over town. They serve cheap but fancy coffee and offer all the light bites, pastries, and trendy ambience you need. The **Mikel Coffee** chain is a bit pricier and more posh.

For Greek coffee made the traditional way—water, grounds, and sugar combined in a *briki* (copper or brass pitcher) and slowly heated in a tray of hot sand—visit **Mokka**, near Central Market (44 Athinas, tel. 210-321-6892). Even if you find Turkish coffee too strong, give Greek coffee a try, as it's much milder.

Wine and Ouzo Tasting

By the Glass wine bar is a jazz-cool, relaxed place where you can enjoy a quiet table or sit at the bar and learn from the server about Greek wines. They serve plates of mixed Greek cheeses and meats, salads, and other upscale nibbles to complement your wine tasting. Panos speaks Eng-

lish and is happy to construct a "flight of Greek wines." Their menu includes countless wines by the tiny glass for a euro or two each (daily 12:00-24:00, between the Plaka and the National Garden at Y. Souri 3, tel. 210-323-2560).

EATING

Brettos—the oldest distillery in Athens, dating from 1909—is a popular stop for tourists and locals wanting to taste various shots and wines by the glass. While buried in the Plaka kitsch, it seems a world apart once you step inside and grab a stool under huge old casks (daily 10:00-24:00, just off Adrianou at Kydathineon 41, tel. 210-323-2100).

Karayiannis Ouzo Bar, in the thick of the Central Market and run by Kostas, is great for a drink and snack. Pay about €3 for an ouzo and little plate of *mezes* to enjoy while you observe the action (on a side aisle, midway down the fish section in the Central Market, Mon-Sat 7:30-15:00, closed Sun). For more on the market, see page 60.

EATING

SHOPPING AND NIGHTLIFE IN ATHENS

Athens may not be a top shopping destination, but it does offer plenty of options for visitors who want to pick up good Greek souvenirs. On the other hand, Athens *is* known for its lively after-hours scene. In this chapter, you'll find tips for shopping and for enjoying the city after dark.

Shopping in Athens

Most shops catering to tourists are open long hours daily (souvenir stores in the Plaka can be open past midnight). Those serving locals are open roughly 9:00 to 20:00 on weekdays, have shorter hours on Saturday, and are closed on Sunday. Afternoon breaks are common, and some places close early a few nights a week.

For details on getting a VAT (Value-Added Tax) refund on your purchases, see page 466.

Shopping Areas: The main streets of the Plaka—especially **Adrianou** and **Pandrossou**—are crammed with crass tourist-trap shops selling cheap plaster replicas of ancient artifacts, along with calendars, magnets, playing cards, postcards, and shockingly profane T-shirts. Competition is fierce, so there's room to bargain, especially if you're buying several items.

For upscale shopping at mostly international chain stores, stroll the pedestrianized **Ermou street** between Syntagma Square and Monastiraki (described in more detail on page 776). You'll find more local flavor at Greek shops such as **Kem** (handbags; Kornarou 1, just off Ermou), **Folli Follie** (jewelry, handbags, and accessories; Ermou 18), and the clothing stores **Regalinas** (Ermou 37) and **Bill Cost** (Ermou 14).

While tourists and big-money Athenians strut their stuff on Ermou, many locals prefer the more authentic shops on the streets

Shops
1. Kem (Handbags)
2. Folli Follie (Jewelry, etc)
3. Regalinas (Clothing)
4. Bill Cost (Clothing)
5. Monastiraki Flea Market
6. Attica Dep't Store
7. Byzantino (2, Jewelry)
8. Olympico (Jewelry)
9. Melissinos Art (Sandals)
10. Peri Lesvou (Edibles)
11. Zouridakis (Edibles)
12. Matsouka (Edibles)
13. Le Chocolat (Edibles)
14. Pantopolion (Edibles)
15. Eleftheroudakis (Books)
16. Public (Books, Electronics, etc.)

Performance & Cinema
17. To Dora Stratou Theater
18. To Aigli Village Cinema
19. Cine Paris
20. To Cine Theseion

Athens Shopping & Nightlife

Bars & Cafés

㉑ Oineas Restaurant
㉒ James Joyce Irish Pub
㉓ Six D.o.g.s
㉔ Brettos Distillery
㉕ By the Glass Wine Bar
㉖ A for Athens
㉗ 360 Cocktail Bar
㉘ Grand Bretagne Hotel Rooftop Bar
㉙ Thissio View
㉚ Athenswas Hotel Bar
㉛ Herodion Hotel Bar

SHOPPING AND NIGHTLIFE

just to the north, such as Perikleous, Lekka, and Kolokotroni. You can also find upscale fancy boutiques in the swanky **Kolonaki** area.

Monastiraki Flea Market: This famous flea market stretches west of Monastiraki Square, along Ifestou street and its side streets.

You'll see plenty of souvenir shops, but the heart of the market is Avissinias Square, filled with antique shops selling furniture, household items, jewelry, dusty books, knickknacks, and stuff that might raise eyebrows at the airport. It's a fun place for tourists and pickpockets to browse, but isn't ideal for buying gifts for friends back home. There's something going on every day, but the market is best and most crowded on Sundays, when store owners lay out all of the stuff they have been scouting for all week. If buying here, make sure to bargain (Sun flea market open 8:00-15:00, packed with locals by 10:00, Metro: Monastiraki or Thissio). Tucked in among the souvenir and T-shirt stores is a good specialty food shop (described later, under "Specialty Foods").

Department Store: The largest department store in Athens is **Attica,** which feels pretty much like a US department store and has a cafeteria on the top floor but no views (Mon-Fri 10:00-21:00, Sat 10:00-19:00, closed Sun, near Syntagma Square at 9 Panepistimiou, tel. 211-180-2600).

Jewelry

Serious buyers tell me that Athens is the best place in Greece to purchase jewelry, particularly at the **shops along Adrianou.** The choices are much better than you'll find elsewhere, and—if you know how to haggle—so are the prices. The best advice is to take your time, and don't be afraid to walk away. The sales staff gets paid on commission, and they hate to lose a potential customer. Most stores have similar selections, which they buy from factory wholesalers. If feeling shy about bargaining, ask "Do you have any discounts?" to start the conversation.

For something a bit more specialized (with high prices), visit **Byzantino,** which made the jewelry worn by Greek dancers in the closing ceremonies of the 2000 Sydney Olympics. They create pricey handmade replicas of museum pieces, along with some original designs (daily 10:00-21:00, Adrianou 120, tel. 210-324-6605, www.byzantino.com, run by Kosta). A second location is nearby at the corner of Pandrossou and Aiolou.

Olympico creates their own modern pieces in the Greek style, along with museum copies. They also sell pieces made by artisans from all over Greece (daily 10:00-21:00, Adrianou 122, tel. 210-324-8697, George).

The gift shop at the **Benaki Museum of Greek History and Culture** (described on page 63) is also popular for its jewelry.

Handmade Sandals

The best place to buy real leather sandals in Athens is **Melissinos Art,** the famous "poet sandal-maker" of Athens. You'll find an assortment of styles in basic shades of tan for about €40 per pair. The price goes up if you want to customize a pair with leather or beading in various colors, and you'll have to wait up to a day (daily 10:00-20:00, just off Monastiraki Square at the edge of Psyrri, Ag. Theklas 2, tel. 210-321-9247, www.melissinos-art.com).

Stavros Melissinos—who's also a poet—ran this shop for decades. Now that he's retired, his son Pantelis (also a painter and playwright) has taken over the family business. When the Beatles came to his shop in 1968, Stavros was asked why he didn't ask for their autographs. He replied, "Why did they not ask for mine? I will be around long after the Beatles." He was right.

Religious Items

Icons and other Greek Orthodox objects can make good souvenirs. For the best selection, visit the shops near the cathedral, along Agia Filotheis street (most are closed Sat-Sun, described on page 81).

Specialty Foods

All over Athens you'll see specialty food stores selling locally produced edibles, such as olive oil, wine and liqueurs, mustards, and sweets like boxed baklava, *loukoumi* (a.k.a., Greek delight), and jars of "spoon sweets" (jam-like spreads).

The best place to shop for these is where the locals do—near the Central Market. Specialty grocers and spice shops cluster around Athinas and Evripidou streets, including **Peri Lesvou,** which sells items produced on the island of Lesbos (Mon-Sat 9:00-17:00, closed Sun, Athinas 27, tel. 210-323-3227) and **Zouridakis,** featuring products from Crete (Mon-Sat 8:00-15:00, closed Sun, Evripidou 25, tel. 210-321-1109).

For chocolate and other Greek goods, check out **Matsouka** and its offshoots, dominating a block of Karageorgi Servias, around the corner from Syntagma Square (with other branches around the city). Matsouka sells nuts, candies, dried fruit, honey, olive oil, and other food items while their shop **Le Chocolat,** next door, sells Greek chocolates for €22-28/kilo (you can also buy French and Belgian chocolates here). Even if not buying, step inside to take a deep whiff. Notice the case of fancy desserts. Greeks bring these to a home when they're invited for a visit instead of, say, a bottle of wine. Across the street is their spice shop (all open daily 8:00-

Worry Beads

As you travel through Greece, you may notice Greek men spinning, stroking, and generally fidgeting with their worry beads.

Greeks use these beaded strings to soothe themselves and get focused—especially during hard times. Loosely based on prayer beads, but today a secular hobby, worry beads make for a fun Greek souvenir. You'll see them sold all over central Athens.

Many major faiths employ some version of stringed beads as a worship aid, typically to help keep track of prayers while calming and focusing the mind. Think of the Catholic rosary, Muslim prayer beads, and the long, knotted rope belts worn by medieval monks. Hindus and Buddhists also make use of beads. Greeks—likely inspired by Muslims during the nearly 400 years of Ottoman rule—adopted the habit, but it no longer carries any religious overtones.

The most typical type of worry bead is the *komboloï,* a loop with an odd number of beads (it can be any number, as long as it's odd). The top of the loop may have a fixed "main bead" (or two), also called the "priest." The newer *begleri*—popular only since the 1950s—is a single string with an even number of beads (so it can be comfortably balanced in the hand).

The beads are made from a variety of materials. The basic tourist version is a cheap "starter set" made from synthetic materials, similar to marbles. You'll pay more for organic materials, which are considered more pleasant to touch: precious stones, bones, horn, wood, coral, mother-of-pearl, seeds, and more. The most prized worry beads are made of amber. Most valuable are the hand-cut amber beads, which are very soft and fragile; machine-cut amber is processed to be stronger.

When buying, go ahead and try several different strings to find one that fits well in your hand; tune in to the smoothness of the beads and the sound they make when clacking together.

There is no "right" or "wrong" way to use your worry beads—everyone finds a routine that works for them. Some flip or spin the beads in their hands, while others sit quietly and count the beads over and over. There are as many ways to use worry beads as there are Greeks. Their seemingly nervous habit appears to have the opposite effect—defusing stress and calming the nerves.

22:00, main shop at 10 Karageorgi Servias, chocolate shop at #3; another Le Chocolat location is a block away at 14 Voulis, on the corner of Karageorgi Servias, tel. 210-331-4770).

If you're wandering the Monastiraki flea market area, stop in at **Pantopolion** to sample products from all over Greece (daily 9:00-22:00, Ifestou 9, tel. 210-325-4890).

Nightlife in Athens

Athens is a thriving, vibrant city...and the Athenians know how to have a good time after hours. I've provided some ideas for how to spend an evening, from folk performances to outdoor movies, enjoying rooftop cocktails, or simply strolling around and finding a scene that appeals to you.

Athens is most inviting from May through October (but not in miserably hot August), when al fresco activities such as outdoor cinema, festivals (including the Athens & Epidavros Festival), folk-dancing shows at Dora Stratou Theater, and outdoor sidewalk cafés and bars are in full swing.

In the heat of summer, some clubs close down to relocate to outdoor venues on the coast. In the winter, your options are limited to indoor venues (concerts and other performances). But folk musicians, who tend to spend their summers in small towns and islands, hibernate in Athens in winter—offering ample opportunities to hear traditional music. A number of tavernas feature live music and dancing locals year-round, providing a wonderful setting for a late dinner.

Events Listings: Athens has a constantly rotating schedule of cultural activities, such as concerts to suit every audience. For local events, look for publications such as the English-language version of the daily newspaper *Kathimerini* (www.ekathimerini.com) and the bimonthly Greek lifestyle magazine *Odyssey* (www.odyssey.gr).

Festivals

Athens' biggest party is the **Athens & Epidavros Festival,** held every June and July. The festival's highlights are its world-class performances of dance, music, and theater at the ancient Odeon

of Herodes Atticus, nestled spectacularly below the flood-lit Acropolis. Outdoor performances at other venues enliven the already hopping city. Performances also take place at the famous Theater of Epidavros on the Peloponnese (these extend into August).

SHOPPING AND NIGHTLIFE

Tickets go on sale about three weeks in advance. You can buy them online, over the phone, and at the festival box office (Mon-Fri 9:00-17:00, Sat 9:00-15:00, closed Sun, in the arcade at Panepistimiou 39, opposite the National Library, tel. 210-327-2000, www.greekfestival.gr). Same-day tickets are also sold at the theater box office.

For a rundown of other festivals in Athens throughout the year, see page 510.

Folk Dancing

The **Dora Stratou Theater** on Filopappos Hill is the place to go to see authentic folk dancing. The theater company—the best in Greece—was originally formed to record and preserve the country's many traditional dances. Their repertoire includes such favorites as the graceful *kalamatianos* circle dance, the *syrtaki* (famously immortalized by Anthony Quinn in *Zorba the Greek*), and the dramatic solo *zimbetikos* (€15, 1.5-hour performances run late May-late Sept, generally Wed-Fri at 21:30, Sat-Sun at 20:15, no shows Mon-Tue, morning tel. 210-324-4395, evening tel. 210-921-4650, www.grdance.org).

The theater is on the south side of Filopappos Hill. If you're taking the Metro, get off at Petralona (10-minute walk) rather than the farther Akropoli stop (20-minute walk). To walk to the theater from below the Acropolis, figure at least 20 minutes (entirely around the base of Filopappos Hill, signposted from western end of Dionysiou Areopagitou).

Other Outdoor Venues

The rebuilt ancient theater at the foot of the Acropolis, the **Odeon of Herodes Atticus,** occasionally hosts concerts under the stars. The theater atop **Lykavittos Hill** is another outdoor favorite. Both of these are used in summer for the Athens & Epidavros Festival.

Outdoor Cinema

Athens has a wonderful tradition of outdoor movies. Screenings take place most nights in summer (around €8, roughly June-Sept, sometimes in May and Oct depending on weather; shows start around 20:00 or 21:00, depending on when the sun sets; many offer a second, later showing). Drinks are served at these "theaters," which are actually compact open-air courtyards with folding chairs. Movies typically are shown in their original language, with Greek subtitles (though children's movies might be dubbed in Greek). Of Athens many outdoor cinema venues, these are particularly well known, convenient, and atmospheric. Call or check online to see what's playing.

Aigli Village Cinema is a cool, classic outdoor theater in the National Garden (at the Zappeion), playing the latest blockbusters with a great sound system (tel. 210-336-9369, www.aeglizappiou. gr).

Cine Paris, in the Plaka, shows movies on the roof with Acropolis views (overlooking Filomousou Square of Kidathineon 22, tel. 210-322-2071, www.cineparis.gr).

Cine Theseion, along the Apostolou Pavlou pedestrian drag in the Thissio neighborhood, enjoys grand floodlit Acropolis views from some of its seats—one of the reasons it was voted the "best outdoor cinema in the world." It shows both classic and current movies (Apostolou Pavlou 7, tel. 210-347-0980 or 210-342-0864, www.cine-thisio.gr).

Apostolou Pavlou Promenade and Thissio

A peaceful pedestrian lane circles the Acropolis, providing locals and visitors alike a delightful place for an evening stroll. This promenade is what I call the "Acropolis Loop" (consisting of Dionysiou Areopagitou to the south and Apostolou Pavlou to the west). As the sun goes down, it's busy with locals (lovers, families, seniors, children at play) and visitors alike.

The promenade cuts through the Thissio district, just beyond the Agora, where the tables and couches of trendy clubs and cocktail bars clog the pedestrian lanes under the Acropolis. More upscale than the Plaka, Thissio gives you an easy escape from the tired tourism of that zone. Thissio is basically composed of three or four streets running into Apostolou Pavlou (part of the "Acropolis Loop"). Iraklidon street is a tight lane with people socializing furiously at café tables squeezed under trees. Akamantos street, while still colorful, is a bit more sedate. Backgammon boards chatter, TVs blare the latest sporting events, and young Athenians sip their iced coffees en masse. As the sun sets and the floodlit temples of the Acropolis ornament the horizon, you understand why this quiet and breezy corner is such a hit with locals enjoying an evening out.

Come here just to stroll through the hippest café scene in town, to enjoy a drink and some great people-watching, or to see a movie under the stars (at Cine Theseion, listed earlier).

To reach Thissio, walk the pedestrian lane around the Acropolis from either end. It makes a wonderful destination after the more peaceful stretch from the Acropolis Museum (Metro: Akropoli). Or ride the Metro to Thissio, then follow the crowds uphill along the broad Apostolou Pavlou walkway toward the Acropolis. For more details about this main drag, see page 48.

Other Fun Nightlife Spots

Athens abounds with bar/cafés serving drinks in lively and atmospheric settings (including on rooftops boasting grand views). I've listed a few good areas to explore. Note that although bars are supposed to be nonsmoking, many places don't adhere to this rule. Expect to leave most bars smelling of smoke.

Psyrri: Immediately north of Thissio, this area is downscale and more cutting-edge than its neighbor...seedy-chic. Until recently it was a grimy area of workshops and cottage industries, famous locally as a onetime hotbed of poets, musicians, revolutionaries, and troublemakers. Now it's one of central Athens' top after-hours zones. The streets are crammed with dumpsters, broken-down cars, and pungent odors, and the crumbling buildings are slathered with graffiti ("Gate 13" and "Gate 7" graffiti, nearly ubiquitous in Athens, is the work of rival soccer fans).

The center of this district is Iroon Square, with several cute bar/cafés spilling into the square. Nearby Lepeniotou and Aisopou streets are good to explore for their creatively decorated places, including **Oineas Restaurant,** with retro wall art (Aisopou 9, tel. 210-321-5614). For something completely un-Greek, head to **James Joyce Irish Pub** to drink a pint of your favorite Irish brew (Astiggos 12, tel. 210-323-5055). For more recommendations, see page 178 of the Eating in Athens chapter.

Around Monastiraki Square: Right on Monastiraki Square, several rooftop bars offer some of the best views of the city (described later). Near the square is **Six D.o.g.s** bar, hiding down some stairs in a nondescript alley. This sunken open-air courtyard with high stone walls, leafy trees overhead, and seating on multilevel terraces serves up Hawaiian cocktails and plenty of atmosphere (6 Avramioutou—from Monastiraki Square go up Athinas, take a right on Agias Irinis, then a left into the alley, tel. 210-321-0510). Also in Monastiraki, Adrianou street has a line of inviting restaurants and cafés with outdoor seating—some with spectacular Acropolis views.

Agia Irini Square: The square surrounding the Church of St. Irene offers one of the most delightful wine-and-coffee scenes in the center. Day or night you'll find the place filled with locals enjoying the stylish, modern bar/cafés and classy ambience.

Near the Old Parliament: Several bars are scattered along the streets surrounding the Old Parliament building and Kolokotronis Square (just off Stadiou). This area offers a quieter, darker feel than the neighborhoods above and serves a more professional-feeling clientele. Just wander the streets—Anthimou Gazi, Christou Lada, and Kolokotroni—to find a spot that suits your tastes.

Plaka: Although the Plaka is jammed full of tourists and

€30 ΑΘΗ
ΑΤΗ

0115023 ‖‖‖

Ισχύει για:
ΡΟΜΑΪΚΗ ΑΓΟΡΑ

Valid for:
ROMAN AGORA

Για την είσοδο

0115023 ‖‖‖ ΑΘΗ ΑΤΗ

Ισχύει για:
ΒΙΒΛΙΟΘΗΚΗ ΑΔΡΙΑΝΟΥ

Valid for:
THE LIBRARY OF HADRIAN

Για την είσοδο

0115023 ΑΤΗ

Ισχύει για:
ΟΛΥΜΠΙΕΙΟ

Valid for:
OLYMPIEION

Για την είσοδο

‖‖‖ 115023 ΑΘΗ ΑΤΗ

ΑΘΗΝΑ
ΑΚΡΟΠΟΛΗ ΚΑΙ ΚΛΙΤΥΕΣ
ΑΡΧΑΙΑ ΑΓΟΡΑ
(ΚΑΙ ΜΟΥΣΕΙΟ ΣΤΟΑΣ ΑΤΤΑΛΟΥ)
ΡΟΜΑΪΚΗ ΑΓΟΡΑ
ΒΙΒΛΙΟΘΗΚΗ ΑΔΡΙΑΝΟΥ
ΟΛΥΜΠΙΕΙΟ
ΚΕΡΑΜΕΙΚΟΣ
(ΚΑΙ ΜΟΥΣΕΙΟ ΕΝΤΟΣ ΤΟΥ ΧΩΡΟΥ)
ΛΥΚΕΙΟ ΑΡΙΣΤΟΤΕΛΟΥΣ

ATHENS
ACROPOLIS AND SLOPES
ANCIENT AGORA
(AND THE MUSEUM OF THE STOA OF ATTALOS)
ROMAN AGORA
THE LIBRARY OF HADRIAN
OLYMPIEION
KERAMEIKOS
(AND MUSEUM IN THE SITE)
LYKEION OF ARISTOTLE

Ισχύει για:
ΚΕΡΑΜΕΙΚΟΣ (ΚΑΙ ΜΟΥΣ.
ΕΝΤΟΣ ΤΟΥ ΧΩΡΟΥ)

Valid for:
KERAMEIKOS
(AND MUSEUM IN THE SITE)

Για την είσοδο

‖‖‖ 0115023 ΑΘΗ ΑΤΗ

Ισχύει για:
ΛΥΚΕΙΟ ΑΡΙΣΤΟΤΕΛΟΥΣ

Valid for:
LYKEION OF ARISTOTLE

Για την είσοδο

‖‖‖ 11502

ΑΘΗ ΑΤΗ

— ΤΑΧΥΤΥΠΟ ΕΛ.Ο/PRINT ΠΑΡΑ —

few locals, it couldn't be more central or user-friendly, with live traditional music spilling out of seemingly every other taverna. One particularly pleasant area to explore is the stepped lane called Mnisikleous (see page 173). For drinks, I enjoy **Brettos** distillery (with a casual atmosphere surrounded by large casks) and **By the Glass** (a sophisticated wine bar serving good food). Both are described on page 183.

Gazi: This neighborhood, west of Kermikos Cemetery, feels more local and authentically lively—but young. You'll find clubs, bars, and restaurants on the streets spiraling out from its main square (which, conveniently, surrounds the Keramikos Metro stop). For recommended restaurants in this area, see page 180.

Kolonaki: This upscale and stylish district, at the foot of Lykavittos Hill, is Athens' top area for yuppie nightlife.

Exarchia: The very grungy student/anarchist zone that stretches north of Kolonaki is rougher around the edges than the other places I describe here. But adventurous travelers might enjoy exploring the area...with care. (First, read the description on page 62.)

Rooftop Bars

A touristy-yet-appealing way to spend an evening is at one of Athens' many rooftop bars, all with views of floodlit monuments.

The rooftop of the **A for Athens** hotel hosts both locals and tourists who come to gawk at its views. Thanks to its prime spot on Monastiraki Square, it offers dramatic views of the Acropolis looming above the city. If this place is too crowded, try the **360 Cocktail Bar** on the same square (but with less impressive panoramas).

For a similarly great view and €15 cocktails, visit the rooftop restaurant and bar of the **Hotel Grande Bretagne,** across the street from Syntagma Square (for details on the restaurant, see page 178). If strolling the pedestrian promenade through Thissio, consider a stop at the **Thissio View** restaurant and bar (Apostolou Pavlou 25).

There are also several rooftop bars at hotels near the Acropolis Museum, including the Modern Restaurant, on top of the **Athenswas Hotel** (5 Dionysiou Areopagitou) and the Point a Bar at the **Herodion Hotel** (4 Rovertou Galli). You'll be in the company of other tourists, and views are less impressive, as you're looking at the backside of the Acropolis, but these spots are convenient to some of my recommended accommodations in Makrigianni and Koukaki.

ATHENS CONNECTIONS

Athens is the transportation hub for all of Greece. Because Athens has a good public transportation system, don't rent a car until you are ready to leave the city—you absolutely do *not* want to drive in Athens traffic. If you're venturing to landlocked destinations beyond Athens, the best option for the rest of your trip is to travel by car. Buses can get you just about anywhere for a reasonable fare, but connections to remote areas can be long and complicated, and straightforward schedule information is hard to come by. Most recommended sights beyond Athens do not have train service: The Greek train system is slated to be privatized (if they can find anyone willing to buy it), and it will take years before it is up to Western European standards. Boats and planes are options for reaching the islands. For specifics on transportation beyond Athens, see the "Connections" sections in each of the following chapters. For general information on transportation by plane, boat, bus, and car, see the Practicalities chapter.

By Plane

ELEFTHERIOS VENIZELOS INTERNATIONAL AIRPORT

Athens' airport is at Spata, 17 miles east of downtown (airport code: ATH, tel. 210-353-0000—press 2 for English, www.aia.gr). This slick, user-friendly airport has two sections: B gates (serving European/Schengen countries—no passport control) and A gates (serving other destinations, including the US). Both sections feed into the same main terminal building (with a common baggage claim, ATMs, shops, car-rental counters, information desks, and additional services). On the top floor (above entrance/exit #3), is a

Public Transit to/from Piraeus

mini museum of Greek artifacts dug up from the area around the airport.

Getting from the Airport to Downtown

Your best route into the city depends on where you want to go: If you're headed to Syntagma Square, the bus is generally better (cheapest, very frequent, and scenic). For Monastiraki, Psyrri, or the Makrigianni area south of the Plaka, the Metro is more direct—and isn't susceptible to traffic jams. Electronic boards in the baggage and arrivals halls show when the next buses and trains are leaving.

By Bus: Buses wait outside exit #5. Express bus #X95 costs €5 and operates 24 hours daily between the airport and Syntagma Square (3-5/hour, roughly 1 hour depending on traffic; tel. 185, www.oasa.gr). The downtown bus stop is on Othonos street, along the side of Syntagma Square; get off after the bus takes a 180-degree turn around a big square filled with palm trees.

By Metro: Line 3/blue zips you downtown in 45 minutes for €8 (2/hour, direction: Agia Marina, daily 6:30-23:30; €14 for 2 people, €20 for 3, half-price for people under 18 or over 65, ticket good for 70 minutes on other Athens transit; consider the €20 three-day tourist ticket, which includes round-trip airport transfer by Metro or bus as well as unlimited in-city travel on all public transit—see page 36).

To reach the Metro from the airport arrivals hall, go through exit #3, cross the street, go up the escalator, and cross the skybridge to the rail terminal. Buy tickets (machines take cash only), and follow signs down to the platforms. Stamp your ticket in a validation machine before you board. In downtown Athens, this train stops at Syntagma (where you can transfer to line 2/red) and Monastiraki (where you can transfer to line 1/green).

To return to the airport by Metro, you can catch a train from Syntagma (2/hour, 5:30-24:00). Keep in mind that some Metro trains terminate at Doukissis Plakentias. If so, just hop off and wait—another train that continues to the airport will be along within about 10 minutes.

By Taxi: A well-marked taxi stand outside exit #3 offers fixed-price transfers that include all fees (€38 to central Athens, covers up to 4 people, fare goes up between 24:00 and 5:00).

By Car Service: Alpha Transfer Service can take you between the airport and your Athens hotel (€40 for car, €80 for 9-seat minivan, book at least one day in advance, mobile 693-229-5395, www.athenstourtaxi.com, atsathens@gmail.com, Panagiotis and Konstantinos Tyrlis). You can also book transport between Athens and other parts of Greece.

Getting from the Airport to the Port of Piraeus

To reach Piraeus, take bus #X96 outside airport exit #5 (€5, runs 24 hours daily, 2-4/hour, 1-1.5 hours depending on traffic; stops at Piraeus' Karaiskaki Square, then at the Metro station; tel. 185, www.oasa.gr). A taxi from the airport to the port costs about €48.

By Boat

ATHENS' PORT: PIRAEUS

Piraeus, a city six miles southwest of central Athens, has been the port of Athens since ancient times. Today it's also the main port for services to the Greek islands, making it the busiest passenger port in the Mediterranean.

Orientation to Piraeus

All ferries, hydrofoils, catamarans, and cruise ships use Piraeus' Great Harbor (Megas Limin). To the east are two smaller harbors used for private yachts: Limin Zeas and the picturesque Mikrolimano, or "Small Harbor."

The vast Great Harbor area is ringed by busy streets. At the northeast corner is the hub of most activity: the Metro station, housed inside a big yellow Neoclassical building with white trim (sometimes labeled "Electric Railway Station" on maps). Trainspotters with time to kill can visit the free and good little electric-railway museum inside. Next door to the Metro station is

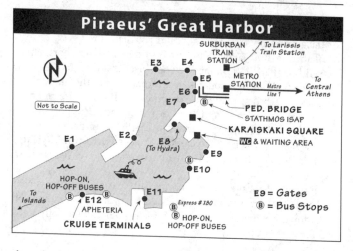

Piraeus' Great Harbor

the suburban train station. A modern pedestrian bridge connects the Metro station to the harbor and serves as a handy landmark.

Just down the street is Karaiskaki Square, which juts out into the harbor. Cheap eateries, flophouse hotels, and dozens of travel agencies round out the dreary scene. The port does have several air-conditioned waiting areas and WCs (between gates E8 and E9) and big electronic display boards showing gate numbers and times for upcoming departures. The port area supposedly has free Wi-Fi, but don't count on it working.

Gates: Twelve "gates" (docks) stretch for about three miles around the harbor, numbered in clockwise order. Gate assignments depend on both the destination and the company operating the line, but, very roughly, you can expect the following:

- **E1:** Dodecanese Islands
- **E2:** Crete; North Aegean Islands (Samos, Ikaria, Chios, Mytilene)
- **E3:** Crete and Kithira (vehicle entrance)
- **E4:** Kithira (vehicle exit)
- **E5:** Bus Terminal
- **E6:** Cyclades (including **Mykonos** and **Santorini**), pedestrian walkway to Metro
- **E7:** Cyclades (including high-speed boats to **Mykonos** and **Santorini**)
- **E8:** Saronic Gulf Islands (Argosaronikos in Greek, including **Hydra,** Spetses, Paros, and Ermioni)
- **E9:** Cyclades (including **Mykonos** and **Santorini**), Samos, Ikaria
- **E10:** Vehicle exit from E9
- **E11:** Cruise Terminal A
- **E12:** Cruise Terminal B

CONNECTIONS

These departure gates are prone to change—check your ticket for the gate number, and ask a local if you're unsure.

Information: Official tourist information is in short supply here, although a TI kiosk may be open just outside Gate 11/Cruise Terminal A. Your best sources of information are the many travel agencies scattered around the area; all have a line on current boats, where they leave from, and how to get tickets. The port police, with several offices clearly marked in English, can be helpful (tel. 210-414-7800). You can also call the Piraeus Port Authority ship-schedule line at toll tel. 14541. The port authority website is www.olp.gr.

Baggage Storage: A bag storage/Internet access shop is near the Metro station. Go under the pedestrian bridge; it's about 50 yards down on the main street (€5 for 6 hours; open daily until 22:00).

Getting from Piraeus to the Islands

For tips on buying tickets and the lowdown on Greece's ferry network, see page 494. It's smart to know ahead of time which gate your ferry leaves from (see above).

Arriving at the Piraeus Metro station (end of the line), walk out the side door (with your back to the tracks, it's to the left) and into a chaotic little square. Head up the escalator and walk to the far end of the pedestrian bridge, overlooking the water. You're standing above gates E6 and E7. Gates with higher numbers are to your left; those with lower numbers are to your right. (For example, Hydra-bound boats usually depart from gate E8, to your left on the far side of the tree-filled park.) Once you have your bearings, descend to the port and walk to your gate. If your boat leaves from gates E1 or E2 on the north side of the port (the Dodecanese Islands, plus some boats to Crete or the North Aegean Islands), turn right and walk to gate E5 (near the end of the pedestrian bridge) to catch a free shuttle bus.

From Piraeus by Boat to: Hydra (6-8/day June-Sept, 4/day Oct-May, 1.5-2 hours, €28), **Mykonos** (generally 3/day in high season—1 fast boat, 3 hours, €60; 2 slow boats, 5.5 hours, €40; off-season likely 1 slow boat daily), **Santorini** (generally 3/day in high season—2 fast boats, 5 hours, €60; 1 slow boat, 8 hours, €40; off-season likely 1 slow boat daily). The frequency and prices listed here are approximate; schedules can change from season to season, and boats can get canceled on short notice—confirm everything locally.

Getting from Piraeus' Ferry Terminals to Athens

By Train: Metro line 1/green conveniently links Piraeus with downtown Athens (€1.20, good for 70 minutes including transfers, departs about every 10-15 minutes between 6:00 and 24:00). The

Metro station is in a big, yellow Neoclassical building near gate E6 (linked to the harbor by the pedestrian bridge). Buy your ticket from a machine (which makes change but takes only coins) rather than waiting in line. Before boarding, validate your ticket in one of the boxes near the platform. In about 20 minutes, the Metro reaches the city-center Monastiraki stop, near the Plaka and many recommended hotels and sights. (For Syntagma, Akropoli, and Syngrou-Fix Metro stops, ride one more stop to Omonia to transfer to line 2/red.) Warning: The Metro line between Piraeus and downtown Athens teems with pickpockets—watch your valuables and wear a money belt.

A **suburban train** also connects Piraeus' train station with Athens, but there's no reason to take it (less frequent, more transfers).

By Taxi: A taxi between Piraeus and downtown Athens should cost €15-20 (including €1.20 port surcharge), and can take anywhere from 20-40 minutes, depending on traffic and on your starting/ending point at Piraeus.

By Bus to Bus Terminal A (Kifissou): For long-distance buses to the Peloponnese (see page 202), you'll need to connect through Athens. To reach Athens' Bus Terminal A (Kifissou), take bus #420 (€1.20, buy ticket at kiosk, cannot buy onboard, 1-2/hour, catch bus at stop across the street from Gate E6).

Getting from Piraeus' Cruise Terminals to Athens

If arriving at one of the cruise terminals, it's a long walk (20-40 minutes) or a bus ride (#843) to the Metro station. The following options are easier ways to get downtown.

By Bus: Several buses run from near the cruise terminals to Athens, including express bus #X80 to Dionysiou Areopagitou (near the Acropolis Museum) and Syntagma Square (1 hour), bus #040 to Makrigianni (near the Acropolis Museum) and the National Garden (near Syntagma Square, 1-1.5 hours), and bus #49 to Omonia Square, a 15-minute walk from the National Archaeological Museum (1.5 hours). Buses heading to Athens originate from the stop called Apheteria (ΑΦΕΤΗΡΙΑ, "starting point"), on the main road between the two cruise terminals (opposite side of street from harbor; check posted schedules for departures). Except for the #X80, you must buy tickets before you board (look for the kiosk near the stop).

By Hop-on, Hop-off Bus: Several companies offer indistinguishable all-day hop-on, hop-off bus tours that include a 70-minute itinerary around Piraeus and link to a separate 1.5-hour bus route around Athens (CitySightseeing, tel. 210-922-0604, www. citysightseeing.gr; Athens Open Tour, tel. 210-881-5207, www. athensopentour.com).

By Taxi or Private Car: Taxis wait outside the cruise terminals, or you can hire a private car and driver to pick you up from Piraeus and take you on an excursion around town (try one of my recommended drivers listed on page 39).

Getting from Piraeus to the Airport

From Piraeus, you can reach the airport by taxi (around €48) or by bus #X96, which goes directly to the airport. In Piraeus bus #X96 stops along the top of Karaiskaki Square (Plateia Karaiskaki/ΠΛ. ΚΑΡΑΙΣΚΑΚΗ stop, between gates E7 and E8), and also in front of the Metro station (Stathmos ISAP/ΣΤΑΘΜΟΣ ΗΣΑΠ stop; €5, runs 24 hours daily, 2-4/hour depending on time of day, 1-1.5 hours depending on traffic).

By Bus

Athens has two major intercity bus stations. Frustratingly, both are far from downtown, and neither is conveniently reached by Metro. Buses serving the south, including the Peloponnese, use the bus station called Kifissou, or "Terminal A." Most buses serving the north, including Delphi, use the station called Liossion, or "Terminal B." (There has been some talk of combining these two stations, but progress is slow.)

Although most destinations in this book are served by at least one daily direct bus from Athens, connecting between destinations outside Athens can involve several changes (as noted in each chapter). Even though all Greek buses are operated by ΚΤΕΛ (KTEL), there's no useful general website or phone number (each region has its own website for its own schedules; some are better than others). There is a list of local phone numbers at www.ktelbus.com, but you'll need to know the name of the province where you are traveling. You can get details for buses originating in Athens by phoning 14505. For more information about taking buses in Greece, try this helpful, unofficial website in English: http://livingingreece.gr (under "Best of..." click on "KTEL Buses of Greece").

TERMINAL A (KIFISSOU)

This bus station is about three miles northwest of the city center. Getting here on public transit is a pain involving a Metro-plus-bus connection (Metro to Omonia then bus #51). It's easier to spring for a taxi ride (pay no more than €15 from central Athens). Buses from here head to southwest Greece.

In the station's vast ticket hall (follow signs to ΕΚΔΟΤΗΡΙΑ), the counters are divided by which region they serve; if you aren't sure which one you need, ask at the information desk near the main door. Beyond the ticket hall are a cafeteria, a restaurant, and a supermarket, and the door out to the buses. This immense bus barn is crammed with well-labeled bus stalls, which are organized—like the ticket windows—by region. Taxis wait out in front of the ticket hall, as well as under the canopy between the ticket hall and the bus stalls.

By Bus from Terminal A to: Nafplio (roughly hourly direct, 2.5 hours, €15), **Epidavros** (2-3/day, 2.5 hours, €12), **Mycenae** (go to Nafplio first, then 2-3/day, none on Sun, 45 minutes, €3.20), **Olympia** (2/day direct, 5.5 hours, €32, more with transfers), **Monemvasia** (3-4/day, 6 hours total, €32), **Kardamyli** (1/day, transfer in Kalamata, 5-6 hours). Terminal A info: Tel. 210-512-4910 (ticket office at 59 Sokratous street, Omonia Square, tel. 210-523-7889; open Mon-Fri 7:00-17:15, Sat 7:30-15:30, closed Sun).

TERMINAL B (LIOSSION)

Smaller, more manageable, and a bit closer to the city center, Liossion (lee-oh-SEE-yohn) is in northwest Athens, a 15-minute, €8 taxi ride from the Plaka. You can also take the Metro to Attiki and then take any bus going north on Liossion street several stops to Praktoria. Buses from here head northwest.

By Bus from Terminal B to: Delphi (5/day, 3 hours, €17).

By Train

In Athens, most trains use **Larissis Station,** just north of downtown (on Metro line 2/red). Greek trains are of limited usefulness to travelers sticking to the destinations described in this book. As the government is planning to privatize the system, many routes have been cut, especially on the Peloponnese. The train does serve areas north of Athens well (such as Thessaloniki), but is essentially useless if connecting south. For places in this book, it's better to take buses or to drive.

Surviving trains are operated by Greek Railways (www.trainose.gr or call customer service, which has English-speaking staff—open 24 hours, tel. 14511). For more extensive travels beyond Greece, you can study your options at www.ricksteves.com/rail.

By Car

RENTING A CAR

Syngrou avenue is Athens' "rental car lane," with all the established, predictable big companies (and piles of little ones) competing for your business. Syngrou is an easy walk from the Plaka and recommended hotels (it's especially near those in Makrigianni and Koukaki). Budget travelers can often negotiate great deals by checking with a few rental places and haggling. Or consider local company **Swift/Avanti,** run by Elias and Salvador, who can help you drive out of central Athens to avoid the stress of city-center driving (1-day rental: €40-60 depending on size of car and season, unlimited mileage; 3-day rental: from €96 for compact; extra charge to drop car outside of Athens; open Mon-Sat 9:00-19:00, until 17:00 in winter, open Sun and after hours by request; tel. 210-933-8252, mobile 693-667-4476, www.greektravel.com/swift, elimano95@gmail.com).

ROUTE TIPS FOR DRIVERS

Avoid driving in Athens as much as possible—traffic is stressful, and parking is a headache. Before you leave Athens, get detailed directions from your rental agency on how to get back to their office and drop off your car.

Here's your strategy for getting out of the city: If you're heading north, such as to **Delphi,** aim for expressway 1 northbound (toward Lamia; see specific directions on page 360). To head for the **Peloponnese,** go westbound on expressway 6, which feeds into expressway 8 to Corinth (the gateway to the Peloponnese). The handy E-75 expressway (a.k.a. Kifissou avenue), which runs north-south just west of downtown Athens, offers an easy connection to either of these.

Assuming you pick up your car on or near Syngrou avenue, and traffic isn't that heavy, the best bet (with the fewest traffic lights and turns) is usually to simply head south on Syngrou. As you approach the water, the road forks; follow signs toward *Piraeus* on the left. After the merge, get into the right lane and be ready to hop on E-75 northbound. Then watch for your exit: for the Peloponnese, exit for expressway 6 (which merges into expressway 8 to Corinth); for Delphi, continue straight north to expressway 1.

THE PELOPONNESE

ΠΕΛΟΠΟΝΝΗΣΟΣ /
Πελοπόννησος

The Peloponnese

NAFPLIO

ΝΑΎΠΛΙΟ / Ναύπλιο

The charming Peloponnesian port town of Nafplio is small, cozy, and strollable. Though it has plenty of tourism, Nafplio is both elegant and proud. It's a must-see on any Greek visit because of its historical importance, its accessibility from Athens (an easy 2.5-hour drive or bus ride), and its handy location as a home base for touring the ancient sites of Epidavros and Mycenae (each a short drive away and described in the next two chapters). Nafplio has great pensions, appealing restaurants, fine beaches, a thriving evening scene, and a good balance of real life and tourist convenience.

Nafplio is understandably proud of its special footnotes in Greek history. Thanks to its highly strategic position—nestled under cliffs at the apex of a vast bay—it changed hands between the Ottomans and the Venetians time and again. But Nafplio ultimately distinguished itself in the 1820s by becoming the first capital of a newly independent Greece, headed by President Ioannis Kapodistrias. Although those glory days have faded, the town retains a certain genteel panache.

Owing to its prestigious past, Nafplio's harbor is guarded by three castles: one on a small island (Bourtzi), another just above the Old Town (ancient Akronafplia), and a third capping a tall cliff above the city (Palamidi Fortress). All three are wonderfully floodlit at night. If you're not up for the climb to Palamidi, explore Nafplio's narrow and atmospheric back streets, lined with elegant Venetian houses and Neoclassical mansions, and dip into its likeable museums.

PLANNING YOUR TIME

Nafplio is light on sightseeing opportunities, but heavy on ambience. Two nights and one day is more than enough time to enjoy everything the town has to offer. With one full day in Nafplio,

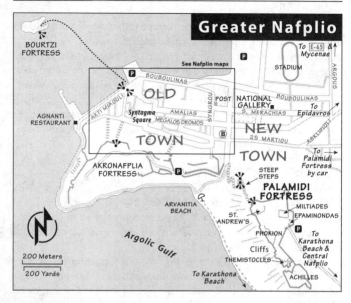

Greater Nafplio

BOURTZI
FORTRESS

To E-65 &
Mycenae

See Nafplio maps

STADIUM

P

ARGOUS

OLD

BOUBOULINAS

P

POST

SYNGROU

NATIONAL
GALLERY

BOUBOULINAS

P. MERACHIAS

To
Epidavros

AGNANTI
RESTAURANT

Syntagma
Square

AMALIAS

ASKLIPIOU

MEGALOS DROMOS

TOWN

NEW

B

25 MARTIOU

AKTI MIAOULI

TOWN

AKRONAFPLIA
FORTRESS

P

STEEP
STEPS

To
Palamidi
Fortress
by car

PALAMIDI
FORTRESS

ARVANITIA
BEACH

ST.
ANDREW'S

MILTIADES

EPAMINONDAS

PHOKION

P

Argolic Gulf

Cliffs

THEMISTOCLES

To
Karathona
Beach &
Central
Nafplio

200 Meters

200 Yards

To Karathona
Beach

ACHILLES

consider the arduous hike up to the Palamidi Fortress first thing
in the morning, before the worst heat of the day (bring water and
wear good shoes; to save time and sweat, you can also drive or taxi
there). Then get your bearings in the Old Town by following my
self-guided walk, and visit any museums that appeal to you. In the
afternoon, hit the beach. (If you get a late start, do the hike in the
early evening.)

Nafplio also serves as an ideal launch pad for visiting two of
the Peloponnese's best ancient sites (each about a 30-minute drive
and covered in the next two chapters): the best-preserved ancient
theater anywhere, at **Epidavros;** and the older-than-old hilltop
fortress of **Mycenae.** It's worth adding a day to your Nafplio stay
to fit these in. If you have a **car,** you can see both of these (and
drive up to the Palamidi Fortress) in a full day; for an even more
efficient plan, consider squeezing them in on your way into or out
of town (for example, notice that Mycenae is between Nafplio and
the major E-65 expressway to the north). These sites are also reachable by **bus.** While it's possible to do them both by bus on the same
day, for a more relaxed approach consider two full days in Nafplio,
spending a half-day at each site, and two half-days in the town.

Orientation to Nafplio

Because everything of interest is concentrated in the peninsular
Old Town, Nafplio feels smaller than its population of 15,000. The
mostly traffic-free Old Town is squeezed between the hilltop Ak-

NAFPLIO

ronafplia fortress and the broad seafront walkways of Bouboulinas and Akti Miaouli; the core of this area has atmospherically tight pedestrian lanes, bursting with restaurants and shops. Syntagma Square (Plateia Syntagmatos) is the centerpiece of the Old Town. From here traffic-free Vasileos Konstantinou—called "Big Street" (Megalos Dromos) by locals—runs east to Syngrou street, which separates the Old Town from the New Town. The tranquil upper part of the Old Town, with some of my favorite accommodations, is connected by stepped lanes.

TOURIST INFORMATION

Nafplio's TI is just inside Town Hall, on Town Hall Square (daily 9:00-13:00 & 16:00-20:00, tel. 27520-24444). Check locally to confirm opening hours for sights and museums given in this chapter. If side-tripping out to Epidavros or Mycenae in the off-season, call to double-check opening times.

Note that the town's name can be spelled in a number of ways in English: Nafplio, Nauplio, Navplio, Naufplio, Nauvplio, and so on—and all these variations may also appear with an "n" at the end (Nafplion, etc.).

ARRIVAL IN NAFPLIO

By Car: Parking is free, easy, and central along the port, which runs in front of the Old Town (look for the big lots). If you're staying higher up, ask your hotel about more convenient parking (for example, near the old, abandoned Hotel Xenia on the road up to the Akronafplia fortress).

By Bus: The bus station is conveniently located on Syngrou street right where the Old Town meets the New; from here all my recommended accommodations are within a 10-minute walk.

HELPFUL HINTS

Festivals: Nafplio hosts a classical music festival in late June. It features a mix of Greek and international performers playing at such venues as the Palamidi and Bourtzi fortresses (details at TI). The town is also a good base for seeing drama and music performances at the famous Theater of Epidavros during the Athens & Epidavros Festival (weekends in July-Aug; see page 191). The local bus company operates special buses to the festival.

Post Office: The post office is at the corner of Syngrou and Sidiras Merarchias (Mon-Fri 7:30-20:30, Sat 7:30-14:30, closed Sun).

Bookshops: Odyssey sells international newspapers, maps, local guidebooks, and paperbacks in English (long hours daily, on Syntagma Square next to the National Bank building, tel. 27520-23430).

Local Guide: Patty Staikou is a charming Nafplio native who enjoys sharing her town and nearby ancient sites with visitors (about €50/hour, she'll meet you at Epidavros or Mycenae, mobile 697-778-3315, staipatt@yahoo.gr).

Travel Agency and Car Rental: Stavropoulos Tours, conveniently located near the bus station, can help you book flights and boat tickets anywhere in Greece (handy for trips you may be planning within the Aegean Islands or to Hydra), and provides bus information (Mon-Fri 9:30-14:30 & 18:30-21:30, Sat 9:30-14:30, closed Sun, also closed Mon in winter, credit cards accepted with small fee, 24 Plapouta street, tel. 27520-25915, mobile 694-777-9162, www.stavropoulostours.gr, helpful Theodore). Several **car rental** places are nearby (across from the Land Gate on Syngrou street).

Nafplio Walk

This self-guided walk, which takes about 1.5 hours, will give you a feel for Nafplio's pleasant Old Town.

• *We'll begin on the harborfront square opposite the fortified island, marked by a sturdy obelisk.*

❶ Square of the Friends of the Greeks (Plateia Filellinon)

This space is named for the French soldiers who fell while fighting for Greek independence in 1821. On the memorial ❷ **obelisk,** a classical-style medallion shows brothers in arms: Hellas and Gallia (Greeks and French). On the other side is the French inscription.

You might see a cruise ship docked here on the **waterfront.** The port was deepened a few years back to accommodate a busy cruise industry (bigger ships, however, still drop anchor around the bend).

Plenty of Nafplio bars, cafés, restaurants, and tavernas face the harbor. The embankment called ❸ **Akti Miaouli** promenades to the left with a long line of sedate al fresco tables. (These places are worth an extra euro or two for the view.) The promenade becomes a scenic shoreline path that continues all the way around the point to Arvanitia Beach, where a road returns to town up and over the saddle between the two fortresses.

The ❹ **Bouboulinas** promenade heads in the other direction

NAFPLIO

Nafplio Walk

1. Square of the Friends of the Greeks
2. Obelisk
3. Akti Miaouli Promenade
4. Bouboulinas Promenade
5. Church of St. Mary Above All Saints
6. Antica Gelateria di Roma
7. Syntagma Square
8. Archaeological Museum
9. National Bank of Greece
10. "Big Street"
11. Worry-Bead Shop & Komboloï Museum
12. Town Hall Square
13. To National Gallery
14. St. George Square
15. Church of St. Spyridon
16. Staikopoulou Street

(to the right, as you face the water)—first passing fine and recommended fish tavernas and then a string of bars.

From the harbor, you can also see the three Venetian forts of Nafplio (and another across the bay). The mighty little fortress is-

land just offshore, called **Bourtzi,** was built during the first Venetian occupation (15th century) to protect the harbor. Most of what you see today is an 18th-century reconstruction from the second Venetian occupation. A shuttle boat departs from here to visit the island. It's a fun little trip, but there's little to see beyond a pleasant city view (see page 222 for details).

Capping the hill high above is the **Palamidi Fortress** (highest, to the left). Locals claim that the Palamidi Fortress, built in just three years (1711-1714), is the best-preserved Venetian fort in the Mediterranean. It can be reached by climbing nearly a thousand stone stairs...or by paying €7 for a taxi. (I taxi up and walk down.) The view is rewarding, but the building itself is a bulky, impressive, empty shell. Below the Palamidi Fortress and to the right is Nafplio's ancient acropolis, the **Akronafplia fortress,** built upon the remains of an ancient fort. The big stones at the base of its wall date from the third century B.C.

Across the bay and in the distance beyond the island fort of Bourtzi is a **fourth Venetian fort,** dramatically capping a hill. This 300-year-old fort is built upon the ancient Acropolis of Argos (which dates from the Mycenaean Age, about 1500 B.C.).

With all this defensive investment, you can imagine how much Venice valued this strategic city as a trade and naval station. Today, locals still call the bay "Porto Catena." That's Italian for "Chain Port," as chains once were strung from the island fort to the mainland in order to control ship traffic.

• *With your back to the water, walk up the street to the right of Hotel Grande Bretagne (Farmakopoulou). After a block, on the first corner (left), is a popular gelateria. Resist temptation for just a minute and first head across the small square to the...*

NAFPLIO

❺ Church of St. Mary Above All Saints

This church has a proud history: It originally dates from the 15th century; today's building is from the 18th century; and just a few years ago, they peeled back, then reapplied, all the plaster. The priest at this church is particularly active, keeping it open late into the evening (long after many other Nafplio churches have closed). Outside the door he posts a daily message—a thought to ponder or a suggested prayer.

Step inside—it's generally open. The flat ceiling with the painted Trinity in three circular panels shows a Venetian influence—most Greek Orthodox churches of this period are domed. The more typical iconostasis, a wall of Greek Orthodox icons, separates worshippers from priests. As is standard in Greek churches, the icon in the center changes with the season. In the front left corner are Q-tips and little plastic baggies for taking home priest-blessed oil. ("If you believe, then it heals.") A glass case in the same corner shows off relics (mostly bones of saints) and little treasures (such as the Ostrich Egg, painted in Russia and symbolic of the Resurrection). There are a few more museum cases on the right. If you're so moved, drop in a coin for a candle (near the entry) and light up a prayer. Notice the heavy-duty venting for the busy candle trays and the icon above the candles featuring the saint-protected city of Nafplio.

The mural just outside the church (on the wall, to the right of the door as you leave) is something of a nationalistic history of Greece in a nutshell. Follow it, starting with Adam and Eve to the Golden Age of ancient Greece (featuring Socrates, Plato, Aristotle, and others), the founding of Christianity and the Greek church, the building of the monasteries at Meteora, the Ottoman occupation (see the Greek priest being hanged by a Turk), independence (with a banner that says "democracy" in Greek), World Wars I and II (find the Nazi with a gun and a Greek resistance hero mightily perched on a rock), and finally, the Greek version of heaven, which looks like Meteora.

• *Now dip into...*

❻ Antica Gelateria di Roma

Greece has great honey-dripping desserts, but nobody does ice cream like the Italians. This popular, fun-loving, air-conditioned ice-cream parlor is run by Marcello and family, who offer a taste of Italy: gelato, fruit-based *sorbetto*, as well as other treats such as biscotti, *limoncello*, and cappuccino. This is one holdover from the Venetian occupation that no local will complain about. (For more details on this *gelateria*, see page 233.)

• *Gelato in hand, exit Marcello's; go left behind the church and into the big square.*

❼ Syntagma Square (Plateia Syntagmatos)

Like the main square in Athens, Nafplio's central plaza is dubbed "Constitution Square," celebrating the 1843 document that estab-

lished a constitutional monarchy for Greece. Nafplio was one of the first towns liberated from the Ottoman Turks (1822), and became the new country's first capital. The square is a delightful mix of architectural styles, revealing the many layers of local history.

Survey this scene in a counterclockwise spin-tour, starting on your immediate right. The big building flying the Greek flag was originally the Venetian arsenal. Of course, wherever Venice ruled, you'll find its symbol: the winged lion of its patron saint, Mark (over the door). The building is stout with heavily barred windows because it once stored gunpowder and weapons. Today it houses the town's ❽ **Archaeological Museum** (described later, under "Sights in Nafplio").

Just to the left of the museum is a domed former **mosque.** In 1825, with the Muslim Ottomans expelled, this building was taken over and renovated to house independent Greece's first parliament. (Now it serves as a conference center.)

The big ❾ **National Bank of Greece** harkens back to the very earliest Greek civilizations, with its dark-red columns that taper

toward the base, as if they were tree trunks stood on their heads (shaped and painted just like the ones in the circa-1500 B.C. Minoan palaces on Crete). In front of the bank stands another Venetian winged lion from the old fortress. The second former

mosque fronting this square (see red tile domes at the far end) was converted after independence into Greece's first primary school; today it's a gallery and theater. To the left, look up past the popular cafés and restaurants to appreciate the square's series of stately Neoclassical buildings. The square is a popular hangout for parents

NAFPLIO

enjoying coffee while their kids run wild—future soccer stars-in-training.

• *Head across the square and walk down the pedestrian street (opposite the side you entered).*

⓾ The "Big Street" (Megalos Dromos)

Nafplio's main drag, connecting the main square with Town Hall Square, is named for King Constantine (Vasileos Konstantinou). Locals know it as Megalos Dromos ("Big Street").

The town is something of a shoppers' paradise—many streets are crammed with shops selling everything from the usual tacky tourist trinkets to expensive jewelry, all aimed at the fat wallets of Athenian weekenders. This is a fine scene in the early evening when everyone's out strolling.

• *Turn right at the first corner up the narrow alley (Soutsou), then turn left onto touristy Staikopoulou. After about a block, on the left (at #25), is a...*

⓫ Worry-Bead Shop

This shop features a remarkable selection of worry beads—the cheapest, synthetic sets cost about €8; the priciest, which can cost hundreds of euros, are antique or made of amber (for more information on worry beads, see page 190). The **Komboloï Museum** upstairs shows off a few small rooms of the owner's vast collection, while a handful of English labels explain how variations on worry beads are used by many different faiths (€2, generally open 9:30-21:00). A few doors farther down you'll find the shops of an olive-tree woodcarver and a sandalmaker.

• *At the next intersection, turn left and walk one block back down to the "Big Street." Turn right onto the "Big Street" and follow it until you emerge into...*

⓬ Town Hall Square

A statue marks the one-time location of the palace of **King Otto** (ΟΘΩΝ), the first head of state of post-Ottoman Greece. (The great powers—England, France, and Russia—insisted that the newly independent Greeks have a monarchy, so Otto was imported from Bavaria.) He wasn't here for long, though: An enthusiastic student of classical history, Otto was charmed by the idea of reviving the greatness of ancient Athens, and moved the capital to Athens after just one year. (The palace that stood here burned down in 1929.)

Otto, looking plenty regal, gazes toward the New Town. Fifty yards in front of Otto (on the right) is the Neoclassical "first high school of Greece"—today's Town Hall, and home to the TI. The monument in front celebrates a local hero from the war against the Ottomans. Until recently this square was named "Three Admirals Square"—remembering those three great European powers that helped the Greeks overthrow their Ottoman rulers in the 1820s.

• *At the far end of Town Hall Square, you hit the busy...*

Syngrou Street and the New Town

This thoroughfare separates the Old Town from the New. Out of respect for the three-story-tall Old Town, no new building is allowed to exceed that height—even in the New Town.

In the square across the street, a statue honors **Ioannis Kapodistrias,** the president of Greece's short-lived republic (back when Nafplio was the capital). He faces the Old Town...and Otto, who stepped in when the president's reign was cut tragically short. (We'll get the whole story later.)

Just behind Kapodistrias is a family-friendly **park.** If you want a cheap and fast meal, consider grabbing a bite at one of the family-filled gyros and souvlaki eateries surrounding the park (cheap meals: order and pay at the bar, then find a bench in the park). Goody's (on the left, by the post office) is the local kids' favorite hamburger joint, found all over Greece.

A few minutes' walk straight ahead, past the end of the park, is the ⓭ **National Gallery,** which shows off evocative artwork from the Greek War of Independence (described later, under "Sights in Nafplio").

Back on Syngrou street, the commotion surrounds Nafplio's tiny but busy **bus station.** KTEL (or ΚΤΕΛ in Greek) is the national bus company; in the office here, you can buy tickets from the counter, or get friendlier customer service from the ticket machine out front.

At the next corner we'll turn right. But first, 50 yards ahead to the left, you'll see the ruined remains of Nafplio's **Land Gate,** part of the city's 18th-century Venetian fortifications. Take a little loop from here through the gate and study the amazing Venetian stone defensive work around and above you.

• *Return to the corner, and head back into the Old Town on Plapouta street. Walk to...*

⓮ St. George Square

The focal point of the square, Nafplio's *mitropolis* (equivalent to a Catholic cathedral), is dedicated to St. George and was the neigh-

borhood church for King Otto (whose palace was once on Town Hall Square, which we walked through earlier). Step into the church's dark interior (noticing the clever system that prevents the doors from slamming) to see a gigantic chandelier hovering overhead.

Back outside, surveying St. George Square, you get a feel for an old Nafplio neighborhood. Like most of the Old Town, well-worn Neoclassical buildings date from the boom that followed the city's rise to prominence when it was

Greece's first capital. During the 1820s and 1830s, Nafplio became a haven to refugees from other lands still threatened by the Ottomans.

• *Walk a block slightly uphill (toward the fortress) and turn right on Papanikolaou street.*

Upper Streets of the Old Town

Strolling this quiet lane, note that the Neoclassical grid-planned town is to your right, while the higgledy-piggledy Ottoman town climbs the hillside (with winding and evocative lanes and stepped alleys) on your left. Consider as you walk how Greece's struggling economy leaves so many buildings with such potential in abandoned shambles.

Straight ahead (100 yards away) stands the white bell tower marking the ⓯ **Church of St. Spyridon** and its square. Facing the square (on the left, hiding in a niche in the wall, near the steps) is the first of several 18th-century Turkish fountains you'll see. When the Ottomans controlled Greece, they still used the Arabic script you see here, rather than the Latin alphabet used for modern Turkish. This panel names the guy who paid for the fountain, tells when he had it built (1734-1735), and why (to provide water for his horses). Other fountains have similar tributes, verses from the Quran, or jaunty greetings.

Continue straight along the side of the church to another Ottoman fountain (on the left)—with its characteristic cypress-tree-and-flowers decor.

Between here and the door of the church (on the right) is the spot marking the rough equivalent—to the Greeks—of Ford's Theater (where Lincoln was assassinated). Ioannis Kapodistrias was elected the first president of independent Greece in 1828. But just three years later, in 1831, he was shot and stabbed in this spot by Mani landowners who feared his promises of land reform. This led to chaos, less democratic idealism, and the arrival of Greece's imported Bavarian royalty (King Otto, whom we met earlier).

Pop into the church if it's open. Across from the church is a collapsing *hamam*, a Turkish bath from the 18th century.

• *At the next corner (Kokkinou street), turn right and climb down the slippery marble steps to Staikopoulou street (where we saw the worry bead shop earlier). This time we'll take it left, back to Syntagma Square.*

⓰ Staikopoulou Street

This bustling pedestrian drag is lined with grill restaurants (the harborfront is better for fish) and their happy hustlers, and another fine Ottoman fountain (on the right after a block).

A couple of blocks down, head right and back into Syntagma Square. Find the tiny black cube in the center and sit on it. Apart from being a handy meeting point for the town's kids and a stand for the community Christmas tree, it means absolutely nothing.

• *Your walk is over. From here you can enjoy the rest of the city. In addition to the museums we've already passed (which you can circle back to now), a few more sights—including a folklore museum and a war museum—are within a few blocks. Adventurers may want to head to any of Nafplio's Venetian forts (see page 222). Or, if you're ready to relax, hit the beach (all described under "Sights and Activities in Nafplio," next).*

Sights and Activities in Nafplio

MUSEUMS

▲▲Nafplio Archaeological Museum

Nafplio's top museum gives a concise overview of prehistoric Greece and the Mycenaean civilization. Visit here for a great warm-up before you go to Mycenae.

Cost and Hours: €6; generally Tue-Sun 8:00-15:00, closed Mon; at the bottom of Syntagma Square, tel. 27520-27502, www.culture.gr.

Visiting the Museum: The museum occupies the top two floors of the grand Venetian arsenal on the main square.

The delightful little collection (starting on the ground floor, well-described in English) was excavated from nearby tombs. While nothing here is from Mycenae itself, many of the artifacts date from the same late Bronze Age (c. 1500 B.C.)—a reminder that the region is rich in late Bronze Age sites. The display runs in chronological order, with Stone Age tools suddenly giving way to dolphin frescoes inspired by the Minoan civilization on Crete. Eye-catching jewelry includes a bull-shaped crystal bead (look for the magnifying glass inside a glass case) and strings of gold beads.

The star of the museum stands in the center: the "Dendra Panoply," a 15th-century B.C. suit of bronze armor that was discovered in a Mycenaean chamber tomb. Also found at the site (and displayed here) is a helmet made from boar tusks. Experts consider this the oldest surviving suit of armor in all of Europe.

The second floor displays artifacts from the Age of Homer to the Roman occupation. Particularly striking are the ceremonial

terra-cotta masks along one wall. Dating from the seventh century B.C., these likely were designed to scare off evil spirits. Check out the display of rare glasswork from the first century A.D.—somehow these pieces have survived two millennia without getting smashed.

▲National Gallery
(Alexandros Soutzos Museum, Nafplio Annex)

Housed in a grandly restored Neoclassical mansion, this museum features both temporary and permanent exhibits. The permanent collection, displayed upstairs, is de-voted to Romantic artwork (mostly paintings) stemming from the in-spirational Greek War of Indepen-dence (1821-1829), which led to Nafplio's status as the first capital of independent Greece. The small, manageable collection is arranged thematically. The English descriptions here are worth reading, as they explain the historical underpin-nings for the art, illuminating com-mon themes such as the dying hero, naval battles, and the hardships of war. The art itself might not be technically masterful, but the pa-triotism shimmering beneath it is stirring even to non-Greeks.

Cost and Hours: €3, free on Mon; open Mon and Wed-Sat 10:00-15:00, Wed and Fri also 17:00-20:00, Sun 10:00-14:00, closed Tue; a 5-minute walk into the New Town from the bus sta-tion along major road called Sidiras Merarchias, at #23, tel. 27520-21915, www.culture.gr.

Peloponnese Folklore Foundation Museum

Dedicated to Peloponnesian culture, this modern exhibit fills two floors with clothing, furniture, and jewelry that trace the cultural history of Nafplio and the surrounding region. While not ex-plained in a particularly engaging way, the interesting collection—which ranges from colorful and traditional costumes, to stiff urban suits, to formal gowns, to looms and spinning wheels—is at least well-displayed.

Cost and Hours: €2; Mon-Sat 9:00-14:30, Sun 9:30-15:00, fun gift shop with Greek crafts, Vasileos Alexandrou 1, tel. 27520-28379, www.pli.gr.

War Museum (Nafplio Branch)

This small exhibit, operated and staffed by the Greek armed forces, is best left to ardent Greek patriots and military buffs; for most others it's not worth the small admission fee. It displays old illus-trations and photos of various conflicts (some providing a peek into Nafplio's past cityscape), plus weapons and uniforms (with some English descriptions). The top floor, dedicated to the modern era, displays some interesting WWII-era political cartoons from the Greek perspective.

NAFPLIO

Cost and Hours: €3; Tue-Sun 9:00-19:00, off-season until 17:00, closed Mon, on Amalias, tel. 27520-25591, www.warmuseum.gr.

NAFPLIO'S THREE VENETIAN FORTRESSES

In the days when Venice was the economic ruler of Europe (15th-18th centuries), the Venetians fortified Nafplio with a trio of

stout fortresses. These attempted—but ultimately failed—to fend off Ottoman invasion. Conquered by the Ottomans in 1715, Nafplio remained in Turkish hands until the Greeks retook the city in 1822. Today all three parts of the Venetian fortifications are open to visitors (with nothing to see but stones and views). These are listed in order from lowest to highest.

Bourtzi

While this heavily fortified island—just offshore from Nafplio's waterfront—looks striking, there's not much to do here (pictured above). Still, it's a pleasant vantage point, offering fine views back on the city.

Cost and Hours: Boats depart regularly from the bottom of the square called Friends of the Greeks/Plateia Filellinon, €4.50 round-trip, won't run with fewer than 4 people, check sign on promenade for next departure, once on island it's free to enter the fortress, tel. 69777-16998.

Akronafplia

Nafplio's ancient acropolis, capping the low hill just behind the Old Town, is fairly easy to reach (a manageable but sometimes-steep

10- to 15-minute uphill hike—from the Old Town, just find your way up on any of a number of narrow stepped lanes, then bear left to reach the main road that leads up into the eastern end of the fortress). The earliest surviving parts of this fortress date back to the third century B.C., but the Venetians brought it up to then-modern standards in the 15th century. Up top, there's little to see aside from a few ruins (free to enter and explore anytime). The top of the park-like hill is flanked by two modern hotels: At the east end (toward

Palamidi), stands the deserted and decaying Hotel Xenia; and at the west end (below a little heliport at the end of the road), the top-of-the-top Nafplia Palace hotel entices you to enjoy a drink from its terrace café. You can avoid the hike up by riding the elevator from the top of the Old Town to this hotel (see map on page 212).

▲▲Palamidi Fortress

This imposing hilltop fortress, built by the Venetians between 1711 and 1714, is the best-preserved of its kind in Greece. Palamidi tow-

ers over the Old Town, protected to the west by steep cliffs that plunge 650 feet to the sea. From its highest ramparts, you can spot several Aegean islands and look deep into the mountainous interior of the Peloponnesian Peninsula.

Cost and Hours: €8, €4 off-season daily 8:30-sunset (or earlier), tel. 27520-28036. If you plan to go in the afternoon, call first to confirm the closing time.

Getting There: You can reach the fortress the old-fashioned way: by **climbing** the loooong flight of 999 steps that leads up from the road to Akronafplia fortress (near the top end of Polyzoidou street, just outside the Old Town). The toughest part of the climb is the heat: Bring water, and either get an early start or go later in the day.

Alternatively, you can catch a **taxi** to the top for about €7 one-way (and perhaps take the steps down). If you have a car, you can **drive** to the top and park for free: Follow signs east of town for the beach at Karathona/Καραθωνα, and after ascending the hill, watch for the turn-off on the right up to *Palamidi/ Παλαμηδη*.

Services: WCs are just outside the St. Andrew's Bastion, near the ticket kiosk for hill climbers, and in the parking lot.

Visiting the Fortress: The fortress is actually a collection of fortresses or bastions within its exterior walls. Notice how the various bastions could defend themselves against each other if attackers breached the outer walls or one of the bastions was taken. You can navigate with the pamphlet included with your ticket and by following the handy signs and info posts you'll see throughout. St. Andrew's Bastion is the main bastion to visit. I'd study this one and then just explore the other bastions with a sense of fun and wonder.

St. Andrew's Bastion (Agios Andreas) is the best preserved and offers great views over the rooftops of old Nafplio. Inside, find

the small church. Behind it, under the first archway, is a tiny entrance leading to the cell of the miserable little Kolokotronis Prison (you'll need to crouch and scramble to get inside). While untrue, Greeks love the legend that the Greek hero, Theodoros Koloko-

tronis, was imprisoned here by his political opponents after playing a key role in liberating Greece from Ottoman rule. Back outside, scamper up the giant vaults, which form an angled approach up to the ramparts. Imagine that the entire vault structure functioned as a cistern. Enjoy the views.

ACTIVITIES

Beaches

When ready for some beach time or a swim you have three good choices in and near Nafplio (all free, with easy parking and showers): Arvanitia (in town), Karathona (1.5 miles away via a lovely walk), and Tolo (6 miles away, with good bus connections).

Arvanitia Beach, on the backside of the peninsula, is a 10-minute walk from the Old Town (walk over the saddle between

the two forts or along the pedestrian path leading from the Old Town and around the peninsula). It's a small, pebbly beach with clear, deep water. Crowded in summer, it's popular with the young crowd and has a bar and a free open-air gym workout zone in the parking lot.

Karathona Beach is for more serious beach-going. This half-mile-long sandy beach with shallow water is popular with families, dotted with beachfront tavernas, and lined with palm trees. From Nafplio's Arvanitia Beach you can walk there in 30 minutes along the delightful seafront lane.

Tolo Beach, the best beach of all with nice sand and shallow water, is farther away (6 miles from Nafplio, hourly buses from bus

NAFPLIO

station). You'll find plenty of services (hotels, restaurants, rental paddle boats, and a small town of shops and cafés).

Walking

One of the great delights of a Nafplio visit is to take a stroll along the waterfront. Locals are understandably proud of their tree-lined, peaceful, and scenic walking and jogging lane that circles the peninsula from the town center to Arvanitia Beach and Karathona Beach. Start on the promenade nearest the island fort and walk out onto the spit, and then continue around the peninsula to Arvanitia Beach. For a longer walk, continue another 1.5 miles from Arvanitia to Karathona Beach, passing beneath the Palamidi Fortress on the way. While you can circle back to the town center from Karathona Beach via the New Town, most people prefer to retrace their steps along the waterfront.

Wine Tasting at the Karonis Wine Shop

Dimitri Karonis specializes in Greek wines and ouzo, and gives serious wine shoppers an informative wine tasting (Mon-Sat 8:30-14:00 & 18:00-21:30, closed Sun, near Syntagma Square at Amalias 5, call or email ahead to set up more in-depth tasting for €5-8, tel. 27520-24446, karonisd@otenet.gr).

SIGHTS NEAR NAFPLIO

Both of these ancient attractions are within a half-hour drive of Nafplio (in different directions) and covered in the next two chapters.

▲▲▲Epidavros

This ancient site, 23 miles (by car) east of Nafplio, has an underwhelming museum, forgettable ruins...and the most magnificent theater of the ancient world. It was built nearly 2,500 years ago to seat 15,000. Today it's kept busy reviving the greatest plays of antiquity. You can catch musical and dramatic performances from July through August. Try to see Epidavros either early or late in the day; the theater's marvelous acoustics are best enjoyed in near-solitude.

NAFPLIO

▲▲▲Mycenae

This was the capital of the Mycenaeans, who won the Trojan War and dominated Greece 1,000 years before the Acropolis and other Golden Age Greek sights. The classical Greeks marveled at the huge stones and workmanship of the Mycenaean ruins. Visitors

today can still gape at the Lion's
Gate; peer into a cool, ancient
cistern; and explore the giant
tholos tomb called the Treasury
of Atreus. The tomb, built in the
15th century B.C., is like a huge
underground igloo, with a vast
subterranean dome of cleverly
arranged stones.

Nightlife in Nafplio

Nafplio enjoys a thriving after-hours scene with several nightlife
microclimates—the age of the clientele varies every few blocks. I
enjoy simply joining the evening strolling scene at all these places.
For the best sunset stroll, head down the promenade Akti Miaouli
and then out on the spit to the tiny lighthouse. Poke around to find
the café or bar that appeals to you most for a pre- or post-dinner
drink. Note that there are no true dance clubs in Nafplio, which
has a strict noise ordinance: No loud music in the Old Town after
23:00. (Instead, huge seasonal outdoor clubs sprout along the roads
leading out of town.) A few zones to consider:

Akti Miaouli Promenade: The upper crust enjoys the cafés
lining the promenade Akti Miaouli. Prices are higher, but the
water views (with the illuminated island fortress) might be worth
the expense. At its farthest southern end is a lively playground and
a fun, youthful place for drinks. This promenade leads to the breakwater spit and then to the path leading both romantically and scenically around the peninsula.

Bouboulinas Promenade and Beyond: Beyond the fish
restaurants are several café/bars—once *the* place to be seen, they
now provide a peaceful setting for a drink. A block beyond the
Bouboulinas promenade is a stretch of teen-friendly fast-food places (Trendy Grill, pizza, bakery), described later under "Eating in
Nafplio."

Syntagma Square and Nearby: People of all ages seem to enjoy
the floodlit marble drawing-room vibe of Syntagma Square. Cafés

and restaurants with ample, atmospheric al fresco seating surround
a relaxed open area with people at
play. Kids happily run free in the
square, playing soccer into the wee
hours. From Syntagma, the street
called Konstantinou is home to
several popular café/bars. To find
them, just follow the noise.

Arvanitia Beach: BluBlanc Beach Bar comes out of hibernation every summer at Arvanitia Beach, transforming it from a popular swimming spot by day into a dance party at night (May-Sept, tel. 27520-96031).

Cinema: The local cinema (at Kolokotronis Park) plays movies in their original languages with Greek subtitles. In summer, the theater moves nearby into the open air.

Sleeping in Nafplio

Nafplio enjoys an abundance of excellent accommodations. Because this is a chic getaway for wealthy Athenians, many of the best beds are in well-run, boutique-ish little pensions. (Some of the smaller pensions are run by skeleton staffs, so don't expect 24-hour reception; let them know what time you'll arrive so they can greet you.) The many options allow hotel seekers to be picky.

It's boom or bust in Nafplio. At the busiest times (June, July, especially Aug, and weekends year-round), hotels are full and prices go up; outside these times, hoteliers are lean and hungry, and rates become soft. Don't be afraid to ask for a deal, especially if you're staying more than a couple of nights. If your hotel doesn't include breakfast, most cafés in town sell a basic breakfast for €5-6.

Most of these accommodations are uphill from the heart of the Old Town. The good news: They provide fresh breezes, have almost no mosquitoes, and offer a quiet retreat from the bustling old center. The bad news: You'll climb a few flights of stairs to reach your room.

$$$ Amfitriti Palazzo's seven plush rooms, highest up, have balconies with sweeping views and fun classy-mod decor, with some rooms built right into the rock (Db-€85-110, family room-€130, price depends on type of room; cheaper off-season, if you stay 3 nights or more, or for early and direct booking; top of the hill—just under the old wall, tel. 27520-96250, www.amfitriti-pension.gr, info@amfitriti-pension.gr, Evangelia and family).

$$$ Amymone Pension (Αμυμώνη) and **Adiandi Hotel** (Αδιάντη) are a pair of super-stylish, trendy boutique hotels that share an owner and are a few doors apart along one of Nafplio's most inviting restaurant lanes. The anything-but-cookie-cutter rooms all have different color schemes, decor, and boldly painted headboards made from recycled materials, such as doors. Their junior suites have balconies, sitting areas, and computers. The very central location can come with more noise than my other listings, and both hotels have lots of stairs with no elevator. The Amymone has eight rooms (Db-€65-120 depending on size, Othonos 39, tel. 27520-99477 or 27520-22073, info@amymone.gr), while the Adi-

---

Sleep Code

Abbreviations   **(€1=about $1.10, country code: 30)**
S=Single, **D**=Double/Twin, **T**=Triple, **Q**=Quad, **b**=bathroom
  $$$ Higher Priced—Most rooms €80 or more
   $$ Moderately Priced—Most rooms €55-80
    $ Lower Priced—Most rooms €55 or less
Unless otherwise noted, breakfast is included, English is spoken, and free Wi-Fi and/or a guest computer is generally available. Many places accept credit cards, and rooms generally have air-conditioning. Prices can change; verify current rates online or by email. For the best prices, always book directly with the hotel.

---

andi has seven rooms (Db-€90-120 depending on size, Othonos 31, same telephone as above, info@hotel-adiandi.com).

$$$ Ippoliti Hotel (ΙΠΠΟΛΥΤΗ) is a classy business-hotel splurge, with 19 elegantly decorated, hardwood-floor rooms with antique touches. In summer, breakfast is served on the patio beside the small swimming pool (Db-€100-180 depending on size and season, elevator, small gym, near waterfront at Ilia Miniati 9, at corner with Aristidou, tel. 27520-96088, www.ippoliti.gr, info@ippoliti.gr).

$$ Pension Marianna is my choice for the most welcoming place in town. The friendly Zotos brothers—Petros, Panos, and Takis—offer genuine hospitality, fair rates, and comfortable rooms in their stony little paradise. It's scenically situated just under the lower Akronafplia wall, well worth the steep climb up the stairs from the Old Town. The 26 rooms—some with views and/or little balconies—are scattered throughout several levels. Atop it all is an airy terrace where you can enjoy a breakfast made up of organic products from their nearby farm (mention this book for these prices: Sb-€50, small Db-€55, bigger Db-€65, Tb-€70, Qb-€80; breakfast-€5, no elevator, Potamianou 9, tel. 27520-24256, www.hotelmarianna.gr, info@hotelmarianna.gr). Park above town at the giant, abandoned Hotel Xenia at the Akronafplia fortress and walk a few steps down.

$$ Byron Hotel is a traditional, family-run standby with 18 simple, older-feeling rooms in a scenic setting up some stairs above the Old Town (Sb-€45, Db-€60-80 depending on size and views, Tb-€90, Platonos 2, tel. 27520-22351, www.byronhotel.gr, byronhotel@otenet.gr, Greek Aris and Swiss Monica).

$$ Pension Rigas is a gem with seven cozy, charmingly rustic rooms in a refurbished old building with exposed stone and beams, hardwood floors, high ceilings, and lots of character. Its comfy lobby and small patio area provide a convivial space for guests to

NAFPLIO

share travel stories (Sb-€35, Db-€40-70 depending on size and season—the €40 Db is tiny but adequate, extra bed-€5, Kapodis-triou 8, tel. 27520-23611, www.pension-rigas.gr, regaspension@ hotmail.com, run by friendly Australian Lena).

$$ Hotel Leto Nuevo is partway up the slopes of the Ak-ronafplia fortress. Its 18 boutiquish rooms all have sea views and either a bathtub or rain shower; ask about elusive and popular room #121, which is higher up (Sb-€50, Db-€65-75 depending on size, extra bed-€15, €10 less without breakfast, Zigomala 28, tel. 27520-28093, www.letohotelnafplio.gr, info@letohotelnafplio.gr, Thana-sis and Athina).

$$ Chroma Design Hotel and Suites has seven colorful, trendy rooms in a renovated old mansion, higher up along some stairs (standard Db-€60-70, superior Db with balcony-€80, junior suite with balcony and sea view-€100, lovely garden area, rooftop view terrace, corner of Zigomala and Kokkinou, tel. 27520-27686, www.thehouseprojecthotels.com, info@thehouseprojecthotels.com, Aggeliki and Ioanna). They also run the **$$ Aroma Guesthouse,** with four romantic rooms overlooking a pleasant small square along a pedestrian street (Db-€60-70, attic Db-€90, on Papanikolaou, near the Church of St. Spyridon, reception at Chroma, same con-tact info as Chroma).

$ Pension Filyra (Φιλύρα) has six tastefully and colorfully decorated rooms at a nice price in a few buildings in the heart of the Old Town (Db-€40-50 depending on size, attic suite with kitch-enette and low beams-€60, rates can be €10 more on weekends, discount for stays of 3 or more nights, your room is stocked with a basic continental breakfast, Aggelou Terzaki 29, tel. 27520-96096, www.pensionfilyra.gr, info@pensionfilyra.gr).

$ Pension Anapli is a cute little place with seven colorful, dressed-up rooms with iron-frame beds (Db-€45, Db with bal-cony-€50, €10 extra on weekends, Fotomara 21, tel. 27520-24585, www.pension-anapli.gr, info@pension-anapli.gr).

Eating in Nafplio

Nafplio is bursting with tempting eateries. Because most of them cater to Athenians on a weekend break, they aim to please repeat customers. This also means that prices can be a bit high. In two high-profile restaurant zones—the tavernas along Staikopoulou street (just above Syntagma Square) and the fish restaurants on Bouboulinas street (along the waterfront)—waiters compete des-perately for the passing tourist trade. While I'd avoid the places on Staikopoulou, if you want seafood, the Bouboulinas fish joints are the best in town. I've focused most of my coverage on the tight pedestrian lanes between these two areas, toward the water from

1. Amfitriti Palazzo Hotel
2. Amymone Pension & Adiandi Hotel
3. Ippoliti Hotel
4. Pension Marianna
5. Byron Hotel
6. Pension Rigas
7. Hotel Leto Nuevo
8. Chroma Design Hotel & Suites
9. Aroma Guesthouse
10. Pension Filyra
11. Pension Anapli
12. Mezedopoleio O Noulis Rest.
13. Taverna Paleo Arhontiko
14. Epi Skinis Restaurant
15. Alaloum Restaurant
16. Aiolos Taverna
17. To Omorfo Tavernaki
18. Bouboulinas Eateries
19. Agnanti Restaurant
20. Trattoria La Gratella
21. Mitato Souvlaki
22. Gyro Grill & Pizza Alpha
23. Trendy Grill Strip
24. Karonis Wine Shop
25. Supermarket
26. Antica Gelateria di Roma
27. Odyssey Bookshop
28. Travel Agency

NAFPLIO

Syntagma Square, where values are good and ambience is excellent. Several places offer live traditional Greek music (generally weekends in summer after 20:30 or 21:00; get details from your hotel).

RESTAURANTS

Mezedopoleio O Noulis—run by Noulis, the man with the mighty moustache shown on the sign—serves up an inviting range of *mezedes* (appetizers). Three or four *mezedes* constitute a tasty meal for two people. This authentic-feeling place offers a rare chance to sample *saganaki flambé* (fried cheese flambéed with Metaxa brandy, €7). As Noulis likes to do it all himself, don't come here if you're in a hurry (€4-7 starters, €8-13 seafood and meat dishes; mid-May-Sept Mon-Sat 13:00-15:00 & 19:00-23:00, closed Sun; Oct-mid-May Tue-Sun 13:00-16:00, closed Mon; cash only, no reservations, Moutzouridou 21, tel. 27520-25541).

Taverna Paleo Arhontiko ("Old Mansion") is a favorite town hangout for its classic homestyle Greek dishes, reasonable prices, lovely ambience, and live music (nightly from 21:00 in summer). It gets packed on weekends, when reservations are recommended (€3-5 appetizers, €6-12 main dishes, daily 12:00-16:00 & 19:30-

Nafplio Hotels & Restaurants

24:00, at corner of Ypsilandou and Siokou, tel. 69818-68914, Anja and Tassos).

Epi Skinis ("On Stage") is a cozy dining room decorated with playbills and other theater paraphernalia that's run by Yannis (the son of a theater director). It feels a bit classier than the tavernas nearby and serves Greek and Mediterranean dishes with a creative twist (€3-8 starters, €8-17 main dishes, Thu-Tue 13:00-24:00, closed Wed, Amalias 19A, tel. 27520-21331, www.episkinis.eu).

Alaloum Restaurant serves inventive Greek and Mediterranean dishes and a famous "mother-in-law's salad." The portions are huge and sharing is encouraged (sit inside or out, €10 plates of the day, Wed-Mon 13:00-24:00, closed Tue and in June, D. Ipsilantou 3, tel. 27520-29883). Michalis organizes live music most weekends in summer at around 21:00.

Tavernas on Olgas Street: The lane called Olgas, tucked away in a grid of streets just two blocks up from the waterfront, is filled with charming, family-run tavernas serving Greek classics to happy tourists. At any of these, you can choose between a cozy, rustic interior or outdoor tables. Window-shop along here and consider these two good options: **Aiolos** (good mixed-grill platters, drunken chicken, *saganaki,* and *sousamotiro*—fried cheese with sesame seeds, Olgas 30, tel. 27520-26828) or **To Omorfo Tavernaki,** literally "The Beautiful Little Tavern" (traditional home-style Greek dishes, Kotsonopoulou 1, tel. 27520-25944, Tsioli family).

Fish Restaurants on Bouboulinas: As you stroll the harborfront, you'll soon come upon the fishy aromas and aggressive come-ons of the town's best seafood eateries (all open daily, roughly 12:00-24:00). Wherever you choose to dine, part of the fun is the strolling scene. Seafood here is typically priced by the kilogram or half-kilogram (figure about 250-300 grams for a typical portion—around €10-20 for a seafood entrée, or about €6-15 for a meat dish). **Arapakos Restaurant,** more elegant than the others with a dressy interior and great outdoor tables, is understandably favored by the town's big shots (Bouboulinas 81, tel. 27520-27675, www.arapakos.gr/index-arapakos-en.htm). **Savouras** (ΣΑΒΟΥΡΑΣ, at #79) is also highly regarded.

Peaceful and on the Water: **Agnanti** is worth considering if you want to be alone with the sea and great views. Just beyond the breakwater spit at Nafplio's "Sea Gate," offering only outside tables, it's like eating on a dock (€5-11 starters and salads, €11-15 main dishes, seafood pasta is a favorite, open daily for lunch and dinner, closed Nov-Feb, walk a few minutes down Akti Miaouli Promenade and look for stone building after path veers left, tel. 27520-29332, mobile 69329-06593, Andrew).

Italian: **Trattoria La Gratella** is your best bet if you crave Italian. They serve tasty and reasonably priced pizza, pasta, and secondi (€8-15) with a bright and modern interior and nice outdoor tables (June-Oct Mon-Thu 17:00-24:00, Fri-Sun 12:00-24:00; Nov-May daily 12:00-24:00; Olgas 44, tel. 27520-28350).

CHEAP GYRO PITA AND SOUVLAKI JOINTS

Each of these places serves souvlaki and gyro pita sandwiches and more for a quick €3 meal. You can sit inside or out on the sidewalk, or get takeaway.

Mitato Souvlaki is an inviting little joint just steps off the main square (daily 11:30-24:00, off Syntagma Square behind National Bank building at Staikopoulou 14, tel. 27520-21159).

Dining in Kolokotronis Park: Several cheap, family- and student-style diners line the park (along Sidiras Merarchias street, just beyond Town Hall Square), all with noisy indoor seating and peaceful options in the park. **Gyro Grill** offers perhaps the cheapest hot dinner in town. **Pizza Alpha** is a few doors down.

Trendy Grill Strip: This thriving strip of eateries is where high-school kids take their dates (facing the harbor and parking, just east of the Bouboulinas promenade). Along with **Trendy**—the busiest souvlaki joint in town—you'll find **Pizza Scuola** and the **Mesali Bakery** (with classic Greek sweets and baklava).

Picnics: The **Carrefour Express** supermarket is the most convenient of several supermarkets in town (Mon-Sat 8:00-21:00, closed Sun, 50 yards behind the post office at corner of Syngrou and Flessa).

DESSERT

Antica Gelateria di Roma is *the* place to go for a mouthwatering array of *gelati* (dairy-based ice cream) and *sorbetti* (fruit-based sorbet) made fresh on the premises daily by Italian gelato master Marcello Raffo, his wife Monica, and his sister Claudia. The Raffos also offer other Italian snacks and drinks (daily 9:00-24:00, free Wi-Fi, Farmakopoulou 3, at corner with Kominou, tel. 27520-23520).

Nafplio Connections

BY BUS

The tiny bus station is convenient and central, and has a printed schedule in English. Their website has an English option and sells tickets (www.ktel-argolidas.gr). While the ticket agent can give information, confirm your plans (and transfers) with your driver or other passengers.

Direct buses go to **Athens** (nearly hourly, 2.5 hours), **Epidavros** (2-3/day, 1/day late on Sun, 45 minutes), and **Mycenae** (2-3/day, none Sun, 45 minutes).

Journeys to other Peloponnesian destinations require multiple transfers; get an early start, and be prepared for frustrations and delays: **Tripoli** (2/day, 1.5 hours—transfer point for many other destinations), **Monemvasia** (1/day, 4.5 hours, change in Tripoli and Sparta), **Olympia** (2/day, 5 hours, change in Tripoli). For these destinations, KTEL, the national bus system, has a minimal website (www.ktelbus.com); for better information, try this helpful unofficial website in English: http://livingingreece.gr (under "Best of..." click on "KTEL Buses of Greece").

BY TAXI

To cut some time off the trip to the ancient sites, you can take a taxi to **Mycenae** or **Epidavros** (€50-70 round-trip for either one, with one-hour wait, bargain hard for the best price).

BY BOAT

To reach long-distance boats connecting to **Hydra** and the other islands in the nearby Saronic Gulf, you'll first need to get to the ports of Tolo, Ermioni, or Metochi. For specifics on ferry connections from these ports to Hydra, see page 388 of the Hydra chapter.

Getting to the Ports: Infrequent excursion boats (2-3/week) to Hydra operated by Pegasus Tours leave from the port at **Tolo,** a short drive or bus ride (20 minutes) from Nafplio. These boats usually leave fairly early in the morning, so stop by the bus station in Nafplio to check morning bus times and to get your ticket.

Hellenic Seaways ferries leave from farther away in **Ermioni** (a.k.a. Hermioni), about 1.5 hours southeast of Nafplio. Buses that are supposedly going to Ermioni usually go instead to Kranidi, a larger town about six miles from Ermioni's port (3/day Mon-Sat, 1/day Sun, 2 hours; this Nafplio-Kranidi bus connection may require a transfer at the town of Ligourio—pay careful attention so as not to miss the change). From Kranidi, it's about a €15-20 taxi ride to the dock at Ermioni (try to split the fare with other Ermioni-bound travelers).

Passenger ferries (either the Freedom Boat or Metoxi Express) leave from even farther away in **Metochi,** which is best reached by car (allow 2 hours).

ROUTE TIPS FOR DRIVERS

Nafplio is a quick and easy drive from Athens—about 2 hours, much of it on toll highways. (When asked about the poor little road connecting the city to the toll highway, locals explain it's intentional...to keep the Athenians out.) To reach **Monemvasia** from Nafplio (3-4 hours), consider taking the scenic route described on page 329.

EPIDAVROS

ΕΠΙΔΑΥΡΟΣ / Επιδαυρος

Nestled in a leafy valley some 20 miles east of Nafplio, Epidavros was once the most famous healing center in the ancient Greek world. It was like an ancient Lourdes, a place of hope where the sick came to be treated by doctor-priests acting on behalf of Asklepios, the god of medicine.

The site began as a temple to Apollo, god of light, who was worshipped here in Mycenaean times. By the fourth century B.C., Apollo had been replaced by his son, Asklepios (who was said to have been born here). Because pilgrims prayed to Asklepios for health, a sanctuary was needed, with a temple, altars, and statues to the gods. The sanctuary reached the height of its popularity in the fourth and third centuries B.C., when it boasted medical facilities, housing for the sick, mineral baths, a stadium for athletic competitions, and a theater.

These days the famous theater is Epidavros' star attraction. It's the finest and best-preserved of all of Greece's ancient theaters—and that's saying something in a country with 132 of them. Epidavros also has some (far) less interesting sights. The once-great sanctuary is now little more than a lonely field of rubble. The small Archaeological Museum displays a few crumbled fragments of statuary. But the theater alone makes Epidavros worth the side-trip.

GETTING THERE

By Car: From **Nafplio** it's a 30-minute **drive** to the east, along winding roads. There's plenty of free parking at the site.

Head east out of Nafplio and follow the signs. If you're connecting Epidavros and Mycenae (see next chapter; allow 60 minutes), you can avoid driving all the way back into Nafplio by watching carefully for signs to either site, which direct you to a roundabout outside central Nafplio.

Be aware that names on signs can vary. Epidavros can be spelled "Epidaurus" in English. Confusingly, many locations in this area carry the name Epidavros/Επιδαυρος. Don't be distracted by signs to Nea ("New") Epidavros/Νεα Επιδαυρος, or Palea ("Old") Epidavros/Παλαιά Επιδαυρος, which will route you to a modern coastal town far from the theater.

By Bus: From **Nafplio,** buses run to Epidavros (Mon-Sat 2-3/day—buses usually leave Nafplio at 10:30, 12:30, and 14:30; 1/day late on Sun; possibly fewer buses Oct-April, 45 minutes). Return buses from Epidavros to Nafplio typically leave in the afternoon (3/day, last bus usually around 18:00). Confirm bus schedules locally.

It's possible to see both Epidavros and Mycenae in one long day from Nafplio by bus (in summer): If the schedule hasn't changed, you could take the 10:00 bus from Nafplio to Mycenae, spend about 2.5 hours at the site, and return to Nafplio on the 13:00 bus; then catch the 14:30 bus to Epidavros, tour the site, and return to Nafplio on the last bus, arriving back in the city about 19:00 (this wouldn't work on Sun, when there are no buses to Mycenae). Taking the bus to Epidavros first and then to Mycenae doesn't work as well (giving you only 30 minutes at Mycenae).

From **Athens,** buses head to Nafplio, then continue on to Epidavros (2-3/day, 2.5 hours, may require transfer in Nafplio—ask when you buy your ticket).

By Taxi: You can get to Epidavros by **taxi** from Nafplio (€50-70 round-trip with one-hour wait).

ORIENTATION TO EPIDAVROS

Cost: €12 (€6 off-season) includes the theater, Archaeological Museum, and the rest of the Sanctuary of Epidavros archaeological site.

Hours: Daily April-Oct 8:00-20:00 (in theory), off-season 8:00-15:00. Tel. 27350-22009, www.culture.gr. Off-season and during holidays, because of the tough economy, sights can close suddenly: Check locally before planning your day.

Length of This Tour: Unfortunately, Epidavros is not really "on the way" to anything else. Budget two to three hours for the round-trip excursion from Nafplio. You can see the entire site in an hour, but it's delightful to linger at the theater.

Services: There's not much here. A simple café/restaurant is along the lane between the parking and ticket office. WCs are near the parking lot, and more are near the museum.

Performances: The theater is still used today for performances on summer weekends during the annual Athens & Epidavros Festival (generally July-Aug Fri-Sat at around 21:00; ideally buy tickets the day before, schedule at www.greekfestival.gr).

Special buses run from Athens and Nafplio on performance nights.

Starring: The most intact (and most spectacularly situated) theater from ancient Greece.

SELF-GUIDED TOUR

From the parking lot, follow signs up the lane to the ticket desk. Buy your ticket and enter. The theater, sanctuary, and museum are all a couple of minutes' walk from one another. The stunning theater is 90 percent of the experience: Climb the seats, take some photos, try out the acoustics—and that's it. Then zip through the little museum and wander the grounds beyond.

• *From the entry gate, climb the stairs on the right up to the theater. Enter the theater, stand in the center of the circular "orchestra" and take it all in. (I've marked your spot with a weathered marble stump, where fellow theatergoers might be posing, singing, or speaking.)*

Theater of Epidavros (c. 300 B.C.)

This magnificent sight is built into the side of a tree-covered hill. The perfect symmetry of its two tiers of seating stands as a tribute

to Greek mathematics. It's easy to locate the main elements of a typical Greek theater: the round **orchestra,** the smaller **stage** area *(skene),* and the **seating** *(kavea).*

The audience sat in the bleacher-like seats (made of limestone blocks) that were set into the hillside, wrapping partially around the performers. Together, the lower rows and 21 upper rows (added by the Romans, c. 50 B.C.) seated up to 15,000. The spectators looked down on the orchestra, a circular area 70 feet across where the group of actors known as the chorus sang and danced. Behind the orchestra are the rectangular foundations of the *skene* (which is often covered with a modern stage.) The *skene* had a raised stage where actors performed, a back wall for scenery, dressing rooms in the back, and various doorways and ramps where actors could make dramatic entrances and exits. The *skene* was not very tall, so spectators in the upper seats could look over it during the performance, taking in the view of the valley below.

The ancient acoustical engineering is remarkable. The acoustics are superb—from the orchestra, whisper to your partner on the top row. (The center stone marks where an altar to Dionysus, the god of wine and theater, once stood.)

Picture a typical performance of a Greek tragedy here at this

Greek Theater

The Greeks invented modern theater, and many plays written 2,500 years ago are still performed today.

Greek drama began in prehistoric times with the songs, poems, and rituals performed to honor Dionysus, the god of wine and orgiastic revelry. By the sixth century B.C., these fertility rites developed into song competitions between choruses of men who sang hymns about Dionysus, heroes, and gods. The contests were held at religious festivals as a form of worship.

Later, Athenian playwrights (such as Thespis, the first "thespian") introduced actors who acted out the story through spoken monologues, alternating with the chorus' songs. Over time, these monologues became dialogues between several actors, and the spoken scenes became as important as the songs of the chorus. Plays evolved from Dionysian hymns to stories of Dionysus to stories of all sorts—myths of gods and heroes, and comedies about contemporary events. By the Golden Age (c. 450-400 B.C.), Athens was the center of a golden age of theater, premiering plays by Sophocles, Euripides, and Aristophanes.

Greek plays fall into three categories. Tragedies, the oldest and most prestigious, were super-serious plays about gods and legends that usually ended with the hero dying. Comedies, which emerged during the Golden Age, were witty satires about contemporary people and events. "Satyr plays" spoofed the seriousness of tragedies—things like Oedipus with a massive strap-on phallus.

Greek drama, like Greek art and philosophy, put human beings at center stage. The theaters were built into the natural slopes of hillsides, giving the audience a glimpse of human emotions against the awesome backdrop of nature. The plays showed mortals wrestling with how to find their place in a cosmos ruled by the gods and Fate.

EPIDAVROS

theater. Before the show began, spectators filed in the same way tourists do today, through the passageway between the seating and the *skene*. The performance began with a sober monologue by a lone actor, setting the scene. Next, the chorus members entered in a solemn parade, singing as they took their place in the orchestra circle. Then the story unfolded through dialogue on the stage, interspersed with songs by the chorus members. At play's end, the chorus sang a song summing up the moral of the play, then paraded out the way they came.

The chorus—a group of three to fifty singers—was a key part of Greek plays. They commented on the action through songs, accompanied by flute or lyre (small harp), and danced around in the orchestra (literally, "dancing space").

For about seven centuries (c. 300 B.C.-A.D. 400), the theater at Epidavros hosted song contests and plays, until the Christian Emperor Theodosius II closed the

sanctuary in the fifth century. Over time, the theater became buried in dirt, preserving it until it was unearthed in almost original condition in 1881. Today it is once again a working theater.

Even if you're not here for one of the theater's official performances, you can still enjoy the show: Tourists often take turns performing monologues, reciting poems, or just clapping to try out the acoustics. If there's an actor inside you, speak up. Try reciting any of the ancient Greek passages presented in the sidebar on the next page.

When you've finished your turn on stage, climb the stairs to the seats to join the spectators. From up here can you fully appreciate the incredible acoustics—not to mention the remarkable scale and intactness of the place. No matter how high you climb, you can hear every word of the naturally amplified performances down

below...all while enjoying the backdrop of sweeping mountains and olive groves.

• *Walk down the stairs across from the theater to find the...*

Archaeological Museum

The exhibits in this dusty little old-school museum come with English de-

Greek Monologues

To get you into the theatrical mood, here are a few (condensed) passages from some famous Greek plays.

Oedipus Rex (or Oedipus Tyrannus), by Sophocles

A man unwittingly kills his father, sleeps with his mother, and watches his wife commit suicide. When he learns the truth, he blinds himself in shame and sorrow:

"With what eyes could I ever behold again my honored
father or my unhappy mother, both destroyed by me?
This punishment is worse than death, and so it should be.
I wish I could be deaf as well as blind, to shut out all sorrow.
My friends, come bury me, hide me from every eye,
cast me into the deepest ocean and let me die.
Anything so I can shake off this hated life.
Come friends, do not be afraid to touch me, polluted as I am.
For no one will suffer for my sins—no one but me."

Antigone, by Sophocles

The heroine Antigone defies the king in order to give her brother a proper burial. Here she faces her punishment:

"O tomb, my bridal chamber, where I go most miserably,
before my time on earth is spent!
What law of heaven have I broken?!
Why should I ever beseech the gods again,

scriptions. The first room (of three) displays various *steles* (inscribed stone tablets). Some of these document successful cases where patients were healed here by the god Asklepios. Others are rules governing the hospital. The only people to be excluded from the sanctuary were the terminally ill and pregnant women (both were considered too high-risk—their deaths would sully the sanctuary's reputation). The room also holds a case displaying some medical instruments that'll make you glad you were born after the invention of anesthetics. (You can see small pots for measuring dosages.)

The second room has many (headless) statues of gods who were invoked in the healing process—most of them textbook examples of that wonderfully relaxed *contrapposto* (S-shaped) stance that was revived centuries later by Renaissance sculptors (find the statue striking an especially sassy pose). The columns and cornice on display were part of the sanctuary's impressive entryway (propylaea).

The star of the final room is an extremely well-preserved capital from a Corinthian column. The builders of the temple buried it on the site, perhaps as an offering to the gods. Archaeologists who dug it up in the 19th century were astonished at its condition; it may have been the prototype for all the capitals in the temple complex.

if I am to be punished for doing nothing but good.
If I am guilty, I accept my sin.
But if it is my accusers that are wrong,
I pray that they do not suffer any more than the evils they
have inflicted upon me."

Plutus, by Aristophanes

In this comedy, a man befriends a blind beggar who is actually
Plutus, the god of wealth, in disguise. He helps Plutus regain his
sight by bringing him to Epidavros. (If the monologue lacks some
of Aristophanes' famed side-splitting humor, maybe it's because
I left out the bit about cutting a huge fart in the presence of the
god Asklepios.)

"Having arrived at the Temple of Asklepios, we first led
our patient to the sea to purify him. Back at the temple, we gave offerings of bread and wheat cake, then
bedded down. During the night, the god Asklepios
appeared, sitting on the bed. He took a clean rag and
wiped Plutus' eyelids. He then whistled, and two huge
snakes came rushing from the temple and licked the patient's eyelids. As quick as you could drain 10 shots of
wine, Plutus stood up—he could see! Asklepios disappeared with the snakes, and, as dawn broke, we clapped
our hands with joy and gave praise and thanks to the
mighty god."

The room also displays two replicas of small, square reliefs (left
wall) showing the god Asklepios
on his throne. Asklepios is often
depicted as a kindly, bearded
man, carrying a staff with a snake
wound around it, the forerunner
of today's medical symbol.

• *Up the stairs, to the left as you leave
the museum (and only WC within
the site), is the sprawling field of
ruins called the...*

EPIDAVROS

Sanctuary of Epidavros

While Epidavros' theater is stunning, the ruins of the sanctuary
itself (in a huge open field between the theater and parking lot)
are a distant also-ran compared with those at other great ancient
sites, such as Delphi and Olympia. The various ruins are well-described in English, but precious little survives. Walking roughly
400 yards from the museum to the far end of the site, you'll pass

the hotel, baths, dining hall, stadium, circular temple *(tholos)*, dormitory (stoa of Abaton), and foundations of the Temple of Asklepios—in that order.

Considering that the sanctuary was a kind of healing resort with a mix of doctors and priests to serve the visitors or patients, it needed a hotel. Only the footprint of a 160-room, luxury two-floor-tall spa hotel survives. You can see the stone foundations (the wood-and-tile superstructure is long gone) and thresholds with hinge holes.

Logically there would be a bathhouse and restaurant for so many important guests. And the scant remains of those are seen next. Beyond them stretches a fine stadium. Every four years, Epidavros' 6,000-seat stadium was used for the Festival of Asklepios (similar to other ancient Greek athletic competitions).

Archaeologists are reconstructing one important building beyond the stadium. The circular building, or *tholos,* had a labyrinth in its basement. Some believe the sick would go here to meditate with snakes. Exactly why and what happened is still a mystery.

The sick would then spend the night in the stoa of Abaton (the large dormitory building just beyond the *tholos*). Here they would likely pray for a miracle while meditating on the experience they had with the snakes. Perhaps they hoped to be visited in a dream by Asklepios, who could give them the secret to their cure. Stories of the miracles people experienced here spread far and wide, making Epidavros very popular.

Like a square memorial, just to the right is the covered foundation of the Temple of Asklepios—the center of this sacred complex.

EPIDAVROS

MYCENAE

MYKΉΝΕΣ / Μυκήνες

Mycenae—a fortress city atop a hill—was the hub of a mighty civilization that dominated the Greek world between 1600 and 1200 B.C., a thousand years before Athens' Golden Age. The Mycenaeans were as distant and mysterious to the Golden Age Greeks as Plato and Socrates are to us today. Ancient Greek tourists visited the dramatic ruins of Mycenae and concluded that the Mycenaeans must have been the heroes who'd won the Trojan War, as related in Homer's epic poems, the *Iliad* and the *Odyssey*. They thought of the Mycenaeans as their ancestors, the first "Greeks."

Following the same ancient sandal-steps as the ancient Greeks, today's visitors continue to enjoy Mycenae's majestic set-

ting of mountains, valleys, and the distant sea. Exploring this still-impressive hilltop, you'll discover the famous Lion Gate, a fine little museum, an enormous domed burial chamber... and distant echoes of the Trojan War.

When it comes to unraveling the mystery of the Mycenae-

ans, modern historians—armed with only the slimmest written record—are still trying to sort out fact from legend. They don't know exactly who the Mycenaeans were, where they came from, or what happened to them. Here are the sketchy (and oft-disputed) details:

Around 1600 B.C., a Bronze Age civilization originating in Asia Minor developed an empire of autonomous city-states that covered the southern half of mainland Greece and a few islands. Their capital was the city of Mycenae, which also gave its name to the people and the era. From contact with the sophisticated Minoan people on the isle of Crete, the militaristic Mycenaeans borrowed elements of religion and the arts.

Sometime about the year 1200 B.C., the aggressive Mycenaeans likely launched an attack on Troy, a rich city on the northwest coast of Asia Minor (present-day Turkey). After a long siege, Troy fell, and the Mycenaeans became the undisputed rulers of the Aegean. Then, just as suddenly, the Mycenaeans mysteriously disappeared, and their empire crumbled. Whether the Mycenaeans fell victim to a sudden invasion by the Dorians (a Greek tribe), an attack of the mysterious tribes later dubbed the "Sea People," a drought, or internal rebellion—no one knows. Whatever the reason, by 1100 B.C., Mycenae was abandoned and burned, and Greece plunged into four centuries known as the Dark Ages.

Nearly three millennia later, in 1876, German archaeologist Heinrich Schliemann excavated this site and put it back on the archaeologists' (and tourists') map. Today a visit to Mycenae is a trip back into prehistory to see some of the oldest remains of a complex civilization in all of Europe—a thousand years older than Athens' Acropolis.

GETTING THERE

By Car: Mycenae is 18 miles north of Nafplio (follow signs to Athens, on the way to the major E-65 expressway). From the modern town of Mycenae/Μυκήνες (near the larger town of Fichti/Φιχτι), the ruins are about two miles north, dramatically perched atop a hill. If you're connecting Mycenae and Epidavros by car (allow 60 minutes), you can avoid driving all the way back into Nafplio by watching carefully for signs to either site, which direct you to a roundabout outside central Nafplio. At Mycenae, drivers can use the free parking lot near the entrance to the ruins and museum; if it's full, park along the road leading to the lot.

By Bus: Buses run from Nafplio directly to ancient Mycenae (Mon-Sat 2-3/day—likely at 10:00, 12:00, and 14:00; no buses on Sun; possibly fewer buses Oct-April, 45 minutes), but the timing for the return trip makes taking a bus a pain. You'll have either just 30 minutes to see the site (not enough) or 2.5 hours (a little too much for some people). For advice about connecting Mycenae and Epidavros in one bus-based day trip from Nafplio, see page 236. If you do take the bus, confirm that your bus goes to the archaeological site; other buses take you only as far as Fichti, two miles away.

By Taxi: You can take a taxi to Mycenae from Nafplio (about €50-70 round-trip with time to sightsee; best to arrange your return in advance. If you need to arrange a return taxi from Mycenae on the spot, call mobile 694-643-1726).

ORIENTATION TO MYCENAE

Cost: €12 (€6 off-season) ticket includes archaeological site, museum, and Treasury of Atreus up the road.

Hours: Roughly May-Oct daily 8:00-20:00; closes an hour or two earlier in fall; Nov-April daily 7:30-15:00 or 8:30-16:00, may close Sun. As at other archaeological sites in Greece, Mycenae's hours can change without notice. Tel. 27510-76585 or 27520-27502, www.culture.gr.

Services: WCs are just above the museum, but none are on the actual site. A stand in the parking lot sells basic snacks.

Planning Your Time: As with most ancient sites with a museum, decide whether to see the museum first (to help reconstruct the ruins) or the site first (to get the lay of the land). To explore the cistern, bring a flashlight. To complement the information in this self-guided tour, read the chapter on Athens' National Archaeological Museum, where many Mycenaean artifacts are now displayed (see page 141).

Length of This Tour: Allow an hour for the site, a half-hour for the museum, and a half-hour for the Treasury of Atreus. Mycenae makes for a handy half-day side-trip from Nafplio. Drivers can combine it with the Theater of Epidavros for a full day of ancient site-hopping.

Pronunciation: Mycenae is pronounced my-SEE-nee by English-speakers; Greeks call the town Mykenes/Μυκήνες (mee-KEE-nehs), also spelled Mikenes. The ancient people are known as the Mycenaeans (my-seh-NEE-uhns).

Starring: The hilltop fortress at the center of the most ancient, powerful, and enigmatic of ancient Greek civilizations.

SELF-GUIDED TOUR

The three main sightseeing areas at Mycenae are a few minutes' walk from one another. The **archaeological ruins** consist of the walled city of Mycenae atop the hill called the acropolis. Here you'll find the famous Lion Gate entrance, Grave Circle A (which yielded precious artifacts), and the ruins of the palace. Below the site is the **museum,** housing artifacts that were found here. Finally, as impressive as anything here is the **Treasury of Atreus**—a huge domed tomb located about 300 yards downhill from the main site (along the main road). A handful of other ruins and tombs are scattered around the area, but stick to these three to start your visit.

Note that some of the ruins (confusingly) have different names—for example, the Treasury of Atreus is also known as the Tomb of Agamemnon.

• *Buy your ticket for the archaeological site and enter, climbing the ramp up the acropolis.*

MYCENAE

Archaeological Site

• *You'll enter the fortified complex through the...*

❶ Lion Gate and Wall

The grand Lion Gate (c. 1300 B.C.) guards the entrance to this fortress city on a hill. Above the doorway, two lionesses flank a column, symbolically protecting it the way the Mycenaean kings once protected the city. The lions' missing heads may have once turned outward, greeting visitors. The heads were made of stone or possibly of gold (anything made of a precious material like that would have been plundered long ago).

The lions form a triangle above the massive lintel (the crossbeam above the door). Mycenaean architects used the weak corbelled arch, less sturdy than the rounded Roman arch developed later. A simple horizontal stone spans the door, while heavy stones above it inch in to bridge the gap. The lintel is slightly arched to distribute the weight to the sides and add to its strength.

Apart from its rather fragile technology, Mycenaean architecture is really massive. The lintel weighs 18 tons—as much as a WWII B-17 bomber. The exterior walls that girdle the base of the hill (c. 1300 B.C.) were about 40 feet high, 20 feet thick, and 3,000 feet long. They were built with an estimated 14,000 boulders weighing 5 to 10 tons each. Marveling at the enormous scale, classical-era Greeks figured the legendary Perseus (who slew the Medusa) must have built the city with the help of the giant one-eyed Cyclopes, and dubbed the style "cyclopean." In reality, the Mycenaeans probably lifted these big stones into place the same way the Egyptians built the pyramids—by building ramps and rolling the stones up on logs drawn by oxen or horses.

Pass through the gate. Carved into the stone are **post-holes** that held the wooden door. Just as you emerge, look left to see a square **niche** in the wall—this could have been a small shrine where statues of the gods who guarded the gates were displayed, or just a simple closet. Poke your head in to study the stonework.

• *Head up the ramp. About 30 yards ahead, you'll see (below and on the right) a circular wall that encloses rectangular graves. Walk a bit higher up the path and look down for the best view.*

Mycenae

25 Meters
25 Yards

UNDERGROUND CISTERN

EASTERN SPUR

⑥ Escape Route Door

⑦ Cistern Entrance

⑧ NORTH GATE

RAMPARTS

⑤ Houses & Storerooms Ruins

TOP OF THE ACROPOLIS

④ Top of the Acropolis

③ Royal Palace & Throne Room

THRONE ROOM

ROYAL PALACE

MUSEUM

⑨

TOUR ENDS

GRAVE CIRCLE A

②

① LION GATE

RAMPARTS

GIFT SHOP

WC

THOLOS TOMB OF AEGISTHUS

THOLOS TOMB OF CLYTEMNESTRA

TICKETS

👣 TOUR BEGINS

GRAVE CIRCLE B

To ⑩

🅿

① Lion Gate & Wall	⑥ Escape Route Door
② Grave Circle A	⑦ Cistern Entrance
③ Royal Palace & Throne Room	⑧ North Gate
④ Top of the Acropolis	⑨ Museum
⑤ Houses & Storerooms Ruins	⑩ To Treasury of Atreus

MYCENAE

❷ Grave Circle A (c. 1550 B.C.)

Judging from what was dug up in this round cluster of graves, Mycenaean royalty were buried here. The rectangular holes are called shaft graves, which were cut into the rock up to 20 feet deep. There are six such shaft graves here, each of which contained several bodies (19 total—9 women, 8 men, and 2 children). The bodies were found embalmed and lying on their backs along with their most precious belongings, with their heads facing east—toward

the rising sun—indicating a belief in an afterlife. Gravestones atop the graves (like the one displayed in the museum) were decorated with a spiral, possibly a symbol of continuous existence.

In 1876 these graves were unearthed by the famed German archaeologist Heinrich Schliemann. Schliemann had recently discovered the long-lost city of Troy, finally giving some historical credibility to Homer's tales. He next turned his attention to Mycenae, the legendary home of Agamemnon. In Grave Circle A, he found a treasure trove of gold swords, spears, engraved cups, and ritual objects buried with the dead—30 pounds in all, confirming Homer's description of Mycenae as a city "rich in gold."

The prize discovery was a gold mask showing the face of a bearded man. Masks like this were tied onto the faces of the deceased. This one was obviously for an important warrior chieftain. Schliemann was convinced the mask proved that Homer's tales of the Trojan War were true, and he dubbed it the "Mask of Agamemnon." This mask and other artifacts are now in the National Archaeological Museum in Athens.

Could it really be the Mask of Agamemnon? No. Not only is it unlikely that Agamemnon ever really existed, but the mask is from the 16th century B.C.—at least 300 years before the legendary king supposedly burned Troy.

The Mycenaeans practiced several different types of burial: interred in a pit (for the poorest), encased in a ceramic jar called a cist grave (for wealthier folks), laid in a shaft grave (for royalty), or placed in an elaborate domed chamber called a *tholos* (like the Treasury of Atreus, which we'll visit at the end of this tour).

• *Continue to climb up the paths, zigzagging past the ruins of former houses and shops, to the top of the acropolis. On the right, below you, are the rectangular foundations of the former...*

MYCENAE

Mycenae and Troy: Fact or Fiction?

Several sites at Mycenae bear legendary names—"Agamemnon's Palace," the "Tomb of Clytemnestra," the "Tomb of Agamemnon," and so on. Although these names are fanciful with no basis in fact, real-life Mycenae does sound eerily similar to the legends found in writings attributed to the poet Homer (c. 850 B.C.) and other ancient scribes.

The tales of the Trojan War are set during the time when the Mycenaeans dominated the Greek world and had the power to conquer Troy. They tell of the abduction of the beautiful Helen (who had "the face that launched a thousand ships") by Paris, a prince of Troy. Outraged at the loss of his bride, Menelaus, king of Sparta, convinced his brother Agamemnon, king of Mycenae, to lead the Greeks in an attack on Troy. But the winds were not favorable for launching the fleet. An oracle told Agamemnon that he had to sacrifice his daughter to get underway, so he lied to his wife, Clytemnestra, and ordered the priests to kill their daughter.

After the sacrifice, the Greek ships finally made it to Troy. When a long siege failed to defeat the Trojans, Odysseus suggested tricking the enemy by building a wooden idol (the famous "Trojan horse"), leaving it outside the city walls, and pretending to withdraw. The Trojans took the bait, brought the horse inside, and were met with an unpleasant surprise: The greatest warriors of Greece emerging from inside the horse to complete the conquest of Troy. The famous heroes of the Trojan War include Achilles and Ajax on the Greek side, and Paris' brother Hector—all of whom died by the war's end.

Homer's *Odyssey* tells of the homeward journey of Odysseus, who survived the war, only to wander for 10 years, thwarted by the god Poseidon, before finally reaching home. Agamemnon's fate is also told in the epic. After sacking Troy, Agamemnon returned to Mycenae with his Trojan concubine, where he was murdered by his wife (who was still brooding over her daughter's sacrifice and not very happy about the new competition). Not that Clytemnestra was a dutiful spouse—her new lover helped her murder Agamemnon and the concubine.

Metaphorically, Agamemnon's tragic story matches that of the historical Mycenaeans—no sooner had they returned home victorious from Troy than their own homes were destroyed. These legends of ancient Mycenae were passed down through oral tradition for centuries until, long after the fall of both Troy and Mycenae, they were preserved for posterity in Homer's *Iliad* and *Odyssey* as well as other ancient epics.

❸ Royal Palace and Throne Room (Megaron)

Kings ruled the Mycenaeans from this palace, which consisted of a line of several rectangular rooms (about all that remains today are the outlines of the rooms).

Imagine entering the palace and walking through a series of rooms. You'd start in an open-air courtyard—that's the biggest rectangle to the far right (west, toward the parking lot). Then you'd enter the palace itself, passing between two columns (see the remaining bases) onto a covered porch. Next, at the far end of the porch, was a small anteroom. Finally, you'd spill into the main hall—the throne room—at the east end. This great hall, or *megaron*, contains the outlines of a round hearth, which is where a fire burned. Here you could make burnt offerings to the gods. The four remaining bases around the hearth once held four inverted columns that supported the roof, which had a sunroof-type hole to let out the smoke. Against the wall to the right (the south wall) sat the king on his throne—the very center of power of the Mycenaean empire. The walls and floors were brightly painted with a pattern of linked spirals.

The same type of palace was found in every Mycenaean city, and later became the standard layout of the Greek temple—courtyard, colonnaded porch, small room *(pronaos)*, and main hall with its sacred *cella* area toward the back, where only the priest could go.

• *While we're on the top of the acropolis, check out the view and imagine the city/fortress at its peak. Facing the distant bay, find the Acropolis of Argos in the distance, and imagine the torches and bronze plates once used to reflect and flash messages across long distances.*

❹ The Top of the Acropolis: Mycenae the Fortress-City

Mycenae was a combination citadel, palace, residence, and administrative capital of the extended empire of Mycenaean cities. But first and foremost, it was a fortress, occupying a superb natural defensive position guarding a major crossroads in Greece. The hill is flanked by steep ravines. To the south there are spacious views across the fertile plains of Argos to the Argolic Gulf, giving the inhabitants ample time to prepare for any attack by sea. The cone-shaped hill in the dis-

tance ringed with walls near the top was the fortress of Argos. The port of Mycenae controlled trade on the road from Corinth to Nafplio, and sea trade from Nafplio to points beyond.

In case of siege, Mycenae could rely on natural springs located on the mountainside to the east (away from the entrance—near the eucalyptus trees, a little above acropolis level, with a patch of exposed reddish hillside behind it). The water was channeled through clay pipes underground to a cistern dug inside the acropolis.

Though Mycenae was fundamentally a fortress, up to 60,000 people lived here.

• *Work your way eastward (farther away from the entrance, and a bit downhill), noticing natural defenses provided by cliffs on the right, before descending to...*

The Cistern and Other Sights at the East End

The ruins at this end were once mostly ❺ **houses and storerooms.** At the far eastern end, notice the doorway in the wall (now covered with a gate). This was ❻ an **escape route** out the back.

Find the gaping cave-like opening of the ❼ **cistern,** where 99 (slippery!) steps lead 50 feet down. Peering inside, you can see...absolutely nothing, unless you've packed a flashlight. The cistern stored water from springs within the hillside, in case of siege or drought.

• *Head back toward the entrance—but bear to the right, following the north (outer) wall. Look for a gate on the right.*

This ❽ **North Gate,** smaller than the Lion Gate, has a similar rectangular crossbeam shape and heavy lintel. The wooden door is a reconstruction similar to the original, fit into the original holes cut in the lintel stone. Next to the North Gate is a niche in the wall (similar to the one at the Lion Gate) to display guardian gods.

• *Exit through the North Gate, and bear left/downhill along the serpentine path to the **museum**, the modern building on the hillside below.*

❾ Museum

Whereas the ruins give a sense of the engineering sophistication of these people, the museum emphasizes their artistic, religious, literary, and cultural sides. You'll see various funeral objects from the graves, plus everyday objects that show influences from the Egyptian, Minoan, and Hittite cultures.

• Follow the one-way, counterclockwise route through the collection, beginning in the...

Entrance Hall

The model of the Mycenae acropolis in the center of the room helps you visualize the city as it once was. Otherwise, the information posted here is pretty dull (on one side, a description of myths relating to this city; on the other, a dry history of the excavation).

• From the entrance hall, move into the next room, where you'll find...

Religious Symbols

This room shows off religious items found in temples. Snakes were believed to have sacred connections and were used for bridging the worlds of the living and the dead. The mysterious two-foot-tall figurines were likely used by priests in rituals to scare away evil. Pottery items found in homes were simply practical in an age without plastic storage. Notice the well-preserved elegant designs and colors that were baked into the clay.

• Descend to the lower level to see...

Funeral Objects

This room is filled with items found in tombs from about 1500 B.C. In the octagonal case, you'll see reproductions of the famous

Mask of Agamemnon and other golden items (such as crowns and medallions). These objects were discovered here in graves. (The originals are now in Athens' National Archaeological Museum.) On the wall behind the mask is a highly decorated funeral *stele* (gravestone) from Grave Circle B.

Diagrams below the artifacts show where each object on display was found in relation to the skeleton of the deceased. Back then, you *could* take it with you. Those with the means were sure to pack along jewelry, tools, kitchen utensils, even children's toys and sippy cups.

The miniature furniture was necessary for packing light. Tiny figurines may have represented the Goddess Earth. Notice the small baby coffin (a clay box with a lid, immediately left of the entry door).

• As you continue into the next room, notice (on your left) a big clay urn used as a coffin for burial, with a band of spiral designs across the middle.

Many funeral objects (such as this urn) were engraved with a spiral pattern—possibly a symbol of the never-ending path of life.

Mycenaean Writing and Everyday Objects

In the case at the end of the room's partition are fragments of clay tablets inscribed in the Mycenaean written language known to scholars as Linear B. Each character represented a syllable. These fragments concern distinct subjects, including "Religion," "Lists of Names," "Products," inventories, and so on. Very few written documents survived from the Mycenaean era—no literature or history or stories—so we know very little of the Mycenaeans' inner thoughts.

On the other side of the partition, a glass case displays sealstones, used to put a person's mark in wax or clay on a sealed document or box, to ensure it reached the intended recipient unopened. The Mycenaeans led an active trading life, and every businessman would have had one of these. The red one on top, in the center (#14), has the symbol from the Lion Gate on it.

To the left a large map shows the vast Mycenaean trading world. The Mycenaeans were seafarers, bringing back gold from Egypt, lapis lazuli from Afghanistan, amber from Scandinavia, ivory from Syria, jewelry from Spain, and more. Near the door, the display on "Women of the Mycenaean World" makes it clear they had plenty of toiletry and jewelry items: combs, tweezers, mirrors, beads, pendants, and so on.

• *Leaving the museum, climb the long stairway back up to the parking lot. (Just below the WC next to the museum, on your right, is the broken but interesting* **Tholos Tomb of the Lions**.) *At the parking lot, continue to the last area, one of the highlights of Mycenae: the tomb known as the* **Treasury of Atreus**. *It's located about 300 yards south of the ruins, along the road back toward the modern town of Mycenae. You can walk there in less than 10 minutes. Or, if you have a car, stop at the Treasury on your way out of the site—there's a small parking lot there. Follow the crowds gradually uphill from the parking lot, and show your entry ticket once more to get to the...*

⑩ Treasury of Atreus (a.k.a. Tomb of Agamemnon, 13th century B.C.)

Mycenae's royalty were buried in massive beehive-shaped underground chambers called *tholoi*, which replaced shaft graves (like the ones at Grave Circle A) beginning in the 15th century B.C.

The entryway to this *tholos* itself is on a grand "cyclopean" scale—110 feet long and 20 feet wide. Imagine entering in a funeral

procession carrying the body of the king. The walls rise at a diagonal up to the entrance, giving the illusion of swallowing you up as you enter.

The lintel over the doorway is mind-bogglingly big—26 feet across by 16 feet by 3 feet—and weighs 120 tons. (For comparison, the biggest stones of the Egyptian pyramids were 30 tons.) Notice before entering the hints of doorway hinges and ornamental pillars that once stood here.

Step inside and hear the 3,300-year-old echoes of this domed room. The round chamber is 47 feet in diameter and 42 feet tall,

with an igloo-style dome made of 33 rings of corbelled (gradually projecting) stones, each weighing about 5 tons. The dome was decorated with bronze ornaments (you can see a few small nail holes where they were attached in the fifth row of stones up). The soot on the dome is from the campfires of fairly recent shepherds.

Kings were elaborately buried in the center of the room along with their swords, jewels, and personal possessions. There is also a side chamber (the door to the right) whose purpose can only be guessed at. After the funeral was over, the whole structure was covered with a mountain of dirt. But grave robbers got in anyway, and modern archaeologists have not found any bodies or treasures.

So why didn't the dome collapse? The weight of the dome is distributed by two triangular niches—one over the main lintel, and one over the side doorway. Notice how the lintel has a crack in it. That crack is to the side of the doorway, right where the triangular niche spills all the weight of the dome onto it. Without this arch, the lintel would have cracked in the center and the dome would have collapsed. Look carefully at the smaller triangle above the smaller arch to find its little crack (on the left). Again, without the arch, the weight over the door would have caused the lintel to break—and you wouldn't be standing here marveling at 3,300-year-old Mycenaean engineering.

• *Our tour's over. While only about 10 percent of the site has been excavated, I've Mycenae-n enough.*

OLYMPIA

ΑΡΧΑΊΑ ΟΛΥΜΠΊΑ / Αρχαία Ολυμπία

A visit to Olympia—most famous as the site of the original Olympic Games—offers one of your best opportunities for a hands-on experience with antiquity. Take your mark at the original starting line in the 2,500-year-old Olympic Stadium. Visit the Temple of Zeus, former site of a gigantic statue of Zeus that was one of the Seven Wonders of the Ancient World. Ponder the temple's once-majestic columns—toppled like towers of checkers by an earthquake—which are as evocative as anything from ancient times. Take a close look at the Archaeological Museum's gold-medal-quality statues and artifacts. And don't forget to step back and enjoy the setting itself. Despite the crowds that pour through here, Olympia remains a magical place, with ruins nestled among lush, shady groves of pine trees.

The modern-day town of Olympia (pop. 11,000) is far less inspiring—a concrete community custom-built to cater to the needs of the thousands of tourists who flock here year-round to visit the site. For convenience while sightseeing, you might want to spend one night in town; more time isn't necessary (though limited bus connections might require a two-night stay). While not romantic, Olympia is tidy, straightforward, functional, and pleasant enough.

Orientation to Olympia

The Sanctuary of Olympia sits in the fertile valley of the Alphios River in the western Peloponnese, nine miles southeast of the regional capital of Pyrgos. The archaeological site curves along the southeastern edge of the tidy modern village of Archaia (Ancient) Olympia. The town's layout is basically a low-lying, easy-to-manage grid, five streets wide by eight streets long. The main road (called Praxitelous Kondyli) runs from Pyrgos in the north and leads right into a parking lot (and bus stop) at the south end of town. From here the museum and site are due east, over the Kladeos River.

Tourist Information: There's no TI, but your hotelier should be able to answer most questions. For current hours of the main sights, you can check local guide Niki Vlachou's **Olympia Travel Guide,** which contains updated information on sights—opening times, entry fees, discounts, etc.—and a detailed interactive map of the area (www.olympiatravelguide.com).

ARRIVAL IN OLYMPIA

By Bus: The bus drops you off just before the retail strip on the main street, a quick walk from the well-signed sights.

By Car: For driving directions into and out of Olympia, see "Route Tips for Drivers" on page 286. Parking is free and easy. It's fine to park on the streets in town. The best parking lots are near the Archaeological Museum, behind the main road next to the train station (see map on next page). Avoid the bus lot near the Museum of the History of the Olympic Games in Antiquity, where you may get a ticket.

By Cruise Ship: For options on reaching Olympia from the cruise-ship port of Katakolo, see page 285.

HELPFUL HINTS

Services: Olympia's main street has wide sidewalks, countless gift shops, and ample hotels, eateries, minimarkets, ATMs, and other tourist services.

Taxis: There's a taxi stand in town a block off the main street on the shady, angled side street called Georgiou Douma (tel. 26240-22555).

Local Guide: Consider hiring fantastic **Niki Vlachou** to show you around Olympia's ruins and museums (reasonable and negotiable rates, contact for exact price; also arranges transportation, wine tastings, olive press visits, cooking classes, and meals in local homes; mobile 697-242-6085, www.olympictours.gr, niki@olympictours.gr).

Don't count on finding a local guide to hire once you arrive—unlike many other popular ancient sites, the Sanctuary of Olympia is not surrounded by hopeful guides-for-hire.

Sights in Olympia

There are three parts to an Olympia visit: The Sanctuary of Olympia archaeological site, the Archaeological Museum, and the smaller Museum of the History of the Olympic Games in Antiquity (with the tiny adjacent Museum of the History of Excavations).

OLYMPIA

Olympia Town

To Pyrgos,
Katakolo (Cruise Port),
Patra & Athens

200 Meters
200 Yards

To Flokas,
Kalamata
& ⑩

MUSEUM
OF MODERN
OLYMPIC GAMES
(CLOSED)

BARELA

TSOUREKA

To
Pyrgos
Ⓑ

TRAIN
STATION

AVGERINOU

AP. KOSMOPOULOU

SPILIOTOPOULOU

① ⑤

③

⑧
②
STEFANOPOULOU

KONDYLI (MAIN STREET)

⑨

Ⓣ

GEORGIOU DOUMA

⑦

Ⓟ

④

MODERN
TOWN

PRAXITELOUS

AEMILIOU KOUNTSE

Ⓟ

ARCHIMEDES
MUSEUM

POST

PIER DE COUBETAIN

BUS STOP
Ⓑ From Pyrgos

KOSMOPOULOU CHAR.

Kladeos River

ARCHAEO-
LOGICAL
MUSEUM

Ⓟ

WC

MUSEUM OF THE
HISTORY OF
EXCAVATIONS

MUSEUM OF THE
HISTORY OF THE
OLYMPIC GAMES
IN ANTIQUITY

CAFÉ

TICKETS

To Miraka
& ⑥

ENTRANCE
GATE

SACRED
WAY

SANCTUARY
OF
OLYMPIA

① Hotel Pelops
② Neda Hotel
③ Kronio Hotel
④ Pension Posidon
⑤ Hotel Inomaos
⑥ To Bacchus Tavern/Rooms
⑦ Aegean Restaurant
⑧ Anesi Restaurant
⑨ Homemade Pies
⑩ To Europa Hotel/Restaurant
& Taverna Thea

▲▲▲THE SANCTUARY OF OLYMPIA AND ARCHAEOLOGICAL MUSEUM

Olympia was the mecca of ancient Greek religion—the location of its greatest sanctuary and one of its most important places of worship. In those times, people didn't live here: The sanctuary was set aside as a monastery and pilgrimage site; the nearest city was 30 miles away. Ancient Greeks came here only every four years, during the religious festival that featured the Olympic Games. The heart of the sanctuary was a sacred enclosure called the Altis—a walled-off, rectangular area that housed two big temples, multiple altars, and statues to the gods.

Whereas Delphi served as a pilgrimage destination mostly for groups of wealthy men on a particular mission, every four years Olympia drew 40,000 ordinary dudes (men only) for a Panhellenic party: the Olympic Games.

Cost: A €12 combo-ticket covers both the site and museum (€6 off-season). Entry is free for ages 18 and under (be prepared to show ID).

Hours: Generally daily April-Aug 8:00-20:00, Sept 8:00-19:00, Oct 8:00-18:00, and Nov-March 8:30-15:00. Schedules vary by season and can change without warning, so confirm these times locally—either with your hotelier or at signs outside the sights. Recommended local guide Niki Vlachou maintains www.olympiatravelguide.com with up-to-date hours, and will answer questions free of charge (see listing under "Helpful Hints," earlier).

Getting There: If staying in Olympia, it's an easy five-minute **walk** from the town center to either the site or the Archaeological Museum. If arriving by **car,** park for free near the Archaeological Museum at one of two small lots at the east edge of town, south of the train station (see map on page 257; do not park near the site where the tour buses park, as you may get a ticket). To reach the museum and site from the parking lots, follow the path away from town, walking several hundred yards and crossing the Kladeos River. Up the stairs is the museum. For the site, take the path opposite the museum entry and walk another five minutes.

Information: The kiosk next to the site ticket booth sells guidebooks to the site and museum for €9. Tel. 26240-22742, www.culture.gr.

Planning Your Time: I recommend walking the archaeological site first, then touring the Archaeological Museum to reconstruct what you've seen. If you're passing the Archaeological Museum en route to the site anyway, buy your combo-ticket at the museum and stop in to see the site model in the entryway (described on page 274), which will spark your imagination as you stroll the site. Allow 1.5 hours for the site, and an hour for the Archaeological Museum.

Try to visit in the early morning or late afternoon (though the site can be very hot in the afternoon). These sights are most crowded between 10:00 and 13:00 (especially the Archaeological Museum). Off-season, it's best to visit the site and museum in the morning, in case they close at 15:00.

If coming into Olympia late in the day, you can use your museum/site combo-ticket to tour one place in the late afternoon and the other the next morning (one entry per place).

If you have all day for sightseeing, first hit the small Museum of the History of the Olympic Games in Antiquity (described on page 280), which provides background on the ancient games that'll help enliven your visit to the site (allow about a half-hour for this museum).

Services: The site has WCs just inside the entrance and near the far end of the Sacred Way. No food is allowed inside the site, though you can (and should) bring a water bottle. An open-air café is located between the site and the museum. The museum has a shop, WCs, and a café (outside, to the right as you face the entrance).

Sanctuary of Olympia (The Site)

This center of ancient Greek religion dedicated to Zeus hosted the Olympic Games for more than a thousand years (c. 776 B.C.-A.D. 393). As you wander among these sporting arenas, temples, and statues, contemplate how the 100-meter dash was much more than a mere running race to the people of this civilization: It was a spiritual exercise that expressed the most cherished values of Western civilization.

❍ Self-Guided Tour

Buy your tickets at the site entrance, then head through the gate. Walk straight ahead, passing WCs on the right, then bear left with the path (passing an orientation board), which leads you down into the ancient world of Olympia. This main path is called the Sacred Way. (Note that the main entry may have shifted about 30 yards to the left by the time you visit; wherever you enter, make your way to this spot along the Sacred Way.)

• *Look to your left (through the trees) to catch glimpses of...*

❶ Kronos Hill

This hill was sacred to the ancient Greeks, who believed it to be the birthplace of Zeus—and the place where as a clever baby he escaped his father, Kronos, who'd tried to eat him. Zeus later overthrew Kronos and went on to lead the pantheon of

Sanctuary of Olympia

1 View of Kronos Hill
2 Gymnasium
3 Palaestra
4 Workshop of Pheidias
5 Temple of Zeus
6 Bouleuterion
7 Pedestal of Nike
8 Winner's Circle
9 Bases of Zanes & Row of Treasuries
10 Krypti
11 Stadium & Finish Line
12 Metroon
13 Nymphaeum
14 Altar of Hera
15 Temple of Hera
16 Philippeion

Kronos Hill

STARTING BLOCKS

ALTAR

STADIUM

JUDGES' BOX

12 9 10 11

HIPPODROME

gods. (Other versions of the myth place this event on Mt. Olympus, in northern Greece, where the gods eventually made their home.) The hill was scorched by devastating wildfires in August 2007—imagine how close the flames came to enveloping this ancient site. Locals replanted the hill, and it's once again green.

• *The Sacred Way leads down into a wide field scattered with ruins. To the left of the path was an enclosed area filled with various temples and altars; to the right were buildings for the athletes, who trained and lived in a complex of buildings similar to today's Olympic Village.*

Head to the right along the small path just before the two long rows of stubby columns. They mark the eastern edge of what was once the...

❷ Gymnasium

This was the largest building in the whole sanctuary, built in the fourth century B.C. The truncated Doric columns once supported a covered arcade, one of four arcades that surrounded a big rectangular courtyard. Here athletes trained for events such as the sprint, discus throw, and javelin throw. The courtyard (about the size of six football fields, side-by-side along the Sacred Way) matched the length of the Olympic Stadium, so athletes could practice in a space similar to the one in which they would compete.

Because ancient Greeks believed that training the body was as important as training the mind, sports were a big part of every boy's education. Moreover, athletic training doubled as military training (a key element in citizenship)—so most towns had a gymnasium. The word "gymnasium" comes from the Greek *gymnos* ("naked"), which is how athletes trained and competed. Even today, the term "gymnasium" is used in many European countries (including Greece) to describe what Americans call high school.

Athletes arrived in a nearby town a month early for the Games, in order to practice and size up the competition. The Games were open to any free-born Greek male (men and boys competed separately), but a good share of competitors were from aristocratic homes. Athletes trained hard. Beginning in childhood, they were given special diets and training regimens, often subsidized by their city. Many became professionals, touring the circuit of major festivals.

• *At the far end of the gymnasium ruins, stairs lead to a square space ringed by twin rows of taller, more intact columns. This is the...*

The Ancient Olympic Games

The Olympic Games were athletic contests held every four years as a way of honoring Zeus, the king of the gods. They were the culmination of a pilgrimage, as Greeks gathered to worship Zeus, the Games' patron.

The exact origins of the Games are lost in the mists of time, but they likely grew from a local religious festival first held at the Sanctuary of Olympia in about 1150 B.C. According to one legend, the festival was founded by Pelops, namesake of the Peloponnese; a rival legend credits Hercules. Sporting events became part of the festivities. A harmonious, healthy body was a "temple" that celebrated its creator by performing at its peak.

The first Olympic Games at which results were recorded are traditionally dated at 776 B.C. The Games grew rapidly, attracting athletes from throughout the Greek world to compete in an ever-growing number of events (eventually taking up to five days in all). They reached their height of popularity around 400 B.C. Of the four major Greek games (including those at Delphi—see page 350—Corinth, and Nemea), Olympia was the first, biggest, and most prestigious.

Besides honoring Zeus and providing entertainment, the Games served a political purpose: to develop a Panhellenic ("all-Greek") identity among scattered city-states and far-flung colonies. Every four years, wars between bickering Greeks were halted with a one-month "sacred truce" so that athletes and fans could travel safely to Olympia. Leading citizens from all corners would assemble here, including many second- and third-generation Greeks who'd grown up in colonies in Italy, France, or Africa. Olympia was geographically central, and for the length of the festivities, it was the symbolic heart of Greece.

This went on for 1,169 years, finally concluding in A.D. 393. Olympia today lives on in the spirit of the modern Olympic Games, revived in Athens in 1896. Every other year, athletes from around the world gather and compete in contests that challenge the human spirit and, it's hoped, foster a sense of common experience. Whether we're cheering on an American swimmer, a Chinese gymnast, or a Jamaican sprinter to go faster, longer, and better than any human has before, the Games bring the world together for a few weeks, much as they united the Greek world in this tranquil pine grove so many centuries ago.

❸ *Palaestra*

Adjoining the gymnasium was this smaller but similar "wrestling school" (built around 300 B.C.). This square courtyard (216 feet on each side—about one acre), also surrounded by arcades, was used by athletes to train for smaller-scale events: wrestling, boxing, long jump (performed while carrying weights, to build strength), and *pankration,* a kind of ancient "ultimate fighting" with only two rules: no biting and no eye-gouging.

Picture athletes in the courtyard working out. They were always naked, except for a layer of olive oil and dust for a bit of protection against scrapes and the sun. Sometimes they exercised in time with a flute player to coordinate their movements and to keep up the pace. Trainers and spectators could watch from the shade of the colonnades. Notice that the columns are smooth (missing their fluting) on the lower part of the inside face. This way, when it rained, athletes could ex-

ercise under the arcade (or take a breather by leaning up against a column) without scraping themselves on the grooves.

In the area nearest the Sacred Way, notice the benches where athletes were taught and people gathered for conversation. You can still see the bathtubs that athletes used to wash off their oil-dust coating. (They also used a stick-like tool to scrape off the oily grime.)

Besides being training facilities, *palaestrae* (found in almost every city) were also a kind of health club where men gathered to chat.

• *Exit the* palaestra *on the left to continue down the Sacred Way, then take the next right. Climb the stairs at the far end, and peek into the ruined brick building that was once the...*

❹ Workshop of Pheidias

In this building, the great sculptor Pheidias (c. 490-430 B.C.) created the 40-foot statue of Zeus (c. 435 B.C.) that once stood in the Temple of Zeus across the street (for details on how he constructed it, see the sidebar on page 266). The workshop was built with the same dimensions as the temple's *cella* (inner room) so that Pheidias could create the statue with the setting in mind. Pheidias arrived here having recently completed his other masterpiece, the colossal *Athena Parthenos* for the Parthenon in Athens (see page 106). According to ancient accounts, his colossal Zeus outdid even that great work.

How do we know this building was Pheidias' place? Because archaeologists found sculptors' tools and molds for pouring metals, as well as a cup with Pheidias' name on it (all now displayed in the museum). After the last ancient Games were held, this workshop was turned into a Christian church (fourth century A.D.—notice the semicircular part at the end facing east, which was added as an altar; see "Olympia's Legacy" on page 274).

• Head right out of the workshop, then loop back around to the left, past a large, open, rubble-strewn field (to the right) with dozens of thigh-high

Ionic capitals. This was the site of the massive **Leonidaion**, *a luxury, four-star hotel with 145 rooms (and private baths) built in the fourth century B.C. to house dignitaries and famous athletes during the Games.*

Cross the Sacred Way, then head left up the ramp/stairs toward Olympia's main sight: the ruins of the Temple of Zeus, marked by a single standing column.

❺ Temple of Zeus

The center of ancient Olympia—both physically and symbolically—was the massive temple dedicated to Zeus, king of the gods and patron of the Games. It was the first of the Golden Age temples, one of the biggest (not much smaller than the Parthenon), and is the purest example of the Doric style.

The temple was built in the fifth century B.C. (470-455 B.C.), stood for a thousand years, and then crumbled into the evocative pile of ruins we see today, still lying where they fell in the sixth century A.D.

Step into the rubble field in front of the temple, walking between big gray blocks, two-

Statue of Zeus

Imagine yourself as a visitor to the Temple of Zeus in ancient times. You'd enter the temple from the east end (the end opposite the Sacred Way). Peering to the far side of the temple, you'd see the monumental statue of Zeus sitting 40 feet high on a golden throne. The statue gleamed gold and white, with colored highlights. In his right hand Zeus held a winged statue of Nike (goddess of victory), and in his left hand was a scepter topped with an eagle. Zeus completely filled the space. His head almost touched the ceiling (which was higher than the exterior columns), and his arms almost touched the sides, making the colossal statue appear even bigger. A cistern of olive oil on the temple floor reflected golden hues onto the statue.

Pheidias made the statue with a core of wood. He covered that with plates of ivory (soaked, carved, and worked into shape) to make Zeus' skin and 500 pounds of gold plates for the clothes and the throne. (Such statues, when decorated with gold and ivory—as many religious statues in ancient Greece were—are called "chryselephantine.") Pheidias' assistants painted the throne with scenes of the gods.

The statue was considered by ancient people as one of the Seven Wonders—a list of tourist musts that also included the Colossus of Rhodes and the pyramids of Egypt. We know the general outlines of the statue because it appeared on coins of the day.

We also know that the statue stood for 900 years, but no one knows what became of it. It may have been melted down by Christians or destroyed in the earthquakes that toppled the temple. Others think the pieces were carried off to Constantinople and accidentally burned in that city's catastrophic fire of A.D. 476.

ton column drums, and fallen 12-ton capitals. They're made not of marble but of cheaper local limestone. Look closely and you can see the seashell fossils in this porous (and not terribly durable) sedimentary rock. Most of the temple was made of limestone, then covered with a marble-powder stucco to make it glisten as brightly as if it were made of pure marble. The pediments and some other decorations were made of expensive white marble from the isle of Paros.

An olive tree near the temple's southwest corner (to your left) marks the spot of the original tree (planted by Hercules, legends say) from which the winners' wreaths were made. Then as now, olives were vital to Greece, providing food, preservatives, fuel, perfumes...and lubrication for athletes.

You're standing near the back (west) end of the temple, near its most sacred part: The *cella*, where Pheidias' statue of Zeus stood. The interior of the temple is closed indefinitely; to get a good look you'll have to head back to the path that runs along what was once the south porch of the temple—the side facing away from Kronos Hill.

As you walk around the temple, try to reconstruct it in your mind. It was huge—about half an acre—and stood six stories tall. The lone standing column is actually a reconstruction (of original pieces, cleaned and restacked), but it gives you a sense of the scale: It's 34 feet tall, 7 feet thick, and weighs 9 tons. This was one of 34 massive Doric columns that sur-

rounded the temple: 6 on each end and 13 along the sides (making this a typical peripteral/peristyle temple, like Athens' Parthenon and Temple of Hephaistos in the Ancient Agora).

The columns originally supported a triangular pediment at each end (now in the Archaeological Museum), carved with scenes of the battle of the Lapiths and centaurs (west end) and Pelops and the chariot race (east end, which was the main entrance).

Along the south side of the temple, you'll see five huge fallen columns, with their drums lined up in a row like dominos. To the right of the path are the ruins of the ❻ **Bouleuterion,** the council chamber where, by stepping on castrated bulls' balls, athletes took

an oath not to cheat. As this was a religious event, and because physical training was a part of moral education, the oaths and personal honor were held sacred.

Continue down the path to the front (east) end of the temple and duck off the path to the left to find the 29-foot-tall, white-marble, triangular ❼ **Pedestal of Nike.** It's missing its top, but it once held a famous statue (now in the museum) of the goddess Nike, the personification of victory.

She looked down upon the ❽ **Winner's Circle,** here at the main entrance to the temple, where Olympic victors were announced and crowned. As thousands gathered in the courtyard below, priests called the name of the winner, who scaled the steps to the cheers of the crowd. The winner was crowned with a wreath of olive (not laurel) branches, awarded a statue in his honor—and nothing more. There were no awards for second and third place and no gold, silver, or bronze medals—those are inventions of the modern Olympics. However, winners were usually showered with gifts and perks from their proud hometowns: free food for life, tax exemptions, theater tickets, naming rights for gymnasiums, statues, pictures on ancient Wheaties boxes, and so on.

In the courtyard you can see pedestals that once held statues of winners, who were considered to be demigods. The inscriptions listed the winner's name, the date, the event won, his hometown, and the names of his proud parents.

The ruined building directly east of here was the Echo Hall, a long gallery where winners were also announced as if into a microphone—the sound echoed seven times.

• *With the main entrance of the Temple of Zeus at your back, walk out to the path, passing several of the inscribed pedestals. Turn left at the tree, then follow the right fork until you bump into the low wall at the base of Kronos Hill. The foot of that hill is lined with a row of pedestals, called the...*

❾ Bases of Zanes and Row of Treasuries

These 16 pedestals once held bronze statues of Zeus (plural "Zanes"). At the ancient Olympic Games, as at the modern ones,

it was an honor just to compete, and there was no shame in not finishing first. Quitters and cheaters were another story. The Zeus statues that once lined this path were paid for with fines levied on cheaters, whose names and ill deeds were inscribed in the bases. As people entered the stadium (straight ahead), they'd spit on the names on the bases. Offenses ranged from doping (using forbidden herbs) or bribing opponents, to failing to train in advance of the Games or quitting out of cowardice. Drinking animal blood—the Red Bull of the day—was forbidden. Official urine tasters tested for this ancient equivalent of steroids.

Just behind the statues (and a few feet higher in elevation) is a terrace that once held a row of treasuries. These small buildings housed expensive offerings to the gods. Many were sponsored by colonies as a way for Greeks living abroad to stay in touch with their cultural roots.

• *Turn right and pass under the arch of the...*

❿ Krypti

As you enter the stadium through this tunnel, imagine yourself as an athlete who has trained for years and traveled for days, car-

rying the hopes of your hometown on your shoulders...and now finally about to compete. Built around 300 B.C., this tunnel once had a vaulted ceiling; along the walls are niches that functioned as equipment lockers. Just like today's NFL players, Olympia's athletes psyched themselves up for the big contest by shouting as they ran through this tunnel, then emerging into the stadium to the roar of the crowd.

• *On your mark, get set, go. Follow the Krypti as it leads into the...*

⓫ Stadium

Line up on that original marble-paved starting line from the ancient Olympic Games and imagine the scene. The place was filled

with 45,000 spectators—men, boys, and girls—who sat on the manmade banks on either side of the track. One lone adult woman was allowed in: a priestess of the goddess Demeter Chamyne, whose altar rose above the sea of testosterone from the north (left) bank (still visible today).

The stadium (built in the fifth century B.C.) held no seats except those for the judges, who sat in a special box (visible on the south bank, to your right). These Hellanodikai ("Judges of the Greeks") kept things on track. Elected from local noble families and carefully trained over 10 months for just a few days of Games, these referees were widely respected for their impartiality.

The stadium track is 192 meters (640 feet) from start to finish line. The Greek word *stadion* literally means a course that is 600 traditional Olympic feet long, supposedly first marked out by Hercules. The line at the near (west) end marked the finish, where all races ended. (Some started at this end as well, depending on how many laps in the race, but most started at the far end.) The racers ran straight up and back on a clay surface, not around the track. There were 20 starting blocks (all still visible today), each with two grooves—one for each foot (athletes competed barefoot). Wooden starting gates (similar to those used in horse races today) made sure no one could jump the gun.

The first Games featured just one event, a sprint race over one length of the stadium, or one *stadion*. Imagine running this distance in 19.3 seconds, as Usain Bolt of Jamaica did at the 2012 Olympic Games. Over time, more events were added. There were races of two *stadia* (that is, up and back, like today's 400-meter event), 24 *stadia* (similar to today's 5K race), and a race in which athletes competed in full armor, including shields.

At the height of the Games (c. 400 B.C.), there were 13 events held over five days (most here in the stadium). Besides footraces, you'd see events such as the discus, javelin, boxing, wrestling, long jump, *pankration* (a wrestling/boxing/martial arts mix), and the pentathlon. (The decathlon is a modern invention.) During the 2004 Games in Athens, the shot-put competition was held in this stadium. South of the stadium was the hippodrome, or horse-racing track, where riding and chariot races took place.

Compare this stadium and the events held here with the gladiatorial contests in ancient Rome several centuries later: In the far more massive Colosseum, the sensationalistic events weren't about honor, athletic glory, or shared humanity, but a bloody fight to the death, staged to remind the citizens of the power of the state. Good thing it's the Greek games we now emulate.

• *Backtrack through the tunnel and continue straight past the pedestals for the Zeus statues. You'll bump into some rectangular foundations, the ruins of the...*

⑫ Metroon and the Altar of Zeus

The Metroon (mid-fourth century B.C.) was a temple dedicated to the mother of the gods, Rhea (also known as Cybele). The site also honored the mother-goddess of the earth, worshipped as "Gaia."

Somewhere near here once stood the Altar of Zeus, though no one knows exactly where—nothing remains today. At this altar the ancient Olympians slaughtered and burned animals in sacrifice to Zeus on a daily basis. For special festivals, they'd sacrifice 100 cattle (a "hecatomb"), cook them on the altar, throw offerings into the flames, and feast on the flesh, leaving a pile of ashes 25 feet high.

In the middle of the wide path, under an olive tree, is a **sunken apse,** only recently excavated. It's actually the foundation of a 3,000-year-old house—i.e., more than 1,000 years older than the ancient ruins we've seen elsewhere—more evidence that this site was important long before the Olympic Games and the Golden Age of ancient Greece.

• *To the right are the ruins of a semicircular structure built into the hillside, the...*

⓯ Nymphaeum

This was once a spectacular curved fountain, lined with two tiers of statues of emperors, some of which are now in the Archaeological Museum. The fountain provided an oasis in the heat and also functioned as an aqueduct, channeling water throughout the sanctuary. It was built toward the end of the sanctuary's life (around A.D. 150) by the wealthy Roman Herodes Atticus (who also financed construction of the famous theater at the base of the Acropolis in Athens—see page 96).

When the Romans conquered Greece, in the second century B.C., they became fans of Greek culture, including the Olympics. The Romans repaired neglected buildings and built new structures, such as this one. But they also changed (some say perverted) the nature of the Games, transforming them from a Greek religious ritual to a secular Roman spectacle. Rome opened up the Games to any citizen of the Empire, broadening their appeal at the cost of their Greekness.

Rome's notorious Emperor Nero—a big fan of the Olympics—attended the Games in the mid–first century A.D. He built a villa nearby, started music contests associated with the Games, and entered the competition as a charioteer. But when he fell off his chariot, Nero ordered the race stopped and proclaimed himself the winner.

• *Directly in front of the Nymphaeum are the rectangular foundations of what was once the...*

⓮ Altar of Hera

These humble foundations provide a bridge across millennia, linking the original Olympics to today's modern Games. Since 1936,

this is where athletes have lit the ceremonial Olympic torch (for both the summer and winter Games). A few months before the modern Games begin, local women dress up in priestess garb and solemnly proceed here from the Temple of Hera. A curved, cauldron-shaped mirror is used to focus the rays of the sun, igniting a flame. The women then carry the flame into the stadium, where runners light a torch and begin the long relay to the next city to host the Games—a distance of more than 6,000 miles to Rio de Janeiro, Brazil, site of the 2016 Summer Games, and more than 9,000 miles to Pyeongchang, South Korea, where the 2018 Winter Games will take place.

• *Fifteen yards farther along are the four standing Doric columns that mark the well-preserved...*

⓯ Temple of Hera

First built in 650 B.C., this is the oldest structure on the site and one of Greece's first monumental temples. The temple originally hon-

ored both Hera and her husband Zeus, before the Temple of Zeus was built.

The temple was long but not tall, giving it an intimate feel. Its length-to-width ratio (and number of columns: 6 on the short sides, 16 on the long ones) is 3:8, which was considered particularly harmonious and aesthetically pleasing, as well as astronomically significant (the ancients synchronized the lunar and solar calendars by making the year three months longer every eight years).

The temple was originally made of wood. Over time, the wooden columns were replaced with stone columns, resulting in a virtual catalog of the various periods of the Doric style. The columns are made from the same shell-bearing limestone as most of the site's buildings, also originally covered in marble stucco.

Inside, a large statue of Hera once sat on a throne with Zeus standing beside her. Hera's priestesses wove a new dress for the statue every four years. The temple also housed a famous statue of Hermes and was topped with the Disk of the Sun (both are now in the museum).

Though women did not compete in the Olympics, girls and maidens competed in the Heraean Games, dedicated to Hera. The Heraean Games were also held here every four years, though not in the same years as the Olympics. They were open only to unmarried virgins—no married women allowed. Wearing dresses that left one shoulder and breast exposed, the girls raced on foot (running five-sixths of a *stadion*, or 160 meters/525 feet). Like the men, the winners received olive wreaths and fame, as well as a painted portrait displayed on a column of the Temple of Hera.

• *Walking out the back of Hera's temple, you'll reach our last stop: a round temple with three reconstructed Ionic columns. This was the...*

⓰ Philippeion

The construction of the Philippeion marked a new era in Greece: the Hellenistic era. (Compare these gracefully slender Ionic columns to the earlier, stouter Doric columns of the Temple of Hera—in the centuries between when they were built, Greek ideals of proportion had shifted away from sturdiness and strength to a preference for elegant beauty.)

Philip of Macedon built this monument to mark his triumph over the Greeks. The Macedonians spoke Greek and had many similar customs, but they were a kingdom (not a democracy), and the Greeks viewed them as foreigners. Philip conquered Greece around 340 B.C., thus uniting the country—by force—while bringing its Classical Age to an end.

The temple—the first major building visitors saw upon entering the sacred site—originally had 18 Ionic columns of limestone and marble stucco (though today it appears dark, as the gleaming stucco is long gone). Inside stood statues of Philip and his family, including his son, the man who would bring Greece to its next phase of glory: Alexander the Great.

Just north of the Philippeion, bordering the Sacred Way and difficult to make out, are the scant remains of the Prytaneion, the building that once housed the eternal Olympic flame.

Olympia's Legacy

After the Classical Age, the Games continued, but not in their original form. First came Alexander and a new era of more secular values. Next came the Romans, who preserved the Games but also commercialized them and opened them up to non-Greeks. The Games went from being a somber celebration of Hellenic culture to being a bombastic spectacle. The lofty ideals for which the games were once known had evaporated—along with their prestige. As Rome/Greece's infrastructure decayed, so did the Games. A series of third-century earthquakes and the turmoil of the Herulian invasion (in A.D. 267) kept the crowds away. As Greece became Christian, the pagan sanctuary became politically incorrect.

The last ancient Games (the 293rd) were held in A.D. 393. A year later, they were abolished by the ultra-Christian emperor Theodosius I as part of a general purge of pagan festivals. The final blow was delivered in 426, when Theodosius II ordered the temples set ablaze. The remaining buildings were adopted by a small early Christian community, who turned Pheidias' workshop into their church. They were forced to abandon the area after it was hit by a combination of earthquakes (in 522 and 551) and catastrophic floods and mudslides. Over the centuries, two rivers proceeded to bury the area under 25 feet of silt, thus preserving the remaining buildings until archaeologists started excavations in 1875. They finally finished digging everything out in 1972.

• *The **Archaeological Museum** is 200 yards to the north and well-signed.*

Archaeological Museum

Many of Olympia's greatest works of art and artifacts have been removed from the site and are now displayed, and well-described in English, in this compact and manageable museum.

 ❷ **Self-Guided Tour:** This tour takes you past the highlights, but there's much more to see if you have time. As you enter, ask for the free pamphlet that includes a map of the museum (and the site).

• *In the entrance lobby, to the right of the ticket desk, is a...*

 ❶ **Model of the Site, Reconstructed:** Looking at Olympia as it appeared in its Golden Age glory, you can see some of the artifacts that once decorated the site (and which now fill this museum). On the Temple of Zeus, notice the pediments, topped with statues and tripods. Southeast of the temple is the Pedestal of Nike, supporting the statue of Nike. Find Pheidias' workshop and the Temple of Hera, topped with the Disk of the Sun. We'll see all of these items on this tour.

• *Continue straight ahead into the main hall. On the right wall are...*

 ❷ **Statues from the West Pediment of the Temple of Zeus:** These statues fit snugly into the 85-foot-long pediment that stood

Olympia Archaeological Museum

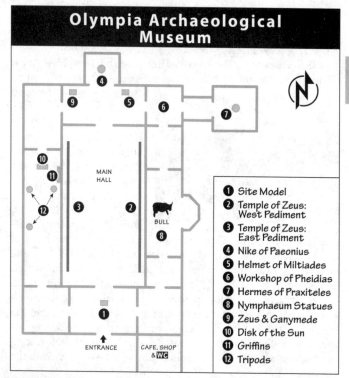

MAIN HALL

BULL

ENTRANCE

CAFE, SHOP & WC

1. Site Model
2. Temple of Zeus: West Pediment
3. Temple of Zeus: East Pediment
4. Nike of Paeonius
5. Helmet of Miltiades
6. Workshop of Pheidias
7. Hermes of Praxiteles
8. Nymphaeum Statues
9. Zeus & Ganymede
10. Disk of the Sun
11. Griffins
12. Tripods

over the back side of the temple (facing the Sacred Way). Study the scene depicting the battle of the Lapiths and centaurs: The centaurs have crashed a human wedding party in order to carry off the women. See one dramatic scene of a woman and her horse-man abductor just left of center. The Lapith men fight back. In the center, a 10-foot-tall Apollo stands calmly looking on. Fresh from their victory in the Persian Wars, the Greeks were particularly fond of any symbol of their struggle against "barbarians."

The statues from the West Pediment are gorgeous examples of the height of Golden Age sculpture: Notice the harmony of the poses and how they capture motion at the perfect moment without seeming melodramatic. The bodies, clearly visible under clothing, convey all the action, while the faces (in the statues that still have them) are stoic.

• *On the opposite side of the hall are...*

❸ **Statues from the East Pediment of the Temple of Zeus:** Olympic victors stood beneath this pediment—the temple's main

entrance—as they received their olive wreaths. The statues tell the story of King Pelops, the legendary founder of the Games. A 10-foot-tall Zeus in the center is flanked by two competing chariot teams. Pelops (at Zeus' left hand, with the fragmented legs)

prepares to race King Oenomaus (at Zeus' right) for the hand of the king's daughter Hippodamia (standing beside Pelops). The king, aware of a prophecy predicting that he would be murdered by his son-in-law, killed 13 previous suitors after defeating them in chariot races. But Pelops wins this race by sabotaging the king's wheels (that may be what the crouching figure is up to behind the king's chariot), causing the king to be dragged to his death by his horses (just like that chariot race in *Ben-Hur*). Pelops becomes king and goes on to unify the Peloponnesian people with a festival: the Olympic Games.

As some of the first sculpture of the Golden Age (made after the Persian invasion of 480 B.C.), these figures show the realism and relaxed poses of the new age (note that they're missing those telltale Archaic-era smiles). But they are still done in the Severe style—the sculptural counterpart to stoic Doric architecture—with impassive

faces and understated emotion, quite different from the exuberant West Pediment, made years later. Still, notice how refined the technique is—the horses, for example, effectively convey depth and movement. But seen from the side, it's striking how flat the sculpture really is.

• *Continue straight ahead, where you'll see a statue rising and floating on her pedestal. She's the...*

❹ **Nike of Paeonius:** This statue of Victory (c. 421 B.C.) once stood atop the triangular Pedestal of Nike next to the Temple of Zeus. Victory holds her billowing robe in her outstretched left hand and a palm leaf in her right as she floats down from Mt. Olympus to proclaim the triumph of the Messenians (the Greek-speaking people from southwest Peloponnese) over Sparta.

The statue, made of flawless pure-white marble from the island of Paros, is the work of the Greek sculptor Paeonius. It was damaged in the earthquakes of A.D. 522 and 551, and today, Nike's wings are completely missing. But they once stretched behind and above her, making the statue 10 feet tall. (She's about seven feet today.) With its triangular base, the whole monument to Victory would have been an imposing 36 feet tall, rising above the courtyard where Olympic winners were crowned.

• *In the glass case to the right as you face Nike are two bronze helmets. The green battered one (#2) is the...*

❺ Bronze Helmet of Miltiades: In September of 490 B.C., a huge force of invading Persians faced off against the outnum-

bered Greeks on the flat plain of Marathon, north of Athens. Although most of the Athenian generals wanted to wait for reinforcements, Miltiades convinced them to attack. The Greeks sprinted across the plain, into the very heart of the Persians— a bold move that surprised and routed the enemy. According to legend, the good news was carried to Athens by a runner. He raced 26 miles from Marathon to Athens, announced "Hurray, we won!"...and dropped dead on the spot.

The legend inspired the 26-mile race called the marathon— but the marathon was not an Olympic event in ancient times. It was a creation for the first modern Games, revived in Athens in A.D. 1896.

• *Pass the helmet and walk into the room with the Zeus statue painting.*

❻ Workshop of Pheidias Room: The poster shows Pheidias' great statue of Zeus, and a model reconstructs the workshop where he created it. In the display case directly to the left as you enter, find exhibit #10, the clay cup of Pheidias. The inscription on the bottom (hence the mirror) reads, "I belong to Pheidias." The adjacent case holds clay molds that were likely used for making the folds of Zeus' robe. The case in the opposite corner contains lead and bronze tools used by ancient sculptors to make the statues we've seen all day.

OLYMPIA

• *The room hiding behind the Zeus poster contains...*

❼ Hermes of Praxiteles: This seven-foot-tall statue (340-330 B.C.), discovered in the Temple of Hera, is possibly a rare original by the great sculptor Praxiteles. Though little is known of this fourth-century sculptor, Praxiteles was recognized in his day as the master of realistic anatomy and the first to sculpt nude women. If this statue looks familiar, that's because his works influenced generations of Greek and Roman sculptors, who made countless copies.

Hermes leans against a tree trunk, relaxed. He carries a baby—the recently orphaned Dionysus—who reaches for a (missing) object that Hermes is distracting him with. Experts guess the child was probably groping for a bunch of grapes, which would

have hinted at Dionysus' future role as the debauched god of wine and hedonism.

Circle the statue counterclockwise and watch Hermes' face take on the many shades of thoughtfulness. From the front he appears serene. From the right (toward the baby), he seems sad. But from the left (toward his outstretched arm), there's the hint of a smile. (And, from the back, nice cheeks!)

The statue has some of Praxiteles' textbook features. The body has the distinctive S-curve of Classical sculpture (head tilted one way, torso the other, legs another). Hermes rests his arm on the tree stump, over which his robe is draped. And the figure is interesting from all angles, not just the front. The famous Praxiteles could make hard, white, translucent marble appear as supple, sensual, and sexual as human flesh.

• *Back in the Pheidias room, consider detouring left to see more statues, from the Roman Nymphaeum fountain. (If you're in a rush, skip this section and head for the Disk of the Sun.)*

❽ Nymphaeum Statues: The grand semicircular fountain near the Temple of Hera had two tiers of statues, including Roman emperors and the family of the

statue's benefactor, Herodes Atticus. Here you can see some of the surviving statues, as well as a bull (in the center of the room) that stood in the middle of the fountain. The bull's inscriptions explain the fountain's origins. Compared to the energetic statues we just saw from the west pediment of the Temple of Zeus, these stately statues are static and lackluster.

The next (smaller) room holds more Roman-era statues, from the Metroon and the Temple of Hera.

• *Return to the Workshop of Pheidias Room, then backtrack past the helmets and Nike to find the glass case with the smaller-than-life-size...*

❾ Statue of Zeus Carrying Off Ganymede: See Zeus' sly look as he carries off the beautiful Trojan boy Ganymede to be his cup-bearer and lover. The terra-cotta statue was likely the central roof decoration (called an *akroterion*—see the nearby diagram) atop one of the treasury houses.

• *Continue into the long hall with the large, decorated terra-cotta pediments, reminding us that these temples were brightly painted, not the plain-white marble we imagine them today.*

❿ Disk of the Sun: This terra-cotta disk—seven and a half feet across and once painted in bright colors—was the *akroterion* that perched atop the peak of the roof of the Temple of Hera. It stood as a sun- or star-like icon meant to ward off bad juju and symbolize Hera's shining glory.

• *Along the left wall is an assortment of cool-looking...*

⓫ Griffins: Because Greeks considered the lion the king of the beasts, and the eagle the top bird, the half-lion-half-eagle griffin was a popular symbol of power for the ancient Greeks, even if no such animal actually existed.

• *The rest of this long room contains several...*

⓬ Tripods: These cauldrons-with-legs were used as gifts to the gods and to victorious athletes. For religious rituals, tripods were used to pour liquid libations, to hold sacred objects, or to burn incense or sacrificial offerings. As ceremonial gifts to the gods, tripods were placed atop and around temples. And as gifts to athletes, they were a source of valuable bronze (which could easily be melted down into some other form), making for a nice "cash" prize.

OTHER OLYMPIA MUSEUMS

Three small museums in Olympia are worth considering: Two of them are perched on a low hill above the southern parking lot—one tiny and skippable, the other a bit bigger and more worthwhile.

They're housed in what used to be Olympia's original archaeological museum and the town's first hotel for antiquity-loving tourists. Today the core of Olympia's collection is displayed at the newer, more modern museum described earlier, but the old hotel building still houses a fine exhibit that nicely complements the other attractions here. Finally, the Archimedes Museum in Olympia town will appeal to engineering nuts.

You may also see signs pointing to the Museum of the Modern Olympic Games, housed in a low building in the middle of town, but it's currently closed (supposedly for a badly needed renovation), and locals don't expect it to open anytime soon.

▲▲Museum of the History of the Olympic Games in Antiquity

Most people are familiar with the modern-day Olympics, but the games played by those early Olympians were a very different operation. The collection offers a handy "Ancient Olympics 101" lesson that helps bring the events to life. If you can spare the 30-45 minutes it takes to see this museum, stop by here first to get your imagination in gear before seeing the ancient site.

Just inside the entrance are models of the site from four different eras. The rooms around the perimeter of the building tell the story of the original Games—you'll see the awards and honors for the victors, and, in the corner, a beautiful mosaic floor (c. A.D. 200) depicting some of the events. The main central hall focuses on the athletic events themselves, displaying ancient discuses, javelin heads, halters (weights used in the long jump), and large shields that were carried by fully armor-clad runners in some particularly exhausting footraces.

Cost and Hours: €2 ticket also includes Museum of the History of Excavations; Mon 10:00-17:00, Tue-Fri 8:00-15:00, closed Sat-Sun; WCs outside building behind excavations museum.

Museum of the History of Excavations

This one-room exhibit, in the small building near the Museum of the History of the Olympic Games in Antiquity, explains the various waves of excavations that have taken place since the site of Olympia was reidentified in the mid-18th century. While early investigations were done by archaeologists from France (in the 1820s) and Germany (in the 1870s), most of the site was systematically uncovered to the point you see today by Germans between 1936 and 1966. (When Berlin hosted the 1936 Olympics, Germany took a special interest in the history of the original Games.) You'll see old maps, photos, and archaeologists' tools.

Cost and Hours: €2, same ticket and hours as Museum of the History of the Olympic Games in Antiquity.

Archimedes Museum

Located on the main drag in Olympia, this museum shows off replicas of ancient Greek technologies, such as the Archimedes screw, the crane used to build the Parthenon, the Antikythera mechanism (ancient computer thought to have been used in astronomy), and the pantograph (the original photocopier). The models (and museum) were created by Konstantinos Kotsanas, who studied mechanical engineering at a university in Patra.

Cost and Hours: Free, donations accepted, daily 10:00-20:00, off-season until 15:00.

Sleeping in Olympia

Olympia's impressive archaeological site and museum—and the town's inconvenient location far from other attractions—make spending the night here almost obligatory. Fortunately, there are just enough good options to make it worthwhile, including one real gem (Hotel Pelops). If you have a car, consider sleeping above Olympia in the more charming village of Miraka.

IN OLYMPIA

For locations, see the map on page 257.

$$ Hotel Pelops is Olympia's top option, with 18 comfortable rooms—try this place first. Run by the warm, welcoming Spiliopoulos clan—father Theodoros, Aussie mom Susanna, and children Alkis, Kris, and Sally—the hotel oozes hospitality. They're generous with travel advice and include free tea and coffee in each room. On the wall of the breakfast room, look for the three Olympic torches that family members have carried in the official relay: Tokyo 1964, Mexico City 1968, and Athens 2004 (Sb-€40-48, Db-€50-58, Tb-€70-78, elevator, fee for cooking classes—arrange well in advance, Varela 2, tel. 26240-22543, www.hotelpelops.gr, hotelpelops@hotelpelops.gr).

$$ Neda Hotel has 44 in-need-of-modernization rooms. But there are two reasons to consider staying here: It's the only place in town with a swimming pool (decent size, surrounded by chaises, café tables, and a small bar), and its top-floor dining room, where the buffet breakfast is served, has outdoor seating and lovely views of Olympia (Sb-€55, Db-€65, Tb-€80, elevator, Karamanli 1, tel. 26240-22563, www.hotelneda.gr, info@hotelneda.gr, Tyligadas family).

> ## Sleep Code
>
> **Abbreviations**   (€1 = about $1.10, country code: 30)
> **S**=Single, **D**=Double/Twin, **T**=Triple, **Q**=Quad, **b**=bathroom
> **Price Rankings**
>   **$$ Higher Priced**—Most rooms €50 or more
>   **$ Lower Priced**—Most rooms less than €50
> Unless otherwise noted, breakfast is included, English is spoken, and free Wi-Fi and/or a guest computer is generally available. Many places accept credit cards, and rooms generally have air-conditioning. Prices can change; verify current rates online or by email. For the best prices, always book directly with the hotel.

$ Kronio Hotel, run by friendly Panagiotis Asteris, rents 23 straightforward rooms along the main street; all but one have balconies and bathtubs (Sb-€40, Db-€48, Tb-€64, elevator, Tsoureka 1, tel. 26240-22188, www.hotelkronio.gr, hotelkronio@hotmail.com).

$ Pension Posidon is a good budget option, with 10 simple but clean rooms in a homey, flower-bedecked house just two blocks above the main street (Sb-€35, Db-€40, Tb-€50, most rooms have balconies, breakfast-€5, rooftop patio, Stefanopoulou 9, tel. 26240-22567, mobile 69732-16726, www.pensionposidon.gr, info@pensionposidon.gr, Liagouras family).

$ Hotel Inomaos has 25 basic crank-'em-out rooms on the main street, each with a no-nonsense balcony (Sb-€25, Db-€35, Tb-€45, Qb-€55, elevator, tel. 26240-22056, inomaos@hol.gr).

NEAR OLYMPIA, IN MIRAKA

The village of Miraka, which sits on a hill above Olympia, is the site of the ancient settlement of Pissa (Archea Pissa/Αρχαια Πισα). Today it offers an authentic-feeling Old-World village experience and a scenic perch with fine views over the fire-charred (but gradually reviving) olive groves in the valley below.

$$ Bacchus Tavern (also a recommended restaurant) rents 11 modern, comfortable rooms in a traditional village a 10-minute drive above Olympia. This is a luxurious-feeling retreat from the drabness of modern Olympia (Db-€69, Tb-€75, across-the-street apartments with kitchen-€85, Qb with Jacuzzi-€95, €10 cheaper in off-season, inviting terrace and swimming pool, tel. 26240-22298, mobile 69371-44800, https://bacchuspensionolympia.reserve-online.net, bacchuspension@gmail.com, Kostas).

Getting There: It's about a 10-minute drive from Olympia's town center: Take the main road out of town toward Pyrgos, then turn right toward Tripoli and twist uphill on the new, modern

highway. After the fourth tunnel, exit to the left and curve around
to reach Miraka. Bacchus Tavern is on the right as you enter town
(look for the parking lot).

Eating in Olympia

Because its restaurants cater to one-nighters, Olympia has no interest in creating return visitors—making its cuisine scene uniformly
dismal in the middle of town. For something more special, it's
worth the drive (or taxi ride) to one of the more interesting places
in the hills above town. See the map on page 257 for locations.

IN THE TOWN CENTER

The shady, angled side-street called Georgiou Douma is lined with
touristy places serving mediocre food; but if you're attracted to the
area's convenient location and leafy scene, try **Aegean** (Αιγαίο),
right off the main street, where the meals are cooked by the owner
(good €12 salads, €10-18 main dishes, open daily for lunch and
dinner, closed Nov-March, tasty vegetarian options, tel. 26240-
22540).

Anesi, located just outside the tourist zone, has zero atmosphere but is the local favorite for grilled meat (€3 starters, €6-7
main dishes, open daily for lunch and dinner, closed Nov-Dec, one
block off main street at corner of Avgerinou and Spiliopoulou, tel.
26240-22644).

Fresh Cheese Pies: Takis opens at 6:00 and closes when he runs
out of his freshly baked pies, made with handmade dough and various fillings (€1.50, along the main street, look for the sign that says
Homemade).

IN THE HILLS ABOVE OLYMPIA

The town's best dining experiences are up in the hills above town,
where locals head to enjoy the food and views. The two places to the
west are a five-minute ride out of town—you could walk to either
of these with enough time (20-30 minutes each way), but I'd drive
or spring for a taxi. Bacchus, to the north, is far beyond walking
distance.

West of Town

Europa Hotel's elegant garden restaurant, on the hills overlooking
Olympia, is a 20-minute uphill hike or a 5-minute drive/taxi ride
(it's well-signed; from middle of town, follow the small road behind Hotel Hercules). Chef Alki practices his art on fresh products
from the hotel's farm. His "farm dish" consists of layers of Talagani
cheese and roasted vegetables—a refreshing break from traditional
Greek salad; the grilled meats and fish are savory and satisfying.

Drink in the magnificent terrace dotted with olive trees, rose bushes, and grapevine arbors—in the fall, Alki will cut off clumps of grapes and bring them to your table for dessert (€3-7 starters, €5-7 salads, €7-14 main dishes, open daily for dinner starting at 19:00, 1 Drouva street, tel. 26240-22650).

Taverna Thea (ΘΕΑ), a few more minutes farther into the hills, is a homier (and cheaper) alternative to dining at the Europa Hotel. Greek Andreas and Swedish Erika proudly serve a standard menu plus some regional specialties to happy locals, who usually gather in the garden terrace after dark, and in-the-know tourists who enjoy the balcony views earlier in the evening (€3-6 salads and starters, €6-10 main dishes, fresh fish, open daily for dinner starting at 18:00, tel. 26240-23264). From the middle of town, follow signs to Europa Hotel (listed above); near the top of the hill, take the fork to the right, following *Krestena, Floka,* and/or *theatre*/ΘΕΑΤΡΟ signs, then stay on the same road as it crests the hill, while looking for the ΤΑΒΕΡΝΑ sign on the left, across the street from the taverna itself.

East of Town

Bacchus Tavern, with a striking setting and pleasant decor that mingles new and old, is the best eatery in the area. The Zapantis family is proud of their traditional, homemade Greek cuisine with creative flair. Olympians favor their lamb baked in oregano and olive oil. Ask owner Kostas how he used water from the swimming pool to save his tavern from the 2007 wildfires (€3-7 salads and starters, €7-14 grilled dishes, €12-17 fixed-price meals, good vegetarian options, daily 12:00-24:00, Fri-Sun only in Jan-Feb, tel. 26240-22298). For driving directions, see the Bacchus Tavern hotel listing, earlier.

Olympia Connections

For all connections, you'll transfer first in **Pyrgos** to the west (about hourly Mon-Fri, 6-8/day Sat-Sun, last bus at 22:15, 35 minutes, €2.20).

From Pyrgos you can connect to **Athens** (8/day, 4-5 hours), **Patra** (8/day, 2 hours, onward connections to **Delphi**), **Kalamata** (2/day, 2.5 hours, onward connections to **Kardamyli, Gythio,** and **Sparta**—connect to **Monemvasia**), and **Tripoli** (3-4/day, 3 hours, onward connections to **Nafplio**). For the Pyrgos bus station, call 26210-20600. For schedules, see the KTEL website for this region (www.ktelileias.gr). For better information, try this helpful, unofficial website in English: http://livingingreece.gr (under "Best of..." click on "KTEL Buses of Greece").

BY CRUISE SHIP

Cruise ships stop at the village of Katakolo (kah-TAH-koh-loh), about 18 miles west of Olympia. Along the waterfront is a pedestrian promenade with several restaurants. This is a good place to try seafood and kill time before reboarding your ship.

Getting to Olympia from Katakolo

By Train: Trains run from Katakolo to Olympia, but not on a predictable schedule. Generally one train leaves Katakolo in the early morning (before 9:00), and one train returns from Olympia in the late morning (before noon), but more trains may be added if several large ships are in town. Since there's no way to look up an updated schedule, it's best to go straight from your ship to the train station to ask. The station is about a 10-minute walk from the port parking lot: Head down Katakolo's tacky tourist street a few blocks until you reach the park. The train platform and ticket booth are to the right. The train ride takes about 50 minutes, followed by an additional 10-minute walk from the Olympia train station to the site (€10 round-trip, buy tickets at booth—not on train, double-check return times, tel. 26210-22525, https://tickets.trainose.gr).

By Big Bus: For the same price you can also take a big bus from one of several agencies on the main street (€10 round-trip; ask how much time you'll have in Olympia—most offer between 1.5 and 3 hours, you'll want at least 2). These places understand how much you don't want to miss your boat—and all but guarantee you won't. But note that you may have to wait up to 30 minutes in Katakolo until they collect enough passengers to make the trip worthwhile. If there's a train leaving soon after you dock, I'd take that instead.

By Tour: Olympic Traveller offers a package combining round-trip transport to Olympia with a two-hour guided tour of the site and museum, likely with recommended local guide Niki Vlachou (€45/person, groups never larger than 25, mobile 697-320-1213, www.olympictraveller.com, info@olympictraveller.com). For €20 less you can skip the guided tour in Olympia, but enjoy a narrated ride, quick pick-up times (they won't dally at the port waiting for the bus to fill up), and guaranteed on-time return to your cruise ship.

By Taxi: Taxis descend upon the dock, hoping to pick up passengers; the round-trip fare for a one-hour visit to Olympia runs €80, while a two-hour visit costs €100 (talk to a few drivers to find a good match). For the best prices and service, book in advance. Consider Takis Tsaparas (mobile 694-543-4913, www.taxikatakolon.gr).

By Rental Car: If you want to drive, avoid the sleazy rental agency on the main street as you leave the dock. Try Avis, just uphill from the main street, marked with a big red sign (€40/day plus gas for smallest manual-transmission car with air-con, best to book ahead in July-Aug, tel. 26210-42200, mobile 694-700-2290, www.katakolo-rentacar.com, helpful Kostas). The route is an easy 30-minute drive that bypasses any towns; ask the rental agent for directions.

Wine Tasting and a Beach: If you don't want to visit Olympia, one option is to ride the hop-on, hop-off tourist train, which stops at Mercouri winery and at rocky Agioas Andreas Beach, which has several restaurant/beach bars. Catch it in Katakolo, in the square next to the church at the end of the promenade (€6, every 30 minutes, last train one hour before cruise ships leave, Katakolo Train Tours, tel. 694-777-8842).

ROUTE TIPS FOR DRIVERS

Olympia is situated in the hilly interior of the Peloponnese, connected to the outside world by one main highway, called E-55. You can take this west to **Pyrgos** (30 minutes), where E-55 forks: Take it north to **Patra** (2 hours from Olympia) and **Delphi** (3.5 hours from Olympia—see Delphi's "Route Tips for Drivers" on page 360); or south to **Kalamata** (2.5 hours from Olympia) and on to **Kardamyli** (3.5 hours from Olympia). Or, from Olympia, you can take E-55 east on its twisty route to **Tripoli** (2.5 hours), then get on the major E-65/A-7 expressway to zip to **Nafplio** (3.5 hours from Olympia) or **Athens** (4.5 hours from Olympia).

Near Olympia: Patra

The big port city of Patra (Πάτρα, sometimes spelled "Patras" in English, pop. 170,000) is many visitors' first taste of Greece, as it's the hub for boats arriving from Italy (and from the Ionian Islands, such as Corfu). While it's not a place to linger, Patra has rejuvenated its main thoroughfare to become a fairly enjoyable place to kill a little time waiting for your boat or bus.

Patra sprawls along its harborfront, which is traced by the busy road called Othonos Amalias. Patra's transit points line up along here (from north to south, as you'll reach them with the sea on your right): the North Port Terminal for some local ferries, a ragtag main bus station, the low-profile train station, and the South Port Terminal where ferries from Italy dock.

Visiting Patra: Patra has several enjoyable pedestrian zones that bustle with a lively, engaging chaos you'll find only in a Mediterranean port town. Stretching west from the bus station, the pedestrianized Riga Fereou (two blocks inland from Othonos Amalias) is where locals spend their time eating, drinking coffee, and shopping. Riga Fereou intersects with another pedestrian zone, called Agiou Nikolaou. Both streets are lined with al fresco cafés, restaurants, and shops—and are fine places to feel the pulse of urban Greece.

Patra has several worthwhile sights. The **archaeological museum,** housed in a modern building on the north side of town, displays artifacts from the city and surrounding area, and focuses on themes of private life, public life, and cemeteries (about 1.5 miles from city center—best to take a taxi or drive, tel. 26136-16100, www.patrasmuseum.gr). The town **castle,** built by the Emperor Justinian in the sixth century, is reachable from a staircase at the top of Agiou Nikolaou (tel. 26106-23390). Near the castle, the impressively restored **ancient *odeon*** (theater) dates from Roman times (tel. 26102-20829). And along the waterfront, south of the main transit zone, the vast **Church of Agios Andreas** is the city's *mitropolis* (like a cathedral). See www.patrasinfo.com for more information on these sights and the town itself.

Sleeping in Patra: If you're stuck here overnight, these options are handy to the boats, buses, and trains: **$$ Olympic Star** (luxurious touches, four blocks up from the port and just below the old town and castle, Agiou Nikolaou 46, tel. 26106-22939, www.olympicstar.gr) or **$$ Hotel Acropole** (business-class rooms across from train station, Agiou Andreou 32, tel. 26102-79809, www.acropole.gr).

Patra Connections: You can sail by **boat** from Patra to several towns in Italy, including Bari, Ancona, and Venice; many boats stop at the Greek island of Corfu en route (check Superfast Ferries—www.superfast.com, Minoan Lines—www.minoan.gr, and ANEK Lines—www.anek.gr). **Buses** connect Patra directly to Athens and Pyrgos (with onward connections to Olympia).

KARDAMYLI AND THE MANI PENINSULA

ΚΑΡΔΑΜΎΛΗ / Καρδαμύλη •
ΜΆΝΗ / Μάνη

The Mani Peninsula is the southernmost tip of mainland Greece (and of the entire European continent, east of Spain)—and it really does feel like the end of the road. Sealed off from the rest of Greece by a thick ring of mountains, the peninsula has seen its population ebb and flow throughout history with tides of refugees fleeing whatever crises were gripping the rest of Greece. The only part of Greece that never completely fell to the Ottoman invaders, the Mani became the cradle of the 1821 revolution that finally brought independence to the Greeks.

In the Mani, travelers discover a timeless region of rustic villages and untrampled beaches. A day's drive around this desolate, rural peninsula offers dramatic mountain scenery and bloody history all tied up in a hardscrabble and evocative package—making hedonism on the Mani coast feel all the more hedonistic. At the end of the day, you can retire to charming Kardamyli.

PLANNING YOUR TIME

Two nights and a full day is a minimum for this area. To really be on vacation, add more nights. Sleep in Kardamyli. With one day, first take my self-guided walk of Kardamyli to get your bearings, then head up to Old Kardamyli. In the afternoon, go for a hike or hit the beach. With a second day and a car, drive the Mani Peninsula. Those with three days here can do the driving tour at a more leisurely pace, saving the Pyrgos Dirou Caves and the detour to Kastania for a separate side-trip from Kardamyli (or as a detour en route to or from Monemvasia).

Instead of returning to Kardamyli, you can head from the Mani loop directly to Monemvasia.

Kardamyli

The village of Kardamyli (kar-dah-MEE-lee) is the gateway to the Mani Peninsula and its best home base. It's an anti-resort that delicately mixes boutique hotels and conscientious travelers with real-world Greece. Relax and tune in to the pace of country life. On Kardamyli's humble but fascinating main drag, locals-only mom-and-pop shops mingle with trendy tourist stalls.

Little Kardamyli is one of the oldest city names in Greek history. In the *Iliad*, Homer described "well-peopled" Kardamyli as one of seven cities presented to the Greek hero Achilles to persuade him to return to the siege of Troy. Achilles' son Pyrrhus sailed to Kardamyli, then walked to Sparta to claim the hand of Ermioni. And the legendary Gemini twins—Castor and Pollux—are said to be buried here.

Kardamyli is wedged between the sparkling pebble beaches of the Messenian Gulf and towering Mount Profitas Ilias (7,895 feet)—the Peloponnese's highest peak, which is snowcapped from November to early May. Between the sea and the distant mountaintop, dramatic hills and cliffs are topped with scenic villages, churches, and ruined towers. As throughout the rest of the Mani, in the sixth century A.D. Kardamyli's residents fled from pirates into these hills—returning to sea level only in the 18th century, after the construction of Old Kardamyli's defensive tower house made it safe.

Visitors can enjoy hiking into the hills, learning about the region's rough-and-tumble history at Old Kardamyli, swimming at the town's Ritsa Beach, and driving deeper into the Mani Peninsula, but the real charm of Kardamyli is its low-key ambience—the place works like a stun gun on your momentum. On my last trip, I could have stayed here for days, just eating well and hanging out. It's the kind of place where travelers plan their day around the sunset.

Orientation to Kardamyli

Tiny Kardamyli—with about 200 year-round residents—swells with far more visitors in the summer months. The town is compact, gathered around a convenient central spine (the main road running south from Kalamata). Kardamyli is small enough to feel like a cozy village, but big enough to serve the needs of its many visitors—with small grocery stores, ATMs, a post office, and more.

Tourist Information: Because Kardamyli has no TI, hoteliers pick up the slack, sometimes offering free hiking maps and usually eager to direct visitors to the best restaurants and activities. The helpful official town website has lots of good information, including accommodations (www.kardamili-greece.com, run by energetic Luna).

Arrival in Kardamyli: For specifics on driving into town, see "Route Tips for Drivers" on page 303.

Local Guide: Elias Polimeneas is a soulful native who proudly introduces visitors to his town and region. If you'd like to explore Kardamyli with a Kardamylian, or see the Mani Peninsula, Elias is your man (reasonable and negotiable rates, tel. 27210-73453, antoniasapartments@yahoo.gr).

Kardamyli Walk

You could walk from one end of Kardamyli to the other in ten minutes, but you'd miss the point. Slow down, and keep an eye out for intriguing pockets of traditional Greek village culture. This leisurely self-guided stroll lasts about an hour.

• *Begin at the beginning of town, by the...*

Village Church

The modern Church of St. Mary, with its thriving congregation, is the heart of this town. Notice the loudspeakers outside, which allow overflow crowds to take part in the service on very important days, such as Easter. Kardamyli takes its Easter celebration very seriously: On Good Friday, a processional passes through the town and the priest blesses each house. At midnight on Holy Saturday, everyone turns off their lights and comes to this main square. The

priest emerges from the church with a candle, passing its flame through the candle-carrying crowd, who then take the light home

Kardamyli

1. Hotel Anniska
2. Hotel Liakoto
3. Hotel Esperides
4. Antonia's Apartments
5. Gorgones Studios
6. Olympia Koymanakou Rooms
7. Vardia Hotel
8. To Kalamitsi Hotel
9. Rogi Ouzerie
10. Taverna Perivolis
11. Harilaos Restaurant
12. Aquarella Café & Cocktail Bar
13. Tikla Café
14. To Kastro Taverna
15. Elies Restaurant
16. Taverna Dioskouroi
17. Lola Frozen Yogurt
18. Androuvista Café
19. Maistros Café
20. Grocery Stores

with them...gradually illuminating the entire town. And then the fireworks begin.

Before we head into the middle of town, walk a few yards up the main street, away from the main square, and look for a worn wooden fence on the right (before the two grocery stores). Behind the fence is the **Botana Herb Shop,** a celebration of what grows in the hills above Kardamyli. Owner Yiannis Dimitreas, a walking encyclopedia on local foraging, offers free tastes of his organic produce—marinated olives, fresh olive oil, and local honey—and also sells homemade herbal teas, soaps, and skin creams (generally daily 9:00-14:30 & 18:00-20:00, tel. 27210-73367, mobile 69726-90170).

• *Extending toward town from the church is the leafy...*

Main Square

Most of the year, this spot is a popular playground for Kardamylian kids, who play under the eucalyptus trees (on the site of the

ancient gymnasium). But on New Year's Day, a local club fills the square with truckloads of snow from the mountains, turning it into a playground for giddy grown-ups as well.

Walk to the end of the square. In the little park is the town water spigot and an oddball collection of **monuments.** Find the busts of two almost comically medal-laden generals who fought in the Greek Revolution and Macedonian Wars. The modern sculpture between them, called *Unity,* evokes the many fortified towers that dot the Mani Peninsula. Despite the vendettas that frequently cropped up among the peninsula's inhabitants, today Maniots generally feel united with one another.

Across the street, on the pedestal, is a **monument to the heroes** who have fought for Greek unity and independence since antiquity. Next to the palm branch is the Greek motto "Freedom or Death." While two wars are highlighted in the wreath below (the 1821 Greek War of Independence, and the 1912-1913 First Balkan War), the monument is a reminder that the ideals behind those conflicts date back to the ancients.

The cobbled path just behind this monument takes hikers (in about 10 minutes) to the restored ruins and museum of **Old Kardamyli** (described later).

Back across the street, in the small square with the fountain, notice the inviting café tables. At the end of the square, look down the street to the **waterfront.** The primary school (with a flag in its yard) stands on the water side of the square. The school has a disproportionate number of Albanian kids, because as a couple of generations of young people moved to Athens in search of work, Albanian workers migrated here to do stone work and other manual labor jobs. And most recently, Greeks who are struggling eco-

nomically are unable to afford a family.

Now look in the opposite direction, up at the **hillsides.** From here you can see two of the most popular nearby hiking destinations: On the left is the little hilltop church of Agia Sophia, and to the right is the village of Petrovouni. An enjoyable three-hour loop covers both of these sights (described later, under "Hiking").

• *Across from the end of the park begins the commercial zone of...*

Kardamyli's Main Street

The next few blocks reveal a fascinating blend of traditional Greek village lifestyles side-by-side with a pleasantly low-key tourism. In

most Greek towns with such a fine seaside setting, the beaches are lined with concrete high-rise hotels, and the main streets are a cavalcade of tacky T-shirt shops. But the people of Kardamyli are determined to keep their town real—a hard-fought local law prohibits new construction over a certain height limit

(ruling out big resorts), and the town has made long-term sustainability a priority over short-term profit. (It also helps that the beach has pebbles instead of sand, which keeps away the party crowds.) Its residents have created a smart little self-sustaining circle: The town keeps its soul even as it profits from visitors...allowing it to attract the caliber of travelers who appreciate Kardamyli for what it is.

Take a walk down the main street for examples of both faces of Kardamyli. Notice that (with the exception of the empty red eyesore a half-block down) all of the buildings are traditionally built, using stone from this area. Even newer buildings (such as the café right at the start of the street) match the old style. As you stroll you'll see:

Maistros Café (on the left, with breakfast and backgammon): This is Kardamyli's closest thing to a place where the "old boys" hang out.

The **pharmacy** (left, after the handy little supermarket): Pop inside to see how tastefully it's been renovated.

Psaltiras Wine and Olive Oil Shop (left): Nicos Psaltiras speaks English and loves to share his quality local products.

To Aloni Bar (on the right): Take a break at this cool hangout with billiards.

2407 Kardamili Mountain Shop (left): Named for the height in meters of the tallest mountain in the Peloponnese, this is the go-to place for outdoor equipment, bike rentals, and advice on walks and treks. See www.2407m.com for their weekly schedule of excursions and tours.

Souvlaki Shop (left): Here you'll find local-style "fast food."

Androuvista Café (left): This delightful little café bakes its much-loved walnut cake daily.

Blauel Olive Shop (right): This shop is a pioneer in organic olive oil production. Katerina loves offering tasty samples.

The **butcher** (left): Peek inside to see a classic butcher block and a row of hooks with tools and smocks. Local shepherds produce lots of goats.

Lola Frozen Yogurt (right): Try this fun stop with a peaceful courtyard out back.

Mountain Herbs Shop (left): Pop in for homegrown goodies—and possibly some samples of olive oils and honeys.

Finish your Main Street stroll with the **bank** (with ATM), **real estate office** (one of two in town for visitors smitten with the desire to have a vacation home here), **TI, City Hall, hardware store** (while shepherds can pick up their goat and cow bells here, it does a more brisk business supplying out-of-towners working on their fixer-upper retirement/vacation properties), **Rogi Bar** (famous for its cocktails), and the old-school **newsstand.**

• *Now backtrack a block past the City Hall and go left (toward the water) at the Piraeus Bank to find yourself among...*

Kardamyli's Back Streets

As you step off the main drag, notice how civilization seems to melt away as back streets quickly turn into cobbles, then gravel, then red dirt.

Continuing down the road

past small shops to the sea, you'll see some signs advertising **rooms** (ΔΩΜΑΤΙΑ, *dhomatia*) for visitors—a great value for cheap sleeps. If you look like you need a roof over your head tonight, someone might offer you a room as you pass.

• *Continue down to the water, walk out on to the concrete pier, and look around at...*

Kardamyli's Waterfront

Until a few generations ago, no roads connected Kardamyli to the rest of civilization. This pier was the main way into and out of the area, providing a link to the big city of Kalamata and bustling with trade and passengers. The old smokestack (to the right as you face the water) marks the site of a once-thriving olive-oil factory. The oil was shipped from this pier. (The factory has been deserted since the 1950s, and much of the original equipment is rusty but intact. There's talk of turning it into a museum.)

Between the 1950s and the 1970s, the ever-improving network of roads made this port obsolete. Today only one professional fishermen works out of Kardamyli. He brings his catch right here to the pier to sell to locals, tourists, and restaurateurs. The little diving board is a favorite for kids. The small harbor across the bay has only a few boats. Even without its traditional industries, Kardamyli still thrives, and most of its traditional lifestyles remain intact...thanks in part to respectful visitors like you.

Above the harbor the Mirginos Tower completes the ring of fortifications that starts at the other end of town at Old Kardamyli. The little island offshore (Miropi) holds the barely visible ruins of an old church.

• *Our walk is finished—time to take a deep breath of sea air, relax, and soak in the slow pace of Kardamyli life. There are a couple of relaxing bars with fine sea views within a few steps.*

Sights in Kardamyli

OLD KARDAMYLI

The fortified compound of Old Kardamyli perches just above today's modern town. On the ancient Mani Peninsula, "old" is relative—this settlement, marked by a fortified tower, was established by the first families (who were forced into the hills in the Middle Ages by pirates) to return to flat ground at the end of the

17th century. After sitting in ruins for centuries, the complex has recently been partially restored and converted into a little museum about the Mani Peninsula and its traditional architecture. It's worth the 10-minute hike through an olive grove to poke around the fortified cluster and visit the museum.

The trail to Old Kardamyli begins just behind the monument to the heroes along the main street (see my self-guided walk, earlier). From here it's an up-and-down 10-minute walk—just follow the cobbled path, lined with lampposts, which leads through an up-close slice of traditional village life and an olive grove. As you approach the site, behind the ruined building on the right is an old cistern once used to draw and carry water back home. Curl around the right side of Old Kardamyli to hike up into the complex. Standing inside the fortified complex, imagine the stark reality of life within these walls, where a church, olive press, iron smith, garden, and cistern were the necessities for the frightened community to survive.

Passing through the archway, on the right you'll see the **Church of St. Spyridon** (circa 1750). Though it's not open to visitors, the exterior is interesting for its bell tower and its (typical-in-Greece) use of fragments of older buildings in its construction (such as the 3,500-year-old Mycenaean-age sill, wall chunks plundered by the Venetians, and Byzantine marble frames that surround the door and windows). Over the window and door, notice the crowned double-headed eagle, a symbol of the Byzantine Empire and the Orthodox Christian Church.

Now head toward the tower complex itself. The **Mourtzinos Tower** was built by the powerful Troupakis family at the begin-

ning of the 18th century. It's named after the leader of the Troupakis clan, who was known for his scowling face *(mourtzinos),* during the War of Independence.

Attached to the tower, the former **Troupakis residence** now houses a multilevel museum (€2, Tue-Sun 8:30-15:00, closed Mon). Poke into all the little doors to see exhibits about the Maniots' terraces, cisterns, beekeeping, agricultural production, salt pans, and quarries. On the top floor you can learn about the different subregions of the Mani.

The cute little blue-and-white church just uphill from the complex, **Agia Sophia,** marks the beginning of a cobbled path that leads up, up, up to the distant church on the hilltop (also called Agia Sophia). High above on the bluff was the site of the acropolis of Homeric-era Kardamyli (from 1250 b.c.). You can do the whole strenuous loop up to the church, then walk around to the adjacent village of Petrovouni (see "Hiking," later). Or, for just a taste, hike about five minutes up the cobbled trail to find two graves burrowed into a rock (on the right, behind the green gate). These are supposedly the **graves of Castor and Pollux,** the "Gemini twins" of mythology. These brothers of Helen of Troy had different fathers. When Castor died, Pollux—who was immortal because he was fathered by Zeus—asked his dad to bond the brothers together in immortality. Zeus agreed and turned them into the Gemini constellation. These brothers, so famous for their affection for each other, remain in close proximity even in death: Notice the connecting passage at the back of the graves.

BEACHES

Many visitors come to Kardamyli to enjoy the beach. Most simply head for nearby **Ritsa Beach,** a pleasant pebbly stretch that be-

gins just beyond the village church. You can swim anywhere along its length, but most beach bums prefer the far end, where the water gets deeper quicker (no showers).

Ritsa Beach is bookended by twin restaurants with outdoor seating. **Elies,** at the far end, is everyone's favorite (see page 302).

If you have a car and want to get out of town, you could daytrip to two more good sand/fine gravel beaches that lie to the south, near the hamlet of Neo Proastio on the way to Stoupa: **Foneas Beach** (a cove flanked by picturesque big rocks) and **Delfinia Beach.** The resort town of **Stoupa** also has some good sandy beaches and a promenade perfect for strolling.

As elsewhere in Greece, water shoes are recommended to avoid stepping on spiny sea urchins. Locals claim that the water's warm enough for swimming year-round, except in March, when it's chilled by snowmelt runoff from the mountains.

HIKING

Hiking vies with beach fun as Kardamyli's biggest attraction. Especially in spring and fall, visitors head away from the sea to explore

the network of color-coded trails that scramble up the surrounding hills. Many of these follow the ancient *kalderimi* (cobbled paths) that until fairly recently were the only way of traveling between villages. Ask your hotel for a map that explains the routes and codes; for serious hikes, buy a more detailed hiking map. As the hikes tend to be strenuous—uphill and over uneven terrain— wear good shoes and bring along water and snacks (some walks do pass through villages where you can buy food and drinks).

The most popular destinations sit on the hillsides just behind Kardamyli: the hilltop church of **Agia Sophia** and the village of **Petrovouni.** You can hike to either one or (with more time and stamina) do a loop trip that includes both. Consider this plan: Start by visiting Old Kardamyli, then continue past the smaller blue-and-white Agia Sophia church and the ancient graves of Castor and Pollux (described earlier) to the higher church of Agia Sophia. Then, if your energy holds, follow the path around to Petrovouni, from which you can head back down into Kardamyli. The paths are very steep (there's about a 650-foot elevation gain from Kardamyli to Petrovouni), and the round-trip takes about 1.5 hours at a good pace with few breaks (follow the yellow-and-black markings). Other trips lead farther into the hills, to the remote village of **Exohori.** To avoid brutal heat in the summer, time your hike to finish by 10:00.

Sleeping in Kardamyli

Most of Kardamyli's accommodations cater to British, European, and Australian tourists who stay for a week or more. Rather than traditional hotels, you'll find mostly "apartments" with kitchenettes, along with simpler and cheaper rooms *(dhomatia)*. While some places do offer breakfast, most charge extra, assuming that you'll make your own in your kitchenette or get a pastry and a coffee at a bakery or café. If you want breakfast, be sure to tell your host the day before (they'll likely buy fresh bread for you in the morning).

Sleep Code

Abbreviations   **(€1=about $1.10, country code: 30)**
S=Single, **D**=Double/Twin, **T**=Triple, **Q**=Quad, **b**=bathroom
Price Rankings
   $$$ Higher Priced—Most rooms €70 or more
     $$ Moderately Priced—Most rooms between €50-70
       $ Lower Priced—Most rooms €50 or less
Unless otherwise noted, breakfast is included, English is spoken, and free Wi-Fi and/or a guest computer is generally available. Many places accept credit cards, and rooms generally have air-conditioning. Prices can change; verify the hotel's current rates online or by email. For the best prices, always book directly with the hotel.

IN THE TOWN

$$$ Hotel Anniska and **Hotel Liakoto** ("Sunny Place") rent nicely appointed, luxurious-feeling apartments with kitchenettes. The Anniska has 22 apartments that share an inviting lounge and a delightful sea-view terrace (studio-€95 July-mid-Sept, €80 off-season; one-bedroom apartment-€125, €95 off-season; optional breakfast-€9.50, free Wi-Fi in reception area, tel. 27210-73601). The Liakoto's 25 apartments cluster around a swimming-pool courtyard oasis, and many have sea views that turn golden at sunset (€10 more than Anniska's rates, tel. 27210-73600). Both hotels are run by friendly British-Australian-Greek couple Ilia and Gerry (www.anniska-liakoto.com, anniska@otenet.gr).

$$$ Hotel Esperides has 19 rooms and apartments with kitchenettes, all surrounding a pleasant garden veranda just a few steps up from the main road. You'll enjoy a friendly welcome and lots of travel advice (studio-€85 Aug, €75 July and Sept, €65 April-June and Oct, one-bedroom apartments about €15-25 more, closed Nov-March, breakfast-€9, arrange arrival time in advance because reception isn't open 24 hours, tel. 27210-73173, www. hotelesperides.gr, info@hotelesperides.gr).

$$ Antonia's Apartments sit among the olive trees, just up from Ritsa Beach and a short walk from the town center. Its two newer apartments in the tower house are stylishly furnished with thoughtful touches that put them several notches above the norm. The two older units, while more old-fashioned, are a bit bigger, with two separate bedrooms. All four apartments have sea-view verandas (Db-€60-70 mid-July-Aug, €45-50 Sept-mid-July, €10-20 more for bigger apartments that fit 3-5 people, discounts for stays of more than 3-4 days, lending library, tel. 27210-73453, antoniasapartments@yahoo.gr, lovingly tended by recommended local guide Elias).

$ Gorgones Studios (Οι Γοργόνες, a.k.a. Les Sirènes) has 10 well-priced rooms over a busy restaurant. The rooms are simple, but all have kitchenettes and balconies overlooking Kardamyli's little harbor (Db-€50 July-Aug, €40 in spring and fall, €35 in winter; good windows block out most of the dining noise, tel. 27210-73469, mobile 69323-34855, Haralambea family).

$ Dhomatia: You'll see signs advertising rooms (ΔΩΜΑΤΙΑ) all over town. Though air-conditioning is a safe bet, rooms are generally quite simple, with kitchenettes but no breakfast. English can be limited, credit cards aren't accepted, and value can vary. If you're in a pinch, check out a few, pick the best, and don't be afraid to haggle. Try warm and welcoming **Olympia Koymanakou,** who rents five rooms on the cobbled lane just up the road from the harbor and speaks just enough English (Sb-€30; Db-€45 July-Aug, €35 off-season; shared kitchen, Paraleia street, tel. 27210-73623, www.koumanstudios.gr).

JUST OUTSIDE KARDAMYLI

These enjoyable retreats sit a bit farther from Kardamyli's main street. While walkable, they're more enjoyable if you have a car (especially the Kalamitsi).

$$$ Vardia Hotel is a stony retreat huddled on a hilltop just above town. All of its 18 rooms have balconies overlooking town and the sea beyond, and a steep, stony path leads from the hotel's grand-view veranda directly to Old Kardamyli (studio-€80 July-Aug, €70 off-season; one-bedroom apartment-€115 July-Aug, €100 off-season; two-bedroom apartment-€165 July-Aug, €135 off-season; breakfast-€7.50, tel. 27210-73777, mobile 69783-83404, www.vardia-hotel.gr, info@vardia-hotel.gr).

$$$ Kalamitsi Hotel is a charming enclave hovering above its own bay, beach, and olive grove a two-minute drive down the road from Kardamyli (toward Areopoli). In addition to 20 rooms in the main building, it has 15 bungalows that bunny-hop across its plateau (Sb-€90 July-mid-Sept, €70 off-season; Db-€110 July-mid-Sept, €90 off-season; suite-€160 July-mid-Sept, €130 off-season; bungalows-€120 July-mid-Sept, €100 off-season; breakfast-€10, dinner-€20, tel. 27210-73131, www.kalamitsi-hotel.gr, info@kalamitsi-hotel.gr).

Eating in Kardamyli

Kardamyli prides itself on pleasing a huge group of return visitors, who come here on holiday year after year. Consequently, quality

is high and value is good. When you ask locals where to dine, they shrug and say, "Anywhere is good"...and you sense it's not just empty town pride talking. As you dine, notice the dignified European visitors conversing quietly around you...and try to imitate them.

IN TOWN

Rogi (Ρογί) isn't technically a restaurant (it's billed as an *ouzerie*), but it's got some of the best food you'll find in town. Vassili's lovingly prepared meal-sized *mezedes* are modern twists on traditional Mani cuisine—and everything on the plate has likely come from within a two-mile radius. Vassili also serves the town's best (and strongest) cocktails: Try the "Mediterranean mojito," made with local liquor, lemon, and fresh basil instead of rum, lime, and mint (€7-9 meals, 8:00 until late, on southern end of main street, tel. 27210-64102).

Taverna Perivolis, run by Peter and his Greek-Australian family, lacks a view but offers good value in a garden setting. Their list of daily specials often includes *pastitsio* (Greek lasagna) and freshly grilled meat (€5-7 starters, €7-10 main dishes, daily 19:00-24:00 except likely closed Mon off-season, tel. 27210-73713). It's near the water, across the street from the deserted factory.

ON THE WATER, WITH SEA VIEWS

These three places are side-by-side overlooking the harbor and designed for enjoying sea views. All have fine interiors if the weather is disagreeable. The first is a serious restaurant, while the next two are bars that serve food.

Harilaos Restaurant seems to be open when others are not. It's bright and elegant, boasts fine views over the harbor, and serves fresh fish and classic Greek dishes (tel. 27210-73373).

Aquarella Café and Cocktail Bar is youthful and hip, taking full advantage of its romantic seaside setting with sofas under trees and backgammon boards. Relax with drinks and snacks—there are even cigars on the menu. They serve breakfast and are open nightly until late.

Tikla Café, with a stylish covered terrace and a stony-mod interior, offers a short menu of updated Greek cuisine (€5-8 salads and savory pies, €3-4 Continental breakfast, €12 two-person American breakfast, free Wi-Fi, long hours daily but may close 14:00-18:00 at slow times, tel. 27210-73223). It's also a fine café/bar for just hanging out with good coffee, cocktails, and music until noon.

JUST OUTSIDE KARDAMYLI

Kastro Taverna is a gourmet's delight and a splurge for your taste buds (but no pricier than most other restaurants in town). Sitting amid an olive grove just outside of town toward Kalamata, it's a 15-minute walk or quick drive from the town center. The trek is worth it—the chef uses local products for his daily specials, including meat and produce from his farm in the hills above town. A highlight is the *keftedes* (meatballs) in a savory tomato sauce, but it's hard to go wrong with anything on the menu. Choose between the cozy fireplace interior and the broad veranda with distant sea views (€3-6 starters, €7-10 main dishes, serves dinner daily starting at 19:00, open only on weekends in winter, tel. 27210-73951).

Elies (Ελιές), with what most locals consider the best lunch around, is a 15-minute walk up from the town center, on Ritsa Beach. Relax with beachgoers at pastel tables in the shade of olive trees, and enjoy their excellent Greek cuisine. They serve simple, traditional Greek dishes for lunch from April through October and offer a fancier dinner menu from June through September (daily, tel. 27210-73140). Kids enjoy their playground.

Taverna Dioskouroi sits in a lovely setting on the headland overlooking Kardamyli's adorable little harbor, on the southern end of the village (€3-9 starters, €6-12 main dishes, daily specials, live music at sunset up to three nights per week, long hours daily, on the right 200 yards south of the village, tel. 27210-73236).

OTHER OPTIONS

Breakfast: If you're not eating breakfast at your hotel consider these options. Bohemian-chic **Aquarella** and smarter **Tikla** are side-by-side (see "On the Water," above). Several places mentioned on my self-guided walk offer breakfast fare: **Lola Frozen Yogurt** (dainty setting, garden tables out back) has light bites and good coffee, **Androuvista Café** serves walnut cake, a beloved local specialty, and **Maistros Café,** on the main square, is an old-school cafeteria with local clientele and full array of breakfast options (see page 294). Or consider a neighboring place with tables actually on the square.

Cafés: Kardamyli enjoys a wide range of delightful cafés with traditional/chic decor and basic food; several line the main drag. Most of these have indoor and outdoor seating and serve drinks as well as light food, including breakfast.

Picnics: Two grocery stores at the entrance to town can help you flesh out your meal (both open long hours daily). For a fast bite, the **souvlaki shop** on the main street is good (see page 294).

Kardamyli Connections

Kardamyli's biggest disadvantage is its tricky-to-reach position on the far-flung Mani Peninsula. The nearest major city (with good bus connections to the rest of Greece) is Kalamata, about 24 twisty miles to the north. Kardamyli is connected to **Kalamata** by bus (4/day Mon-Fri—first bus around 7:30, last at around 20:30; 3/day Sat-Sun, 1 hour; in Kardamyli, catch bus at main square). For Kalamata bus information, call 27210-22851. KTEL, the national bus system, has a minimal website (www.ktelbus.com); for better information, try this helpful, unofficial website in English: http://livingingreece.gr (under "Best of...," click on "KTEL Buses of Greece").

You can also get to Kalamata by taxi—a handy option for catching early buses out of Kalamata off-season, when buses from Kardamyli to Kalamata might not run early enough (€45; try local guide Elias Polimeneas—see page 290).

ROUTE TIPS FOR DRIVERS
The Mani Peninsula's mountains make driving slow going. The most straightforward approach to Kardamyli is from the city of Kalamata: As you enter Kalamata, follow signs reading *Port, Seafront,* or *Areopoli*. Once past the port, keep driving in the same direction, with the water on your right. The road to Kardamyli is badly signed—you might see directions in Greek for Καρδαμύλη (Kardamyli) or Μάνη (Mani)—but as long as you keep the water on your right, you'll end up on the highway. (A bypass may be completed by the time you visit, allowing you to skirt Kalamata.) Heading south from Kalamata, you'll twist over a suddenly remote-feeling terrain of dramatic mountains and emerge overlooking a grand bay with views over Kardamyli.

After going through Kardamyli, the road continues south, passing near—or directly through—a string of scenic villages before climbing back up over mountains and around a dramatic bay to the regional capital of Areopoli.

From Areopoli you can head east to Gythio and then on to Monemvasia (about 2 hours total), or head south for a loop of the Mani on lesser roads. For all the details on the Mani loop, see the self-guided driving tour on the next page.

The Mani Peninsula

The Mani Peninsula is where the rustic charm of Greece is most apparent. For many travelers, this peninsula is the rural slice of Greek coast-and-mountains that they came to this country to see.

The region's dramatic history has left behind a landscape that's at once eerily stark and remarkably scenic. While mountains edged with abandoned terraces hint that farming was once more extensive, olives have been the only Mani export for the last two centuries. Empty, ghostly hill towns cling barnacle-like onto distant ridges, still fortified against centuries-old threats. Cisterns that once caught rainwater to sustain hardy communities are now mucky green puddles that would turn a goat's stomach. The farther south you go, the bleaker conditions become. And yet many Mani towns feature sumptuous old fresco-slathered churches...pockets of brightness that survive in this otherwise parched land.

This region is difficult to fully experience without a car. To really delve into this rustic corner of Greece, follow this loop drive from Kardamyli.

Mani Pensula Driving Tour

To hit all the places described here in one day, you'll need to get an early start and not linger too long in any one place. If you prefer a later start or a more relaxed day, you could skip Kastania or the cape (saving you about an hour). The major towns worth stopping at on this self-guided driving tour are Agios Nikolaos, Areopoli, and Gerolimenas.

Tips: The light inside old churches can be very dim—if you have a flashlight, bring it along to illuminate the frescoes. Along the way, be prepared for stunning coastal vistas equal to California's Big Sur or the French Riviera. But keep a firm grip on the wheel—the route is a string of hairpin curves, missing guardrails, and blind corners in ancient stone villages. Allow time to pull over frequently for photos and to soak it all in.

• *Head south from Kardamyli on the main road. After a few miles you'll pass the attractive little resort town of* **Stoupa.** *While Kardamyli turns its back to the sea, Stoupa embraces it—with a fine sandy beach arcing right through its center. (Stoupa also works as a separate jaunt from Kardamyli.)*

Just after Stoupa, keep an eye out for the turnoff for our first stop,

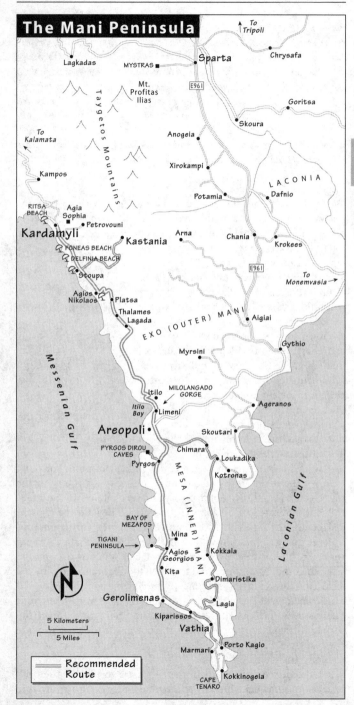

The Mani Peninsula

To Tripoli

Lagkadas

MYSTRAS

Sparta

Chrysafa

Mt. Profitas Ilias

E961

Goritsa

Taygetos Mountains

Anogeia

Skoura

To Kalamata

Xirokampi

LACONIA

Kampos

Potamia

Dafnio

RITSA BEACH

Agia Sophia

Petrovouni

Kardamyli

Kastania

Arna

Chania

Krokees

FONEAS BEACH

DELFINIA BEACH

Stoupa

E961

To Monemvasia

Agios Nikolaos

Platsa

Thalames

Lagada

EXO (OUTER) MANI

Aigiai

Gythio

Myrsini

Messenian Gulf

Itilo

MILOLANGADO GORGE

Itilo Bay

Limeni

Ageranos

Areopoli

Skoutari

PYRGOS DIROU CAVES

Chimara

Pyrgos

Loukadika

Kotronas

MESA (INNER) MANI

Laconian Gulf

BAY OF MEZAPOS

Mina

TIGANI PENINSULA

Agios Georgios

Kokkala

Kita

Gerolimenas

Dimaristika

Kiparissos

Lagia

Vathia

Marmari

Porto Kagio

CAPE TENARO

Kokkinogeia

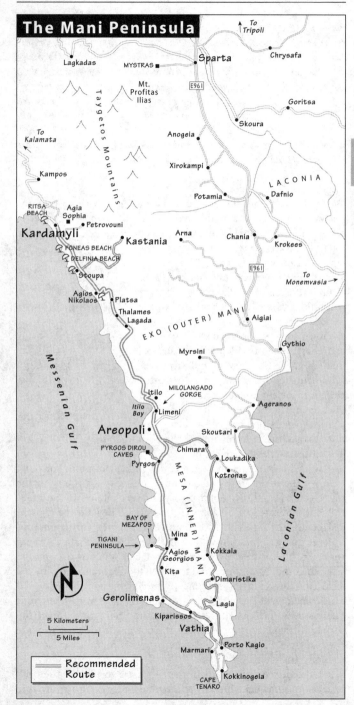

N

5 Kilometers

5 Miles

Recommended Route

KARDAMYLI & MANI PENINSULA

Kastania (Καστανια). The turnoff might not be well-signed: Look for the road up through the olive orchard, on the left, opposite the prominent rocky hill (if you pass a low yellow/orange sign on the left reading ΕΡΓΟ, you've gone a tad too far; follow any signs to Neochori, which is en route). Leaving the main road, head uphill, passing through two other villages along the way. Keep going, following the well-traveled blacktop. Because Kastania is a time-consuming detour from the main road (allow 90 minutes for the round-trip, 30 minutes to walk around), you might want to skip it for now and consider making it a separate side-trip from Kardamyli or a detour en route to Monemvasia.

Kastania

Wedged in a gorge, the village of Kastania offers you a rare opportunity to explore a traditional Mani village that's completely off the tourist track. It may feel sleepy today, but Kastania was once a local powerhouse. During the 19th-century Greek War of Independence, it boasted no fewer than 400 "guns" (as Maniots called their menfolk), gathered under a warlord whose imposing family tower still stands over the town square. The town also had many churches, some of which still feature remarkably well-preserved old frescoes. (Unfortunately, the churches are often closed. If you come across one that doesn't look open, try the door. If it's locked and you see people nearby, ask if they know how to get inside—sometimes there's a key hidden somewhere close by.)

Kastania is nestled in a strategically hidden location: You don't even see the town until you're right on top of it. As you enter the town, you'll pass the first of many Byzantine churches on the left—this one dedicated to St. John (Ag. Ioannis). Beyond the church, just before the two signs (one brown, one blue), turn right and squeeze past the buildings into what seems to be an alley. It's actually the link to the main square, which is watched over by the Church of the Assumption and the town's tower house (built by the local Dourakis clan and now mostly ruined, but may be renovated to become one of seven planned Mani museum towers). Park your car wherever you can near the square, and poke into one of the very traditional cafés for a coffee. The one at the top of the square is a real time warp, where old-timers gather around simple tables, smoking and chatting.

Consider hiking uphill from the square to take in the back streets and some deep breaths of mountain air. Along a rustic lane near the old cistern at the upper end of town is the **Church of St. Peter** (Ag. Petros), which dates from around 1200 and is the oldest of the town's Byzantine churches. It appears to be cobbled together using bits and pieces of antiquity. If it's open, go inside—it's richly adorned with frescoes that have told Bible stories to

this community since the 14th century. While the lighting may be jerry-rigged and a destructive mold has hastened the aging of its precious art, the spiritual wonder of the place remains intact. The olive-oil lamp burns 24 hours a day, tended by a caretaker family. Even if the church is closed, stop to enjoy the views over town from this perch.

• *Back in your car, backtrack to the main road and turn left (south). Continue driving...*

From Stoupa to Areopoli

As you drive you may notice rooftop **solar panels** attached to cylindrical tanks—an efficient way to heat water in this sunny climate. All along the route, set on roadside pedestals, are those little **miniature churches** you've seen throughout Greece. Most of these are "votive churches," erected as a thank-you gesture to God by someone who was spared in an accident. Little churches with a photograph of a person, however, are memorials to someone killed in an accident.

Heading south, you'll pass another fine beach town, **Agios Nikolaos** (St. Nicholas). About a kilometer (half-mile) off the road, this is a little fishing port with wild rocks, a tiny bell tower, a scrawny lighthouse, a tough fleet of little fishing boats, and harborfront restaurants selling fresh fish to stray travelers. The waterfront eatery **Vesuvius** here has a ladder down to the sea from its terrace, so you can combine swimming, basking, and eating.

After Agios Nikolaos the road begins to curve up the mountain, passing through **Platsa** (with the interesting church of St. John/Ag. Ioannis). If the church is open, poke inside to see the ceiling fresco with Jesus surrounded by zodiac symbols—a reminder of the way early Christians incorporated pre-Christian mythology. Higher up, the village of **Thalames**—its square shaded by a giant plane tree—is known for its olive-oil production (several shops on the square sell it). Then, in **Lagada,** watch (on the left) for the re-

KARDAMYLI & MANI PENINSULA

History of the Mani Peninsula

The Mani feels as wild as its history. The region was supposedly first developed around 200 B.C. by breakaway Spartans (from the famously warlike city to the north). Spartan stubbornness persisted in the Mani character for centuries—and made Maniots slow to adopt Christianity. In the 10th century, St. Nikon finally converted the Maniots, and a flurry of Byzantine church-building followed.

Most coastal Mani towns (including Kardamyli) were slowly deserted in the Middle Ages as marauding pirate ships forced people to flee into the hills. There they hid out in villages tucked in the folds of the mountains, far from the coast. (Later, in the 18th century, the construction of protective tower houses allowed Maniots to tentatively begin to return to their coastal settlements.)

Fertile land here was at an absolute premium and hotly contested. In the 17th and 18th centuries, this hostile corner of Greece was known to travelers as the "land of evil counsel" *(Kalavoulia)*

because of its reputation for robbery and piracy—a more reliable way to survive than trying to eke out an honest living by farming. Maniots banded together in clans, whose leaders built the characteristic tower settlements *(kapitanias)* that are a feature of the region. Each *kapitania* controlled its own little city-statelet of land. Some larger towns were occupied by several rival *kapitanias*. Honor was prized even more than arable land, and each clan leader had a chip on his shoulder the size of a big slab of feta cheese. Vendettas and violent bickering between clans—about control of territory or sometimes simply respect—became epidemic. If Greece had

markably well-preserved Byzantine church, lavishly decorated with terra-cotta designs.

As you ascend ever higher, notice how the landscape fades from green to brown. From here on out, the Mani becomes characteristically arid. You'll also begin to see **terraces** etched into the mountainsides, a reminder of how hard Maniots had to work to earn a living from this inhospitable land. They'd scrape together whatever arable soil they could into these little patches to grow olive trees and wheat. Some of the larger stone walls surrounding the terraces demarcate property boundaries.

Soon you cross the "state line" that separates the Exo (Outer) a Tombstone and an O.K. Corral, this is where they'd be.

When they weren't fighting each other, the Maniots banded together to fight off foreign invaders. Locals brag that the feisty Mani—still clinging to the stubborn militarism of the ancient Spartans—remained the only corner of Greece not fully under the thumb of the Ottoman Turks. During nearly four centuries of Turkish rule, the sultan struck a compromise to appoint more or less Ottoman-friendly Maniots as regional governors. After a failed Greek uprising against the Turks in the late 18th century, Greeks from all over the country flooded into the Mani to escape harsh Ottoman reprisals. As the population boomed, competition for the sparse natural resources grew even fiercer.

Perhaps not surprisingly, the hot tempers of the Maniots made the peninsula the crucible for Greek independence. On March 17, 1821, Maniot Petros Mavromichalis, the Ottoman-appointed governor *(bey)*, led a spirited rebellion against his Turkish superiors. Mavromichalis succeeded in taking Kalamata six days later, and the War of Independence was underway. What began in the remote hills of the Mani quickly engulfed the rest of Greece, and by 1829 the Ottomans were history and Greece was free.

Looking around today at the barren landscape of the Mani Peninsula, which now barely supports 5,000 people, it's hard to believe that 200 years ago it sustained a population of almost 60,000. Over time that number was depleted by blood feuds, which raged into the early 20th century. The end of Ottoman rule in the early 19th century and the devastating Greek Civil War of the mid-20th century sparked population shifts out of the region, as Maniots sought easier lifestyles elsewhere in Greece, or set out for the promise of faraway lands, primarily America, the UK, and Australia. But these days, as the Mani emerges as a prime tourist destination, many Maniot emigrants are returning home—bringing back with them an array of accents from around the world.

Mani from the Mesa (Inner) Mani—its southern tip and most striking area.

As you reach the lip of the dramatic Milolangado Gorge, the

town of **Itilo** (EE-tee-loh) comes into view. Like Kardamyli, this town was mentioned in Homer's *Iliad*. The fortifications on the southern side of the gorge belong to Kelefa Castle, built by the Ottomans in 1670 in a short-lived attempt to control the rebellious Maniots. Enjoy the views before heading down to Itilo Bay, where you'll pass the settlements of Neo ("New") Itilo and Limeni (birthplace of the war hero Petros Mavromichalis, whom we'll meet shortly). From the bayside road, adventure-seekers enjoy hiking the 3.5 miles up into the gorge itself.

• *Continuing up the other side of the gorge, and then cresting the top, you'll shortly arrive in...*

Areopoli

Areopoli (ah-reh-OH-poh-lee)—named after Ares, the ancient god of war—is the de facto capital of the Inner Mani. Less charming but more lived-in than other Mani towns, Areopoli is the region's commercial center.

As you arrive from Itilo, signs direct you to the town center and its modern main square, **Plateia Athanaton** (where you should

be able to find a place to park). Dominating the square is a statue of Petros Mavromichalis (1765-1848). This local-boy-done-good was selected to rule the region by the Ottoman overlords, who assumed they could corrupt him with money and power. But they underestimated his strong sense of Mani honor. On March 17, 1821, Mavromichalis gathered a ragtag Maniot army here in Areopoli and marched north to Kalamata, launching the War of Independence. Mavromichalis looks every inch a warrior, clutching a mighty curved sword, with a pistol tucked into his waistband.

The square hosts a lively market on Saturday mornings. At other times, everything else of interest is to be found about 500 yards west of here, around the old main square, **Plateia 17 Martiou.** If Mavromichalis jumped off his pedestal, marched to the candy-colored cafés, and headed left, he'd reach the old center of town: a stony fortified village settlement circling a stone church. This is the spot where Petros mustered his men for the march to Kalamata, a moment commemorated by a plaque on the northern wall. The square is

dominated by the 18th-century Church of Taxiarhes ("Archangels"), sporting an impressive four-story bell tower. The carvings above the main door (around the left side) show the archangels

Gabriel and Michael, flanked by the saints Georgios and Dimitrios on horseback. Under the bell tower is a private war museum of rough artillery. Just behind the church (ΑΡΤΟΠΟΙΕΙΟ sign, near the well), find the rustic bakery run by Milia, who makes bread and savory pies in a wood-fired oven. For an edible souvenir, survey the bags of cookies on the rack by the door.

With your back to the war museum's doorway, take the path straight in front of you, skirting around the ruins of the war tower of Petros Mavromichalis. Follow this alley as it winds its way next to a church. At the end

of the alley, jog left, then right. On this second alley are the Church of St. John and the Pikoulakis Tower—home to the two-room **Mani Museum of Religion,** which documents the long history of Christianity on the peninsula (closed Mon, tel. 27330-29531).

• *Your next stop is the Pyrgos Dirou Caves, about six miles south of Areopoli. (If you're skipping the caves, follow signs toward* Kotronas/ Κότρωνας *just south of Areopoli—take the left turn at the fork—and pick up this tour at "The Eastern Mani," later.)*

Continuing south of Areopoli, follow the signs for Gerolimenas/ Γερολιμενας *at the fork (to the right), then follow signs to Pyrgos; the turnoff for the caves is marked with a blue sign in the center of town. If you go past Pyrgos and reach the turnoff sign for* Γκλεζι, *you've gone too far—backtrack into Pyrgos. The cave entry is along a small bay, reached by a steep road that twists down to the water.*

▲Pyrgos Dirou Caves (a.k.a. Diros Caves and Vlychada Cave)

These remarkable cave formations—discovered by locals in the 1870s and opened to the public in 1963—rank among Europe's best. The formations range from stout stalactites and stalagmites to delicate hair-like structures—many of them surprisingly colorful, thanks to reddish iron deposits.

Cost and Hours: €12, daily Oct-April 8:30-15:30, May-Sept 9:00-17:00, tel. 27330-52222. Because this is a very popular attraction, you might be in for a wait during busy summer months (lines are worst from noon to 14:00 and any time in August). Figure about an hour total to tour the caves (not counting wait time).

Visiting the Caves: Buy your ticket at the gate, then walk five minutes down to the cave entrance to wait for your appointed entry time (if the gate's open, you can also drive right down to the cave entrance after getting your ticket). The temperature in the caves is usually between 60 and 65 degrees Fahrenheit—you may want a sweater. (Be sure to pick up the English brochure, which says about as much as your Greek guide.)

After you've boarded a little boat, your guide poles you along underground canals, softly calling out (usually in Greek only) the creative names for each of the spectacular formations: "Hercules' columns," "palm forest," "golden rain," "crystal lily," and so on. Stalactites drip down directly overhead, and damp cave walls, beautifully lit, are inches away—you'll need to duck or bend from time to time as the boat glides through some of the narrower passageways. In some places the water beneath you is 100 feet deep...you're actually floating near the ceiling of a vast, flooded cavern. (Life preservers are provided.) Pinch yourself: This isn't a movie or a Disney ride, but the real deal. After your three-quarter-mile boat trip, you return to dry land and walk another quarter-mile for up-close views of more limestone formations.

Museum: If you have more time and interest after your cave visit, consider touring the little museum on the hillside between the entrance and ticket office. It shows off human bones and Neolithic artifacts found in similar caves in this area (€2, Tue-Sun 8:30-15:00, closed Mon, well-described in English).

The Eastern Mani

To experience the Mani's most rugged and remote-feeling area, cross over the spine of the peninsula to the eastern coast. The few

tourists you encounter melt away the farther south you drive, until it's just you, sheer limestone cliffs, fortified ghost towns, olive trees, and tumbling surf. Here the terrain seems even more desolate than what you've seen so far.

As you explore the countryside you'll notice huge building projects, hotel developments springing up like mushrooms, and decadent private mansions. (Athenian big shots like to have a Mani escape.) The impressive stonework is generally done by Albanian workers. Mixed in are tiny 13th-century Byzantine churches clinging to the stark land like barnacles and lots of mobile "honey farms." Bee farmers chase the sage and thyme, setting up their hives where the pollen is best. The honey of the Mani is the most expensive and prized in Greece. With so much to see, you'll need to drive carefully. You don't want to become just another of the many roadside shrines.

After taking the left turn for **Kotronas/Κότρωνας** just south of Areopoli, head overland through stark scenery. Cresting the hills at **Chimara/Χιμαρα,** you'll begin to glimpse the Mani's east coast. At **Loukadika/Λουκαδικα,** bear right (south) along the main road toward **Kokkala/Κοκκαλα,** and you'll soon find yourself traversing the top of a cliff above some of the best scenery on the Mani. Heading south you'll see more and more fortified towers climbing up the rocky hillsides. Imagine that each of these towers represents the many ruthless vendettas that were fought here.

Approaching **Dimaristika/Διμαριστικα,** notice the three tower settlements that dot the hill at three different levels. It's easy to imagine why the Ottomans never took this land—the villages could see them coming by ship from miles away and bombard them with cannonballs. And if the Ottomans managed to make landfall, they'd have to climb up, up, up to overtake the forts. It just wasn't worth the trouble.

The village of **Lagia/Λαγια** was supposedly the site of the last Mani vendetta, a scuffle in the 1930s. The town seems almost abandoned today, but most of these houses are owned by Maniots who now live in Athens and come back for the holidays. On the square (along the main road through town) is a monument honoring Panagiotis Vlahakos, a villager who died in a 1996 conflict over a small Aegean island (called Imia in Greek, or Kardak in Turkish) claimed by both Greece and Turkey. The Ottomans left this country close to two centuries ago, but Greek-Turkish relations are still raw.

• *Leaving Lagia, continue straight ahead. After about five minutes, you'll reach a fork. If you're ready to head back around to the western Mani coast, take the left turn (direction: Lagia—and skip down to the "Vathia" section of this tour). But to reach the most distant corner of mainland Greece, Cape Tenaro, bear right toward the long list of Greek names (including Kokkinogeia/Κοκκινόγεια). Switchback your way tightly down toward the sea, always following signs for* Kokkinogeia/Κοκκινόγεια; *if highway signs are missing, look for smaller hiking-route signs that mark the* Tenaro Archaeological Site (*not* Porto Kagio). *After cresting the small isthmus over to the west side of the cape, you'll pass near Marmari/Μαρμαρι (but not through it; it'll be below and to the right as you follow hikers' signs to take an uphill left fork).*

Then keep following signs to Tenaro/Ταίναρο. *You'll come to the literal end of the road.*

Imagine the work it takes to eke out a subsistence living in this godforsaken corner of Greece, and spending your days digging up stones to build the fortified tower houses you see capping the hills.

Cape Tenaro (a.k.a. Cape Matapan): Greece's "Land's End"

Drive out to the tip of the rocky promontory known as the "Sanctuary of the Dead." As the farthest point of the known world, this

was where the ancient Greeks believed that the souls of the deceased came to enter the underworld. An underwater cave here was thought to belong to Hades, god of the underworld. It was also the site of a temple and oracle devoted to Poseidon, the god of the sea (marked today by a ruined Christian church).

Visitors can still explore the scant unexcavated ruins of an ancient town that was called Tenaron (mentioned in the *Iliad*). An inviting restaurant also offers travelers a good opportunity for a break.

Just below the parking lot are the ruins of an early Christian church, likely constructed using giant blocks scavenged from

the temple upon which it sits. To visit the poorly marked ruins of Tenaron, walk down from the parking lot toward the water, then bear right around the far side of the bay. You'll soon be able to pick out the footprints of ancient Greek and Roman structures. Hiding behind one

of these low walls, about a five-minute walk around the tiny bay, is a surprisingly intact floor mosaic from a Roman villa, just sitting out in the open. If you've got time to kill and are up for a longer hike, trudge another 30 minutes out to a lighthouse at the end of the world. A busy shipping channel lies just offshore; you can count the vessels heading east to Athens or to ports to the west.

• *Retrace your tracks back to civilization. Reaching the main road, turn left and head back up the west coast of the Mani (toward Vathia/Βαθειά). Soon you'll be treated to views of the classic Mani ghost town. Drive 100 yards past the town for the best view. Then return and park near the double phone booth. From there you can walk into the stony village. Circle it clockwise (a former donkey mill is inside the first house on the left). Consider how a settlement like this with no roads and only footpaths can't survive in the modern age.*

Vathia

The most dramatic of all the Mani tower villages, Vathia is Vendetta-ville—it seems everyone here barricaded themselves in forts.

The more towers a town had, the more dangerous it was—and it's hard to imagine cramming more towers into a single town than they did in Vathia. Built on a rocky spur and once famed for its olive oil, Vathia was an extreme example of what can happen when neighbors don't get along. The 80-some houses were split north/south into two rival camps, which existed in a state of near-permanent hostility. Now Vathia is mostly uninhabited. Once-intimidating towers are now haunting ruins, held together with boards and steel cables.

• *Driving north, you'll pass through the larger town of Kiparissos—originally Kenipolis ("New City"), which was settled by those who left ancient Tenaron—then turn off (signs in Greek only) to reach the town center and port of...*

Gerolimenas

Gerolimenas (yeh-roh-LEE-meh-nahs, roughly "sacred port"), nestled at the back of a deep sheltered bay, is a cute fishing town

kept alive by tourism. The waterfront is lined with cafés and restaurants, and the water is good for a swim—making it an all-around enjoyable place to take a break and watch the surf.

• *Continue back out to the main road, toward* **Kita.**

This town was the setting for the Mani's final major feud in 1870, which raged for weeks until the Greek army arrived, artillery in tow, to enforce a truce.

For one last little detour, hang a left turn at the village of Agios Georgios (toward Μέζαπος/*Mezapo/Beach), and go a bit more than a mile down to the...*

Bay of Mezapos

At the cove at Mezapos (MEH-zah-pohs), carved out of limestone by the surf, boats bob picturesquely in the protective harbor, watched over by an extremely sleepy hamlet. Mezapos was once a notorious haven for pirates. It's easy to see why, if you look across the bay to see the long, naturally fortified peninsula aptly named Tigani ("frying pan"). This was once thought to be the site of the Frankish castle of Maina (roughly, "clenched fist"), which some believe to be the namesake of the Mani.

• *Continuing north you'll first pass the village of Pyrgos—where you turned off earlier to see the caves—then arrive back at Areopoli. From here retrace your steps around Itilo Bay back to Kardamyli; or, if you're continuing onward, head east just beyond Areopoli to reach Monemvasia.*

MONEMVASIA

ΜΟΝΕΜΒΑΣΊΑ / Μονεμβασία

Monemvasia (moh-nehm-VAH-see-ah), a gigantic rock that juts improbably up from the blue-green deep just a few hundred yards offshore, is a time-warp to the medieval Peloponnese. Its little Lower Town hamlet hides on the seaward side of the giant rock, tethered to the mainland only by a skinny spit of land. This remarkably romantic walled town—with the remains of an even bigger Upper Town scattered along the peak high above—is a stony museum of Byzantine, Ottoman, and Venetian history dating back to the 13th century. Summiting Monemvasia is a key experience on any Peloponnesian visit.

Monemvasia means "single entry"—and the only way to get here is to cross the narrow causeway. At the mainland end of the causeway is the nondescript town of Gefyra (YEH-fee-rah), a smattering of hotels, restaurants, shops, and other modern amenities that offer a handy 21st-century base and springboard for exploring the Rock.

Heading to or from Monemvasia, consider a stop at Mystras, near Sparta. Although the town of Sparta has little of touristic interest, the site of Mystras has well-preserved Byzantine churches (dating from the 13th to 14th century) that evoke the grandeur of the Byzantine Empire before it fizzled.

PLANNING YOUR TIME

It takes only a couple hours to see Monemvasia—a stroll through the Lower Town, a hike to the Upper Town, and you've done it all. Though doable as a day trip from Kardamyli or Nafplio (3-4 hours by car each way), I don't recommend it. Spending the night in Monemvasia (or mainland Gefyra) allows you to linger on the floodlit cobbles and makes the long trip down here more worthwhile.

Monemvasia Overview

To Sparta

THE ROCK

CHURCH OF AGIA SOPHIA

ACROPOLIS

UPPER TOWN

Cliffs

Ⓑ

LOWER TOWN
(SEE DETAIL MAP)

Sea of Crete

GEFYRA

Not to Scale

Ⓑ SHUTTLE BUS STOPS

MONEMVASIA

❶ Hotel Panorama
❷ The Flower of Monemvasia Hotel
❸ Hotel Pramataris
❹ Anastatios Sofos Rooms & Supermarket
❺ Taverna Scorpios
❻ Taverna Asterias
❼ Grill House
❽ Malvasia Travel Agency & Bus Stop
❾ Post Office, ATMs & Bakery

Orientation to Monemvasia

Monemvasia is moored to the mainland at the village of Gefyra, where most of its services are located. The road into Gefyra from Sparta becomes the main street, where you'll find—clustered where the road bends left toward the Rock—the post office, a few ATMs, and an excellent bakery (with a supermarket just up the street). The Malvasia Travel Agency sells bus tickets and serves as the town's bus stop (located at the start of the causeway across from the shuttle bus stop).

After passing through Gefyra, the main road leads to the causeway across to the Rock (Vraxos). The hamlet of Monemvasia itself, which locals call To Kastro ("The Castle"), is out of sight around behind the Rock. To Kastro is divided into the Lower Town (with shops, hotels, and restaurants) and the ruins of the Upper Town high above. Only a dozen or so people actually live in Monemvasia, and it's fair to say every business there caters to tourists.

ARRIVAL IN MONEMVASIA

A road runs around the base of the Rock from the causeway to Monemvasia's Lower Town. To get from Gefyra on the mainland to the Lower Town, you have three options: walk (across the causeway, then around the Rock, about 20 minutes); drive (go all the way to the castle gate and then circle back to grab the closest roadside parking spot); or take a shuttle bus (see next).

HELPFUL HINTS

Gefyra-Monemvasia Shuttle Bus: Use this handy service to avoid the long, hot and boring walk between Gefyra and old Monemvasia (2/hour, leaves Gefyra on the half hour from 8:00-24:00 and from the castle a few minutes later, €1 each way, just hop on and pay driver, bus is signed *Kastro,* which means castle).

Name Variation: In English the town's name can also be spelled Monemvassia, Monembasia, or Monembacia. During the Venetian period it was called Malvasia.

Addresses: Locals don't bother with street numbers, or even names—both Monemvasia and Gefyra are small enough that everyone knows where everything is. If you can't find something, just ask around. On the Rock, businesses are only allowed on the main drag.

Don't Needlessly Fry: If climbing to the top of the Rock in the summer, make a point to do it early or late if possible, as it can be brutally hot in mid-day.

Monemvasia Walk

There are only two things to see in Monemvasia: the walled Lower Town and the castle ruins of the Upper Town high above (free and open 24 hours daily). This self-guided walk covers both. Note: The Upper Town may be closed for renovation when you visit—check locally.

Lower Town

Begin outside the 17th-century **main gate,** designed by the Ottomans who were occupying the town at the time (and who knew a thing or two about designing— and breaching—gates like this one). The only public WCs are to the right, in front of the gate.

Look up to the cliff and down to the sea, appreciating how successfully the crenellated wall protected this mighty little nugget

Monemvasia's History

Mighty Monemvasia, a Gibraltar-like rock with a Crusader-style stone town at its base, has ruins scattered all across its Masada-like plateau summit.

Monemvasia's Upper Town may have been founded in the sixth century A.D. by refugees fleeing Slavic raids into the Peloponnese. Gradually the settlement spread down the hill and, thanks to its uniquely well-defended position, became a powerful town. It was a center of both trade and military importance, with merchants living below and the nobility living above. In the declining days of the Byzantine Empire (1262-1460), when nearby Mystras was its ecclesiastical base, Monemvasia was its main city and one of the great commercial centers of the Byzantine world, with a thriving population in the tens of thousands. It was known for its Malvasia wine, a lightly fortified red that was prized at the royal courts of Europe. Over the next several centuries, highly strategic Monemvasia changed hands again and again—mostly back and forth between the Venetians and the Ottomans. While most of the buildings that survive today date from the second period of Venetian rule (1690-1715), foundations and architectural elements from each chapter survive.

By the 18th century, Monemvasia slipped into decline... until it was rediscovered by tourists in the 1970s. Today Monemvasia is a leading destination both for international visitors and for wealthy Athenians, who are converting its old houses into weekend retreats.

of Byzantine power. There are only four entrances: two on this side, one on the opposite side, and one from the sea. Combine that with the ridiculously easy-to-defend little causeway (once equipped with a drawbridge) and the perfect bird's-eye view from the top of the Rock (ideal for spotting would-be invaders from miles and miles away), and Monemvasia was a tough nut to crack.

Enter the gate. (The stairway inside leads left up to a terrace with a monument noting the fact that the 20th-century poet Yiannis Ritsos—beloved by Greeks but unknown abroad—spent much of his life here.) Inside the gate, notice that the road jogs, preventing you from even getting a peek at the town until you emerge on the other side—another defensive measure. And then...

You're at the start of Monemvasia's narrow, cobbled **main street.** Bear uphill (left) at the fork, through a gauntlet of tourist shops, hotel offices (renting rooms in buildings scattered all over town), and cafés with inviting terraces stretching toward the sea. Elsewhere in town, doors and windows are small, but here—on what's always been the main commercial drag—the wide, arched windows come with big built-in counters for displaying wares. Enjoy this atmospheric lane, scouting cafés and restaurants for later (see "Eating in Monemvasia").

At the **Edodimopolio local products shop** (on the left, near the entry gate), energetic Fotini stocks all sorts of gifty edibles and is happy to offer samples of her honey-wine and olive oil.

The lane leads to the town's **main square,** Plateia Dsami—literally "Mosque Square," a very rare-in-Greece tip of the hat to Ottoman rule. The namesake mosque still stands (the blocky building with the small red dome, on the right). In the middle of the square, notice two symbols of the town: a cannon (Monemvasia was nothing if not well-defended) and a well. Monemvasia is honeycombed with cisterns for catching rainwater...the one thing that a city clinging to a rock floating in the sea needs to survive. Virtually every house—in both the Upper and Lower Towns—had a roof designed to catch water, with pipes plumbed into its walls and its own cellar cistern.

Walk to the edge of this square and survey the rooftops of the **Lower Town.** Notice a unique feature of Monemvasia houses:

sharply angled rooflines, which allowed built-in tile gutters to carefully channel water into those cellar cisterns. Houses are built of stone quarried from right here on the Rock—a very efficient way to get building materials. Whereas the stone walls of many houses are exposed today, historically most houses were covered with plaster (some still are), which once gave the skyline Santorini-like soft edges.

Now turn around and face the Rock and the **Upper Town.**

Monemvasia: Lower Town

① Byzantino Hotel
② Malvasia Hotel
③ Matoula & To Kanoni Restaurants
④ Voltes Mezedopolio Restaurant
⑤ Enetiko Café Cocktail Bar
⑥ Edodimopolio Local Products Shop
⑦ To Gefyra Hotels & Eateries

AGIA SOFIA

To Tower Ruins & Great Views

To Acropolis Ruins & Great Views

STEEP PATH

UPPER TOWN

LOWER

TOWN

AYLOS NIKOLAOS

TOWN WALL

PANAYIA MYRTIDIOTISSA

PANAYIA KHRYSAFIOTISSA

CHRISTOS ELKOMENOS

BISHOP'S RESIDENCE

Main Square

CANNON

FORMER MOSQUE & ARCH. MUSEUM

MAIN GATE

P

B WC

To Gefyra & ⑦

Shuttle Bus to Gefyra

100 Meters
100 Yards

Notice the stoutly walled, zigzagging path that climbs the cliff face. Halfway up and a little to the right, notice the small cave (with the white entrance) burrowed into the cliff—a humble chapel reached by a precarious footpath. You can see from here that most of the Upper Town is in ruins...but it is fun to explore (described later).

Before leaving the square, do a little sightseeing. The old mosque—which has also served as a church, prison, and coffee shop—today hosts a modest **archaeological museum** (€2, Tue-Sun 9:00-15:00, closed Mon, tel. 27320-61403). The one-room display, though sparse, is well-presented and well-described in English: pottery fragments, the stone chancel screen (iconostasis) from a long-gone Byzantine church, and an explanation of how many ancient architectural elements were scavenged to build early Christian churches.

Across from the mosque/museum is the whitewashed, 11th-century **Church of Christos Elkomenos** ("Christ in Pain"). In its day, this was a very important Byzantine church. (The twin plat-

forms in the rear are said to be for the thrones used when the emperor and empress visited from Constantinople.) While this was originally a Byzantine church, the Venetians substantially expanded it: Notice the elaborately carved lintel above the entrance, a sure sign of Venetian influence. The peacock relief above the lintel was added after independence (1820s), as was the bell tower. If open (generally daily 9:00-14:00 & 16:00-20:00), step into the tidy white interior for a serene visit to an Orthodox church. If you're so moved, drop a coin in the box, light a candle, and say a prayer. Hiding behind the marble iconostasis (peek behind the curtain) is a small reminder of the church's humble Byzantine origins: old amphitheater-like stone risers where bishops once stood.

The artistic highlight of the entire region is in a small chapel to the right: a precious icon of the Crucifixion dating from around 1300, the peak of the Byzantine Renaissance. As this is the world in which El Greco trained, you could consider it "proto-El Greco." The emotions portrayed were ground-breaking for the age (English description outside the door). This icon was stolen in the 1970s, making headlines across the country and is displayed now only with high security.

Although it's a little town today, Monemvasia was one important enough to be a bishopric. Back outside, to the right as

you face the church, notice the entrance to the bishop's former residence—with the Venetian coat of arms (the winged lion of St. Mark) above the door. You'll also see that the church is attached by an archway to a small chapel.

Before huffing up to the Upper Town, poke around the Lower Town's twisty lanes. Descend through the archway to the right of the church. The steps lead down through a maze of steeply cobbled streets to the sea wall. A gate (tiny and therefore easy to

MONEMVASIA

defend) at the center of the wall leads out to a rocky platform with ladders into the sea for swimmers (there's a handy shower here).

As you explore, keep a few things in mind: The streets of Monemvasia are a variety of architectural influences: Byzantine,

Venetian, and Ottoman. Wandering the streets of the Lower Town, you might notice pointed archways or large lintels (stones over windows), which are distinctively Venetian; or occasional tulip-shaped windows (curling on top with a little peak in the middle), which are unmistakably Turkish. Notice the many arched passageways spanning narrow lanes—the only way a crowded, walled town could grow. Quite a few houses are still in ruins, but with Monemvasia's tourism on the rise, many of these are

now being excavated and rebuilt. Because the town is protected, restoration requires navigating a lot of red tape and giving painstaking attention to historical accuracy.

You'll notice lots of little churches. In Byzantine times, ecclesiastical and political power overlapped, and building a church gave a wealthy family more prestige and power. Also, a trading town like this would have been home to communities from different lands—each with its own style of worship and particular church.

Each significant site around town is numbered and explained by posted information...but there's no need to get bogged down by those details. Just have fun with the perfect medieval streetscapes awaiting discovery around each turn.

When you're ready to climb the Rock, be sure you're prepared: Wear good shoes and bring sun protection (there's very little shade up there) and water (there are no shops up top, but you can buy water at gift shops along the Lower Town's main drag). Before hiking up, confirm with any local that the Upper Town is actually open. Then make your way to the top of town and huff up the steep path to the...

Upper Town

The ruins of the Upper Town are spread across a broad, rolling plateau at the summit of the Rock. Unlike the well-preserved Lower Town, very little of the Upper Town has survived intact. The last weary resident left the plateau nearly a century ago, and it is now a wasteland of ruined old buildings, engulfed by a sea of shrubs and wildflowers that seem to sprout from the rocks. As you explore up here, watch your step—sudden cliffs and open cisterns could bring your vacation to a sudden and tragic end.

Nearing the top of the trail, curl through yet another defensive gateway. The door here, with its metal casing, is likely 18th-century Ottoman—and is probably the best artifact surviving in the Upper Town. Emerging onto the top, get oriented using four points: the collection of buildings at the gate (with fine views onto the Lower Town from the tiny square); the Church of Agia Sophia (directly above you—just follow the trail up); the acropolis at the highest point (to the left); and the promontory (overlooking the sea at the far right). The best way to enjoy the top of the Rock is to let your inner child take over for a king- or queen-of-the-castle scramble across the ramparts and ruins.

Hike up to the 12th-century Byzantine **Church of Agia Sophia.** Thanks to recent erosion, the church hangs precariously (and

scenically) close to the edge of a sheer cliff. Like so many buildings here, the church has elements from various eras of history: a Byzantine core (it retains its original octagonal design), with Ottoman elements (most now gone, but you can still see the prayer niche, or mihrab), and a triple-arched loggia grafted onto the front in the 16th century by the Venetians. The interior was whitewashed when it was converted into a mosque under Turkish rule, but fragments of original frescoes survive.

From here you can climb higher up the hill for good **views** back down onto the church. If you want to lengthen your hike, you

can climb all the way to the acropolis, the fortification near the peak of the Rock (visible from here). Or, for an easier walk, head downhill to the crenellated watchtower area out toward the sea; this promontory has the best views back up to the church.

As you explore the site, remember that this was regarded as the mightiest fortress in Byzantine Greece. Not surprisingly, it was never captured in battle—only by a protracted starve-'em-out siege. Monemvasia's Achilles' heel was its dependence on the mainland for food. And though some basic supplies were cultivated atop the Rock, it wasn't enough to sustain the entire town for very long.

Back at the entrance gateway, consider heading right along the wall (as you face the Lower Town and water) for good views

back down onto the Lower Town. If you continue farther along this path, you'll reach an old Turkish house, and then the granddaddy of all the town's cisterns: a **cavernous vaulted hall.**

Our tour of the Rock is finished. When you're done enjoying the views and the evocative ruins, head back down the way you came up.

Evenings in Monemvasia

Monemvasia is touristy yet peaceful and romantic after dark, with several bars and cafés open late. In the Lower Town, everything of interest is along the one business street or on the town square. My choice for a drink is the **Enetiko Café Cocktail Bar** (about 100 yards in from the gate, with great cocktails, a chill vibe, and a view terrace).

The long walk between the mainland and the old town is lit but nerve-wracking, with cars dodging pedestrians. I'd take advantage of the shuttle bus that goes on the half-hour until midnight (see page 319). Evenings along the harborfront in **Gefyra** can be delightful, too, with plenty of places for a drink or meal.

Sleeping in Monemvasia

Peak-season demand drives prices up in July and August—especially on weekends when this is a popular retreat for Athenians. Off-season, you can usually get a deal.

ON THE ROCK

Sleeping in Monemvasia's old Lower Town, romantic and appealing to many, is a lot of work because you can't park nearby. Various hotels rent rooms scattered through old buildings. All of them have decor that mixes new and old, with old-fashioned Monemvasia flourishes (such as low platform beds, tight bathrooms, head-banging archways, and stone shower enclosures without curtains). Keep in mind that Monemvasia is a honeycomb of cobblestone alleys and stairs. Luggage with wheels won't work here. If you stay on

---

Sleep Code

Abbreviations   (€1=about $1.10, country code: 30)
S=Single, **D**=Double/Twin, **T**=Triple, **Q**=Quad, **b**=bathroom
Price Rankings
  $$$ Higher Priced—Most rooms €100 or more
   $$ Moderately Priced—Most rooms between €70-100
    $ Lower Priced—Most rooms less than €70

Unless otherwise noted, breakfast is included, English is spoken, and free Wi-Fi and/or a guest computer is generally available. Many places accept credit cards, and rooms generally have air-conditioning. Prices can change; verify the hotel's current rates online or by email. For the best prices, always book directly with the hotel.

---

the Rock, be prepared to carry your luggage to your hotel (drivers might want to cram essentials into a day pack).

I've listed two "hotels" that are actually a reception desk near the entry gate managing mostly elegantly remodeled rooms scattered throughout the Lower Town. Review their websites and compare what they offer.

$$ Byzantino Hotel rents 25 tastefully old-fashioned rooms in the Lower Town (Db-€60-80 with no view, €80-90 with sea view, €100-135 with sea view and balcony, breakfast-€5 at their café, tel. 27320-61351, www.hotelbyzantino.com, hotelbyzantino@yahoo. gr). Avoid the pricey rooms in their Lazareto Hotel, outside the Lower Town, just across the causeway from the mainland.

$$ Malvasia Hotel is a collection of 50 rustic but atmospheric rooms around town. About half of them have been beautifully renovated with no loss of charm (Db-€50-100 depending on season, view, and room condition; tel. 27320-61323, www. malvasiahoteltraditional.gr, malvasia@otenet.gr).

IN GEFYRA

Sleeping in the mainland town of Gefyra lacks the romance of spending the night in old Monemvasia, but it's less expensive and easier. The following listings are each a solid value if rooms in Monemvasia are booked up, or for those who'd rather trade atmosphere for the convenience of parking a few steps from their room.

$ Hotel Panorama is well-run by friendly Angelos and Rena Panos. At the top of Gefyra, a 10-minute hike up from the main street, it's quiet and comes with great views. Its 27 comfy rooms all have balconies (Sb-€50, Db-€60, sea-view Db-€70, Tb-€75, sea-view Tb-€85, family room-€100, rooms €15-20 more in Aug, no elevator, tel. 27320-61198, www.panoramahotel-monemvasia. gr, info@panoramahotel-monemvasia.gr).

$ The Flower of Monemvasia is a pleasant family-run hotel along the main road near the causeway with 20 rooms, each with a balcony (Db-€30-50, third person-€18, about €16 more per room in Aug and on holiday weekends, soft rates, cheaper in winter, pricier suites, breakfast optional, no elevator, tel. 27320-61395, www.flower-hotel.gr, info@flower-hotel.gr).

$ Hotel Pramataris offers 22 good-value rooms across the street from The Flower of Monemvasia. Most rooms have balconies and views of the Rock (Db-€40-60 depending on season, no elevator, tel. 27320-61833, www.pramatarishotel.gr, hotelpr@hol.gr).

$ Anastatios Sofos is the cheaper option, with eight bare-bones rooms along the main road (Db-€40 July-Aug, otherwise €35, no breakfast, tel. 27320-61202, speaks just enough English).

Eating in Monemvasia

ON THE ROCK

Both of these eateries are along the main pedestrian artery of Monemvasia's Lower Town, just before the main square.

Matoula (Ματούλα), with its delightful vine-shaded terrace looking out to sea, is the most appealing of the restaurants on the Rock. Amid all of the pretense of this town, it serves good traditional Greek dishes at fine prices. Consider the daily specials and *barbounia* (red mullet), or ask owner Venetia about the daily specials (€4 starters, €8-14 main dishes, seafood splurges, daily 12:00-late, tel. 27320-61660).

To Kanoni ("The Cannon"), next door to Matoula, is another good choice, with a cozy interior and a scenic upper veranda (€4-7 starters, €8-16 main dishes, pricier seafood dishes, daily 10:00-late, tel. 27320-61387, say hi to Petros). I like the tables on the cool rooftop terrace with a view down on the old square.

Voltes Mezedopolio, a cozy little place just inside the gate, is run by two hardworking brothers and make a good stop for *mezes* (€5 plates to enjoy family-style). The restaurant has no view, but the atmosphere is friendly and the prices are very good.

IN GEFYRA

A collection of interchangeable eateries cluster like barnacles at the Gefyra end of the causeway. In good weather, it's pointless to eat anywhere here without a view of the Rock. I like to walk along the water (on either side of the causeway) and survey the options.

At **Taverna Scorpios,** Vasillis cooks and Julie takes good care of diners at rustic white tables under a blue canopy. It has a castaway ambience and my favorite views of the Rock (€3-6 starters, €5-11 main dishes, daily 12:00-24:00, tel. 27320-62090).

Taverna Asterias is a place where your chair can settle into the pebbles of the beach while friendly Spiro cooks fresh fish daily for lunch and dinner. When it's cold, dine indoors by the cozy open fireplace (to the left of the causeway as you face the Rock, tel. 27320-62049).

Fast Food and Picnics: For a quick snack, the **Grill House** is a hit for its souvlaki and gyros (eat-in with the local teenagers or take-away; located in the center a block from the causeway). The bakery on Gefyra's main street (near the post office) is wonderful, and the supermarket just up the side street from there will help you round out your moveable feast for the top of the Rock. While you can buy basic drinks and snacks in Monemvasia's Lower Town, there's no grocery store there—do your shopping in Gefyra.

Monemvasia Connections

By Bus: Monemvasia is not well connected by bus and has no bus station. Buses stop across the street from the Malvasia Travel Agency, just before the causeway; you can buy tickets on the bus or at the travel agency (recommended a day in advance in busy times, tel. 27320-61752).

Four to five buses leave for **Sparta** each day (likely at 5:15, 7:15, 14:15, and 17:30; Mon and Thu-Fri also at 8:30; 2 hours); these continue on to **Tripoli** (4 hours total) and then **Athens** (6 hours total). You'll need to change in Sparta to reach just about anywhere else, such as **Areopoli** on the Mani Peninsula (3.5 hours from Sparta). Change in Tripoli for **Nafplio** (1.5 hours from Tripoli).

By Shared Taxi: Hotels can arrange a shared taxi to **Athens** (€40/person, 4 hours, departs early each morning).

ROUTE TIPS FOR DRIVERS

Monemvasia's a bit out of the way, but the trek is worth it. Allow 3 hours from **Kardamyli** (consider a pit stop in Gythio, a workaday port town with fine harborfront restaurants, about 1.5 hours from Monemvasia) or roughly 3 hours from **Nafplio** (on the fast road via Sparta and Tripoli). If you pass through Sparta en route, you can easily fit in a visit to the nearby Byzantine city and churches of Mystras (see next section).

You can speed on the highway for most of the route between Nafplio and Monemvasia, but you'd be missing one of the most stunning scenic drives in Greece: The coastal road between Nafplio and cute little Leonidio is very pretty, and the twisty cliffside uphill from (or downhill to) Leonidio is jaw-dropping. The mountain town of Kosmas is good for a quick break. Between Monemvasia and Kosmas, look for signs to Skala and Vrontamas. The route requires a little planning (as roads aren't well marked) and isn't for the squeamish. Even with a GPS on board, it's a good idea to ask your hotelier for route tips.

Sparta and Mystras

Located roughly between Kardamyli, Monemvasia, and Nafplio, the town of Sparta (which is nothing much) is near the site of Mystras, which is worth a stop. Its impressive Byzantine churches are fine examples of the empire's last Golden Age.

SPARTA (ΣΠΑΡΤΗ)

Sparta—where mothers famously told their sons to "come home with your shield...or on it"—is a classic (and, I hope, thought-provoking) example of how little a militaristic society leaves as a legacy for the future.

The ancient Sparta that dominated Greek affairs in the sixth and fifth centuries B.C. isn't one visitors can experience: The various excavation sites around town go down no farther than the level of Roman Sparta, which was built on the foundations of the classical city from the first century B.C.

One reason why so little remains is that the town was abandoned in the 13th century, and its buildings were dismantled for reuse in the construction of nearby Mystras. Sparta was reestablished in 1834 on the initiative of King Otto and his Bavarian court, whose classical education had given them a strong appreciation of Sparta's place in history. Otto ordered his planners to create a city of wide boulevards and parks; today Sparta looks more like 19th-century Bavaria than the home of Spartan hero King Leonidas.

Sparta, built on a grid system, is easier to navigate than many Greek cities. Coming from Monemvasia or Gythio, you'll enter on Palaeologou and head through town, past the main square, until the main drag reaches a statue of King Leonidas. (Below the statue is written his famous taunt before the Persians slaughtered him and his last 300 troops in 380 B.C.: "Come and get it.") A block before the statue, in the median, a monument honors 27 centuries of hometown athletes—medalists in Olympic Games from 720 B.C. to A.D. 1996 (mostly for running and wrestling).

The acropolis of ancient Sparta is signposted from the statue of Leonidas. It's a pleasant 10-minute walk, but the ruins that lie scattered among the olive trees are Roman-era or later. The main feature of the excavations is an impressive Roman theater; however, much of its stone seating was removed and used in the defensive wall built around the city's acropolis in the fourth century A.D.

MYSTRAS (ΜΥΣΤΡΑΣ)

Mystras, four miles west of Sparta, is the most important Byzantine site in Greece. It was here, in the foothills of the Taygetos Mountains, that the Byzantine Empire enjoyed a final dazzling period of creative energy (1262-1460) before it was swallowed up by the Ottomans.

The main attractions in Mystras are its churches—regarded as some of the finest surviving examples of late Byzantine architecture in Greece. The extravagantly decorated frescoes were painted by the empire's greatest artists (although their names sadly went unrecorded). Because of ongoing restoration work, some of the churches may be closed when you visit.

Cost and Hours: €12, €6 off-season Mon-Sat 8:00-20:00, Sept until 13:30, Oct until 17:30, Nov-March until 15:00; Sun 8:00-15:00 year-round; tel. 27310-23315. There's a good restaurant a block below the entrance. The only WC in the site is before entering.

Background

The last rulers of the Byzantine Empire were the Palaiologos "despots"—but they were not tyrants; the name comes from a subdivision of the Byzantine church called a "despotate." Under the Palaiologos family, Mystras became the Byzantine Empire's cultural and intellectual capital. It was home to many great artists and to the philosopher Plethon, who was responsible for the revival of Plato's teachings. Plethon and other scholars based here had a major impact on the Italian Renaissance, especially after he visited Florence in 1438.

After the fall of Constantinople to the Ottomans in 1453, the Byzantine emperors retreated here, and Mystras became the last outpost of their empire. But Mystras' Golden Age came to end when the city surrendered to the Turks a few years later in 1460.

While Mystras is many centuries old, it was a thriving center until more modern times: Mystras had about 15,000 people living within its walls even during Muslim Ottoman rule (1460-1828). During that period, the sultan appointed the Orthodox patriarch, who was allowed to carry on if he didn't cause trouble. You'll see only one mosque in the entire site (built for the sultan's bureaucracy).

Then, with Greek independence in the early 1800s, the Ottomans were expelled. King Otto consolidated power in part by dissolving the Orthodox monasteries and nationalizing the Greek Orthodox Church. He shut down Mystras and turned the great city into a quarry, providing stone for the building of modern Sparta. (He dreamed of making Sparta and Athens twin cities for his new Greece.) It's interesting to note that ancient Sparta served as a quarry for the building of Mystras, and then Mystras served as a quarry for the rebuilding of 19th-century Sparta.

Visiting the Site

The gangly site stretches halfway up the mountain. Tour groups start at the top entrance (about a mile up the road) and see Mystras as a long downhill walk—convenient if you can find a ride to the top entrance. But I'll assume you'll park at the main (bottom) entry and see the site by zigzagging uphill and then retracing your steps back down to leave. Here are the main stops from the bottom to the top.

Metropolitan (Cathedral): The cathedral was built in 1270 and dedicated to St. Demetrius. Stepping into the courtyard, you see columns recycled from ancient Sparta, the bishop's residence, and a fountain built with a mishmash of ancient plunder. Inside the cathedral are more ancient columns. The double-headed eagle relief set into the floor in the center commemorates the coronation of the last Byzantine emperor, which took place here in 1449. (Since ancient times, the double-headed eagle has been the symbol of anyone considering himself the successor of the Roman Emperor—like Byzantine emperors, Habsburg rulers, and Holy Roman Emperors.)

Museum: From the courtyard, steps lead to a small museum (featuring old holy books, marbles, artifacts from local graves). Before leaving the courtyard enjoy the uphill view of the rest of Mystras. The lower zone was for the common people and merchants (and this cathedral). The upper zone was for the nobility and ruling elite. The intact building directly above is the Palace of the Despots (described later). Imagine the despot surveying his realm from that perch.

Churches of Theodoros and Aphentiko: Beyond the Metropolitan, a path slopes gently uphill to the right. This takes you to the churches of Agios Theodoros and Aphentiko, nestled below a grove of tall cypress trees. It's worth the detour just to admire the frescoes and the magnificent, multiple red-tiled domes of the Aphentiko.

Convent and Church of Pantanassa: Opposite the Metropolitan, a steep path leads up toward the imposing Church of Pantanassa. The only living part of Mystras, it's home to six sweet, elderly, black-veiled nuns who live in a row of small rooms (on the left as you enter the church's walled compound). They tend the flower gardens and produce linen embroidered with Byzantine motifs, sold in the small shop at the end of the row. (A sister told me they actually have me and my guides on their prayer list in thanks for the thoughtful visitors who come here with this book and on our tours and buy their handmade embroidery work. Please, buy their delightful little souvenirs...I can use the prayers.) The church here is home to Mystras' best collection of frescoes and more columns and capitals plundered from ancient Sparta.

Monemvasia Gate: From the convent, retrace your steps to the main path and continue uphill through the well-fortified gate (the name means "only one entrance"). The gate provided the only access between the lower town and the upper town, where the noble and powerful lived.

Palace of the Despots: The original palace is the closest wing of the building on the right, which was built by the Crusaders. Although the palace has been closed to the public for many years, you can check out the pointed Gothic arches of the top floor windows—a favorite motif found at other Crusader castles around the Peloponnese. In the final decades of their rule, the Palaiologos despots built the second wing. Its massive central hall, which covers the entire second floor, served as their throne room.

St. Nicholas Church, Church of St. Sofia, Top Entry, and Crusader Castle: The top part of the site is a long climb (not worth the sweat for many if it's hot). The St. Nicholas Church (which comes first) is most interesting and worth hiking up to see. It was built in the early 1600s, during Ottoman rule. Near the top entry is the Church of St. Sofia. High above, capping the mountain, stands the Crusader Castle, built in 1249 and offering a commanding view into a 400-yard-deep gorge and out across the Peloponnese.

MONEMVASIA

BEYOND
ATHENS

DELPHI
ΔΕΛΦΟΊ / Δελφοί

Perched high on the southern slopes of Mt. Parnassos, and over-looking the gleaming waters of the Gulf of Corinth, Delphi (Greeks pronounce it "dell-FEE," not "DELL-fye") is without doubt the most spectacular of Greece's ancient sites.

Back then, Delphi was famous throughout the world as the home of a prophetess known as the oracle (a.k.a. the Pythia). As the mouthpiece of Apollo on earth, she told fortunes for pilgrims who came from far and wide seeking her advice on everything from affairs of state to wars to matrimonial problems. Delphi's fame grew, and its religious festivals blossomed into the Pythian Games, an athletic contest that was second only to the Olympics.

Today Delphi offers visitors several worthwhile sights. The archaeological site contains the ruins of the Sanctuary of Apollo. Next door is the great Archaeological Museum, where statues and treasures found on the site help bring the ruins to life. And a short walk from the site are still more ruins—including the Kastalian Spring and the photogenic Sanctuary of Athena (pictured on pre-vious page), taking you back to Delphi's prehistoric origins.

It's possible to visit Delphi as a day trip from Athens, but it's more relaxed as an overnight stop, allowing you to enjoy the pleasant modern town and craggy mountainside setting (suitably awesome for the mysterious oracle). Though the town is crammed with tourists, it still feels laid-back, offering sweeping vistas of the valley below and the Gulf of Corinth in the distance. (It's hard to find a hotel or restaurant that doesn't boast grand views.)

Delphi Overview

Phaedriades Rocks

SANCTUARY OF APOLLO
See detail map

STADIUM

Kastalian Spring

To Itea & Patra

MUSEUM OF DELPHIC FESTIVALS

GYMNASIUM

To Athens

TOWN HALL

ARCHAEOLOGICAL MUSEUM

APOLLONOS ST.

PAVLOU

FILELLINON

FRID.

SANCTUARY OF ATHENA (THOLOS)

DELPHI TOWN

200 Meters
200 Yards

→ ONE-WAY STREET

1 Hotel Leto
2 Hotel Acropole
3 Pitho Rooms
4 Hermes Hotel
5 Tholos Hotel & Taverna Vakchos

6 Sibylla Hotel
7 To Patriko Mas
8 Taverna Dion
9 Taverna Gargadouas
10 In Delphi Taverna (Bus Tickets & Info)

DELPHI

Especially after a stay in bustling Athens, Delphi is an appealing place to let your pulse slow.

Orientation to Delphi

Visitors flock from all over Greece to walk the Sacred Way at Delphi. Many don't bother to spend the night. But the town, a half-

mile west of the archaeological site and museum, is a charming place in its own right. Delphi, sometimes spelled Delfi or Delfoi in English (pop. 2,300), was custom-built to accommodate the hordes of tourists. The main street, Vasileos Pavlou-Frideri-kis, is a tight string of hotels, cafés, restaurants, and souvenir shops. Two other streets run roughly parallel to this main drag at different levels (Apollonos is one block uphill/north, and Filelli-non is one block downhill/south), connected periodically by steep stairways. The three streets converge at the eastern end of the town.

TOURIST INFORMATION

Delphi has no TI. The Town Hall office on the main drag posts current hours for the museum and site (at Pavlou-Friderikis 12, on the sanctuary end of town). If it's open, you may be able to pry more information out of the staff inside. Its entryway has a model of the Sanctuary of Apollo in ancient times—before you head out to the site, stop here to give it a good look; compare it to the map on page 341 to locate what you'll see later.

ARRIVAL IN DELPHI

Delphi is three hours north of Athens, and is reachable by bus or by car.

By Bus: Buses to Delphi depart Athens from Terminal B—described on page 203—roughly five times a day (check local schedules—you can get one at the Athens TI or go to www.ktel-fokidas.gr; online tickets available). Most buses have air-conditioning but no WC and make a café rest stop en route. The drive takes you past Thiva (ancient Thebes) and has nice views of Mt. Parnassos as you approach.

Buses drop you off at the sanctuary (east) end of town. It's smart to buy your return ticket as soon as you arrive, because buses can fill up. Buy tickets from the In Delphi taverna (signed ἐN ΔΕΛΦΟἰζ): From the stop, walk toward town past a storefront or two, staying on the right (uphill) side of the road. The restaurant doubles as the town's ersatz bus station; waiters sell bus tickets and can tell you today's schedule. You can also buy advance bus tickets at www.ktel-fokidas.gr (for more on buses back to Athens, see "Delphi Connections," later).

Many Athens-based companies offer convenient one-day **package tours** to Delphi, which include transportation, a guided tour, and lunch. Ask at your Athens hotel for details.

By Car: For tips on getting to Delphi by car, see "Route Tips for Drivers" at the end of this chapter. While it's possible to park at the site/museum, space is limited, so it's best to leave your car in town and walk (10 minutes). Park anywhere in town where the street doesn't have a double-yellow line.

HELPFUL HINTS

Unpredictable Hours: Don't count on the opening hours given here: They're likely to fluctuate. Check locally before planning your day.

Services: The main drag, Pavlou-Friderikis, has just about everything you might need, including a **post office** (at the east end, Mon-Fri 8:00-14:00, closed Sat-Sun), **ATMs,** and several cafés and shops advertising **Internet access.**

Local Guide: Penny Kolomvotsou is a great guide who can resur-

Delphi: From Legend to History

Delphi's origins are lost in the mists of time and obscured by many different, sometimes conflicting, legends.

The ancients believed that Delphi was the center of the world. Its position was determined by Zeus himself, who released two eagles from the opposite ends of the world and noted where they met.

It was here that a prophetess (the sibyl) worshipped Gaia, the mother of the gods. A serpent (python) guarded the ravine of the Kastalian Spring. Apollo, the god of the sun and music, arrived in the guise of a dolphin (*delfini,* hence Delphi) and killed the snake. The sibyl's role was later taken on by an oracle priestess, the Pythia, and she and the place now served Apollo.

Historically speaking, the site was probably the home of a prophetess as early as Mycenaean times (1400 B.C.). The worship of Apollo grew, and the place gained fame for the oracle and for its religious festivals. Every four years, athletes and spectators gathered here to worship Apollo with music and athletic competitions: the Pythian Games, which soon rivaled the Olympics. The Sanctuary of Apollo reached the height of its prestige between the sixth and fourth centuries B.C., by which time Delphi so dominated Greek life that no leader would make a major decision without first sending emissaries here to consult the oracle. The sanctuary was deemed too important to be under the control of any one city-state, so its autonomy was guaranteed by a federation of Greek cities.

Even when Greece was conquered by the Macedonians (Alexander the Great) and Romans, the sanctuary was preserved and the conquerors continued to consult the oracle. For a thousand years, Apollo spoke to mortals through his prophetess, until A.D. 394, when Christians shut down the pagan site.

DELPHI

rect the ruins at Delphi and tailor each tour to your particular interests (reasonable prices, great with families, mobile 694-464-4427, kpagona@hotmail.com). Penny can also arrange activities in Delphi such as horseback riding, hiking, and pottery classes.

Weather: Delphi is in the mountains and can be considerably cooler and rainier than Athens. Check the forecast (ask at your hotel) and dress accordingly, especially off-season.

Sights in Delphi

Delphi's most important sights are its archaeological site (with the Sanctuary of Apollo) and the adjacent Archaeological Museum. Nearby are other Sanctuary of Apollo sites (Kastalian Spring, the gymnasium, and the Sanctuary of Athena). The skippable Museum of Delphic Festivals is in Delphi town.

▲▲▲THE SANCTUARY OF APOLLO AND ARCHAEOLOGICAL MUSEUM

Ancient Delphi was not a city, but a sanctuary—a place of worship centered on the Temple of Apollo, where the oracle prophesied.

Surrounding the temple is what remains of grand monuments built by grateful pilgrims. And the Pythian Games produced what are perhaps the best-preserved theater and stadium in Greece.

Planning Your Time: Allow 1.5-2 hours for the archaeological site (hiking to the stadium alone is nearly a half-hour round-trip) and another 45-60 minutes for the museum. You can do the archaeological site and the museum in either order. Crowds and weather might help you decide. If it's hot or raining, do the museum first to hedge your bets for better conditions for the site. With all things being equal, I recommend doing the site first: You'll have more energy for the climb (there's a 700-foot elevation gain from the entrance to the stadium), and later, when you tour the museum, you can more easily imagine the original context of the items on display. On your way to the site, stop at the museum to check the day's opening hours, posted on the wall just up the steps (before the ramp). If arriving later in the day, consider visiting one sight when you arrive and the other the next morning: Your combo-ticket is good over two days (but only one visit per sight).

To visit the other sights to the east of the Sanctuary of Apollo, allow another 30-45 minutes by foot (though you can view two of them, distantly, from in front of the site).

Cost and Hours: It's €12 to enter both the site and museum (€6 off-season or if visiting only one or the other; 18 and under free—be prepared to show ID). Both the site and museum are open daily 8:00-20:00 in summer (generally April-Oct). In winter, both are open daily 8:00-15:00 (generally Nov-March, but winter schedule can be extended). Upon your arrival in Delphi, confirm opening times either with your hotel or in person by stopping by the museum or site. Tel. 22650-82312, www.culture.gr.

Sudden Closures: Parts of the site—especially the path to the stadium, above the theater—can be closed after heavy rains (to keep visitors safe from possible rock slides).

Getting There: The archaeological site and museum are about

Delphi's Sanctuary of Apollo

- **STANDING RUINS**
- **ORIGINAL FOOTPRINT**

TOUR ENDS

THEATER

FOOTBRIDGE

TEMPLE OF APOLLO

POLYGONAL WALL

SACRED WAY

SACRED WAY

ROMAN FORUM

20 Meters
20 Yards

TOUR BEGINS

WC

Path to Museum, Café
← & Delphi Town

TICKETS **WATER REFILL STATION**

To Other →
Delphi Sites

DELPHI

1. Roman Forum
2. Bull of the Corcyreans
3. Trojan Horse Replica
4. Kings and Queens of Argos Monument
5. Treasuries
6. Omphalos
7. Treasury of the Athenians
8. Polygonal Wall
9. Rock of the Sibyl
10. Sphinx of Naxos
11. Athenian Stoa
12. Tripod of Plataea
13. Great Altar of Apollo
14. Pillar of Prusias II & Other Sights
15. Acanthus Column of Dancers
16. Temple of Apollo
17. Theater
18. Viewpoint
19. To Stadium

a half-mile east of the modern town of Delphi. Parking is limited, so it's best to leave your car in town and walk (10 minutes). You'll reach the museum first; to reach the site, continue along the path past the museum.

Services: A WC and a café (with a wide selection of slushie-style drinks and little else) are outside the museum. At the site itself, you'll find only a water refill station to the right of the ticket booth (you can bring a water bottle but no food inside the site). The sanctuary's WC is just above the entrance, up the first set of stairs, after you've scanned your ticket (inhaling the fumes there is not guaranteed to give you any prophetic visions).

Photography: Photos are allowed, but you cannot use a flash in the museum.

The Sanctuary of Apollo

Looking up at the sheer rock face, you see the ruins clinging to a steep slope. From here you ascend a switchback trail that winds up, up, up: through the ruins to the Temple of Apollo, the theater, and the stadium, 700 feet up from the road. Every pilgrim who visited the oracle had to make this same steep climb.

❍ Self-Guided Tour

• *Start up the path, going to the right up a set of stairs (WCs at the top). After you double back on the switchback path, you enter a rectangular area with 10 gray columns, marking the...*

❶ Roman Forum

This small public space stood outside the sanctuary's main gate. The columns supported an arcade of shops (check out the illustration on the information plaque). Here pilgrims could pick up handy last-minute offerings—small statues of Apollo were popular—before proceeding to their date with the oracle. At festival times, crowds of pilgrims (all of them men) gathered here for parades up to the temple, theater, and stadium.

Gaze up at the hillside and picture the ruins as they were 2,000 years ago: gleaming white buildings with red roofs, golden statues atop columns, and the natural backdrop of these sheer gray-red rocks towering up 750 feet. It must have been an awe-inspiring sight for humble pilgrims, who'd traveled here to discover what fate the fickle gods had in store for them.

The men began their ascent to the oracle by walking through the original entrance gate, between 10-foot walls, entering the sanctuary on the street known as the Sacred Way.

• *A huge wall once enclosed the whole sanctuary, forming a rough rectangle, with the Temple of Apollo in the center. As you climb the five steps out of the forum, you're passing through a gate in the walls and beginning your walk along the...*

Sacred Way

The road is lined with ruins of once-glorious statues and monuments financed by satisfied pilgrims grateful for the oracle's advice. Immediately to the right is a pedestal of red-gray blocks, 17 feet long. This once held a huge bronze statue, the ❷ **Bull of the Corcyreans** (c. 580 B.C.), a gift from the inhabitants of Corfu to thank the oracle for directing them to a great catch of tuna fish.

A dozen or so steps farther along (left side) was an even bigger statue, a colossal bronze replica of the ❸ **Trojan Horse.**

Just beyond that (right side) is a semicircle 40 feet across, which was once lined with 10 statues of the legendary ❹ **Kings and Queens of Argos,** including Perseus, Danae, and Hercules.

Next comes a row of so-called ❺ **Treasuries** (left side), small buildings that housed precious gifts to the gods. These buildings and their contents were paid for by city-states and kings to thank the oracle and the gods for giving them success (especially in war). From the outside they looked like mini temples, with columns, pediments, statues, and friezes. Inside they held gold, jewels, bronze dinnerware, ivory statues, necklaces, and so on. The friezes and relief sculptures that once adorned the Sikyonian and Siphnian Treasuries are now in the museum.

• *At the corner where the path turns to go uphill is a cone-shaped stone called an...*

❻ Omphalos

The ancients believed that Delphi was the center of the world and marked that spot with a strange cone-shaped monument called an omphalos (navel). The omphalos was also a symbolic tombstone for the python that Apollo slew.

Several omphalos stones were erected at different places around the sanctuary. The original was kept inside the Temple of Apollo. A copy graced the temple's entrance (it's now in the museum). Another copy stood here along the Sacred Way, where this modern replica is today.

As the center of the world, Delphi was also the starting point

DELPHI

for history. From here the oracle could predict the course of human destiny.

• *Rounding the bend and gazing uphill, you'll face the...*

❼ Treasury of the Athenians

The Athenians built this temple to commemorate their victory over the Persians (ancient Iranians) at the Battle of Marathon in

490 B.C. The tiny inscriptions on the blocks honor Athenian citizens with praise and laurel-leaf wreaths, the symbol of victory at Delphi's Pythian Games. When the ruins were rebuilt (1904-1906), the restorers determined which block went where by matching up pieces of the inscriptions.

The structure's ceremonial entrance (east end) has two Doric columns of expensive marble from Paros. They support six metopes (reconstructed; the originals are in the museum) that feature the Greeks battling the legendary Amazon women—symbolizing the Greek victory over the barbaric Persians at Marathon.

• *Follow the path as it continues uphill. By now you have a great view to the left of the...*

❽ Polygonal Wall and Other Ancient Features

The retaining wall (sixth century B.C.) supports the terrace with the Temple of Apollo. It runs across the hillside for some 250 feet at heights of up to 12 feet. It has survived in almost perfect condition because of the way that the stones were fitted together (without mortar). This created a "living" wall, able to absorb the many

earthquakes for which the region is renowned (earthquakes caused the other buildings here to crumble).

Near the wall, just above the Treasury of the Athenians, the 10-foot ❾ **Rock of the Sibyl** hearkens back to the murky prehistoric origins of this place as a sacred site. According to legend, the oracle's predecessor—called the sibyl—sat atop this rock to deliver her prophecies, back when the area was sacred to Gaia, the mother of the gods.

Just behind that rock, near the stubby white column (walk up the path to get a better view), is a pile of rocks with a black slab pedestal. This was once a 35-foot-tall pillar holding the statue of the ❿ **Sphinx of Naxos** (c. 570-560 B.C., now in the museum). Inhabitants of the isle of Naxos used their best marble for this gift to the oracle, guaranteeing them access to her advice even during busy times.

A few more steps up, the three white fluted Ionic columns along the wall belonged to the ⓫ **Athenian Stoa,** a 100-foot-long

open-air porch. Here the Athenians displayed captured shields, ships' prows, and booty from their naval victory over Persia at the decisive Battle of Salamis (480 B.C.). It was the oracle of Delphi who gave Athens the key to victory. As the Persian army swarmed over Greece, the oracle prophesied that the city of Athens would be saved by a "wooden wall." The puzzled Athenians eventually interpreted the oracle's riddle as meaning not a city wall, but a fleet of wooden ships. They abandoned Athens to the Persian invaders, then routed them at sea. Once the enemy was driven out, Greece's cities ceremonially relit their sacred flames from the hearth of Delphi's temple.

• *Continue up the Sacred Way and follow it as it turns left, up the hill. As you ascend, along the right-hand side you'll pass a square gray-block pedestal that once supported a big column. This monument, the ⓬ Tripod of Plataea, was built to thank the oracle for victory in the Battle of Plataea (479 B.C., fought near Thebes), which finally drove the Persians out of Greece. The monument's 26-foot bronze column of three intertwined snakes was carried off by the Romans to their chariot-racing track in Constantinople (now Istanbul), where tourists can snap photos of what's left of it.*

At the top of the path, turn left and face the six Doric columns and ramp that mark the entrance to the Temple of Apollo. In the courtyard in front of the temple are several noteworthy ruins.

The Temple Courtyard

Take in the temple and imagine the scene 2,000 years ago as pilgrims gathered here at the culmination of their long journey. They'd come seeking guidance from the gods at a crucial juncture in their lives. Here in the courtyard they prepared themselves before entering the temple to face the awe-inspiring oracle.

Opposite the temple entrance, pilgrims and temple priests offered sacrifices at the (partially restored) ⓭ **Great Altar of Apollo.** Worshippers would enter the rectangular enclosure, originally made of black marble with white trim. Inside they'd sacrifice an

DELPHI

animal to Apollo—goats were especially popular. One hundred bulls (a hecatomb) were sacrificed to open every Pythian Games.

To the right of the temple (as you face it) once stood several monuments that dazzled visitors. Imagine a 50-foot **Statue of Apollo Sitalkas** towering over the courtyard, where only a humble rectangular base remains today. Next to it is the still-impressive 20-foot-tall rectangular **⑭ Pillar of Prusias II.** Atop this was a statue of a second-century king on horseback who traveled here from Turkey to consult the oracle. To the right of the pillar are **three round column stubs** that once held ceremonial tripods. Behind them rose the tall **⑮ Acanthus Column of Dancers,** three young women supporting a tripod (now in the museum).

• *But these sights paled in comparison to the...*

⑯ Temple of Apollo

This structure—which in its day must have towered over the rest of the site—was the centerpiece of the whole sanctuary. It was dedi-

cated to the god who ruled the hillside, and it housed the oracle who spoke in his name. This was the third and largest temple built on this site (completed 330 B.C.), replacing earlier versions destroyed by earthquake and fire. It was largely funded by Philip of Macedon and dedicated in the time of Alexander the Great.

The temple was gleaming white, ringed with columns, with a triangular pediment over the entrance and a roof studded with statues. Above the entrance, the pediment statues showed Apollo arriving in Delphi in a four-horse chariot (now in the museum). The six huge Doric columns that stand near the entrance today (reassembled in 1904) were complemented by 15 columns along each side. (Sections from a toppled column lie on the hillside below the temple's left side, near the Polygonal Wall, giving an idea of the temple's scale; to see this, backtrack down the hill.) Though the temple appeared all white, it was actually constructed with a darker local limestone. The columns were coated with a stucco of powdered marble to achieve the white color. Only the pediments and other decorations were made from costly white marble shipped in from the isle of Paros.

The Oracle

The oracle was a priestess of Apollo who acted as a seer by "channeling" the god's spirit. Always female, she was usually an older empty-nester with a good reputation, but we don't know any of Delphi's oracles by name. These women were not the focus—rather, they were vessels for the words of Apollo as interpreted by priests.

Early on, there was one oracle, who prophesied only on auspicious days. At Delphi's peak, two or three oracles worked shifts every day. The oracle purified herself in the Kastalian Spring, dressed in white, and carried a laurel branch—a symbol of Apollo. Why the oracle sat on a tripod—a ritual cauldron on three legs—no one knows for sure. (For more on tripods, see page 279.)

The oracle presumably prophesied in a kind of trance, letting the spirit of Apollo possess her body and speaking as if she were the god himself. Many think she was high on vapors that rose from the natural chasm in the inner sanctum floor. Science has found no evidence of the supposed chasm, though ravines and springs nearby do emit psychotropic gases. The trance might also have been caused by the oracle eating or inhaling burned laurel leaves. Regardless of the source, the oracle's ultimate message was tightly controlled by the priests.

The oracle addressed all kinds of questions. Travelers came to Delphi before journeys. Rulers came to plan wars. Explorers wanted advice for getting newfound colonies off to a good start. Philosophers asked the oracle to weigh in on ethical dilemmas. Priests sought approval of new rituals and cults. Ordinary people came because their marriages were rocky or simply to have their fortunes told.

Apollo was considered a god of peace, order, and personal virtue. As the priestess of Apollo, the oracle could address moral questions and religious affairs. And because Delphi was considered the center of the world, the words of the oracle were the source of fate and the fortunes of men.

Many famous people made the pilgrimage. A young Socrates was so inspired by the phrase "Know Thyself" (inscribed on the Temple of Apollo) that he pursued the path of self-knowledge. The oracle was visited by foreign kings such as Midas (of the golden touch) and the ancient billionaire Croesus (of "rich-as" fame). The historian Plutarch served here as a priest, interpreting the oracle's utterances. Roman Emperor Nero visited, participated in the Pythian Games, and was warned about his impending assassination. Alexander the Great asked the oracle whether he'd be successful in conquering the world. When the oracle hesitated, Alexander grabbed her by the hair and wouldn't let go. The helpless oracle cried, "You're unstoppable." Alexander said, "I have my answer."

Imagine yourself an ancient pilgrim finally preparing to meet the oracle after the long trek to the center of the world. You've just bathed with the priests at the Kastalian Spring in the ravine east of the sanctuary. You've paraded ceremonially to the temple, up the same Sacred Way tourists walk today. At the Great Altar, you just offered a sacrifice, likely of goat (a loaf of bread was the minimum cover charge). At last, you're about to enter the temple with the priests, climbing the ramp and passing through the columns to learn your fate. Inscribed at the entrance are popular proverbs, including "Know Thyself," "Nothing in Excess," and "Stuff Happens."

Inside, the temple is cloudy with the incense of burning laurel leaves. You see the large golden statue of Apollo and the original omphalos stone, a reminder that you've arrived at the center of the world. After offering a second sacrifice on the hearth of the eternal flame, it's time to meet the oracle.

The priests lead you into the *adyton*—the farthest back, holiest chamber of the *cella*. There, amid the incense, is the oracle—an older woman, dressed in white, seated in the bowl of a tripod, perhaps with an unsettling gleam in her eye. The tripod may be balanced over a hole in the floor of the temple, exposing a natural ravine where a spring bubbles up. While you wait, the priests present your question to the oracle. She answers—perhaps crying out, perhaps muttering gibberish and foaming at the mouth. The priests step in to interpret the oracle's meaning, rendering it in a vague, haiku-like poem.

Then you're ushered out of the temple, either enlightened or confused by the riddle. For many pilgrims—like Socrates, who spent much of his life pondering the oracle's words—a visit to Delphi was only the beginning of their life's journey.

• *Uphill, to the right of the Temple of Apollo, stands Delphi's stone theater. Climb up—I'll meet you there.*

⓱ Theater

One of Greece's best-preserved theaters (fourth century B.C.) was built to host song contests honoring Apollo, the god of music. With 35 rows of white stone quarried from Mt. Parnassos, it could seat 5,000. The action took place on the semicircular area (60 feet across, surrounded by a drainage ditch)

known as the orchestra. As at most ancient theaters, it would have been closed off along the street by a large structure that created a backdrop for the stage and served as the theater's grand entryway. The famous *Bronze Charioteer* statue (now in the museum) likely stood outside the theater's entrance, in the middle of the road, greeting playgoers. The theater was designed so that most spectators could look over the backdrop, taking in stunning views of the valley below even as they watched the onstage action.

The theater's original and main purpose was to host not plays, but song contests—a kind of "Panhellenic Idol" competition that was part of the Pythian Games. Every four years, singer-songwriters from all over the Greek-speaking world gathered here to perform hymns in honor of Apollo, the god of music. They sang accompanied by flute or by lyre—a strummed autoharp, which was Apollo's chosen instrument.

Over time, the song competition expanded into athletic contests (held at the stadium), as well as other events in dance and drama. The opening and closing ceremonies of the Pythian Games were held here. One of the games' central features was a play that re-enacted the dramatic moment when Apollo slew the python and founded Delphi...not unlike the bombastic pageantry that opens and closes today's Olympic Games.

• *A steep path continues uphill to a stunning...*

⑱ View from Above the Theater

With craggy cliffs at your back, the sanctuary beneath you, and a panoramic view of the valley in the distance, it's easy to see why the

ancients found this place sacred.

We're 1,800 feet above sea level on the slopes of Mt. Parnassos (8,062 feet). The area's jagged rocks and sheer cliffs are made of gray limestone, laced with red-orange bauxite, which is mined nearby. The cliffs have striations of sedimentary rocks that have been folded upward at all angles by seismic activity. The region is crisscrossed with faults (one runs right under the temple), pocked with sinkholes, and carved with ravines.

Two large sections of rock that jut out from the cliff (to the left) are known as the Phaedriades Rocks, or "Shining Ones," because of how they reflect sunlight. At the foot of one of the rocks lies the sanctuary. Between the two rocks (east of the sanctuary) is the gaping ravine of the Kastalian Spring.

Looking down on the entire sanctuary, you can make out its shape—a rough rectangle (640 feet by 442 feet—about twice as big as a football field) enclosed by a wall, stretching from the top of

Delphi's Decline and Rediscovery

After reaching a peak during the Classical Age, the oracle's importance slowly declined. In Hellenistic times, traditional religions like Apollo-worship were eclipsed by secular philosophy and foreign gods. By the third century B.C., the oracle was handling more lonely-hearts advice than affairs of state. The Romans alternated between preserving Delphi (as Hadrian did) and looting its treasuries and statues. Nero famously stole 500 statues for his home in Rome (A.D. 66), and Constantine used Delphi's monument to decorate his new capital. As Rome crumbled, barbarians did their damage. Finally, in A.D. 394, the Christian Emperor Theodosius I closed down the sanctuary, together with all the other great pagan worship centers.

The site was covered by landslides and by the village of Kastri until 1892, when the villagers were relocated to the modern village of Delphi, about a half-mile to the west. Excavation began, the site was opened to tourists, and its remaining treasures were eventually put on display in the museum.

DELPHI

the theater down to the Roman Forum. Trace the temple's floor plan: You'd enter where the columns are, pass through the lobby *(pronaos)*, into the main hall *(cella)*, and continue into the back portion *(adyton)*, where the oracle sat (they say) above a natural chasm.

In the distance, looking south, is the valley of the Pleistos River, green with olive trees. Beyond that (though not visible from this spot) are the turquoise waters of the Gulf of Corinth.

• *If you're winded, you can make your way back down now. But you've come so far already—why not keep going? Hike another 10 minutes up the steep, winding path to the...*

⓭ Stadium

Every four years, athletes and spectators from across Greece gathered here to watch the same kinds of sports as at the ancient Olympics. The Pythian Games (founded at least by 582 B.C.) were second only to the (older, bigger) Olympic Games in prestige. They were one of four Panhellenic Games on the athletics calendar (Olympia, Corinth, Nemea, and Delphi).

The exceptionally well-preserved stadium was built in the fifth century B.C. (Though you aren't allowed to walk through its center, you can still get a good look down into it from the far end.) It was remodeled in the second century A.D. by the wealthy Herodes

Atticus, who also built a theater in Athens and a fountain in Olympia (the Nymphaeum). There was stone seating for nearly 7,000, which was cushier than Olympia's grassy-bank stadium. Among the seats on the north side, you can still make out the midfield row of judges' seats. The track—580 feet long by 84 feet wide—is slightly shorter than the one at Olympia. The main entrance was at the east end; the thick pillars once supported a three-arched entry. The starting lines (one at either end, depending on the length of the race) are still here, and you might be able to make out the postholes for the wooden starting blocks.

The Pythian Games lasted about a week and were held in the middle of a three-month truce among warring Greeks that allowed people to train and travel safely. Winners were awarded a wreath of laurel leaves (as opposed to the olive leaves at the Olympic Games) because Apollo always wore a laurel-leaf wreath. For more on the types of events held here during the games, see the Olympia chapter.

• *Wind your way back down to the exit. The museum is located 200 yards west of the Sanctuary of Apollo. Before heading in that direction, you might consider venturing a little farther out of town to reach the Kastalian Spring, gymnasium, and/or Sanctuary of Athena (all described later, under "Other Delphi Sights").*

Archaeological Museum

Delphi's compact-but-impressive museum houses a collection of ancient sculpture matched only by the National Archaeological and Acropolis museums in Athens.

○ Self-Guided Tour: Follow the one-way route, looking for the following highlights. Everything is well described in English.

• *Scan your ticket and head into the...*

❶ First Room: This room holds the earliest traces of civilization at Delphi. Near the entry, find the picture depicting French architect Albert Tournaire's romantic rendering of how the Sanctuary of Apollo would have looked at its ancient peak. Also in this room is a giant bronze cauldron, which was once adorned with grotesque griffin heads.

• *Proceed into the next room, then turn right to find the...*

❷ **Sphinx of Naxos (c. 570-560 b.c.):** This marble beast—a winged lion with a female face and an Archaic smile—was once brightly painted, standing atop a 40-foot Ionic column in the sanctuary. The myth of the sphinx is Egyptian in origin, but she made a splash in Greek lore when she posed a famous riddle to Oedipus at the gates of Thebes: "What walks on four legs in the morning, two at noon, and three at night?" Oedipus solved it: It's a man—who crawls in infancy, walks in adulthood, and uses a cane in old age.

• *Across the room, find the...*

❸ **Frieze from the Siphnian Treasury:** This shows how elaborate the now-ruined treasuries in the sanctuary must have been. The east frieze (left wall) shows Greeks and Trojans duking it out. The gods to the left of the battle are rooting for the Trojans, with the Greek gods to the right. The north frieze (back wall) features scenes from the epic battle between the Greek gods and older race of giants.

• *Backtrack into the previous room, then turn right. You're face-to-face with...*

❹ **Twin Kouros Statues (c. 600-580 b.c.):** These statues have the typical features of the Archaic period: placid smiles, stable poses facing the front, braided dreadlocks, and geometrical anatomy. These sturdy seven-foot-tall athletes are the legendary twins of Argos, who yoked themselves to their mother's chariot and pulled her five miles so she wouldn't be late for the female Games (the Heraia). Upon arrival, the exhausted twins fell into a sleep so deep they never woke up.

• *In the small room behind the twins (to the right) is what's left of a...*

❺ **Silver Bull:** These silver-and-gold plates are the surviving fragments that once covered a life-size bull statue from the sixth century b.c. This bull and the other objects in the room were buried in ancient times (perhaps for safekeeping) and were discovered in the 20th century in a pit along the Sacred Way, near the Treasury of the Athenians.

• *In the room after the twins, find the...*

❻ **East Pediment of the Temple of Apollo:** This is what greeted visitors as they stood before the temple entrance. Though it's mostly fragments today, in the center you can make out some of

Delphi's Archaeological Museum

1 First Room
2 Sphinx of Naxos
3 Frieze from the Siphnian Treasury
4 Twin Kouros Statues
5 Silver Bull
6 East Pediment of the Temple of Apollo
7 Metopes from the Treasury of the Athenians
8 Acanthus Column of Dancers
9 Daochos Monument
10 Roman Period Artifacts
11 Bronze Charioteer

the four horses that pulled Apollo in his chariot. To the right, a lion jumps on an animal's back and takes it down.

• Continue into the next room, then turn left to find the...

7 Metopes from the Treasury of the Athenians (510-480 b.c.): These carvings from the sanctuary's small surviving treasury include (among other themes) six of the Twelve Labors of Hercules. In the most intact carving (directly to the left as you enter),

Hercules is the one with curly hair and beard, inscrutable Archaic smile, and lion skin tied preppy-style around his neck.

• *Proceed through the next three rooms (the third of which has an exhibit with some pieces from the round tholos monument, at the Sanctuary of Athena). You'll wind up in a room with two monuments from the era of Alexander the Great, which once stood side by side in the sanctuary.*

❽ Acanthus Column of Dancers: This giant leafy sculpture sat atop a 40-foot column to the right of the Temple of Apollo (on

the same level as the theater). The three dancing girls originally carried a bronze tripod on their shoulders. Scholars now believe that this tripod supported the **omphalos**—the gigantic pinecone-shaped stone, which represented the "navel" of the world. The omphalos, now resting next to the column, is not the original stone marking the center of the earth, but a Roman-era copy. Nearby is the bottom of the column, which appears to be sprouting out of the ground.

• *Then, as now, next to the column stand statues from the...*

❾ Daochos Monument (c. 336-332 b.c.): Out of the nine original statues (count the footprints), today seven survive (OK, six—one is just a sandal). They have the relaxed poses and realistic detail of Hellenism. Daochos (center, wearing a heavy cloak) was a high-ranking army commander under Alexander the Great. His family flanks him, including two of the three sons who were famous athletes, all of whom won laurel crowns at the same Pythian Games. Nude Agelaos (also in the center, armless, with sinuous *contrapposto*) won running contests in Delphi. Aghias (to the right, with two partial arms and genitals) swept all four Panhellenic Games in *pankration*, a brutal sport that combined wrestling and boxing with few holds barred.

• *Across the room and facing these gents, notice the sculpture of bearded, balding Socrates, who was inspired by the mystery of this place. The next room features artifacts from the...*

❿ Roman Period (191 b.c.-a.d. 394): The Romans made Delphi their own in 191 b.c. and left their mark. On the left you'll see the **frieze** that decorated the proscenium of the theater and (high on the wall) an inscription from the proud Emperor Domitian, crowing that he had repaired the Temple of Apollo.

Across the room is the **top of a pillar,** one erected by the arrogant King Perseus in anticipation of a military victory. Instead, the king was soundly defeated by Aemilius Paulus, who topped the pedestal with his own equestrian victory statue (pictured nearby) and adorned it with this frieze of scenes depicting Perseus' defeat. This sculpture is particularly exciting for historians, as it's the oldest relief work (in Western history, at least) narrating an actual event. For centuries after this, battles would be recounted in similar 3-D carvings (think of Trajan's Column in Rome or Nelson's Column in London).

Also worth noting here is the **circular altar** decorated with a graceful relief sculpture showing young women gussying up the sanctuary for a festival performance.

At the end of the room are two noteworthy sculptures. The small, lightly bearded head dubbed the "Melancholy Roman" (likely Titus Quinctius Flamininus, who proclaimed autonomy for the Greek state in 197 B.C.) demonstrates a masterful sense of emotion. Standing next to him is a full-size nude statue (minus its forearms) of Emperor Hadrian's young lover, **Antinous.** The handsome curly-haired youth from Asia Minor (today's Turkey) drowned in the Nile in 130 B.C. A heartbroken Hadrian declared Antinous a god and erected statues of him everywhere, making him one of the most recognizable people from the ancient world. Notice the small holes around his head, which were used to affix a bronze laurel wreath. Next to the sculpture, find the photo of excited archaeologists unearthing this strikingly intact specimen.

• *The grand finale is the museum's star exhibit, the...*

❶ Bronze Charioteer: This young charioteer has just finished his victory lap, having won the Pythian Games of 474 B.C. Standing ramrod straight, he holds the reins lightly in his right hand, while his (missing) left hand was raised, modestly acknowledging the crowd.

This surviving statue was part of an original 3-D ensemble that greeted playgoers at the entrance to the theater. His (missing) chariot was (probably) pulled by four (mostly missing) horses, tended by a (missing) stable boy. Nearby, a case displays scant surviving chunks of the cart, the horse, and the stable boy's arm.

The statue is life-size (5'11") and lifelike. His fluted robe has straps around the waist and shoulders to keep it from ballooning out in the wind. He has a rounded face, full lips, awestruck eyes

(of inset stones and enamel), and curly hair tied with the victor's headband.

The most striking thing is that—having just won an intense and dangerous contest—his face and attitude are calm and humble. The statue was cast when Greece was emerging from the horrors of the Persian invasion. The victorious chari-

oteer expresses the sense of wonderment felt as Greece finally left the battle behind, gazed into the future, and rode triumphantly into the Golden Age.

As you exit the museum, examine the small model (in the lobby) of the sanctuary as it appeared in ancient times.

OTHER DELPHI SIGHTS

The related Sanctuary sites, especially the Temple of Athena Pronea, are worth a visit. There are also a number of hikes from Delphi—ask your hotelier for ideas.

Sanctuary of Apollo Sites

These three sites, located along the main road beyond (to the east of) the site, are associated with the Sanctuary of Apollo and free to view. I've listed them in order, from nearest to farthest (you can walk to any of them, or you can simply view the gymnasium and the Sanctuary of Athena from the road in front of the site and museum).

Kastalian Spring: On the left side of the road, 800 yards past the archaeological site (around the jutting cliff), a spring bubbles forth from the ravine between the two Phaedriades Rocks. It was here that Apollo slew the python, taking over the area from the mother of the gods. Pilgrims washed here before consulting the oracle, and the water was used to ritually purify the oracle, the priests, and the Temple of Apollo. Inside are two ruined fountains (made of stone, with courtyards and benches to accommodate pilgrims) that tapped the ancient sacred spring, but because of rock slides, the ravine is closed to visitors (you can still see and hear the gurgling spring water).

Gymnasium: On the right side of the road, look for running tracks and a circular pool, where athletes trained for the Pythian Games. Access to this site may or may not be possible.

Sanctuary of Athena Pronea: Farther along (also on the

right side of the road) is a cluster of ruined temples. Because of the area's long association with Gaia, Athena was worshipped at Delphi along with Apollo. The star attraction is the *tholos* (c. 380 B.C.), a round structure whose exact purpose is unknown. Although presumably less important than the Sanctuary of Apollo, its three reconstructed columns (of 20 Doric originals that once held up a conical roof) have become the most-photographed spot in all of Delphi.

Museum of Delphic Festivals

Perched high on the hill above the town of Delphi, this old mansion explains the quest of beloved poet and resident Angelos Sikelianos to create a new "Delphic Festivals" tradition in the 1920s. There's not much to see, aside from photos, costumes, and props of the event—which was held twice (in 1927 and 1930)—and some artifacts from Sikelianos' life. It's only worthwhile as an excuse for a strenuous hike (or quick drive) above town to grand vistas.

Cost and Hours: €1, open hours vary—ask your hotelier to call ahead to make sure someone's there, tel. 22650-82175.

Sleeping in Delphi

Spending the night in Delphi is a pleasant (and much cheaper) alternative to busy Athens. The town is squeezed full of hotels, which makes competition fierce and rates very soft—hoteliers don't need much of an excuse to offer a discount in slow times. When I've given a price range, it's based on demand (busiest April-May and Sept-Oct).

$$ Hotel Leto is a class act, with 22 smartly renovated rooms right in the heart of town (Sb-€50, twin Db-€65, superior Db-€70, Tb-€90, prices fluctuate with demand, 10 percent discount with this book if you book directly with hotel, elevator, Apollonos 15, tel. 22650-82302, www.leto-delphi.gr, info@leto-delphi.gr, Petros).

$$ Hotel Acropole is a big but welcoming group-oriented hotel along the lower road. It's quieter and has better vistas than my other listings. Some of the 42 rooms feature view terraces for

Sleep Code

Abbreviations   (€1=about $1.10, country code: 30)

S=Single, **D**=Double/Twin, **T**=Triple, **Q**=Quad, **b**=bathroom

Price Rankings

$$ **Higher Priced**—Most rooms €50 or more

$ **Lower Priced**—Most rooms less than €50

Unless otherwise noted, breakfast is included, English is spoken, and free Wi-Fi and/or a guest computer is generally available. Many places accept credit cards, and rooms generally have air-conditioning. Prices can change; verify current rates online or by email. For the best prices, always book directly with the hotel.

no extra charge; try to request one when you reserve (Sb-€54, Db-€65, family suite with fireplace-€150, 10 percent discount with this book, elevator, 13 Filellinon, tel. 22650-82675, www.delphi.com.gr, delphi@delphi.com.gr, say hi to Effie).

$ Pitho Rooms ("Python") has eight good rooms above a gift shop on the main street. Your conscientious hosts, George and Vicky, pride themselves on offering a good value; they'll make you feel like part of the family (Sb-€40, Db-€50, Tb-€65, Qb-€75, show this book for these prices, no elevator, Pavlou-Friderikis 40A, tel. 22650-82850, www.pithohotel.gr, pitho_rooms@yahoo.gr).

$ Hermes Hotel explodes with polished wood, cut glass, artwork, and sculptures in its public areas. Upstairs, its 36 rooms have spare but stately furniture; nearly all face the valley and have balconies (Sb-€30-35, Db-€45-50, price depends on season and demand, elevator, Pavlou-Friderikis 37, tel. 22650-82318, www.hermeshotel.com.gr, info@hermeshotel.com.gr).

$ Tholos Hotel has 20 quasi-Scandinavian rooms on the upper street, some with view balconies (Sb-€25, Db-€35, breakfast-€5, no elevator, Apollonos 31, tel. 22650-82268, www.tholoshotel.com, hotel_tholos@yahoo.gr).

$ Sibylla Hotel rents eight simple rooms at youth-hostel prices without a hint of youth-hostel grunge. No elevator, no air-conditioning...just good value. All have balconies: four with valley views, four over the street (Sb-€24, Db-€30, Tb-€40, no breakfast, mini fridge, ceiling fans, Pavlou-Friderikis 9, tel. 22650-82335, www.sibylla-hotel.gr, info@sibylla-hotel.gr, Christopoulos family).

Eating in Delphi

Delphi's eateries tend to cater to tour groups, with vast dining rooms and long tables stretching to distant valley-and-gulf views. The following restaurants distinguish themselves by offering high

DELPHI

quality and good value. Look for the regional specialty, fried *for-maela* cheese (spritz it with fresh lemon juice, then dig in). All of my listings are open daily for both lunch and dinner (around 12:00 until 22:30 or 23:00). Some places close for a midafternoon siesta (roughly 16:00-18:30).

Taverna Vakchos is homey and woody, with down-home, family-run charm. The focus is on tasty traditional dishes, such as *kokoras kokkinisto* (rooster cooked in red wine) and baked lamb with lemon sauce. For dessert, try the locally produced farm-fresh yogurt with honey or ask what topping is in season (€4-6 starters, €5-8 pastas and salads, €8-18 main dishes, Apollonos 31, tel. 22650-83186).

To Patriko Mas ("Our Family's Home") is a bit more upscale, with a classy stone-and-wood interior and a striking outdoor terrace clinging to the cliff face (€4-7 starters, €8 salads, €8-20 main dishes plus some splurges, reservations suggested for view table, Pavlou-Friderikis 69, tel. 22650-82150, Konsta family).

Taverna Dion serves standard Greek fare at reasonable prices and specializes in grilled meats (€4-8 starters and salads, €6-10 main dishes, €9 fixed-price meals include 3 plates plus dessert, Apollonos 30, tel. 22650-82790).

Taverna Gargadouas is proud *not* to cater to tour groups (it's too small). This simple taverna has a blaring TV in the corner and locals mixed in with the tourists, all here for affordable, unpretentious, traditional cuisine (€4-7 starters, €6-10 main dishes, €12 fixed-price meals, on main drag at end of town farthest from sanctuary, tel. 22650-82488).

Picnics: Grocery stores and bakeries are well-marked along the main street. And though picnics are not allowed inside the archaeological site, you could choose a perch along the road overlooking the vast valley.

Delphi Connections

BY BUS

Delphi's one disadvantage, from a traveler's perspective, is its distance from the other attractions described in this book. Delphi is well-connected by bus to **Athens** (roughly 5/day—check times locally, 3-hour trip, €17 one-way). Connecting to the **Peloponnese** is long and complicated. For the eastern Peloponnese (such as **Nafplio**), it's best to go via Athens (see Athens bus connections on page 202). To the western Peloponnese, you'll connect through **Patra** (one bus per day from Delphi, departs around 13:15 Mon-Sat, 15:45 on Sun, 3 hours, €15 one-way). From Patra you can continue on to **Olympia** (via Pyrgos) or **Kardamyli** (via Kalamata). Either

DELPHI

is a very long trip, and the Delphi-Kardamyli trip can't be done in one day.

For bus information, go to www.ktel-fokidas.gr (online tickets available) or try this helpful unofficial website in English: http://livingingreece.gr (under "Best of...," click on "KTEL Buses of Greece").

ROUTE TIPS FOR DRIVERS

From Athens to Delphi: Head north (toward *Lamia/Λαμία*) on national road 1/expressway E-75 (one toll booth). Take the second exit for *ΘΕΒΑ/Theba/Thiva*, which is also marked for *Livadia/Λιβαδειά* (another toll booth). From the turnoff, signs lead you (on road 3, then road 48) all the way to *Delphi/Δελφοί*. As you get farther up into the mountains, keep an eye out for ski resorts—Athenians come here to ski from December to March.

From Delphi to the Peloponnese: As with the bus, for sights in the eastern Peloponnese (such as **Nafplio** or **Monemvasia**), it's faster to backtrack through Athens. (See page 204 for driving tips.)

To reach the western Peloponnese (such as **Olympia** or **Kardamyli/Mani Peninsula**), first follow the twisting road from Delphi down toward Itea (*Ιτέα*) on the Gulf of Corinth, then follow signs toward *Galaxidi/Γαλαξίδι* (a charming port city worth a quick stop). Trace the gulf on a magnificently scenic, two-hour westward drive along road E-65 (toward *Nafpaktos/Ναύπακτος*). Take your time and use the pullouts to enjoy the views. In Antirrio, follow signs for *Patra/Πάτρα* across the Rio-Antirrio suspension bridge (€13.20 toll) to the town of Rio. You'll enter the Peloponnese just north of the big port city of Patra (*Πάτρα*, described on page 286); skirt this city and head south another 1.5 hours along road E-55 toward *Pyrgos/Πύργος*—be sure to get on the faster highway, with a green sign, instead of the slower regional road. (Note that attempting to "shortcut" through the middle of the Peloponnese takes you on some very twisty, slow, and poorly signed mountain roads—avoid them unless you value scenery more than time.)

Once at Pyrgos, you can head east/inland to Ancient Olympia (*Αρχαία Ολυμπία*, well-marked with brown signs); or continue south to Kiparissia and Pilos, then eastward to Kalamata/*Καλαμάτα* (about two hours beyond Pyrgos; note that the Kalamata turnoff, just before Kiparissia, is not well-marked). From Kalamata, continue south another hour to Kardamyli.

DELPHI

GREEK ISLANDS

For many people, Greece is synonymous with islands. If you need a vacation from your busy mainland Greek vacation, the islands exert an irresistible pull.

Explore a tight, twisty maze of whitewashed cubic houses with vibrant trim. Dig your toes into the hot sand while basking under a beach umbrella. Go for a dip in the crystal-clear, bathwater-warm Aegean. Nurse an iced coffee along a bustling harborfront, watching fishermen clean their catch while cuddly kittens greedily beg below. Indulge in fresh seafood at a rustic seaside taverna, and chat with the big personality whose family has owned the place for generations, all while watching the sun gradually descend into the sea. The Greek islands really do live up to their worldwide acclaim.

While I appreciate a healthy dose of restorative island time, I prefer to spend the bulk of my Greek vacation visiting the country's amazing wealth of ancient sites. That's why I've focused this book on the bustling capital of Athens and Greece's "heartland," the Peloponnese, where—compared to the islands—prices are much lower, tourism is less suffocating, and travelers have more exciting opportunities to peel back layers of history. Still, a visit to Greece isn't complete without at least one island stay. This book covers three island destinations: Hydra, Mykonos, and Santorini.

GREECE'S ISLAND GROUPS

Greece's roughly 3,000 islands and islets (227 of which are inhabited) are scattered far and wide across the eastern Mediterranean. Most are in the Aegean Sea (south and east of mainland Greece), while a few are in the Ionian Sea (west of the mainland). The islands are divided into distinct clusters:

The **Ionian Islands,** closer to Albania and Italy than to Athens, are Greece's northwest gateway to the Adriatic and the rest of Europe—they've had more foreign invaders and rulers (from Venice, France, Britain, Russia, Austria, and so on) than anywhere else in the country. The main island is Corfu (Kerkyra in Greek), with a bustling, architecturally eclectic main town and a lush, green islandscape dotted with attractions and beaches.

The **Saronic Gulf Islands** (Argosaronikos), conveniently wedged between the Peloponnese and Athens, ooze lots of island charm and give you a chance to get away from it all without actually going very far. **Hydra,** my favorite, is in this group.

The **Sporades Islands,** due east of Athens, are dominated by the giant Evia island, which is attached to the mainland by a bridge. Thickly forested and less touristed by international visitors, the Sporades are a popular and handy weekend getaway for Athenians.

The **Cycladic Islands** (or simply Cyclades)—a bit farther south, between Athens and Crete—are the prototypical "Greek islands," boasting chalk-white houses with colorful windowsills and doorways; rocky, sun-parched landscapes; delightful beaches; old-fashioned white windmills topped with tufts of grass like unkempt hair; and an almost overwhelming crush of international visitors. **Mykonos** and **Santorini** are the two best and most famous of the Cyclades. Near Mykonos is the archaeological site of **Delos** (one of the most important locales of the ancient world).

The **Dodecanese Islands,** at the sunny, southeastern end of the Greek lands, are more rustic and less developed than the Cyclades. Their proximity to Turkey and historic ties to Venice give them a hybrid Turkish-Venetian flavor (though the population is mostly ethnic Greek, these islands merged with Greece only after World War II). Rhodes, with an appealing and very real-feeling old town, is the biggest of these islands.

The **North Aegean Islands,** relatively untrampled and remote-feeling, lie roughly between Turkey and Thessaloniki (at the northern end of mainland Greece). The southernmost of these, Samos, is a particularly handy springboard for Turkey, as it's very close to the Turkish port city of Kuşadası (near the remarkable ancient site of Ephesus).

Crete is Greece's biggest island and practically a ministate of its own (in fact, from 1897 to 1913 it was an autonomous state within the Ottoman Empire). While many of Greece's smaller islands merit a day or two of fun in the sun, Crete could occupy even a busy traveler for a week or more. Historically, Crete was home to the Minoans—the earliest advanced European civilization, peaking around 1950 B.C., centuries before "the ancient Greeks" of Athens. While Crete's modern main city, Iraklio, is drab and uninviting, the rest of the island offers an engaging diversity of attractions: Minoan ruins, scenic mountains, enticing beaches, characteristic rustic villages, and dramatic caves and gorges (including the famous Samaria Gorge).

CHOOSING AN ISLAND

For this book I've chosen to cover three of the most popular escapes. **Hydra** is my favorite, thanks to its speedy connections to Athens and the Peloponnese, its relaxing car-free ambience, its easily reached beaches, and its charming harbor that invites you to just linger. Two of the most popular Greek islands are Mykonos and Santorini; both are relatively well connected to Athens. **Mykonos** is an adorable, windmill-topped fishing village slathered in white and thronged by a hard-partying international crowd, enjoying its many beaches and side-tripping to the ruins on nearby Delos. **Santorini** is the most geologically interesting of all the Greek islands, and arguably the most picturesque, with idyllic villages perched on the rim of a collapsed and flooded volcano crater.

If you're choosing just one island, I'd go with Hydra. Farther-flung Mykonos and Santorini can easily be connected in a loop—they are linked to Athens' port (Piraeus), and to each other, by various boats and flights. If your travels take you to islands beyond these three, pick up another guidebook to supplement the information here.

While each Greek island has its own personality and claims to fame, most offer the same basic ingredients: a charming fishing village, once humble and poor, now a finely tuned machine for catering to (and collecting money from) a steady stream of tourists; a rugged interior and rough roads connecting coastal coves; appealing beaches with rentable umbrellas and lounge chairs, presided over by tavernas and hotels; maybe a few dusty museums collecting ancient artifacts or bits and pieces of local folklore; and occasionally a good or even great ancient site to tour.

Many islands have a main town, which is sometimes named for the island itself, or might be called Chora or Hora (Χώρα), which literally means "village." This is generally the hub for transportation, both to other islands (port for passenger ferries and cruise ships) and within the island (bus station and taxi stand). Some islands—such as Rhodes, Corfu, and Crete—have sizeable cities as their capitals.

GETTING AROUND THE GREEK ISLANDS

Many passenger boats crisscross the Aegean Sea, making it quick and fairly easy to reach your island getaway. Be warned, however, that gathering ferry information takes some work, as routes can be covered by multiple companies and schedules can change. Prior to your trip, look up schedules online, then confirm the details on arrival in Greece at any travel agency (or two or three,

as you may get slightly different information from different agencies). For more tips on schedules and tickets, see page 494; for connections from Piraeus (Athens' port), see page 200. Note that boats can be cancelled due to bad weather (more likely in the off-season).

To save time, consider flying between Athens and Mykonos or Santorini. Compared to boats, flights are less likely to get delayed or cancelled, tend to offer more frequent connections, and are much faster—but usually more expensive. Two major Greek carriers that offer daily flights from Athens to many Greek islands are **Olympic Airlines** (tel. 210-355-0500, toll-free tel. 801-801-0101 within Greece, US tel. 855-359-6200, www.olympicair.com) and **Aegean Airlines** (tel. 210-626-1000, toll-free tel. 801-112-0000 within Greece, www.aegeanair.com). Also consider **Astra Airlines** (tel. 231-048-9392, www.astra-airlines.gr) and **Sky Express** (tel. 281-022-3500, www.skyexpress.gr).

The Greek islands are made-to-order for cruising and a major destination for cruise ships. If you're coming on a cruise, your challenge is to beat the hordes: You'll arrive in town at precisely the same time as 2,000 other visitors, all hoping to fit the maximum amount of sightseeing, shopping, or beach time in a single day. Get as early a start as possible, and explore the back lanes and beaches when the main drag gets too congested.

If you're not cruising, it's smart to be aware of when ships are scheduled to show up. If you're planning to visit outlying sights or beaches, do it when the ships are in port—by the time you return to town in the afternoon, the cruise-ship passengers will be loading up to leave again.

ISLAND ACCOMMODATIONS

Greek-island accommodations range from rustic *dhomatia* to chic designer hotels with spectacular views. Even out-of-the-way islands get heavy tourist traffic in the summer, so options abound. Some travelers just show up on the boat and are greeted at the dock by locals offering cheap beds; this can be a decent way to find accommodations if you're not too picky (be very clear on the location before you agree to take a room).

At the busiest times (July-Sept, peaking in Aug), visitors can outnumber beds; to get your choice of accommodations, book ahead. Expect to pay (sometimes wildly) inflated prices in high season—in the most popular destinations, such as Mykonos and Santorini, prices for even budget hotels can more than double. Prices for other services—such as car rentals and restaurant meals—also increase when demand is high. For the best combination of still-good weather, fewer crowds, and more reasonable prices, visit just before or after these busy times.

Whenever you visit, enjoy your time here and simply give yourself over to the Greek islands. With a few exceptions, the "sights" (museums and ruins) are not worth going out of your way for—you're here to relax on the beach and explore the charming towns. Make the most of it.

GREEK ISLANDS

HYDRA

ΎΔΡΑ / Ύδρα

Hydra (pronounced EE-drah, not HIGH-drah)—less than a two-hour boat ride from Athens' port, Piraeus—is a glamorous getaway that combines practical convenience with idyllic Greek island ambience. After the noise of Athens, Hydra's traffic-free tranquility is a delight. Donkeys rather than cars, the shady awnings of well-worn cafés, and memorable seaside views all combine to make it clear...you've found your Greek isle.

The island's main town, also called Hydra, is one of Greece's prettiest. Its busy but quaint harbor—bobbing with rustic fishing boats and luxury yachts—is surrounded by a ring of rocky hills and blanketed with whitewashed homes. From the harbor, a fleet of zippy water taxis whisks you to isolated beaches and tavernas. Hydra is an easy blend of stray cats, hardworking donkeys, welcoming Hydriots (as locals are called), and lazy tourists on "island time."

One of the island's greatest attractions is its total absence of cars and motorbikes. Sure-footed beasts of burden—laden with

everything from sandbags and bathtubs to bottled water—climb stepped lanes. While Hydra is generally quiet, dawn teaches visitors the exact meaning of "cockcrow." The end of night is marked with much more than a distant cock-a-doodle-doo; it's a dissonant chorus of catfights, burro honks, and what sounds like roll call at an asylum for crazed roosters. After the animal population gets all that out of its system, the island slumbers a little longer.

Hydra's Hystory

Though it may seem tiny and low-key, overachieving Hydra holds a privileged place in Greek history. The fate of Hydriots has always been tied to the sea, which locals have harnessed to their advantage time after time.

Many Hydriot merchants became wealthy running the British blockade of French ports during the Napoleonic Wars. Hydra enjoyed its glory days in the late 18th and early 19th centuries, when the island was famous for its shipbuilders. Hydra's prosperity earned it the nickname "Little England." As rebellion swept Greece, the island flourished as a safe haven for those fleeing Ottoman oppression.

When the Greeks launched their War of Independence in 1821, Hydra emerged as a leading naval power. The harbor, with its twin forts and abundance of cannons, housed and protected the fleet of 130 ships. Hydriots of note from this period include the naval officer Andreas Miaoulis, who led the "firebrands" and their deadly "fireships," which succeeded in decimating the Ottoman navy (see page 374); and Lazaros Kountouriotis, a wealthy shipping magnate who donated his fleet to the cause (see page 379).

Greece won its independence, but at a great cost to Hydra, which lost many of its merchant-turned-military ships to the fighting...sending the island into a deep economic funk. During those lean postwar years, Hydriots again found salvation in the sea, farming the sponges that lived below the surface (sponge divers here pioneered the use of diving suits). Gathering sponges kick-started the local economy and kept Hydra afloat.

In 1956 Sophia Loren came here to play an Hydriot sponge diver in the film *Boy on a Dolphin,* propelling the little island onto the international stage. And the movie's plot—in which a precious ancient sculpture is at risk of falling into the hands of a greedy art collector instead of being returned to the Greek government—still resonates with today's Greeks, who want to reclaim their heritage for the Acropolis Museum.

Thanks largely to the film, by the 1960s Hydra had become a favorite retreat for celebrities, well-heeled tourists, and artists and writers, who still draw inspiration from the idyllic surroundings. Canadian songwriter Leonard Cohen lived here for a time—and was inspired to compose his beloved song "Bird on the Wire" after observing just that here on Hydra. Today visitors only have to count the yachts to figure out that Hydra's economy is still based on the sea.

Little Hydra—which has produced more than its share of military heroes, influential aristocrats, and political leaders—is packed with history. Rusted old cannons are scattered about town; black, pitted anchors decorate squares; and small museums hold engaging artifacts. But most visitors enjoy simply being on vacation here. Loiter around the harbor. Go on a photo safari for donkeys and kittens. Take a walk along the coast or up into the hills. Head for an inviting beach, near or far, to sunbathe and swim. Hang out past your bedtime in a cocktail bar. Hydra's the kind of place that makes you want to buy a bottle of ouzo and toss your itinerary into the sea.

PLANNING YOUR TIME

While Hydra can be done as a long day trip from Athens, it's better to spend at least two nights to take full advantage of the island's many dining options, and to give yourself a whole day to relax. Even if you're visiting Mykonos, Santorini, or other Greek islands, Hydra has a totally different vibe and is still the best place I know of to take a vacation from your Greek vacation.

To get your bearings, take my brief self-guided walk as soon as you arrive. While the walk gives you the historic context of the town, it also points out practical stops that will make your stay more efficient and enjoyable (and finishes at a wonderful little bakery). You'll still have ample time for your choice of activities—dipping into a museum that tickles your curiosity, enjoying a drink at a café, going for a hike into the hills, walking along the water to nearby villages and beaches, or catching a shuttle boat or water taxi for a spin around the island.

Orientation to Hydra

Remember, Hydra is the name of both the island and its main town (home to about 90 percent of the island's 3,000 residents). Hydra

town climbs up the hill in every direction from the port.

Branching off from the broad café-lined walkway at the bottom of the harbor are four major streets. In order from the boat dock, these are called Tompazi, Oikonomou, Miaouli, and Lignou. Not that street names mean much in this town—locals ignore addresses, and few lanes are labeled. Though the island is small, Hydra's streets twist defiantly to and fro. If seeking a specific location, use the map in this chapter or ask a local. (Note that, like our map on page 372, most maps of

Hydra Island

Saronic Gulf

To Poros & Piraeus

Cape Zourva

To Ermioni, Metochi & Spetses

Mandraki Bay

KAMINIA
VLYCHOS

HYDRA TOWN

LIMNIONIZA

BISTI

MOLOS

NISIZA

2 Miles

2 Kilometers

AG. NIKOLAOS

- • • FERRY BOATS
- • • • • WATER TAXI
- — — TRAILS
- ♣ BEACHES

Hydra show the harbor—which is actually to the north—at the bottom.) Expect to get lost in Hydra...and enjoy it when you do.

Consider venturing beyond Hydra town to settlements and beaches elsewhere on the island. The most accessible is the tiny seaside hamlet of Kaminia, which lies just over the headland west of the harbor (with a good recommended restaurant).

TOURIST INFORMATION

Hydra has no TI, but most of the hoteliers I've listed here are happy and willing to help. You can also check www.hydra.gr and the more basic www.hydra.com.gr.

ARRIVAL ON HYDRA

All ferry boats dock in the heart of Hydra town's harbor, along its eastern edge (for details on how to get to Hydra, see "Hydra Connections" at the end of this chapter). Nearly all of my recommended accommodations are within a 10-minute walk of the harbor. At the port you can hire a donkey to carry your bags (€10-15, establish the price up front). If you ask, better hotels will often meet you at the boat and help with your bags.

GETTING AROUND HYDRA

As there are no cars, your options are foot, donkey, or boat. You'll walk everywhere in town. You can hike to neighboring beaches, but it's fun to hop a **shuttle boat** (about €3 to Vlychos, departures

about every 30 minutes in high season from in front of Hotel Sophia) or take a **water taxi** (much more expensive unless you're a
small group—same rate for one person or eight). You'll see the red
taxi boats stacked and waiting near the donkeys on the harborfront. Sample taxi fares: €10 to Kaminia, €15 to Vlychos (there's
a fare board lashed to the pole by the taxi dock, with the English
translation hiding on the back side). To get back to town by water
taxi, call 22980-53690.

HELPFUL HINTS

Post Office: The post office (Mon-Fri 7:30-14:00, closed Sat-Sun)
  faces the outdoor market (just inland from the harbor).

Drinking Water: The island's name means "water" in ancient
  Greek, but it was named a long, long time ago: Today there's
  no natural water source on Hydra (other than private cisterns).
  Until recently, water was barged in daily. But with EU help,
  Hydra now has a seawater desalination plant, giving the island
  a reliable water supply and drinkable tap water.

Hydra Harbor Walk

Hydra clusters around its wide harbor, squeezed full of fishing
boats, pleasure craft, luxury yachts, and the occasional Athens-
bound ferry. Get the lay of the land with this lazy 30-minute self-
guided stroll.

• *Begin at the tip of the port (to the right, as you face the sea). Climb the
stairs (by the cactus) to the cannon-studded turret. From here you have
a fine...*

View of the Harbor

The harbor is the heart and soul of Hydra. Imagine it as an ancient
theater: The houses are the audience, the port is the stage, the boats

are the actors...and the Saronic
Gulf is the scenic backdrop.

This little town has a history
rich with military might, political power, and artistic sophistication. Looking at the arid, barren mountains rising up along
the spine of the island, it's clear
that not much grows here—so
Hydriots have always turned to
the sea for survival. As islanders grew wealthy from the sea trade,
prominent local merchant families built the grand mansions that
rise up between the modest whitewashed houses blanketing the
hillsides. One of these—the Lazaros Kountouriotis Historical

HYDRA

Hydra Town

50 Meters
50 Yards

HYDRA

AGIOS CONSTANTINOS

RAFALLA ST.

AGIOS DIMITRIOS

KOULOURA

AGIOS ANATHANSIOS

SACHTOYRI ST.

OIKONOMOU

AGIA BARBARA

ANALIPSIS

TOMPAZI

BAKERY

HELLENIC SEAWAYS OFFICE

DONKEYS

WATER TAXIS

METOCHI BOATS

HYDROFOILS & CATAMARANS

MERCHANT MARINE ACADEMY

HISTORICAL ARCHIVES MUSEUM

WALK BEGINS

ANDREAS MIAOULIS MONUMENT

To Mandraki Bay

1 Hotel Leto
2 Phaedra Hotel
3 Hotel Miranda
4 Hotel Sophia
5 Mistral Hotel
6 Greco Hotel
7 Ippokampos Hotel
8 Alkionides Pension
9 Nereids Guest House
10 Pension Erofili
11 Pension Achilleas & Spalieri's Dhomatia
12 Psaropoula Restaurant
13 Taverna Gitoniko
14 Veranda Restaurant
15 Nero Gatto
16 The Onion Souvlaki
17 Café Isalos
18 Flora's Pastry Shop
19 To Kodylenia's Taverna
20 Pirate Bar
21 Amalour Bar
22 Hydronetta Bar
23 Gardenia Cinema

To
Kaminia
via High Road

AGIOS
GEORGIOS

RAFALIAS
PHARMACY

LAZAROS
KOUNTOURIOTIS
HISTORICAL
MANSION

Square of the
Five Prime
Ministers

Votsi
Square

MIAOULI

LIGNOU
STAIRS

WALK
ENDS

SAHINI ST.

CATHEDRAL
(MITROPOLIS)

MARKET

POST

VOTSI

BYZANTINE
MUSEUM

VLYCHOS
SHUTTLE BOATS

MONASTERY
OF THE
DORMITION

ACROPOLIS

HARBOR

SCHOOL OF
FINE ARTS

To
Kaminia, Vlychos &
via Coastal Path

SPILIA
"BEACH"

HYDRA

Saronic Gulf

To
Blsti &
Ag. Nikolaos
Beaches
via
Water Taxi

To
Vlychos Beach
via Shuttle Boat

To Piraeus
(Athens)

To
Ermioni & Metochi
(Peloponnese)

Mansion—is open to the public (the yellow mansion with the red roof, high on the hill across the harbor and to the right, with the small red bell tower nearby; described later).

Another mansion, the rough-stone four-story building directly across from the port (behind the imposing zigzag wall), now houses Hydra's School of Fine Arts. Artists—Greek and foreign—have long swooned over the gorgeous light that saturates Hydra's white homes, brown cliffs, and turquoise waters.

Look directly across the mouth of the harbor. Along the base of the walkway, under the seafront café tables, is the town's closest "beach," called Spilia ("Cave")—a concrete pad with ladders luring swimmers into the cool blue. For a more appealing option, you can follow the paved, mostly level path around this point to the fishing hamlet of Kaminia (with a scenic recommended restaurant) and, beyond that, to Vlychos (for the best beach around). Visually trace the ridgeline above that trail, noticing the remains of two old windmills—a fixture on many Greek islands, once used for grinding grain and raw materials for gunpowder. The windmills' sails are long gone, but the lower one was restored for use as a film prop (for the Sophia Loren film *Boy on a Dolphin*). Crowning the hill high above are the scant ruins of Hydra's humble little acropolis.

• *Turn your attention to the centerpiece of this viewpoint, the...*

Andreas Miaoulis Monument

The guy at the helm is Admiral Andreas Miaoulis (1768-1835), an Hydriot sea captain who valiantly led the Greek navy in the revolution that began in 1821. This war sought to end nearly four centuries of Ottoman occupation. As war preparations ramped up, the wealthy merchant marines of Hydra transformed their vessels into warships. The Greeks innovated a clever and deadly naval warfare technique: the "fireship." (For details, see page 378.) While this kamikaze-burning strategy cost the Greeks a lot of boats, it was even more devastating to the Ottoman navy—and Miaoulis' naval victory was considered a crucial turning point in the war. For three days each June, Hydra celebrates the Miaoulia Festival, when they set fire to an old ship to commemorate the burning of the Ottoman fleet.

On the monument, the cross that hangs from the steering column represents the eventual triumph of the Christian Greeks over the Muslim Ottomans. Miaoulis' bones are actually inside the stone pedestal under the statue.

• *Head back down the stairs and begin walking along the harborfront.*

Along the Harbor

About 50 yards down is the stout stone mansion that houses the **Historical Archives Museum.** This small but good collection (described on page 378) does its best to get visitors excited about Hydra's history. The gap after the museum is filled with monuments honoring Hydriot heroes. The green plaque in the pillar is a gift from Argentina to honor an Hydriot aristocrat who fought in the Argentinean war for independence. The next building is the Merchant Marine Academy, where Hydra continues to churn out sailors—many of whom often hang around out front. (During the WWII occupation of Greece, this building was used as a Nazi base.) Next, the row of covered metal benches marks the embarkation point for the ferries ("Flying Dolphin" hydrofoils and "Flying Cat" catamarans) that connect Hydra to Athens and other Greek islands for those of us who lack yachts of our own.

Notice the three flags to the right—specifically, the **flag of Hydra.** Dating from the uprising against the Ottomans, it's loaded with symbolism: the outline of the island of Hydra topped with a flag with a warrior's helmet, a cross, and an anchor—all watched over by the protective eye of God. The inscription, Η ΤΑΝ Η ΕΠΙ ΤΑΣ, means "with it or on it," and evokes the admonition of the warlike Spartans when sending their sons into battle with their huge shields: Come back "with it," victorious and carrying your shield; or "on it," dead, with your shield serving as a stretcher to carry your body home.

When you reach the corner of the harbor, you'll likely see **donkeys and mules** shooing flies as they wait to plod into town with

visitors' luggage lashed to their backs. The donkeys are not just a touristy gimmick, but also a lifestyle choice: Hydriots have decided not to allow any motorized vehicles on their island, keeping this place quiet and tranquil, and reducing pollution (now just donkey poop). This means that, aside from a few garbage trucks, these beasts of burden are the only way to get around. It's not unusual to see one with a major appliance strapped to its back, as it gingerly navigates the steps up to the top of town. Locals dress their burros up with rugs, beads, and charms. Behind each mule-train toils a human pooper-scooper. On Hydra a traffic jam looks like a farm show. And instead of the testosterone-fueled revving of moped engines, Hydra's soundtrack features the occasional distant whinnying of a donkey echoing over the rooftops.

In the same corner as the donkeys is the dock for the feisty fleet of red **water taxis.** These zip constantly from here to remote points around the island. Meanwhile, simple fishing boats squeeze between the luxury yachts to put in and unload their catch...eyed hungrily by scrawny cats.

Hang a right and continue along the bottom of the harbor. At this corner (next to the Alpha Bank) is Sahtouri street, which soon becomes Tompazi, and quickly devolves into a twisty warren of lanes with many hotels. Continue along the harbor, past a tiny dead-end lane leading to a good bakery. As you stroll, window-shop the **cafés** and choose one to return to later. Overhead, notice the ingenious rope system the seafaring Hydriots have rigged so that they can quickly draw a canopy over the seating area—like unfurling the sails on a ship—in the event of rain...or, more common here, overpowering sunshine. Next, skinny Oikonomou street leads to shops and the open-air Gardenia Cinema. A few steps farther, another narrow lane leads to the post office, public WC, and Hydra's ramshackle little market hall.

Hydra is known for its **jewelry.** A few shops right here on the harbor, such as Zoe's and Elena Votsi, sell the handiwork of Hydriot designers and artists (Votsi is locally famous as the designer of the 2004 Olympic medals). Many Hydra hoteliers supplement their income by running jewelry and souvenir shops, often with the same name as their hotels (good to know if you need to find your hotelier at midday). The next street, Navarhou Miaouli, bustles with appealing **tavernas.**

Shuttle boats line up along the next stretch of the quay. They offer cheap rides to points around the island—a service much appreciated by the owners of Hydra's many remote cafés and tavernas (but which annoys the water-taxi drivers).

• *Near the far corner of the harbor stands a symbol of Hydra, the clock tower of the...*

Monastery of the Dormition

Hydra's ecclesiastical center is dedicated to the Dormition of the Virgin. "Dormition"—as in "sleep"—is a Greek euphemism for death. Orthodox Christians believe Mary died a human death, then (like her son) was resurrected three days later, before being assumed into heaven.

Go through the archway under the tower, and you'll emerge into what was, until 1832, an active monastery. The double-decker arcade of cells circling the courtyard was once the monks' living quarters; it now houses the offices of the city government and mayor.

The monastery's church, which doubles as Hydra's *mitropolis* (cathedral), is free to enter. Stepping inside, it's clear that this was a wealthy community—compare the marble iconostasis, silver chandelier, gorgeous *Pantocrator* dome decoration, rich icons, and frescoes with the humbler decor you'll see at small-town churches elsewhere in Greece. Just inside the door (to the left), the icon of the Virgin and Child is believed to work miracles. Notice the many votive rings and necklaces draping it as a thank-you for prayers answered.

Back in the courtyard, you'll see war memorials and monuments to beloved Hydriots. The humble Byzantine Museum (also called the "Ecclesiastical Museum"—up the stairs across the courtyard) has a few rooms of glittering icons, vestments, and other paraphernalia from this monastery and church (€4 off-season, some English labels, Tue-Sun 10:00-14:00, closed Mon).

• *If the doorway's open under the museum, exit here onto Votsi street (otherwise, return to the harborfront, then hang a left up the next street). From this spot (either straight ahead or around the right side of the yellow butcher's shop) stairs head to the upper reaches of town, and eventually lead over the headland and down to the village and little harbor of Kaminia. For now though, keep to the left, walking toward the orange-tree-filled square.*

Upper Town Squares

Tidy **Votsi Square** has lots of cats. Hydriots love their cats, perhaps because they share a similar temperament: tender, relaxed, but secretly vigilant and fiercely independent. At the bottom of the square (on the left) is Flora's Pastry Shop, where we'll finish our stroll.

For now, keep walking about 100 feet above the square until the lane hits the old-time **Rafalias Pharmacy.** The pharmacy is an institution in town, and Vangelis Rafalias has kept it just as his grandfather did. He welcomes the browsing public, so take a look. Just inside the window, on the far right wall, is a photo of Jackie Onassis visiting Hydra.

With your back to the pharmacy, one lane leads to the left, heading uphill to the site of the original town, which was positioned inland to be safely away from marauding pirates. We'll head in the other direction, right, and slightly downhill, rounding the building on the left to the little **Square of the Five Prime Ministers.** The monument, with five medallions flanked by cannons, celebrates the five Hydriots who were chosen for Greece's highest office in the nearly two centuries since independence. It's an impressive civic contribution from a little island town, perhaps due to Hydra's seafaring wealth and its proximity to the Greek capitals (Nafplio, then Athens). From here, narrow, stepped, cobblestone lanes invite exploration of Hydra's quiet side.

But for now, continue left and downhill, back to Votsi Square. The recommended **Flora's Pastry Shop** (signed ΖΑΧΑΡΟΠΛΑΣΤΕΙΟ) is at the bottom of the square, on the right. Treat yourself to a homemade ice cream or baklava. Or, for something more traditional, try the local favorite—*galaktoboureko* (gha-lahk-toh-boo-re-KOH), which is cinnamon-sprinkled egg custard baked between layers of phyllo.

Sights and Activities in Hydra

MUSEUMS
▲Historical Archives Museum
This fine little museum, in an old mansion right along the port, shows off a small, strangely fascinating collection of Hydra's history and has good English descriptions throughout.

Cost and Hours: €5, includes temporary art exhibits, daily June-Sept 9:00-16:00 & 19:30-21:30, Oct-May 9:00-16:00, along the eastern side of the harbor near the ferry dock, tel. 22980-52355, www.iamy.gr.

Visiting the Museum: The core of the exhibit is upstairs. At the top of the stairs, look straight ahead for a tattered, yellowed **old map** by Rigas Feraios from 1797.

Depicting a hypothetical and generously defined "Hellenic Republic," it claims virtually the entire Balkan Peninsula (from the Aegean to the Danube) for Greece. The map features historical and cultural tidbits of the time (such as drawings of coins from various eras), making it a treasure trove for historians. Drawn at a time when the Greeks had been oppressed by the Ottomans for centuries, the map—with 1,200 copies printed and distributed—helped to rally support for what would become a successful revolution starting in 1821.

The stairwell to the top floor is lined with portraits of **"firebrands"**—sailors (many of them Hydriots) who burned the Ottoman fleet during the war. They were considered the "body and soul" of the Greek navy in 1821. To learn more about their techniques, head behind the map and into the room on the left; in its center, find the **model of a "fireship"** used for these attacks. These vessels were loaded with barrels of gunpowder, with large ventilation passages cut into the deck and hull. Suspended from the masts were giant, barbed, fishing-lure-like hooks. (Two actual hooks flank the model.) After ramming an enemy ship and dropping the hooks into its deck to attach the two vessels, the Greek crew would light the fuse and escape in a little dinghy...leaving their ship behind to become a giant firetrap, engulfing the Ottoman vessel in flames. Also in this room are nautical maps and models and paintings of other Hydriot vessels.

In the biggest room (immediately behind the old map), you'll see a Greek urn in the center containing the actual, embalmed **heart** of local hero Andreas Miaoulis. On the walls are portraits of V.I.H.s (very important Hydriots). Rounding out the collection is a room filled with **weapons** and 18th- and 19th-century **Hydriot attire.**

Lazaros Kountouriotis Historical Mansion

Because of Hydra's merchant-marine prosperity, the town has many fine aristocratic mansions...but only this one is open to the public.

Lazaros Kountouriotis (koon-doo-ree-OH-tees, 1769-1852) was a wealthy Hydriot shipping magnate who helped fund the Greek War of Independence. He donated 120 of his commercial ships to be turned into warships, representing three-quarters of the Greek navy. Today Kountouriotis is revered as a local and national hero, and his mansion offers visitors a glimpse into the lifestyles of the 18th-century Greek rich and famous.

Cost and Hours: €4, daily June-Aug 10:00-14:00 & 18:00-21:00, Sept 10:00-14:00 & 17:00-20:00, April-May and Oct 10:00-14:00, Nov-March by appointment only, on the hillside above town, signposted off the stepped Lignou street—turn right past Veranda Restaurant, tel. 22980-52421.

Visiting the Mansion: The main building of Kountouriotis' former estate is a fine example of aristocratic Hydriot architecture of the late 18th century, combining elements of Northern Greek, Saronic Gulf Island, and Italian architecture. The house has changed little since its heyday.

You'll enter on the second floor, with several period-decorated rooms. These reception rooms have beautiful wood-paneled ceilings, and are furnished with all the finery of the period. Included is the statesman's favorite armchair, where you can imagine him spending many hours pondering the shape of the emerging Greek nation. Then you'll head outside and upstairs to see a collection of traditional costumes and jewelry from throughout Greece, labeled in English. The lower floor displays the art of the local Byzantinos family: father Pericles (hazy Post-Impressionistic landscapes and portraits) and son Constantinos (dark sketches and boldly colorful modern paintings).

BEACHES

Although Hydra's beaches are nothing to get excited about, there's no shortage of places to swim. There's one swimming spot in Hydra town—the rest are reachable by foot, shuttle boat, or water taxi. Three decent beaches within a pleasant, easy walk of Hydra are Mandraki Bay, Kaminia Castello, and Vlychos. Distant beaches on the southwestern tip of the island (Bisti and Ag. Nikolaos) really get you away from it all, but are best reached by boat.

Spilia

The only spot to swim in town is Spilia ("Cave"), at the western entrance to Hydra harbor. There you'll find steps that lead down to a series of small concrete platforms with ladders into the sea—but no showers or changing rooms. (Spilia appears to belong to the adjacent café, but anyone is welcome to swim here.)

Mandraki Bay

This pebble beach is to the east of Hydra, near the main coastal path (30-minute walk from the eastern end of the harbor, €3 shuttle boat from Hydra). If it's sun you're after, Mandraki is best earlier in the day, as the hills around it bring shade in the late afternoon. The beach is dominated by a hotel that closed during the economic crisis, so it may not be as well maintained.

Kaminia Castello Beach

To the west of town is the delightful little harbor of Kaminia (15-minute walk). Just beyond that you'll find a restaurant and bar called Castello above the small Kaminia Castello Beach. While handy, the beach can be overwhelmed by the musical taste of the kids who run the bar, and is often crowded with lots of families. For walking directions, see "Walks," below.

Vlychos Beach

Located past Kaminia, Vlychos is my favorite. Like a little tropical colony, 20 thatched umbrellas mark a quiet stretch of pebbly beach. You'll pay €3 for a lounge chair and €3 for an umbrella. There's a café, Marina Taverna, for a meal (open daily for lunch

and dinner, tel. 22980-
52496), and showers at the
beach of the nearby hotel.
In peak tourist season,
a shuttle boat zips from
Hydra to Vlychos twice
an hour until sunset (confirm last boat time, €3).
The 40-minute walk from
Hydra to Vlychos is great
(described next).

WALKS
From Hydra to Kaminia and Vlychos
The walk from Hydra town to the cute cove of Kaminia and the
excellent beach at Vlychos (both described earlier) is one of my favorites. While the walk leads to two beaches, it's perfectly pleasant
whether or not you take a dip.

For the easy approach, simply follow the mostly level coastal
path that runs west from Hydra town to the villages of Kaminia
and Vlychos. As you curve out of Hydra, you'll pass the town's
best-preserved windmill, which was reconstructed for the 1957 Sophia Loren film *Boy on a Dolphin*. Up the steps to the windmill is a
statue honoring the film that attracted many celebrities to Hydra.

Continuing along the path, you'll find yourself in delightful
Kaminia after about 15 minutes, where two dozen tough little
fishing boats jostle within a breakwater. With cafés, a tiny beach,
and a good taverna (see page 387), this is a wonderful place to
watch island life go by.

Continue through Kaminia where the donkey path climbs a
cliff, passing Kaminia Castello Beach. Soon you're all alone with

great sea views. Ten minutes
or so later, you round a bluff,
descend into a ravine, cross an
Ottoman-style single-arched
bridge, and drop into **Vlychos,**
with its welcoming little beach.

From Vlychos, a higher
trail leads inland back to Hydra.
Leaving Vlychos, go under the
Ottoman Bridge, across the
footbridge, and straight onto the
path (30 minutes to reach the top of Hydra town, lit at night).

The Hydra-Kaminia High Road: For an alternate route to Kaminia, find way up Hydra's maze of stepped lanes that lace the
hills just west and south of town. Here, shabby homes enjoy grand

views, tethering off-duty burros seems unnecessary, and island life trudges on, oblivious to tourism. Feel your way up and over the headland, then descend into Kaminia. Along the way, look for dry, paved riverbeds, primed for the flash floods that fill village cisterns each winter. (You can also climb all the way up to the remains of Hydra's humble acropolis, topping the hill due west of the harbor.)

More Walks and Hikes

Beyond walking to a nearby beach, Hydra is popular for its network of ancient paths that link the island's outlying settlements, churches, and monasteries. Most of the paths are well maintained and clearly marked. Ask your hotel for a trail map; serious hikers should buy a detailed hiking map (€6, sold locally). If you do venture into the hills, wear sturdy shoes, sunscreen, and a hat, and take your own water and picnic supplies.

Nightlife in Hydra

Locals, proud of the extravagant yachts that flock to the island, like to tell of movie stars who make regular visits. But the island is so quiet that by midnight, all the high-rollers seem to be back onboard watching movies.

And yet there are plenty of options to keep visitors busy. People enjoy watching a film at the town's outdoor cinema or nursing a drink along the harborfront—there are plenty of mellow cocktail bars proudly serving "Paradise in a Glass" for €8.

Pirate Bar is run by a hardworking family serving homemade breakfast and lunch until 17:00 and fine cocktails until late. It sits on a prime spot on the water, at the little lane just past Lignou. The son, Zeus, runs the night shift and is famous for his Lychee Martini. This is a mellow, trendy spot to be late at night (tel. 22980-52711).

Amalour Bar, run by Vasilis, is "the place to fall in love" (or just enjoy wonderful music and good drinks). There's no sea view here—just cool music played at the right volume inside, and tables outside tumbling down a cobbled lane. It's mellow tunes until midnight, and then harder music (€6 cocktails during the 20:00-23:00 nightly "happy hour," just up Tompazi street from the harbor, mobile 697-746-1357).

Hydronetta Bar, catering to a younger crowd with young-

er music, offers great sea
views from under the
"Sofia Loren windmill,"
with a bunch of roman-
tic tables nestled within
the ramparts and cannons
(tel. 22980-54160). Reach
it by walking along the
coastline past Spilia Beach
and through the Sunset
Restaurant. This and the

neighboring Spilia cocktail bar charge €9 for cocktails and are the
most touristy of Hydra's nightlife choices.

Gardenia Cinema is part of a great Greek summer tradition:
watching movies in the open air. Hydra's delightful outdoor theater, lovingly run by the local cinema club, is right in the center of
town on Oikonomou street; it shows movies in the original language on summer weekends (€8, runs for 40 nights in the height of
summer, nightly at 21:00 and 23:00, tel. 22980-53105).

Sleeping in Hydra

Hydra has ample high-quality accommodations. Unfortunately,
the prices are also high—more expensive than anywhere on the
Peloponnese, and rivaling those in Athens. Prices max out in the
summer (June-mid-Sept), and I've generally listed these top rates.
Outside of these times, most accommodations offer discounts—always ask. Longer stays might also garner you a deal. If you arrive
with no reservation and sniff around, you can generally find a rough
little place with soft prices renting doubles for around €60: Look in
the harborfront for signs offering rooms. Some cheaper hotels don't
provide breakfast, in which case you can eat for about €6 at various
cafés around town. Communication can be challenging at a few of
the cheaper places (as noted). The only hotel with an elevator is the
Leto (though no hotel has more than three stories). Because Hydra
has a labyrinthine street plan and most people ignore street names,
I list no addresses, so use the map on page 372 and follow signs
posted around town. Most accommodations in Hydra close for the
winter (typically Nov-Feb, sometimes longer).

$$$ Hotel Leto is the island's closest thing to a business-
class hotel, offering great service with a professional vibe, 21 well-
appointed rooms, and inviting public spaces (Db-€165-185, Tb-
€204-228; rate depends on room type, season, and demand; higher
prices for rooms with snazzy marble bathrooms, small elevator, spa
treatments, tel. 22980-53385, www.letohydra.gr, info@letohydra.
gr, Alexandros Sofianos).

Sleep Code

Abbreviations (€1=about $1.10, country code: 30)

S=Single, **D**=Double/Twin, **T**=Triple, **Q**=Quad, **b**=bathroom

Price Rankings

  $$$ Higher Priced—Most rooms €120 or more

   $$ Moderately Priced—Most rooms €80-120

    $ Lower Priced—Most rooms €80 or less

Unless otherwise noted, breakfast is included, English is spoken, and free Wi-Fi and/or a guest computer is generally available. Many places accept credit cards, and rooms generally have air-conditioning. Prices can change; verify current rates online or by email. For the best prices, always book directly with the hotel.

$$$ Phaedra Hotel rents seven spacious and tasteful rooms in what was once a carpet factory. Helpful owner Hilda takes pride in her hotel, and it shows (Sb-€110, standard Db-€140, superior Db with balcony-€170, family studio-€220, superior 2-bed 2-bath suite with private veranda-€300, prices soft off-season, great breakfast, open year-round, tel. 22980-53330, mobile 697-221-3111, www.phaedrahotel.com, info@phaedrahotel.com).

$$$ Hotel Miranda, in a sea captain's house from the early 19th century, is filled with an elegant nautical charm that feels almost New England-y—it's the most atmospheric of my listings. Its 10 stylish rooms are bright with whitewashed stone, and surround a classy terrace (Sb-€100, Db-€130, superior Db with sea view-€200, tel. 22980-52230, www.mirandahotel.gr, mirandahydra@hol.gr).

$$ Hotel Sophia is a plush little boutique hotel right above the harbor restaurant strip. It's been family-run since 1934; today English-speaking sisters Angelika and Vasiliki are at the helm. The six thoughtfully appointed rooms, while a little tight, are stony-chic, with high ceilings, heavy exposed beams, tiny-but-posh bathrooms, and good windows that manage to block out most of the harbor noise. All the rooms have access to a little balcony, giving you a royal box seat overlooking all the harbor action (Db-€90-110, loft Db-€100-135, rates depend on season and length of stay, 10 percent discount with this book if paying cash and staying at least two nights, cheaper off-season, closed Nov-March, tel. 22980-52313, www.hotelsophia.gr, hydra@hotelsophia.gr). Ask to see the family museum filled with items from the original hotel.

$$ Mistral Hotel is a well-run place offering 17 rooms in a comfortable, modern-equipped, ivy-covered stone building with a central lounge and a breezy courtyard. It's a fine value at the very quiet top part of town (Db-€100, big Db with view-€150, free Wi-Fi in lobby and courtyard, tel. 22980-52509, www. hotelmistral.gr, info@hotelmistral.gr, Theo and Jenny serve a particularly good breakfast).

$$ Greco Hotel rents 19 rooms set above one of the shadiest, lushest gardens in town. It's where lovely owner Maria Keramidas serves a homemade buffet breakfast...and where you'll be tempted to just relax and do nothing all afternoon (Sb-€80, Db-€80-110, Tb-€100-130, prices depend on season and length of stay—email for best price, closed Nov-March, tel. 22980-53200, www.grecohotel. gr, grecohotelhydra@gmail.com; Maria speaks little English, but son Alkis is around to help).

$$ Ippokampos Hotel has 16 pleasant rooms around a cocktail-bar courtyard. The four top-floor rooms open right onto a seaview patio. The suite is a few notches up in quality and amenities, with its own private veranda (Sb-€50-75, Db-€80-90, Db suite-€130-160, Tb-€85-115, prices very soft for second-floor rooms depending on demand and length of stay, bar closes at 23:00, hotel closed Nov-March, tel. 22980-53453, www.ippokampos. com, ippo@ippokampos.com, Sotiris and Voula).

$ Alkionides Pension offers 10 smartly renovated rooms around a beautiful and relaxing courtyard, and is buried in Hydra's back lanes (Db-€70, Tb-€100, apartment-€100, extra person-20 percent more, no breakfast, tel. 22980-54055, mobile 697-741-0460, www.alkionidespension.com, info@alkionidespension.com, Kofitsas family).

$ Nereids Guest House is a bit farther from the harbor than my other listings, but the nine stony rooms offer good atmosphere and space for the price (Db-€65, Tb-€80, cheaper off-season, no breakfast, two minutes past Greco Hotel, tel. 22980-52875, www. nereids-hydra.com, nereids@otenet.gr).

$ Pension Erofili is a reliable budget standby in the heart of town, renting 12 basic but tasteful rooms just off (or over) a relaxing little courtyard (Db-€55—this special price with this book if you reserve directly with hotel, Tb-€65, apartment-€90, cheaper off-season, expansive homemade breakfast-€8, tel. 22980-54049, mobile 697-768-8487, www.pensionerofili.gr, info@pensionerofili. gr, George and Irene).

$ Pension Achilleas rents 13 decent rooms in an old mansion with a relaxing courtyard terrace and a gorgeous seaview roof patio. Request one of the upstairs rooms (they're brighter), and try to land one with a balcony (Sb-€50, Db-€75, Tb-€90, apartment-€150, cheaper off-season, cash only, breakfast-€7, tel. 22980-52050, www.achilleaspension.gr, kofitsas@otenet.gr, Dina speaks only a little English).

$ Spalieri's Dhomatia has five rooms in a cheery home with a welcoming garden courtyard. The units, though simple, are spacious. Staying with the Spalieri family provides a homier experience than at most other places in town (D-€70, Tb-€90, breakfast-€6, next to Pension Achilleas, tel. 22980-52894, mobile 694-414-1977, www.hydra.com.gr/spalieri, minimal English).

Eating in Hydra

There are dozens of places to eat, offering everything from humble gyros to slick modern-Mediterranean cuisine. Harbor views come with higher prices; places farther inland typically offer better value.

IN HYDRA TOWN

Psaropoula Restaurant, at the southwest corner of the harbor, fills a top-floor terrace in a prime spot overlooking all of the action. They specialize in seafood but also have pasta and meat dishes. Ask to see what's cooking in the kitchen, or peek inside their drawers full of fresh fish to see what looks good for dinner (€4-8 starters, €8-15 seafood starters, €8-20 main dishes, €15-25 seafood dishes, daily 12:00-23:00, reservations smart in summer—especially for prime view tables, tel. 22980-52573).

Taverna Gitoniko is a Hydra institution. Offering wonderful hospitality, delicious food, and delightful rooftop-garden seating, this tricky-to-find taverna is worth seeking out for a memorable meal. Christina and her son work magic with the produce they snap up fresh from the market—everything is good here. Order a selection of creative first courses and check their daily specials (€4-6 starters, €6-10 main dishes, seafood splurges, daily for lunch and dinner, closed Nov-Feb, Spilios Haramis, tel. 22980-53615).

Veranda Restaurant, perched on a terrace with fine views over the town and harbor, wins the best ambience award. It's great on a summer evening; enjoy a cold drink before selecting from a menu that offers pasta served a dozen different ways and a creative assortment of salads (€9-16 seafood starters and pastas, €10-25 meat and seafood dishes, better-than-average wine list, daily 18:00-late, halfway up the steps on Sahini lane or up a long staircase from the Lignou steps, reservations smart in summer, tel. 22980-52259, Andreas).

Nero Gatto is a modern Italian eatery, with tables inside or out on lively Tompazi street. Here you'll find good food, a friendly owner, and just the right mix of trendy and casual (€7-10 salads and starters, €10 pizzas, €9-15 pastas, €12-20 meat dishes, open daily 14:00-late, closed mid-Oct-mid-April, a minute up from the harbor on Tompazi, tel. 22980-54024).

Tavernas on Miaouli Street: This street leading up from the port (to the left of the monastery bell tower) is crammed with appealing little tavernas that jostle for your attention with outdoor seating and good food.

Souvlaki: For a quick, cheap (€2.50) meal, souvlaki is your best bet. For a civilized, sit-down souvlaki experience, drop by **The Onion Souvlaki** (Και Κρεμμύδι), a cute eatery filling a charming corner up Tompazi street, next to the Amalour Bar.

Cafés on the Harbor: Enjoy the scene as you nurse a drink here—drivers rolling their pushcarts, donkeys sneezing, taxi-boat drivers haggling, big boats coming and going. For a meal, try **Café Isalos** ("Waterline"), with a fun menu of light bites (€7-10 salads and sandwiches, €11-16 pizzas, good €3 iced coffees). In the early evening, watch for yachts trying to dock; some are driven by pros and others aren't, providing a comedic scene of naval inexperience.

Dessert: **Flora's Pastry Shop** is a hardworking little bakery cranking out the best pastries and homemade ice cream on the island. Flora has delightful tables that overlook Votsi Square, just behind the monastery. She sells all the traditional local sweets, including honey treats such as baklava. Many of her ingredients come from her farm on the nearby island of Dokos (daily 7:00-24:00).

EATING NEAR HYDRA, IN KAMINIA

A great way to cap your Hydra day is to follow the coastal path to the rustic and picturesque village of Kaminia, which hides behind the headland from Hydra. Kaminia's pocket-sized harbor shelters the community's fishing boats. Here, with a glass of ouzo and some munchies, as the sun slowly sinks into the sea and boats become silhouettes, you can drink to the beauties of a Greek isle escape. Consider combining with a late-afternoon stroll (along the seafront, see page 371).

Kodylenia's Taverna is perched on a bluff just over the Kaminia harbor. With my favorite irresistible dinner views on

Hydra, this scenic spot lets you watch the sun dip gently into the Saronic Gulf, with Kaminia's adorable port in the foreground. Owner Dimitris takes his own boat out early in the morning to buy the day's best catch directly from the fishermen. For meals, you can sit out on the shady covered side terrace above the harbor—check the chalkboard to see what's freshest today. For drinks, sit out front on the porch. Relax and take in a sea busy with water taxis, ferries that connect this oasis with

Athens, old freighters—like castles of rust—lumbering slowly along the horizon, and cruise ships anchored as if they haven't moved in weeks (€4-9 starters, €9-14 main dishes—visit their display case and see what's cooking, for a seafood meal figure €12-60 per person depending on what you order, daily 12:00-23:30, may close earlier off-season, closed Dec-Feb, tel. 22980-53520).

Hydra Connections

GETTING BETWEEN ATHENS AND HYDRA

Hydra is easily reached from Athens's port at Piraeus via the Hellenic Seaways ferry, either the "Flying Dolphin" hydrofoil or the slightly larger "Flying Cat" catamaran (6-8/day June-Sept, 4/day Oct-May, 1.5-2 hours, €28). If traveling to Hydra from Athens, then on to the Peloponnese, note that it's not necessary to return to Athens to pick up a car. You can go by ferry from Athens to Hydra, then continue by ferry from Hydra to Ermioni on the coast of the Peloponnese, where you can pick up a rental car (described later).

When to Buy Tickets: Because these boats are virtually the only game in town, it's wise to book in advance (at least a week ahead in summer). They can sell out during summer weekends, when boats are packed with Athenians headed to or from their Hydra getaway. Outside of summer, it's safe to assume that tickets will be available up to a day or two in advance.

Where to Buy Tickets: If you reserve ahead online on the **Hellenic Seaways website** (www.hellenicseaways.gr), there are a few ways to get your actual ticket. You can either check in online (anytime between 30 minutes and 48 hours before departure) and have an eticket sent to you. Or you can pick up a paper ticket at a travel agency, a Hellenic Seaways ticket office, or at a self-service machine at Piraeus.

It's also possible to buy a ticket in person soon after you arrive in Greece (tickets sold for the same price at any **travel agency**). Check the cancellation policy before buying your ticket.

In Hydra you can buy tickets at the **Hellenic Seaways office,** just down an alley near the Alpha Bank (open long hours daily in summer, tel. 22980-54007 or 22980-53812).

Boat Cancellations: Be aware that boats can be delayed, or even cancelled, if the weather's bad enough (mostly a concern in off-season). For more advice on navigating the Greek ferry system, see page 494.

GETTING BETWEEN HYDRA AND THE PELOPONNESE

You have several options for connecting Hydra and the Peloponnese via several spots on the coast of the peninsula: Metochi, Ermioni, or Tolo. Drivers can leave their cars in long-term parking at either Metochi (frequent crossings to Hydra on small passenger boats, just show up) or Ermioni (larger, less-frequent ferries, can be booked in advance). You can also connect Nafplio and Ermioni by public transportation (with some effort) or pick up a rental car in Ermioni to begin a tour of the Peloponnese. Another option is to day-trip from Tolo (near Nafplio) to Hydra.

Metochi (Drivers Only): Metochi is the spot on the mainland closest to Hydra (under 2 hours from Nafplio, 3 hours from Athens). It's at the end of a dirt road with nothing there except a couple of ticket stands and a small boat pier. You can park on the road or in the small dirt lot for free, or use the pay lot (€5/day). Both the **Freedom Boat** (mobile 694-424-2141, www.hydralines.gr) and **Metoxi Express** (tel. 22980-53000, www.hydracelebrity.gr) sail to Hydra quickly and frequently (€6.50, hop on the one that's leaving next, about hourly in summer, less frequent in spring and fall, 20 minutes, no boats Jan-March). Another option is a **water taxi** (these may be waiting in Metochi, otherwise call Hydra's sea taxi service at tel. 22980-53690, about €40 but confirm upfront).

Ermioni (Drivers and Those Without Cars): Ermioni (a.k.a. Hermioni) is an actual town with some amenities, and a little closer to Nafplio (1.5 hours). It's a 25-minute boat ride between Ermioni and Hydra on a Hellenic Seaways ferry (€8, 3-4/day in summer, fewer off-season, www.hellenicseaways.gr).

If you're visiting Hydra early in your trip and then continuing to the Peloponnese, a good plan is to ride the ferry from Athens to Hydra, then take the ferry from Hydra to Ermioni, where you can rent a car (try Pop's Car, www.popscar.gr, ask about fee for dropping the car in Athens or at the airport; you can also ask your Hydra hotelier to help with car rental).

Without a car, you can connect Ermioni and Nafplio by taxi and bus, though this is more complicated than it should be (see "Nafplio Connections" on page 233).

Tolo, near Nafplio (Day Trippers Only): Pegasus Tours operates an excursion boat from the port at Tolo, near Nafplio, but it runs only a few times a week, can be cancelled on short notice (if not enough passengers—mainly off-season), and requires an early-morning (though short) bus ride. Stopping in both Spetses and Hydra, it's a good option only for travelers without a car who can't devote an overnight to Hydra (3 boats/week in July-mid-Sept, 2/week May-June and mid-Sept-Oct, €34, tel. 27520-59430, www.pegasus-cruises.gr, easiest to book through Stavro-poulos Tours in central Nafplio—see page 211). For information on reaching Tolo, see page 224.

HYDRA

MYKONOS

ΜΥΚΟΝΟΣ / Μυκονοσ

Mykonos (MEE-koh-nohs) is the very picture of the perfect Greek island town: a humble seafront village crouched behind a sandy harbor, thickly layered with blinding-white stucco, bright-blue trim, and bursting-purple bougainvilleas. (Thank goodness for all that color; otherwise, this island—one of Greece's driest—would be various shades of dull brown.) On a ridge over town stretches a trademark row of five windmills, overlooking a tidy embankment so pretty they call it "Little Venice."

Mykonos' more recent status as a fashionable, jet-set destination and a mecca for gay holiday-makers also gives it a certain hip

cachet. These days, weary fisherfolk and tacky trinket stalls share the lanes with top-end fashion boutiques. Prices are stunningly high here, and the island is crammed full of fellow vacationers, particularly in August (try to come in spring or fall, if you can). But the Mykonians have taken all of the changes in stride. Fishermen still hang out on the benches by the harbor, wearing their traditional caps (Mykonian men are famous among Greeks for their baldness).

Mykonos does have some museums, but they merely provide an excuse to get out of the sun for a few minutes. The real attraction here is poking around the Old Town streets: shopping, dining, clubbing, or—best of all—simply strolling. The core of town is literally a maze, designed by the Mykonians centuries ago to discourage would-be invaders from finding their way. That tactic also works on today's tourists. But I can think of few places where getting lost is so enjoyable.

If you manage to break free, wander up to the windmills for the view, or head to one of the many enticing sandy beaches around the island. Near Mykonos, accessible by an easy boat trip, is the island of Delos—one of the Greek islands' top ancient sites. Delos hosts the remains of what was one of the most important places in the ancient Greek world: the temples honoring the birthplace of the twin gods Apollo and Artemis (it later became a bustling shipping community). Delos was a pilgrimage site for believers who came from all over to worship this "birthplace of light." Judging by the present-day sun-worshippers who scramble for the best patch of sand on Mykonos each summer, things haven't changed much around here.

PLANNING YOUR TIME

Mykonos, a delightful place to be on vacation, merits at least a full day and two overnights. The easiest plan is to simply explore the Old Town lanes; the restless can dip into a museum or two, but they're all skippable. If you want to get out of town, you can tour the archaeological site at Delos (easy 30-minute boat trip each way, figure 3-4 hours round-trip total) or head for the beaches. As Mykonos has better beaches and fewer interesting in-town sights than many other Greek isles, it's the perfect place to squeeze in some quality beach time.

Be warned that the island can be painfully crowded in peak season, roughly July through mid-September, and worst in August. During this time hotel prices skyrocket, and the beaches (and everything else) are uncomfortably packed with people. In winter (around Nov-March), the island essentially shuts down, as many restaurants and hotels close for the season.

Orientation to Mykonos

Mykonos' main town is called Chora (or Hora, Χώρα; roughly "village") but it's often referred to as "Mykonos town."

Mykonos town is the main point of entry for the island. The Old Town clusters around the south end of the Old Port—the harbor area bookended by two piers. To the north is the Old Port pier and bus station, and to the southwest is the pier for boats to Delos and the Sea Bus. Beyond that pier, to the south, is the Little Venice quarter and the windmill ridge. Squeezed between the harbor and the main road (passing above town on the gentle hill) is the Old Town's tight maze of whitewashed lanes.

While some streets have names, others don't, and in any case, locals never use those names—they just know where things are. If you can't find something, ask.

TOURIST INFORMATION

Mykonos doesn't have a TI. Hoteliers, travel agents, and other friendly locals can answer basic questions. Look for promotional but helpful town maps, or consult www.mykonos.gr, the island's official website. Another helpful website is www.e-mykonos.gr.

ARRIVAL IN MYKONOS

By Boat: Most travelers coming by boat arrive at the **New Port,** a mile north of the Old Town (most ships from Piraeus and Santorini and many cruise ships). From the New Port you have several options for getting to the Old Town: Easy and pleasant, the Sea Bus water taxi runs between the New Port and Mykonos town (may stop at the Old Port en route; €2, 1-2/hour, runs 7:00-23:00, tel. 69788-30355). By land you can take a taxi (€8-10 one-way), ride a public bus to the Old Port bus station (2/hour, €1.60), or, if arriving on a cruise, take the cruise line's shuttle bus (cost varies from free up to €10 round-trip). Alternatively, you could do the dreary 20- to 25-minute walk along the coast into town (turn right, follow the

MYKONOS

water, and just keep going—you can see the gaggle of white houses across the bay).

A few smaller, passenger-only ferries from other islands dock at the **Old Port,** while some cruise-ship tenders use its southern pier (described below). To reach the Old Town from the Old Port, walk five minutes along the harborfront promenade past a stretch of beach, then down a shop-lined lane to the main harborfront.

If your cruise ship is tendered, you'll disembark at the **pier** extending out from the Old Town's sandy harbor (where boats to Delos come and go). Just walk down the pier and you're at the harbor (there's a public WC on the right, along the water).

By Plane: Mykonos is well connected by air to Athens, but also (thanks to its worldwide popularity as a vacation spot) to many other European cities (airport code: JMK, tel. 22890-22327). Mykonos' small airport sits just two miles outside of town, easily connected by a short taxi ride (€10). There are also infrequent public buses—worthwhile only if a bus happens to be there when you arrive. Some hotels can arrange airport transfers.

GETTING AROUND MYKONOS

Mykonos is a fun and easy island to explore, with several very different but equally inviting beach coves within a short drive.

By Taxi: A taxi can take you to points around the island; however, Mykonos generally doesn't have enough taxis to accommodate demand, so you may have to wait in line, especially in peak season. Fares are reasonable; figure €12-20 one-way to most beaches listed in this chapter, except Super Paradise, which is more like €25 (note that taxis here do not use meters but set fares for different destinations). There are no cars allowed in Mykonos town, so you'll wait for a taxi at one of two places: the stand behind the large building labeled *Remezzo* (behind the Archaeological Museum at the north end of town) or at the Fabrika bus stop at the south end of town (described below). Rather than paying the taxi to wait for you at the beach, hail or call one when you're ready to leave (tel. 22890-22400). You can also ask a taverna at the beach to call for you. If you call for a taxi, there's a surcharge of several euros.

By Bus: Mykonos' bus network is well designed for connecting travelers to the island's many fine beaches. Buses are frequent, though they might leave you a short walk from the beach itself. And because this is a party island, buses run late into the night in peak season. Schedules are posted on chalkboards at stops, and many hotels post copies of the schedule near reception. Rides cost between €1.60 and €2.30 depending on the destination (may be pricier after midnight); buy your ticket from the bus driver or at a ticket kiosk.

There are two bus stations in Mykonos town. **Fabrika** station is at the south end of town (away from the harbor), where several Old Town streets funnel gradually uphill to the main road that passes above. From Fabrika you can catch buses to the beaches I've described in this chapter: **Ornos/Agios Ioannis** (1-2/hour), **Paradise** (2/hour), **Platis Gialos** (2/hour), and **Paraga** (hourly in high season, fewer in off-season).

The **Old Port** station is at the northeast edge of the Old Town by the pier. This station serves buses to the New Port and the eastern half of the island (the large town of Ano Mera, plus the smaller towns of Kalafati and Elia).

By Motorized Scooter or All-Terrain Vehicle (ATV): On Greek islands, tourists are notorious for renting a scooter or an ATV, overestimating their abilities to control a machine they've never driven before, and denting someone's fender or leaving a strip of knee or elbow skin on the pavement...or worse. That said, and keeping in mind the risks inherent in renting wheels here, it can be an affordable, efficient, and memorably fun way to connect distant beaches. If I were renting a scooter or an ATV on a Greek isle, I'd do it here, where the roads are not too heavily trafficked (you'll pass more fellow scooters and ATVs than cars), and idyllic beaches are a short ride away.

Travel agencies all over town rent both types of wheels for reasonable all-day rates (€10-25/day for a scooter or an ATV, some places may charge €7-10/day extra for insurance). Two people can ride one machine, but both should ask for helmets (you'll see many riders without them, but it's stupidly risky not to wear one, and most rental agencies are happy to loan you one).

Once on the road, be especially careful on turns, where centrifugal forces suddenly make it more difficult to steer. Be aware that even distances that appear short can take time to reach on a slow-moving ATV; figure 15-20 minutes from Mykonos town to any of the beaches I list in this chapter (Super Paradise is the farthest). Note: You'll see ads for renting a "bike," but this refers to motorized scooters—the island is hilly and arid enough to make actual bicycling undesirable for all but the most serious cyclists.

By Car: You can rent a car for as little as €35 per day, depending on demand; look for car-rental signs at several agencies around town, and negotiate a good bargain if you're here outside peak season.

By Private Tour: Greek Travelling offers private guided tours of Mykonos and Delos, including transfers from your boat if arriving by cruise ship (contact them to customize a tour and for prices, mobile 69732-01213, www.greektravelling.com, info@ greektravelling.com, Niki and Christos).

MYKONOS

HELPFUL HINTS

Unpredictable Hours: Don't count on the opening hours given here: they're likely to fluctuate. Check locally before planning your day.

English Bookstore: The **International Press Newsstand,** in the Old Town (a couple of streets in from the center of the harbor), stocks a good selection of international (including English-language) paperbacks, magazines, and newspapers (long hours daily, Kampani 5, tel. 22890-78507).

Services: You'll find travel agencies, ATMs, launderettes (€10 drop-off service), minimarkets, pharmacies, Internet cafés, and other helpful services scattered around the Old Town. For the highest concentration of services (and tattoo parlors), head for the area around the Fabrika bus station, at the south end of the Old Town (near where it meets the main road).

Open-Air Cinema: In summer, locals and vacationers sit back and enjoy the movies under the palm trees at **Ciné Manto,** in a lovely garden smack in the middle of town (films shown in original language—usually English, June-Sept only, usually two showings a night—check signs around town for times, café, tel. 22890-26165).

Sights in Mykonos

▲▲Old Town

Mykonos' Old Town seems made for exploring. Each picture-perfect lane is slathered with a thick, bulbous layer of stucco, giving

the place a marshmallow-village vibe. All that white is the perfect contrast to the bright-blue sky and the vivid trim. Sometimes described as "cubist" for its irregular jostle of angular rooflines, Mykonos' townscape is a photographer's delight. Enjoy getting lost, then found again. Try wandering aimlessly for a while—you may be amazed how quickly you find yourself going in circles. To get your bearings, look at a map and notice that three "main" roads (still barely wide enough for a moped) form a U-shaped circuit facing the harbor: Kouzi Georgouli, Enoplon Dynameon, and Matogianni.

Or just relax along the sandy **harbor.** The pier for excursion boats to Delos (described later) sticks straight out; nearby is an impossibly picturesque white chapel with sky-blue trim. Nurse an iced coffee or a beer at a rustic café table and watch the tide of tourists wash over local village life. Glancing offshore, you'll see humble fishing boats bobbing in the foreground, with 2,000-passenger cruise ships looming in the distance. Along the sandy harbor, fisherfolk sort and clean their catch at the marble table (while stray cats gather below), and old-timers and kids alike toss fishing lines into the water. You may even see one of the resident pelicans—Petros, Nikolas, or Irini. (Ever since a local fisherman found an ailing pelican and nursed it back to health half a century ago, these odd birds have been the town's mascots.)

The piazza known as **Manto Square** is at the east end of the sandy harbor. It's marked by a bust of Manto Mavrogenous (1796-1848), a heroine of the Greek War of Independence. A wealthy aristocrat of Mykonian heritage, she spent her fortune supplying Greek forces in a battle against their Turkish rulers. Mavrogenous ended her life destitute on the island of Paros, never regretting the sacrifices she made for Greece's freedom.

▲▲Windmills

Mykonos is infamously windy, and Mykonians have special names for the different winds that blow through: "the bell-ringer," "the chair-thrower," and "the unseater of horsemen." As in many Greek

island towns, Mykonos' old-fashioned windmills harnessed this natural power in order to grind grain to supply its ships. Five of them (plus the bases of two more) stand proudly along a ridge called Kato Myloi at the

top of town, overlooking the Little Venice area. While there's nothing to see inside these buildings, they make for a fine photo op and great views over town.

To enter a windmill, head to the opposite (east) end of the Old Town, where the **Boni Myli windmill** is open to visitors (June-Sept daily 16:00-20:00, closed Oct-May, tel. 22890-22591).

MYKONOS

Mykonos Town

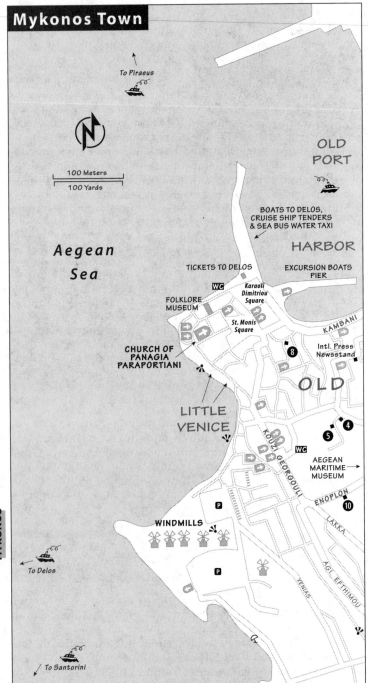

To Piraeus

N

100 Meters
100 Yards

OLD PORT

Aegean Sea

BOATS TO DELOS,
CRUISE SHIP TENDERS
& SEA BUS WATER TAXI

HARBOR

TICKETS TO DELOS

EXCURSION BOATS
PIER

WC

Karaoli
Dimitriou
Square

FOLKLORE
MUSEUM

St. Monis
Square

KAMBANI

CHURCH OF
PANAGIA
PARAPORTIANI

Intl. Press
Newsstand

8

OLD

LITTLE
VENICE

4
5

WC

AEGEAN
MARITIME
MUSEUM

KOUZI GEORGOULI

ENOPLON

10

LAKKA

P

WINDMILLS

P

AGI. EFTHIMOU

XENIAS

To Delos

To Santorini

MYKONOS

1. Hotel Carbonaki
2. Elena Hotel
3. The Matogianni Hotel
4. Fresh Hotel
5. Terra Maria Rooms
6. Hotel Philippi
7. To Maereio
8. Fish Tavern Kounelas
9. Komninos Traditional Healthy Flavors
10. Supermarket

MYKONOS

▲Little Venice (Mikri Venetia)

Along the bay at the western edge of town, just below the windmills, wealthy local shipping merchants built a row of fine man-

sions, with brightly painted wooden balconies, that seem to rise from the deep. While "Little Venice" is a bit of a misnomer (where are the canals?), this is a particularly scenic corner of town. At the head of this area, a stately Catholic church (the only one on Mykonos, which boasts some 400 little Orthodox chapels) marks a square filled with restaurant tables.

The embankment here is lined with cocktail bars and cafés (I particularly like **Scarpa, Galleraki,** and **Caprice**), crowded every night with throngs of visitors enjoying the island's best spot to watch the sunset—one of the highlights of visiting Mykonos.

▲Church of Panagia Paraportiani

Huddled at the tip of land between Little Venice and the harbor, this unusual church is a striking architectural oddity—a hodge-

podge of five small chapels that gradually merged together, then were draped in a thick layer of whitewashed stucco. While it's a much-touted landmark (and one of the island's most-photographed spots), there's little to see beyond the initial, otherworldly appear-

ance. One of the chapel interiors is open most days, where a local woman sells votive candles and fills the small space with the rich aroma of incense.

Archaeological Museum

This small museum, just uphill from the Old Port, displays artifacts found on the nearby island of Rinia, which became the burial isle for Delos when residents of that sacred island's cemeteries were relocated by the Athenians in the sixth century B.C. (see sidebar on page 408). With limited English labels and almost no descriptions, most of what's here—intricately carved stone grave markers, vases, jewelry, and statue fragments—is pretty dull. One item, however, makes a visit worth considering: a large vase (in room just beyond entry, dead center along the back wall) clearly showing the Trojan Horse filled with Greek soldiers sporting gleeful archaic smiles, and cartoon-like panels telling the story of the massacre that followed when they jumped out. Dating from roughly 670 B.C., it's the oldest depiction of the Trojan Horse ever found. Unlike the museum's other pieces, it wasn't excavated from the Rinia graves, but found right here on Mykonos, discovered in 1961 by a (surely very surprised) farmer who'd set out to dig a well.

Cost and Hours: €2, April-Sept Tue-Sun 9:00-16:00, off-season until 15:00, closed Mon year-round, tel. 22890-22325. Ask for the free brochure when you enter.

Aegean Maritime Museum

This tight but endearing collection traces the story of the local mercantile shipping industry. A desert isle of history in a sea of wealthy tourism, this little place takes its subject very seriously. In its three rooms you'll find amphora jugs, model ships, and more. The tranquil garden in back displays the actual, original lighthouse from the island's Cape Armenistis, as well as replicas of ancient sailors' gravestones. The good English descriptions offer a fine history lesson for those willing to read them.

Cost and Hours: €4, April-Oct daily 10:30-13:00 & 18:30-21:00, closed Nov-March, Enoplon Dynameon 10, tel. 22890-22700.

Lena's House

Part of the Folklore Museum, this little museum shows part of a typical middle-class Mykonian house dating from the late 19th century, complete with original furnishings and artwork. The rest of the house is occupied by the Maritime Museum next door.

Cost and Hours: Free, donations appreciated; April-Sept Mon-Sat 18:30-21:30, Sun 19:00-21:00; closed Oct-March; tel. 22890-22390.

Mykonos Folklore Museum

Housed in a typically Cycladic former sea captain's residence just up the bluff from the harbor, this museum displays a random mix of traditional folk items from around the island, as well as a typical kitchen and bedroom.

Cost and Hours: Free; April-Sept Mon-Sat 10:30-14:00 & 17:30-20:30, closed Sun; closed Oct-March; tel. 22890-22591.

BEACHES

Mykonos' array of beaches rivals that of any Greek island. Each beach seems to specialize in a different niche: family-friendly or party; straight, gay, or mixed; nude or clothed; and so on. (Keep in mind that in Greece, even "family-friendly" beaches have topless sunbathers.) Get local advice to find the one that suits your beach-bum preferences, or choose from one of the options listed here (all of my suggestions are within a 10- to 20-minute drive, ATV/scoot-

MYKONOS

er outing, or bus ride from town). To connect the beaches, you'll drive up and down over the steep, dusty, dirty, desolate spine of this arid island. You can also connect the southern beaches—Platis Gialos, Paraga, Paradise, Super Paradise, Agrari, and Elia—by regular shuttle boat for around €3 (none from Mykonos town).

All of these beaches rent comfortable lounge chairs with umbrellas out on the sand (around €15-30 for two chairs that share

an umbrella; more at exclusive beaches). Just take a seat—they'll come by to collect money. Be warned that in peak season (July and especially Aug), all beaches are very crowded, and it can be difficult to find an available seat.

Mykonos' beaches are lined with cafés and tavernas, with typical Greek-island menus...sometimes functional, sometimes surprisingly good. These can offer a welcome break from the sun.

Agios Ioannis

This remote-feeling patch of sand—my favorite beach on the island—is tucked behind a mountain ridge, and best gives you

the feeling of being on a castaway isle. You'll enjoy views across to the important isle of Delos. From Mykonos town go to Ornos, then head toward Kapari; on your way down the hill, turn off on the left at the low-profile beach signs (one directs you to Πύλη, one of the restaurants on the beach). You'll drop down the road to an idyllic Robinson Crusoe spot where a few restaurants share a sandy beach.

For the even more secluded **Kapari** beach, continue down the road past the Agios Ioannis turnoff, then swing right at the white church.

Ornos

Easy to reach since it's in a sizeable town in the middle of the island, this very family-friendly beach is also one of the more functional of those I list (and has better lounge-chair values)—but is least memorable. The whole place has an unpretentious charm.

Psarou and Platis Gialos

These two beaches, along the next cove to the east of Ornos, are much more densely developed. At each one a tight line of hotels arcs along the top of a crowded patch of sand. Psarou is considered a somewhat exclusive, favorite retreat of celebrities, while Platis Gialos feels more geared toward families (the far end from the bus stop/parking is less claustrophobic).

Paradise

This famous "meat-market" beach is a magnet for partiers in the Aegean, and even more of a destination than the other beaches listed here. Located at the southern tip of the island, Paradise (a.k.a. Kalamopodi) is presided over by hotels that run party-oriented bars for young beachgoers—perfect if you want to dance in the sand all night to the throbbing beat with like-minded backpackers from around the world. As you approach, the last stretch is through thick, high grasses, giving the place an air of secrecy; then you'll pass long rows of lockers before popping out at the party.

The next cove over hosts **Super Paradise** (Plintri) beach, which has eclipsed the original as the premier party beach on the island.

Sleeping in Mykonos

Mykonos is an expensive place to overnight—especially in peak season (mid-July through August, sometimes extending all the way from mid-June to mid-September). During these premium times, even "budget" hotels dramatically increase their rates... which means you should lower your value-for-money expectations. If you can come just before or after this busy period, you can save more than half. If you do come in peak season, book as far ahead as possible—that's when most of the smaller hotels get filled up with repeat customers, here on their annual visit. If you show up without a reservation, try the room-finding service near

MYKONOS

Sleep Code

Abbreviations   **(€1=about $1.10, country code: 30)**
S=Single, **D**=Double/Twin, **T**=Triple, **Q**=Quad, **b**=bathroom
Price Rankings
   $$ **Higher Priced**—Most rooms €160 or more
    $ **Lower Priced**—Most rooms less than €160
Unless otherwise noted, breakfast is included, English is spoken, and free Wi-Fi and/or a guest computer is generally available. Many places accept credit cards, and rooms generally have air-conditioning. Prices can change; verify current rates online or by email. For the best prices, always book directly with the hotel.

---

the bus stop at the Old Port; expect to pay at least €80 for a basic double that may not be in the most central location.

In this party town, nighttime noise—dance clubs, people carousing in the streets, and so on—is epidemic; plan to wear earplugs, and if you're a light sleeper, try requesting a hotel's quietest room. I've tried to recommend places on streets that are less raucous than the norm, but they're also very central, so no promises.

$$ Hotel Carbonaki is a family-run hotel near the top of town, with 22 nicely appointed rooms around an oasis courtyard with a Jacuzzi. It's the most inviting of the places I've found in this price range (high season: Sb-€120-150, Db-€150-190; off-season: Sb-€55-95, Db-€66-125; higher rates are for busier weeks, closed Nov-Feb; breakfast-€10, Panachrantou 23, tel. 22890-24124, www.carbonaki.gr, info@carbonaki.gr, Theodore and the Rousounelos family).

$$ Elena Hotel has 30 modern rooms, helpful staff, and a pleasant veranda lounge/breakfast area with a bit of a sea view. It's a little more peaceful, set slightly away from the Old Town crowds (July-mid-Sept: Db-€200; late May-June: Db-€155; mid-Sept-late May: Db-€100; €20 more for sea-view room, breakfast-€15, Rochari street, tel. 22890-23457, www.elenamykonos.gr, info@elenamykonos.gr).

$$ Fresh Hotel's 10 rooms, some with balconies, are thoroughly modern, with posh bathrooms. While it hardly has any public spaces, its sleek garden restaurant (which can be a little noisy) serves as an ersatz lounge (late July-late Aug: Db-€160-180, rest of summer: Db-€100-140, May-June: Db-€60-120, off-season: Db-€53-80, €10 less without breakfast, closed Dec-Feb, N. Kalogera 31, tel. 22890-24670, www.hotelfreshmykonos.com, info@hotelfreshmykonos.com).

$$ Terra Maria is a decent option, with a pleasant white-on-white decor (high season: Db-€160-190, off-season: Db as low as €60, price depends on room type, breakfast-€10, N. Kalogera 18, tel. 22890-24212, www.terramariahotel.com, mykonos@terramariahotel.com).

$$ Hotel Philippi has 14 rooms huddled around a garden in the heart of the Old Town (high season: Db-€180, mid-season: Db-€80-120, low season: Db-€50-60, rates flex with size of room and demand—and are fairly soft off-season, small breakfast-€4, full breakfast-€9, closed Nov-March, N. Kalogera 25, tel. 22890-22294, www.philippihotel.com, chriko@otenet.gr, Chris).

$ The Matogianni Hotel offers trendy pizzazz at reasonable prices. Hiding on a quiet lane near the harborfront, it boasts a long, pleasant front porch filled with wicker chairs (Db-€120-180 in high season, much lower off-season, ground-floor rooms about €20 cheaper, price depends on demand and length of stay—email or call for best rates, cash preferred, may close Dec-Jan, Matogianni street, tel. 22890-22217, www.matogianni.gr, info@matogianni.gr; friendly, helpful Nancy).

Eating in Mykonos

The twisting streets of the Old Town are lined with tourist-oriented restaurants. Don't look for good values here—Mykonos is ex-

pensive. Simply choose the spot with the menu and ambience that appeal to you: with a sea view, out on a busy pedestrian lane, or in a charming garden courtyard.

The many tavernas and cafés that face the sandy harbor are touristy and overpriced, but it's hard to argue with their appeal. Consider enjoying a *freddo cappuccino* or *frappé*—if not a full meal—from this comfortable perch, which offers the best people-watching (and sometimes cat-and pelican-watching) in town. The harborfront has the workaday action, while the places in Little Venice are more romantic—especially at sunset. A few steps inland, tucked in the town's winding

back lanes, are countless charming restaurants filling hidden gardens under trellises of bougainvillea. Take mental notes as you explore by day, then come back to the place that most appeals. I've also suggested a few places that are worth seeking out for dinner.

Inside cozy little **To Maereio** (Τό Μαερειό), in-the-know diners choose from a small but reasonably priced, inventive menu that includes some Mykonian specialties (daily from 19:00, little outside seating, near Hotel Philippi at Kalogera 16, tel. 22890-28825).

Fish Tavern Kounelas is your top bet for seafood, where they grill the fresh fish right out on the tiny alley (daily from 18:30, near St. Monis Square—look for blue-and-white *KOUNELAS* signs, tel. 22890-28220).

M-Eating serves up spendy but good modern Mediterranean cuisine. Most diners vie for their outdoor covered terrace seating; you might have better luck snagging one of the few small tables inside (daily from 19:00, reservations smart, 10 Kalogera, tel. 22890-78550, www.m-eating.gr).

Bakery: Locals still shop at **Psillos,** a family-run, unsigned hole-in-the-wall where they bake everything on site. Grab something from the bins of breads, cookies, and other items lining the wall, or try a meat or cheese pie (€2). It offers a bit of affordability and local flavor in the center of this pricey, touristy town (daily until 15:00, find it between Fresh and Terra Maria hotels on Klaous street).

Mykonos Connections

BY BOAT

All bigger boats and car ferries leave from the New Port, about a mile north of town (see page 393 for information on how to get there from Mykonos town). That includes most boats to Piraeus and Santorini. The rest of the boats leave from the Old Port. Be sure to check locally to confirm which port your ferry is departing from. For ferry tips and ferry-company contact info, see page 494.

To Piraeus: Generally 3/day in high season (1 fast boat, 3 hours, €60; 2 slow boats, 5.5 hours, €40). Off-season (Oct-March) there is likely one slow boat daily (confirm, especially Jan-March).

To Santorini: Generally 2-3/day April-mid-Oct, none in winter, 3 hours, 1-2 stops en route, €60.

MYKONOS

Near Mykonos: Delos

Popular as Mykonos is today, it was just another island centuries ago, and the main attraction was next door: the island of Delos, worth ▲. In antiquity, Delos lived several lives: as one of the Mediterranean's most important religious sites, as the "Fort Knox" of Greek city-states, and as one of the ancient world's busiest commercial ports. Its importance ranked right up there with Athens, Delphi, or Olympia. Today the island is a ghost town—only ruins and a humble museum remain. Highlights of your visit include the much-photographed lion statues, some nice floor mosaics, the view from Mt. Kynthos, and a windswept setting pockmarked with foundations that hint at Delos' rich history.

ORIENTATION TO DELOS

Cost and Hours: €12 admission (€6 off-season), plus cost of the boat trip (see below); open daily from the arrival of the first boat to the departure of the last one; tel. 22890-23413.

Warning: Delos is an uninhabited island with virtually no shade and only a small museum and café. Wear good shoes, and bring sun protection and plenty of water.

Getting There: Delos is reachable by a 30-minute boat ride from Mykonos. Boats depart Mykonos from the pier extending straight out from the Old Town; buy the €19 round-trip ticket at the kiosk at the base of the pier (generally departing Mykonos at 9:00, 10:00, and either 11:00 or 11:30; returning from Delos at 12:00, 13:30, and either 14:30 or 15:00). You can take any boat back. There may also be a late-afternoon boat from Mykonos (around 16:00) that returns in the early evening (around 18:30). Times can change depending on weather, cruise-ship arrivals and departures, and other factors, so be sure to check locally.

Tours: Local guides meet arriving boats (€10 for a 1-1.5 hour tour—you'll need more time to actually hike around the site and see the museum). Travel agencies in Mykonos town sell package excursions to Delos that include the boat, museum entry, and a guided tour (overpriced at roughly €40, though these tours last longer than those offered by on-site guides).

The Rise and Fall of Delos

Delos enters history 3,000 years ago as a sacred place where a number of gods were worshipped. Blessed with a prime location (midway between the mainland of Greece and Asia Minor—today's Turkey—and in the center of the Greek islands), but cursed with no natural resources, the barren island survived as a religious destination for pilgrims bringing offerings to the gods.

According to myth, the philandering Zeus impregnated the mortal Leto. Zeus' furious wife, Hera, banished Leto from the earth, but Zeus implored his brother Poseidon to create a refuge for her by raising up the underwater world of "Invisible" (Greek *Adelos*) to create an island that was "Visible" *(Delos)*. Here Leto gave birth to twins—Apollo (god of the sun) and Artemis (goddess of the moon). Their human followers built temples in their honor (ninth century B.C.), and pilgrims flocked here with offerings.

As Athens began to assert control over the Aegean (sixth century B.C.), it made sure that spiritually influential Delos stayed politically neutral. The Athenians ordered a "catharsis" (purification) of the island, removing dead bodies from the cemeteries. Later, they also decreed that no one could be born or die there—that is, there were to be no permanent residents. The Delians were relocated to an adjacent larger island called Rinia. Ostensibly, this was to keep Delos pure for the gods, but in reality it removed any danger of rivals influencing the island's native population.

Because of its neutral status and central location, Delos was chosen in 478 B.C. as the natural meeting place for the powerful Delian League—an alliance of Greek city-states formed to battle the Persians and to promote trade. The combined wealth of the league was stored here in the fabulously rich bank of Delos. But all that changed in 454 B.C., when Pericles moved the treasury to Athens, and Delos reverted to being a pilgrimage site.

Centuries later, under the Romans, Delos' course changed dramatically once more. Thanks to its strategic location, the island was granted the right to operate as a free port (167 B.C.). Almost overnight, it became one of the biggest shipping centers in the known world, complete with a town of 30,000 inhabitants.

Then, in 88 B.C., soldiers from the Kingdom of Pontus, an enemy of Rome, attacked and looted the town, slaughtering 20,000 of its citizens. Delos never really recovered. Plagued by pirate attacks and shifting trade routes, Delos faded into history. Its once-great buildings were left to decay and waste away. In 1872, French archaeologists arrived (so far, scientists have excavated about one-fifth of the site), and Delos' cultural treasures were revealed to the modern world.

Services: A small building next to the museum sells coffee, juice, and basic snacks. Behind the café are WCs.

Length of This Tour: Most visitors find that 1.5-2 hours on the island is plenty to wander the site and see the museum.

◑SELF-GUIDED TOUR

• *From the boat dock, walk to the entrance, buy your ticket, pick up the helpful included map, and enter the gate.*

Pause and survey the site. The commercial harbor was to your right, and the sacred harbor to your left. Ahead and to the right are the foundations of shops and homes that once constituted one of the Aegean's finest cities. Standing above those ruins is Mount Kynthos, its hillsides littered with temple remains. The Agora of the Competaliasts—one of the main squares in town—is straight ahead (with the museum building poking up behind). The religious area (with the temples of Apollo) is ahead and to the left, at the end of the Sacred Way. And far to the left was the Sacred Lake (now a patch of trees), overlooked by the iconic row of lions.

• *Start by wandering through the long rows of foundations on your right. You can circle back to these at the end or poke around now in case you run out of steam later.*

❶ Residential and Commercial District

Most of these remains were either homes or shops. In the second century B.C. (when Delos was a bustling commercial port), the

streets were lined with some 3,000 shops where you could buy just about anything, and the hillsides above were covered with the elaborate homes of wealthy merchants and shippers. Delos was considered the most important commercial center in the known world. (One of its primary commodities was human beings—it was a major center in the ancient slave trade.) The city was cosmopolitan, with 30,000 residents and distinct ethnic groups, each with its own linguistic and cultural neighborhood (Greeks, Syrians, Beirutis, Italians, and so on). Remains of these same neighborhoods can still be seen today.

Delos

STANDING RUINS
ORIGINAL FOOTPRINT

200 Meters
200 Yards

Aegean Sea

To Mykonos

STADIUM

GYMNASIUM

To Synagogue

LAKE HOUSE

HIPPODROME

ESTABLISHMENT OF THE POSEIDONIASTS FROM BEIRUT

LIONS OF THE NAXIANS

ROMAN WALL

AGORA OF THE ITALIANS

CAFÉ & WC

SANCTUARY OF ARTEMIS

MUSEUM

RELIGIOUS CENTER

COLOSSUS APOLLO

SANCTUARY OF DIONYSUS & MONUMENT OF CARYSTIUS

Sacred Harbor

STOA OF PHILIP V

SACRED WAY

ENTRANCE & TICKETS

RESIDENTIAL & COMMERCIAL DISTRICT

BOAT DOCK

Commercial Harbor

TERRACE OF FOREIGN GODS

THEATER QUARTER

THEATER

HOUSE OF THE DOLPHINS

CISTERN

HOUSE OF THE MASKS

TEMPLE OF ZEUS & ATHENA

Mt. Kynthos

❶ Residential & Commercial District
❷ Agora of the Competaliasts
❸ Sanctuaries of Apollo & Artemis
❹ Lions of the Naxians
❺ Sacred Lake
❻ Museum
❼ Temple of Zeus & Athena
❽ House of the Dolphins
❾ House of the Masks

MYKONOS

Poke into some of the **house foundations**. Homes were generally organized around a central courtyard above a giant cistern. Look for fragments of elaborate mosaic floors (intact portions are on display inside the museum), as well as marble structures that once decorated the place. The city even had a surprisingly advanced sewer system. Because wood was rare on the arid Cycladic Islands, most buildings were constructed from dry-stone walls; wood was a status symbol, used only by the wealthiest to show off. Delos had some of the biggest homes of ancient Greece, not necessarily because of wealth, but because they could build big here without fear of the devastating earthquakes that plagued other locations. The Greeks attributed this to divine intervention (modern seismologists have found that Delos sits away from major fault lines).

• *Now head toward the agora that's near the ticket building.*

❷ Agora of the Competaliasts

This was the main market square of the Roman merchants who worshipped the deities called *lares compitales,* who kept watch over the crossroads. This is not *the* agora, but one of many agoras (marketplaces) on Delos—a reminder that several different communities coexisted in this worldly trading city.

• *Just above the upper-left corner of this agora, the Sacred Way leads off to the left. Follow the same path ancient pilgrims walked as they approached the temples of Apollo (look for the blue arrows to guide you). Along the left side of the road runs the long ledge of the pediment (with recognizable triglyphs) from the **Stoa of Philip V** (what we see here as the "bottom" actually ran along the top of the building). At the end of the Sacred Way is the...*

Religious Center

Both the ❸ **Sanctuary of Apollo** and, beyond that, the **Sanctuary of Artemis** consisted of several temples and other ceremonial buildings. In its day, Apollo's sanctuary had three large, stern Doric temples lined with columns. The biggest temple was nearly 100 feet long. The nearby Porinos Naos served as the treasury of the Delian League. Other treasuries once held untold riches—offerings to the gods brought by devout pilgrims.

• *Follow the route to the right, then left, then left again around the Sanctuary of Apollo. Before heading off to the right down the main path, pause at the giant marble pedestal that once held the...*

Colossus Apollo Statue

The 35-foot statue (seventh century B.C.) was a gift from the Naxians and was carved from a single block of marble. It's long gone now, but a few bits of its fingers are on display in the museum.

• *Continue down the path, beyond the Sanctuary. You'll pass the foundations that surround the spacious **Agora of the Italians** (on the right) on the way to the...*

❹ Lions of the Naxians

This row of five sphinx-like lion statues is the main, iconic image of this site. These are replicas, but five of the original statues (sev-

enth century B.C.) are in the museum. One of the originals was stolen by the Venetians, "repaired" with an awkwardly too-big head, and still stands in front of Venice's Arsenal building.

• *Northwest of the lions, up a small hill, are four columns marking the* **Establishment of the Poseidoniasts from Beirut,** *the religious and commercial center for merchants and other businessmen from Berytus, in ancient Syria. Below the columns is the...*

❺ Sacred Lake

This was supposedly the source of Zeus' seed. When Leto was about to give birth to Zeus' children (according to the "Hymn to Delian Apollo," attributed to Homer), she cried out: "Delos, if you would be willing to be the abode of my son Apollo and make him a rich temple, your people will be well-fed by strangers bringing offerings. For truly your own soil is not rich." The Sacred Lake was drained by French archaeologists to prevent the spread of bacterial disease.

• *Walk around the Sacred Lake. At the top, stop by the* **Lake House,** *providing a glimpse of a second-century B.C. Delian home. Now hike up toward the museum. Just before the museum, a path detours to the left far into the distance. You can follow it to find the remains of the gymnasium, stadium, and the Jewish synagogue.*

Olympics-style games were held at Delos' **stadium** *every five years. Like the more famous games at Olympia and Delphi, these were essentially religious festivals to the gods, particularly Dionysus. Pilgrims from across the Greek world gathered to celebrate with sports, song contests, theatrical performances, and general merrymaking.*

Make your way to the...

❻ Museum

This scantily described collection includes statuary, vases, and other items (though there is talk of building a new, modern museum here). Inside the door is a model of the site in its heyday. Most of the site's best pieces are in the National Archaeological Museum in Athens, but a few high-lights remain, including a beautifully carved stone table, five of the original Lions of the Naxians (in a room of their own), the fingers of Colossus Apollo (in the central hall, near the front door), and—perhaps the best part—several bits of striking floor mosaics.

For more body parts of other gods, exit the museum straight out, then go slightly left to stand in front of the **Monument of Carystius** (once part of the Sanctuary of Dionysus), with its large (broken-off) penis-on-a-pillar statues.

• *Past the museum, the path splits. If you stay right you'll wind back to the start. Or you can go left, which starts a hike up the hill toward more remains of houses and temples all the way up to Mount Kynthos (allow about 45 minutes). If you are short on time, you can skip the final stair climb to the summit. Otherwise, take the stairs up to…*

Mount Kynthos

At 370 feet, the island's highest point feels even taller on a hot day. To ancient Greeks, this conical peak looked like the spot from which Poseidon had pulled this mysterious isle up from the deep. Up here are the remains of the ❼ **Temple of Zeus and Athena.** As you observe the chain of islands dramatically swirling around Delos, you can understand why most experts believe that the Cycladic Islands got their name from the way they circle (or cycle around) this oh-so-important islet.

• *Head back downhill, toward the theater and harbor. On your way down you'll pass the ❽ House of the Dolphins, with mosaics of cupids riding dolphins, and the ❾ House of the Masks, with a beautiful mosaic of a tambourine-playing Dionysus riding a leopard. As you return to the boat, you'll see the remains of a giant cistern and the 5,500-seat theater…starring a 360-degree view of the Cycladic Islands.*

SANTORINI

ΣΑΝΤΟΡΙΝΗ / Σαντορίνη;
a.k.a. Thira (ΘΗΡΑ / Θηρα)

Santorini is one of the Mediterranean's most dramatic islands: a flooded caldera (a collapsed volcanic crater) with a long, steep, multicolored arc of cliffs, thrusting up a thousand feet above sea level. Sometimes called "The Devil's Isle," this unique place has captured visitors' imaginations for millennia and might have inspired the tales of Atlantis. But the otherworldly appeal of Santorini (sahn-toh-REE-nee) doesn't end with its setting. Perched along the ridgeline is a gaggle of perfectly placed whitewashed villages punctuated with azure domes that make this, undeniably, one of Greece's most scenic spots. If this place didn't exist, some brilliant fantasy painter would have to conjure it up.

The island's main town, Fira (**Φηρα**, FEE-rah)—with Santorini's handiest services and best museum—is both functional and scenic. While Fira is dramatic, the town of Oia (**Οια**, EE-ah), on the northern tip of the island, with its chalk-white houses and vivid domes, is even more so—it's the place you imagine when you think "Santorini." Strolling through Oia is like spinning a postcard rack—it's tempting to see the town entirely through your camera's viewfinder.

Not surprisingly, Santorini is hugely popular and can be very crowded—and expensive—in high season (roughly July through September, peaking mid-July-August). Tourism has made the island wealthy. It's one of the few places in Greece where the population isn't aging (as young people don't have to move away to find satisfying work). Fortunately, it's not difficult to break away from the main tourist rut and discover some scenic lanes of your own. In both Fira and Oia, the cliffside streets are strewn with countless cafés, all of them touting "sunset views"...the end of the day is a main attraction here.

SANTORINI OVERVIEW

The five islands that make up the Santorini archipelago are known to Greeks as Thira (Θηρα, THEE-rah). Most of the settlement is on the 15-mile-long main island, also called Thira. But most travelers call it Santorini (a Venetian bastardization of "Santa Irene," after a local church), and I do too. The west side of Santorini is a sheer drop-off (i.e., into the mouth of the former volcano), while the east side tapers more gradually to the water (the former volcano's base).

The primary tourist towns are on the steep western side of Santorini: The town of Fira is the island's capital and transportation hub, but the main attraction is Oia, a village six miles to the northwest. The relatively level east and south areas have the ancient sites and the best beaches.

PLANNING YOUR TIME

Santorini deserves at least two nights and a full day divided between Oia and Fira. Fira is the handiest home base (with the best transportation connections and services), but to really soak it in, hang your hat in Oia.

If your time on Santorini is short, make a beeline (by bus or taxi) to Oia to get your fill of classic Santorini views. Try to catch the sunset from somewhere along the caldera ridge (which spot is best depends on the time of year; in mid-summer, Oia's tops). You can fill any additional time in Fira, where the only worthwhile sight is the manageable, well-presented Museum of Prehistoric Thira. It's also fun to explore some of the steep lanes below Fira's Orthodox cathedral.

On a longer visit, consider renting a car or taking a bus or taxi to other points on the island: ancient sites, wineries, red- and black-sand beaches, and traditional villages. Another option is a boat trip to the active volcano crater and hot springs in the middle of the caldera.

Don't rely on the opening hours for museums and archaeological sites given in this book. Though they were accurate at press time, they may change at the whims of the government and the Greek economy. Check locally before planning your day.

ARRIVAL IN SANTORINI
By Boat

Boats arrive in one of two places on Santorini: Ferries from Athens and the other islands arrive at the New Port at Athinios, about five miles south of Fira; cruise ships usually tender passengers to the Old Port, directly below Fira.

By Ferry at the New Port (Athinios): From the Athinios port, a serpentine road climbs up the hill. Taxis and buses meet arriving boats to take new arrivals into Fira, where you can connect to other points on the island (taxi-€20; bus-€2.30, pay driver). As these buses can be very crowded in peak season, don't dawdle: Get on the bus as quickly as possible (marked *Local Bus*). You may also be accosted by transfer companies offering shared shuttle-bus rides into town (€20/2 people).

Visible from the road above Athinios, the ringed-off area in the bay just below the switchbacks is the site of the *Sea Diamond* shipwreck—a cruise ship that sank here in 2007; all but two of the 1,195 passengers were rescued. The ship rests in 450 feet of water. Concerned that it might slip deeper and that it's polluting the bay, islanders are hoping to pull it up.

For boat connections from Athinios, see page 438.

By Cruise Ship: Cruise ships generally anchor in the caldera below Fira. Passengers taking excursions get the first tenders,

When Santorini Blew Its Top

Situated on an edgy stack of tectonic plates, Santorini was created by volcanic activity that lasted more than two million years. The island once had a tidy conical shape, but around 1630 B.C., it exploded in what's called the "Minoan eruption"— one of the largest in human history. It blew out 24 cubic miles of volcanic material—at least four times the amount ejected by the 1883 explosion of Krakatoa in today's Indonesia.

The volcano likely warned Santorini's inhabitants with a major earthquake and an initial small eruption before the full-scale eruption. No human skel-

etons and few valuable items from that time have been found here, suggesting that islanders were able to pack up and evacuate. Good thing. Soon afterward, large amounts of ash and pumice blasted out of the crater, and superheated pyroclastic flows swept down the island's slopes. Eventually the emptied-out volcano collapsed under its own weight, forming the flooded caldera (meaning "cauldron") that we see today.

The volcano's collapse displaced enough seawater to send a tsunami screaming south toward Crete, less than 70 miles away. Archaeologists think that the tsunami (and perhaps earthquakes near the same time) caused severe hardship, eventually leading to the downfall of the Minoan civilization.

The volcano isn't done. Two little islets emerged from the bay quite recently, by geological standards—Palea Kameni ("Old Burnt Island") in 197 B.C., and Nea Kameni ("New Burnt Island") in A.D. 1707. To this day, these islets sometimes sputter and steam, and earthquakes still wrack the entire archipelago (including a devastating one in 1956). The last small eruption (on Nea Kameni) was in 1950. Today, the hot springs on Palea Kameni are a popular tourist attraction.

Although the historic eruption devastated the island, it also created its remarkable shape and left behind a unique ecosystem and agricultural tradition (see sidebar on page 429). The volcanic soil was also the basis for a local industry. The upper layer of pumice and volcanic ash was quarried, pulverized, and mixed with lime to create a very strong concrete (produced until recently in the blocky building on the cliff near Fira—visible from the bay below). Santorini is the country's sole source of this material.

On scenic, seismic Santorini, you're on special ground... carved out more than four millennia ago by one very big bang.

which go to the New Port at Athinios (described earlier). Note that after your excursion, the bus drops you off in Fira (for info on returning to your ship, see below).

To Fira: Independent day-trippers are tendered to the Old Port directly below Fira. From the Old Port there are three different ways to reach Fira's town center on the cliff above: Take a cable car, hike up, or ride a donkey. The **cable car** is the easiest option (€5 each way, €2.50 more with luggage, daily 7:00-21:00, every 20 minutes, more frequent with demand, 3-minute ride to the top). But, because the cable car is small (6 cars take 6 passengers each, maximum 36 people/trip), you might be in for a long wait if you arrive on a big ship. **Hiking** up the 587 steep steps is demanding, and you'll share them with fragrant, messy donkeys. You can pay €5 to ride up on a **donkey,** but the stench and the bumpy ride make this far less romantic than it sounds.

Once at the **top** (the cable-car and donkey trail converge near the same point), you're smack in the middle of town. If you go south (left from cable-car exit) down Gold Street—true to its name, it's lined with jewelry and tourist-trinket shops—you'll eventually reach the Orthodox cathedral, some recommended eateries and accommodations, and Santorini's best museum (the Museum of Prehistoric Thira). Or, if you want to escape some of the crowds and browse the scenic veil of cafés that cascade down the cliff, head right from the cable-car exit and find the stairs going down (on the left).

To return to the Old Port, you can take the cable car (possibly long lines; get there early to get back to your ship), ride a donkey, or walk down.

To Oia: To head straight to Oia from Fira's Old Port, shop around once on shore for local transport. A typical package, costing around €25, includes a fast boat from the Old Port to Ammoudi (Oia's port), a bus ride up the hill to Oia, several hours to explore Oia and have lunch, then a 30-minute bus ride back to Fira Town. Once there, you can sightsee in Fira or line up for the often-lengthy wait for the cable car back down to the Old Port, where you'll board your ship's tender.

By Plane

Santorini's airport sits along the flat area on the east (back) side of the island, about four miles from Fira (airport code: JTR, tel. 22860-28400; www.santorini-airport.com). It's connected to Fira by taxi (€15-20 depending on amount of luggage) or bus (€1.80, roughly hourly, 15 minutes).

GETTING AROUND SANTORINI

By Bus: Fira is the bus hub for the island. The bus station is a block off the main road, near the south end of town (just downhill from the Orthodox cathedral and Museum of Prehistoric Thira). Buy tickets on the bus and get information at the kiosk at the far end of the lot. Buses can be extremely crowded, especially in peak season. Get there early or you may have to stand. For bus connections, see "Fira Connections" on page 430.

By Taxi: Just around the corner from Fira's bus station, along the main road, is a taxi stand. Rates are high (around €20 to Oia, Athinios port, or Perissa; €15 to Kamari's beaches; €25 to Akrotiri). You can also call for a taxi (tel. 22860-22555 or 22860-23951). In peak season, taxi lines can be long. Consider renting a car or asking your hotel if they can get a driver for you.

By Car: Driving around Santorini is easy. Roads are windy but wide (enough), drivers are aggressive but not reckless, towns are well signposted, and parking is usually free and easy. Traffic, however, can be a big problem at certain times of day and in peak season. You'll find many car-rental (plus ATV and scooter) places in town, or ask your hotel to help. In July and August, it's smart to book ahead (about €50-70/24 hours). Outside those times, you can usually rent a car on the spot (€40-50/24 hours).

By Guided Tour: Greek Travelling offers small-group and private guided tours of Santorini (geared toward cruise-ship passengers), including visits to Oia, a winery, a beach, and more (contact them about tours, options, and prices, mobile 697-320-1213, www.greektravelling.com, info@greektravelling.com, Niki and Christos).

Fira

The island's main town, Fira, is a practical transit hub with an extraordinary setting. Sitting at a cliff-clinging café terrace and sipping an iced coffee gives you the chance to watch thousands of cruise-ship passengers flood into town each morning (on the cable-car and donkey trail), then recede in the afternoon. All of this built-in business has made

Fira a bit greedy; its so-called Gold Street, starting at the cable-car station, is lined with aggressive jewelry salespeople and restaurants with great views, high prices, and low quality.

But if you can ignore the tackiness in this part of town, you'll discover that Fira has a charm of its own—particularly in the cozy labyrinth of streets that burrow between its main traffic street and the cliff edge, and on the steeply switchbacked lanes that zigzag down the side of the cliff. Fira is also home to a pair of cathedrals (Orthodox and Catholic) and the island's top museum (the excellent Museum of Prehistoric Thira).

Remember that Fira is not the setting of all those famous Santorini photos—those are taken in Oia (described later).

Orientation to Fira

The core of Fira is squeezed between the cliff and the main road through town, called 25 Martou. This street—with a taxi stand, TI kiosk, various scooter/ATV/car-rental places, Internet cafés, and other services—is busy and not particularly charming. One block down (away from the caldera) is the road to Oia. The bus station is behind the taxi stand. Most places of interest to visitors are in the cluster of narrow streets between the bus station (along the main road near the south end of town) and the cable-car station (along the cliff near the north end of town)—a distance you can easily cover in about a 10-minute walk.

Even where street names exist, locals ignore them. Making navigation even more confusing, it's a very vertical town—especially along the cliff. Use a map, and don't be afraid to ask for directions.

TOURIST INFORMATION

Fira has the island's **TI kiosk,** which is small and fairly useless (open in peak season Mon-Fri 10:00-20:00, closed Sat-Sun, along the main road, about 50 yards toward the town center from the bus station). Otherwise, ask around at local travel agencies or other businesses for help.

HELPFUL HINTS

Laundry: Most launderettes in town offer drop-off service for €10-15 (generally closed Sun; ask at your hotel for the nearest location). **Penguin** has both self-service and full-service (€7 wash, €6 dry, €1.70 soap, same cost to drop off, Mon-Sat 9:00-22:00, closed Sun, on 25 Martou toward Oia side, tel. 22860-22168).

Bookstore: Books & Style, on 25 Martou, has a decent selection of books in English (long hours daily, tel. 22860-24510)

Fira

To Firostefani, Imerovigli & Oia via Cliff-Top Trail

To Oia, Folklore Mus. & ⑤ via Main Road

100 Meters
100 Yards

⑲

CATHOLIC CATHEDRAL

MEGARO GYZI CULTURAL MUSEUM

CABLE CAR

ARCHAEOLOGICAL MUSEUM

SANTOZEUM

⑭

⑬

⑫

STAIRWAY/ DONKEY TRAIL

OLD PORT

Cliffs

Aegean Sea

③

⑱

④ ① ⑮
⑨ ⑧
⑪ ⑦ ⑩

ORTHODOX CATHEDRAL

⑥

ℹ️ ⑯

TAXI STAND
Ⓣ Ⓑ BUS STATION
WC

MUSEUM OF PREHISTORIC THIRA

Cliffs

②
⑰

To New Port (Athinios) & Akrotiri

EPITROU STAVROU

AGIOU MINA

IPAPANTIS

25 MARTOU (MAIN ROAD)

① Villa Renos
② Kamares Apartments
③ Scirocco Apartments
④ Studios Caldera
⑤ To Galatia Villas
⑥ Villa Roussa
⑦ Koukoumavlos Restaurant
⑧ Archipelagos Restaurant
⑨ Sphinx Restaurant
⑩ Naoussa Restaurant
⑪ Cori Rigas Art Café
⑫ Argo Restaurant
⑬ Nikolas Restaurant
⑭ Dionysos Restaurant
⑮ The Ouzerie
⑯ Mama's House Restaurant
⑰ Supermarket
⑱ Bookstore
⑲ Laundry

SANTORINI

Grocery Store: Carrefour, at the south end of town, is sizeable (Mon-Sat 8:00-21:00, Sun 9:30-14:30).

Folk Theater: For evening entertainment, consider the **White Door Theater,** which puts on a faux Greek wedding, with traditional music and dance and, of course, plate breaking. The audience, acting as guests at the wedding, is invited to participate (€45 includes tapas dinner, runs May-Oct at 21:00, tel. 22860-21770, www.whitedoorsantorini.com).

Sights in Fira

▲▲Museum of Prehistoric Thira

While no competition for Greece's top archaeological museums, this little one is Santorini's best, presenting items found in the prehistoric city buried under ash near Akrotiri. (A visit is particularly worthwhile if you plan to see the excavated ruins of that city at the southern end of the island—see page 435.) That settlement was the largest city outside Crete in the Minoan-era world, dating back to the earliest documented civilization in the Aegean (third to second millennium B.C.)—impossibly ancient, even to the ancients. The people who lived here fled before Santorini blew its top (likely around 1630 B.C.—see sidebar on page 417), leaving behind intriguing artifacts of a civilization that disappeared from the earth not long after. Most of those artifacts have been moved off-site, either to this museum or to the biggies in Athens. Everything in this manageable museum is described in English and well-presented in modern, air-conditioned comfort.

Cost and Hours: €6, Wed-Mon 8:00-15:00, closed Tue, entrance across from taxi stand, tel. 22860-23217, www.culture.gr.

Visiting the Museum: The model of the Akrotiri site in Room D puts the items in context. From here follow the letters counterclockwise through the exhibit, starting with the Early Cycladic figures and vessels, dating from 2700-2300 B.C. The stiff figurines, with their arms crossed, perplex archaeologists, who speculate that they might represent the Mother Goddess worshipped here.

The majority of the museum's pieces date from the Late Cycladic Period (mid-17th century B.C.), when Akrotiri peaked just before its residents fled the erupting volcano. Although they took valuable items (such as jewelry) with them, they left behind easily replaceable everyday objects and, of course, immovable items such as wall frescoes. These left-behind items form the core of the collection.

Primitive cooking pots, clay ovens, and barbeque grills, along with bronze vases, daggers, tongs, and fishing hooks, offer clues to the Aegean lifestyle. The Thirans were traders rather than warriors, so many items reflect their relatively comfortable lifestyle, connection with the wider world, and consumer society. One plaster cast shows the shape left by a (now-deteriorated) three-legged wooden table that could have passed for Baroque from the 17th century A.D.—but it's from the 17th century B.C.

The stack of metal weights illustrates the evolution of standardization during early trading. Also look for the three **large containers,** each one marked differently to suggest its contents—for example, a vessel that held water was decorated with reeds (aquatic plants).

The museum's highlights are the vibrantly colorful, two-dimensional **wall frescoes.** Local artists likely executed these wall

paintings, but their naturalistic style was surely influenced by the wider Minoan culture. In keeping with the style of Crete (the home of the Minoans), men appear brown, and the women, white. (If you've been to the National Archaeological Museum in Athens, you might recognize this style of fresco from that museum's collection, which includes wall paintings of antelopes, swallows, and young men boxing, all from this same Akrotiri site—see page 435.) The wall frescoes from the House of the Ladies show exquisitely dressed women. In one, an older woman leans over and appears to be touching the arm of another (now-missing) woman and holding a dress in her right hand. Farther along you'll see a fragment of another wall fresco showing blue monkeys. Because monkeys are not indigenous to Greece, these images offer more evidence that the Cycladic and Minoan people traveled far and wide, and interacted with exotic cultures.

Between these frescos, the **vessels** (such as beautiful vases decorated with dolphins and lilies) give us a glimpse of everyday life back then. Look for the ritual vessel shaped like a boar's head.

In the final display case (near the exit) is an exquisite miniature **golden ibex**—one of the few items of great value that was left behind by fleeing islanders.

SANTORINI

▲▲▲Sunset from Fira

While Oia is more famous for its sunsets, Fira's are nothing to sneeze at. If you're on Santorini for just one sunset, ask around about where viewing is best (for some of the year, the last dramatic moments of Fira's sunsets are blocked by the island of Thirassia). If your hotel doesn't offer a perch over the caldera, scout out a bar or restaurant during the day so you'll know where you want to sit well before the magic hour.

Orthodox Cathedral of Candelmas (Panagia Ypapantis)

This modern cathedral, which caps Fira like a white crown, has a grandly painted interior that's worth a look. The cliff-hanging lanes just in front are some of Fira's most enjoyable (and least crowded) to explore.

Archaeological Museum

This museum pales in comparison to the Museum of Prehistoric Thira. Its dusty cases are crammed with sparsely-described jugs, statues, and other artifacts from ancient Thira, described on page 436 (in contrast to the older Minoan pieces from Akrotiri). Skip it unless you're an archaeologist.

Cost and Hours: €3, Tue-Sun 8:00-15:00, closed Mon, just up the street from the top cable-car station, tel. 22860-22217.

Catholic Cathedral

Directly up the stairs from the top cable-car station, this cathedral is the heart of the island's Catholic community—a remnant of the island's past Venetian rule. Compare this rare Catholic cathedral with the giant Orthodox cathedral at the other end of town: Inside this one are pews; few wall paintings; and none of the tall, skinny candles that are a mainstay of Orthodox worship. Next door is a Dominican monastery and church.

Megaro Gyzi Museum

Hiding in the alleys behind the Catholic cathedral, this modest but endearing local history museum celebrates Santorini life. You'll see photographs of the town from the early to mid–20th century (including scenes before and after the devastating 1956 earthquake), an archive of historic manuscripts and documents, modern paintings of Santorini, and samples of the various types of volcanic rock found on the island. Find the 1870 clipping from a London newspaper article about "Santorin," and, next to it, an engraving of a

SANTORINI

smoldering islet in the caldera. Linger over the evocative etchings of traditional Santorini lifestyles.

Cost and Hours: €3, May-Oct Mon-Sat 10:00-22:00, Sun 10:00-16:00, closed Nov-April, tel. 22860-23077, www.santorini.com/museums.

OUTSIDE OF TOWN
Folklore Museum of Santorini

With bits and pieces left over from a bygone era, this museum gives visitors a sense of how Santorini sustained itself before tourism. The highlight is a restored 19th-century cave house decorated with items from that period (furniture, pots, utensils, and even a toilet). It's especially interesting if you happen to be staying in a renovated cave house. You'll also find various workshops (including those of a carpenter, shoemaker, and blacksmith), a *canava* (wine cellar), and a small chapel—a modern example of those people built in their homes so they could pray for the safe return of family members who went off to sea for months or years.

Cost and Hours: €3, April-Oct daily 10:00-14:00, closed Nov-March, tel. 22860-22792, www.santorinisfolkmuseum.com. If the place isn't busy (and it rarely is), ask whoever's manning it for a tour, which brings everything to life.

Getting There: It's a 10-minute walk from the center of Fira, on the northern (Oia) end of town: Find the road to Oia (one block east of 25 Martou) and follow it past several ATV/scooter rental outfits and a launderette or two; after the road bends left, it's a few more minutes (look for *MUSEUM* sign on right).

Hike to Oia

With a few hours to spare, you can venture out on one of Greece's most scenic hikes. While the main road connecting Fira to Oia is drab and dusty, a wonderful cliff-top trail links the two towns, offering fantastic views most of the way. From Fira head north through the adjoining villages of Firostefani and Imerovigli, then continue along the lip of the crater all the way to Oia. It's about 5 miles (plan on at least 4 hours one-way), fairly strenuous (with lots of ups and downs), and offers little or no shade in hot weather, so don't attempt it unless you're in good shape and have the right gear (good shoes, water, food, sun protection). Get an early start. You can catch a bus or taxi back to Fira when you're done.

Boat Excursions

Several outfits offer sunset cruises and excursions to the volcano and hot springs from Fira. See page 436.

SANTORINI

Sleep Code

Abbreviations   **(€1=about $1.10, country code: 30)**
S=Single, **D**=Double/Twin, **T**=Triple, **Q**=Quad, **b**=bathroom
Price Rankings
 $$$ **Higher Priced**—Most rooms €180 or more
  $$ **Moderately Priced**—Most rooms €130-180
   $ **Lower Priced**—Most rooms €130 or less
Unless otherwise noted, English is spoken and free Wi-Fi and/
or a guest computer is generally available. Many places accept
credit cards, and rooms generally have air-conditioning. Prices
change; verify current rates online or by email. For the best
prices, always book directly with the hotel.

Sleeping in Fira

For a true getaway with maximum views and charm, sleep in Oia
(recommendations on page 433). But Fira has its own share of
breathtaking views, and is handier because it's the bus hub for the
island.

Note that rates on this popular island skyrocket in peak season
(July-Sept). To widen your budget options, consider sleeping outside pricey Fira and Oia (for example, Firostefani and Imerovigli—
sleepy villages just north of Fira, easily reached via the Fira-Oia
bus—offer rooms with equally good caldera views at significantly
lower prices). With a car, you can save even more by staying outside
these main towns (for example, near the beaches on the "back" of
the island). But given that the spectacular views are one of the main
reasons you came here, if you can afford it I'd recommend springing for a place with a caldera view.

PLACES WITH CALDERA VIEWS

All of these feature fantastic views of the caldera and have peaceful
terraces from which to watch the sunset.

Most of these places spill down the cliffs from town and involve lots of stairs and steep climbs. To avoid so much climbing,
try Villa Renos (some stairs) or Kamares Apartments (a couple of
minutes south of the Old Town). Note that taxis can only take you
to the top of the hill; you'll have to walk from there.

To reach the paths to the terrace hotels (all of my listings except Kamares Apartments), turn right from the bus station and
walk uphill along the street toward the big, white Orthodox cathedral. Go through the gap between the church and Atlantis Hotel
to reach a view terrace. From here, two paths lead down. You can
either turn left down the lane from the view terrace (to the left of
the Sphinx restaurant if facing the caldera) or walk about 50 yards

to the right (along the front of the church) to find the small stepped lane just to the left of the red doorway for Palea Kameni Bar; this lane leads down to Villa Renos. Either path bottoms out at a lower cliffside lane leading (on the right) to Studios Caldera and Scirocco Apartments.

$$$ Villa Renos, just below the cathedral, has nine well-appointed rooms that have more of a hotel vibe than the rest of my listings. It's a class act all around, well-run by Vassilis Matekas, who used to live in Rhode Island (July-Sept: Db-€310; May-June and early Oct: Db-€275; April and late Oct: Db-€190; March and Nov: Db-€165; closed Dec-Feb, pricier deluxe rooms and suites, includes great homemade breakfast that changes every day, tel. 22860-22369, www.villarenos.gr, hrenos@otenet.gr).

$$$ Kamares Apartments surround an oasis of white-on-white stucco, with six large rooms, each with its own Jacuzzi (some inside the room, some outside). It's at the very south end of town, meaning it's sheltered from some of central Fira's nightlife noise (Aug: Db-€306, Tb-€345; June-July and Sept: Db-€261, Tb-€319; April-May and Oct: Db-€178, Tb-€207, Qb rooms available, includes breakfast, free Wi-Fi on terrace, tel. 22680-28110, www.kamares-apartments.gr, info@kamares-apartments.gr).

$$ Scirocco Apartments, run by a Greek-German couple (Eleftherios and Anja Sirigos), rents straightforward rooms, some of them "cave houses" burrowed right into the cliffside. All rooms have sinks and are stocked with basic dishware, while some have bigger kitchenettes; all enjoy either a private or shared terrace and the swimming pool on the lowest level (July-late Sept: Db-€170; May-June and late Sept-mid-Oct: Db-€140; April and late Oct: Db-€75; more for larger units, extra bed-€40, cash only, breakfast-€10, closed Nov-March, free Wi-Fi on terrace, tel. 22860-22855, www.scirocco-santorini.com, info@scirocco-santorini.com).

$$ Studios Caldera has seven basic rooms with classic cliff views, and a Jacuzzi perfectly positioned to enjoy them—but its biggest plus might be lovely Koula, who runs the place with a gracious hospitality (July-Aug: Db-€150-170, June and Sept: €130-150, off-season: €70-100, these prices if you book directly with the hotel and mention Rick Steves, prices vary with size of room, breakfast-€10, closed Nov-Dec, tel. 22860-25166, www.calderastudios.com, calderastudios2010@gmail.com).

WITHOUT CALDERA VIEWS BUT CHEAPER

If you're willing to give something up—view, luxury, and/or in-town convenience—you'll pay lower rates.

Close to Town: **$ Galatia Villas** is calm and out of the way of the Fira's stifling crowds, with 10 tasteful rooms—four larger stu-

SANTORINI

dios and six doubles—plus a small swimming pool. Technically in Kontorhori, the next village over (around the corner from the Folklore Museum), it's about a 10-minute walk to Fira's action along a busy road (July-mid-Sept: Db-€100-120, June and mid-Sept-mid-Oct: Db-€90-100, cheaper off-season, tel. 22860-24524, www.galatiavillas.gr, info@galatiavillas.gr).

In Town: **$ Villa Roussa** offers 12 basic, worn, but clean budget rooms tucked in a dreary modern building overlooking a parking lot, behind the taxi stand and bus station. Some rooms have balconies, but not caldera views—which are a short walk away, over the ridge (July-Aug: Db-€65-85, June and Sept: €50-65, Oct-May: €35-50, prices fluctuate with demand, extra bed-€20, no breakfast but shared kitchen, free transfer from airport, tel. 22860-23220, www.villaroussa.gr, villaroussa@gmail.com, well-run by Peter Pelikanos).

Eating in Fira

Eating in Fira ranges from expensive (with a view overlooking the caldera)...to much cheaper (at a more typical Greek taverna)...to cheapest (grabbing a souvlaki to eat on a stool or to go). In general, places that are closest to the cable car lure in cruise passengers with great views, but—because they know cruisers are in town for only a few hours—have little incentive to put out good food. Natives and lingering travelers do better by dining at the places a 5- to 10-minute walk farther from the cable car.

WITH A CALDERA VIEW

Near the Orthodox Cathedral: The streets just under the Orthodox cathedral (the gigantic white-domed building at the south end of town) are lined with several expensive, trendy eateries with good food...you're paying a premium for the high-rent location (€10-15 starters, €20-30 main dishes, all open daily until late in summer, most close off-season). **Koukoumavlos** is particularly well regarded but more expensive than the other two (dinner only from 19:00, tel. 22860-23807); **Archipelagos** specializes in Greek standards and pasta (tel. 22860-23673); and **Sphinx** has a broader Mediterranean menu that includes a fair bit of Italian (tel. 22860-23823).

On the cheaper side is **Naoussa,** a family-friendly place churning out big plates of sloppy Greek food (€6-10 starters, €10-15 main dishes, daily 12:00-24:00, just down the path from the Atlantis Hotel, tel. 22860-24869).

The steep streets below these restaurants are filled mostly with hotels, but some turn their breakfast terraces into cafés; exploring this area to find your favorite perch for a cup of coffee is a fun activ-

Island Cuisine in a Desert

Santorini has an unusual approach to cuisine, dictated (like all facets of life here) by its volcanic geology. Most produce on the island is never watered...which is even more surprising when you think that Santorini—and the neighboring island of Anafi—are the only places in Europe technically classified as having a desert climate. But the island's very steep cliffs trap passing clouds, so on most mornings there's a fine layer of dew covering the ground—just enough to keep plants growing. Residents claim that this approach, along with the volcanic soil, makes their produce taste particularly sweet. Santorini specialties include grapes, tomatoes, eggplant, and cucumbers.

You'll find the predictable Greek classics on most menus, but also look for some local dishes. A Santorinian salad uses the island's cherry tomatoes and cucumbers; tomato croquettes are also popular. Fava is a chickpea spread similar to hummus. Because the main settlements of Santorini are perched on the tops of cliffs—with challenging access to the sea—fish isn't as integral to the cuisine as on other islands and is quite expensive. If you want fresh seafood, it's best to descend from the cliffsides and dine by the water, such as in Akrotiri in the south or on Ammoudi Bay in the north.

ity (I particularly like the **Cori Rigas Art Café** at the Cori Rigas Apartments, along the lower cliffside lane).

Near the Cable Car: **Argo,** also along the cliffs, serves traditional Greek food specializing in fish. Reserve ahead for the upper deck, with the best caldera views (€4-12 starters, €10-18 main dishes, open long hours daily, along the donkey path just below Gold Street, tel. 22860-22594).

IN THE OLD TOWN

Nikolas oozes a family-run taverna vibe, with one big room crammed with tables overseen by the namesake patriarch; the menu consists of stick-to-your-ribs Greek classics (€4-5 starters, €8-12 main dishes, daily 12:00-22:00, tel. 22860-24550).

Dionysos, just down the street from Nikolas, has nice energy out on its vast terrace (€4-8 starters, €8-20 main dishes, daily 12:00-23:30, tel. 22860-23845).

The Ouzerie (Το Ουζερι) offers sea views from its outside tables, albeit ones looking east, rather than into the caldera. That means it doesn't work well at sunset (unless you're trying to avoid the crowds), but it's great for lunch or after dark. Try some of their local specialties, such as meatballs in an ouzo sauce and the *tomatokeftedes* starter—fried tomatoes with onions and herbs (€5-10 *me-*

zedes and starters, €7-15 main dishes, daily 11:00-24:00, in square that's up the stairs, next to Orthodox cathedral, tel. 22860-21566).

Mama's House, set a few steps down from the main road near the taxi stand, is a good budget choice with unpretentious Greek fare and American-style breakfast (€4-8 starters, €8-15 main dishes, daily 8:00-24:00, shorter hours off-season, tel. 22860-21577).

Souvlaki: The local favorites for souvlaki are **Lucky's** for its quality and **Obelix** for its sizeable menu.

Fira Connections

From Fira by Bus to: Oia (2-3/hour, 25 minutes, €1.80), **Athinios/New Port** (coordinated to meet boats, 20 minutes, €2.30; for boat connections from Athinios, see page 438), **airport** (roughly hourly, 15 minutes, €1.80), **Kamari** and its nearby beaches (2-3/hour, 10 minutes, €1.80), **Akrotiri** with its archaeological site and nearby red-sand beach (2/hour, 30 minutes, €2), and **Perissa** with its black-sand beaches and access to the Ancient Thira archaeological site (2-3/hour, 30 minutes, €2.30). Bus information: tel. 22860-25404, www.ktel-santorini.gr.

Oia

Oia (EE-ah, not OY-ah; sometimes spelled "Ia" in English) is the classic, too-pretty-to-be-true place you imagine when someone says "Greek islands." This idyllic ensemble of whitewashed houses and blue domes is delicately draped over a steep slope at the top of a cliff. And in their wisdom, the locals have positioned their town just right for enjoying a sunset over the caldera. On a blue-sky day or at sunset, there's no better place in Greece to go on a photo safari. In fact, if you can't snap a postcard-quality photo here, it's time to retire your camera.

Oia wasn't always this alluring. In fact, half a century ago it was in ruins—devastated by an earthquake on July 9, 1956. When rebuilding, natives seized the opportunity to make their town even more picture-perfect than before—and it paid off. Though far from undiscovered, Oia is the kind of place that you don't mind sharing with boatloads of tourists. And if you break away from its main streets, you can find narrow, winding lanes that take you far from the crowds.

GETTING THERE

To reach Oia from the island's transport hub at Fira, you can take the bus (see "Fira Connections," earlier), a taxi (€20 one-way), hike (see page 425), or drive.

Orientation to Oia

Oia lines up along its cliff. The main pedestrian drag, which traces the rim of the cliff, is called Nikolaou Nomikou. Oia's steep seaward side is smothered with accommodations and restaurants, while the flat landward side is more functional. The town is effectively traffic-free except for the main road, which sneaks up on Oia from behind, opening onto the town's bus stop (several parking areas are along the road). From here, it's a few short, nondescript blocks toward the cliff and its million-dollar views.

Sights in Oia

▲▲▲Oia Photo Safari

The main sight here is the town itself, and the best advice is to just get lost with your camera cocked. Shoot the classic, blue-domed postcard views, but also wander around to find your own angle on the town. At the far tip of Oia, venture down, then up, to reach the old turret-like viewpoint, which faces the windmills on the horizon and affords you a breathtaking 360-degree view.

Why all the whitewash? For one thing, white reflects (rather than absorbs) the powerful heat of the sun. White is the color of the mineral lime mixed with water, which makes a good antiseptic (islanders used it to paint their houses so it would naturally disinfect the rainwater that was collected on rooftops). Later, white evolved into an aesthetic choice...and a patriotic one: During the 400-year Ottoman occupation, Greeks were not allowed to fly their blue-and-white flag. But here in Oia—with its white houses, blue domes, and the blue sea and sky—the whole village was one big defiant banner for Greece.

The most interesting houses are the ones burrowed into the

Oia

To Tholos & Mavopetra Beach

To Fira and the rest of Santorini

To Tholos & Mavopetra Beach

AGIOS GEORGIOS

100 Meters

100 Yards

MAIN ROAD

AGIOS NIKOLAOS

2

3

STAIRWAY

ARMENI BEACH

BUS STOP **B** **WC**

NOMIKOU

4

1

PANAGIA OF PLATSANI

Main Square

Cliffs

POST

MARITIME MUSEUM

5

To Agios Ioannis & Ammoudi Port via Road

Cliffs

Aegean Sea

TURRET VIEWPOINT

Cliffs

To Oia Town via Road

AMMOUDI PORT

SANTORINI

1 Chelidonia Traditional Villas

2 Thea Studios

3 Flora Café

4 Floga Restaurant

5 Kyprida Restaurant

side of the rock wall. These "cliff houses," surrounded by air-filled pumice, are ideally insulated—staying cool in summer and warm in winter. While cliff houses were once the poorest dwellings in town, today only millionaires can afford to own them (and most are rented out as very pricey accommodations).

▲▲▲Oia Sunset

As the best place on Santorini to enjoy the summer sunset, Oia becomes even more crowded when the sun starts to go down. Shutterbugs jockey for position on the town's best viewpoints, and all that white captures the swirling colors of the sky for a fleeting mo-

ment. Many travelers plan their day around being here at sunset. Before you plant yourself for the evening at a bar or restaurant advertising sunset views, make sure you really are positioned to see the sun dip down, as the sunset's position on the horizon shifts with the seasons.

Naval Maritime Museum

Every Greek island seems to have its own maritime museum, and Oia hosts Santorini's. With two floors of old nautical objects and basic English labels, the collection includes roomfuls of old ship paintings, letters and documents, model ships, and well-endowed mastheads. It's the only museum in town, but it's nothing to jump ship for, unless you're a sailor or need a place to get out of the sun.

Cost and Hours: €3, Wed-Mon 10:00-14:00 & 17:00-20:00, closed Tue and Nov-March, well-signposted a block off the main clifftop drag, tel. 22860-71156.

Sleeping in Oia

Several places rent out appealing "cliff houses" just down from the main cliffside road. They range from smaller rooms or studios for two people, to larger units sleeping four or more. Though expensive, these provide an unforgettable experience.

$$$ At **Chelidonia Traditional Villas,** friendly Greek-Austrian couple Triantaphyllos and Erika Pitsikali rent 13 traditional apartments surrounded by burgeoning bougainvillea and burrowed into the cliff face right in the heart of town. Triantaphyllos grew up in one of these houses, bought the others from his grandparents and cousins, and renovated them himself, retaining as much as he could of the original (large) footprint. Promising "panorama and privacy," this place lets you be a temporary troglodyte (June-Sept: studio-€215, villa-€245, suite-€295; March-May and Oct-Nov: studio-€195, villa-€225, suite-€280, no breakfast but kitchen in units, tel. 22860-71287, www.chelidonia.com, erika@chelidonia.com).

$$ Thea Studios offers the same caldera views as other more expensive places but with fewer frills (no swimming pool or Jacuzzi, no breakfast, etc.). The eight rooms, though basic, are clean, pleasant, a decent size, and come with kitchenettes. Note that one of the standard doubles doesn't have a separate shower (the showerhead is above the bathroom sink and toilet); if that's a problem, make sure to clarify what you're getting (mid-June-mid-Sept: standard Db-€155, superior Db-€170, Qb loft apartment-€200-230, cheaper off-season, closed Nov-March, guests have access to pool at nearby Lioyerma Pool Bar, tel. 22860-71290, www.theasantorini.com, info@theasantorini.com, managed by Marcos and Torun).

Eating in Oia

Dining with a view is a no-brainer here—it's worth the too-high prices to enjoy caldera views with your meal or drink. The cliffside places are pretty interchangeable, but if you can't make up your mind, consider one of these. (I'd recommend against taking a dinner table at Kastro, the can't-miss-it restaurant that is perfectly situated for sunset views most of the year—but has mediocre food at terrible prices.)

Flora Café is an affordable alternative to the budget-busting places along the cliff. Set along the main drag (at the Fira end of town), it's essentially a classy snack bar with a pleasantly casual setting and friendly service (€4-8 small dishes and sweets; €8-12 pizzas, meatballs, and pasta; daily 9:00-24:00, tel. 22860-71424, Flora).

Floga dishes up traditional Greek food with a modern spin. It's a few steps below the main drag at the Fira end of town, with dramatic caldera views—albeit not of the sunset (€8-13 starters, €16-25 main dishes, daily specials, daily 8:00-24:00, tel. 22860-71152).

Kyprida Restaurant, serving traditional Cypriot cuisine, is set a couple of blocks back from the cliff edge, but its top terrace still has a fine sunset view (€5-9 starters, €11-20 main dishes, daily 12:00-24:00, live music on Wed nights and also Sat in summer, closed off-season, tel. 22860-71979).

More Sights on Santorini

Santorini has several worthwhile sights outside Fira and Oia, do-able by bus or taxi but best by car. These include a string of beaches along its eastern side, two major archaeological sites, a lighthouse on a bluff, wineries, and boat trips around the caldera. Both archaeological sites have a history of unexpected closures, so carefully confirm in town that they're open before you set out.

Beaches

The volcanic composition of the island has created some unusual opportunities for beach bums. There are volcanic black-sand beaches near **Kamari** (tidy and more upscale-feeling) and **Perissa** (more popular with backpackers)—both on the east coast, but separated from each other by a mountain (connectable by boat or 3-hour hike). Red-sand beaches are near the town of **Akrotiri** (facing away from the caldera along the southern arc of the island).

▲Akrotiri Archaeological Site

Just before Santorini's massive c. 1630 B.C. eruption, its inhabitants fled the island, leaving behind a city that was soon buried (and preserved) in ash—much like Pompeii, just 1,700 years earlier. (Consider this: The Minoan-era civilization that lived here was as ancient to the Romans as the Romans are to us; many scholars think this may have been what started the legend of Atlantis.) That city, near the modern-day town of Akrotiri, is still being dug up, with more than 30 buildings now excavated and viewable in a well-designed structure that makes it easy to explore the ruins. Keep in mind that only 3 percent of the site has been unearthed—this city was huge. Ramps let you climb around and through the streets of the prehistoric city, where careful observers can pick out sidewalks, underground sewage systems, and some ceramic vases left behind. However, the most interesting items discovered here—wonderful wall frescoes, fancy furniture, painted ceramics—are on display elsewhere, mainly at Fira's Museum of Prehistoric Thira (see page 422) and the National Archaeological Museum in Athens.

Cost and Hours: €12; €6 off-season, April-Oct daily 8:00-20:00; Nov-March Tue-Sun 8:00-15:00, closed Mon; one-hour guided tours-€10, one-on-one guide-€60, tel. 22860-81939.

Getting There: Without a car, Akrotiri is reachable by frequent buses from Fira (2/hour, 30 minutes, €2) or taxi (€25).

Eating: For some of the freshest seafood on the island, try **The Dolphins** on Akrotiri Beach, a delightful family-run fish tavern with palapa-covered tables on a pier and more seating along the water (daily 12:00-23:00, turn left out the Akrotiri ruins and walk

SANTORINI

down into the village, tel. 22860-81151; mom and sons run the place, dad fishes).

Other Stops in the Area: The **lighthouse** at Faros, at the southwest tip of the island, has amazing views (also a good place to watch the sunset at certain times of year—ask at your hotel). You can also visit one of the **beaches** that dot the southeastern end of the island, such as Red Beach or White Beach, or stop at a **winery**—Santo and Venetsanos are both on the way back to Fira (both described later).

Ancient Thira

Dramatically situated on a mountaintop between Perissa and Kamari, this site dates from a more recent civilization. It was settled post-volcano by Dorians from Sparta, likely in the ninth century B.C., and continued to thrive through the Hellenistic, Roman, and Byzantine periods. This place is less distinctive than the Akrotiri site and is only worth a visit by archaeology completists. If you've toured other Greek ruins from this era—in Athens, Delphi, Olympia, Epidavros, and so on—you'll see nothing new here. You can reach the Ancient Thira site from Kamari, which has regular bus excursions.

Cost and Hours: €4, April-Oct Tue-Sun 8:00-15:00, closed Mon, call Archaeological Museum in Fira for more information—tel. 22860-22217, http://odysseus.culture.gr.

Getting There: Besides driving or taxi, you can take a bus to Kamari, then either walk 30 minutes or catch an hourly minibus from the TI in that town. Hardy hikers can also huff up from Perissa on a very twisty serpentine path.

Volcanic Islets and Other Caldera Trips

A popular excursion is to sail from the Old Port below Fira out to the active volcanic islets in the middle of the caldera. The quickest trips include a hike to the crater on **Nea Kameni** (€15, 2 hours); longer tours allow time for a swim in the shallow, muddy hot springs on **Palea Kameni** (€18, 3 hours) and a visit to **Thirassia,** the island across the caldera (€23, 5.5 hours; skippable, as Thirassia doesn't have much to offer). The "sunset tour" includes a visit to the volcano and hot springs, followed by a boat trip under the cliffs of Oia for the sunset with a glass of wine (€30, 5 hours). It's cool to get a volcano's-eye view of the inside of the caldera, and the hike on the crater is exciting if you've never climbed around a lava field before. Various travel agencies around Santorini sell these trips—look for ads locally. Luxe catamarans do similar trips leaving from the port

Santorini Wines

While Greece isn't particularly acclaimed for its wines, Santorini's are well-respected. The discovery of ancient grape seeds at Akrotiri proved that the winemaking tradition here dates back more than 3,500 years. Today, the most common local grapes are Assyrtiko, one of the best Greek varietals; they produce a dry white wine with minerality and acidity. The growing vines are twisted into a round basket shape called *ampelies,* with the grapes tucked inside to protect them from the strong sunlight and fierce winds. The shape also helps retain moisture from nighttime fog on this otherwise arid isle, and does such a good job that the grapes don't need to be watered. Connoisseurs say that the terroir created by Santorini's porous volcanic soil gives the wine a special flavor. Two of the most renowned Santorini wines are Vinsanto (sweet dessert wine made from a blend of sun-dried grapes) and Nykteri (dry white wine produced in one day; the name means "night work"). Several shops in Fira or Oia offer wine tasting, or you can visit one of the wineries on the island (I've listed a few).

of Vlychada for a higher-end, higher-priced experience with fewer passengers (€100-150/person; they'll pick you up from your hotel to take you to the port; multiple outfits, so ask at your hotel or a travel agency).

Wineries

Santorini, one of Greece's most high-profile wine producers, has a dozen or so wineries that are open to the public. If visiting during the harvest (around mid-August), you may even find a winery that lets you stomp some grapes.

The most famous winery is **Santo,** just up the road from the New Port, on the road between Fira and Akrotiri. It's a cooperative working with all the island's wineries—the biggest operation like this in the Cyclades. Established in 1947, it produces 500,000 bottles a year, 70 percent of which are consumed in Greece. Despite the cruise-ship tour crowds that descend on this place (it can be mobbed), Santo offers a good opportunity to taste Santorini's wine while enjoying great views. They also offer a video on winemaking and tours (tours are €5.50/person, last about 20 minutes, and run about 10:00-15:00 depending on their availability; winery open daily May-Sept 9:00-22:00, July-Aug until 23:00, shorter hours off-season and closed on Mon Dec-Feb, tel. 22860-22596, www.santowines.gr). For people staying in Oia, **Sigales** is a good nearby winery (tel. 22860-71644, www.sigalas-wine.com).

To learn about the history of winemaking on Santorini, consider a visit to the Cave Wine Museum at **Koutsoyannopoulos.** The included audioguide tells the history of the winery (which

SANTORINI

dates back to 1880), explains how grapes have been grown, transferred, and crushed through the years, and discusses the challenges facing wine producers on this hot, dry island. With its cheesy sets and fake figures, the museum is a bit old-school, though it is interesting to see the equipment that was used back in the day (€8, includes audioguide and four tastings, daily 9:00-19:00, off-season until 16:00, last entry one hour before closing, tel. 22860-31322, www.wine-museum-koutsoyannopoulos.gr).

An interesting contrast to Koutsoyannopoulos is **Venetsanos,** a sleek modern facility. The founder, George Venetsanos, was a real pioneer when he built this winery in 1947, using a system of interconnected equipment to turn grapes into wine, then flowing the final product from fermentation tanks through a series of pipes that ran down the hillside and straight into barrels on ships docked at the port. To see some of the original equipment and walk through the winery's tunnels, request a tour (€2.50, 10-15 minutes). Or you can pay about €6 for four tastings, served to you either on the terrace with gorgeous caldera views or in the tasting room (May-Oct daily 10:00-22:00, Nov-March Wed-Sun only 11:00-20:00, tel. 22860-21100, www.venetsanoswinery.com).

Santorini Connections

Remember, the New Port is a 20-minute bus ride away from Fira, and buses can be very crowded in summer—allow enough time to make your connection. For ferry tips and ferry-company contact info, see page 365.

By Boat from the New Port (Athinios): Santorini is connected daily to **Piraeus** in Athens (slow boat: 1/day year-round, 8 hours, €40 on Blue Star; fast boat: generally 2/day April-Oct, 5 hours, €60 on Hellenic Seaways or SeaJet), **Mykonos** (generally 2-3/day April-mid-Oct, 3 hours, €60), and other Cycladic Islands, as well as to **Crete** (1/day April-Oct, 2 hours).

GREEK HISTORY AND MYTHOLOGY

Our lives today would be quite different if it weren't for a few thousand Greeks who lived in the small city of Athens about 450 years before Christ was born. Democracy, theater, literature, mathematics, science, philosophy, and art all flourished in Athens during its 50-year "Golden Age"—a cultural boom time that set the tone for the rest of Western history to follow.

Greece's history since Classical times may be less familiar to most visitors, but it's fascinating nonetheless. From pagan to Christian to Muslim, to the freedom-fighters of the 19th century and the refugees of the 20th century, Greece today is the product of many different peoples, religions, and cultures.

THE PRE-GREEK WORLD:
THE MINOANS (2000-1450 B.C.)

The incredible civilization that we now call Classical Greece didn't just pop out of nowhere. Cursed with rocky soil, isolated by a rugged landscape, and scattered by invasions, the Greeks took centuries to unify. The civilization of Golden Age Greece was built on the advances of earlier civilizations: Minoans, Mycenaeans, Dorians, and Ionians—the stew of peoples that eventually cooked up what became Greece.

A safe, isolated location on the island of Crete, combined with impressive business savvy, enabled the Minoans to dominate the pre-Greek world. Unlike most early peoples, they were traders, not fighters. With a large merchant fleet, they exported wine, olive oil, pottery, and well-crafted jewelry, then returned home with the wealth of the Mediterranean.

Today we know them by the colorful frescoes they left behind on the walls of prosperous, unfortified homes and palaces. Surviving frescoes show happy people engaged in everyday life: la-

Ancient Greek World

dies harvesting saffron, athletes leaping over bulls, and charming landscapes with animals.

The later Greeks would inherit the Minoans' business skills, social equality, love of art for art's sake, and faith in rational thought over brute military strength. Some scholars hail the Minoans as the first truly "European" civilization.

Between about 1450 and 1150 B.C., the Minoan civilization suddenly collapsed, and no one knows why (volcano? invasions?). Physically and economically weakened, they were easily overrun and absorbed by a tribe of warlike people from the mainland—the Mycenaeans.

Minoan-Era Sights

- Frescoes from Akrotiri on the island of Santorini, in the National Archaeological Museum in Athens, and the Museum of Prehistoric Thira in Fira

MYCENAE (1600-1200 B.C.)

After the fall of the Minoans, the Greek mainland was dominated by the Mycenaeans (myseh-NEE-uhns), a fusion of local tribes centered in the city of Mycenae (my-SEE-nee). Culturally, they were the anti-Minoans—warriors not traders, chieftains not bureaucrats. Their ruins at the capital of Mycenae (about two hours by bus southwest of Athens, or a half-hour's drive north of Nafplio) tell the story. Buildings are fortress-like, the city has thick defensive walls, and statues are stiff and crude. Early Greeks called Mycenaean architecture "cyclopean," because they believed that only giants could have built with such colossal blocks. Mycenaean kings were elaborately buried in cemeteries and tombs built like subterranean stone igloos, loaded with jewels, swords, and precious objects that fill museums today.

The Mycenaeans dominated Greece during the era of the legends of the Trojan War. Whether or not there's any historical truth to the legends, Mycenae has become associated with the tales of Agamemnon, Clytemnestra, and the invasion of Troy.

Around 1100 B.C., the Mycenaeans—like the Minoans before them—mysteriously disappeared, plunging Greece into its next, "dark," phase.

Mycenaean Sights
- The citadel at Mycenae, with its Lion Gate, Grave Circle A, palace, and *tholos* tombs
- Mask of Agamemnon and other artifacts at the National Archaeological Museum in Athens
- Dendra Panoply, a 15th-century B.C. suit of bronze armor in the Nafplio Archaeological Museum

THE GREEK DARK AGES (1200-700 B.C.)
Whatever the reason, once-powerful Mycenaean cities became deserted, writing was lost, roads crumbled, trade decreased, and

bandits preyed on helpless villagers. Dark Age graves contain little gold, jewelry, or fine pottery. Divided by mountains into pockets of isolated, semi-barbaric, warring tribes, the Greeks took centuries to unify and get their civilization back on track.

It was during this time that legends passed down over generations were eventually compiled (in the ninth century B.C.) by a blind, talented, perhaps nonexistent man that tradition calls Homer. His long poem, the *Iliad*, describes the battles and struggles of the early Greeks (perhaps the Mycenaeans) as they conquered Troy. The *Odyssey* tells of the weary soldiers' long, torturous trip back home. The Greeks saw these epics as perfect metaphors for their own struggles to unify and build a stable homeland. The stories helped shape a collective self-image.

Dark Age Sights
- The Kastalian Spring and omphalos monuments at Delphi

Heart of Greek Ancient World

ARCHAIC PERIOD (700-480 B.C.)

Tradition holds that in 776 B.C., Greek-speaking people from all over the mainland and islands halted their wars and gathered in Olympia to compete in the first Olympic Games. Bound by a common language and religion, Greece's scattered tribes began settling down.

Living on islands and in valleys, the Greek-speaking people were divided by geography from their neighbors. They naturally formed governments around a single city (or polis) rather than as a unified empire. Petty warfare between city-states was practically a sport.

Slowly, the city-states unified, making alliances with one another, establishing colonies in what is now Italy and France, and absorbing culture from the more sophisticated Egyptians (style of statues) and Phoenicians (alphabet). Scarcely two centuries later, Greece would be an integrated community and the center of the civilized world.

Statues from Archaic times are crude, as stiff as the rock they're carved from. Rather than individuals, they are generic people: called either kore (girl) or kouros (boy). With perfectly round heads, symmetrical pecs, and a navel in the center, these sturdy statues reflect the order and stability the troubled Greeks were striving for.

By the sixth century B.C., Greece's many small city-states had coalesced around two power centers: oppressive, no-frills, and militaristic Sparta; and its polar opposite, the democratic, luxury-loving, and business-friendly Athens.

Archaic Sights

- Dipylon Vase (National Archaeological Museum in Athens) and other geometric vases in various museums
- Kouros and kore statues (National Archaeological Museum in Athens, Acropolis Museum in Athens, Archaeological Museum in Delphi)
- The Olympic Stadium and Temple of Hera in Olympia
- *Sphinx of Naxos* (Archaeological Museum in Delphi)
- *Lions of the Naxians* statues on the island of Delos

PRE-GOLDEN AGE: THE RISE OF ATHENS AND THE PERSIAN WARS (480-450 B.C.)

In 490 B.C., an enormous army of Persians under King Darius I swept into Greece to punish the city of Athens, which had dared

to challenge his authority over Greek-speaking Ionia (in today's western Turkey). A few thousand plucky Athenians raced to head off the Persians in a crucial bottleneck valley, at the Battle of Marathon. Though outnumbered three to one, the crafty Greeks lined up and made a wall of shields (a phalanx) and pushed the Persians back. An excited Greek soldier ran the 26.2 miles from the city of Marathon to Athens, gasped the good news...and died.

In 480 B.C., Persia attacked again. This time all of Greece put aside its petty differences to fight the common enemy as an alliance of city-states. King Leonidas of Sparta and his 300 Spartans made an Alamo-like last stand at Thermopylae that delayed the invasion. Meanwhile, Athenians abandoned their city and fled, leaving Athens (and much of the lower mainland) to be looted. But the Athenians rallied to win a crucial naval victory at the Battle of Salamis, followed by a land victory at the Battle of Plataea, driving out the Persians.

Greek Mythology

The following were the stars among a large cast of characters—gods, beasts, and heroes—who scampered through the Greek mindscape, mingled with mortals, and inspired so much classical art and literature.

The Gods

The major Greek gods (the Olympians) lived atop Mount Olympus, presided over by Zeus, king of the gods (and father of many of them). Each god had a distinct personality, unique set of talents, and area of responsibility over the affairs of the world (they specialized). Though they were immortal and super-powerful, these gods were not remote, idealized deities; instead, like characters in a celestial soap opera, they displayed the full range of human foibles: petty jealousies, destructive passions, broken hearts, and god-sized temper tantrums. They also regularly interacted with humans—falling in love with them, seducing them, toying with them, and punishing them. The Romans were so impressed by the Greek lineup of immortals that they borrowed them, but gave them new names (shown in parentheses below).

Zeus (Jupiter): Papa Zeus liked the ladies, and often turned himself into some earthly form (a bull, a cloud, or a swan) to hustle unsuspecting mortal females. Statues depict him wearing a beard and sometimes carrying a spear. He is also symbolized by a thunderbolt or an eagle.

Hera (Juno): The beautiful queen of the gods was the long-suffering wife of philandering Zeus. She was also—whether ironically or fittingly—the goddess of marriage.

Hades (Pluto): The king of the underworld and lord of the dead is depicted as sad, with a staff.

Poseidon (Neptune): The god of the sea, he was also responsible for earthquakes, earning him the nickname "Earth Shaker." He is often shown holding a trident.

Apollo: The ruler of the Sun, he drives the Sun's flaming chariot across the sky each day, and represents light and truth. He is also the god of music and poetry.

Hermes (Mercury): The messenger of the gods sports a helmet and shoes with wings. He delivers a lot of flowers in his current incarnation as a corporate logo.

Ares (Mars): The god of war (and Aphrodite's boyfriend), he dresses for battle and carries a spear.

Dionysus (Bacchus): The god of wine and college frats holds grapes and wears a toga and a laurel wreath.

Athena (Minerva): The virginal goddess of wisdom was born from the head of Zeus, and is depicted carrying a spear. Athens is named for her and the Parthenon was built in her honor.

Artemis (Diana): The goddess of the moon and hunting, she was the twin sister of Apollo. She carries a bow and arrow.

Aphrodite (Venus): The goddess of love and beauty, she was born of the sea. This good-looking lady was married to the crippled god Hephaistos, but was two-timing him with Ares.

Eros (Cupid): The god of desire is depicted as a young man or a baby with wings, wielding a bow and arrows.

Hestia (Vesta): Modestly dressed veiled goddess of the home and hearth, she oversaw domestic life.

Hephaistos (Vulcan): Poor cuckolded Hephaistos was lame and ugly, but useful. Blacksmith to the gods, he was the god of the forge, fire, and craftsmen.

Demeter (Ceres): Goddess of the seasons, the harvest, and fertility, she is shown holding a tuft of grain.

The Beasts

Pan (Faun): Happy Pan, with a body that's half man (on top) and half goat, was the god of shepherds and played a flute.

Centaur: This race of creatures, human on top and horse below, was said to be wise.

Satyr: Like Pan, satyrs were top-half man, bottom-half goat. And they were horny.

Griffin: With the head and wings of an eagle and the body of a lion, griffins were formidable.

Harpy: Creatures with the head of a woman and the body of a bird, harpies were known for stealing.

Medusa: With writhing snakes instead of hair, she had a face that turned people to stone. She was slain by Perseus.

Pegasus: The winged horse was the son of Poseidon and Medusa.

Cyclops: A race of one-eyed giants, they were known for their immense strength.

Minotaur: This beast with the head of a bull lived in the labyrinth at Knossos, the palace on Crete.

The Heroes

Hercules: This son of Zeus was born to a mortal woman. The strongest man in the world performed many feats of strength and tested negative for steroids. To make Hercules atone for killing his family in a fit of madness, the gods forced him to perform Twelve Labors, which included slaying various fierce beasts and doing other chores. He often wore a lion's skin.

Amazons: A race of powerful female warriors. Classical art often depicts them doing battle with the Greeks.

Prometheus: He defied the gods, stealing fire from them and giving it to humans. As punishment, he was chained to a rock, where an eagle feasted daily on his innards.

Jason: He sailed with his Argonauts in search of the Golden Fleece.

Perseus: He killed Medusa and rescued Andromeda from a serpent.

Theseus: He killed the Minotaur in the labyrinth on Crete.

Trojan War Heroes: This gang of greats includes Achilles, Ajax, Hector, Paris, Agamemnon, and the gorgeous Helen of Troy.

Athens was hailed as Greece's protector and policeman, and the various city-states cemented their alliance (the Delian League) by pooling their defense funds, with Athens as the caretaker. Athens signed a 30-year peace treaty with Sparta...and the Golden Age began.

Pre-Golden Age Sights

- Severe-style statues, such as the *Artemision Bronze* (Athens' National Archaeological Museum) and *Bronze Charioteer* (Olympia)
- Olympia's Temple of Zeus and the bronze helmet of Miltiades

GOLDEN AGE ATHENS (450-400 B.C.)

Historians generally call Greece's cultural flowering the "Classical Period" (approximately 500-323 B.C.), with the choice cut being the two-generation span (450-400 B.C.) called the "Golden Age."

After the Persian War, the Athenians set about rebuilding their city (with funds from the Delian League). Grand public buildings and temples were decorated with painting and sculpture. Ancient Athens was a typical city-state, with a population of at least 100,000 gathered around its acropolis ("high town"), which was the religious center and fort of last defense. Below was the agora, or marketplace, the economic and social center. Blessed with a harbor and good farmland, Athens prospered, exporting cash crops (wine and olive oil, pottery and other crafts) to neighboring cities and importing the best craftsmen, thinkers, and souvlaki. Amphitheaters hosted drama, music, and poetry festivals. The marketplace bustled with goods from all over the Mediterranean. Upwardly mobile Greeks flocked to Athens. The incredible advances in art, architecture, politics, science, and philosophy set the pace for all of Western civilization to follow. And all this from a Greek town smaller than Muncie, Indiana.

Athens' leader, a charismatic nobleman named Pericles, set out to democratize Athens. As with many city-states, Athens' government had morphed from rule by king, to a council of nobles, to rule by "tyrants" in troubled times, and finally to rule by the people. In Golden Age Athens, every landowning man had a vote in the Assembly of citizens. It was a direct democracy (not a representative democracy, where you elect others to serve), in which every man was expected to fill his duties of voting, community projects, and

GREEK HISTORY

A Who's Who of Classical Age Greeks

Socrates (c. 469-399 B.C.) questioned the status quo, angered authorities, and calmly accepted his own death rather than change his teachings.

Plato (c. 424-348 B.C.) was Socrates' follower (and note-taker), and focused on elucidating nonmaterial, timeless mathematical ideas.

Aristotle (c. 384-322 B.C.) was Plato's follower and championed the empirical sciences, emphasizing the importance of the physical world as a means of knowledge.

Pericles (c. 495-429 B.C.) was a charismatic nobleman who promoted democracy.

Pythagoras (c. 580-500 B.C.) gave us $a^2 + b^2 = c^2$.

Euclid (c. 335-270 B.C.) laid out geometry as we know it.

Diogenes (c. 412-323 B.C.) lived homeless in the Agora, turning from materialism to concentrate on ethical living.

Aristophanes (c. 446-386 B.C.), **Sophocles** (c. 496-406 B.C.), and **Euripides** (c. 480-406 B.C.) wrote comedies and tragedies that are still performed today.

Hippocrates (c. 460-370 B.C.) made medicine a hard science. He rejected superstition and considered disease a result of natural—rather than supernatural—causes.

Pheidias (c. 480-430 B.C.) designed the statuary of the Parthenon and several monumental statues.

Praxiteles (c. 400-330 B.C.) sculpted lifelike yet beautiful human figures.

military service. Of course, Athens' "democracy" excluded women, slaves, freed slaves, and anyone not born in Athens.

Perhaps the greatest Greek invention was the very idea that nature is orderly and man is good—a rational creature who can solve problems. Their concept of the "Golden Mean" reveals the value they placed in balance, order, and harmony in art and in life. At school, both the mind and the body were trained.

Philosophers debated many of the questions that still occupy the human mind. Socrates questioned traditional, superstitious beliefs. His motto, "Know thyself," epitomizes Greek curiosity about who we are and what we know for sure. Branded a threat to Athens' youth, Socrates willingly obeyed a court order to drink poison rather than compromise his ideals. His follower Plato wrote down many of Socrates' words. Plato taught that the physical world is only a pale reflection of true reality (the way a shadow on the wall is a poor version of the 3-D, full-color world we see). The greater reality is the unseen mathematical orderliness that underlies the fleeting physical world. Plato's pupil Aristotle, an avid biologist, emphasized study of the physical world rather than the intangible one. Both Plato and Aristotle founded schools that would attract Europe's great minds for centuries. And their ideas would resurface much later, after Europe experienced a resurgence of humanism and critical thought.

Greeks worshipped a pantheon of gods, viewed as supernatural humans (with human emotions) who controlled the forces of nature. Greek temples housed a statue of a god or goddess. Because the people worshipped outside, the temple exterior was the important part and the interior was small and simple. Generally, only priests were allowed to go inside, where they'd present your offering to the god's statue in the hope that the god would grant your wish.

Most temples had similar features. They were rectangular, surrounded by rows of columns, and topped by slanted roofs. Rather than single-piece columns, the Greeks usually built them of stacked slices of stone (drums), each with a plug to keep it in line. Columns sat on a base, and were topped with a capital. The triangle-shaped roof formed a gable—typically filled with statues—called the pediment. A typical pediment might feature a sculpted gang of gods doing their divine mischief. Beneath the pediment was a line of carved reliefs called metopes. Under the eaves, a set of sculpted low-relief panels—called the frieze—decorated one or more sides of the building.

Classical art is known for its symmetry, harmony, and simplicity. It shows the Greeks' love of rationality, order, and balance. Greek art of this era featured the human body in all its naked splendor. The anatomy is accurate, and the poses are relaxed and natural. Greek sculptors learned to capture people in motion, and to show them from different angles, not just face-on. The classic Greek pose—called *contrapposto*, Italian for "counter-poise"—has a person resting weight on one leg while the other leg is relaxed or moving slightly. This pose captures a balance between timeless stability and fleeting motion that the Greeks found beautiful. It's also a balance between down-to-earth humans (with human flaws and quirks) and the idealized perfection of a Greek god.

Golden Age Sights
- The Acropolis in Athens, with the Parthenon, Erechtheion, Propylaea, Temple of Athena Nike, and Theater of Dionysus
- The Agora, Athens' main square—crossed by the Panathenaic Way and frequented by all the Golden Age greats
- Temple of Hephaistos, in the Agora

Greek Columns

DORIC   IONIC   CORINTHIAN

Classical Greek architecture evolved through three orders: Doric (strong-looking columns topped with simple and stocky capitals), Ionic (thinner columns with rolled capitals), and Corinthian (even thinner columns with leafy, ornate capitals). As a memory aid, remember that the orders gain syllables as they evolve: Doric, Ionic, Corinthian. The differences between the three orders point to how the Greek outlook mirrored its developing culture: Having mastered the ability to show balance and harmony in its finest Doric temples (the Parthenon being the cream of the crop), the Corinthian order caught on as architects began to prefer a more elegant look. The Corinthian order, developed to look good from all sides (Ionic columns didn't work well on corners), and to give temple interiors a foresty look, could only have come from the Hellenistic era, when Greek tastemakers preferred their art and architecture ornate and lavish.

• Panathenaic Stadium in Athens
• Sanctuary of Apollo at Delphi
• Workshop of Pheidias at Olympia
• Museum of Cycladic Art in Athens (top-floor exhibit)

LATE CLASSICAL PERIOD: THE DECLINE OF ATHENS (400-323 B.C.)

Many Greek city-states came to resent the tribute money they were obliged to send to Athens, supposedly to protect them from an invasion that never came. Rallying behind Sparta, they ganged up

on Athens. The Peloponnesian War, lasting a generation, toppled Athens (404 B.C.), drained Greece, and ended the Golden Age. Still more wars followed, including struggles between Sparta and Thebes. In 338 B.C., Athens, Sparta, and all the rest of the city-states were conquered

GREEK HISTORY

Alexander's Empire

Areas of Greek Settlement

MACEDONIA • Byzantium

Sparta • Athens ASIA MINOR

Mediterranean Sea

PALESTINE

Alexandria •

EGYPT

ARABIA

Caspian Sea

• Babylon

PERSIA

Persian Gulf

INDIA

by powerful Greek-speaking invaders from the north: the Macedonians.

Late Classical Sights

- Bronze statue of a youth at Athens' National Archaeological Museum
- *Statue of Hermes,* perhaps by Praxiteles, in Olympia

HELLENISM (323-100 B.C.)

"Hellenism," from the Greek word for "Greek," refers to the era when Greece's political importance declined but Greek culture was

spread through the Mediterranean and Asia by Alexander the Great.

After King Philip of Macedonia conquered Greece, he was succeeded by his 20-year-old son, Alexander (356-323 B.C.). Alexander had been tutored by the Greek philosopher Aristotle, who got the future king hooked on Greek culture. According to legend, Alexander went to bed each night with two things under his pillow: a dagger and a copy of the *Iliad.* Alexander loved Greek high culture, but was also pragmatic about the importance of military power.

In 334 B.C., Alexander and a well-trained army of 40,000 headed east. Their busy itinerary included conquering today's Turkey, Palestine, Egypt (where he was declared a living god), Iraq, and Iran, and moving into India. Alexander was a daring general, a benevolent conqueror, and a good administrator. As he conquered, he founded new cities on the Greek model, spread the Greek language, and opened Greek schools. After eight years on the road, an exhausted Alexander died at the age of 32, but by then he had created the largest empire ever. (What have you accomplished lately?)

Hellenistic art reflects the changes in Greek society. Rather than noble idealized gods, the Hellenistic artists gave us real people with real emotions, shown warts-and-all. Some are candid snapshots of everyday life, like a boy stooped over to pull a thorn from his foot. Others show people in extreme moments as they struggle to overcome life's obstacles. We see the thrill of victory and the agony of defeat. Arms flail, muscles strain, eyes bulge. Clothes and hair are whipped by the wind. Figures are frozen in motion, in wild, unbalanced poses that dramatize their inner thoughts.

For two centuries much of the Mediterranean and Asia—the entire known civilized world—was dominated by Greek rulers and Greek culture.

Hellenistic Sights

- Stoa of Attalos, in Athens' Agora, built by a Grecophile from Pergamon
- *Artemision Jockey, Fighting Gaul,* and other statues in Athens' National Archaeological Museum
- Head of Alexander the Great in Athens' Acropolis Museum
- Theater (and sanctuary) of Epidavros
- Philippeion temple in Olympia

ROMAN GREECE (146 B.C.-A.D. 476)

At the same time that Alexander was conquering the East, a new superpower was rising in the West: Rome. Eventually, Rome's le-

gions conquered Greece (146 B.C.) and the Hellenized Mediterranean (31 B.C.). Culturally, however, the Greeks conquered the Romans.

Roman governors ruled cosmopolitan Greek-speaking cities, adopting the Greek gods, art styles, and fashions. Greek-style temple facades, with their columns and pediments, were pasted on the front of (Roman-arch) temples as a veneer of sophistication. Greek statues dotted Roman villas and public buildings. Pretentious Romans sprinkled their Latin conversation with Greek phrases as they enjoyed the plays of Sophocles and Aristophanes. Many a Greek slave was more cultured than his master, reduced to the role of warning his boss not to wear a plaid toga with polka-dot sandals.

Athens was a major city in the cosmopolitan Roman world. Paul—a Jewish Christian with Roman citizenship—came to Athens (A.D. 49) to spread the Christian message from atop Mars Hill. The Bible makes it clear (Acts 17) that the sophisticated Athenians were not impressed.

Athens, with its prestigious monuments, was well-preserved under the Romans, but as Rome began to collapse, it became less able to protect and provide for Greece. In A.D. 267, Athens suffered a horrendous invasion by barbarian Herulians, who left much of the city in ashes. Other barbarian invasions followed.

In A.D. 476, even the city of Rome fell to invaders. As Christianity established itself, Greece's pagan sanctuaries were closed. For a thousand years Athens had carried the torch of pagan and secular learning. But in A.D. 529, the Christian/Roman/Byzantine Emperor Justinian closed Athens' famous schools of philosophy... and the "ancient" world came to an end.

Greek culture would live on, resurfacing throughout Western history and eventually influencing medieval Christians, Renaissance sculptors, and Neoclassical architects, including the ones who designed Washington, DC in the Greek style.

Roman Sights
- Roman Forum (and Tower of the Winds) in Athens
- Temple of Olympian Zeus and Arch of Hadrian in Athens
- Odeon of Agrippa and Statue of Hadrian, in Athens' Agora
- Hadrian's Library (near Monastiraki) in Athens
- Temple of Roma and Monument of Agrippa, on the Acropolis in Athens
- Odeon of Herodes Atticus (built by a wealthy ethnic-Greek/ Roman-citizen) in Athens
- Mars Hill (the rock where the Christian Apostle Paul preached to the pagans) in Athens
- Nymphaeum in Olympia
- Many Greek buildings and artworks that were renovated in Roman times

BYZANTINE GREECE (A.D. 323-1453)
With the fall of Rome in Western Europe, Greece came under the sway of the Byzantine Empire—namely, the eastern half of the ancient Roman Empire that *didn't* "fall" in A.D. 476. Byzantium remained Christian and enlightened for another thou-

Byzantine Empire

Venice
Ravenna
Rome
Constantinople
Nicaea
Athens
Antioch
Jerusalem

Areas of
Greek Settlement

GREEK HISTORY

sand years, with Greek (not Latin) as the common language. The empire's capital was Constantinople (modern Istanbul), founded in A.D. 330 by Roman Emperor Constantine to help manage the fading Roman Empire. For the next thousand years, Greece's cultural orientation would face east.

Though ostensibly protected by the Byzantine emperor in Constantinople, Greece suffered several centuries of invasions (A.D. 600-900) by various Slavic barbarians. The Orthodox Church served as a rallying point, and the invaders were eventually driven out or assimilated.

After A.D. 1000, Greece's economic prosperity returned—farms produced, the population grew, and cities engaged in trade—and Athens entered a second, more modest, Golden Age (c. 1000-1200). Greece reconnected with the rest of Western Europe during the Crusades, when Western soldiers traveled through Greek ports on their way to Jerusalem. This revived East–West trade, which was brokered by Venetian merchants who were granted trading rights to establish ports in Greek territory.

This Golden Age is when many of Athens' venerable Orthodox churches were built. Christian pilgrims from across the Byzantine Empire flocked to Athens to visit the famous church housed within the (still-intact) Parthenon. Byzantine mosaics, featuring realistic plants, animals, and people, were exported to the West.

The Byzantine Empire—and, by extension, Greece—was weakened by the disastrous Fourth Crusade (1204), in which greedy Crusaders looted their fellow Christian city of Constantinople. Following this, Western Crusaders occupied and ruled many parts of Greece, including Athens, and Byzantine Christians battled Crusading Christians at Monemvasia. Meanwhile, the Ottomans were whittling away at the empire's fringes. In 1453, Constantinople fell to the Ottoman Turks.

Byzantine-Era Sights
• Athens' old Orthodox churches, including the Church of Kapnikarea (on Ermou street), Agios Eleftherios (next to the cathedral), and Holy Apostles (in the Agora)
• Byzantine and Christian Museum in Athens
• Icons of the Eastern Orthodox Church
• Monemvasia fortress
• Churches and palaces at Mystras

ISLAMIC/OTTOMAN GREECE (1453-1821)
Under the Ottomans, Greece was ruled by Islamic Turks from their capital of Constantinople. Like many other temples-turned-churches, Athens' Parthenon (still intact) became a mosque, and a minaret was built alongside it.

Greek Christians had several choices for surviving the new regime. Some converted to Islam and learned Turkish, while others faked their conversion and remained closet Christians. Some moved to the boonies, outside the reach of Ottoman administrators. Many of Greece's best and brightest headed to Western Europe, helping to ignite the Renaissance (which revived the Classical achievements of ancient Athens). Most Greeks just stayed put, paid the "Christian tax," and lived in peace alongside the Ottomans. The Ottomans were (relatively) benevolent rulers, and the Greek language and Orthodox Christianity both survived.

Greece found itself between the powerful Ottomans and powerful merchants of Venice. This made Greece a center for East–West trade, but also a battleground. Venetian traders (backed by their military) occupied and fortified a number of Greek seaports in order to carry on trade throughout the Ottoman Empire. In 1687, the Venetians attacked Ottoman-controlled Athens. The Ottomans hunkered down on the Acropolis, storing their gunpowder in the Parthenon. A Venetian cannonball hit the Parthenon, destroying it and creating the ruin we see today. Venetian looters plundered the rubble and carried off statues as souvenirs.

Ottoman-Era Sights
• Benaki Museum of Islamic Art in Athens
• The Tzami, a former mosque on Monastiraki Square in Athens
• Venetian fortresses (including those in Nafplio) established in Byzantine times

GREEK INDEPENDENCE AND NEOCLASSICISM (1800s)

After centuries of neglect, Greece's Classical heritage was rediscovered, both by the Greeks and by the rest of Europe. Neoclassicism was all the rage in Europe, where the ancient Greek style was used to decorate homes, and create paintings and statues. In 1801-1805, the British Lord Elgin plundered half of the Parthenon's statues and reliefs, carrying them home for Londoners to marvel at.

Greeks rediscovered a sense of their national heritage, and envisioned a day when they could rule themselves as a modern democracy. In 1821, the Greeks rose up against rule from Constantinople. It started with pockets of resistance by guerrilla Klepht warriors from the mountains, escalating into large-scale massacres on both sides. The Greeks' struggle became a cause célèbre in Europe, attracting Romantic liberals from England and France to take up arms. The poet Lord Byron died (of a fever) near the Gulf of Patra while fighting for Greece.

At one point the rebels gained control of the Peloponnese and declared Greek independence. The Greeks even sank the flagship of the Ottoman fleet in 1822, earning international respect for their nascent rebellion. But tribal rivalries prevented the Greeks from preserving their gains. With Egyptian reinforcements, the Ottomans successfully invaded the Peloponnese and captured several cities. An Egyptian army in Europe was too much to take for Britain, France, and Russia, who intervened with their navies and saved Greek independence.

By 1829, the Greeks had their freedom, a constitution, and—for the first time—a unified state of "Greece," based in Nafplio. But after its first president, Ioannis Kapodistrias, was assassinated in 1831, the budding democracy was forced by Europe's crowned heads to accept a monarch: 17-year-old King Otto from Bavaria (crowned in 1832). In 1834, historic Athens was chosen as the new capital, despite the fact that it was then a humble village of a few thousand inhabitants.

Over the next century, Greece achieved a constitution (or *syntagma*, celebrated by Syntagma Square in Athens, as well as Nafplio and many other cities) and steered the monarchy toward modern democracy. Athens was rebuilt in the Neoclassical style. Greek engineers (along with foreigners) built the Corinth Canal. The

Greek nation expanded, as Greek-speaking territories were captured from the Ottomans or ceded to Greece by European powers. In 1896, Greece celebrated its revival by hosting the first modern Olympic Games.

19th-Century Neoclassical Sights

- Syntagma Square, Parliament, and the evzone at the Tomb of the Unknown Soldier, in Athens
- National Garden in Athens
- Patriotic paintings in the Nafplio Annex of the National Gallery
- Zappeion exhibition hall in Athens
- Athens' Panathenaic Stadium (ancient stadium renovated for the first modern Olympics in 1896)
- Cathedral in Athens
- Museum of Greek Folk Art (17th-19th century) in Athens
- Corinth Canal

20th CENTURY

Two world wars and the Greek Civil War caused great turmoil in Greece. During World War I, Greece remained uncommitted until the final years, when it joined the Allies (Britain, France, Italy, Russia, and the US) against Germany.

World War I scrambled the balance of power in the Balkans. Greece was given control of parts of western Turkey, where many ethnic Greeks lived. The Turks, having thrown out their Ottoman rulers, now rose up to evict the Greeks, sparking the Greco-Turkish War (1919-1922) and massacres on both sides. To settle the conflict, a million ethnic Greeks living in Turkish lands were shipped to Greece, while Greece sent hundreds of thousands of its ethnic Turks to Turkey. In 1923, hordes of desperate refugees poured into Athens, and the population doubled overnight. Many later immigrated to the US, Canada, and Australia. Today there are more than a million Greek Americans living in the US.

In World War II Greece sided firmly with the Allies, heroically repulsing Mussolini's 1940 invasion. But Adolf Hitler finished the job, invading and occupying Greece for four brutal years of repression and hunger.

Making the situation worse, the Greek Resistance movement (battling the Nazis) was itself divided. It broke out into a full-fledged civil war (1944-1949) between Western-backed patriots and Marxist patriots.

World War II and the Greek Civil War left Greece with hundreds of thousands dead, desperately poor, and bitterly divided. Thanks to America's Marshall Plan (and tourism), the economy recovered in the 1950s and '60s, and Greece joined the NATO alliance. Along with modernization came some of Europe's worst pollution, which eroded the ancient monuments.

Politically, Greece would remain split between the extreme right (the ruling monarchy, military, and the rich) and the extreme left (communists, students, and workers), without much room in the middle. The repressive royalist regime was backed heavily by the United States, which made Greece the first battleground in the Cold War (the Truman Doctrine). By the 1960s, when the rest of Europe was undergoing rapid social change, the Greek government was still trying to control its society with arrests and assassinations. When the royalists began losing control, a CIA-backed coup put the military in charge (1967-1974). They outlawed everything from long hair and miniskirts to Socrates and the theme song from *Zorba the Greek* (because its composer was accused of being a communist).

For Greece, 1974 was a watershed year. In the midst of political turmoil, Turkey invaded the Greek-friendly island of Cyprus (sparking yet more decades of bad blood between Turkey and Greece). The surprise attack caught the Greek military junta off guard, and they resigned in disgrace. A new government was elected with a new constitution. Guided by two strong (sometimes antagonistic) leaders—Andreas Papandreou and Constantine Karamanlis—Greece inched slowly from right-wing repression toward open democracy. Greece in the 1970s and '80s would suffer more than its share of assassinations and terrorist acts. But the economy grew, and Greece joined the European Union (1981) and adopted the euro (2002).

20th-Century Sights
• National War Museum in Athens
• Central Market in Athens
• Greek flag atop the Acropolis in Athens (reminder of resistance leaders who flew it there during the Nazi occupation in World War II)

GREECE TODAY
After adopting the euro, the Greek economy boomed. EU subsidies flowed in for major infrastructure projects, such as highways and high-speed rail. As host of the 2004 Summer Olympics, Athens cleaned up its city and installed a new airport and Metro. But the worldwide recession that started in 2008 hit Greece hard.

Suddenly, international investors dumped Greek bonds, since the national debt was larger than the country's gross domestic product (for more on the economic crisis in Greece, see page 20). In 2010, Greece received an unprecedented €110 billion bailout from the EU and the International Monetary Fund—and then needed an even bigger rescue package—€130 billion—just two years later. A third bailout—worth up to €86 billion—was approved in 2015. The bailouts required severe economic reforms, sending the economy into recession and pushing the unemployment rate over 25 percent.

The already-volatile political scene became even more stirred up as Greeks argued about how to grapple with their financial crisis. Financial markets and European leaders feared a Greek exit from the euro, which could have caused a breakup of the currency.

With support from what was then a thin majority of Greeks (cautiously) willing to stomach more budget cuts rather than abandon the euro, in 2012 the center-right New Democracy party—led by Prime Minister Antonis Samaras—forged a coalition with the Socialists and some smaller political groups. But the new government didn't take hold. Samaras failed to get support for a bailout referendum and resigned in summer 2015.

Samaras' successor, Alexis Tspiras (from the left-wing Syriza party), has made the Greek debt crisis a top priority. But with the bailout money going toward paying international loans, rather than making its way into Greece's economy, some analysts now say a Greek exit from the eurozone wouldn't be such a bad thing, because most international banks and vulnerable euro countries have taken steps to reduce their risk.

Greece is seriously hampered by widespread governmental corruption and a bloated (indeed, "Byzantine") bureaucratic system that's tangled itself in red tape. Recent administrations have had some success with attempts to combat the corruption, but few Greeks are optimistic that the bureaucracy is headed toward efficiency.

Immigration is another hotly debated topic. People are divided over how the nation can and should accommodate the thousands of economic and political refugees who arrive here, both legally and illegally. Alarmingly, this has bolstered support for far-right, brazenly racist extremists. The neo-fascist political organization Golden Dawn won seven percent of the popular vote in 2015. Greeks also argue among themselves about the nation's high military spending, the draft, and excessive privileges for the Greek Orthodox church. Meanwhile, relations with Turkey—its next-door neighbor across the Aegean pond—remain strained.

On my last visit, I was constantly surprised by how sunny most Greeks remain amid the current upheaval—as if a certain optimism and resilience were just part of the Greek character. Given that their language and culture have survived for more than two millennia—despite being conquered by Romans, Turks, and Nazis—Greeks seem confident that they'll survive this, too.

Greece Today Sights

- Ermou street pedestrian zone in Athens
- Renovated Monastiraki Square in Athens
- Acropolis Museum in Athens (pictured on previous page)
- Athens' Metro and airport
- 2004 Olympic Games sights, including new stadium, in Athens

To learn more about Greek history, consider *Europe 101: History and Art for the Traveler,* by Rick Steves and Gene Openshaw (available at www.ricksteves.com).

PRACTICALITIES

This chapter covers the practical skills of European travel: how to get tourist information, pay for things, sightsee efficiently, find good-value accommodations, eat affordably but well, use technology wisely, and get between destinations smoothly. To study ahead and round out your knowledge, check out "Resources."

Tourist Information

The Greek **national tourist office** has a helpful website with lots of information and downloadable maps and brochures (www. visitgreece.gr). Other good websites include www.culture.gr (Greek Ministry of Culture, with information on major archaeological sites and museums), www.thisisathens.org (City of Athens Convention and Visitors Bureau), and www.athensguide.com (guide to Athens by travel writer Matt Barrett).

In Greece, tourist offices are often marked *EOT* (for the Greek phrase "Greek Tourism Organization"). Unfortunately, budget cuts have forced many towns to close their TIs. The offices that are still open can usually give you a free map, a few local tips, and some assistance with bus connections. Occasionally you'll find a well-run office (such as in Athens). In general, though, your hotelier may end up being your best source of information.

Travel Tips

Emergency and Medical Help: In Greece, dial 100 or 112 for English-speaking help for any emergency or 171 or 1571 for the Tourist Police. To summon an ambulance, call 166.

The Tourist Police serves as a contact point between tourists and other branches of the police and is also responsible for handling problems such as disputes with hotels, restaurants, and other tourist services (available 24 hours daily; Athens office located south of the Acropolis in Koukaki at Veikou 43, office tel. 210-920-0724).

If you get sick, do as the locals do and go to a pharmacist for advice. Or ask at your hotel for help—they'll know the nearest medical and emergency services.

Theft or Loss: To replace a passport, you'll need to go in person to an embassy (see page 509). If your credit and debit cards disappear, cancel and replace them (see "Damage Control for Lost Cards" on page 465). File a police report, either on the spot or within a day or two; you'll need it to submit an insurance claim for lost or stolen valuables, and it can help with replacing your passport or credit and debit cards. For more information, see www.ricksteves.com/help. To minimize the effects of loss, back up your digital photos and other files frequently.

Borders: If you enter Greece from most European countries (those that are part of Europe's open-borders Schengen Agreement), you won't need to go through customs. But if you arrive on a direct flight from the US, or from the neighboring countries of Turkey, Macedonia, Albania, and Bulgaria (which aren't part of the EU pact), you'll have to clear customs.

Time Zones: Greece, which is one hour ahead of most of continental Europe, is generally seven/ten hours ahead of the East/West Coasts of the US. The exceptions are the beginning and end of Daylight Saving Time: Europe "springs forward" the last Sunday in March (two weeks after most of North America) and "falls back" the last Sunday in October (one week before North America). For a handy online time converter, try www.timeanddate.com/worldclock.

Business Hours: Most shops catering to tourists are open long hours daily. In Athens stores are generally open weekdays from 9:00 to 20:00. Afternoon breaks are common, and some places close early a few nights a week.

Saturdays are virtually weekdays, with earlier closing hours. Sundays have the same pros and cons as they do for travelers in the US: Sightseeing attractions are generally open, while shops and banks are closed, public transportation options are fewer, and there's no rush hour. Friday and Saturday evenings are lively; Sunday evenings are quiet.

Lower Your Expectations: The Greeks have been through the economic wringer over the past few years. Budget cuts have reduced staffing to a minimum at museums, ancient sites, and the few TIs that are still operating. Opening hours can be short, and the staff may be grumpy. Don't take it personally.

Watt's Up?: Europe's electrical system is 220 volts, instead of North America's 110 volts. Most newer electronics (such as laptops, battery chargers, and hair dryers) convert automatically, so you won't need a converter, but you will need an adapter plug with two round prongs, sold inexpensively at travel stores in the US. Avoid bringing older appliances that don't automatically convert voltage; instead, buy a cheap replacement in Europe. Travel hairdryers and other small appliances are sold at Public stores (ask your hotelier for the closest branch; there's a hard-to-miss location on Syntagma Square).

Bathroom Etiquette: There's a reason every bathroom in Greece has a small wastebasket next to the toilet—bad plumbing. Don't flush toilet paper; use the wastebasket instead.

Discounts: Youth, student, and senior discounts aren't listed in this book. However, many sights offer discounts for seniors (loosely defined as those who are retired or willing to call themselves a senior), groups of 10 or more, families, and students or teachers with proper identification cards (www.isic.org). Always ask. Children under 18 get in free at all museums and archaeological sites run by the Ministry of Greek Culture, including the Acropolis. Some discounts are available only for citizens of the European Union (EU).

Online Translation Tips: You can use Google's Chrome browser (available free at www.google.com/chrome) to instantly translate websites. With one click, the page appears in (very rough) English translation. You can also paste the URL of the site into the translation window at www.google.com/translate. The Google Translate app converts spoken English into most European languages (and vice versa) and can also translate text it "reads" with your mobile device's camera.

Money

This section offers advice on how to pay for purchases on your trip (including getting cash from ATMs and paying with plastic), dealing with lost or stolen cards, VAT (sales tax) refunds, and tipping.

PRACTICALITIES

> ## Exchange Rate
>
> ### 1 euro (€)=about $1.10
> To convert prices in euros to dollars, add about 10 percent: €20=about $22, €50=about $55. (Check www.oanda.com for the latest exchange rates.) Just like the dollar, one euro (€) is broken down into 100 cents. Coins range from €0.01 to €2, and bills from €5 to €500 (bills over €50 are rarely used).

WHAT TO BRING

Bring both a credit card and a debit card. You'll use the debit card at cash machines (ATMs) to withdraw local cash for most purchases, and the credit card to pay for larger items. Some travelers carry a third card, in case one gets demagnetized or eaten by a temperamental machine.

For an emergency stash, bring several hundred dollars in hard cash in $20 bills. If you need to exchange the bills, go to a bank; avoid using currency-exchange booths because of their lousy rates and/or outrageous (and often hard-to-spot) fees.

CASH

Cash is highly preferable in Greece. Small businesses (hotels, mom-and-pop-cafés, shops, etc.) require payment in cash. Some vendors will charge you extra for using a credit card, some won't accept foreign credit cards, and some won't take any credit cards at all. Cash is the best—and sometimes only—way to pay for cheap food, bus fare, taxis, and local guides.

Throughout Europe, ATMs are the standard way for travelers to get cash. They work just like they do at home. To withdraw money from an ATM (surprisingly labeled *ATM* in the Greek alphabet), you'll need a debit card (ideally with a Visa or MasterCard logo for maximum usability), plus a PIN code (numeric and four digits). For increased security, shield the keypad when entering your PIN code, and don't use an ATM if anything on the front of the machine looks loose or damaged (a sign that someone may have attached a "skimming" device to capture account information). Try to withdraw large sums of money to reduce the number of per-transaction bank fees you'll pay.

When possible, use ATMs located outside banks—a thief is less likely to target a cash machine near surveillance cameras, and if your card is munched by a machine, you can go inside for help. Stay away from "independent" ATMs such as Travelex, Euronet, YourCash, Cardpoint, and Cashzone, which charge huge commissions, have terrible exchange rates, and may try to trick users with "dynamic currency conversion" (described at the end of "Credit and Debit Cards," next).

Although you can use a credit card to withdraw cash at an ATM, this comes with high bank fees and only makes sense in an emergency.

While traveling, if you want to monitor your accounts online to detect any unauthorized transactions, be sure to use a secure connection (see page 485).

Pickpockets target tourists. To safeguard your cash, wear a money belt—a pouch with a strap that you buckle around your waist like a belt and tuck under your clothes. Keep your cash, credit cards, and passport secure in your money belt, and carry only a day's spending money in your front pocket.

CREDIT AND DEBIT CARDS

Your debit card is particularly essential in Greece. Many businesses—except for the pricier and more touristy hotels and restaurants—don't accept credit cards (and Visa and MasterCard are preferred over American Express).

In Greece, I use my credit card sparingly: to book hotel reservations, to buy advance tickets for events or sights, or to cover major expenses (such as car rentals or plane tickets), and to pay for things online or near the end of my trip (to avoid another visit to the ATM). While you could instead use a debit card for these purchases, a credit card offers a greater degree of fraud protection.

Ask Your Credit- or Debit-Card Company: Before your trip, contact the company that issued your debit or credit cards.

• Confirm that your card **will work overseas,** and alert them that you'll be using it in Europe; otherwise, they may deny transactions if they perceive unusual spending patterns.

• Ask for the specifics on transaction **fees.** When you use your credit or debit card—either for purchases or ATM withdrawals—you'll typically be charged additional "international transaction" fees of up to 3 percent (1 percent is normal) plus $5 per transaction. If your card's fees seem high, consider getting a different card just for your trip: Capital One (www.capitalone.com) and most credit unions have low-to-no international fees.

• Verify your daily **ATM withdrawal limit** and if necessary, ask your bank to adjust it. I prefer a high limit that allows me to take out more cash at each ATM stop and save on bank fees; some travelers prefer to set a lower limit in case their card is stolen. Note that foreign banks also set maximum withdrawal amounts for their ATMs.

• Get your bank's emergency **phone number** in the US (but not its 800 number, which isn't accessible from overseas) to call collect if you have a problem.

• Ask for your credit card's **PIN** in case you need to make an emergency cash withdrawal or encounter Europe's chip-and-PIN system; the bank won't tell you your PIN over the phone, so allow time for it to be mailed to you.

Magnetic-Stripe versus Chip-and-PIN Credit Cards: While much of Europe is shifting to a chip-and-PIN security system for credit and debit cards, Greece still uses the old magnetic-stripe technology. (European chip-and-PIN cards are embedded with an electronic security chip, and require a four-digit PIN to make a purchase.) If you happen to encounter chip and PIN, it will probably be at payment machines, such as those at toll roads or unattended gas pumps. On the outside chance that a machine won't take your card, find a cashier who can make your card work (they can print a receipt for you to sign), or find a machine that takes cash. Most travelers who use only magnetic-stripe cards don't run into problems. Still, it pays to carry euros; remember, you can always use an ATM to withdraw cash with your magnetic-stripe debit card.

If you're concerned, ask if your bank offers a chip-and-PIN card. Andrews Federal Credit Union (www.andrewsfcu.org) and the State Department Federal Credit Union (www.sdfcu.org) offer these cards and are open to all US residents.

Dynamic Currency Conversion: If merchants or hoteliers offer to convert your purchase price into dollars (called dynamic currency conversion, or DCC), refuse this "service." You'll pay even more in fees for the expensive convenience of seeing your charge in dollars. If your receipt shows the total in dollars only, ask for the transaction to be processed in the local currency. If the clerk refuses, pay in cash—or mark the receipt "local currency not offered" and dispute the DCC charges with your bank.

Some ATMs and retailers try to confuse customers by presenting DCC in misleading terms. If an ATM offers to "lock in" or "guarantee" your conversion rate, choose "proceed without conversion." Other prompts might state, "You can be charged in dollars: Press YES for dollars, NO for euros." Always choose the local currency in these situations.

DAMAGE CONTROL FOR LOST CARDS

If you lose your credit, debit, or ATM card, you can stop people from using your card by reporting the loss immediately to the respective global customer-assistance centers. Call these 24-hour US numbers collect: Visa (tel. 303/967-1096), MasterCard (tel. 636/722-7111), and American Express (tel. 336/393-1111). In Greece, to make a collect call to the US, dial 00-800-1311. Press zero or stay on the line for an English-speaking operator. European toll-free numbers (listed by country) can be found at the websites for Visa and MasterCard.

Try to have this information ready: full card number, whether you are the primary or secondary cardholder, the cardholder's name exactly as printed on the card, billing address, home phone number, circumstances of the loss or theft, and identification verification (your birth date, your mother's maiden name, or your Social Security number—memorize this, don't carry a copy). If you are the secondary cardholder, you'll also need to provide the primary cardholder's identification-verification details. You can generally receive a temporary card in Europe within two or three business days in Europe (see www.ricksteves.com/help for more).

If you report your loss within two days, you typically won't be responsible for any unauthorized transactions on your account, although many banks charge a liability fee of $50.

TIPPING

Tipping in Greece isn't as automatic and generous as it is in the US. For special service, tips are appreciated, but not expected. As in the US, the proper amount depends on your resources, tipping philosophy, and the circumstances, but some general guidelines apply.

Restaurants: At Greek restaurants that have waitstaff, locals generally round up their bill after a good meal (usually about 10 percent). For more on tipping in restaurants, see page 479.

Taxis: For a typical ride, round up your fare a bit (for instance, if the fare is €4.50, pay €5). If the cabbie hauls your bags and zips you to the airport to help you catch your flight, you might want to toss in a little more. But if you feel like you're being driven in circles or otherwise ripped off, skip the tip.

Services: In general, if someone in the service industry does a super job for you, a small tip of a euro or two is appropriate...but not required. If you're not sure whether (or how much) to tip for a service, ask a local for advice.

GETTING A VAT REFUND

Wrapped into the purchase price of your Greek souvenirs is a Value-Added Tax (VAT) of about 23 percent. You're entitled to get most of that tax back if you purchase more than €120 (about $130) worth of goods at a store that participates in the VAT-refund scheme. Typically, you must ring up the minimum at a single retailer—you can't add up your purchases from various shops to reach the required amount.

Getting your refund is straightforward and, if you buy a substantial amount of souvenirs, well worth the hassle. (Note that if the store ships the goods to your US home, VAT is not assessed on your purchase.) You'll need to:

Get the paperwork. Have the merchant completely fill out the necessary refund document, called a "Tax-Free Shopping Cheque." You'll have to present your passport. Get the paperwork done before you leave the store to ensure you'll have everything you need (including your original sales receipt).

Get your stamp at the border or airport. Process your VAT document at your last stop in the European Union (such as at the airport) with the customs agent who deals with VAT refunds. Arrive an additional hour before you need to check in for your flight to allow time to find the local customs office—and to stand in line. It's best to keep your purchases in your carry-on. If they're too large or dangerous to carry on (such as knives), pack them in your checked bags and alert the check-in agent. You'll be sent (with your tagged bag) to a customs desk outside security; someone will examine your bag, stamp your paperwork, and put your bag on the belt. You're not supposed to use your purchased goods before you leave. If you show up at customs wearing your chic Greek shirt, officials might look the other way—or deny you a refund.

Collect your refund. You'll need to return your stamped document to the retailer or its representative. Many merchants work with services, such as Global Blue or Premier Tax Free, that have offices at major airports, ports, or border crossings (either before or after security, probably strategically located near a duty-free shop). These services, which extract a 4 percent fee, can refund your money immediately in cash or credit your card (within two billing cycles). If the retailer handles VAT refunds directly, it's up to you to contact the merchant for your refund. You can mail the documents from home, or more quickly, from your point of departure (using an envelope you've prepared in advance or one that's been provided by the merchant). You'll then have to wait—it can take months.

CUSTOMS FOR AMERICAN SHOPPERS

You are allowed to take home $800 worth of items per person duty-free, once every 31 days. You can take home many processed and packaged foods: vacuum-packed cheeses, dried herbs, jams, baked goods, candy, chocolate, oil, vinegar, mustard, and honey. Fresh fruits and vegetables and most meats are not allowed, with exceptions for some canned items. As for alcohol, you can bring in one liter duty-free (it can be packed securely in your checked luggage, along with any other liquid-containing items).

To bring alcohol (or liquid-packed foods) in your carry-on bag on your flight home, buy it at a duty-free shop at the airport. You'll increase your odds of getting it onto a connecting flight if it's packaged in a "STEB"—a secure, tamper-evident bag. But stay away from liquids in opaque, ceramic, or metallic containers, which usually cannot be successfully screened (STEB or no STEB).

For details on allowable goods, customs rules, and duty rates, visit http://help.cbp.gov.

Sightseeing

Sightseeing can be hard work. Use these tips to make your visits to Greece's finest sights meaningful, fun, efficient, and painless.

PLAN AHEAD

Set up an itinerary that allows you to fit in all your must-see sights. For a one-stop look at opening hours in Athens, see the "Athens at a Glance" sidebar on page 52. Because these hours can vary, it's best to confirm opening hours when you arrive in town by checking with the TI or your hotelier.

Don't put off visiting a must-see sight—you never know when a place will close unexpectedly for a holiday, strike, or restoration. Many museums are closed or have reduced hours at least a few days a year, especially on holidays such as Christmas, New Year's, and Labor Day (May 1). A list of holidays is on page 510; check online for possible museum closures during your trip.

Most of Greece's ancient sites and archaeological museums are operated by the government and can be affected by budget cutbacks and strikes. In general, hours at sights are longer during peak season (April-October) and on weekends, and shorter on weekdays and in the off-season. The timing of this seasonal switch can be unannounced and differs between sights. Year-round, if things are slow, places may close early with no advance notice. It's smart to arrive well in advance of listed closing times, and to hit your must-see sights in the morning, especially if traveling outside of summer.

The Ministry of Greek Culture website (www.culture.gr) purports to list the latest hours for virtually all of the major sights—including Athens' Acropolis, Ancient Agora, Acropolis Museum, and the National Archaeological Museum, plus the attractions at Delphi, Olympia, Epidavros, and Mycenae—but you'll get more reliable, up-to-date information by asking your hotelier or calling the sights directly.

Going at the right time helps avoid crowds. This book offers tips on the best times to see specific sights. Try visiting popular sights very early or very late. Evening visits are usually peaceful, with fewer crowds.

All museums and archaeological sites run by the Ministry of Greek Culture, including the Acropolis, are free on national holidays and every first Sunday from November through March. Children under 18 always get in free to these sights.

Study up. To get the most out of the self-guided tours and sight descriptions in this book, read them before you visit. The

Acropolis is much more entertaining if you've polished up on Doric architecture the night before.

AT SIGHTS

Most of Greece's artifacts have been plunked into glass cases labeled with little more than title and date. Sights run by the Greek Ministry of Culture provide a free information pamphlet, though usually only by request.

More than most destinations in Europe, Greece demands (and rewards) any effort you make to really understand its treasures. If you read up on Greek history and art, the artifacts come to life; without this background, visiting Greece's museums can quickly become an unforgiving slog past stiff statues and endless ceramic vases.

It can also help to put your imagination into overdrive. As you stroll Athens' Ancient Agora, mentally clad the other tourists in robes. Approach the temple at Delphi as if you were about to learn your fate from an oracle; enter the stadium at Olympia ready to race its length in front of a huge crowd. At museums, imagine being the archaeologist who unearthed the intact glass vessels, intricate golden necklaces, and vases inscribed with the faces of people who lived four millennia ago.

Many major ancient sites have both an archaeological site and a museum for the artifacts and models. You can choose between visiting the museum first (to mentally reconstruct the ruins before seeing them) or the site first (to get the lay of the ancient land before seeing the items found there). In most cases, I prefer to see the site first, then the museum. However, crowds and weather can also help determine your plan. If it's a blistering hot afternoon, tour the air-conditioned museum first, then hit the ruins in the cool of evening (if opening hours allow). Or, if rain clouds are on the horizon, do the archaeological site first, then duck into the museum when the rain hits.

Here's what you can typically expect:

Entering: Be warned that you may not be allowed to enter if you arrive 30 to 60 minutes before closing time. And guards start ushering people out well before the actual closing time, so don't save the best for last.

Some important sights have a security check, where you must open your bag or send it through a metal detector. Some sights require you to check daypacks and coats. (If you'd rather not check your daypack, try carrying it tucked under your arm like a purse as you enter.)

Ancient sites are meticulously monitored; you're sure to hear the tweets of many whistles aimed at visitors who've crossed a barrier or climbed on a ruin. The Greeks take their ancient artifacts

PRACTICALITIES

very seriously. Posing with ancient statues—or even standing next to them for a photo—is strictly forbidden.

Photography: If the museum's photo policy isn't clearly posted, ask a guard. Generally, taking photos without a flash or tripod is allowed. Some sights ban photos altogether.

Temporary Exhibits: Museums may show special exhibits in addition to their permanent collection. Some exhibits are included in the entry price, while others come at an extra cost (which you may have to pay even if you don't want to see the exhibit).

Expect Changes: Artwork can be on tour, on loan, out sick, or shifted at the whim of the curator. Pick up a floor plan as you enter, and ask museum staff if you can't find a particular item.

Audioguides and Tours: In Greece, audioguides are rare, but good guidebooks are available.

I've produced free downloadable audio tours for my Athens City Walk, and for the Acropolis, Ancient Agora, and National Archaeological Museum; look for the 🎧. For more on my audio tours, see page 10.

You can usually hire a live local guide at the entrance to major ancient sites or museums at a reasonable cost (prices are soft and negotiable; save money by splitting the guide fee with other travelers). I list recommended guides in the "Helpful Hints" section of many chapters. Two notable exceptions are Olympia, where guides are sparse, and the Acropolis, where the loitering guides are generally of poor quality.

Services: Important sights may have an on-site café or cafeteria (usually a handy place to rejuvenate during a long visit). The WCs at sights are free and generally clean.

Before Leaving: At the gift shop, scan the postcard rack or thumb through a guidebook to be sure that you haven't overlooked something that you'd like to see.

Every sight or museum offers more than what is covered in this book. Use the information in this book as an introduction—not the final word.

Sleeping

I favor hotels and restaurants that are handy to your sightseeing activities. Rather than list hotels scattered throughout a city, I choose hotels in my favorite neighborhoods. My recommendations run the gamut, from dorm beds to fancy rooms with all of the comforts.

A major feature of the Sleeping sections of this book is my extensive and opinionated listing of good-value rooms. I like places that are clean, central, relatively quiet at night, reasonably priced, friendly, small enough to have a hands-on owner and a stable staff, run with a respect for Greek traditions, and not listed in other guidebooks. (In Greece, for me, six out of these eight criteria means it's a keeper.) I'm more impressed by a convenient location and a fun-loving philosophy than flat-screen TVs and a pricey laundry service.

Book your accommodations well in advance, especially if you want to stay at one of my top listings or if you'll be traveling during busy times. See page 510 for a list of major holidays and festivals in Greece; for tips on making reservations, see page 474.

Some people make reservations as they travel, calling hotels a few days to a week before their arrival. If you'd rather travel without any reservations at all, you'll have greater success snaring rooms if you arrive at your destination early in the day. If you anticipate crowds (weekends are worst) on the day you want to check in, call hotels at about 9:00 or 10:00, when the receptionist knows who'll be checking out and which rooms will be available. If you encounter a language barrier, ask the fluent receptionist at your current hotel to call for you.

RATES AND DEALS

I've described my recommended accommodations using a Sleep Code (see sidebar). The prices I list are for one-night stays in peak season, generally include breakfast, and assume you're booking directly with the hotel (not through an online hotel-booking engine or TI). Booking services extract a commission from the hotel, which logically closes the door on special deals. Book direct. Don't be surprised if you're quoted higher prices than those listed in this book; starting in 2016, hotel taxes are expected to go up significantly.

My recommended hotels each have a website (often with a built-in booking form) and an email address; you can expect a response in English within a day (and often sooner).

Given Greece's economic crisis, some hoteliers may be willing to make a deal (less likely on the islands). If you're on a budget, it's smart to email several hotels to ask for their best price. Comparison-shop and make your choice. This is especially helpful when dealing with larger hotels that use "dynamic pricing," a computer-generated system that predicts the demand for particular days and sets prices accordingly: High-demand days can be more than double the price of low-demand days. This makes it impossible for a guidebook to list anything more accurate than a wide range of prices. I regret this trend. While you can assume that hotels listed in this book are good, it's difficult to say which ones are the better value unless you email to confirm the price.

As you look over the listings, you'll notice that some accommodations promise special prices to Rick Steves readers. To get these rates, you must book directly with the hotel (that is, not

Sleep Code

(€1=about $1.10, country code: 30)

Price Rankings

To help you easily sort through my listings, I've divided the accommodations into three categories, based on the highest price for a basic double room with bath during high season:

$$$ Higher Priced
$$ Moderately Priced
$ Lower Priced

I always rate hostels as $, whether or not they have double rooms, because they have the cheapest beds in town.

Prices can change without notice; verify the hotel's current rates online or by email. For the best prices, always book directly with the hotel.

Abbreviations

To pack maximum information into minimum space, I use the following code to describe accommodations in this book. Prices listed are per room, not per person. When a price range is given for a type of room (such as a double room listing for €80-120), it means the price fluctuates with the season, size of room, or length of stay; expect to pay the upper end for peak-season stays.

S = Single room (or price for one person in a double)
D = Double or twin room. "Double beds" can be two twins sheeted together and are usually big enough for nonromantic couples
T = Triple (generally a double bed with a single)
Q = Quad (usually two double beds; adding an extra child's bed to a T is usually cheaper)
b = Private bathroom with toilet and shower or tub

According to this code, a couple staying at a "Db-€85" hotel would pay a total of €85 (about $94) for a double room with a private bathroom. Unless otherwise noted, breakfast is included, basic English is spoken, and free Wi-Fi and/or a guest computer is generally available. Many places accept credit cards, and rooms generally have air-conditioning.

through a booking site like TripAdvisor or Booking.com), mention this book when you reserve, and then show the book upon arrival. Rick Steves discounts apply to readers with ebooks as well as printed books. Because I trust hotels to honor this, please let me know if you don't receive a listed discount. Note, though, that discounts understandably may not be applied to promotional rates.

In general, prices can soften if you do any of the following: offer to pay cash, stay at least three nights, or mention this book. You can also try asking for a cheaper room or a discount, or offer to skip breakfast. I'd avoid bargaining for rock-bottom rates. Unlike international chain hotels, Greece's mom-and-pop hoteliers have been hit hard by these rough economic times.

Remember that some hotels in Greece, especially smaller places, may require payment in cash.

TYPES OF ACCOMMODATIONS
Hotels

You'll usually see the word "hotel," but you might also see the traditional Greek word *Xenonas* (ΞΕΝΩΝΑΣ/Ξενώνασ). In some places, especially Nafplio, small hotels are called *pensions*.

In this book, the price for a double room ranges from about $45 (very simple, toilet and shower down the hall) to $400 (maximum plumbing and more), with most clustering at about $90. You'll pay more at hotels in Athens and on the islands, less on the Peloponnese.

In general, a triple room is cheaper than the cost of a double and a single. Traveling alone can be expensive: A single room can be close to the cost of a double.

A satisfying Greek breakfast with cheese, ham, yogurt, fresh bread, honey, jam, fruit, juice, and coffee or tea is standard and is sometimes included in hotel prices. More expensive hotels also tend to serve eggs and cereal.

Greece's hotels differ from American-style hotels in several ways. Most bathrooms come with just a shower (if you want a bathtub, ask for one when you reserve). You may see signs requesting that you discard toilet paper in the bathroom wastebasket. Hotel elevators, while becoming more common, are often very small—pack light, or you may need to send your bags up separately.

If visiting areas with mosquitoes (such as Kardamyli and Monemvasia), avoid opening your windows, especially at night. If your hotel lacks air-conditioning, request a fan. Many hotels furnish a small plug-in bulb that helps keep the bloodsuckers at bay. If not already plugged into the electric socket, it may be on a table or nightstand. Some may have a separate scented packet that you have to unwrap and insert into the device.

Hotels in Greece are required by law to be nonsmoking, but enforcement is spotty. Hoteliers are obsessive about eliminating any odors, but if your room smells like the Marlboro man slept there, ask to be moved.

If you're arriving in the morning, your room probably won't be

Making Hotel Reservations

Reserve your rooms several weeks in advance—or as soon as you've pinned down your travel dates. Note that some national holidays merit your making reservations far in advance (see page 510).

Requesting a Reservation: It's easiest to book your room directly through the hotel's website. (For the best rates, be sure to use the hotel's official site and not a booking agency's site.) If there's no reservation form, or for complicated requests, send an email (see sample request). Most recommended hotels take reservations in English.

The hotelier wants to know:
- the number and type of rooms you need
- the number of nights you'll stay
- your date of arrival (use the European style for writing dates: day/month/year)
- your date of departure
- any special needs (such as bathroom in the room or down the hall, cheapest room, twin beds vs. double bed)

Mention any discounts—for Rick Steves readers or otherwise—when you make the reservation.

Confirming a Reservation: Most places will request a credit-card number to hold your room. If they don't have a secure online reservation form—look for the *https*—you can email it (I do), but it's safer to share that confidential info via a phone call or two emails (splitting your number between them).

Canceling a Reservation: If you must cancel, it's courteous—and smart—to do so with as much notice as possible, especially

ready. Drop your bag safely at the hotel and dive right into sight-seeing.

Hoteliers can be a great help and source of advice. Most know their city well, and can assist you with everything from public transit and airport connections to finding a good restaurant, the nearest launderette, or Wi-Fi hotspot.

Even at the best places, mechanical breakdowns occur: Air-conditioning malfunctions, sinks leak, hot water turns cold, and toilets gurgle and smell. Report your concerns clearly and calmly at the front desk. For more complicated problems, don't expect instant results.

If you suspect night noise will be a problem (if, for instance, your room is over a noisy café), ask for a quieter room in the back or on an upper floor. To guard against theft in your room, keep valuables out of sight. Some rooms come with a safe, and other hotels have safes at the front desk. I've never bothered using one.

Checkout can pose problems if surprise charges pop up on

PRACTICALITIES

From:	rick@ricksteves.com
Sent:	Today
To:	info@hotelcentral.com
Subject:	Reservation request for 19-22 July

Dear Hotel Central,

I would like to reserve a room for 2 people for 3 nights, arriving 19 July and departing 22 July. If possible, I would like a quiet room with a double bed and private bathroom inside the room.

Please let me know if you have a room available and the price.

Thank you!
Rick Steves

for smaller family-run places. Be warned that cancellation policies can be strict; read the fine print or ask about these before you book. Internet deals may require prepayment, with no refunds for cancellations.

Reconfirming a Reservation: Always call or email to reconfirm your room reservation a few days in advance. For *dhomatia* (privately rented rooms) or very small hotels, I call again on my day of arrival to tell my host what time I expect to get there (especially important if arriving late—after 17:00).

Phoning: For tips on calling hotels overseas, see page 486.

your bill. If you settle your bill the afternoon before you leave, you'll have time to discuss and address any points of contention (before 19:00, when the night shift usually arrives).

Above all, keep a positive attitude. Remember, you're on vacation. If your hotel is a disappointment, spend more time out enjoying the city you came to see.

Dhomatia (Rooms)

Rooms in private homes (similar to B&Bs, called *dhomatia/* ΔΩΜΑΤΙΑ/δωμάτια in Greece) offer double the cultural intimacy for a good deal less than most hotel rooms. You'll usually have air-conditioning, your own bathroom, and a minifridge, but expect simple, stripped-down rooms, and little or nothing in the way of a public lounge. Hosts generally speak English and are interesting conversationalists. Your stay probably won't include breakfast, but you'll have access to a kitchen.

Local TIs may have lists of *dhomatia* and can book a room for

Keep Cool

If you're visiting Greece in the summer, an air-conditioned room can be a godsend. Most air-conditioners have similar symbols and features: fan icon (click to toggle through wind power, from light to gale); louver icon (choose steady airflow or waves); snowflake and sunshine icons (cold air or heat, depending on season); clock ("O" setting: run X hours before turning off; "I" setting: wait X hours to start); and the temperature control (21 or 22 degrees Celsius is comfortable; also see the thermometer diagram on page 516). When you leave your room for the day, turning off the air-conditioning is good form.

you, but you'll save money by booking direct with the *dhomatia* listed in this book.

Hostels

A hostel provides cheap dorm beds where you sleep alongside strangers for about $25 per night. Travelers of any age are welcome if they don't mind dorm-style accommodations and meeting other travelers. Most hostels offer kitchen facilities, guest computers, Wi-Fi, and a self-service laundry. Nowadays, concerned about bedbugs, hostels are likely to provide all bedding, including sheets. Family and private rooms may be available on request.

Independent hostels tend to be easygoing, colorful, and informal (no membership required); www.hostelworld.com is the standard way backpackers search and book hostels, but also try www.hostelz.com and www.hostels.com.

Official hostels are part of Hostelling International (HI) and share an online booking site (www.hihostels.com). HI hostels typically require that you either have a membership card or pay extra per night.

OTHER ACCOMMODATION OPTIONS

Renting an apartment, house, or villa can be a fun and cost-effective way to go local. Websites such as Booking.com, Airbnb, VRBO, and FlipKey let you browse properties and correspond directly with European property owners or managers.

Airbnb and Roomorama also list rooms in private homes. Beds range from air-mattress-in-living-room basic to plush-B&B-suite posh. If you want a place to sleep that's free, Couchsurfing.org is a vagabond's alternative to Airbnb. It lists millions of outgoing members, who host fellow "surfers" in their homes.

Eating

Greek food is simple...and simply delicious. Unlike the French or the Italians, who are forever experimenting to perfect an intricate

cuisine, the Greeks found an easy formula and stick with it—and it rarely misses. The four Greek food groups are olives (and olive oil), salty feta cheese, ripe tomatoes, and crispy phyllo dough. Virtually every dish you'll have here is built on a foundation of these four tasty building blocks.

When restaurant-hunting, choose a spot filled with locals, not the place with the big neon signs boasting, "We Speak English and Accept Credit Cards." Venturing even a block or two off the main drag leads to higher-quality food for a better price.

Menus are usually written in both Greek and English. Many tavernas will have a display case showing what they've been cooking for the day, and it's perfectly acceptable to ask for a look and point to the dish you want. This is a good way to make some friends, sample a variety of dishes, get what you want (or at least know what you're getting), and have a truly memorable meal. Be brave.

Smoking is banned in enclosed spaces, such as restaurants and bars. As a result, many smokers occupy outdoor tables—often that's where you'll want to sit too. Despite the law, many bars and some restaurants allow smoking inside, too.

Restaurant hours can be informal. While the opening times I've listed are reasonably reliable, closing times often depend on how busy a place is—if you arrive too late on a slow day, you may find the place shuttered.

If a tourist complains about Greek food, they'll usually say something like, "It was fish with heads and the same salads every day." Remember that eating in a foreign land is sightseeing for your taste buds. Greece has local specialties that are good, memorable, or both. At least once, seek out and eat or drink the notorious "gross" specialties: ouzo, eggplant, fish eggs, octopus, and so on. You've heard references to them all your life—now's your chance to actually experience what everyone's talking about. *Kali orexi! (Bon appétit!)*

TYPES OF RESTAURANTS

Greeks like to eat late: Dine at 18:00, and you'll be surrounded by other tourists; stick around until 21:00, and they'll all have been

The Good and Bad of Online Reviews

User-generated travel review websites—such as TripAdvisor, Booking.com, and Yelp—have quickly become a huge player in the travel industry. These sites give you access to actual reports—good and bad—from travelers who have experienced the hotel, restaurant, tour, or attraction.

My hotelier friends in Europe are in awe of these sites' influence. Small hoteliers who want to stay in business have no choice but to work with review sites—which often charge fees for good placement or photos, and tack on commissions if users book through the site instead of directly with the hotel.

While these sites work hard to weed out bogus users, my hunch is that a significant percentage of reviews are posted by friends or enemies of the business being reviewed. I've even seen hotels "bribe" guests (for example, offer a free breakfast) in exchange for a positive review. Also, review sites are uncurated and can become an echo chamber, with one or two flashy businesses camped out atop the ratings while better, more affordable, and more authentic alternatives sit ignored farther down the list. (For example, I find review sites' restaurant recommendations skew to very touristy, obvious options.) And you can't always give credence to the negative reviews: Different people have different expectations.

Remember that a user-generated review is based on the experience of one person. That person likely stayed at one hotel and ate at a few restaurants, and doesn't have much of a basis for comparison. A guidebook is the work of a trained researcher who has exhaustively visited many alternatives to assess their relative value. I recently checked out some top-rated TripAdvisor listings in various towns; when stacked up against their competitors, some are gems, while just as many are duds.

Both types of information have their place, and in many ways, they're complementary. If a hotel or restaurant is well reviewed in a guidebook or two and also gets good ratings on one of these sites, it's likely a winner.

replaced by locals. Especially in cities, popular restaurants tend to stay open until midnight or even past that.

When you sit down, you'll be asked if you want a basket of (generally fresh, good) bread, often with your napkins and flatware tucked inside. You'll pay a bread and cover charge of about €0.50-1 (usually noted clearly on the menu). A small dessert (that you didn't order) may appear at the end of your restaurant meal—often a tiny pastry, candied fruit, or shot of grappa. It's included in the price of your meal. You are welcome to linger as late as you want—don't feel pressured to eat quickly and turn over the table.

In addition to the traditional Greek restaurant *(estiatorio)*, you'll also encounter these places:

Taverna: Common, rustic neighborhood restaurant with a smaller menu, slinging the Greek favorites. These tend to be cheaper, to cater to locals' budgets.

Mezedopolio: Eatery specializing in small plates/appetizers/ *mezedes.*

Ouzerie: Bar that makes ouzo, often selling high-quality *mezedes*—or even meals—to go along with it.

If you're looking for fast food, in addition to the usual international chains (McDonald's and Starbucks), there are some Greek versions. Grigoris Coffee Right is the local version of Starbucks, and Goody's is the Greek take on McDonald's. Everest is open 24/7, selling sandwiches and savory pies to go.

Tipping: Tipping is an issue only at restaurants that have table service. If you order your food at a counter, don't tip. At Greek restaurants that have waitstaff, service is generally included, although it's common to round up the bill after a good meal (about 10 percent; so, for an €18.50 meal, pay €20). It's considered bad form to leave a single euro, though; if a bill is €10, leave a €2 tip.

GREEK CUISINE

Although the Greeks don't like to admit it, their cuisine has a lot in common with Turkish food, including many of the same dishes. (This is partly because they share a similar climate, and partly because Greece was under the Ottoman Empire for nearly 400 years.) Some names—such as moussaka—come directly from Turkish. You'll find traces of Italian influences as well, such as *pastitsio*, the "Greek lasagna."

My favorite fast, cheap, and filling Greek snack is souvlaki pita, a tasty shish kebab wrapped in flat bread. Souvlaki stands are all over Greece (see sidebar on page 175). On the islands, eat fresh seafood. Don't miss the creamy yogurt with honey. Feta cheese salads and flaky nut-and-honey baklava are two other tasty treats. Dunk your bread into *tzatziki* (TZAHT-zee-kee), the ubiquitous and refreshing cucumber-and-yogurt dip. (Tourists often call it *tzitziki*, which sounds like the Greek word for crickets—a mispronunciation which endlessly amuses local waiters.)

Here are more flavors to seek out during your time in Greece.

Olives

As you'll quickly gather when you pass endless tranquil olive groves on your drive through the countryside, olives are a major staple of Greek food—both the olives themselves and the oil they produce. Connoisseurs can distinguish as many varieties of olives as there are grapes for wine, but they fall into two general categories: those for eating and those for making oil.

Greeks are justifiably proud of their olive oil: Their country is the third-largest producer in the European Union, and they consume more olive oil per capita than any other Mediterranean nation—almost seven gallons per person a year. Locals say that the taste is shaped both by the variety and the terrain where the olives are grown. Olive oils from the Peloponnese, for example, are supposed to be robust with grassy or herbaceous overtones. Pay attention, and you'll notice the differences as you travel. Common, edible Greek olives include the following:

Amfissa: Found in both black and green varieties, grown near Delphi. These are rounder and mellower than other varieties.

Halkithiki: Large, green olives from northern Greece, often stuffed with pimento, sun-dried tomato, feta cheese, or other delicacies.

Kalamata: Purple and almond-shaped, the best-known variety. These come from the southern Peloponnese and are cured in a red-wine vinegar brine.

Throubes: Black, wrinkled olives, usually from the island of Thassos, that stay on the tree until fully ripe. Dry-cured, they have an intense, salty taste and chewy texture.

Tsakistes: Green olives grown mainly in Attica (near Athens) that are cracked with a mallet or cut with a knife before being steeped in water and then brine. After curing, they are marinated in garlic and lemon wedges or herbs.

Cheese

Feta: Protected by EU regulations, it's made with sheep's milk, although a small percentage of goat's milk can be added (but never cow's milk). Feta comes in many variations—some are soft, moist, and rather mild; others are sour, hard, and crumbly.

Graviera: A hard cheese usually made in Crete from sheep's milk, it tastes sweet and nutty, almost like a fine Swiss cheese.

Kasseri: The most popular Greek cheese after feta, it's a mild, yellow cheese made from either sheep's or goat's milk.

Pies

Flaky phyllo-dough pastries (*pita,* not to be confused with pita bread) are another staple of Greek cuisine. These can be ordered as a starter in a restaurant or purchased from a bakery for a tasty bite on the run. They can be made out of just about anything, but the most common are ***spanakopita*** (spinach), ***tiropita*** (cheese), ***kreatopita*** (beef or pork), ***meletzanitopita*** (eggplant), and ***bougatsa*** (with a sweet cream filling).

Salads and Starters (Mezedes)

Mezedes (meh-ZEH-dehs), known internationally as *meze,* are a great way to sample several tasty Greek dishes. This "small plates" approach is common and easy—instead of ordering a starter and a main dish per person, get two or three starters and one main dish to split.

Almost anything in Greece can be served as a small-plate "starter" (including several items listed in other sections here—olives, cheeses, and main dishes), but these are most common:

Bekri meze: Literally "drunkard's snack"—chunks of chicken, pork, or beef cooked slowly with wine, cloves, cinnamon, bay leaves, and olive oil.

Dolmathes: Stuffed grape (or cabbage) leaves filled with either meat or rice and served hot or cold.

Greek salad (a.k.a. *horiatiki,* "village" salad): Ripe tomatoes chopped up just so, rich feta cheese (usually in a long, thick slab that you break apart), olives, and onions, all drenched with olive oil. You'll find yourself eating this combination again and again—yet somehow, it never gets old.

Keftedes: Small meatballs, often seasoned with mint, onion, parsley, and sometimes ouzo.

Melitzanosalata: Cooked eggplant with the consistency of mashed potatoes, usually well-seasoned and delicious.

Pantzarosalata: Beet salad dressed with olive oil and vinegar.

Papoutsaki: Eggplant "slippers" filled with ground beef and cheese.

Roasted red peppers: Soft and flavorful, often drizzled with olive oil.

Saganaki: Cooked cheese, often breaded, sometimes grilled and sometimes fried, occasionally flambéed.

Soutzoukakia: Meatballs with spicy tomato sauce.

Taramosalata: Smoky, pink, fish-roe mixture with the consistency of mashed potatoes, used as a dip for bread or vegetables.

Tirokafteri: Feta cheese that's been softened and mixed with white pepper to give it some kick, served either as a spread or stuffed inside roasted red peppers.

Tzatziki: A pungent and thick sauce of yogurt, cucumber, and garlic. It seems like a condiment but is often ordered as a starter, then eaten as a salad or used to complement other foods.

Soups

Summertime visitors might be disappointed not to find much soup on the menu (including *avgolemono,* the delicious egg, lemon, and rice soup). Soup is considered a winter dish and is almost impossible to find in warm weather. If available, Greek chicken soup *(kotosoupa)* is very tasty. *Kremithosoupa* is the Greek version of French

PRACTICALITIES

onion soup, and *kakavia* is a famous fish soup often compared to bouillabaisse.

Main Dishes

Here are some popular meat and seafood dishes you'll likely see.

Meats

Arnaki kleftiko: Slow-cooked lamb, usually wrapped in phyllo dough or parchment paper. Legend says it was created by bandits who needed to cook without the telltale signs of smoke or fire. (Baked fish, and other meats, may also be served *kleftiko*.)

Gyros: Literally "turn," a gyro is not a type of meat but a way of preparing it—stacked on a metal skewer and vertically slow-roasted on a rotisserie, then shaved off in slices. In Greece it's usually made from chicken or pork, and often served wrapped in a pita, making a handy to-go sandwich.

Moussaka: A classic casserole with layers of minced meat, eggplant, and potatoes and a topping of cheesy Béchamel sauce or egg custard.

Pastitsio: A layered baked dish called the "Greek lasagna." Ground meat is sandwiched between two layers of pasta with an egg-custard or Béchamel topping.

Souvlaki: Pork or chicken cooked on a skewer, often eaten with pita bread or a rice pilaf.

Stifado: Beef stew with onions, tomatoes, and spices such as cinnamon and cloves. It was traditionally made with rabbit *(kouneli)*.

Fish and Seafood

Barbounia: Red mullet that is usually grilled or fried and is always expensive. These small fish are bony, but the flesh melts in your mouth.

Gavros: An appetizer similar to anchovies. Squeeze lemon luxuriously all over them, and eat everything but the wispy little tails.

Htapothi: Octopus, often marinated and grilled, then drizzled with olive oil and lemon juice.

Psari plaki: Fish baked in the oven with tomatoes and onions.

Sweets

Baklava: Phyllo dough layered with nuts and honey.

Ekmek: A cake made of thin phyllo fibers soaked in honey, then topped with custard and a layer of whipped cream.

Karydopita: Honey-walnut cake made without flour.

Kataifi: Thin fibers of phyllo (like shredded wheat) layered with nuts and honey.

Loukoumades: The Greek doughnut, soaked in honey or sugar syrup.

Meli pita: Honey-cheese pie, traditionally served at Easter.

DRINKS

Wine: This is a rough land with simple wines. A local vintner told me there's no fine $50 bottle of Greek wine. I asked him, "What if you want to spend $30?" He said, "Fine, you can buy three $10 bottles."

There are two basic types of Greek wines: *retsina* (resin-flavored, rarely served) and nonresinated wines. **Retsina wine,** a post-WWII rotgut with a notorious resin flavor, has long been famous as the working man's Greek wine. It makes you want to sling a patch over one eye and say, "Arghh." The first glass is like drinking wood. The third glass is dangerous: It starts to taste good. If you drink any more, you'll smell like it the entire next day. Why resin? Way back when, Greek winemakers used pine resin to seal the amphoras that held the wine, protecting the wine from the air. Discovering that they liked the taste, the winemakers began adding resin to the wine itself.

If pine sap is not your cup of tea, there are plenty of other **wine options.** With its new generation of winemakers (many of them trained abroad), Greece is receiving more recognition for its wines. More than 300 native varietals are now grown in Greece's wine regions. About two-thirds of the wine produced in Greece is white. The best known are Savatiano (the most widely grown grape used for *retsina* and other wines), Assyrtiko (a crisp white mostly from Santorini), and Moschofilero (a dry white from the Peloponnese). Red wines include Agiorgitiko (a medium red also from the Peloponnese; one carries the name "Blood of Hercules") and Xynomavro (an intense red from Naoussa in Macedonia). Greeks also grow Cabernet Sauvignon, Merlot, Chardonnay, and other familiar varieties.

Here are a few wine terms that you may find useful: *inos* (οίνος—term for "wine" printed on bottles), *krasi* (spoken term for "wine"), *ktima* (winery or estate), *inopolio* (wine bar), *lefko* (white), *erithro* or *kokkino* (red), *xiro* (dry), *agouro* (young), *me poli soma* (full-bodied), *epitrapezio* (table wine), and O.P.A.P. (an indication of quality that tells you the wine came from one of Greece's designated wine regions).

Beer: Greeks are proud of their few local brands, including Alpha, Fix, Vergina, and Mythos.

Spirits: Beyond wine and beer, consider special Greek spirits. Cloudy, anise-flavored **ouzo,** supposedly invented by monks on Mount Athos, is worth a try even if you don't like the taste (black licorice). Similar to its Mediterranean cousins, French *pastis* and Turkish *raki,* ouzo turns from clear to milky white when you add ice or water (don't drink it straight). Greeks drink it both as an aperitif and with food. I like to sip it slowly in the early evening while sharing several *mezedes* with my travel partner. Some of the bestselling brands are Ouzo 12, Plomari Ouzo, and Sans Rival Ouzo.

Even better is **tsipouro.** Similar to Italian grappa, this brandy is distilled from leftover grape skins; it is sometimes flavored with anise. Stronger and purer than ouzo, it's best drunk with water on the rocks. Some of the best are Barbayanni, Tsilili, and Adolo.

Metaxa is to be savored after dinner. This rich, sweet, golden-colored liqueur has a brandy base blended with aged wine and a "secret" herbal mixture.

If you're traveling on the Peloponnese, try **Tentura,** a regional liqueur flavored with cloves, nutmeg, cinnamon, and citrus. It packs a spicy kick.

Coffee: All over Greece, Starbucks-style coffee houses have invaded Main Street. But in some places you can still find traditional **Greek coffee,** made with loose grounds. It's similar to Turkish coffee, but milder, as the beans are roasted at a lower temperature. Traditionally it is heated up in a small copper or brass pitcher (called a *briki*) in a tray of hot sand. When you get your coffee, let the grounds settle to the bottom of the cup, and avoid this highly caffeinated "mud" unless you want a jolt. It's usually served with a glass of water.

You can order your coffee *pikro/sketos* (bitter/plain), *metrio* (semi-sweet), or *gliko* (sweet). Most people take theirs *metrio.* Don't ask for a regular coffee, as almost nobody will understand what you mean.

Especially in the summer, cafés are filled with Greeks sipping **iced coffee** drinks. *Freddo cappuccino* (iced cappuccino) is the drink of choice, though you will also usually find the *frappé* (iced Nescafé; order it black or white—with milk), *freddo espresso* (iced espresso), and *freddo Mokka.*

Water: Water is served in bottles. It's generally cheap and rarely carbonated.

Staying Connected

Staying connected in Europe gets easier and cheaper every year. The simplest solution is to bring your own device—mobile phone, tablet, or laptop—and use it just as you would at home (following the tips on the next page, such as connecting to free Wi-Fi whenever possible). Another option is to buy a European SIM card for your mobile phone—either your US phone or one you buy in Europe. Or you can travel without a mobile device and use European landlines and computers to connect. Each of these options is described below, and you'll find even more details at www.ricksteves.

PRACTICALITIES

Tips on Internet Security

Using the Internet while traveling brings added security risks, whether you're getting online with your own device or at a public terminal using a shared network.

First, make sure that your device is running the latest version of its operating system and security software. Next, ensure that your device is password- or passcode-protected so thieves can't access your information if your device is stolen. For extra security, set passwords on apps that access key info (such as email or Facebook).

On the road, use only legitimate Wi-Fi hotspots. Ask the hotel or café staff for the specific name of their Wi-Fi network, and make sure you log on to that exact one. Hackers sometimes create a bogus hotspot with a similar or vague name (such as "Hotel Europa Free Wi-Fi"). The best Wi-Fi networks require entering a password.

Be especially cautious when checking your online banking, credit-card statements, or other personal-finance accounts. Internet security experts advise against accessing these sites while traveling. Even if you're using your own mobile device at a password-protected hotspot, any hacker who's logged on to the same network may be able see what you're doing. If you do need to log on to a banking website, use a hard-wired connection (such as an Ethernet cable in your hotel room) or a cellular network, which is safer than Wi-Fi.

Never share your credit-card number (or any other sensitive information) online unless you know that the site is secure. A secure site displays a little padlock icon, and the URL begins with *https* (instead of the usual *http*).

com/travel-tips/phones-tech. The Greek phone company is known by its initials: OTE.

USING YOUR OWN MOBILE DEVICE IN EUROPE

Without an international plan, typical rates from major service providers (AT&T, Verizon, etc.) for using your device abroad are about $1.50/minute for voice calls, 50 cents to send text messages, 5 cents to receive them, and $20 to download one megabyte of data. But at these rates, costs can add up quickly. Here are some budget tips and options.

Use free Wi-Fi whenever possible. Unless you have an unlimited-data plan, you're best off saving most of your online tasks for Wi-Fi. You can access the Internet, send texts, and even make voice calls over Wi-Fi.

Many cafés (including Starbucks and McDonald's) have hotspots for customers; look for signs offering it and ask for the Wi-Fi password when you buy something. You'll also often find

How to Dial

Many Americans are intimidated by dialing European phone numbers. You needn't be. It's simple, once you break the code.

Dialing Rules

Here are the rules for dialing, along with examples of how to call one of my recommended hotels in Athens (tel. 210-324-9737).

Dialing Internationally to Greece

Whether you're phoning from a US landline, your own mobile phone, a Skype account, or a number in another European country (e.g., Turkey to Greece), you're making an international call. Here's how to do it:

1. Dial the international access code (011 if calling from a US or Canadian phone; 00 if calling from any European phone number outside of Greece). If dialing from a mobile phone, you can enter a + in place of the international access code (press and hold the 0 key).
2. Dial the country code (30 for Greece).
3. Dial the phone number.

Examples:

- To call my recommended hotel from a US or Canadian phone, dial 011, then 30, then 210-324-9737.
- To call from any European phone number (outside of Greece),

Wi-Fi at TIs, city squares, major museums, public-transit hubs, airports, and aboard buses.

Sign up for an international plan. Most providers offer a global calling plan that cuts the per-minute cost of phone calls and texts, and a flat-fee data plan that includes a certain amount of megabytes. Your normal plan may already include international coverage (T-Mobile's does).

Before your trip, call your provider or check online to confirm that your phone will work in Europe, and research your provider's international rates. A day or two before you leave, activate the plan by calling your provider or logging on to your mobile phone account. Remember to cancel your plan (if necessary) when your trip's over.

Minimize the use of your cellular network. When you can't find Wi-Fi, you can use your cellular network—convenient but slower and potentially expensive—to connect to the Internet, text, or make voice calls. When you're done, avoid further charges by manually switching off "data roaming" or "cellular data" (in your device's Settings menu; if you don't know how to switch it off, ask your service provider or Google it). Another way to make sure you're not accidentally using data roaming is to put your device in

dial 00, then 30, then 210-324-9737.
- To call from any mobile phone (except a Greek one), dial +, then 30, then 210-324-9737.

Dialing Within Greece

To make a domestic call (either from a Greek mobile phone or landline, such as a hotel-room phone), simply dial the phone number. Although Greece technically has "area codes," in practice you need to dial all 10 digits, whether you're calling from across the street or across the country.

Example: To call my recommended Athens hotel from any Greek landline or mobile phone, dial 210-324-9737.

Calling from any European Country to the US

To call the US or Canada from Europe (either from a mobile phone or landline), dial 00 (Europe's international access code), 1 (US/Canada country code), and the phone number, including area code. If calling from a mobile phone, you can enter a + instead of 00.

Example: To call my office in Edmonds, Washington, from anywhere in Europe, I dial 00-1-425-771-8303; or, from a mobile phone, +1-425-771-8303.

"airplane" or "flight" mode (which also disables phone calls and texts, as well as data), and then turn on Wi-Fi as needed.

Don't use your cellular network for bandwidth-gobbling tasks, such as Skyping, downloading apps, and watching YouTube—save these for when you're on Wi-Fi. Using a navigation app such as Google Maps can take lots of data, so use this sparingly.

Limit automatic updates. By default, your device is constantly checking for a data connection and updating apps. It's smart to disable these features so they'll only update when you're on Wi-Fi, and to change your device's email settings from "auto-retrieve" to "manual" (or from "push" to "fetch").

It's also a good idea to keep track of your data usage. On your device's menu, look for "cellular data usage" or "mobile data" and reset the counter at the start of your trip.

Use Skype or other calling/messaging apps for cheaper calls and texts. Certain apps let you make voice or video calls or send texts over the Internet for free or cheap. If you're bringing a tablet or laptop, you can also use them for voice calls and texts. All you have to do is log on to a Wi-Fi network, then contact any of your friends or family members who are also online and signed into the same service. You can make voice and video calls using Skype,

Phoning Cheat Sheet

Just smile and dial, using these rules.

Calling a European number

- **From a mobile phone** (whether you're in the US or in Europe): Dial + (press and hold 0), then country code and number*
- **From a US/Canadian number:** Dial 011, then country code and number*
- **From a different European country** (e.g., German number to French number): Dial 00, then country code and number*
- **Within the same European country** (e.g., German number to another German number): Dial the number as printed, including initial 0 if there is one

* Drop initial 0 (if present) from phone number in all countries except Italy

Calling the US or Canada from Europe

Dial 00, then 1 (country code for US/Canada), then area code and number; on mobile phones, enter + in place of 00

Country	Country Code	Country	Country Code
Austria	43	Italy	39 [2]
Belgium	32	Latvia	371
Bosnia-Herzegovina	387	Montenegro	382
Croatia	385	Morocco	212
Czech Republic	420	Netherlands	31
Denmark	45	Norway	47
Estonia	372	Poland	48
Finland	358	Portugal	351
France	33	Russia	7 [3]
Germany	49	Slovakia	421
Gibraltar	350	Slovenia	386
Great Britain & N. Ireland	44	Spain	34
Greece	30	Sweden	46
Hungary	36 [1]	Switzerland	41
Ireland	353	Turkey	90

[1] For long-distance calls within Hungary, dial 06, then the area code and number.
[2] When making international calls to Italy, do not drop the initial 0 from the phone number.
[3] For long-distance calls within Russia, dial 8, then the area code and number. To call the US or Canada from Russia, dial 8, then 10, then 1, then the area code and number.

Viber, FaceTime, and Google+ Hangouts. If the connection is bad, try making an audio-only call.

You can also make voice calls from your device to telephones worldwide for just a few cents per minute using Skype, Viber, or Hangouts if you prebuy credit.

To text for free over Wi-Fi, try apps like Google+ Hangouts, WhatsApp, Viber, and Facebook Messenger. Apple's iMessage connects with other Apple users, but make sure you're on Wi-Fi to avoid data charges.

USING A EUROPEAN SIM CARD IN A MOBILE PHONE

This option works well for those who want to make a lot of voice calls at cheap local rates. Either buy a phone in Europe (as little as $40 from mobile-phone shops anywhere), or bring an "unlocked" US phone (check with your carrier about unlocking it). With an unlocked phone, you can replace the original SIM card (the micro-chip that stores info about the phone) with one that will work with a European provider.

In Europe, buy a European SIM card. Inserted into your phone, this card gives you a European phone number—and European rates. SIM cards are sold at mobile-phone shops, department-store electronics counters, some newsstands, and even at vending machines. Costing about $5-10, they usually include about that much prepaid calling credit, with no contract and no commitment. You can still use your phone's Wi-Fi function to get online. To get a SIM card that also includes data costs (including roaming), figure on paying $15-30 for one month of data within the country you bought it. This can be cheaper than data roaming through your home provider. To get the best rates, buy a new SIM card whenever you arrive in a new country.

I like to buy SIM cards at a mobile-phone shop where there's a clerk to help explain the options and brands. I've used the Ger-manos (ΓΕΡΜΑΜΟΣ) electronics stores, which have staff who speak English, to buy a SIM card and help me switch my US mo-bile phone to a Greek number. They're all over Greece, including at the Athens airport. Certain brands—including Lebara and Ly-camobile, both of which operate in multiple European countries—are reliable and economical. Ask the clerk to help you insert your SIM card, set it up, and show you how to use it. In some countries you'll be required to register the SIM card with your passport as an antiterrorism measure (which may mean you can't use the phone for the first hour or two).

When you run out of credit, you can top it up at newsstands, tobacco shops, mobile-phone stores, or many other businesses (look for your SIM card's logo in the window), or online.

USING LANDLINES AND COMPUTERS IN EUROPE

It's easy to travel in Europe without a mobile device. You can check email or browse websites using public computers and Internet cafés, and make calls from your hotel room and/or public phones.

Phones in your **hotel room** can be inexpensive for local calls and calls made with cheap international phone cards (sold at many post offices, newsstands, street kiosks, and tobacco shops). You'll either get a prepaid card with a toll-free number and a scratch-to-reveal PIN code, or a code printed on a receipt; to make a call, dial the toll-free number, follow the prompts, enter the code, then dial your number.

Most hotels charge a fee for placing local and "toll-free" calls, as well as long-distance or international calls—ask for the rates before you dial. Since you're never charged for receiving calls, it's better to have someone from the US call you in your room.

You'll see **public pay phones** in post offices and train stations. The phones generally come with multilingual instructions, and work with insertable phone cards (*Telekarta* [THΛEKAPTA] sold at post offices, newsstands, etc.) To use the card, take the phone off the hook, insert the card, wait for a dial tone, and dial away. With the exception of Great Britain, each European country has its own insertable phone card—so your Greek card won't work in a Turkish phone.

Cheap **call shops,** often located in train-station neighborhoods, advertise low international rates. Before making your call, be completely clear on the rates (e.g., if there's a charge per unit, find out how long a unit is).

It's always possible to find public computers: at your hotel (many have one in their lobby for guests to use), or at an Internet café or library (ask your hotelier or the TI for the nearest location). If typing on a European keyboard, use the "Alt Gr" key to the right of the space bar to insert the extra symbol that appears on some keys. If you can't locate a special character (such as @), simply copy it from a Web page and paste it into your email message.

MAIL

You can mail one package per day to yourself worth up to $200 duty-free from Europe to the US (mark it "personal purchases"). If you're sending a gift to someone, mark it "unsolicited gift." For details, visit www.cbp.gov and search for "Know Before You Go."

The Greek postal service works fine, but for quick transatlantic delivery (in either direction), consider a service such as DHL (www.dhl.com). Get stamps for postcards and letters at the neighborhood post office, newsstands within fancy hotels, and some mini-marts and card shops.

Transportation

For connecting most of the destinations in this book (except the islands of Hydra, Mykonos, and Santorini), you have two options: rental car or public bus. (Train service is minimal and not worth your while.)

A **rental car** allows you to come and go on your own schedule, and make a beeline between destinations. Outside of congested Athens, roads are uncrowded, and parking is often free. However, driving in Greece can be stressful, as Greek drivers tackle the roads with a kind of anything-goes, Wild West abandon. And it's more expensive than the bus. But if you're a confident driver, the convenience of driving in Greece trumps the hassles of bus transport.

Greece's network of public **buses** is affordable and will get you most anywhere you want to go. Unfortunately, it's not user-friendly. Particularly outside of Athens, the frequency can be sparse and schedules are hard to nail down. You'd need to allow plenty of time, expect delays, and pack lots of patience to visit all of my recommended destinations.

BUSES

Greek buses are cheap and the fleet is clean, modern, and air-conditioned, but the bus system can be frustrating. Athens has decent bus service to popular destinations such as Delphi, Nafplio, and the port town of Piraeus, but smaller destinations on the Peloponnese are connected by only one or two buses a day.

All buses are run by a central company (KTEL, or ΚΤΕΛ in Greek), but the local offices don't cooperate with each other—each one sets its own schedules, and they often don't coordinate well. Specific bus schedules can be very difficult to pin down, even for buses leaving from the town you're in. (Forget about getting bus schedules for other Greek towns.) Local TIs, where they exist, are unlikely to have the information you need. Don't hesitate to ask your hotelier for help—they're used to it.

KTEL has no helpful website or information office for the entire Greek bus system, but there is a list of local phone numbers at www.ktelbus.com (you'll need to know the name of the province where you are traveling). The KTEL Athens site, www. ktelattikis.gr, is in Greek only, but Matt Barrett's website has schedules for long-distance buses from and to Athens (www. athensguide.com). Or try this helpful unofficial website in English: http://livingingreece.gr (under "Best of..." click on "KTEL Buses of Greece").

Particularly on the Peloponnese, where your journeys likely will require a transfer (or multiple transfers), you frequently won't be able to get the information for the full route from the bus station

PRACTICALITIES

Public Transportation in Greece

To Igoumenitsa

Delphi

Antirrio

Ag. Nikolaos

Rio

Aigio

To Corfu & Italy

Patra

Diakofto

Vouraikos Gorge

COG RAILWAY

Kalavryta

Killini

PELOPONNESE
(PELOPONNISOS)

Pyrgos

Katakolo

Olympia

Tripoli

Sparta

Kalamata

Messenian Gulf

Kardamyli

Ionian Sea

Gythio

Areopoli

MANI PENINSULA

Laconian Gulf

Vathia

10 Kilometers

10 Miles

····· Rail
- - - Bus
········ Boat

at your starting point. For example, to go from Nafplio to Monem-vasia, you'll change at Tripoli, then Sparta. The Nafplio bus station can give you details for the leg to Tripoli, but can't tell you anything about the rest of the journey.

Before you get on a bus, ask the ticket-seller and the conductor explicitly if there are transfers—they might not volunteer these details otherwise. Then pay attention (and maybe even follow the route on a map) to be sure you don't miss your change.

BOATS

Greece has been a great seafaring nation since the days of Odysseus. Today the country's islands are connected to Athens' port (Piraeus, see the Athens Connections chapter for details) and to one another by a variety of ferries, ranging from hulking, slow-moving car ferries to sleek, speedy catamarans. While the decentralized ferry system isn't as straightforward or efficient as many travelers would like it to be, it's still fairly fast and easy to get around by boat in Greece.

Buying Tickets: In peak season (especially July-Aug), some popular connections—such as Piraeus-Hydra—can sell out early; book at least a week in advance. Advance tickets also make sense if you'll be setting sail soon after your arrival in Greece. Outside of peak season, it's generally safe to purchase your ticket from a travel agency or ferry office a day or two before your crossing. Buying from a travel agency can be the easiest way to understand your options, and costs no more than buying online, but beware that some agencies may try to upsell you. Ferries are comfortable; there's no need to spring for business-class seats.

Greek ferry services are operated by multiple companies without a central information service. Good websites for researching connections include www.danae.gr/ferries-Greece.asp, www.greekferries.gr, and www.gtp.gr. Some ferry companies post only their current schedule—if you're looking online in January, you may not find sailing times for June. If you buy tickets online, you'll need to convert your reservation into an actual ticket. Some ferry companies let you do this online through Web check-in (they'll send you an eticket). Otherwise, you'll need to go to a ticket office or travel agency before the boat trip to pick up a paper ticket (you'll need your passport).

Before you buy, make sure you're clear on the ferry company's refund and exchange policies. Since schedules can flex with demand, confirm sailing time a day ahead.

Possible Delays or Cancellations: Smaller high-speed ferries (such as the Hellenic Seaways' "Flying Cat" and SeaJet's Super-Jet or SeaJet2) can be affected by high winds and other inclement weather. Larger ferries, such as the Hellenic Seaways Highspeed,

Ferry Companies in Greece

Company	Phone Number	Website address
Hellenic Seaways	210-419-9000	hellenicseaways.gr
Blue Star Ferries	210-891-9800	bluestarferries.com
ANEK Lines	210-419-7470	anek.gr
Aegean Speed	210-969-0950	aegeanspeedlines.gr
NEL Lines	281-034-6185	ferries.gr/nel
SeaJets	210-412-1001	seajets.gr
Minoan Lines	210-414-5700	minoan.gr
Kallisti Ferries	210-422-2972	ferries.gr/kallisti-ferries

PRACTICALITIES

SeaJet Champion Jet, and the Blue Star ferries are slower, more stable, and less likely to be canceled. In general, cancellations are rare but possible in summer, and more common off-season. If a sailing is canceled, the ferry company will contact you to rebook (for this reason, it's essential to provide a telephone number when you book). Usually you can go later that same day, but it's possible (though rare) to get stranded overnight. Even if the sea is rough, the ships may still run—but the ride can be very rocky. If you're prone to seasickness, be prepared.

Boarding the Ferry: If a place has several ports (such as Mykonos), make sure you know which port your boat leaves from. While ferry companies tell passengers to be at the dock 30 minutes before the boat leaves, most locals amble over to the dock about 10 minutes ahead. The sole advantage to turning up early is the chance to grab a better seat, which only makes a difference if your ferry has open seating, such as the Blue Star ferries (although even if there are assigned seats, they're often ignored). Don't be surprised if boats aren't on time—soak up some sun at the dock while you wait.

On the Ferry: Greece's ferries are very relaxing and can be a lot cheaper than flying, though they take longer. On big, slow-moving car ferries, you can sit outside and watch the islands slide by—but on the fast boats you'll be sitting inside, peering through saltwater-spattered windows.

Bigger ferries move slowly but can run in almost any weather. While the number of cars allowed onboard is limited, they can accommodate about 1,000-2,000 walk-on passengers, and tend to cost less. The smallest, fastest ferries are typically catamarans carrying only about 300-400 passengers, so they are more likely to sell out. While small boats are time-efficient, they have to slow down (or sometimes can't run at all) in bad weather. On some islands, such as Mykonos, bigger ferries arrive at a different point (usually

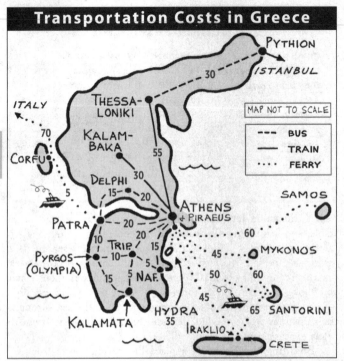

Transportation Costs in Greece

MAP NOT TO SCALE

- - - BUS
—— TRAIN
···· FERRY

farther from the main town) than the smaller boats (which may drop you right in the town center).

You may be able to stow your luggage on a rack on the boarding level of your boat; otherwise you'll haul it up several flights of stairs to the passenger decks. Ferries of all sizes typically are equipped with WCs and charging outlets; many offer Wi-Fi (usually for a fee and with spotty service). You can buy food and drinks on most boats. It's not too expensive, but it's usually not top quality, either. Bring your own snacks or a picnic instead.

RENTING A CAR

If you're renting a car in Greece, bring your driver's license. You're also technically required to have an International Driving Permit—an official translation of your driver's license (sold at your local AAA office for $15 plus the cost of two passport-type photos; see www.aaa.com). While that's the letter of the law, I generally rent cars without having this permit. How this is enforced varies from country to country: Get advice from your car-rental company.

Rental companies require you to be at least 21 years old and to have held your license for one year. Drivers under age 25 may incur a young-driver surcharge, and some rental companies do not rent to anyone 75 or older. If you're considered too young or old, look into leasing (covered later), which has less-stringent age restrictions.

Research car rentals before you go. It's cheaper to arrange most car rentals from the US. Consider several companies to compare rates.

Most of the major US rental agencies (including Avis, Budget, Enterprise, Hertz, and Thrifty) have offices throughout Europe. Also consider the two major Europe-based agencies, Europcar and Sixt. For a friendly local car-rental company in Athens, consider Swift/Avanti (see page 204; www.greektravel.com/swift). It can be cheaper to use a consolidator, such as Auto Europe/Kemwel (www.autoeurope.com) or Europe by Car (www.europebycar.com), which compares rates at several companies to get you the best deal—but because you're working with a middleman, it's especially important to ask in advance about add-on fees and restrictions.

Always read the fine print carefully for add-on charges—such as one-way drop-off fees, airport surcharges, or mandatory insurance policies—that aren't included in the "total price." You may need to query rental agents pointedly to find out your actual cost.

For the best deal, rent by the week with unlimited mileage. To save money on fuel, you can request a diesel car. I normally rent the smallest, least-expensive model with a stick shift (generally cheaper than an automatic). Almost all rentals are manual by default, so if you need an automatic, request one in advance; be aware that these cars are usually larger models (not as maneuverable on narrow winding roads). Because of the size of Greek roads (and Greek parking spaces), it's a good idea to rent a small vehicle.

Figure on paying roughly $230 for a one-week rental. Allow extra for supplemental insurance, fuel, tolls, and parking. For trips of three weeks or more, leasing can save you money on insurance and taxes. Be warned that international trips—say, picking up in Athens and dropping in Istanbul—while efficient, can be expensive (it depends partly on distance).

As a rule, always tell your car-rental company up front exactly which countries you'll be entering. Some companies levy extra insurance fees for trips taken in certain countries with certain types of cars (such as BMWs, Mercedes, and convertibles). Double-check with your rental agent that you have all the documentation you need before you drive off (especially if you're crossing borders into non-Schengen countries, such as Turkey, where you might need to present proof of insurance).

Picking Up Your Car: Big companies have offices in most cities; ask whether they can pick you up at your hotel. Small local rental companies can be cheaper but aren't as flexible.

Compare pickup costs (downtown can be less expensive than the airport) and explore drop-off options. Always check the hours

PRACTICALITIES

PRACTICALITIES

of the location you choose: Many rental offices close from midday Saturday until Monday morning and, in smaller towns, at lunchtime.

When selecting a location, don't trust the agency's description of "downtown" or "city center." In some cases, a "downtown" branch can be on the outskirts of the city—a long, costly taxi ride from the center. Before choosing, plug the addresses into a mapping website. You may find that the "train station" location is handier. But returning a car at a big-city train station or downtown agency can be tricky; get precise details on the car drop-off location and hours, and allow ample time to find it.

When you pick up the rental car, check it thoroughly and make sure any damage is noted on your rental agreement. In Greece, your rental car is likely to come pre-scratched and dented for you (which is actually a plus, in that you're unlikely to get hassled for tiny dings in the vicinity of pre-existing ones). Find out how your car's lights, turn signals, wipers, radio, and fuel cap function, and know what kind of fuel the car takes (diesel vs. unleaded). When you return the car, make sure the agent verifies its condition with you. Some drivers take pictures of the returned vehicle as proof of its condition.

Navigation Options

When renting a car in Europe, for a digital navigator you can use the mapping app that's already on your cellular-connected device, or download a mapping app that's designed to be used offline. As an alternative, you could rent a GPS device (or bring your own GPS device from home).

To use your mobile device for pulling up maps or routes on the fly, for turn-by-turn directions, or for traffic updates, you'll need to go online—so it's smart to get an international data plan (see page 486). But just using GPS to locate your position on a map doesn't require an Internet connection (and therefore doesn't require Wi-Fi or cellular data). This means that once you have the map in your phone, you can navigate with it all day long without incurring data-roaming charges.

Using Your Device's Mapping App: The mapping app you use at home (such as Google Maps or Apple Maps) will work just as well for navigating Europe.

The most economical approach is to download information while you're on Wi-Fi (at your hotel, before setting out for the day). Google Maps' "save map to use offline" feature is useful for this, allowing you to view a map when you're offline (though you can't search for an address or get directions). Apple Maps doesn't offer a save-for-offline feature, though it does automatically cache (save) certain data. So if you bring up the maps you need or plan your route while on Wi-Fi in the morning, the Apple Maps app may end up caching those maps and not using data roaming much during the day.

No matter which app you use, view the maps in standard view (not satellite view) to limit data use. And consider bringing a car charger: Even offline, mapping services gobble up battery life.

Using a Third-Party Offline Mapping App: A number of well-designed apps allow you much of the convenience of online maps without any costly data demands. City Maps 2Go is popular; OffMaps and Navfree also offer good, zoomable offline maps—similar to Google Maps—for much of Europe. You need to be online to download the app, but once that's done, the maps are accessible anywhere (note that you won't get turn-by-turn directions, which require a data connection).

Using GPS: Some drivers prefer using a dedicated GPS unit—not only to avoid using cellular data, but because a stand-alone GPS can be easier to operate (important if you're driving solo). The downside: It's expensive—around $10-30 per day. Your car's GPS unit may only come loaded with maps for its home country—if you need additional maps, ask. And make sure your device's language is set to English. If you have a portable GPS device at home, you can take that instead, but you'll need to buy and download European maps before your trip. This option is far less expensive than renting.

Car Insurance Options

When you rent a car, you are liable for a very high deductible, sometimes equal to the entire value of the car. Limit your financial risk with one of these three options: Buy Collision Damage Waiver (CDW) coverage with a low or zero deductible from the car-rental company, get coverage through your credit card (free, if your card automatically includes zero-deductible coverage), or get collision insurance as part of a larger travel-insurance policy.

Basic **CDW** includes a very high deductible (typically $1,000-1,500). Though each rental company has its own variation, basic CDW costs $10-30 a day (figure roughly 30 percent extra) and reduces your liability, but does not eliminate it. When you reserve or pick up the car, you'll be offered the chance to "buy down" the deductible to zero (for an additional $10-30/day; this is sometimes called "super CDW" or "zero-deductible coverage").

If you opt for **credit-card coverage,** there's a catch. You'll technically have to decline all coverage offered by the car-rental company, which means they can place a hold on your card (which can be up to the full value of the car). In case of damage, it can be time-consuming to resolve the charges with your credit-card company. Before you decide on this option, quiz your credit-card company about how it works.

Driving in Greece

To Meteora
140m
3.75h

To Igoumenitsa
165m • 4.5h

80m • 2h

Delphi

Ag. Nikolaos

Aigio

To Corfu & Italy

Patra

85m • 1.75h

60m • 1.5h

Killini

PELOPONNESE
(PELOPONNISOS)

20m
.5h

Pyrgos

Olympia

75m • 2.5h

45m • .75h

35m • .75h

40m • 1h

Tripoli

m = miles
h = hours

75m • 2h

60m • 1h

35m • 1h

Ionian

Sea

35m • 1.5h

Mystras

Sparta

Kalamata

24m
1h

25m • .75h

Messenian
Gulf

Kardamyli

30m • .75h

Gythio

Areopoli

15m
.5h

MANI
PENINSULA

25m • .75h

Laconian
Gulf

Vathia

10 Kilometers

10 Miles

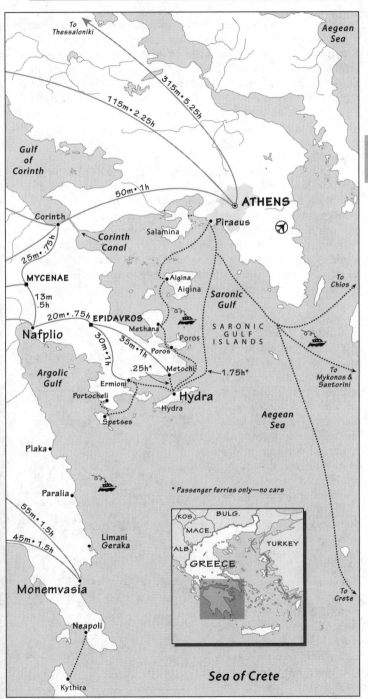

To Thessaloniki

Aegean Sea

315m • 5.25h

115m • 2.25h

Gulf of Corinth

50m • 1h

ATHENS

Corinth

Piraeus

Salamina

2.5m • .75h

Corinth Canal

MYCENAE

13m .5h

Aigina

Aigina

To Chios

Saronic Gulf

20m • .75h EPIDAVROS

Methana

S A R O N I C
G U L F
I S L A N D S

30m • 1h

Poros

Nafplio

35m • 1h Poros

Argolic Gulf

.25h*

Metochi

1.75h*

To Mykonos & Santorini

Ermioni

Portocheli

Hydra

Spetses

Hydra

Aegean Sea

Plaka

* Passenger ferries only—no cars

Paralia

KOS.   BULG.

55m • 1.5h

MACE.

45m • 1.5h

Limani Geraka

ALB.

GREECE

TURKEY

Monemvasia

Neapoli

To Crete

Kythira

Sea of Crete

If you're already purchasing a **travel-insurance policy** for your trip, adding collision coverage is an option. For example, Travel Guard (www.travelguard.com) sells affordable renter's collision insurance as an add-on to its other policies; it's valid everywhere in Europe except the Republic of Ireland, and some Italian car-rental companies refuse to honor it, as it doesn't cover you in case of theft.

For more on car-rental insurance, see www.ricksteves.com/travel-tips/transportation/car-rental-cdw.

Leasing

For trips of three weeks or more, consider leasing (which automatically includes zero-deductible collision and theft insurance). By technically buying and then selling back the car, you save lots of money on tax and insurance. Leasing provides you a brand-new car with unlimited mileage and a 24-hour emergency assistance program. You can lease for as little as 21 days to as long as five and a half months. Car leases must be arranged from the US. One of many companies offering affordable lease packages is Europe by Car (http://europebycarblog.com).

Driving

Statistically, Greece is one of the most dangerous European countries to drive in. Traffic regulations that are severely enforced back home are treated as mere suggestions here. Even at major intersections in large towns, you might not see stop signs or traffic lights; drivers simply help each other figure out who goes next. And yet, like so many seemingly chaotic things in Greece, somehow it works quite smoothly. Still... drive defensively. Greeks won't hesitate to pass you, if they feel you're going too slowly.

Road Rules: The speed limit, almost never posted, can be hard to ascertain on backcountry roads. Generally, speed limits in Greece are as follows: city—50 km/

hour; open roads—90 km/hour; divided highways—110 km/hour, superhighways—130 km/hour. Making matters even more confusing, half of all Greek drivers seem to go double the speed limit, while the others go half the limit. On country roads and highways, the lanes are often a car-and-a-half wide, with wide shoulders, so passing is common—even when there's oncoming traffic in the other lane. Do as Greek drivers do on two-lane roads with wide shoulders—straddle the shoulder if someone wants to pass you.

Don't drink and drive: The legal alcohol limit is lower in Greece than in the US. Be aware of typical European road rules; for example, many countries require headlights to be turned on at all times, and it's generally illegal to drive while using your mobile phone without a hands-free device. In Europe, you're not allowed to turn right on a red light, unless a sign or signal specifically authorizes it, and on expressways it's illegal to pass drivers on the right. Ask your car-rental company about these rules, or check the US State Department website (www.travel.state.gov, search for your country in the "Learn about your destination" box, then click on "Travel and Transportation").

Navigation: The driving directions in this book are intended to be used with a good local map. Pick up a Michelin map in the US or buy one of the good road maps available in Greece (the Road Editions maps are tops). Study it before taking off, especially if you'll be driving solo.

Because road numbers can be confusing and inconsistent, navigate by city names. Know the names of major cities en route to your destination. Often the signs will point only to the next major town, even if your final destination is a big city. Almost all road signs are in Greek and in English, but you should also know the name of your destination using the Greek alphabet—road sign transliteration can be confusing. Most Greek town names can be spelled a number of different ways in the Latin alphabet—don't be too worried about exact spelling, especially at the ends of town names.

Tolls: Special highways called *Ethniki Odos* (National Road) have tolls, which vary and must be paid in cash. This includes the road between Athens and the Peloponnese and part of the stretch between Athens and Delphi.

Fuel: Gasoline (*venzini*, βενζίνη) prices are around $8 a gallon for regular unleaded—labeled *95*, less for diesel, which is around $6.50 per gallon (*ntizel*, ντίζελ). Self-service gas stations are rare. Tell the attendant how much you want to spend and use cash. He's just there to pump gas, so don't expect him to wash your windshield or check your tires.

Parking and Safety: Choose parking places carefully. You'll rarely pay for parking, and parking laws are enforced only sporadically. If you're not certain, ask at your hotel (or ask another local) whether your space is legit. Keep your valuables in your hotel room, or, if you're between destinations, covered in your trunk. Leave nothing worth stealing in the car, especially overnight. If your car's a hatchback, take the trunk cover off at night so thieves can look in without breaking in. Try to make your car look locally owned by hiding the "tourist-owned" rental-company decals and putting a local newspaper in your front or back window. While you should avoid parking lots with twinkly asphalt, thieves break car windows anywhere, even at stoplights.

Drive carefully. If you're involved in an accident, expect a monumental headache—you will be blamed. Small towns come with speed traps.

FLIGHTS

The best comparison search engine for both international and intra-European flights is www.kayak.com. For inexpensive flights within Europe, try www.skyscanner.com or www.hipmunk.com; for inexpensive international flights, try www.vayama.com.

Flying to Europe: Start looking for international flights four to five months before your trip, especially for peak-season travel. Off-season tickets can be purchased a month or so in advance. Depending on your itinerary, it can be efficient to fly into one city and out of another. If your flight requires a connection in Europe, see our hints on navigating Europe's top hub airports at www.ricksteves.com/hub-airports.

Flying Within Europe: A flight may save you both time and money over a bus ride or driving. When comparing your options, factor in the time it takes to get to the airport and how early you'll need to arrive to check in.

Well-known cheapo airlines include easyJet (www.easyjet.com) and Ryanair (www.ryanair.com). For flights within mainland Greece and to the Greek islands, the country's main carriers are **Olympic** (tel. 210-355-0500, toll-free tel. 801-801-0101 within Greece, www.olympicair.com), **Aegean Airlines** (tel. 210-626-1000, toll-free tel. 801-112-0000 within Greece, www.aegeanair.com), **Astra Airlines** (tel. 231-048-9392, www.astra-airlines.gr), and **Sky Express** (tel. 281-022-3500, www.skyexpress.gr). But be aware of the potential drawbacks of flying with a discount airline: nonrefundable and nonchangeable tickets, minimal or nonexistent customer service, and stingy baggage allowances with steep over-age fees. If you're traveling with lots of luggage, a cheap flight can quickly become a bad deal. To avoid unpleasant surprises, read the small print before you book.

These days you can also fly within Europe on major airlines affordably—and without all the aggressive restrictions—for around $100 a flight.

Flying to the US and Canada: Because security is extra tight for flights to the US, be sure to give yourself plenty of time at the airport. It's also important to charge your electronic devices before you board because security checks may require you to turn them on (see www.tsa.gov for the latest rules).

Resources

RESOURCES FROM RICK STEVES

Rick Steves Greece: Athens & the Peloponnese is one of many books in my series on European travel, which includes country guide-

books, city guidebooks (Rome, Florence, Paris, London, etc.), Snapshot guides (excerpted chapters from my country guides), Pocket Guides (full-color little books on big cities, including Athens), and my budget-travel skills handbook, *Rick Steves Europe Through the Back Door.* Most of my titles are available as ebooks. My phrase books—for Italian, French, German, Spanish, and Portuguese—are practical and budget-oriented. My other books include *Europe 101* (a crash course on art and history designed for travelers); *Mediterranean Cruise Ports* and *Northern European Cruise Ports* (how to make the most of your time in port); and *Travel as a Political Act* (a travelogue sprinkled with tips for bringing home a global perspective). A more complete list of my titles appears near the end of this book.

Video: My public television series, *Rick Steves' Europe,* covers Europe from top to bottom with over 100 half-hour episodes. To watch full episodes online for free, see www.ricksteves.com/tv. Or to raise your travel I.Q. with video versions of our popular classes (including my talks on travel skills, packing smart, European art for travelers, travel as a political act, and indi-vidual talks covering most European countries), see www.ricksteves.com/travel-talks.

Audio: My weekly public radio show, *Travel with Rick Steves,* features interviews with travel experts from around the world. A com-

Begin Your Trip at www.RickSteves.com

My mobile-friendly **website** is *the* place to explore Europe. You'll find thousands of fun articles, videos, photos, and radio interviews organized by country; a wealth of money-saving tips for planning your dream trip; monthly travel news dispatches; my travel talks and travel blog; my latest guidebook updates (www.ricksteves.com/update); and my free Rick Steves Audio Europe app. You can also follow me on Facebook and Twitter.

Our **Travel Forum** is an immense yet well-groomed collection of message boards, where our travel-savvy community answers questions and shares their personal travel experiences—and our well-traveled staff chimes in when they can be helpful (www.ricksteves.com/forums).

Our **online Travel Store** offers travel bags and accessories that I've designed specifically to help you travel smarter and lighter. These include my popular bags (rolling carry-on and backpack versions, which I helped design...and live out of four months a year), money belts, totes, toiletries kits, adapters, other accessories, and a wide selection of guidebooks and planning maps.

If you're traveling beyond Greece and will require a rail pass, our website will help you find the perfect fit for your itinerary and your budget: We offer easy, one-stop shopping for rail passes, seat reservations, and point-to-point tickets.

Want to travel with greater efficiency and less stress? We organize **tours** with more than three dozen itineraries and 900 departures reaching the best destinations in this book...and beyond. We offer a 14-day tour of Athens and the Heart of Greece. You'll enjoy great guides, a fun bunch of travel partners (with small groups of 24 to 28 travelers), and plenty of room to spread out in a big, comfy bus when touring between towns. You'll find European adventures to fit every vacation length. For all the details, and to get our Tour Catalog and a free Rick Steves Tour Experience DVD (filmed on location during an actual tour), visit www.ricksteves.com or call us at 425/608-4217.

plete archive of 10 years of programs (over 400 in all) is available at www.ricksteves.com/radio. I've also produced free, self-guided audio tours of the top sights in Athens. Most of this audio content is available for free through my **Rick Steves Audio Europe app,** an extensive online library organized by destination. For more on my app, see page 10.

MAPS

The black-and-white maps in this book are concise and simple, designed to help you locate recommended places and get to local TIs, where you can pick up more in-depth maps of cities and regions (usually free). Better maps are sold at newsstands and bookstores. Before you buy a map, look at it to be sure it has the level of detail you want. The Greek-produced maps by Road Editions are best. Map apps for your smartphone or tablet are also handy (see "Navigation Options," earlier).

APPENDIX

Useful Contacts

Emergency Needs
Police: Tel. 100
Tourist Police: Tel. 171 or 1571 (English-speaking)
Medical or Other Emergency: Tel. 112

Embassies
US Embassy in Athens: Tel. 210-720-2414; after-hours emergency tel. 210-729-4444, consular section open Mon-Fri 8:30-17:00, closed Sat-Sun and last Wed of month (Vasilissis Sofias 91, Metro: Megaro Moussikis, http://athens.usembassy.gov)
Canadian Embassy in Athens: Tel. 210-727-3400, for after-hours emergency help call Canada collect at tel. 1-613-996-8885; open Mon-Fri 8:30-12:30, closed Sat-Sun (Ethnikis Antistaseos 48, www.canadainternational.gc.ca/greece-grece)

Directory Assistance
Operator/Directory Assistance for Greece: Tel. 11888
Operator/Directory Assistance for International Calls: Tel. 139

Holidays and Festivals

This list includes selected festivals, plus national holidays observed throughout Greece. Many sights and banks close on national holidays—keep this in mind when planning your itinerary. Before planning a trip around a festival, verify its dates by checking the festival's website or TI sites (www.visitgreece.gr).

Here are some major holidays:

APPENDIX

Jan 1	New Year's Day
Jan 6	Epiphany
Mid-Jan-March	Carnival season (Apokreo), famous in Patra, peaks on the last Sunday before Lent
Early March	"Clean Monday" (Kathari Deftera), the first day of Lent in the Orthodox church
March 25	Greek Independence Day
Easter Weekend	Orthodox Good Friday through Easter Monday (April 29-May 2, 2016; April 14-17, 2017)
May 1	Labor Day
June	Miaoulia Festival, Hydra (falls on the weekend closest to June 21)
June	Nafplio Festival, classical music, Nafplio
June-Aug	Athens & Epidavros Festival (music, opera, dance, and theater at the Odeon of Herodes Atticus beneath the Acropolis in Athens; drama and music at the Theater of Epidavros—www.greekfestival.gr/en)
July-Aug	Ancient Olympia International Festival (music, dance, and theater at the site of the ancient Olympics)
Aug 15	Assumption
Sept	Athens International Film Festival
Oct 28	Ohi Day (Anniversary of the "No"; commemorates rejection of Mussolini's WWII ultimatum)
Dec 25	Christmas
Dec 26	"Second Day" of Christmas

Recommended Books and Films

To learn more about Greece past and present, check out a few of these books and films.

NONFICTION

Alexander the Great (Paul Anthony Cartledge, 2004). Alexander's legacy comes to life in this engaging history.

Apology (Plato, 390 B.C.). This is a classic for a reason, opening up a window into the Greek mind and soul.

The Cambridge Illustrated History of Ancient Greece (Paul Anthony Cartledge, 1997). Offered in large format, Cartledge's history is packed with gorgeous illustrations.

Colossus of Maroussi (Henry Miller, 1941). Miller tells a sometimes-graphic account of his down-and-out sojourn in Greece in the late 1930s.

A Concise History of Greece (Richard Clogg, 1986). For an overview of the 18th century to modern times, this history is surprisingly succinct.

Dinner with Persephone (Patricia Storace, 1996). This book is more than a memoir about living in Athens—it's one writer's critical look at modern Greek culture and family life.

Eleni (Nicholas Gage, 1983). Gage tells the riveting account of his quest to uncover the truth behind his mother's assassination during Greece's civil war.

The Greeks (H. D. F. Kitto, 1951). Considered the standard text on ancient Greece by a leading scholar, this decades-old work is still quite accessible.

The Greek Way (Edith Hamilton, 1930). Hamilton introduces the world of ancient Greece to the 20th century.

Inside Hitler's Greece (Mark Mazower, 1993). This shocking account of the Nazi occupation of Greece details the background for the country's civil war.

Lives (Plutarch, 100). Written at the start of the second century, *Lives* is an epic attempt to chronicle the ancient world through biography.

Mani: Travels in the Southern Peloponnese (Patrick Leigh Fermor, 1958). This is the definitive book on the "forgotten" side of the peninsula.

Mediterranean in the Ancient World (Fernand Braudel, 1972). Braudel gives a marvelous overview of the ancient Mediterranean.

Mythology (Edith Hamilton, 1942). Along with *The Greek Way*, this is a must-read tome on classic myths and cultures.

The Nature of Alexander (Mary Renault, 1975). This biography from a famous novelist provides insight on Alexander the Great.

The Parthenon Enigma (Joan Breton Connelly, 2014). Connelly uses the temple's dramatic frieze—depicting, she says, human sacrifice—to go deep into the history of the Acropolis.

Persian Fire (Tom Holland, 2005). Holland offers an excellent history of the fifth-century B.C. Persian conflict.

Republic (Plato, 380 B.C.). In this classic, Plato captures the words of Socrates from Golden Age times.

Sailing the Wine-Dark Sea: Why the Greeks Matter (Thomas Cahill, 2003). Cahill astutely probes the relevance of ancient Greek culture to today's world.

The Spartans (Paul Anthony Cartledge, 2002). This history chronicles the rise and fall of the Spartan warriors.

The Summer of My Greek Taverna (Tom Stone, 2002). An American expat recounts his experiences in Greece while running a bar on the island of Patmos.

A Traveller's History of Greece (Timothy Boatswain and Colin Nicolson, 1990). This compact, well-written account covers the earliest times to the present.

FICTION

Corelli's Mandolin (Louis de Bernières, 1993). This novel about ill-fated lovers on a war-torn Greek island was made into a 2001 film starring Nicolas Cage and Penélope Cruz.

Deeper Shade of Blue (Paul Johnston, 2002). Detective Alex Mavros leaves Athens for the island of Trigono to find a missing woman.

Fire from Heaven (Mary Renault, 1969). The most renowned author of historical novels about Greece offers the dramatic story of Alexander the Great.

Gates of Fire (Steven Pressfield, 1998). Pressfield re-creates the Battle of Thermopylae, where 300 Spartans held back the Persian army—for a while.

The Iliad/The Odyssey (Homer, 850 B.C.). This classic epic follows the hero Odysseus through the Trojan War and his return home.

The King Must Die (Mary Renault, 1958). Renault reimagines the Theseus legend in this exciting tale.

The Last Temptation of Christ (Nikos Kazantzakis, 1953). Kazantzakis' literary reinterpretation of the Gospels is hailed internationally as a masterpiece.

Little Infamies (Panos Karnezis, 1903). This fine collection of short stories looks at the lives of Greek villagers with magical realism.

The Magus (John Fowles, 1965). An Englishman plays psychological games with a wealthy recluse on a Greek island.

Middlesex (Jeffrey Eugenides, 2002). An American author of Greek descent explores the Greek immigrant experience in the US, as well as sexual identity.

Stealing Athena (Karen Essex, 2008). The Parthenon plays a pivotal role in the lives of Pericles' mistress, Aspasia, and Lord Elgin's wife, Mary.

Uncle Petros and Goldbach's Conjecture (Apostolos Doxiadis, 1992). A Greek genius is obsessed with trying to prove one of mathematics' great theories.

The Walled Orchard (Tom Holt, 1990). Amusing and well-researched, this novel is the pseudo-autobiography of comic playwright Eupolis.

Zorba the Greek (Nikos Kazantzakis, 1946). A wily old rogue teaches life's lessons to a withdrawn intellectual.

TV AND FILM

300 (2006). Based on a graphic novel, this is a highly fictional and stylized account of the Battle of Thermopylae.

300: Rise of an Empire (2014). Also based on a graphic novel, this movie tells the tale of the final naval battle of Salamis after Thermopylae.

Alexander (2004). Colin Farrell plays the military genius who conquered the known world.

Boy on a Dolphin (1957). A beautiful sponge diver on Hydra, played by Sophia Loren, becomes aware of her cultural heritage.

Clash of the Titans (1981). Featuring an all-star cast including Laurence Olivier, Claire Bloom, and Maggie Smith, this adaptation of the Perseus myth is a classic.

The Guns of Navarone (1961). A team of English commandos tries to take out a WWII German artillery battery.

Mamma Mia! (2008). Filmed in the mainland region of Pelion and on the islands of Skiathos and Skopelos, this musical uses ABBA songs to tell the story of a young woman trying to find her father.

My Big Fat Greek Wedding (2002). Hilarity ensues when a Greek-American woman tries to plan her wedding while contending with her large and boisterous family.

My Family and Other Animals (2005). This film follows the adventures of an English family relocated to Greece in 1939.

Never on Sunday (1960). Melina Mercouri stars as a Greek prostitute who is pursued by an American scholar with classical ideals.

Secrets of the Parthenon (2008). This NOVA episode, available on www.pbs.org, documents the restoration of the Parthenon.

Stella (1955). A young Greek woman must decide between falling in love and retaining her freedom.

The Trojan Women (1971). Euripides' classic tragedy of Troy's female aristocracy in chains features Katharine Hepburn, Vanessa Redgrave, and Irene Pappas.

APPENDIX

Troy (2004). Brad Pitt stars as the petulant warrior Achilles in this adaptation of Homer's epic.

Z (1969). This thriller follows the assassination of a crusading politician—and the rise of the Greek junta—in the 1960s.

BOOKS AND FILMS FOR KIDS

Ancient Civilizations: Greece (Eva Bargallo I Chaves, 2004). Kids can brush up on ancient Greece, including history, art, government, and mythology.

Ancient Greece! 40 Hands-On Activities to Experience This Wondrous Age (Avery Hart and Paul Mantell, 1999). With this book, learn how to make traditional foods, build a model temple, and put on a play.

Greece (Changing Face of...) (Tasmin Osler, 2003). This nonfiction book weaves first-person accounts from modern Greeks with a summary of today's challenges.

Greece in Spectacular Cross-Section (Stephen Biesty, 2006). Kids and grown-ups alike will enjoy these cut-away diagrams re-creating ancient sites.

Hercules (1997). This animated Disney film is loosely based on the hero of Greek legend, Hercules, son of Zeus.

If I Were a Kid in Ancient Greece (Cricket Media, 2012). Kids can put themselves in the sandals of a young Grecian in this fun series.

Percy Jackson and the Olympians (Rick Riordan, 2005). A young boy learns that he is the son of a Greek god in this clever and amusing young adult series. Two *Percy Jackson* films bring the books to life (2010 and 2013).

The Random House Book of Greek Myths (Joan D. Vinge, 1999). Greek gods and goddesses are highlighted in this illustrated primer on Greek mythology.

This Is Greece (Miroslav Sasek, 1966). Reissued in 2009, Sasek's classic picture book captures the essence of ancient and modern Greece.

Conversions and Climate

NUMBERS AND STUMBLERS

- Europeans write a few of their numbers differently than we do. 1 = 1, 4 = 4, 7 = 7.
- In Europe, dates appear as day/month/year, so Christmas 2017 is 25/12/17.
- Commas are decimal points and decimals are commas. A dollar and a half is $1,50, one thousand is 1.000, and there are 5.280 feet in a mile.
- When counting with fingers, start with your thumb. If you

hold up your first finger to request one item, you'll probably get two.
- What Americans call the second floor of a building is the first floor in Europe.
- On escalators and moving sidewalks, Europeans keep the left "lane" open for passing. Keep to the right.

METRIC CONVERSIONS

A kilogram is 2.2 pounds, and 1 liter is about a quart, or almost four to a gallon. A kilometer is six-tenths of a mile. I figure kilometers to miles by cutting them in half and adding back 10 percent of the original (120 km: 60 + 12=72 miles, 300 km: 150 + 30=180 miles).

1 foot = 0.3 meter	1 square yard = 0.8 square meter
1 yard = 0.9 meter	1 square mile = 2.6 square kilometers
1 mile = 1.6 kilometers	1 ounce = 28 grams
1 centimeter = 0.4 inch	1 quart = 0.95 liter
1 meter = 39.4 inches	1 kilogram = 2.2 pounds
1 kilometer = 0.62 mile	32°F = 0°C

CLOTHING SIZES

When shopping for clothing, use these US-to-European comparisons as general guidelines (but note that no conversion is perfect).
- Women's dresses and blouses: Add 30
  (US size 10 = European size 40)
- Men's suits and jackets: Add 10
  (US size 40 regular = European size 50)
- Men's shirts: Multiply by 2 and add about 8
  (US size 15 collar = European size 38)
- Women's shoes: Add about 30
  (US size 8 = European size 38-39)
- Men's shoes: Add 32-34 (US size 9 = European size 41;
  US size 11 = European size 45)

Athens' Climate

First line, average daily high; second line, average daily low; third line, average days without rain. For more detailed weather statistics for destinations in this book (as well as the rest of the world), check www.wunderground.com.

J	F	M	A	M	J	J	A	S	O	N	D
56°	57°	60°	66°	75°	83°	88°	88°	82°	73°	66°	59°
44°	45°	47°	53°	60°	68°	73°	72°	67°	59°	53°	48°
24	22	26	27	28	28	30	30	28	27	24	24

FAHRENHEIT AND CELSIUS CONVERSION

Europe takes its temperature using the Celsius scale, while we opt for Fahrenheit. For a rough conversion from Celsius to Fahrenheit, double the number and add 30. For weather, remember that 28°C is 82°F—perfect. For health, 37°C is just right. At a launderette, 30°C is cold, 40°C is warm (usually the default setting), 60°C is hot, and 95°C is boiling.

Packing Checklist

Whether you're traveling for five days or five weeks, you won't need more than this. Pack light to enjoy the sweet freedom of true mobility.

Clothing

- ☐ 5 shirts: long- & short-sleeve
- ☐ 2 pairs pants or skirt
- ☐ 1 pair shorts or capris
- ☐ 5 pairs underwear & socks
- ☐ 1 pair walking shoes
- ☐ Sweater or fleece top
- ☐ Rainproof jacket with hood
- ☐ Tie or scarf
- ☐ Swimsuit
- ☐ Sleepwear

Money

- ☐ Debit card
- ☐ Credit card(s)
- ☐ Hard cash ($20 bills)
- ☐ Money belt or neck wallet

Documents & Travel Info

- ☐ Passport
- ☐ Airline reservations
- ☐ Rail pass/train reservations
- ☐ Car-rental voucher
- ☐ Driver's license
- ☐ Student ID, hostel card, etc.
- ☐ Photocopies of all the above
- ☐ Hotel confirmations
- ☐ Insurance details
- ☐ Guidebooks & maps
- ☐ Notepad & pen
- ☐ Journal

Toiletries Kit

- ☐ Toiletries
- ☐ Medicines & vitamins
- ☐ First-aid kit
- ☐ Glasses/contacts/sunglasses (with prescriptions)
- ☐ Earplugs
- ☐ Packet of tissues (for WC)

Miscellaneous

- ☐ Daypack
- ☐ Sealable plastic baggies
- ☐ Laundry soap
- ☐ Spot remover
- ☐ Clothesline
- ☐ Sewing kit
- ☐ Travel alarm/watch

Electronics

- ☐ Smartphone or mobile phone
- ☐ Camera & related gear
- ☐ Tablet/ereader/media player
- ☐ Laptop & flash drive
- ☐ Earbuds or headphones
- ☐ Chargers
- ☐ Plug adapters

Optional Extras

- ☐ Flipflops or slippers
- ☐ Mini-umbrella or poncho
- ☐ Travel hairdryer
- ☐ Belt
- ☐ Hat (for sun or cold)
- ☐ Picnic supplies
- ☐ Water bottle
- ☐ Fold-up tote bag
- ☐ Small flashlight
- ☐ Small binoculars
- ☐ Insect repellent
- ☐ Small towel or washcloth
- ☐ Inflatable pillow
- ☐ Some duct tape (for repairs)
- ☐ Tiny lock
- ☐ Address list (to mail postcards)
- ☐ Postcards/photos from home
- ☐ Extra passport photos
- ☐ Good book

Greek Survival Phrases

Knowing a few phrases of Greek can help if you're traveling off the beaten path. Just learning the pleasantries (such as please and thank you) will improve your connections with locals, even in the bigger cities.

Because Greek words can be transliterated differently in English, I've also included the Greek spellings. Note that in Greek, a semicolon is used the same way we use a question mark.

English	Greek	Pronunciation
Hello. (formal)	Gia sas. Γειά σας.	yah sahs
Hi. / Bye. (informal)	Gia. Γειά.	yah
Good morning.	Kali mera. Καλή μέρα.	kah-**lee meh**-rah
Good afternoon.	Kali spera. Καλή σπέρα.	kah-**lee speh**-rah
Do you speak English?	Milate anglika? Μιλάτε αγγλικά;	mee-**lah**-teh ahn-glee-**kah**
Yes. / No.	Ne. / Ohi. Ναι. / Όχι.	neh / **oh**-hee
I understand.	Katalaveno Καταλαβαίνω.	kah-tah-lah-**veh**-noh
I (don't) understand.	(Den) katalaveno. (Δεν) καταλαβαίνω.	(dehn) kah-tah-lah-**veh**-noh
Please. (Also: You're welcome.)	Parakalo. Παρακαλώ.	pah-rah-kah-**loh**
Thank you (very much).	Efharisto (poli). Ευχαριστώ (πολύ).	ehf-hah-ree-**stoh** (poh-lee)
Excuse me. (Also: I'm sorry.)	Sygnomi. Συγνώμη.	seeg-**noh**-mee
(No) problem.	(Kanena) problima. (Κανένα) πρόβλημα.	(kah-**neh**-nah) **prohv**-lee-mah
Good.	Orea. Ωραία.	oh-**reh**-ah
Goodbye.	Antio. Αντίο.	ahd-**yoh** (think "adieu")
Good night.	Kali nikta. Καλή νύχτα.	kah-**lee neek**-tah
one / two	ena / dio ένα / δύο	**eh**-nah / **dee**-oh
three / four	tria / tessera τρία /τέσσερα	**tree**-ah / **teh**-seh-rah
five / six	pente / exi πέντε / έξι	**pehn**-deh / **ehk**-see
seven / eight	efta / ohto εφτά / οχτώ	ehf-**tah** / oh-**toh**
nine / ten	ennia / deka εννιά / δέκα	ehn-**yah** / **deh**-kah
hundred / thousand	ekato / hilia εκατό / χίλια	eh-kah-**toh** / **heel**-yah
How much?	Poso kani? Πόσο κάνει;	**poh**-soh **kah**-nee
euro	evro ευρώ	ev-**roh**
Write it?	Grapsete to? Γράψετε το;	**grahp**-seh-teh toh

English	Greek	Pronunciation
Is it free?	Ine dorean? Είναι δωρεάν;	ee-neh doh-ree-**ahn**
Is it included?	Perilamvanete? Περιλαμβάνεται;	peh-ree-lahm-**vah**-neh-teh
Where can I find / buy...?	Pou boro na vro / agoraso...? Που μπορώ να βρω / αγοράσω...;	poo boh-**roh** nah vroh / ah-goh-**rah**-soh
I'd like / We'd like...	Tha ithela / Tha thelame... Θα ήθελα / Θα θέλαμε...	thah **ee**-theh-lah / thah **theh**-lah-meh
...a room.	...ena dhomatio. ...ένα δωμάτιο.	eh-nah doh-**mah**-tee-oh
...a ticket to ___.	...ena isitirio gia ___. ...ένα εισιτήριο για ___.	eh-nah ee-see-**tee**-ree-oh yah ___
Is it possible?	Ginete? Γίνεται;	**yee**-neh-teh
Where is...?	Pou ine...? Που είναι...;	poo **ee**-neh
...the bus station	...o stathmos ton leoforion ...ο σταθμός των λεωφορίων	oh **stahth**-mohs tohn leh-oh-foh-**ree**-ohn
...the train station	...o stathmos tou trenou ...ο σταθμός του τρένου	oh **stahth**-mohs too **treh**-noo
...the tourist information office	...to grafeio enimerosis touriston ...το γραφείο ενημέρωσης τουριστών	too grah-**fee**-oh eh-nee-**meh**-roh-sis too-ree-**stohn**
toilet	toualeta τουαλέτα	twah-**leh**-tah
men / women	andres / gynekes άντρες / γυναικες	**ahn**-drehs / yee-**neh**-kehs
left / right	dexia / aristera δεξιά / αριστερά	dehk-see-**ah** / ah-ree-steh-**rah**
straight	efthia ευθεία	ehf-**thee**-ah
At what time...	Ti ora... Τι ώρα...	tee **oh**-rah
...does this open / close?	...anigete / klinete? ...ανοίγετε / κλείνετε;	ah-**nee**-yeh-teh / **klee**-neh-teh
Just a moment.	Ena lepto. Ένα λεπτό.	eh-nah lep-**toh**
now / soon / later	tora / se ligo / argotera τώρα / σε λίγο / αργότερα	**toh**-rah / seh **lee**-goh / ar-**goh**-teh-rah
today / tomorrow	simera / avrio σήμερα / αύριο	**see**-meh-rah / **ahv**-ree-oh

In a Greek Restaurant

English	Greek	Pronunciation
I'd like to reserve...	*Tha ithela na kliso...* Θα ήθελα να κλείσω...	thah **ee**-theh-lah nah **klee**-soh
We'd like to reserve...	*Tha thelame na klisoume...* Θα θέλαμε να κλείσουμε...	thah **theh**-lah-meh nah **klee**-soo-meh
...a table for one / two.	*...ena trapezi gia enan / dio.* ...ένα τραπέζι για έναν / δύο.	**eh**-nah trah-**peh**-zee yah **eh**-nahn / **dee**-oh
non-smoking	*mi kapnizon* μη καπνίζων	mee kahp-**nee**-zohn
Is this table free?	*Ine eleftero afto to trapezi?* Είναι ελεύθερο αυτό το τραπέζι;	**ee**-neh eh-**lef**-teh-roh ahf-**toh** toh trah-**peh**-zee
The menu (in English), please.	*Ton katalogo (sta anglika) parakalo.* Τον κατάλογο (στα αγγλικά) παρακαλώ.	tohn kah-**tah**-loh-goh (stah ahn-glee-**kah**) pah-rah-kah-**loh**
service (not) included	*to servis (den) perilamvanete* το σέρβις (δεν) περιλαμβάνεται	toh **sehr**-vees (dehn) peh-ree-lahm-**vah**-neh-teh
cover charge	*kouver* κουβέρ	koo-**vehr**
"to go"	*gia exo* για έξω	yah **ehk**-soh
with / without	*me / horis* με / χωρίς	meh / hoh-**rees**
and / or	*ke / i* και / ή	keh / ee
fixed-price meal	*menu* μενού	meh-**noo**
specialty of the house	*i specialite tou magaziou* η σπεσιαλιτέ του μαγαζιού	ee speh-see-ah-lee-**teh** too mah-gah-zee-**oo**
half-portion	*misi merida* μισή μερίδα	mee-**see** meh-**ree**-dah
daily special	*to piato tis meras* το πιάτο της μέρας	toh pee-**ah**-toh tees meh-rahs
appetizers	*proto piato* πρώτο πιάτο	**proh**-toh pee-**ah**-toh
bread	*psomi* ψωμί	psoh-**mee**
cheese	*tiri* τυρί	tee-**ree**
sandwich	*sandwich or toast* σάντουιτς, τόστ	"sandwich," "toast"
soup	*soupa* σούπα	**soo**-pah
salad	*salata* σαλάτα	sah-**lah**-tah
meat	*kreas* κρέας	**kray**-ahs

English	Greek	Pronunciation
poultry / chicken	*poulerika / kotopoulo* πουλερικά / κοτόπουλο	poo-leh-ree-**kah** / koh-**toh**-poo-loh
fish / seafood	*psari / psarika* ψάρι / ψαρικά	**psah**-ree / psah-ree-**kah**
shellfish	*thalassina* θαλασσινά	thah-lah-see-**nah**
fruit	*frouta* φρούτα	**froo**-tah
vegetables	*lahanika* λαχανικά	lah-hah-nee-**kah**
dessert	*gliko* γλυκό	lee-**koh**
(tap) water	*nero (tis vrisis)* νερό (της βρύσης)	neh-**roh** (tees **vree**-sees)
mineral water	*metalliko nero* μεταλλικό νερό	meh-tah-lee-**koh** neh-**roh**
milk	*gala* γάλα	**gah**-lah
(orange) juice	*himos (portokali)* χυμός (πορτοκάλι)	hee-**mohs** (por-toh-**kah**-lee)
coffee	*kafes* καφές	kah-**fehs**
tea	*tsai* τσάι	**chah**-ee
wine	*krasi* κρασί	krah-**see**
wine (printed on label)	*inos* οίνος	**ee**-nohs
red / white	*kokkino / lefko* κόκκινο / λευκό	**koh**-kee-noh / **lef**-koh
sweet / dry / semi-dry	*gliko / xiro / imixiro* γλυκό / ξηρό / ημίξηρο	lee-**koh** / ksee-**roh** / ee-**meek**-see-roh
glass / bottle	*potiri / boukali* ποτήρι / μπουκάλι	poh-**tee**-ree / boo-**kah**-lee
beer	*bira* μπύρα	**bee**-rah
Here you are. (when given food)	*Oriste.* Ορίστε.	oh-**ree**-steh
Enjoy your meal!	*Kali orexi!* Καλή όρεξη!	kah-**lee** oh-**rehk**-see
(To your) health! (like "Cheers!")	*(Stin i) gia mas!* (Στην υ) γειά μας!	(stee nee) yah mahs
Another.	*Allo ena.* Άλλο ένα.	**ah**-loh **eh**-nah
Bill, please.	*Ton logariasmo parakalo.* Τον λογαριασμό παρακαλώ.	tohn loh-gah-ree-ahs-**moh** pah-rah-kah-**loh**
tip	*bourbouar* μπουρμπουάρ	boor-boo-**ar**
Very good!	*Poli oreo!* Πολύ ωραίο!	poh-**lee** oh-**ray**-oh
Delicious!	*Poli nostimo!* Πολύ νόστιμο!	poh-**lee** **nohs**-tee-moh

INDEX

INDEX

Εθνικό Αρχαιολογικό
National Archaeological

100 1391800 02/06/2018 18:13:54

2 031001 391802

Κανονικό
Standard

Τιμή
Price

10.00

Welcome

11 P1003

MAP INDEX

Our website enhances this book and turns

Explore Europe

At ricksteves.com you can browse through thousands of articles, videos, photos and radio interviews, plus find a wealth of money-saving travel tips for planning your dream trip. And with our mobile-friendly website, you

can easily access all this great travel information anywhere you go.

TV Shows

Preview the places you'll visit by watching entire half-hour episodes of Rick Steves' Europe (choose from all 100 shows) on-demand, for free.

your travel dreams into affordable reality

Radio Interviews

Enjoy ready access to Rick's vast library of radio interviews covering travel

tips and cultural insights that relate specifically to your Europe travel plans.

Travel Forums

Learn, ask, share! Our online community of savvy travelers is a great resource for first-time travelers to Europe, as well as seasoned pros. You'll find forums on each country, plus travel tips and restaurant/hotel reviews. You can even ask one of our well-traveled staff to chime in with an opinion.

Travel News

Subscribe to our free Travel News e-newsletter, and get monthly updates from Rick on what's happening in Europe.

Save time and energy

This guidebook is your independent-travel toolkit. But for all it delivers, it's still up to you to devote the time and energy it takes to manage the preparation and logistics that are essential for a happy trip. If that's a hassle, there's a solution.

Rick Steves Tours

A Rick Steves tour takes you to Europe's most interesting places with great

with minimum stress

guides and small groups of 28 or less. We follow Rick's favorite itineraries, ride in comfy buses, stay in family-run hotels, and bring you intimately close to the Europe you've traveled so far to see. Most importantly, we take away the logistical headaches so you can focus on the fun.

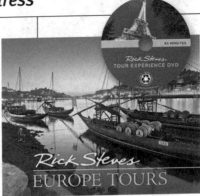

customers—along with us on 40 different itineraries, from Ireland to Italy to Istanbul. Is a Rick Steves tour the right fit for your travel dreams? Find out at ricksteves.com, where you can also get Rick's latest tour catalog and free Tour Experience DVD.

Join the fun

This year we'll take 18,000 free-spirited travelers— nearly half of them repeat

Europe is best experienced with happy travel partners. We hope you can join us.

See our itineraries at ricksteves.com

BEST OF GUIDES

Full color easy-to-scan format, focusing on Europe's most popular destinations and sights.

Best of France
Best of Germany
Best of England
Best of Europe
Best of Ireland
Best of Italy
Best of Spain

COMPREHENSIVE GUIDES

City, country, and regional guides with detailed coverage for a multi-week trip exploring the most iconic sights and venturing off the beaten track.

Amsterdam & the Netherlands
Barcelona
Belgium: Bruges, Brussels, Antwerp & Ghent
Berlin
Budapest
Croatia & Slovenia
Eastern Europe
England
Florence & Tuscany
France
Germany
Great Britain
Greece: Athens & the Peloponnese
Iceland
Ireland
Istanbul
Italy
London
Paris
Portugal
Prague & the Czech Republic
Provence & the French Riviera
Rome
Scandinavia
Scotland
Spain
Switzerland
Venice
Vienna, Salzburg & Tirol

HE BEST OF ROME

ne, Italy's capital, is studded with
san remnants and floodlit-fountain
res. From the Vatican to the Colos-
s, with crazy traffic in between, Rome
nderful, huge, and exhausting. The
s, the heat, and the weighty history

of the Eternal City where Caesars walked
can make tourists wilt. Recharge by taking siestas, gelato breaks, and after-dark
walks, strolling from one atmospheric
square to another in the refreshing evening air.

*d Pantheon—which
st dome until the
y 2,000 years old
y over 1,500).*

*f Athens in the Vat-
ies the humanistic
e.*

*ladiators fought
other, entertaining*

*Rome ristorante.
at St. Peter's
eriously.*

Rick Steves guidebooks are published by Avalon Travel,
an imprint of Perseus Books, a Hachette Book Group company

POCKET GUIDES
Compact, full color city guides with the essentials for shorter trips.

Amsterdam
Athens
Barcelona
Florence
Italy's Cinque Terre
London
Munich & Salzburg

Paris
Prague
Rome
Venice
Vienna

SNAPSHOT GUIDES
Focused single-destination coverage.

Basque Country: Spain & France
Copenhagen & the Best of Denmark
Dublin
Dubrovnik
Edinburgh
Hill Towns of Central Italy
Krakow, Warsaw & Gdansk
Lisbon
Loire Valley
Madrid & Toledo
Milan & the Italian Lakes District
Naples & the Amalfi Coast
Northern Ireland
Normandy
Norway
Reykjavik
Sevilla, Granada & Southern Spain
St. Petersburg, Helsinki & Tallinn
Stockholm

CRUISE PORTS GUIDES
Reference for cruise ports of call.

Mediterranean Cruise Ports
Northern European Cruise Ports

Complete your library with...

TRAVEL SKILLS & CULTURE
Study up on travel skills and gain insight on history and culture.

Europe 101
European Christmas
European Easter
European Festivals
Europe Through the Back Door
Postcards from Europe
Travel as a Political Act

PHRASE BOOKS & DICTIONARIES

French
French, Italian & German
German
Italian
Portuguese
Spanish

PLANNING MAPS

Britain, Ireland & London
Europe
France & Paris
Germany, Austria & Switzerland
Ireland
Italy
Spain & Portugal

Rick Steves books are available from your favorite bookseller.
Many guides are available as ebooks.

Credits

To research and help write this book, Rick relied on...

WRITERS
Cameron Hewitt

Born in Denver and raised in central Ohio, Cameron settled in Seattle in 2000. Ever since, he has spent three months each year in Europe, contributing to guidebooks, tours, radio and television shows, and other media for Rick Steves' Europe, where he serves as content manager. Cameron married his high school sweetheart (and favorite travel partner), Shawna, and enjoys taking pictures, trying new restaurants, and planning his next trip.

Gene Openshaw

Gene has co-authored a dozen Rick Steves books and contributes to many others. For this book, he wrote material on Europe's art, history, and contemporary culture. When not traveling, Gene enjoys composing music, recovering from his 1973 trip to Europe with Rick, and living everyday life with his daughter.

RESEARCHER
Cathy Lu

A researcher and editor at Rick Steves' Europe, Cathy feels very fortunate that she gets to travel and nitpick for a living. Originally from New Jersey, she now lives in Seattle, where she enjoys playing tennis, eating conveyor-belt sushi, engaging in late-night karaoke, and most of all, spending time outdoors with her husband and daughter.

Acknowledgments

Efharisto poli to our tour-guide friends David Willett, Colleen Murphy, and Julie and Reid Coen for their invaluable help in shaping this book. Their travel savvy, knowledge, and understanding of Greek culture—and their never-ending quest to find the perfect ruined temple, secluded beach, bottle of ouzo, and other Back Door experiences—gave this book a firm foundation. Also, many thanks to Kiki Tsagkaraki-Rae for her help with the Greek survival phrases. *Stin i gia mas!*

Avalon Travel
An imprint of Perseus Books
A Hachette Book Group company
1700 Fourth Street
Berkeley, CA 94710

Text © 2016 by Rick Steves. All rights reserved.
Maps © 2016 by Rick Steves' Europe. All rights reserved.
Photos are used by permission and are the property of the original copyright owners.
Printed in Canada by Friesens
Fifth printing March 2018

ISBN 978-1-63121-307-6
ISSN 1947-4725
4th Edition

For the latest on Rick's lectures, books, tours, public-radio show, and public television
series, contact Rick Steves' Europe, 130 Fourth Avenue North, Edmonds, WA 98020,
tel. 425/771-8303, www.ricksteves.com, rick@ricksteves.com.

Rick Steves' Europe

Special Publications Manager: Risa Laib
Managing Editor: Jennifer Madison Davis
Editors: Glenn Eriksen, Tom Griffin, Katherine Gustafson, Suzanne Kotz, Cathy Lu,
  John Pierce, Carrie Shepherd
Editorial & Production Assistant: Jessica Shaw
Editorial Interns: Grace Swanson, Chelsea Wing
Researcher: Cathy Lu
Writers: Cameron Hewitt, Gene Openshaw
Graphic Content Director: Sandra Hundacker
Maps & Graphics: David C. Hoerlein, Lauren Mills, Mary Rostad

Avalon Travel

Senior Editor and Series Manager: Madhu Prasher
Editor: Jamie Andrade
Associate Editor: Sierra Machado
Copy Editor: Maggie Ryan
Proofreader: Janet Walden
Indexer: Beatrice Wikander
Production & Typesetting: Rue Flaherty, Tabitha Lahr, Sarah Wildfang
Cover Design: Kimberly Glyder Design
Maps & Graphics: Kat Bennett, Mike Morgenfeld

Photo Credits

Front Cover: Tholos at Delphi © Christian Delbert/Alamy Stock Photo
Title Page: Views of the Saronic Gulf from Hydra © Sandra Hundacker
Front Matter Color: p. viii, Santorini © Pat O' Connor
Full-page photos: p. 27, Parthenon, Acropolis, Athens; p. 205, Vathia, Mani Peninsula,
  Peloponnese; p. 335, Sanctuary of Athena, Delphi
Additional Photography: Tom Griffin, Cameron Hewitt, Sandra Hundacker, Anne
  Jenkins, Cathy Lu, Gene Openshaw, Rhonda Pelikan, Carol Ries, Rich Sorensen,
  Rick Steves, Gretchen Strauch, Laura VanDeventer, David Willet. Photos are used
  by permission and are the property of the original copyright owners.

More for your trip!
Maximize the experience with Rick Steves as your guide

Guidebooks
Dozens of European city and country guidebooks

Planning Maps
Use the map that's in sync with your guidebook

Rick's TV Shows
Preview where you're going with 3 shows on Greece

Free! Rick's Audio Europe™ App
Get free audio tours for Athens' top sights

Small Group Tours
Including Athens and the Heart of Greece

For all the details, visit ricksteves.com